The Practice of
Biliary Surgery

To our wives, Susan and Hana,
who spent many hours alone, we trust,
while this book was being written.

The Practice of Biliary Surgery

GABRIEL A. KUNE
MBBS FRACS FRCS FACS
Professor of Surgery, University of Melbourne
Consultant Surgeon, Royal Melbourne Hospital and
Repatriation General Hospital, Melbourne
Hunterian Professor, Royal College of Surgeons of England

AVNI SALI
MBBS PhD FRACS
Professorial First Assistant in Surgery
University of Melbourne, and Consultant Surgeon
Repatriation General Hospital, Melbourne

SECOND EDITION

Blackwell Scientific Publications
OXFORD LONDON EDINBURGH
BOSTON MELBOURNE

First published 1972 by
Little Brown, Boston
Second edition published 1980 by
Blackwell Scientific Publications

Printed in Great Britain at
The Alden Press, Oxford
Bound at Kemp Hall Bindery, Oxford

DISTRIBUTORS

USA
  Blackwell Mosby Book Distributors
  11830 Westline Industrial Drive
  St Louis, Missouri 63141

Canada
  Blackwell Mosby Book Distributors
  120 Melford Drive, Scarborough
  Ontario, M1B 2X4

Australia
  Blackwell Scientific Book
  Distributors
  214 Berkeley Street, Carlton
  Victoria 3053

British Library
Cataloguing in Publication Data

Kune, Gabriel A.
  The practice of biliary surgery—2nd ed.
  1. Biliary tract—Surgery
  I. Title   II. Sali, Avni
    617''.556   RD 546

ISBN 0-632-00589-0

Contents

Associate Contributors

BARRIE J. AARONS MBBS FRACS
Consultant Surgeon, Hamilton Base Hospital, Victoria, Australia

HIRAM BADDELEY MBBS DMRD FRCR
Professor of Radiology, University of Queensland, Australia

H. JOACHIM BURHENNE MD
Professor and Head of Department of Diagnostic Radiology, University of
  British Columbia, Canada

S.T. CHOU MB PhD MRC(Path)
Senior Lecturer in Pathology, University of Melbourne, Australia

SAMUEL C. FITZPATRICK CBE MC MBBS FRACS
Late Consultant Surgeon, Hamilton Base Hospital, Victoria, Australia

JOHN M. HAM MD(Syd) FRACS FACS
Associate Professor of Surgery, University of New South Wales, Australia;
Consultant Surgeon, Prince of Wales Hospital, Sydney, Australia

PETER G. JONES MBMS FRCS FRACS FACS
Consultant Surgeon, Royal Children's Hospital, Melbourne, Australia

TREVOR JONES MBBS FRACS
Senior Lecturer in Surgery, University of Melbourne, Australia;
Consultant Surgeon, Repatriation General Hospital and Western General
Hospital, Melbourne, Australia

CLAUDE LIGUORY MD
Endoscopist, University Department of Surgery, Cochin Hospital, Paris

G.B. ONG FRCS FRACS FACS
Professor of Surgery, University of Hong Kong

IAN C. ROBERTS-THOMSON MD FRACP
Gastroenterologist, Royal Melbourne Hospital, Australia;
Endoscopist, Repatriation General Hospital, Melbourne, Australia

Preface

Biliary tract disease remains the commonest abdominal condition that the surgeon, physician, gastroenterologists, or radiologist encounters. In spite of its frequency the most appropriate form of management of some aspects of biliary disease still poses problems. There remain gaps in our knowledge of the cause, pathogenesis, methods of diagnosis, and the most appropriate form of treatment, whether it be medical or surgical. Surgical treatment has its own special problems because of the relative inaccessibility of the bile ducts, which makes accurate operative diagnosis and the actual surgery technically difficult on occasions. Also, alternative modes of treatment have been advocated for the same condition. The penalty for errors in management remains high in terms of patient mortality and morbidity in biliary disease. Thus the clinician who treats a patient with biliary tract disease needs to have current knowledge of diagnosis, medical and surgical treatment, to recommend correct and safe management.

The aim of this book is to present an up-to-date account of the practice of biliary disease within the limits of our present knowledge, based on scientific evidence rather than on clinical impression and personal bias. The approach of this book is essentially clinical and practical. Biliary tract surgery must be effective yet safe, and therefore special attention has been placed on these aspects of management.

Emphasis has also been given to an evaluation of preoperative and peroperative investigations currently in use. When controversy exists between alternative modes of treatment the available evidence for and against each is presented and this is followed by our appraisal of the most appropriate form of management, so that the reader is given a clear direction to pursue yet on the evidence he can still disagree and choose one of the other alternatives.

Since the writing of the first edition there have been major advances in the diagnosis and treatment of biliary tract conditions and these advances have all been incorporated. Thus ultrasonography, computed tomography, endoscopic retrograde cholangiography, and pancreatography have been important additions to the radiology of the biliary tract. Also, percutaneous transhepatic cholangiography has been improved and made safer and all of these investigations have had a major effect on patients with obstructive jaundice as well as on others with various biliary tract disorders. Enormous advances have been made in the understanding of the secretion of bile under normal and abnormal conditions and this had led to the medical treatment of gallstones by oral methods of gallstone dissolution. The non-operative methods of dealing with bile duct stones, such as endoscopic sphincterotomy and removal of stones overlooked at a previous choledochotomy by extraction through the tube track, are also new and these are described in this edition. Advances in choice of surgery and surgical technique in benign biliary stricture, in biliary tumours, and biliary cysts are also included. The current approach to the prevention and treatment of biliary tract infections has been brought up to date. A number of new chapters have been introduced, written by internationally known experts in the field. This includes a consideration of the diagnosis and treatment of acalculous benign biliary disease, of endoscopic sphincterotomy, of the paediatric aspects of biliary disease and of an assessment of the liver in the presence of biliary disease. Hepatobiliary hydatid disease remains a problem in our country and also in other parts of the world and this has also been introduced as a new chapter.

The references have all been revised and there are now 1700 current references in this edition. Most of these references are recent publications. Many of the illustrations have been revised and 100 new illustrations included, so that there are now 254 illustrations in the second edition.

We hope that this edition will remain to be a valuable book to the practising surgeon, the physician, gastroenterologist, and radiologist. It should be of value also to those who are under the unenviable stresses of study for postgraduate medical, surgical, gastroenterological, or radiological diplomas and degrees.

Melbourne 1980   GABRIEL A. KUNE
                                                                              AVNI SALI

Acknowledgements

I am a part of all that I have met
TENNYSON: *Ulysses*

Many of our colleagues in Australia, England, Europe, North America, South America, and Asia have, over the years, contributed directly or indirectly to this book by sharing with us their clinical material, their stimulating ideas, their research projects and the wisdom of their wide clinical experience in diseases of the biliary tract.

In Melbourne we would like to thank Professor Sir Edward Hughes, Mr. Graham McKenzie, Sir Ian Wood, Mr. Douglas R. Leslie, Mr. Donald G. Macleish, Mr. Robert Marshall, Professor Kenneth J. Hardy, Mr. Phillip Hunt, Professor Vernon Marshall, Professor W. S. C. Hare, Professor R. D. Wright, and Professor Jack Nayman. In Adelaide, Professor Ronald Elmslie, Professor James Watts, and Mr. Anthony Slavotinek, while in Sydney, Professor John Ham, in Brisbane, Professor Lawrie Powell and Mr. Cameron Battersby, have been our soul brothers.

In London, Lord Smith of Marlow, one of the master surgeons of this century, whose friendship has always been a great booster. Professor Hugh Dudley of St. Mary's Hospital and Professor Harold Ellis of Westminster Hospital were our stimulants to the scientific approach, as has been Professor Sir Andrew Kay of Glasgow. In Paris, Professor Maurice Mercadier and Professor Lucien Leger, in Marseille, Professor Henri Sarles and in Strasbourg, Professor Louis Hollender gave us that much-needed Gallic touch. Professor Walter Hess of Zurich has remained a generous and experienced adviser and friend.

In the United States, Dr. Kenneth W. Warren of Boston has had the most profound influence on this book. In this regard we would also like to thank Dr. John W. Braasch of Boston; Dr. William P. Longmire Jr. and Dr. George Berci of Los Angeles; Dr. John L. Madden and Dr. Frank Glenn of New York; Dr. Lawrence W. Way of San Francisco; and Dr. Frank G. Moody of Salt Lake City.

In South America we've had wonderful ties with Professor Clemente Morel, Professor Jose Mainetti, and Professor Emilio Etala of Argentina; Professor Raul Praderi of Uraquay; Professor Fernando Paulino, Professor Jose Hilario and Professor Marcel Machado of Brazil; and Professor Jose Klinger of Chile.

We are delighted to have a galaxy of associate contributors. We thank Mr. Barrie Aarons of Hamilton, Victoria and Professor Hiram Baddeley of Brisbane; Professor Joachim Burhenne of British Columbia, Canada; Dr. S. T. Chou of Melbourne, Australia; Mr. Sam Fitzpatrick of Hamilton, Victoria; Professor John Ham of Sydney; Mr. Peter Jones of Melbourne; Mr. Trevor Jones of Melbourne; Dr. Claude Liguory of Paris; Professor G. B. Ong of Hong Kong and Dr. Ian Roberts-Thomson of Melbourne for their superb contributions.

The new illustrations were again drawn with artistry and skill by Mrs. Patricia Baker (*née* Madden) who also drew the illustrations for the first edition of this book. The radiological illustrations were expertly performed by Mrs. Irene Zalstein, clinical photographer.

The entire manuscript was typed by Mrs. Elaine Downard and Mrs. Pamela Sheehan, our secretaries. We are most grateful for their long hours of painstaking and exacting work.

Our relationship with the publishers has always been most cordial and we appreciate their enthusiasm and advice. In particular, we would like to thank Mr. Peter Jones, Director of Blackwell Scientific Publications, Australia and Mr. Per Saugman, Chairman and Managing Director of Blackwell Scientific Publications.

G.A.K.
A.S.

1. Surgical Anatomy

SEGMENTAL ANATOMY OF THE LIVER

A description of the intrahepatic bile ducts is incomplete without an understanding of the segmental anatomy of the liver, which assumes that the organ consists of a number of relatively independent segments with respect to blood supply and biliary drainage. The bile ducts and the branches of the portal vein and hepatic artery have regular patterns of distribution, and vascular and biliary anastomoses between adjacent segments are minimal [17, 19, 20, 26, 27, 49].

The liver is divided into a functional right lobe and left lobe by the lobar fissure, which extends in a plane from the gallbladder fossa to the fossa for the inferior vena cava (Fig. 1.1). This plane, the principal plane, represents a functional division into two lobes, because all left-sided blood vessels and bile ducts in the porta hepatis supply the liver to the left of this plane, and all right-sided blood vessels and bile ducts supply the liver to the right of this plane. This division provides an important difference from the classic anatomical description, which divides the liver into a left lobe and a right lobe along the plane of attachment of the falciform ligament. The classic description is based on arbitrary external landmarks rather than on function.

Each lobe is further divided into two segments by a segmental fissure which runs in a vertical plane from the front of the liver and is obliquely inclined toward the fossa of the inferior vena cava (Fig. 1.1).

There are thus four principal liver segments—right anterior, right posterior, left medial, and left lateral. The bile duct, portal vein, and hepatic artery radicles associated with these segments bear names corresponding to their segments of supply.

Each of the four liver segments is usually supplied by one principal branch of the hepatic artery and the portal vein, and is drained by one principal bile duct. In some instances more than one branch supplies a liver segment; this is most frequently noted in the distribution of the portal vein. The main blood vessels and bile ducts destined for a particular liver segment usually travel together, forming a 'pedicle' for that segment.

The hepatic venous tributaries eventually drain into three main vessels, the left, the middle, and the right hepatic veins. They do not follow the segmental pattern described above, and they drain adjacent segments as they pass upward toward the inferior vena cava, to open into it at the upper margin of the liver. These veins are intrahepatic for most of their course and lie for the most part in an intersegmental plane (Fig. 1.1).

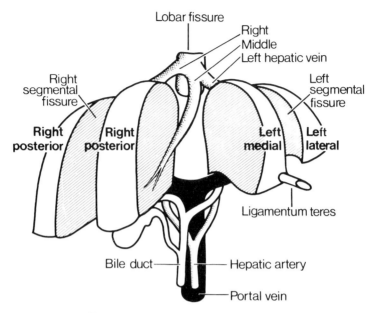

Fig. 1.1. Segmental anatomy of the liver

PROXIMAL BILE DUCTS

The intrahepatic bile ducts and the bile ducts in the porta hepatis are now described within the framework of segmental liver anatomy.

MODE OF UNION OF SEGMENTAL BILE DUCTS

In each segment the small bile ducts join to form one main channel, called the segmental bile duct. Only occasionally are there two such ducts draining one segment. The mode of union of the four segmental bile ducts may vary in different subjects, and this variability is of surgical importance.

FUNCTIONAL LEFT LOBE

The bile ducts which drain the left lobe of the liver unite in one of two ways. In about 75 per cent of cases the left medial and the left lateral segmental bile ducts join to form the left hepatic duct [10, 17, 26, 27]. In approximately 25 per cent of cases more than one duct drains the left medial or the left lateral segment.

Of the greatest significance is that, regardless of the manner of union of the segmental bile ducts, the final common pathway of drainage of the functional left lobe is always a single trunk, the left hepatic duct.

FUNCTIONAL RIGHT LOBE

The biliary drainage of the functional right liver lobe is accomplished in one of two ways (Fig. 1.2). In approximately 75 per cent of cases the right anterior and

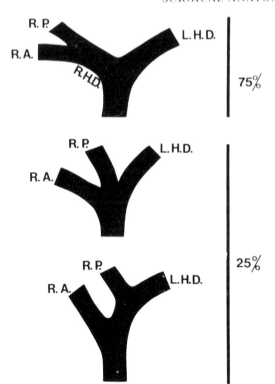

75%

25%

Fig. 1.2. Patterns of union of segmental bile ducts of the right liver lobe. R.A., right anterior bile duct. R.P., right posterior bile duct. R.H.D., right hepatic duct. L.H.D., left hepatic duct. From Kune [27].

the right posterior segmental bile ducts unite to form the right hepatic duct, which then joins the left hepatic duct [10, 17, 26, 27]. In about 25 per cent of cases the right anterior segmental duct does not unite with the right posterior segmental duct. In these, a right hepatic duct does not exist and the two right segmental ducts join the left hepatic duct directly. This may be accomplished as a trifurcation of ducts, or else the right anterior and posterior ducts join the left hepatic duct at separate points. It should be noted that on many cholangiograms the right anterior and right posterior segmental bile ducts *appear* to cross each other, but this is only illusory and due to anteroposterior superimposition of the image (Fig. 1.3).

BILE DUCTS IN THE PORTA HEPATIS

HEPATIC DUCTS
It is important for the surgeon to know how much of the ductal system is outside the liver and thereby surgically accessible (Fig. 1.4). The common hepatic duct is always outside the liver in its entire length. Portions of the left and right hepatic ducts are also extrahepatic, but the length of the extrahepatic segments varies from 1 to 6 cm in different subjects, the majority being from 2 to 4 cm [26, 27]. In some cases small portions of the segmental bile ducts are also outside the liver. In

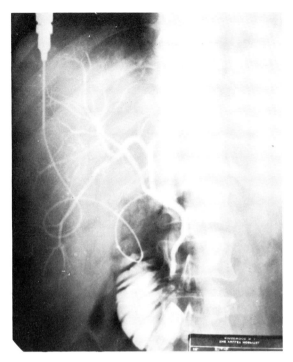

Fig. 1.3. Cholangiogram which *appears* to show that right anterior and right posterior segmental bile ducts cross. This illusion is due to antero-posterior superimposition of the image.

one-quarter of the subjects, in whom a right hepatic duct is not present, parts of the right anterior and right posterior bile ducts are always extrahepatic.

In most cases the hepatic ducts unite close to their exit from the liver. A relatively long extrahepatic course of the left and right ducts and, therefore, a low point of formation of the common hepatic duct is uncommon, but such an arrangement does predispose to duct injury during cholecystectomy.

COMMON HEPATIC DUCT

In almost all subjects the entire length of the common hepatic duct is outside the liver. The length of the duct is determined by the point of cystic duct entry, and is thus extremely variable. The average diameter of the common hepatic duct is 8 mm and the range in different subjects is 4–15 mm [8, 10].

RELATION TO HEPATIC ARTERY AND PORTAL VEIN

The mode of branching and relationship of the hepatic artery, portal vein, and bile ducts in the porta hepatis is so variable that a so-called normal arrangement cannot be described [26]. However, a number of surgically useful generalisations may be made.

The hepatic artery usually divides into its terminal branches well below the point of formation of the common hepatic duct (Fig. 1.5). The hepatic artery branches may be anterior, lateral, or posterior to the bile ducts.

The terminal branches of the portal vein, that is, the left and right main trunks, are at their origin posterior to the bile ducts. In most cases the common hepatic duct is formed at approximately the same level as the point of division of the portal vein. In the majority of cases the left branch of the portal vein turns forward after a short course to the left, thereby hiding the proximal part of the left hepatic duct.

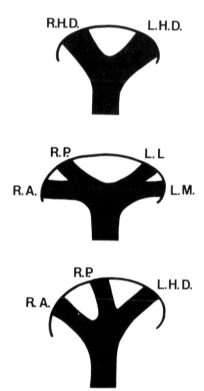

Fig. 1.4. Bile ducts which may be found outside the liver in different subjects. R.H.D., right hepatic duct. L.H.D., left hepatic duct. R.A., right anterior bile duct. R.P., right posterior bile duct. L.L., left lateral bile duct. L.M., left medial bile duct. From Kune [27].

SURGICAL IMPLICATIONS

The concept of lobar and segmental liver structure has had considerable influence on liver surgery, especially on the development of planned lobar and segmental liver resections, but this subject is outside the scope of the present book.

The relatively constant distribution of the intrahepatic segmental bile ducts is of obvious importance in the interpretation of operative cholangiograms when gallstones, strictures, infections, and tumours are present in the liver [26, 27]. Thus, absence of filling or the presence of a filling defect may be seen in a segmental or in a hepatic duct, which may be of diagnostic value.

The ducts that are relatively easy to expose surgically are the common hepatic duct, the right hepatic duct, and the distal portion of the left hepatic duct. The proximal part of the left hepatic duct is frequently hidden by the pars umbilica portion of the left portal vein, from which it needs to be separated [21, 26, 27]. The branches of the hepatic artery may overlie these ducts, but they can be separated by dissection (Fig. 1.5). Following their exposure the correct identification of bile ducts in the porta hepatis may be of utmost importance in certain operations. For example, in major segmental or lobar liver resections the bile ducts must be precisely identified to ensure that the correct duct is ligated [26]. Identification is best performed by a combination of dissection and operative cholangiography.

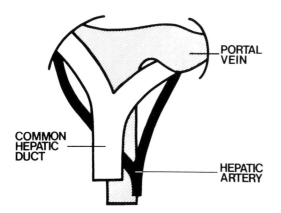

Fig. 1.5. Common type of relationship of the bile ducts, hepatic artery, and portal vein at the porta hepatis. Considerable variation exists in different subjects.

ACCESSORY AND ABERRANT BILE DUCTS

An understanding of so-called accessory and aberrant bile ducts is crucial in biliary surgery. The most important consideration is the recognition and, thereby, the prevention of injury during surgery to bile ducts which have an unusual course.

The vast early literature, particularly before 1950, showing accessory or aberrant bile ducts in anatomical dissections, or in operated cases, has been shown to be almost entirely unreliable by all recent studies. The recognition of segmental bile duct structure, a knowledge of the considerable normal variation in bile duct branching, the consistent use of cholangiography and improvement in anaesthesia allowing meticulous operative dissection, have all helped to reshape this subject completely.

IN PRACTICE SIX TYPES OF BILE DUCT NEED TO BE CONSIDERED

1. Accessory hepatic ducts.
2. Hepatic duct entering cystic duct.
3. Hepatic duct entering gallbladder (cholecystohepatic ducts).
4. Subvesical duct.
5. Cystic duct entering hepatic duct (see p. 14).
6. Absent cystic duct (see p. 17).

ACCESSORY HEPATIC DUCTS

The literature is abundant with reports of so-called accessory hepatic ducts. Thus, in a series of over 1000 cadaveric dissections collected from the early literature an accessory hepatic duct was noted in about 10 per cent of subjects. Most were described as accessory right hepatic ducts. In the majority of these reports a duct was termed accessory if it did not conform to the particular author's concept of 'normality', yet it is now known that the modes of union of hepatic bile ducts are variable and a single 'normal' pattern cannot be described. The area of drainage of these reported 'accessory' ducts in most cases was not determined, nor was it shown that a duct termed accessory was in fact additional to another duct draining the same area of the liver.

In all recent studies which recognise the segmental concept of liver structure so-called accessory hepatic ducts were not found [17, 21, 26, 27]. The type of arrangement, in the past called an accessory hepatic duct, usually corresponds to those cases in which the right hepatic duct is not formed. This arrangement is present in about one-quarter of all normal subjects. In these cases the surgeon encounters three ducts issuing from the liver—the left hepatic duct, the right anterior bile duct, and the right posterior bile duct, and he calls one of these an 'accessory' duct (Fig. 1.6). This error is more likely to occur if the ducts have a long extrahepatic course.

Such ducts, therefore, should *not* be called either accessory or aberrant.

If the surgeon encounters more than two ducts issuing from the liver on no account should he divide or ligate any of them, assuming it to be an 'accessory' duct, because serious consequences of cholangitis, jaundice, or biliary fistula will follow.

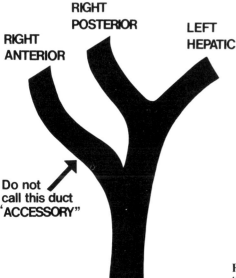

RIGHT POSTERIOR

RIGHT ANTERIOR

LEFT HEPATIC

Do not call this duct "ACCESSORY"

Fig. 1.6. When three ducts issue from the liver, one has been incorrectly called an accessory duct in the past.

Uncommonly, the right hepatic duct or the right anterior bile duct (rarely the right posterior) may have a long extrahepatic course and may become closely related to the cystic duct. In these, the involved duct is in danger of injury during cholecystectomy (Fig. 1.7). Again, the surgeon should not term such a hepatic duct aberrant or accessory, and on no account should he ligate or divide it.

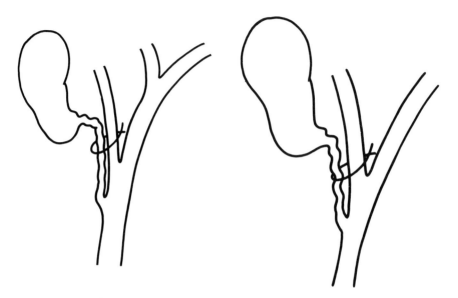

Fig. 1.7. (*left*) Right anterior bile duct close to cystic duct. (*right*) Right hepatic duct close to cystic duct. These ducts are not accessory nor aberrant; both are in danger of injury during cholecystectomy.

HEPATIC DUCTS ENTERING CYSTIC DUCT

Do hepatic ducts of any significant size ever join the cystic duct (Fig. 1.8)? Clearly, this might be important if such a situation were encountered during cholecystectomy. Instances of hepatic ducts entering the cystic duct have been described both in cadaveric specimens and at operation. It was noted in six of the 1200 dissections mentioned earlier, and individual reports of this in dissections or at operation were found in another eight cases. Thus, genuine examples of this arrangement are rare, but well-documented cases have been described [15, 46].

Some of these cases were associated with gallstones as well as fibrosis and induration of the porta hepatis. In some the anatomy of the bile ducts was not always accurately displayed, and also the gallstones may have obliterated or eroded the duct system [65]. In other cases it is possible that in fact the cystic duct joined the hepatic duct, and not the reverse.

The only sure way of recognising the cystic duct at operation in these instances is by its characteristic convoluted cholangiographic picture of the valves of Heister, in contrast to the smooth outline of a hepatic duct. During cholecystectomy if a hepatic duct is found to join the cystic duct the cystic duct should be ligated proximal to the entry of the hepatic duct.

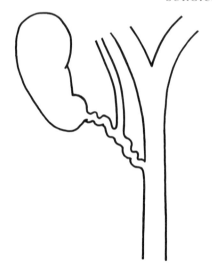

Fig. 1.8. A right-sided hepatic duct opening into the cystic duct. This is rare.

HEPATIC DUCTS ENTERING GALLBLADDER (CHOLECYSTOHEPATIC DUCTS)
Do hepatic ducts of significant size ever enter the gallbladder? In the past large cholecystohepatic ducts were occasionally reported to have been found during the course of anatomic dissections, but in careful recent series no ducts of this kind were seen [13, 17, 21, 26, 27, 35]. Nevertheless, a number of well-documented instances of cholecystohepatic ducts have been found during cholecystectomy [23, 48, 65]. The outstanding feature of these cases is the presence of one or more large gallstones in the gallbladder, as well as induration and fibrosis of the porta hepatis. This suggests that the condition is not congenital but acquired secondarily to erosion and obliteration of the bile ducts by the gallstones and by recurrent attacks of cholecystitis. Very rarely all the hepatic ducts drain into the gallbladder without ever forming a common hepatic duct and then the gallbladder acts as a cistern from which arises the common bile duct [14, 41]. Should sizeable bile ducts of this type be present during cholecystectomy injury to these should not occur if the surgeon follows the rules of careful anatomical dissection as described in the section which deals with the technique of cholecystectomy.

SUBVESICAL DUCT
The subvesical duct is a slender bile duct 1 to 2 mm in diameter which is occasionally seen emerging from the liver in the gallbladder fossa; it passes toward the liver hilum to join the common hepatic or right hepatic duct (Fig. 1.9). A duct of this kind was seen by Healey and Schroy [17] in 35 per cent of their dissections, by Hobsley [21] in 50 per cent, and by Kune [26, 27] in 20 per cent.

In embryology this duct is called the duct of Luschka. It is probably an intrahepatic bile duct which comes to the surface of the liver due to the relative atrophy of liver tissue in the gallbladder fossa during development [38]. Unfortunately, these ducts are still described in some reports as accessory bile ducts [2, 14].

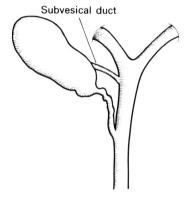

Fig. 1.9. Course of the subvesical duct.

Inadvertent division of this duct during cholecystectomy may be responsible for temporary postoperative drainage of bile from the drain tube, but persistent biliary fistulas or other disastrous consequences of this accident have not been reported. Nevertheless, the presence of this duct in a high proportion of cases and its risky situation in the gallbladder fossa adds emphasis to the need for routine drainage following cholecystectomy. It is probable that some subvesical ducts that were divided during cholecystectomy had been mistaken in the past for examples of cholecystohepatic ducts.

SUMMARY

The term *accessory bile duct* should not be used when more than two large ducts issue from the liver hilum. These ducts are never truly 'accessory' and represent merely one pattern of confluence of the duct system. Whenever these ducts are closely related to the cystic duct they are in danger of injury during cholecystectomy, but they should never be ligated or divided.

Hepatic ducts only very occasionally enter the cystic duct and many of these are probably secondary to erosion and obliteration of the bile ducts by gallstones, rather than congenital aberrations. Large cholecystohepatic ducts are rare and many of these are also secondary to erosion and obliteration of the bile ducts by gallstones.

The slender subvesical duct is frequently present. Because it lies in the gallbladder fossa it may be inadvertently divided during cholecystectomy; this accident may be responsible for temporary postoperative drainage of bile from the drain tube.

The cystic duct entering the right hepatic duct is an uncommon, but normal variant (p. 14). Absence of the cystic duct is rare, and usually secondary to obliteration of the cystic duct by a large gallstone (p. 17).

Almost all of these unusual bile duct arrangements can be recognised during surgery by following the rules of meticulous anatomical dissection and thus preventing the tragedy of an operative bile duct injury.

GALLBLADDER

The gallbladder is an elongated saccular organ with a rounded fundus. The fundus is frequently visible below the margin of the liver. In most patients the surface marking of the fundus is approximately at the junction of the ninth right costal cartilage with the lateral border of the right rectus abdominis muscle. When the gallbladder dilates the fundus is frequently palpable as a rounded superficial swelling, moving downward and slightly inward on respiration.

The body of the gallbladder is found in a groove on the undersurface of the liver as it runs upward and backward, covered by a layer of parietal peritoneum. The body of the gallbladder then leaves the undersurface of the liver and narrows in calibre. Because at this point it has lost its attachment to the liver and is merely enclosed by the two layers of the parietal peritoneum it becomes slightly lax and droopy and is called the infundibulum. When this part is distended by a calculus it forms a pouch-like structure referred to as Hartmann's pouch. The cystic duct issues from the infundibulum. At the junction of the cystic duct and infundibulum the peritoneal covering turns downward to form the free edge of the lesser omentum (Fig. 1.10).

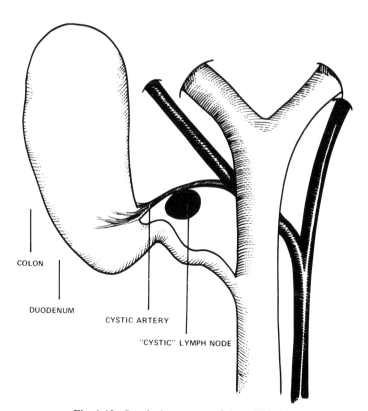

COLON

DUODENUM

CYSTIC ARTERY

"CYSTIC" LYMPH NODE

Fig. 1.10. Surgical anatomy of the gallbladder.

BLOOD SUPPLY AND LYMPHATICS

In the majority of cases (about 80 per cent) the cystic artery is a single trunk which arises from the right hepatic artery and passes to the gallbladder above and behind the cystic duct. In approximately 20 per cent of subjects the cystic artery has an uncommon site of origin or an unusual course, or both [34]. Thus, it may arise from the left hepatic or even from the superior mesenteric artery. In a number of instances the cystic artery crosses in front of the common hepatic duct or even the common bile duct. Two cystic arteries are not uncommon, but three are rare.

In some cases, usually in elderly arteriosclerotic subjects, the right hepatic artery forms a 'loop' toward the neck of the gallbladder (Fig. 1.11). If this situation is unrecognised during cholecystectomy the artery can be inadvertently ligated or damaged, resulting in torrential operative haemorrhage.

A lack of appreciation of the possible variations in the number, origin, and course of the cystic artery may be responsible for unexpected bleeding during cholecystectomy, and the inexpert handling of such an accident may cause an injury of the bile ducts. (See Operative bile duct injuries—post-traumatic biliary strictures, Chapter 6.)

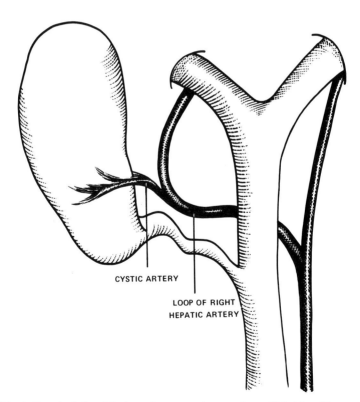

CYSTIC ARTERY

LOOP OF RIGHT
HEPATIC ARTERY

Fig. 1.11. A 'loop' of the right hepatic artery close to the gallbladder. The artery is in danger of injury during cholecystectomy.

Most of the venous return is by small veins which enter the liver directly, but it is not uncommon to find a cystic vein which passes with the cystic artery into the portal vein or into the right branch of the portal vein.

The gallbladder lymphatics drain to the lymph glands alongside the common bile duct near the gastroduodenal artery. Some of the lymphatics pass through a gland situated above the cystic duct, in relation to the cystic artery, and occasionally referred to as the cystic lymph node (Fig. 1.10). Eventually, the lymphatic drainage of the gallbladder is to the coeliac lymph nodes.

RELATIONS OF THE GALLBLADDER

The undersurface of the body of the gallbladder is usually in close relation to the hepatic flexure, and the infundibulum (Hartmann's pouch) is closely related to the duodenum (Fig. 1.10). Occasionally, gallstones are responsible for perforation of Hartmann's pouch and the creation of an internal fistula, which is usually into the duodenum but can also be into the colon.

VARIANTS AND ANOMALIES

Many of the variants and anomalies of the gallbladder are rare and have little surgical importance and will not be considered here.

PHRYGIAN CAP DEFORMITY
Phrygian cap deformity is a folding of the fundus, giving rise to a characteristic radiologic appearance. It has been estimated to be present in about 18 per cent of normal gallbladders, and is not regarded as an abnormality, nor as a cause of symptoms.

HARTMANN'S POUCH
This is a pouch-like dilatation of the infundibulum, usually seen in the presence of gallstones and thought to be an acquired condition secondary to the lodgement of stones in the infundibulum of the gallbladder.

A large Hartmann's pouch may wrap itself around the lateral side of the common bile duct and, if there is a good deal of induration or fibrosis in the area, this may cause difficulties during cholecystectomy. Very occasionally, a large gallstone in Hartmann's pouch may be responsible for recurrent episodes of inflammation and obliteration of the cystic duct. This condition is described later in this chapter (see Fig. 1.16).

INTRAHEPATIC GALLBLADDER
Rarely, the gallbladder fossa is so deep that the liver almost completely surrounds the gallbladder. In these cases cholecystectomy may be accompanied by considerable bleeding from the liver; excision should be carried out as close as possible to the gallbladder in order to minimise haemorrhage.

GALLBALDDER ON A MESENTERY

The gallbladder may hang below the liver by a definite mesentery formed by the peritoneum which normally attaches it to the undersurface of the liver. When such a gallbladder becomes dilated a lump may be felt clinically in an unusual position, such as in the left iliac fossa. Cholecystectomy in these cases is usually a very simple technical exercise.

Torsion of the gallbladder can occur when the organ is on a mesentery of this kind [1, 5]. Very rarely, the gallbladder has no mesentery and no peritoneal attachment to the liver; then it is particularly mobile and liable to torsion.

DOUBLE GALLBLADDER

A true double gallbladder with its own cystic duct is a rare congenital anomaly, and only about 50 cases have been described. Some reputed cases are probably congenital or acquired bile-duct cysts or diverticula (Chapter 8).

ABSENT GALLBLADDER

Absence of the gallbladder is a rare anomaly [11, 51]. It is one of the rare causes of nonvisualisation of the gallbladder on cholecystography and on intravenous cholangiography (Chapter 3).

CYSTIC DUCT

The cystic duct arises from the infundibulum of the gallbladder and when there is a Hartmann's pouch, the duct originates from the upper and left aspect of the pouch. The lumen of the duct is from 2 to 3 mm, though this is variable in different subjects. The mucosa, especially in its proximal part, is thrown into a number of folds known as the valves of Heister, and these produce a characteristic appearance in cholangiograms.

The length and course of the cystic duct, as well as its site and mode of union with the common hepatic duct, are extremely variable. This variability makes it a structure of utmost importance during cholecystectomy.

SITE OF UNION

The cystic duct usually joins the common hepatic duct at some point of its course in the gastrohepatic omentum (Fig. 1.12). This site of union is present in about 80 per cent of subjects [35, 40]. In about 20 per cent the cystic duct joins the bile duct in its retroduodenal or retropancreatic portion.

In about 1 per cent of subjects the cystic duct opens into the right hepatic duct [2, 27]. This may be of significance if met during cholecystectomy, because the right hepatic duct may not be correctly identified. In such cases the right hepatic duct may be inadvertently divided if the left hepatic duct is mistaken for the common hepatic ducts (Fig. 1.13). There is only one recorded case of the cystic duct opening into the left hepatic duct [64].

Independent entry of the cystic duct into the duodenum has been described,

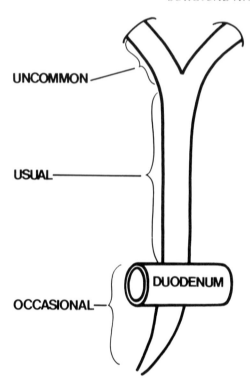

UNCOMMON

USUAL

DUODENUM

OCCASIONAL

Fig. 1.12. Various sites of union of the cystic duct with the bile duct.

but it has never been found in any series of anatomic dissections, and the site of entry must therefore be extremely rare [61].

MODE OF UNION

The mode of union of the cystic duct with the common hepatic duct may be described as angular, parallel, or spiral (Fig. 1.14).

ANGULAR UNION
In angular union the cystic duct approaches the bile duct at an angle and joins it; the angle subtended between the two is dependent on the site of the union. Angular union is the most common arrangement, and in a series of 1000 dissections it was noted in about 75 per cent of instances [26, 27, 40].

PARALLEL UNION
In parallel union the cystic duct approaches the bile duct at an angle, but travels more or less parallel with the common hepatic duct for a variable distance before joining it. A connective tissue sheath commonly surrounds the two ducts over this distance. This arrangement was noted in approximately 20 per cent of the dissections described above.

Parallel mode of union of the cystic duct was brought into prominence in

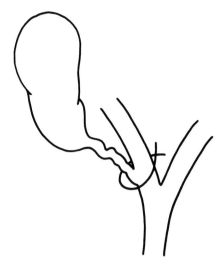

Fig. 1.13. Mode of injury of right hepatic duct during cholecystectomy if the cystic duct opens into it.

relation to operative injuries of the bile ducts by Warren, McDonald, and Kune (1966). In a review of a large series of patients with operative injuries of the bile ducts it was found that in a number the injury occurred when a clamp was applied to the cystic duct, when it was running parallel with the common hepatic duct, and when it had been incompletely mobilised (Fig. 1.15).

SPIRAL UNION
In spiral union the cystic duct approaches the bile duct at an angle and then spirals around it to open at a lower level on its posterior or posteromedial surface. This is the least common arrangement and was seen in about 5 per cent of the dissections. The cholangiogram of a gallstone in the spiral part of the cystic duct can be mistaken for a stone in the common bile duct. Also, those who advocate at cholecystectomy 'flush' ligation of the cystic duct at a point where it joins the bile duct would find this procedure difficult and dangerous. Luckily, 'flush' ligation is quite unnecessary.

ANGULAR   **PARALLEL**   **SPIRAL**

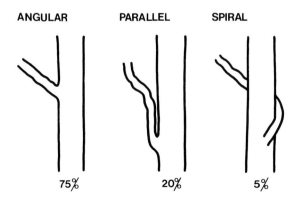

75%   20%   5%

Fig. 1.14. Various modes of union of the cystic duct with the bile duct, and their frequency. From Kune [27].

Fig. 1.15. Possible mechanism of bile duct injury with parallel union of the cystic duct. Clamp applied to the incompletely mobilised cystic duct also includes the adjacent common hepatic duct.

ANOMALIES

ABSENT CYSTIC DUCT

Absence of the cystic duct, which results in the gallbladder opening directly into the bile duct, was not encountered in any of the approximately 1000 anatomic dissections mentioned earlier, though more recently one such case has been described [41]. However, an absent cystic duct has been encountered by the authors on several occasions and cases have been reported by others [3, 4, 48, 58, 60, 65].

In all the reported cases a large gallstone was situated in Hartmann's pouch, and induration and fibrosis of the porta hepatis were noted (Fig. 1.16). It may be

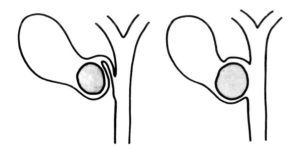

Fig. 1.16. Absent cystic duct. Probable development of this acquired condition is shown. (*left*) Large gallstone in Hartmann's pouch, occluding cystic duct. (*right*) Cystic duct obliterated, resulting in cholecystocholedochal fistula.

assumed that the cystic duct is obliterated and becomes fibrotic by repeated episodes of acute cholecystitis. At the same time the gallstone erodes part of Hartmann's pouch and the adjacent bile duct, resulting in a new opening, in effect a cholecystocholedochal connection. Absence of the cystic duct, with a gallstone overlying the bile duct and the presence of fibrosis and induration of the area, can clearly be a predisposing factor to a bile duct injury during cholecystectomy.

DOUBLE CYSTIC DUCT

Double cystic duct was not encountered in any of the 1000 dissections. A case was described by Milroy in 1947, but the condition must be extremely rare. When the surgeon encounters a situation in which he believes there are two cystic ducts he must be absolutely certain that the second duct is not a hepatic duct running in close relationship with the cystic duct. Far too many letters from surgeons referring cases of operative bile duct injury describe 'a double cystic duct', one of which eventually turns out to be part of the common hepatic duct!

COMMON BILE DUCT

The common bile duct is formed by the union of the common hepatic and cystic ducts and passes down in the free edge of the gastrohepatic omentum and then behind the first part of the duodenum to reach the dorsal aspect of the pancreas. It lies to the right of the hepatic artery and in front of the portal vein. The free edge of the gastrohepatic omentum forms the anterior margin of the aditus of the lesser sac and, therefore, the supraduodenal portion of the common bile duct is readily accessible surgically for palpation and exploration.

The arterial blood supply of the bile duct is by a number of fine vessels arising from the major vessels nearby, and especially from the retroduodenal and gastroduodenal arteries below and from the left and right hepatic arteries above. Very little of the blood supply comes from the trunk of the common hepatic artery, as was previously supposed [7, 43, 44]. Recent work by Northover indicates that the supraduodenal duct is supplied by these small vessels running axially, often along the lateral borders of the bile duct [43]. Often also there is a vessel arising from the coeliac axis or the superior mesenteric artery supplying the back of the supraduodenal bile duct [43]. Damage to this blood supply may be an explanation of the unusual long stricture which can rarely follow bile duct surgery and this may also be the explanation of some of the bile duct problems and strictures which have followed human liver transplantation.

The venous return is to the portal vein via an epicholedochal venous plexus, which has been described as an aid to the identification of the choledochus during operation [52]. These veins can also cause annoying oozing during bile duct surgery.

There are usually a number of lymph glands adjacent to the common bile duct, which eventually drain the lymph to the coeliac glands. One relatively large node is near the upper margin of the pancreas, behind the duodenum, on the

posteroinferior aspect of the gastrohepatic omentum (Fig. 1.17). The common
bile duct is almost always superomedial to this lymph gland in the gastrohepatic
omentum. This gland was termed the common duct gland by Cattell, because it
was an accurate guide to the position of the distal bile duct [6].

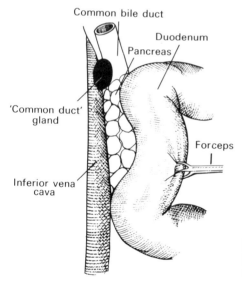

Fig. 1.17. The 'common duct' lymph
gland and its relationship to the bile duct
and pancreas.

WIDTH OF THE SUPRADUODENAL COMMON BILE DUCT

The diameter of the normal common bile duct varies considerably in different
subjects. Thus, direct measurement in 100 post-mortem specimens by Dowdy
and co-workers in 1962 showed the range to be 4 to 13 mm. Kune measured the
width of the supraduodenal common bile duct in 50 post-mortem specimens after
distending the duct at a physiologic pressure, and found that the diameter varied
from 5 to 13 mm [24]. Thus, a bile duct about 13 or 14 mm in diameter is still
within the range of normality. In 100 autopsies Mahour and co-workers found
that the average diameter of the normal bile duct increases with age in both men
and women [32].

Abnormal dilatation of the common bile duct is generally regarded as
important evidence of a pathologic condition within the duct, such as gallstones.
In this regard the observations of Leslie are particularly interesting, for he
meticulously measured the width of the flattened supraduodenal common bile
duct in over 200 operations on the biliary tract and related this to the operative
findings. He found a great variation in the width of normal ducts and an even
greater variation in the width of ducts which contained stones or other forms of
obstruction. There was some overlap between the diameters of normal and
abnormal ducts. Thus, if the width of the duct was less than 9 mm it never
contained a pathologic condition; with widths between 9 and 17 mm a pathologic
condition was sometimes present, and with widths over 17 mm there was almost

always a pathologic condition. The probability that the duct was abnormal was found to rise steeply in ducts over 14 mm in diameter. Ferris and Vibert in 1959 seem to be the only other workers who directly measured the width of the duct at operation, and their findings agree in principle with those of Leslie.

COMMON BILE DUCT GROOVE OF THE PANCREAS

The bile duct passes behind the first part of the duodenum and approaches the second part obliquely as it lies on the dorsal aspect of the pancreas. The duct lies in a groove, called the common bile duct groove of the pancreas [8, 24, 31]. In some cases the bile duct is bare of pancreatic tissue posteriorly as it lies in the groove, but in others there is a thin tongue of pancreas arising from the left edge of the groove which covers the bile duct to a variable extent (Fig. 1.18). When there is a tongue of pancreas covering the bile duct a cleavage plane is almost always present, which allows palpation of this groove from the right side.

With some practice the common bile duct groove may be palpated at operation as shown in Fig. 1.19 [24, 31]. The common bile duct itself cannot be felt, but

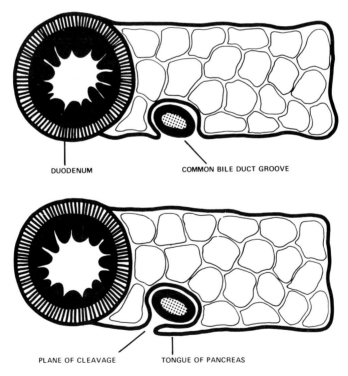

Fig. 1.18. Common bile duct groove of the pancreas. (*top*) Bile duct groove bare of pancreatic tissue posteriorly. (*bottom*) Bile-duct groove partly covered by tongue of pancreas. Modified from Kune [24].

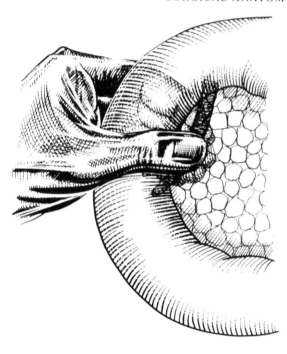

Fig. 1.19. Method of palpation at operation of the common bile duct groove of the pancreas. Modified from Lytle [31].

gallstones lying in this part of the duct may be felt between fingers and thumb. In difficult and doubtful cases this method of palpation is facilitated by division of the peritoneum lateral to the second part of the duodenum and mobilisation of the duodenum and head of the pancreas.

RELATION OF THE COMMON BILE DUCT TO DUODENUM

The common bile duct approaches the second part of the duodenum obliquely and then, before piercing the duodenum, the bile duct comes into close relation with its side wall, so that the two structures run side by side (Fig. 1.28). Over this segment there is no intervening pancreatic tissue and the duodenum and bile duct are separated merely by a layer of connective tissue. The length over which this close relation between the bile duct and duodenum is maintained is variable in different subjects; the range was found to be between 8 and 22 mm [24].

This close relationship between the two structures is the basis of internal choledochoduodenostomy first advocated by Kocher in 1895. This is a transduodenal method of removal of a gallstone impacted in the lower end of the common bile duct by making an anterior duodenotomy and then dividing the duodenal wall posteromedially over the palpable stone. This technique is now not commonly used; most surgeons prefer to remove such a stone through a sphincterotomy incision. Nevertheless, the intimate relationship outside the duodenum between the bile duct and the duodenal wall is comforting for the surgeon performing a transduodenal sphincterotomy, for he may safely extend upward his sphincterotomy incision beyond the intraduodenal part of the sphincter of Oddi without fear of creating a hole in the duodenum, or in the common bile duct.

NARROW PORTION OF DISTAL COMMON BILE DUCT

The external diameter of the bile duct in any one subject is fairly uniform along its entire length. In a few subjects there is a gradual tapering of the lumen from above downward, giving the common bile duct a long, cone-shaped appearance, though in most subjects the lumen of the duct is uniform until just outside its point of entry through the duodenum. The lumen narrows abruptly just proximal to this point and this is associated with a corresponding thickening of its wall, as shown in Fig. 1.20 [16, 22, 24, 27, 55].

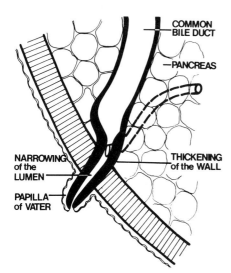

Fig. 1.20. Anatomy of the distal common bile duct. Note the narrow lumen and thick wall of its most distal portion.

The width of this narrow segment varies in different individuals and, as will be seen later, also varies during the various phases of action of the sphincter of Oddi, but it is never wider than the proximal bile duct. The length of this narrow segment varies considerably in different individuals; Hand in 1963 found the range to be 11 to 27 mm, while Kune found a range of 7 to 38 mm [24, 27].

The distal bile duct has a characteristic cholangiographic picture due to this abrupt narrowing of its most distal segment (Fig. 1.21). It should be noted, however, that when a large quantity of dye has already entered the duodenum this narrow distal segment may become obscured.

The thickening that corresponds to this narrow segment is caused by the presence of muscle fibres and connective tissue. This is part of the sphincteric mechanism of the bile duct, known as the sphincter of Oddi; its function is discussed in the section on physiology (Chapter 2).

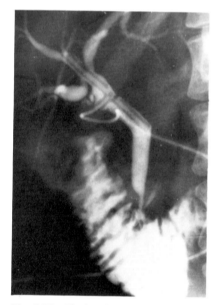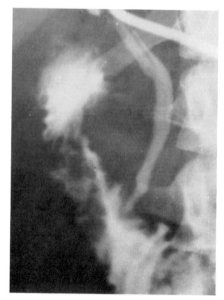

Fig. 1.21. Cholangiograms which show the abrupt narrowing of the lumen of the lower end of the common bile duct. (*left*) Narrowing is eccentric. (*right*) Narrowing symmetrical.

Thus, when a cholangiogram shows a narrow distal bile duct, this in itself should not be interpreted as evidence of biliary tract obstruction, stricture formation, or stenosis, as this is the normal appearance.

When gallstones are arrested in the lower end of the bile duct they are usually just proximal to this narrow segment rather than within it, as is sometimes supposed (Fig. 1.22).

Occasionally, the lumen of this narrow segment has an eccentric position in relation to the wide proximal portion, as seen in the cholangiogram in Fig. 1.23. This may be responsible for difficulties in negotiating the distal common bile duct with probes and other instruments during an exploration of the duct. Mechanical obstruction, such as a gallstone, may be diagnosed in error under these circumstances. An eccentric opening of the narrow distal segment may also be responsible for a false passage, produced when the surgeon is unable to find the lumen of the narrow segment with a probe.

In a number of instances localised dilatation of the common bile duct has been noted just proximal to the narrow segment, producing something which resembles a pouch or a diverticulum [16, 22, 24, 25]. The pouches are more common on the duodenal side of the bile duct and are accentuated by a rise of intraductal pressure (Fig. 1.24). These pouches are of considerable surgical interest, and a number of cases have been described in which gallstones have lodged in them [25]. In some of these, large gallstones have been overlooked at operation, probably because the instruments used to demonstrate their presence slipped past the gallstones (Fig. 1.25). An operative cholangiogram is most helpful in the diagnosis of gallstones lodged in such diverticula [25].

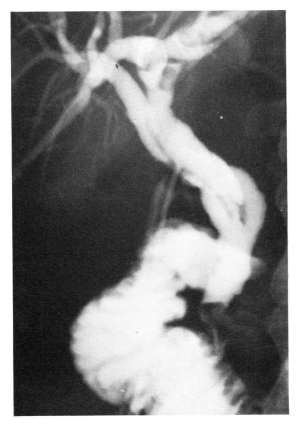

Fig. 1.22. Cholangiogram showing a gallstone arrested just above the narrow distal segment of the bile duct.

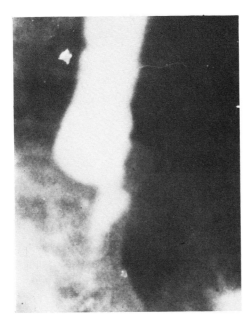

Fig. 1.23. Cholangiogram showing eccentric opening of the narrow distal portion of the common bile duct.

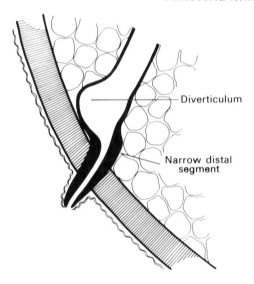

Fig. 1.24. Diverticulum produced just proximal to the narrow distal segment of the common bile duct. Modified from Kune [24].

RELATION OF PANCREATIC DUCT OF WIRSUNG TO COMMON BILE DUCT

The main pancreatic duct, or duct of Wirsung, passes transversely to the right through the body and neck of the pancreas, then turns sharply downward and approaches the distal common bile duct as it lies in the common bile duct groove of the pancreas for a distance which varies in different subjects, but which is

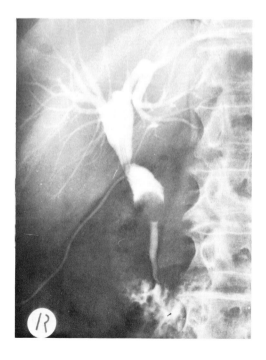

Fig. 1.25. Cholangiogram of a large gallstone arrested in a diverticulum of the lower common bile duct. Note that the narrow distal segment is particularly long. From Kune [25].

about 1–2 cm, and the two ducts run almost side by side, though the pancreatic duct is still more transverse in its direction.

Thus, probing of the pancreatic duct through the duodenal papilla is best done in the direction of the common bile duct. When a fine probe is placed into the papilla of Vater through the duodenum it will spontaneously pass into the pancreatic duct in 80 per cent of instances in which a common channel exists between the two ducts. Similarly, it is technically easier to perform an endoscopic retrograde cannulation of the pancreatic duct than of the common bile duct.

In the majority of cases the pancreatic duct joins the common bile duct to form a common channel (Fig. 1.26). In a series of 540 cases collected from the

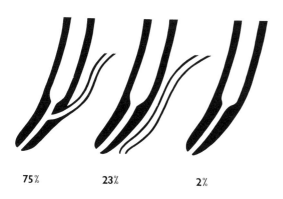

75%   **23%**   **2%**

Fig. 1.26. Various relationships between the common bile duct and the main pancreatic duct, and their frequency. (*left*) A common channel is present. (*centre*) Independent entry of the pancreatic duct into the duodenum. (*right*) Pancreatic duct of Wirsung absent. Replaced by duct of Santorini.

literature a common channel was present in approximately 75 per cent [8, 16, 22, 24, 36, 59]. The length of this common channel is variable, ranging from 1 to 20 mm. When a common channel is present the pancreatic duct joins the common bile duct at its thickened narrow terminal portion and almost always has a posteromedial relation to it (Fig. 1.27). Only very rarely does the main pancreatic duct open anteriorly or laterally into the common bile duct.

This constant relationship between the two ducts, when there is a common terminal channel, is the premise upon which the operation of transduodenal sphincterotomy rests. In this procedure the roof of the duodenal papilla is divided in order not to damage the main pancreatic duct, which opens into the bile duct posteromedially.

In a number of cases the main pancreatic duct runs by the side of the common bile duct, but does not join it, and it has a separate opening on the duodenal papilla (see Fig. 1.26, centre). In the series of 540 cases, reviewed from the literature, this situation was present in about 23 per cent of subjects. In about 2 per cent a pancreatic duct of Wirsung was not present (see Fig. 1.26, right). In these, the duct of Santorini entirely replaced the duct of Wirsung.

PAPILLA OF VATER

SITE OF TERMINATION

The major duodenal papilla is situated on the medial or posteromedial side of the

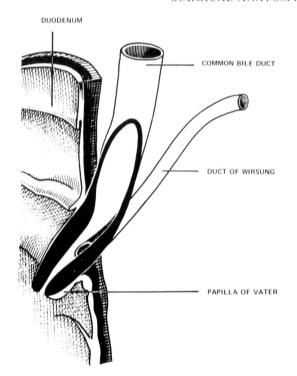

DUODENUM

COMMON BILE DUCT

DUCT OF WIRSUNG

PAPILLA OF VATER

Fig. 1.27. Relationship of the distal common bile duct to the pancreatic duct in the presence of a common channel. Note that the pancreatic duct joins the bile duct at its thickened narrow distal portion.

duodenum. In approximately 95 per cent of subjects the duodenal papilla is located in the midportion, or the distal half of the descending duodenum, as shown in Fig. 1.28 [8, 29]. In about 5 per cent it is found in the third part of the duodenum, although the figure varies according to the mode of investigation [29, 45]. It is also important to remember that with only a little rotation of the duodenal C the bile duct is found to terminate in the proximal part of the third part of the duodenum. It is wrong to speak of an 'anomalous location' of the papilla of Vater under these circumstances and the authors prefer to call it an uncommon, but normal variant. However, the papilla opening into the stomach or the pylorus is a rarity and termination in the first part of the duodenum is also most uncommon [47, 63].

When the surgeon wishes to explore the papilla of Vater, but is uncertain of its position, he should commence the duodenotomy incision in the middle of the descending duodenum, and carry it distally, and this is the position in which the papilla will be found in 95 per cent of cases. The commonest error in performing this procedure is that the duodenotomy incision is made far too proximally.

APPEARANCE OF THE PAPILLA

The major duodenal papilla is a smooth elevation on the duodenal mucosa; it contains the terminal portions of the common bile duct and pancreatic duct of Wirsung, either jointly as a common channel, or running independently.

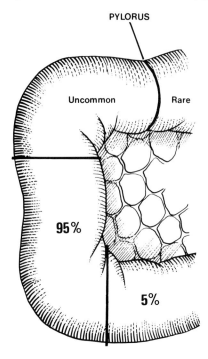

Fig. 1.28. Various locations of the papilla of Vater and their frequency.

With the advent of the technique of endoscopic cannulation of the papilla of Vater for the purpose of retrograde cholangiopancreatography, endoscopists have recently given us an excellent anatomical description of the papilla of Vater and the surrounding structures, which they refer to as the 'papillary apparatus'.

The endoscopists see the papilla as a pink projection of the medial wall of the second part of the duodenum, surrounded by a number of folds, which greatly facilitate its recognition. One may see a longitudinal fold representing the intramural part of the terminal bile duct leading down to the papilla, a transverse fold just above the papilla which may sometimes hide it from view, and a distal longitudinal fold, or frenulum, leading up to the papilla from below.

A prominent papilla of Vater can generally be palpated at operation through the duodenal wall as a nipple-like structure.

When the duodenum is opened an actual papilla is almost always present. It is prominent and easily found in about 60 per cent of subjects [8, 22]. When the papilla is not prominent it may be identified by the endoscopic description, and by running the finger down the medial wall of the duodenum until an elevation is felt which is firmer than the surrounding folds of duodenal mucosa. Compression of the gallbladder or of the common bile duct results in exudation of bile from the duodenal papilla, and this manoeuvre is of help in locating it.

The length of the papilla was found by Dowdy and co-workers in 1962 to vary from 1 to 7 mm, with an average of 3 mm. These workers found that the width of the papilla varied from 3 to 8 mm, with an average of 4 mm.

The actual stoma of the papilla is usually round, but it may be ovoid or slit-like. The diameter of the actual opening is usually 1–2 mm at rest. The size of the opening varies with the various phases of bile emptying. It is distensible, as evidenced by the passage of dilators through it during bile duct exploration.

PERIPAPILLARY DUODENAL DIVERTICULA

Pouches or diverticula of the duodenum found in close relationship to the major duodenal papilla are seen frequently in adults [33, 66].

There, peripapillary diverticula are usually intimately related to the distal common bile duct and the pancreatic duct, so that either or both of these ducts open into or very close to the diverticulum, and therefore their surgical excision may be a hazardous procedure [66]. Complications, such as perforation, are uncommon, but these diverticula have recently been shown to be associated with a higher bacteriological contamination of the common bile duct, and a higher incidence of gallstone disease than matched controls without duodenal diverticula [30, 33, 50].

REFERENCES

1. ASHBY B.S. Acute and recurrent torsion of the gallbladder. *Br. J. Surg.* **52**:182, 1965.
2. BENSON E.A. & PAGE R.E. A practical reappraisal of the anatomy of the extrahepatic bile ducts and arteries. *Br. J. Surg.* **63**:853, 1976.
3. BOGARDUS G.M. & LUNDMARK V.O. The short or absent cystic duct. *Surgery* **65**:274, 1969.
4. CARRIQUIRY L.A., ESTEFAN A. & PRADERI R.C. Ambiente Comun cistico-coledociano. *Cir del Uruguay* **45**:329, 1975.
5. CARTER R., THOMPSON R.J. JR., BRENNAN L.P. & HINSHAW D.B. Volvulus of the gallbladder. *Surg. Gynec. Obstet.* **116**:105, 1963.
6. CATTELL R.B. & BRAASCH J.W. Primary repair of benign strictures of the bile duct. *Surg. Gynec. Obstet.* **109**:531, 1959.
7. DOUGLASS T.C. & CUTTER W.W. Arterial blood supply of the common bile duct. *Arch. Surg.* **57**:599, 1948.
8. DOWDY G.S. JR., WALDRON G.W. & BROWN W.G. Surgical anatomy of the pancreatobiliary ductal system. *Arch. Surg. (Chicago)* **84**:229, 1962.
9. FAHIM R. B., MCDONALD J.R., RICHARDS J.C. & FERRIS D.O. Carcinoma of the gallbladder: A study of its modes of spread. *Ann. Surg.* **156**:114, 1962.
10. FAINSINGER M.H. The radiology of the intrahepatic biliary tree. *S. Afr. J. Med. Sci.* **15**:51, 1950.
11. FERRIS D.O. & GLAZER I.M. Congenital absence of gallbladder. *Arch. Surg. (Chicago)* **91**:359, 1965.
12. FERRIS D.O. & VIBERT J.C. The common bile duct: Significance of its diameter. *Ann. Surg.* **149**:249, 1959.
13. FOSTER J.H. & WAYSON E.E. Surgical significance of aberrant bile ducts. *Am. J. Surg.* **104**:14, 1962.
14. GOOR D.A. & EBERT P.A. Anomalies of the biliary tree. Report of a repair of an accessory bile duct and review of the literature. *Arch. Surg.* **104**:302, 1972.
15. GOURNET C. & DROUARD F. Une observation de canal hepatique aberrant. *Ann. Med. Reins.* **4**:149, 1967.
16. HAND B.H. An anatomical study of the choledochoduodenal area. *Br. J. Surg.* **50**:486, 1963.

17. HEALEY J.E. JR. & SCHROY P.C. Anatomy of the biliary ducts within the human liver. *A.M.A. Arch. Surg.* **66:**599, 1953.
18. HESS W. Surgery of the Biliary Passages and the Pancreas. Van Nostrand, Princeton, N.J., 1965.
19. HJORTSJO C.H. The internal topography of the liver: Studies by roentgen and injection technique. *Nord. Med.* **38:**745, 1948.
20. HJORTSJO C.H. The topography of the intrahepatic duct system. *Acta Anat.* **11:**599, 1951.
21. HOBSLEY M. Intra-hepatic anatomy. A surgical evaluation. *Br. J. Surg.* **45:**635, 1958.
22. HUGHES E.S.R. & KERNUTT R.H. The terminal portion of the common bile duct and of the pancreatic duct of Wirsung. *Aust. New Zeal. J. Surg.* **23:**223, 1954.
23. JACKSON J.B. & KELLY T.R. Cholecystohepatic ducts: Case report. *Ann. Surg.* **159:**581, 1964.
24. KUNE G.A. Surgical anatomy of the common bile duct. *Arch. Surg. (Chicago)* **89:**995, 1964.
25. KUNE G.A. Gall stones in diverticula of the lower common bile duct. *Gut* **6:**95, 1965.
26. KUNE G.A. The anatomical basis of liver surgery. *Aust. New Zeal. J. Surg.* **39:**117, 1969.
27. KUNE G.A. The influence of structure and function in the surgery of the biliary tract. Arris and Gale Lecture, April, 1970. *Ann. R. Coll. Surg. Eng.* **47:**78, 1970.
28. LESLIE D.R. The width of the common bile duct. *Surg. Gynec. Obstet.* **126:**761, 1968.
29. LINDNER H.H., PENA V.A. & RUGGERI R.A. A clinical and anatomical study of anomalous terminations of the common bile duct into the duodenum. *Ann. Surg.* **184:**626, 1976.
30. LOTVEIT T. & AUNE, S. The significance of duodenal diverticula in pancreatitis. *Scand. J. Gastroent.* **9:**32, 1974 (Suppl. 27).
31. LYTLE W.J. The common bile duct groove in the pancreas. *Br. J. Surg.* **47:**209, 1959.
32. MAHOUR G.H., WAKIM K.G. & FERRIS D.O. The common bile duct in man: Its diameter and circumference. *Ann. Surg.* **165:**415, 1967.
33. MCSHERRY C.K. & GLENN F. Biliary tract obstruction and duodenal diverticula. *Surg. Gynec. Obstet.* **130:**829, 1970.
34. MICHELS N.A. The hepatic, cystic and retroduodenal arteries and their relations to the biliary ducts: With samples of the entire celiacal blood supply. *Ann. Surg.* **133:**503, 1951.
35. MICHELS N.A. *Blood Supply and Anatomy of the Upper Abdominal Organs.* Lippincott, Philadelphia, 1955.
36. MILLBOURN E. On the excretory ducts of the pancreas in man, with special reference to their relations to each other, to the common duct and to the duodenum. *Acta Anat.* **9:**1, 1950.
37. MILROY P. An important anomaly of the right hepatic duct and its bearing on the operation of cholecystectomy. *Br. J. Surg.* **35:**383, 1947.
38. MISSEN A.J.B. Aberrations of the biliary passages on the surface of the liver and gall-bladder and in the gall-bladder wall. *Br. J. Surg.* **56:**427, 1969.
39. MOODY F.G., ASCH T. & GLENN F. Intrahepatic cholangiography. *Arch. Surg. (Chicago)* **87:**475, 1963.
40. MOOSMAN D.A. & COLLER F.A. Prevention of traumatic injury to the bile ducts. *Am. J. Surg.* **82:**132, 1951.
41. MOOSMAN D.A. The surgical significance of six anomalies of the biliary duct system. *Surg. Gynec. Obstet.* **131:**655, 1970.
42. NORMAN O. Studies on the hepatic ducts in cholangiography. *Acta Radiol (Stockholm)* (Suppl. 84), 1951.
43. NORTHOVER J.M.A. & TERBLANCHE J. A new look at the arterial supply of the bile duct in man and its surgical implications. *Br. J. Surg.* **66:**379, 1979.
44. PARKE W.P., MICHELS N.A. & GHOSH G.M. Blood supply of the common bile duct. *Surg. Gynec. Obstet.* **117:**47, 1963.

45. PEREIRA-LIMA J., PEREIRA-LIMA L.M., NESTROWSKI M. & CUERVO C. Anomalous location of the papilla of Vater. *Am. J. Surg.* **128**:71, 1974.
46. PRINZ R.A., HOWELL H.S. & PICKLEMAN J.R. Surgical significance of extrahepatic biliary tree anomalies. *Am. J. Surg.* **131**:755, 1976.
47. QUINTANA E.V. & LABAT R. Ectopic drainage of the common bile duct. *Ann. Surg.* **180**:119, 1974.
48. RABINOVITCH J., RABINOVITCH P. & ZISK H.J. Rare anomalies of the extrahepatic bile ducts. *Ann. Surg.* **144**:93, 1956.
49. REIFFERSCHEID M. *Chirgurgie der Leber.* Thieme, Stuttgart, 1957.
50. REILLY P. & KUNE G.A. Perforation of duodenal diverticula. A new hypothesis. *Aust. New Zeal. J. Surg.* **40**:40, 1970.
51. ROGERS H.I., CREWS R.D. & KALSER M.H. Congenital absence of the gallbladder with choledocholithiasis. Literature review and discussion of mechanisms. *Gastroenterology* **48**:524, 1965.
52. SAINT J.H. The epicholedochal venous plexus and its importance as a means of identifying the common bile duct during operations on the extrahepatic biliary tract. *Br. J. Surg.* **48**:489, 1961.
53. SALMON P.R. *Fibre-optic Endoscopy.* Pitman, London, 1974.
54. SCHILLER K.F.R. & SALMON P.R. *Modern Topics in Gastrointestinal Endoscopy.* Heinemann, London, 1976.
55. SCHULENBURG C.A.R. *Operative Cholangiography.* Butterworth, London, 1966.
56. SHAPIRO A.L. & ROBILLARD L. The arterial blood supply of the common and hepatic bile ducts with reference to the problems of common duct injury and repair. *Surgery* **23**:1, 1948.
57. SMITH R. & SHERLOCK S. *Surgery of the Gall Bladder and Bile Ducts.* Butterworth, London, 1964.
58. SPERLING M.J. Absence of the cystic duct. *Arch. Surg. (Chicago)* **88**:1077, 1964.
59. STERLING J.A. The common channel for the bile and pancreatic ducts. *Surg. Gynec. Obstet.* **98**:420, 1954.
60. SUTTON J.P. & SACHATELLO C.R. The confluence stone: A hazardous complication of biliary tract disease. *Amer. J. Surg.* **113**:719, 1967.
61. SWARTLEY W.B. & WEEDER S.D. Choledochus cyst with a double common bile duct. *Ann. Surg.* **101**:912, 1935.
62. WARREN K.W., McDONALD W.M. & KUNE G.A. Bile duct strictures: new concepts in the management of an old problem. In W.T. Irvine (ed.) *Modern Trends in Surgery* (2e). Butterworth, London, 1966.
63. WATSON A. & TORRANCE B. Anomalous insertion of the common bile duct. *Proc. R. Soc. Med.* **68**:747, 1975.
64. WATSON J.F. Anomalous cystic and common bile ducts associated with cholecystitis. *Am. J. Surg.* **118**:459, 1969.
65. WILLIAMS C. & WILLIAMS A.M. Abnormalities of the bile ducts. *Ann. Surg.* **141**:498, 1955.
66. WOLFSON N.S. & MILLER F.B. Anatomic relationship of insertion of the common bile duct into primary duodenal diverticula. *Surg. Gynec. Obstet.* **146**:628, 1978.

2. Applied Physiology

Normal and abnormal function of the biliary apparatus is of great interest to the clinician. During the last decade enormous gains have been made in the understanding of biliary physiology. A number of the difficulties preventing measurement of the various parameters of the biliary system, without disturbances of normal function, have been overcome. Advances resulting from animal experiments must be applied to man with caution, because of known species differences in anatomy and physiology.

This chapter focuses attention on those aspects of biliary function which are of importance in the understanding and management of biliary disorders. The pathophysiology of jaundice, gallstone formation, and the effects of biliary fistulas are covered elsewhere in the relevant sections. Bile secretion and its control are considered first. The mode of emptying of bile into the duodenum is presented in detail, together with current views of bile duct and sphincter of Oddi function, as these have important practical applications. Finally, the physiological basis of reflux of the biliary and pancreatic ducts is discussed and the significance of reflux in the production of biliary or pancreatic disorders is analysed. Functional disorders of the biliary system are dealt with by Professor John Ham in Chapter 12.

SECRETION OF BILE

Bile is unique in being both an exocrine secretion and a major excretory pathway. This dual role of bile accounts for its unusual composition (Table 2.1). It is secreted by the liver continuously. Bile is a watery solution which is concentrated six to tenfold in the gallbladder [40, 198]. The pH of bile varies, although it is generally alkaline [33, 179]. The chief constituents of bile are water, inorganic electrolytes, bile acids, cholesterol, phospholipids, and bile pigments (Table 2.1). It is estimated that 500–1000 ml of bile is produced per day by the hepatocytes and the duct cells [127, 182]. Bile acids are synthesised from cholesterol, and are actively secreted by the hepatocytes into the caniculi which are the most proximal portions of the intrahepatic biliary system [197]. It is the bile acids that are responsible for most of the bile volume and its fluctuation [162]. The active secretion of bile acid results in flow of water and permeable ions, such as sodium, into the bile ductules due to the osmotic effect of the bile acids [173, 174, 175].

Table 2.1. Composition of bile

	Hepatic bile (g%)	Gallbladder bile (g%)
Water	97	92
Bile acids	1	6
Bilirubin	0.04	0.03
Cholesterol	0.06	0.35
Lecithin	0.1	0.7

SYNTHESIS AND METABOLISM OF BILE ACIDS

Bile acids are synthesised in the liver from cholesterol and are the major pathway of cholesterol excretion by the body [12, 128]. The biochemical structure of bile acids is similar to a variety of steroid hormones and cholesterol [12, 168]. The bile acids, cholic and chenodeoxycholic, are produced from cholesterol [12, 168]. In the colon, bacteria convert cholic acid to deoxycholic acid, and chenodeoxycholic acid to lithocholic acid [13, 74, 113]. Cholic acid and chenodeoxycholic acid are the primary bile acids in bile. Deoxycholic acid and lithocholic acid are the secondary bile acids and form approximately 20 per cent of the bile acid in bile, after being absorbed from the bowel. Conjugation of the bile acids to the amino acids, taurine or glycine, occurs in the liver [35, 121, 169]. The salts of these acids are secreted in the bile.

FUNCTION OF BILE ACIDS

Bile acids have long been regarded as possessing a dual function; acting as a solvent for lecithin and cholesterol in bile, and consequently aiding the excretion of these otherwise insoluble endogenous lipids; and also as a solvent for insoluble dietary lipids in the intestine as well as promoting their absorption [25, 77, 78, 85, 87, 88, 170, 171]. Bile acids, cholesterol, and phospholipid are the principal lipids in bile. The phospholipid is almost entirely lecithin [182]. Each of these three substances have part of their molecules soluble in water and part which is soluble in fat solvents [2, 25, 78]. Substances with these properties are called amphiphilic [2, 25, 31, 78]. Bile acids are water soluble because of their structure, but lecithin and cholesterol are not soluble in water [2, 25, 31, 78].

The main function of bile acids in bile is to form mixed micelles or aggregates with lecithin and this maintains cholesterol in solution [25]. Lecithin expands the bile acid micelle and enables it to take up more cholesterol [25]. In addition to their solvent action on dietary lipids, bile acids activate pancreatic lipase and form micelles with the lipids [38, 78, 84]. In the intestine the micelles can be regarded as miniature lipid transporters, ferrying packets of lipid repeatedly to the absorptive membrane of the microvilli of the bowel [17, 158, 196]. However, even with total biliary obstruction or external fistula, at least half the normal dietary load of fat can be absorbed [78, 143, 144]. Bile acids have antibacterial properties which may explain the small number of bacteria in the small intestine [39, 59, 78, 100, 176].

Bilirubin, which is one of the major waste products of haemoglobin, is excreted by the liver [57, 112, 138, 163]. Bilirubin is produced in hepatocytes and is conjugated mainly to glucuronide and smaller amounts of sulphate and to a multitude of other substances [56, 79, 134]. The conjugated bilirubin is actively excreted into bile [5, 57, 95, 163]. Unconjugated bilirubin is weakly acidic, lipid soluble, and only sparingly water soluble compared to the conjugated form which is water soluble [57, 163]. The daily hepatic excretion of bilirubin is approximately 300 mg [14, 72, 182, 202]. The majority of the conjugated bilirubin is excreted in the faeces after conversion to stercobilin and other degradation products [163]. Initially, bilirubin is mainly converted to urobilinogen in the intestine by bacterial action. Urobilinogen and bilirubin are partially absorbed from the gut and are returned to the liver for re-excretion [111, 163]. This process presents a form of enterohepatic circulation. Urobilinogen entering the systemic circulation is excreted in the urine [163].

CONTROL OF BILE SECRETION

It is generally accepted that the regulation of hepatic bile secretion is influenced by neural and hormonal stimuli. The enterohepatic circulation of bile acids also plays a major role in the control of bile secretion.

ENTEROHEPATIC CIRCULATION OF BILE ACIDS

The liver secretes 20–30 g of bile acids per day, but the total body pool of bile acids at any one time is between 3 and 5 g [1, 15, 37, 76, 124, 192]. Bile acids returning to the liver via the portal vein, control hepatic bile acid synthesis from cholesterol through a negative feedback mechanism [11, 55]. The body conserves bile acids mainly by an efficient active transport mechanism in the ileum and by an enterohepatic circulation (Fig. 2.1.).

Once the primary bile acids, cholic and chenodeoxycholic acid, are absorbed they are resecreted by the liver. Passive absorption of bile acid does occur in the intestine, but this is mainly of unconjugated bile acids. Bile acids are deconjugated as a result of bacterial action, mainly in the colon. Each day one-third to one-quarter of the primary bile acid pool is lost or converted by anaerobic bacteria to the secondary bile acids, deoxycholic acid and lithocholic acid [86]. Bacteria convert cholic acid to deoxycholic acid and chenodeoxycholic acid to lithocholic acid. About one-third to one-half of the deoxycholate which is formed is absorbed [86]. Both of these secondary bile acids are resecreted by the liver once they are conjugated to either glycine or taurine.

Bile acids returning to the liver via the portal vein are cleared efficiently by the liver. Less than 5 per cent of the total bile acid entering the liver passes out into

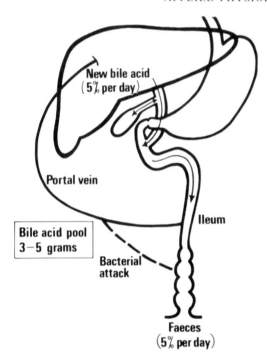

Fig. 2.1. Enterohepatic circulation of bile acids.

the hepatic veins to enter the systemic circulation [135]. Therefore, the serum level of bile acids under normal conditions is extremely low [107, 152, 199]. The bile acids entering the hepatocyte are rapidly secreted into the hepatic canaliculi [135]. A small amount of newly synthesised bile acid is added to this recirculated bile acid. The bile acid pool circulates two or three times during the digestion of a meal, and therefore six to eight times per day [16, 84, 114]. Less than 5 per cent of the secreted bile acid is excreted in the faeces. The normal daily faecal bile acid averages 500–600 mg on a standard diet and therefore this is the amount of bile acid synthesised per day from cholesterol [24, 62, 66, 71, 148]. External drainage of bile due to T-tube drainage, or a biliary fistula, depletes the bile acid pool and stimulates an increase in bile acid synthesis [45, 55, 148, 166, 167, 172].

NEUROHUMORAL CONTROL OF HEPATIC BILE SECRETION

The role of neurohumoral factors in the control of biliary secretion has been principally elucidated by Sali in 1977, although in man much remains unclear, as most of the information is based on animal experiments [148]. It has been shown by Sali and others that cholecystokinin and secretin can influence hepatic bile secretion [65, 70, 91, 98, 145, 148]. Vagus stimulation using insulin administration increases hepatic bile secretion [7, 61, 120, 148, 203]. Hepatic bile secretion is also increased following the ingestion of food. This response most probably results from vagal and hormonal stimulation [58, 61, 97, 103, 151].

BILIARY TRACT PAIN

MODES OF PAIN PRODUCTION

The actual physiological mechanisms responsible for biliary tract pain have been investigated and a number of factors appear to be of importance: distension, spasm, bile duct peristalsis, and the presence of acute inflammation in the vicinity of the biliary tract.

DISTENSION

Sudden distension or stretching of the whole or a portion of the gallbladder or the bile ducts is probably the most important cause of biliary pain [63, 90, 101, 159, 178]. A more gradual distension or stretching may not give rise to pain, but merely to a feeling of discomfort.

Very slow distension may not stimulate the receptor fibres at all; then the sensation of pain or discomfort is absent. It seems to be the *rate* of pressure rise, rather than the actual pressure reached, which is the factor of importance in pain production [93, 101].

SPASM

Spasm of the sphincter of Oddi is probably not in itself responsible for the production of pain, unless this is associated with bile duct distension. Thus, it was found that the administration of morphine to patients who have a T tube in place, will constantly produce spasm of the sphincter of Oddi without pain. However, pain is produced if morphine administration is combined with the infusion of fluid through the T tube, thereby producing distension as well, but pain is not produced by fluid infusion alone.

Cases have been recorded in which a morphine injection precipitated an attack of biliary colic, in the absence of other demonstrable biliary pathology [9, 90]. These cases are sometimes cited as evidence that sphincteric spasm alone may cause pain. Unfortunately, the cases were not documented by cholangiography or by pressure measurements, so that one is unable to draw any conclusions regarding the precise mechanism responsible for the pain.

BILE DUCT PERISTALSIS

True colic of the common bile duct due to excessive peristaltic activity has been postulated as a cause of pain. The sphincter of Oddi is excluded from these considerations. Some evidence indicates that the bile duct is capable of coordinated activity, but it is unlikely that such activity can be responsible for pain (see Discharge of Bile into the Duodenum, later in this chapter).

INFLAMMATION

An acute inflammatory reaction, either within the biliary system or in the overlying peritoneum, may be responsible for pain in a manner similar to that caused by an acute inflammatory process anywhere in the body.

PAIN RECEPTORS OF THE BILIARY SYSTEM

Receptor nerve endings have been demonstrated in all layers of the biliary apparatus [4, 20, 92]. There are thus receptors in the mucosal layer, the submucosal layer (including the myenteric plexus where muscle tissue is present), and the subserosal layer of the visceral peritoneum. In each layer the receptors are in communication with each other and with fibres of other layers, thereby forming a network. Receptors are also present in the parietal peritoneum which overlies the biliary system, but these are not in immediate communication with the receptor fibres of the biliary tract.

AFFERENT NERVE PATHWAYS

The nervous impulse set up by the stimulation of peripheral pain receptors travels toward the central nervous system along one or several pathways (Fig. 2.2).

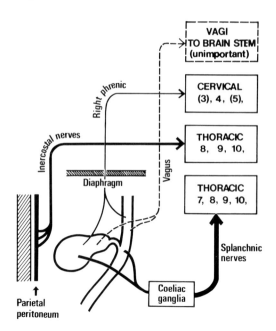

Fig. 2.2. Pain-carrying afferents of the biliary tract.

SPLANCHNIC NERVES

Afferent fibres pass to the coeliac ganglia and then to the right and left splanchnic nerves, entering the sympathetic ganglia at the level of the seventh, eighth, ninth, and tenth thoracic spinal segments. From the spinal cord the fibres pass upward to reach the sensory cortex. The right coeliac ganglion and the right splanchnic nerve carry the greatest proportion of afferent fibres from the biliary tract.

The importance of these fibres in carrying pain sensation was demonstrated by Schein and co-workers [161]. A peridural block of the thoracic sympathetic inflow achieved a marked increase in the perfusion pressure required to cause pain on choledochal distension by fluid administered through a T tube. This sympathetic block had no effect on common duct size nor on sphincteric dynamics.

VAGUS NERVES

Some afferent fibres do pass to the vagi from the anterior and posterior hepatic plexuses, but these are not thought to be important mediators of pain sensation from the biliary tract [4, 63].

RIGHT PHRENIC NERVE

Some pain-carrying fibres pass from the gallbladder and bile ducts to the right phrenic nerve and thus reach the spinal cord at the level of the third, fourth, and fifth cervical segments.

INTERCOSTAL NERVES

The whole of the parietal peritoneum sends afferent pain fibres along the intercostal nerves. Pain sensations arising from receptors overlying the biliary tract are transmitted to the spinal cord through the eighth, ninth, and tenth thoracic intercostal nerves [63].

CORTICAL INTERPRETATION OF BILIARY PAIN

Pain sensation anywhere in the body, including the biliary tract, is a subjective phenomenon. Thus, the assessment of the severity of pain can be difficult in some patients whose pain threshold is unusually low or unusually high.

The afferent pain pathways from the biliary tract are scattered widely over a number of spinal cord segments, which include the seventh, eighth, ninth, and tenth thoracic segments and the fourth cervical segment. The cortical interpretation, i.e. referral of such pain, is also widely scattered and there is great variation in different subjects. Doran in 1967 showed that pain arising from the common bile duct may be variously referred in different patients to the epigastrium, the costal margins, the back, and the scapula [417]. These areas of cortical sensory representation fit in well with the known spinal cord segments of the afferent pain fibres of the biliary tract.

A prospective survey of the sites of most severe pain in gallstone patients has revealed that the majority of patients have upper abdominal pain and, surprisingly, approximately 25 per cent have left costal margin pain [73]. Patients often likened the severity of biliary pain to that of labour pains [49, 73].

The studies of Kjellgren [101] indicated that in some patients, pain identical in character and distribution to biliary tract pain, could be elicited by stimulation of the duodenum or the parietal and visceral peritoneum of the right upper quadrant. These findings may be extended to the common clinical experience of pain arising in the liver, pancreas, stomach, or duodenum, which is similar to biliary tract pain. Thus, pain which resembles biliary pain in a patient whose biliary tract is clinically and radiologically normal must be interpreted with caution, because it may arise from an area other than the biliary tract. This is of particular importance in the diagnosis of the so-called functional disorders of the biliary tract (Chapter 12).

For a long time it was known that pain due to biliary disease may be perceived by the patient in the retrosternal area, or in the precordium, thereby mimicking pain of myocardial ischaemia. Only rarely does pain of myocardial ischaemia become manifest in the area of distribution of biliary tract pain [63, 140, 177, 204]. Occasionally, one reads reports of the cure of supposed angina of effort following cholecystectomy for gallstones. It is almost certain that these instances are merely the result of cortical referral of biliary tract pain to unusual sites, such as the retrosternal or the precordial area.

CLINICAL VARIETIES OF PAIN

BILIARY COLIC AND BILIARY DISCOMFORT

The term biliary colic is a misnomer, because the quality of the pain is not truly like a cramp, nor does it come in waves [60]. It begins suddenly, reaches a peak quickly, and remains for a variable period of a few hours, after which it gradually eases off [49, 73] (Fig. 2.3). In different patients it may be referred to a variety of areas, including the epigastrium or one or both costal margins (though usually it is the right costal margin) [49, 73]. From the front of the abdomen the pain may radiate around the costal margin to the back, or it may pass directly through to the back, or it may radiate to the right, or less frequently to the left shoulder blade. The pain never starts in the back and then radiates through to the front of the abdomen. Some patients experience a pain in the back only. The pain is often aggravated by food and can be relieved by vomiting [73].

This type of pain is produced by the sudden stretching or distension (due to obstruction) of the gallbladder or the bile ducts, or both. Gallstones are by far the commonest cause of biliary colic. However, identical pain may result from other

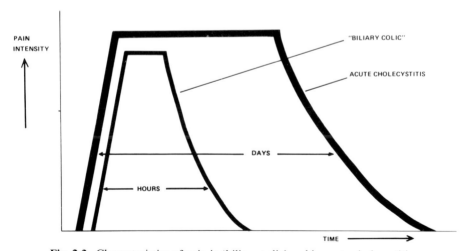

Fig. 2.3. Characteristics of pain in 'biliary colic' and in acute cholecystitis.

causes of obstruction and distension, such as the rupture of a liver hydatid into the biliary tract, producing a sudden flooding of the bile ducts by hydatid elements. Gallbladder stones probably produce pain by distending Hartmann's pouch and also by occluding the gallbladder outlet. The pain eases when this obstruction is relieved by movement of the stone. Similarly, biliary colic may be produced by gallstones in the bile duct which stretch the duct and which also produce obstruction to bile flow. The distribution of this pain is similar to that produced by pain arising in the gallbladder. In this type of obstruction the most severe pain is experienced when complete, sudden bile duct obstruction is associated with suppurative cholangitis, a condition referred to as acute obstructive cholangitis [137] (Chapters 5 & 9).

When the distension is more gradual the patient may experience only discomfort and not actual pain. This discomfort is referred to the same areas of the body as biliary colic. This type of symptom is frequently present with non-malignant biliary strictures. It is likely that the incomplete obstruction in these strictures produces a distension of the ducts which may be aggravated by an increased bile flow or other factors, such as biliary debris, stone formation, or cholangitis, which precipitate the symptom of discomfort.

Very slow distension of the biliary tract, such as gradual obstruction due to a malignant tumour, may produce no pain or discomfort. In some patients even sudden distension may produce no pain, for reasons which at present are uncertain [41]. Thus, sudden complete bile duct obstruction by gallstones has been, on occasion, observed to be completely painless.

ACUTE CHOLECYSTITIS
The pain of acute cholecystitis is probably compounded of two main elements. Acute cholecystitis is almost always associated with a gallstone impacted in Hartmann's pouch. It is supposed that the pain begins as a pain of biliary colic due to a stone in Hartmann's pouch occluding the gallbladder outlet. The obstruction is not relieved and is followed by distension of the gallbladder and then by the onset of acute inflammation in the gallbladder and overlying peritoneum, thereby adding the second element of the pain.

GALLBLADDER FUNCTION

The gallbladder receives bile through the cystic duct and concentrates it by active reabsorption of water and electolytes. Its evacuation is a result of contraction of its musculature. The cine-radiographic studies of Caroli have clearly shown that the gallbladder contracts actively, all its diameters becoming shorter, and that the viscus assumes a spherical shape [26, 27, 28, 190].

The usual stimulus for gallbladder contraction is the presence of food (especially fat) in the duodenum which releases the hormone cholecystokinin into the circulation. This hormone is probably the most important stimulator of gallbladder contraction [51, 80, 185]. The role of the autonomic nervous system is uncertain, but it seems to be concerned with the tonicity of the gallbladder, while the splanchnic nerve reduces the tone [80, 89, 116, 139]. Henri Sarles' group from France has demonstrated the presence of a hormone which is capable of relaxing the gallbladder. They have called this hormone, anticholecystokinin [155].

Gallbladder contraction begins within minutes of the introduction of fat into the duodenum and is maximal after about 10–15 minutes; it is usually concluded within 15–30 minutes. The amount emptied is variable, but is frequently of the order of 50 per cent of the original volume [23, 51].

DISTURBANCE OF GALLBLADDER FUNCTION

EFFECT OF VAGOTOMY
Bilateral truncal vagotomy is followed by dilatation of the gallbladder so that its resting volume is approximately doubled [30, 89, 96, 139, 147]. In contrast to truncal vagotomy, parietal cell vagotomy does not alter the resting gallbladder volume [89, 139]. Progressive dilatation of the gallbladder has also been observed after gastrectomy presumably because, in some cases, the hepatic branches of the anterior vagus are divided during the gastrectomy [32].

It is uncertain whether gallbladder malfunction which follows vagotomy has any clinical significance. It has been suggested that dilatation of the gallbladder may be a factor in gallstone production. A number of workers have noted an increased incidence of gallstones following gastrectomy and also following bilateral vagotomy, but the importance of this factor is probably not great [30, 68, 69, 122, 123, 133, 154].

EFFECT OF TRANSDUODENAL SPHINCTEROTOMY
It has been claimed for some time, on the basis of experimental work in dogs, that section or bypass of the sphincter of Oddi will result in gallbladder stasis and that this will be followed by acute or chronic cholecystitis [67, 106]. It was recommended that cholecystectomy should always be performed when a sphincterotomy is done.

However, others who investigated gallbladder function following section of the sphincter of Oddi found that the gallbladder functioned normally, and also that there did not seem to be an increased incidence of cholecystitis following this procedure [22, 108, 109]. This has also been the experience of the authors, who have studied six patients in whom a transduodenal sphincterotomy was performed without cholecystectomy and whose gallbladders functioned satisfactorily after this procedure, as shown by oral cholecystography.

EFFECT OF INCOMPLETE CYSTIC DUCT OBSTRUCTION
A number of cases have exhibited incomplete non-calculous obstruction to the cystic duct, causing pain which resembles that of biliary colic [3, 23, 64, 81, 191]. The obstruction may be due to a kink or to a fibrotic narrowing of the cystic duct. A purely functional form of incomplete cystic duct obstruction caused by hypertonicity of the cystic duct musculature has also been described, but this entity is doubtful [3]. The reader is also referred to Chapter 12, which deals with acalculous benign biliary disease.

The cholecystogram, in cases of incomplete cystic duct obstruction, shows a normal concentration of dye, but the contents are not adequately expelled after a fatty meal. In attempting to expel its contents the gallbladder assumes a spherical shape; this appearance has been given the fanciful name of the 'fighting gallbladder'. When an injection of cholecystokinin is substituted for the fatty meal the appearance is similar but more rapid in onset, and the patients experience pain of the biliary colic type, which is taken as additional evidence for the presence of this condition [23].

Cholecystectomy seems to be a uniformly successful mode of treatment of this uncommon condition.

DISCHARGE OF BILE INTO THE DUODENUM

The intermittent discharge of bile into the duodenum is accomplished by a coordinated action in which the gallbladder contracts and the sphincter of Oddi relaxes. During this period the motor activity in the second part of the duodenum is inhibited. The most important stimulus for this action is the presence of food (especially fat) in the duodenum, which generates the release of cholecystokinin [28, 51, 187].

Ashkin and others (1978) have shown that the delivery of bile to the duodenum is wave-like and is predominantly controlled by the sphincter of Oddi, and the gallbladder has only a minor role [6]. There is disagreement as to whether there is continuous secretion of bile into the duodenum during overnight fasting in normal people [6, 190].

ROLE OF VAGI AND SPLANCHNIC NERVES

The role of the extrinsic nerves in the discharge of bile in man is uncertain. The vagus is usually ascribed a stimulant action on the biliary musculature, and the splanchnic nerves an inhibitory action [80, 201]. The vagally denervated small intestine has a diminished cholecystokinin–pancreozymin release and, therefore, the vagus may act on the biliary tract indirectly [116]. It is probable that these extrinsic nerves merely modify, but do not determine, the bile-emptying mechanism. Thus, Schein and co-workers found that hepatic plexus vagectomy decreased the sphincteric resistance in some of their patients, but the mode of action of the sphincter of Oddi was not altered [160]. It is very likely that the vagus and splanchnic nerves act in unison with the stimulus of cholecystokinin, as well as with the activity of the intrinsic neuronal plexus of the biliary tract, to achieve the coordinated action of bile discharge into the duodenum [20]. However, there is conflicting evidence suggesting that neural factors may not have a role [180].

BILE DUCT PERISTALSIS

Do the human bile ducts, excluding the sphincter of Oddi, contract actively during the discharge of bile into the duodenum, or are they merely passive conducting tubes? The sphincter of Oddi is excluded from this discussion, because it is clearly the site of active cyclic activity (see Function of the sphincter of Oddi, later in this chapter).

Sporadic reports appear in the literature describing what is thought to be peristaltic activity of the human common bile duct, apparently concerned with the active propulsion of bile into the duodenum [21, 36, 125]. On the other hand, a number of cine-radiographic studies failed to show bile duct peristalsis under any circumstances [29, 80, 129, 159, 185]. The shape of the bile duct is seen to alter frequently, but this is not a coordinated peristaltic movement, but rather kinking of the biliary passages due to outside influences, such as movement of the diaphragm and changes in intra-abdominal pressure. On present evidence it appears that true peristaltic activity, as we know it in the gastrointestinal tract, probably does not take place in the bile duct.

Dunphy and co-workers made interesting experimental and clinical observations regarding the role of the common bile duct in biliary dynamics [47, 48, 147, 195, 205]. They found that longitudinal muscle fibres present in the bile duct do contract, producing a movement which is not true peristalsis, but rather a shortening and lengthening of the duct. This motility has also been shown in *in vitro* experiments using human and dog bile ducts [184]. The motility appears to play a role in the transit of bile into the duodenum. Circumferential scarring or other forms of damage to a segment of the bile duct can interfere with this action and produce a degree of hepatobiliary dysfunction, even though mechanical bile duct obstruction is not present.

A disturbance of this mechanism may provide the answer to a number of otherwise inexplicable situations in which bile transit is disturbed, although mechanical obstruction is not present. Thus, primary choledocholithiasis has been noted in patients who have a thick-walled, chronically inflamed bile duct in the absence of distal duct obstruction (Chapter 5). Jaundice of the obstructive type is sometimes seen in patients who have a bile duct carcinoma with spread of the tumour intramurally, but who at operation still have a reasonable-sized lumen of the duct (Chapter 7). The jaundice sometimes associated with acute or chronic pancreatitis, but without choledocholithiasis, may also be due to this phenomenon because, in these patients, peridochal inflammation is usually present. Similarly, the acute inflammatory process in acute cholecystitis frequently spreads to the area of the common bile duct. In some of these patients a transient type of obstructive jaundice is present and yet, at operation, the bile duct is mechanically patent (Chapter 5).

FUNCTION OF THE SPHINCTER OF ODDI

Although the discharge of bile into the duodenum is a coordinated action involving the whole biliary system the part played by the sphincter mechanisms is of special significance.

SPHINCTERIC MUSCULATURE

It was shown convincingly by Boyden [19] that the distal end of the common bile duct is surrounded by muscle fibres that are exclusive to the bile duct. There is also evidence that this muscle is embryologically different from the intestinal musculature [164]. This intrinsic musculature has some circular fibres, but is composed mainly of longitudinal and oblique fibres. The distal end of the common bile duct, as it passes through the duodenum, is surrounded by a substantial bundle of circular duodenal muscle fibres.

The intrinsic muscle bundles of the bile duct and the muscle fibres derived from the duodenum make up the complex usually referred to as the sphincter of Oddi.

MECHANISM OF SPHINCTERIC ACTION

Scientific opinion has long debated the relative importance of the intrinsic bile duct musculature and that of the duodenal musculature in the control of sphincteric action; careful cine-cholangiographic studies involving flow and pressure measurements have helped to resolve this controversy [29, 75, 80, 94, 102, 105, 110, 129, 132, 165]. All these workers found that the sphincteric and duodenal musculature work together as a synergic unit (Fig. 2.4), so that argument about

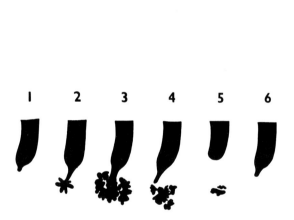

Fig. 2.4. Cine-cholangiography sequence (diagrammatic) showing synergic contraction and relaxation of the sphincter of Oddi and adjacent duodenum, which produce an intermittent discharge of bile into the gut. Note that the sphincter opens from above down and closes from below up. Redrawn from Hess: *Surgery of the Biliary Passages and the Pancreas* (C) 1965, Litton Educational Publishing, with permission.

their relative importance becomes meaningless. Recently, it has been shown with electromyography that the sphincter of Oddi can play a part in biliary flow apart from any duodenal muscular action [157].

For bile to be able to enter the duodenum the sphincter of Oddi must be open and bile duct pressure must be higher than duodenal pressure. The resting choledochal pressure shows great variation in different individuals and also in the same individual at different times. The range of resting pressures lies between 8 and 16 cm of water, but higher and lower figures have been recorded in some normal subjects [34, 75, 93, 102, 104, 131, 181]. The corresponding resting duodenal pressures were found to be always lower by a few centimetres of water [102].

Relaxation of the sphincter of Oddi is associated with relaxation of the adjacent segment of duodenal musculature and results in the discharge of bile into the duodenum. Similarly, contraction of the sphincter is associated with contraction of the surrounding duodenum. The sphincteric area opens from above down and closes from below up. This cycle of contraction–relaxation–contraction and the associated changes in the surrounding duodenum may be initiated by food in the duodenum, by an injection of cholecystokinin, or by any wave of duodenal peristalsis which passes over the sphincter region. This sequence of changes is termed duodenal-sphincteric synergy [29].

Duodenal-sphincteric synergy is shown diagrammatically in Fig. 2.4. Fig. 2.5 is taken from a cine-cholangiography sequence to show the changes in the sphincter and the surrounding duodenum. Note the tremendous variation in the size and shape of the sphincteric region. However, even at the maximal point of relaxation the sphincteric region is still narrower than the bile duct above.

This orderly synergy between the duodenum and the sphincter of Oddi sometimes breaks down, so that the sphincteric region is contracted and the

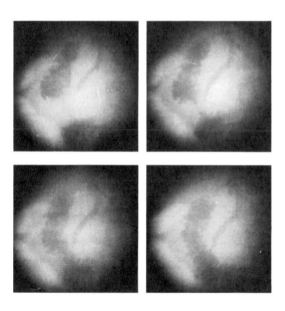

Fig. 2.5. Sequence of frames from cine-cholangiography performed through a T tube and demonstrating duodenal-sphincteric synergy. (*top left*) Synchronous contraction of duodenum and sphincter of Oddi. (*top right*) Slight relaxation of duodenum and sphincteric area. (*bottom left*) Moderate relaxation of duodenum and sphincter. (*bottom right*) Complete relaxation of duodenum and sphincter. From Kune [105]; courtesy of Dr. R.E. Wise, Boston.

duodenum is relaxed. The opposite situation—contraction of the duodenum and relaxation of the sphincter of Oddi—has also been recorded [29, 136]. These occasional aberrations of function are unexplained. It is not known whether under these circumstances both the duodenal and bile duct components of the sphincter participate, or whether these alterations in function are ever responsible for symptoms and functional disorders. Controversy exists regarding the action of cholecystokinin–pancreozymin on the sphincter of Oddi with some results indicating that contraction occurs, whilst others show the opposite finding [141, 142, 153, 156, 183, 186, 195].

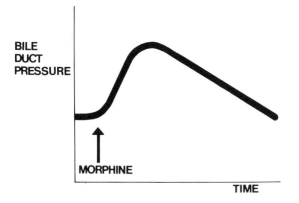

BILE
DUCT
PRESSURE

MORPHINE

TIME

Fig. 2.6. Effect of morphine during a bile duct flow study in which saline is passed into the duct at a steady rate through a T tube.

FACTORS THAT MODIFY SPHINCTERIC ACTION

A number of factors can alter sphincteric action; of these, drugs and operations on the sphincter are of importance.

Drugs. The administration of morphine causes a spasm of the sphincteric region, contraction of the adjacent duodenum, and a rise of bile duct pressure, as shown by cholangiography and by pressure studies [18, 50, 93, 94, 105, 110, 129]. This effect can be seen from a graph of a bile duct flow study, in which morphine was administered to the patient (Fig. 2.6). Fig. 2.7 is a cholangiogram taken at the height of the morphine action, showing spasm of the sphincter of Oddi. Meperidine (demerol, pethidine) has an action similar to morphine derivatives, contrary to the common belief that this drug does not influence the sphincter of Oddi. Pentazocine (fortral) causes the least rise in biliary pressure [50].

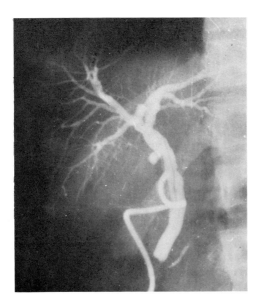

Fig. 2.7. T-tube cholangiogram showing sphincteric spasm produced by morphine. Note spasm of pancreatic duct sphincter also. Contrast medium which had previously refluxed into the pancreatic duct is retained there.

Sphincteric spasm can be relaxed by inhalation of amyl nitrate (Fig. 2.8), by sublingual glyceryl trinitrate, and by ganglion-blocking agents, such as probanthine [75, 94, 105, 129, 146]. However, the effect of these drugs is not uniform; in some subjects only partial relaxation occurs and in others no effect is noted. Although it is unknown if cholecystectomy alters the sphincteric function, it is known that sphincteric activity is still present after this operation [165].

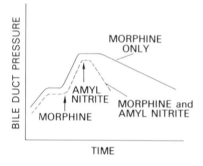

Fig. 2.8. Effects of morphine and amyl nitrite on bile duct pressure during a bile duct flow study in which saline is passed into the duct at a steady rate through a T tube.

Sphincterotomy and sphincteroplasty. Does a single-cut transduodenal sphincterotomy alter the dynamics of bile flow? All recent investigations, with the exception of Boulter (1961), indicate that transduodenal sphincterotomy does not lower the resistance of the sphincter of Oddi [53, 75, 105, 110, 181]. Cine-cholangiography shows that the mechanism of sphincteric action is not altered by sphincterotomy. Operative and postoperative cholangiograms performed after sphincterotomy cannot be distinguished from the cholangiographic appearance of a normal intact sphincter (Fig. 2.9). Drugs, such as morphine, meperidine (demerol, pethidine), and amyl nitrate have an effect entirely similar to that noted in patients with an intact sphincter (Fig. 2.10). Thus, the value of this procedure in augmenting biliary flow and in achieving improved biliary drainage must be seriously questioned.

The augmentation of sphincteric resistance and the alterations of bile flow produced by the more extensive operation of transduodenal sphincteroplasty are uncertain at present because of the lack of sufficient data. Flow studies, pressure measurements, and cine-cholangiography performed by Kune on four patients showed that the resistance of the sphincter is lowered by the procedure, but the sphincter still functions and responds in a manner similar to an intact sphincter [105]. However, it is often seen that after sphincteroplasty the normally narrow segment of the distal bile duct has been significantly widened (Fig. 2.11). This is in accord with the observations of Vajcner, Grossling, and Nicoloff in 1967, who found in eleven patients that transduodenal sphincteroplasty produced a permanent decrease in the resistance of the sphincter of Oddi.

After sphincteroplasty, gastrointestinal reflux into the biliary tract is commonly seen when a barium meal is performed. This indicates that sphincteric resistance has been considerably lowered, allowing reflux to occur. However, even when reflux does occur, bile-duct emptying seems to take place in a manner similar to the intact sphincter.

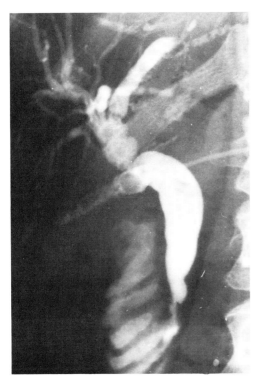

Fig. 2.9. T-tube cholangiogram performed 3 months
after a single-cut trans-
duodenal sphincterotomy.
The appearance of the
sphincter is indistinguishable from that of an intact
sphincter.

These findings indicate that even the most ambitious of sphincteroplasties
will be unable to divide the entire sphincteric mechanism. No matter how
extensive the operation the lower end of the bile duct will still be surrounded by
circular duodenal muscle which will act as a sphincter. However, sphincteroplasty does appear to alter dynamics of bile flow and emptying permanently.

BILIARY-PANCREATIC REFLUX

Few concepts in surgery have stimulated greater interest and controversy than
the proposition that under certain circumstances a continuous system may exist
between the bile and pancreatic ducts, with the possibility of bile reflux into the
pancreatic duct and vice versa.

In the discussion of anatomy in Chapter 1 it was noted that in a large
proportion of individuals the disposition of the ducts is such that a continuous
biliary-pancreatic system could be created under certain circumstances. Now we
shall examine the current physiological evidence of the presence of biliary-pancreatic reflux.

INCIDENCE OF REFLUX

How common is biliary-pancreatic reflux and under what conditions does it
occur?

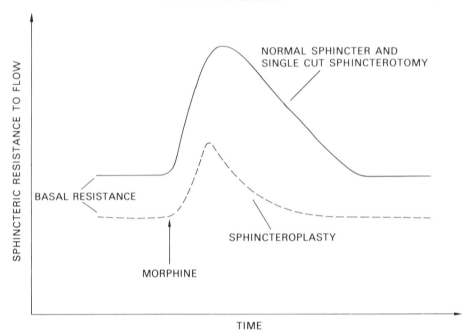

Fig. 2.10. Sphincteric resistance to flow after sphincterotomy and after sphincteroplasty. Note that there is no change after sphincterotomy when compared to the normal sphincter. Basal resistance is lowered after sphincteroplasty, but the sphincter still responds in a normal way to morphine injection.

The incidence of reflux in normal subjects is not known. Reflux is in part dependent on bile duct pressure, because it is uncommon to find it during cine-cholangiography when bile duct pressure is less than 20 cm of water [29, 105, 177]. Normal bile duct pressure is lower than this figure in most subjects. However, reflux was noted on a few occasions during cine-cholangiography by Kune and other workers within the range of physiological pressures [105, 177]. The pressure generated in the bile duct during a contraction of the normal gallbladder is unknown. It is possible that during gallbladder contraction bile duct pressure rises to a level sufficiently high to permit reflux.

Although the incidence of reflux is uncertain in the normal subject there is no doubt that this can be seen during operative and postoperative cholangiography. The incidence of such reflux has been variously reported between 7 and 46 per cent [29, 53, 83, 105]. The reason for this wide variation is that the conditions of study varied. Thus, pancreatic reflux can be obtained more frequently when the pressure of injection of contrast medium is increased. The incidence also increases with the number of pictures taken, reaching a maximum with cine-cholangiography.

MECHANISM OF REFLUX

The precise mechanism of pancreatic reflux has been extensively studied by

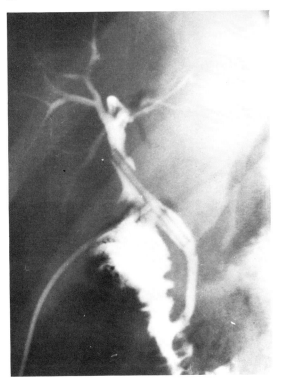

Fig. 2.11. T-tube cholangiogram of a patient 2
months after an extensive
sphincteroplasty showing
that the narrow distal segment of the common bile
duct has been widened by
the operation.

cine-cholangiography combined with manometry. These studies have shown
that reflux of contrast medium into the pancreatic duct may occur in subjects
who have an anatomic common channel. This reflux occurs when bile duct
pressure is high, and at a phase when the sphincter of Oddi is relaxed (Fig. 2.12)
[29, 94, 105, 132]. These observations are diametrically opposed to the original
theories which held that pancreatic reflux occurs during spasm or during some
other form of obstruction of the sphincter [42, 126]. When the sphincteric area is
contracted reflux does not occur, and any contrast material which has already
refluxed into the pancreatic duct remains there until the sphincter of Oddi relaxes
again (Fig. 2.8).

It was noted in Chapter 1 that in the presence of a common channel the
pancreatic duct opens into the thickened distal portion of the bile duct, which is
the area of the sphincter of Oddi (Figs. 1.20 & 1.27). Clearly, contraction of the
sphincter will separate the two channels and relaxation will produce continuity.
From this it follows that all agents which produce sphincteric spasm, such as
morphine, will separate the 'common channel' and oppose reflux. All agents
which produce sphincteric relaxation, e.g. fatty food and amyl nitrate, will
favour reflux.

An unusual mode of pancreatic reflux may occur when the common bile duct
and the duct of Wirsung open independently into the duodenum and this is called
duodenopancreatic reflux. Under these circumstances contrast material in the

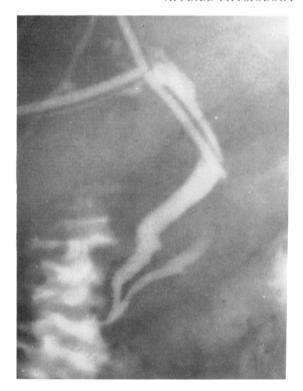

Fig. 2.12. T-tube cholangiogram in a patient with a common channel, showing free biliary-pancreatic reflux when the sphincter area and the adjacent duodenum are relaxed.

duodenum may regurgitate into the duct of Wirsung during a phase of sphincteric and duodenal relaxation [29, 82, 105, 118, 119]. However, no further contrast enters the duct of Wirsung when the sphincter of Oddi is contracted, probably because the sphincter around the pancreatic duct is incorporated within the sphincter of Oddi, and these work in unison. Again, agents which cause sphincteric spasm oppose reflux and those causing relaxation favour it. Fig. 2.13 is a cholangiogram of duodenopancreatic reflux. This duodenal reflux is not influenced by bile duct pressure, and it appears to be solely a physiological phenomenon [105].

CLINICAL SIGNIFICANCE OF REFLUX

Reflux into the pancreatic duct is almost certainly not harmful in itself [54, 105, 188]. However, it is possible that bile salts or some other factor in bile may promote pancreatic cancer [149, 206]. The frequency with which reflux occurs under physiological conditions is uncertain, but it is probable that pressures required to cause reflux can, on occasion, be generated in a normal biliary tract. Reflux has been produced on innumerable occasions during operative and postoperative cholangiography without ill effects. There are no documented case reports to show that acute pancreatitis followed cholangiography. Also, patients who were shown to have pancreatic reflux during cholangiography did not have a

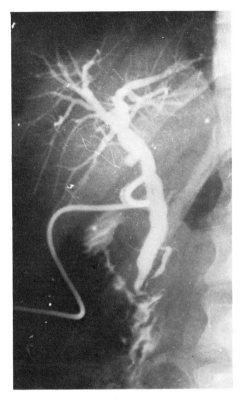

Fig. 2.13. T-tube cholangiogram showing indepen-
dent entry of the pancreatic duct into the duodenum
and the presence of duo-
denopancreatic reflux.

higher incidence of pancreatitis than those who did not show reflux [8, 82, 105].
Recently, two instances of bile reflux without acute pancreatitis based on operative findings have been reported [199]. Bergkvist and Seldinger (1957) found
some increase in the incidence of a 'previous pancreatic affection' in patients who
had reflux on cholangiography, but as their criterion of previous pancreatic
disorder was merely a high urinary diastase level the significance of this finding is
questionable.

   In the past, reflux in itself was regarded as a harmful phenomenon by many
workers, who believed this was an aetiologic factor in pancreatitis [43, 44, 117,
126]. They felt that reflux was potentiated by any form of obstruction, such as
stenosis or spasm of the sphincteric region, and recommended sphincterotomy as
a mode of treatment. These views can now be seriously challenged. First, reflux in
itself does not seem to be harmful. Second, spasm or stenosis of the sphincteric
region is more likely to oppose than to favour reflux. Third, a single-cut sphincterotomy does not seem to influence biliary dynamics to a great extent. Indeed,
the results of sphincterotomy in these conditions have not been encouraging [52,
181, 193, 194].

   It was noted earlier that reflux of duodenal contents into the duct of Wirsung
may occur in instances when the duct of Wirsung and the common bile duct open
into the duodenum independently. Some clinical and experimental evidence has

been presented to implicate duodenopancreatic reflux as an aetiological factor in pancreatitis [118, 119]. At present, however, there is no direct evidence to substantiate this relationship.

Pressures in the duct of Wirsung may exceed bile duct pressure, and on occasion pancreatic juice has been found in the biliary apparatus [46, 54, 200]. The effects of the regurgitation of pancreatic juice into the bile ducts have not been extensively studied, and this avenue of research may shed some light on biliary disorders.

REFERENCES

1. ABAUREE P., GORDON S.G., MANN J.G. & KERN F. JR. Fasting bile salt pool size and composition after ileal resection. *Gastroenterology* **57**:679, 1969.
2. ADMIRAND W.H. & SMALL D.M. The physico-chemical basis of cholesterol gallstone formation in man. *J. Clin. Invest.* **47**:1043, 1968.
3. ALBOT G., OLIVIER C. & LIBAUDE H. Radiomanometric examination of biliary ducts: experience with 418 cases. *Gastroenterology* **24**:242, 1953.
4. ALEXANDER W.F. The innervation of the biliary system. *J. Comp. Neurol.* **72**:357, 1940.
5. ARIAS I.M., JOHNSTON L. & WOLFSON S. Biliary excretion of injected conjugated and unconjugated bilirubin by normal and Gunn rats. *Am. J. Physiol.* **200**:1091, 1961.
6. ASHKIN J.R., LYON D.T., SCHULL S.D., WAGNER C.I. & SOLOWAY R.D. Factors affecting delivery of bile to the duodenum in man. *Gastroenterology* **74**:560, 1978.
7. BALDWIN J., HEER F.W., ALBO R., PELOSO O., SILEN W. & RUBY L. Effect of vagus nerve stimulation on hepatic secretion of bile in human subjects. *Am. J. Surg.* **113**:66, 1966.
8. BARDENHEIER J.A. III, KAMINSKI D.L., WILLMAN V.L. & HANLON C.R. Ten years experience with direct cholangiography. *Am. J. Surg.* **118**:900, 1969.
9. BERGH G.S. The sphincter mechanism of the common bile duct in human subjects. *Surgery* **11**:299, 1942.
10. BERGKVIST A. & SELDINGER S.I. Pancreatic reflux in operative cholangiography in relation to pre- and post-operative pancreatic affection. *Acta Chir. Scand.* **114**:191, 1957.
11. BERGSTRÖM S. & DANIELSSON H. On the regulation of bile acid formation in the rat liver. *Acta Physiol. Scand.* **43**:1, 1958.
12. BERGSTRÖM S. & DANIELSSON H. The formation and metabolism of bile acids. In C.F. Code & B. Heidel (eds.), *Handbook of Physiology*. Section 6, vol. 5, Am. Physiol. Soc., Washington DC, 1968.
13. BERGSTRÖM S. & NORMAN A. Metabolic products of cholesterol in bile and faeces of rat. *Proc. Soc. Exp. Biol. Med.* **83**:71, 1953.
14. BLOOMER J.R., BOYER J.L., KLATSKIN G. Inhibition of bilirubin excretion in man during dehydrocholate choleresis. *Gastroenterology* **65**:929, 1973.
15. BORGSTRÖM B. Digestion and absorption of fat. *Gastroenterology* **43**:216, 1963.
16. BORGSTRÖM B., DAHLQVIST, A., LUNDH G. & SJOVALL J. Studies of intestinal digestion and absorption in the human. *J. Clin. Invest.* **36**:1521, 1957.
17. BORGSTRÖM B., LUNDH G. & HOFMANN A. Site of absorption of conjugated bile salts in man. *Gastroenterology* **45**:229, 1963.
18. BOULTER P.S. Flow studies on the human common duct. With special reference to the effect of sphincterotomy. *Br. J. Surg.* **49**:17, 1961.
19. BOYDEN E.A. The anatomy of the choledochoduodenal junction in man. *Surg. Gynec. Obstet.* **104**:641, 1957.
20. BURNETT W., GAIRNS F.W. & BACSICH P. Some observations on the innervation of the extrahepatic biliary system in man. *Ann. Surg.* **159**:8, 1964.

21. BURNETT W. & SHIELDS R.S. Movements of the common bile duct in man: studies with the image intensifier. *Lancet* **2:**387, 1958.

22. CADILI G. & SOMMARIVA V. Studio colecistografico per os dopo abolizione anatomica e funzionale della sfintere di Oddi. *Minerva Chir.* **13:**215, 1958.

23. CAMISHION R.C. & GOLDSTEIN F. Partial noncalculous cystic duct obstruction (cystic duct syndrome). *Surg. Clin. N. Amer.* **47:**1107, 1967.

24. CAMPBELL C.B. & McIVOR W.E. The modified assay of total faecal bile acid excretion for clinical studies. *Pathology* **7:**157, 1975.

25. CAREY M.C. & SMALL D.M. The characteristics of mixed micellar solution with particular reference to bile. *Am. J. Med.* **49:**590, 1970.

26. CAROLI J. Les Maladies des Voies Biliaires. In J. Carsli (ed.) *Traite des Maladies due Foie, des Voies Biliaires et du Pancréas.* Vigot, Paris, 1951.

27. CAROLI J. & MERCADIER M. Les Dyskinesies Biliaires. Vigot, Paris, 1949.

28. CAROLI J., PLESSIER J. & PLESSIER B. Endogenous cholecystokinin and its inhibitor: method of assessment in humans; its role in normal and pathologic physiology. *Am. J. Dig. Dis.* **6:**646, 1961.

29. CAROLI J., PORCHER P., PEQUIGNOT G. & DELATTRE M. Contribution of cineradiography to study the function of the human biliary tract. *Am. J. Dig. Dis.* **5:**677, 1960.

30. CLAVE R.A. & GASPAR M.R. Incidence of gallbladder disease after vagotomy. *Am. J. Surg.* **118:**169, 1969.

31. COYNE M.J., MARKS J. & SCHOENFIELD L.J. Mechanisms of cholesterol gallstone formation. *Clin. Gastroenterol.* **6:**129, 1977.

32. COX H.T., DOHERTY J.F. & KERR D.F. Changes in the gallbladder after elective gastric surgery. *Lancet* **1:**764, 1958.

33. CRAWFORD N. & BROOKE B.N. The pH buffering power of human bile. *Lancet* **1:**1096, 1955.

34. CUSHIERI A., HOWELL HUGHES J. & COHEN M. Biliary-pressure studies during cholecystectomy. *Br. J. Surg.* **59:**267, 1972.

35. DAM H., KRUSE I., PRANGE I., KALLEHAUGE A.G., FENGLER H.J. & JENSEN M.K. Studies on human bile. III. Composition of duodenal bile from healthy young volunteers compared with composition of bladder bile from surgical patients with and without uncomplicated gallstone disease. *Z. Ernäbrungsw* **10:**160, 1971.

36. DANIELS B.T., McGLONE F.B., JOB T. & SAWYER R.B. Changing concepts of common bile duct anatomy and physiology. *J.A.M.A.* **178:**394, 1961.

37. DANIELSSON H. Present status of research on metabolism and excretion of cholesterol. *Adv. Lipid Research* **1:**335, 1963.

38. DESNUELIE P. Pancreatic lipase. *Adv. Enzymol.* **23:**129, 1961.

39. DICKMAN M.D., CHAPPELKA A.R. & SCHAEDLER R.W. The microbial ecology of the upper small bowel. *Am. J. Gastroenterol.* **65:**57, 1976.

40. DIETSCHY J.M. Recent developments in solute and water transport across the gallbladder epithelium. *Gastroenterology* **50:**692, 1966.

41. DORAN F.S.A. The sites to which pain is referred from the common bile duct in man and its implication for the theory of referred pain. *Br. J. Surg.* **54:**599, 1967.

42. DOUBILET H. Pancreatic reflux deliberately produced. *Surg. Gynec. Obstet.* **84:**710, 1947.

43. DOUBILET H. & MULHOLLAND J.H. Surgical treatment of recurrent pancreatitis by endocholedochal sphincterotomy. *Surg. Gynec. Obstet.* **86:**295, 1948.

44. DOUBILET H. & MULHOLLAND J.H. Eight-year study of pancreatitis and sphincterotomy. *J.A.M.A.* **160:**521, 1956.

45. DOWLING R.H., MACK E., SMALL D.M. & PICOTT J. Effects of controlled interruption of the enterohepatic circulation of bile salts by biliary diversion and by ileal resection on bile salt secretion, synthesis and pool size in the Rhesis monkey. *J. Clin. Invest.* **49:**232, 1970.

46. DREILING D.A., JANOWITZ H.D. & PERRIER C.V. *Pancreatic Inflammatory Disease. A Physiologic Approach.* Hoeber Med. Div., Harper & Row, New York, 1964.

47. Dunphy J.E. Some observations, practical and impractical, on the function of the common bile duct. *J. Roy. Coll. Surg. Edinb.* **11**:115, 1966.

48. Dunphy J.E. & Stephens F.O. Experimental study of the effect of grafts in the common duct on biliary and hepatic function. *Ann. Surg.* **155**:906, 1962.

49. Earlam R.J. & Thomas M. The clinical significance of gallstones and their radiological investigation. *Br. J. Surg.* **65**:164, 1978.

50. Economou G. & Ward-McQuaid J.N. A cross-over comparison of the effect of morphine, pethidine, pentazocine and phenazocine on biliary pressure. *Gut* **12**:218, 1971.

51. Edholm P. Gallbladder evacuation in normal male induced by cholecystokinin. *Acta Radiol. (Stockholm)* **53**:257, 1960.

52. Efron G. The natural history of pancreatitis. *Br. J. Surg.* **53**:702, 1966.

53. Eiseman B., Brown W.H., Virabutr S. & Gottesfeld S. Sphincteromoty—an evaluation of its physiologic rationale. *A.M.A. Arch. Surg.* **79**:294, 1959.

54. Elmslie R., White T.T. & Magee D.F. The significance of reflux of trypsin and bile in the pathogenesis of human pancreatitis. *Br. J. Surg.* **53**:809, 1966.

55. Eriksson S. Biliary excretion of bile acids and cholesterol in bile fistula rats. Bile acids and steroids. *Proc. Soc. Exp. Biol. Med.* **94**:578, 1957.

56. Fevery J., van Damme B., Michiels R., De Groote J. & Heirwegh K.P.M. Bilirubin conjugates in bile of man and rat in the normal state in liver disease. *J. Clin. Invest.* **51**:2482, 1972.

57. Fleischner G. & Arias I.M. Recent advances in bilirubin formation, transport, metabolism and excretion. *Am. J. Med.* **14**:576, 1970.

58. Fletcher D.M. & Clark C.G. Changes in canine bile flow and composition after vagotomy. *Br. J. Surg.* **56**:103, 1969.

59. Floch N.H., Gershengoren W., Elliot S. & Spiro H.M. Bile acid inhibition of the intestinal microflora—a function for simple bile acids? *Gastroenterology* **61**:228, 1971.

60. French E.B. & Robb W.A.T. Biliary and renal colic. *Br. Med. J.* **2**:135, 1963.

61. Fritz M.E. & Brooks F.P. Control of bile flow in the cholecystectomized dog. *Am. J. Physiol.* **204**:825, 1963.

62. Garbutt J.T., Lack L. & Tyor M.P. The enterohepatic circulation of bile salts in gastrointestinal disorders. *Am. J. Med.* **51**:627, 1971.

63. Glenn F. Pain in biliary tract disease. *Surg. Gynec. Obstet.* **122**:495, 1966.

64. Goldstein F. Cystic duct syndrome. In H.L. Bockus (ed.), *Gastroenterology* (2 e). Saunders, Philadelphia, 1965.

65. Gordon E.M., Douglas M.C., Jablonski P., Owens J.A., Sali A & Watts J. McK. The effect of cholecystokinin, pancreozymin, gastrin and secretin on bile secretion in the isolated perfused pig liver. *Surgery* **73**:708, 1972.

66. Gray C.H., Nicholson D.C. & Quencey R.V. Fate of bile in the bowel. In C.S. Code (ed.), *Handbook of Physiology*, Sect. 6, vol. 5. Am. Physiol. Soc., Washington, 1968.

67. Gray S.H., Probstein J.G. & Schar L.A. Chronic cholecystitis produced by division of the sphincter of Oddi. *Arch. Surg.* **59**:1007, 1949.

68. Griffith C.A. Selective gastric vagotomy. Part II: Eliminating undesirable sequelae of total abdominal vagotomy by selective gastric vagotomy. *Western J. Surg.* **70**:175, 1962.

69. Griffith J.M.T. & Holmes G. Cholecystitis following gastric surgery. *Lancet* **2**:780, 1964.

70. Grossman M.I., Janowitz H.D., Ralston H. & Kim K.S. The effect of secretin on bile formation in man. *Gastroenterology* **12**:133, 1949.

71. Grundy S.M., Ahrens E.H. Jr. & Miettinen T.A. Quantitative isolation in gas–liquid chromatographic analysis of total faecal bile acids. *J. Lipid Res.* **6**:397, 1965.

72. Guldhammer E. & Kjeldsen K. Bile flow, pH, electrolytes and bilirubin in hepatic bile flow following choledochotomy. *Acta Chir. Scand.* **133**:483, 1967.

73. GUNN A. & KEDDIE, N. Some clinical observations on patients with gallstones. *Lancet* **2**:240, 1972.
74. GUSTAFSSON B.E., BERGSTRÖM S., LINDSTEDT S. & NORMAN A. Turnover and nature of faecal bile acids in germ free and infected rats fed cholic acid-24-^{14}C. *Proc. Soc. Exp. Biol. Med.* **94**:467, 1957.
75. HAND B.H. Anatomy and function of the extrahepatic biliary system. *Clin. Gastroenterol.* **2**:3, 1973.
76. HARDISON W.G.M. & ROSENBERG I.H. Bile salt deficiency in the steatorrhoea following resection of the ileum and proximal colon. *New Eng. J. Med.* **227**:337, 1967.
77. HASLEWOOD G.A.D. *Bile Salts.* Methuen, London, 1967.
78. HEATON K.W. *Bile Salts in Health and Disease.* Churchill Livingstone, Edinburgh, 1972.
79. HEIRWEGH K.P.M., FEVERY J., MICHIELS R., VAN HESS G.P. & COMPERNOLLE F. Separation by thin layer chromatography and structure elucidation of bilirubin conjugates isolated from dog bile. *Biochem. J.* **145**:185, 1975.
80. HESS W. *Surgery of the Biliary Passages and the Pancreas.* Van Nostrand, Princeton, N.J., 1965.
81. HESS W. Les affections non lithiasigues et non cancéreuses de la vésicule biliaire et du canal cystique: Traitement chirurgical. *Sem. Hop. Paris* **43**:794, 1967.
82. HICKEN N.F. & MCALLISTER A.J. Is the reflux of bile into the pancreatic ducts a normal or abnormal physiologic process? *Am. J. Surg.* **83**:781, 1952.
83. HJORTH E. Contribution to the knowledge of pancreatic reflux as an etiologic factor in chronic affections of the gallbladder. *Acta Chir. Scand. (Suppl. 134)* **96**:1, 1947.
84. HOFMANN A.F. Clinical implications of physico-chemical studies on bile salts. *Gastroenterology* **48**:484, 1965.
85. HOFMANN A.F. Function of bile in the alimentary canal. In C.S. Code (ed.), *Handbook of Physiology*, Sect. 6, *Alimentary canal. 5:Bile, Digestion.* Amer. Physiol. Soc., Washington, 1968.
86. HOFMANN A.F. The enterohepatic circulation of bile acids in man. *Clin. Gastroenterol.* **6**:3, 1977.
87. HOFMANN A.F. & BORGSTRÖM B. Physico-chemical state of lipids in intestinal content during digestion and absorption. *Fedn. Proc.* **21**:43, 1962.
88. HOFMANN A.F. & SMALL D.M. Detergent properties of bile salts: correlation with physiological function. *A. Rev. Med.* **18**:333, 1967.
89. INBERG M.V. & VUORIO M. Human gallbladder function after selective gastric and total abdominal vagotomy. *Acta Chir. Scand.* **135**:625, 1969.
90. IVY A.C. Motor dysfunction of the biliary tract: an analytical and critical consideration. *Am. J. Roentgen.* **57**:1, 1947.
91. JABLONSKI P., SALI A. & WATTS J. McK. Gastrointestinal hormones and bile secretion in the perfused pgi liver: the effects of secretin, cholecystokinin and pentagastrin. *Aust. New Zeal. J. Surg.* **44**:173, 1974.
92. JABONERO V. Études sur le système neurovégétatif péripherique. IV. Innervation intramurale de la vésicule biliaire. *Acta. Anat.* **13**:171, 1951.
93. JACOBSSON B. Determination of pressure in the common bile duct at and after operation. *Acta Chir. Scand.* **113**:483, 1957.
94. JACOBSSON B., LANNER L.O. & RADBERG C. The dynamic variability of the choledocho-pancreatico-duodenal junction. *Acta Radiol. (Stockholm)* **52**:269, 1959.
95. JAVITT N.B. Bile salt regulation of hepatic excretory function. *Gastroenterology* **56**:622, 1969.
96. JOHNSON E.F. & BOYDEN E.A. The effect of double vagotomy on the motor activity of the human gallbladder. *Surgery* **32**:591, 1952.
97. JONES R.S. & GROSSMAN M.I. The choleretic response to feeding in dogs. *Proc. Soc. Exp. Biol. Med.* **132**:708, 1969.
98. JORPES E., MUTT V., JONSON G., THULIN L. & SUNDMAN L. The influence of secretin

and cholecystokinin on bile flow. In W. Taylor (ed.), *The Biliary System*. Blackwell, Oxford, 1965.

99. JOSEPHSON B. The circulation of bile acids in connection with their production, conjugation and excretion. *Physiol. Rev.* **21**:463, 1941.

100. KALSAR M., COHEN R., ARTEAGA I., YAWN E., MAYDRAL L., HOFFERT W.R. & FRAZIER D. Normal viral and bacterial flora of the human small and large intestine. *New Eng. J. Med.* **274**:500, 1966.

101. KJELLGREN K. Persistence of symptoms following biliary surgery. *Ann. Surg.* **152**:1026, 1960.

102. KOCK N.G., KEWENTER J. & JACOBSSON B. The influence of the motor activity of the duodenum on the pressure in the common bile duct. *Ann. Surg.* **160**:950, 1964.

103. KOCOUR E.J. & IVY A.C. The effects of certain foods on bile volume output as recorded in the dog by quantitative methods. *Am. J. Physiol.* **122**:325, 1938.

104. KUNE G.A. Surgical anatomy of common bile duct. *Arch. Surg. (Chicago)* **89**:995, 1964.

105. KUNE G.A. The influence of structure and function in the surgery of the biliary tract. Arris and Gale Lecture, April, 1970. *Ann. R. Coll. Surg. Eng.* **47**:78, 1970.

106. LARGE A.M. Regurgitation cholecystitis and cholelithiasis. *Ann. Surg.* **146**:607, 1957.

107. LaRUSSO N.F., HOFFMAN N.E., KORMAN M.G., HOFMANN A.F. & COWEN A.E. Determinants of fasting and postprandial serum bile acid levels in healthy man. *Digestive Diseases* **23**:385, 1978.

108. LEGER L., MICHON H., GUYET-ROUSSET P. & FUJISHIRO Y. Sphinctérotomie et physiologie vésiculaire. *J. Chir.* **85**:129, 1963.

109. LEMPKE R.E. The sphincter of Oddi and gallbladder function. I. Preservation of function after section and resection of the sphincter. *Ann. Surg.* **152**:815, 1960.

110. LEMPKE R.E. The sphincter of Oddi and gallbladder function. II. The effect of sphincterotomy upon sphincteric resistance. *Ann. Surg.* **158**:9, 1963.

111. LESTER R. Why is conjugation necessary for bilirubin excretion in the biliary system? In W. Taylor (ed.), *The Biliary System*, Blackwell, Oxford, 1965.

112. LEVITT M., SCHACTER B.A., ZIPURSKY A. & ISRAELS L.G. The non erythropoietic component of early bilirubin. *J. Clin. Invest.* **47**:1281, 1968.

113. LINDSTEDT S. & AHRENS E.H. Conversion of cholesterol to bile acids in man. *Proc. Soc. Expt. Biol. Med.* **108**:286, 1961.

114. LOW-BEER T.S., LACK L. & TYOR M.P. Effect of one meal on enterohepatic circulation of bile salts. *Gut* **10**:1050, 1969.

115. MacKAY C. & LEDINGHAM I. In *Jamieson and Kay's Textbook of Surgical Physiology*. Churchill Livingstone, Edinburgh, 1978.

116. MALAGELADA J.R., GO V.L.W. & SUMMERSKILL W.J.H. Altered pancreatic and biliary function after vagotomy and pyloroplasty. *Gastroenterology* **66**:22, 1974.

117. MALLET-GUY P., FEROLDI J. & MICEK F. Maladie du sphincter d'Oddi. *Lyon Chir.* **45**:33, 1950.

118. McCUTCHEON A.D. Reflux of duodenal contents in the pathogenesis of pancreatitis. *Gut* **5**:260, 1964.

119. McCUTCHEON A.D. A fresh approach to the pathogenesis of pancreatitis. *Gut* **9**:296, 1968.

120. McKELVEY S.T.D., KENNEDY T.L. & CONNELL A.M. The pancreatic biliary response to hypoglycaemia following both selective and truncal vagotomy. *Br. J. Surg.* **59**:387, 1972.

121. McLEOD G.M. & WIGGINS H.S. Bile salts in small intestinal contents after ileal resection and in other malabsorption syndromes. *Lancet* **1**:873, 1968.

122. METHENEY D. & LUNDMARK V.O. A review of 155 gastric resections in private practice from 1946 to 1956. *Am. J. Surg.* **94**:357, 1957.

123. MILLER M.C. Cholelithiasis developing after vagotomy. A preliminary report. *Canad. Med. Ass. J.* **98**:350, 1968.

124. MILLER J.R., FARRAR J.T. & SWELL L. Kinetics and pool size of primary bile acids in man. *Gastroenterology* **61**:85, 1971.
125. MIRIZZI P.L. Functional disturbances of the choledochus and hepatic bile ducts. *Surg. Gynec. Obstet.* **74**:306, 1942.
126. MIRIZZI P.L. Biliary lithiasis and pancreatic diseases. *Rev. Gastroent. Mex.* **2**:291, 1946.
127. MOLLOWITZ G. Beobachtungen der Gallesekretion des Menschen. Mitteilung einer neuen Methode zur fortlaufenden. Registrierung der gesamten Galleausscheidung. *Langenbecks Arch. Klin. Chir.* **291**:359, 1959.
128. MOSBACH E.H. Hepatic synthesis of bile acids. Biochemical steps and mechanisms of rate control. *Arch. Intern. Med.* **130**:478, 1972.
129. MYERS R.N., HAUPT G.J., BIRKHEAD N.C. & DEAVER J.M. Cinefluorographic observations of common bile duct physiology. *Ann. Surg.* **156**:442, 1962.
130. NASH T.P. The behaviour of the sphincter of Oddi in health and disease. *Aust. New Zeal. J. Surg.* **31**:40, 1961.
131. NEBEL O.T. Effect of enteric hormones on the human sphincter of Oddi. *Gastroenterology* **68**:692, 1975.
132. NEBESAR R.A., POLLARD J.J. & POTSAID J.J. Cine-cholangiography: some physiologic observations. *Radiology* **86**:475, 1966.
133. NIELSEN J.R. Development of cholelithiasis following vagotomy. *Surgery* **56**:909, 1964.
134. NOIR B.A. & NANET H. Study of the ethyl anthranilate azo derivatives of bilirubin sulphate. Confirmation of the existence of bilirubin sulphate conjugates in bile. *Biochem. Biophys. Acta.* **372**:230, 1974.
135. O'MAILLE E.R., RICHARDS T.G. & SHORT A.H. The influence of conjugation of cholic acid on its uptake and secretion: hepatic extraction of taurocholate and cholate in the dog. *J. Physiol.* **189**:337, 1967.
136. ONO K., WATANABE N., SUZUKI K., TSUCHIDA H., SUGIYAMA Y. & ABO M. Bile flow mechanism in man. *Arch. Surg. (Chicago)* **96**:869, 1968.
137. OSTERMILLER W. JR., THOMPSON R.J., CARTER R. & HINSHAW D.B. Acute obstructive cholangitis. *Arch. Surg. (Chicago)* **90**:392, 1965.
138. OSTROW J.D., JANDL J.H. & SCHMID R. The formation of bilirubin from haemoglobin in vivo. *J. Clin. Invest.* **41**:1628, 1962.
139. PARKIN G.J.S., SMITH R.B. & JOHNSTON D. Gallbladder volume and contractility after truncal selective and highly selective (parietal-cell) vagotomy in man. *Ann. Surg.* **178**:581, 1973.
140. PATTERSON H.A. The relationship between gallstones and heart disease. *Ann. Surg.* **139**:683, 1954.
141. PERSSON C.G.A. & EKMANN M. Effect of morphine, cholecystokinin and sympathomimetics on the sphincter of Oddi and intramural pressure in cat duodenum. *Scand. J. Gastroenterol.* **7**:345, 1972.
142. PLESSIER J. The use of cholecystokinin in the roentgenological examination. Clinical aspects. *Handb. exp. Pharm.* **34**:311, 1973.
143. PORTER H.P., SAUNDERS D.R., BRUNSER O., TYTGAT G.N. & RUBIN C.E. Fat absorption in bile fistula man: a clue to the pathway of normal fatty acid absorption. *Gastroenterology* **58**:984, 1970.
144. PORTER H.P., SAUNDERS D.R., TYTGAT G.N., BRUNSER O. & RUBIN C.E. Fat absorption in bile fistula man: a morphological and biochemical study. *Gastroenterology* **60**:1008, 1971.
145. RAZIN E., FELDMAN M.G. & DREILING D.A. Studies on the biliary flow and composition in man and dog. *J. Mt. Sinai Hosp. N.Y.* **32**:42, 1965.
146. ROBINSON T.M. & DUNPHY J.E. Effect of incomplete obstruction of the common bile duct. *Arch. Surg. (Chicago)* **83**:34, 1961.
147. RUDICK J. & HUTCHISON J.S.F. Evaluation of vagotomy and biliary function by

combined oral cholecystography and intravenous cholangiography. *Ann. Surg.* **162**:234, 1965.

148. SALI A. *Neurohumoral control of hepatic bile secretion.* PhD Thesis, Monash University, Melbourne, 1977.

149. SALI A. Rising incidence of cancer of the pancreas. In G.A. Kune, A. Sali & T. Jones (eds.), *Proc. First Australian Pancreas Congress, Melbourne,* 1978.

150. SALI A., MURRAY W.R. & MACKAY C. Aluminium hydroxide in bile salt diarrhoea. *Lancet* **2**:1051, 1977.

151. SALI A. & WATTS J. MCK. Regulation of hepatic bile flow and its composition. *Aust. New Zeal. J. Surg.* **41**:94, 1971.

152. SANDBERG D.H., SJÖVALL J., SJÖVALL K. & TURNER D.R. Measurement of human bile acids by gas liquid chromatography. *J. Lipid Res.* **6**:182, 1965.

153. SANDBLOM P., VOEGTLIN W.L. & IVY A.C. The effect of cholecystokinin on the choledochoduodenal mechanism (sphincter of Oddi). *Am. J. Physiol.* **113**:175, 1935.

154. SAPALA M.A., SAPALA J.A., SOTO A.D.R. & BOUWMAN D.L. Cholelithasis following subtotal gastric resection with truncal vagotomy. *Surg. Gynec. Obstet.* **148**:36, 1979.

155. SARLES H. Research and the pancreas. In G.A. Kune, A. Sali & T. Jones (eds.), *Proc. First Australian Pancreas Congress, Melbourne,* 1978.

156. SARLES J.C., BIDART J.M., DEVAUX M.A., ECHINARD C. & CATAGNINI A. Action of cholecystokinin and caerulein on the rabbit sphincter of Oddi. *Digestion* **14**:415, 1976.

157. SARLES J.C., MIDEJEAN A. & DEVAUX M.A. Electromyography of the sphincter of Oddi. Technique and experimental results in the rabbit: effect of certain drugs. *Am. J. Gastroenterol.* **63**:221, 1976.

158. SCHAPIRO R.H., HEIZER W.D., GOLDFINGER S.E. & ASERKOFF B.R. Cholestyramine responses to idiopathic diarrhoea. *Gastroenterology* **58**:993, 1970.

159. SCHEIN C.J. & BENEVENTANO T.C. Choledochal dynamics in man. *Surg. Gynec. Obstet.* **126**:591, 1968.

160. SCHEIN C.J., BENEVENTANO T.C., ROSEN R.G., DARDIK M.M. & GLIEDMAN M.L. Hepatic plexus vagectomy as an adjunct to cholecystectomy. *Surg. Gynec. Obstet.* **128**:241, 1969.

161. SCHEIN C.J., TAWIL V.E., DARDIK H. & BENEVENTANO T.C. Common duct dynamics in man. The influence of sympathetic block. *Am. J. Surg.* **119**:261, 1970.

162. SCHERSTEN T., NILSSON S., CAHLIN E., FILIPSON M. & BRODIN-PERSSON G. Relationship between biliary excretion of bile acids and the excretion of water, lecithin and cholesterol in man. *Eur. J. Clin. Invest.* **1**:242, 1971.

163. SCHMID R. Bilirubin metabolism in man. *New Eng. J. Med.* **287**:703, 1972.

164. SCHWEGLER R.A. JR. & BOYDEN E.A. The development of the common bile duct in the human fetus with special reference to the origin of the ampulla of Vater and the sphincter of Oddi. *Surg. Gynec. Obstet.* **68**:17, 193, 1937.

165. SCOTT G.W., SMALLWOOD R.E. & ROLLINS S. The flow through the bile duct after cholecystectomy. *Surg. Gynec. Obstet.* **140**:912, 1975.

166. SHEFER S., HAUSER S., BEKERSKY I. & MOSBACH E.H. Feedback regulation of bile acid biosynthesis in the rat. *J. Lipid Res.* **10**:646, 1969.

167. SHEFER S., HAUSER S., BEKERSKY I. & MOSBACH E.H. Biochemical site of regulation of bile acid synthesis in the rat. *J. Lipid Res.* **11**:404, 1970.

168. SJÖVALL J. Quantitative determination of bile acids on paper chromatograms. *Ark. Kemi.* **8**:317, 1955.

169. SJÖVALL J. Bile acids in man under normal and pathological conditions. *Clin. chim. Acta* **5**:33, 1960.

170. SMALL D.M. The formation of gallstones. *Adv. Internal Med.* **16**:243, 1970.

171. SMALL D.M. Surface and bulk interactions of lipids and water with a classification of biologically active lipids based on these interactions. *Fedn. Proc.* **29**:1320, 1970.

172. SMALL D.M., DOWLING R.H. & REDINGER R.N. The enterohepatic circulation of bile salts. *Archiv. Int. Med.* **130**:552, 1972.

173. SPERBER I. Secretion of organic anions in the formation of urine and bile. *Pharmacol. Rev.* **11**:109, 1959.
174. SPERBER I. Biliary secretion and choleresis. In C. Hogben (ed.), *Drugs and Membranes*; *Proc. First Intern. Pharmacol. Meeting, vol. 4*, 1963.
175. SPERBER I. Biliary secretion of organic anions and its influence on bile flow. In W. Taylor (ed.), *The Biliary System*. Blackwell, Oxford, 1965.
176. STACY M. & WEBB M. Studies on the antibacterial properties of the bile acids and some compounds derived from cholanic acid. *Proc. Roy. Soc. B.* **134**:523, 1947.
177. STEWART J.H. Cardiac therapy. Hoeber, New York, 1952.
178. SULLIVAN F.J., EATON S.B. JR., FERRUCCI J.T. JR., DREYFUSS J.R. & SLOAN R.W. Cholangiographic manifestations of acute biliary colic. *New Eng. J. Med.* **288**:33, 1973.
179. SUTOR D.J. & WILKIE L.I. Diurnal variations in the pH of pathological gallbladder bile. *Gut* **17**:971, 1976.
180. TANSY M.F., INNES D.L., MARTIN J.S. & KENDALL F.M. An evaluation of neural influences on the sphincter of Oddi in the dog. *Am. J. Dig. Dis.* **19**:423, 1974.
181. THISTLETHWAITE J.R. & SMITH D.F. Evaluation of sphincterotomy for the treatment of chronic recurrent pancreatitis. *Ann. Surg.* **158**:226, 1963.
182. THUREBORN E. Human hepatic bile composition changes due to altered enterohepatic circulation. *Acta Chir. Scand.* **303** (suppl. 1), 1962.
183. TOOULI J. & WATTS J. McK. The spontaneous motility and the action of cholecystokinin–pancreozymin, secretin and gastrin on the canine extrahepatic biliary tract. *Br. J. Surg.* **57**:858, 1970.
184. TOOULI J. & WATTS J. McK. Actions of cholecystokinin–pancreozymin, secretin and gastrin on extrahepatic biliary tract motility in vitro. *Ann. Surg.* **175**:439, 1972.
185. TORSOLI A., RAMORINO M.L. & ALESSSANDRINI A. Motility of the biliary tract. *Rendiconti Romani di Gastroenterologia*, **2**:67, 1970.
186. TORSOLI A., RAMORINO M.L. & CARRATU R. The use of cholecystokinin in the roentgenological examination of the extrahepatic biliary tract and intestines. *Handb. exp. Pharm.* **34**:247, 1973.
187. TORSOLI A., RAMORINO M.L., COLAGRANDE C. & DEMAIO G. Experiments with cholecystokinin. *Acta Radiol. (Stockholm)* **55**:193, 1961.
188. TRAPNELL J.E. The pathogenesis of gallstone pancreatitis. *Postgrad. Med. J.* **44**:497, 1968.
189. VAJCNER A., GROSSLING S. & NICOLOFF D.M. Physiologic evaluation of sphincteroplasty. *Surgery* **62**:589, 1967.
190. VAN BERGE HENEGOUWEN G.P. & HOFMANN A.F. Nocturnal gallbladder storage and emptying in gallstone patients and healthy subjects. *Gastroenterology* **75**:879, 1978.
191. VASCOUCELOS D., CASTRO F.L. & CHAVES E. Cystic-cholecystic syndrome due to mechanical blocking. *Rev. Ass. Med. Brasil* **5**:128, 1959.
192. VLAHCEVIC Z.R., BELL C. JR., BUHAC I., FARRAR J.T. & SWELL L. Diminished bile acid pool size in patients with gallstones. *Gastroenterology* **59**:165, 1970.
193. WARREN K.W. Surgical management of chronic relapsing pancreatitis. *Amer. J. Surg.* **117**:24, 1969.
194. WARREN K.W. & KUNE G.A. Surgical treatment of chronic relapsing pancreatitis. In H.R. Hawthorne, A.S. Frobese & J.A. Sterling (eds.), *The Acute Abdomen and Emergent Lesions of the Gastrointestinal Tract*. Thomas Springfield III, 1967.
195. WATTS J. & DUNPHY J.E. The role of the common bile duct in biliary dynamics. *Surg. Gynec. Obstet.* **122**:1207, 1966.
196. WEISS J.B. & HOLT P.R. Controlling factors during intestinal fat absorption. *J. Clin. Invest.* **50**:97a, 1971.
197. WHEELER H.O. Secretion of bile. In L. Shiff (ed.), *Diseases of the Liver*. Lippincott, Philadelphia, 1969.
198. WHEELER H.O. Concentrating function of the gallbladder. *Am. J. Med.* **51**:588, 1971.

199. WHITE T.T. & ALLAN B.J. Two instances of bile reflux without acute pancreatitis. *Surg. Gynec. Obstet.* **146:**917, 1978.
200. WHITE T.T., ELMSLIE R.G. & MAGEE D.F. Observations on the human intraductal pancreatic pressure. *Surg. Gynec. Obstet.* **118:**1043, 1964.
201. WILLIAMS R. Physiology of the gallbladder and bile ducts. In R. Smith & S. Sherlock (eds.), *Surgery of the Gallbladder and Bile Ducts.* Butterworth, London, 1964.
202. WITH T.K. Bilirubin and urobilinoid contents of human bile. *Acta Med. Scand.* **122:**513, 1945.
203. WOLFERT W., HARTMANN W. & HOTZ J. Exocrine pancreatic secretion and output of bile in humans under conditions of hypoglycaemia and administration of atropine. *Digestion* **10:**9, 1974.
204. WRIGHT A.D. Surgery of the biliary tract. *Ann. R. Coll. Surg. Eng.* **27:**373, 1960.
205. WYATT A.P., BELZER F.O. & DUNPHY J.E. Malfunction without constriction of the common bile duct. *Am. J. Surg.* **113:**592, 1967.
206. WYNDER E.L., MABUCHI K., MARUCHI N. & FORTNER J.G. Epidemiology of cancer of the pancreas. *J. Nat. Cancer Inst.* **50:**645, 1973.

3. Radiology of the Biliary Tract

BY HIRAM BADDELEY

Calcification in biliary calculi, the gallbladder, and pancreas or gas lucencies in the bile ducts may be evident on plain abdomen radiographs, but in the majority of patients artificial contrast medium needs to be introduced in order to display disease (Fig. 3.1).

The human gallbladder was first visualised by oral cholecystography in 1924 by Graham and Cole, and this is still the most commonly used investigation for suspected gallbladder disease.

Although infusion cholangiography has been improved by the use of slow infusion and safer contrast media, ultrasound examination is reducing the need for this examination. Ultrasound can demonstrate calculi in a non-radiopacified gallbladder in the majority of cases and is much easier and safer to perform. It may also reveal dilatation of the bile ducts, duct calculi, or pancreatic pathology. The introduction of contrast medium into the biliary system by endoscopic cannulation or by percutaneous needle puncture has proved increasingly valuable in defining pathology, especially in the investigation of jaundiced patients in whom a surgical lesion is suspected.

Computed abdominal tomography has joined scintigraphy and ultrasound examination as another non-invasive method of demonstrating hepatobiliary disease. It can be expected to have a profound effect on biliary and pancreatic diagnosis in the future.

The following techniques will be discussed:
1. Oral cholecystography.
2. Ultrasound examination.
3. Computed tomography.
4. Intravenous cholangiography.
5. Percutaneous transhepatic cholangiography.
6. Endoscopic retrograde cholangiopancreatography.
7. Operative cholangiography.

ORAL CHOLECYSTOGRAPHY

Oral cholecystography has proved to be a simple and accurate method of demonstrating gallbladder disease and, if the gallbladder is well opacified, has a predictive accuracy in the region of 95 per cent for the presence or absence of calculi. Calculi usually show as radiolucent defects within the opaque medium but in some cases they may be calcified and of the same or greater density than the

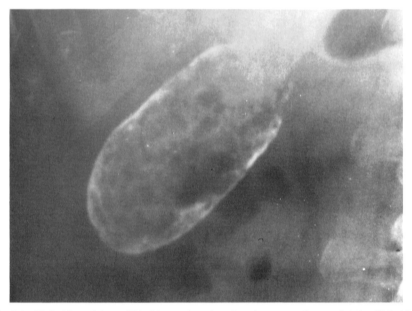

Fig. 3.1. Plain film of the gallbladder region showing the unusual 'porcelain' gallbladder.

contrast medium. Very small calculi can be difficult to demonstrate and overlying bowel gas shadows may simulate lucent calculi.

Oral cholecystographic media are lipid soluble and become bound to serum albumin following absorption from the bowel and prior to conjugation in the liver and excretion in the bile. They are concentrated within the gallbladder due to the reabsorption of water from bile.

Contrast media in current use are iopanoic acid (telepaque) and sodium ipodate (biloptin), usually given as a 3-g dose with 4 g for large patients.

Side-effects such as nausea, diarrhoea, abdominal pain, and skin reactions are not uncommon. Renal failure is a rare complication that has been reported, following large doses of contrast medium, in patients with hepatobiliary disease of increasing severity and with bunamiodyl, a medium which has now been withdrawn from use [15, 51]. Renal complications are more likely to occur if the patient is dehydrated, if there has been a recent intravenous cholangiogram, or if repeat, double, or multiple doses are used [26, 10].

CONTRAINDICATIONS TO ORAL CHOLECYSTOGRAPHY

1. Jaundice—especially if increasing.
2. Liver or renal failure.
3. Sensitivity to cholecystographic media.
4. Proposed thyroid function studies.
5. Immediately following intravenous cholangiography.
6. Previous cholecystectomy.

A preliminary plain film of the gallbladder region is desirable to demonstrate opaque calculi [29]. Three grams of contrast medium are taken with a light evening meal. Fluids should be encouraged but no food should be taken until after the examination. Optimum opacification occurs 14–18 hours after ingestion of most contrast media, although sooner with calcium ipodate.

Radiographs are taken in the prone, supine, and erect positions and, if the gallbladder is well demonstrated, the examination is completed with a film 30 minutes after a fat stimulus. The after-fat film is helpful in the diagnosis of adenomyomatosis and may reveal small calculi [30]. Failure of the gallbladder to contract does not by itself indicate gallbladder pathology. Intravenous cholecystokinin has been used to promote gallbladder contraction during cholecystography [11]. Films taken in the erect position may show a horizontal band made up of many small lucent gallstones floating within the dense contrast medium (Fig. 3.2).

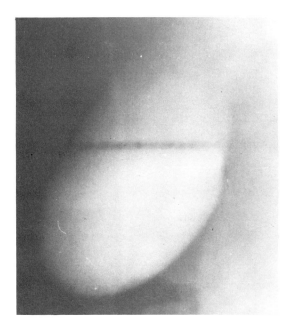

Fig. 3.2. Oral cholecystogram in the erect position showing a horizontal layer made up of many small lucent calculi of similar density floating within dense contrast medium.

NON-VISUALISATION AND FAINT OPACIFICATION OF THE GALLBLADDER

The causes of non-visualisation of the gallbladder are the following:
1. Gallbladder disease and cystic duct obstruction.
2. Vomiting or failure to take medium orally.
3. Obstructive lesions—pharyngeal pouch, achalasia, and pyloric stenosis.
4. Jaundice and impaired liver function.
5. Previous cholecystectomy.
6. Absent or ectopic gallbladder.

Patients with diarrhoea or malabsorption usually manage to absorb sufficient medium for adequate cholecystography [46]. Congenital absence of the gallbladder is exceedingly rare, but an ectopic gallbladder lying within the liver, on the left side of the abdomen or low in the right iliac fossa, may be missed unless a radiograph of the whole abdomen is taken; this will also confirm if the patient took the contrast medium as directed. Acute pancreatitis has been found to interfere with opacification [37].

Tomography of a faint or non-opacified gallbladder may show cystic duct calculi or reveal a gallbladder filled with lucent calculi. Bile duct opacification with non-filling of the gallbladder indicates cystic duct obstruction or gallbladder disease [50].

Only occasionally does a repeat or double dose of contrast medium produce visualisation of a non-opacified gallbladder and ultrasound examination or intravenous cholangiography after 1 week are usually more rewarding. However, the radiodensity of a faintly opacified gallbladder is often enhanced with a repeat or double dose. If multiple doses are used the risk of renal failure must be considered and the patient adequately hydrated.

In the past, the absence of gallbladder opacification was considered to be an indication for cholecystectomy. Occasionally, an apparently normal gallbladder in a patient with adequate liver function may not opacify so that ultrasonography or intravenous cholangiography should be employed to confirm the presence of gallbladder disease prior to surgery [52]. Faint opacification without evidence of gallstones cannot be regarded as indicating gallbladder disease and should also be investigated further with a repeat dose, ultrasound, or cholangiography.

ULTRASOUND EXAMINATION

The development of high-quality grey scale ultrasound equipment in recent years is altering the pattern of biliary diagnosis significantly and, where it is available, is reducing the need for many invasive investigations. It is possible to demonstrate the gallbladder in most patients and the intra- and extrahepatic bile ducts when these are dilated. Masses within the head of the pancreas may also be defined. The examination can be unsatisfactory if there is a great deal of bowel gas or if the patient is obese.

Ultrasound investigation is indicated in patients with suspected gallbladder disease who show no opacification of the gallbladder at oral cholecystography, and may demonstrate calculi correctly in about 90 per cent of non-opacified gallbladders which contain calculi [44]. If ultrasound examination is equivocal then intravenous cholangiography can be used.

The gallbladder is examined with the patient starved and shows as an oval echo-free region under the right lobe of the liver (Fig. 3.3). A contracted gallbladder or one filled completely with gallstones can be difficult to find; however, calculi usually give strong echoes, but with an echo-free area or sonic shadow behind them (Fig. 3.3).

Ultrasound examination is the primary screening investigation of choice in

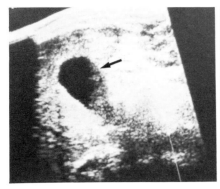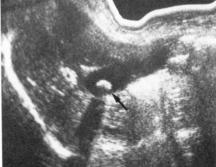

Fig. 3.3. (*left*) Ultrasound of a normal gallbladder (arrow). (*right*) Ultrasound of a gallbladder containing gallstones (arrow).

the jaundiced patient. It may demonstrate dilated intrahepatic ducts, extrahepatic ducts, or gallbladder (over 12 cm in length), thus indicating that jaundice is due to obstruction [65]. Large duct calculi and pancreatic abnormalities may be also visualised. The reader is referred to Chapter 4 regarding the use of ultrasound in the jaundiced patient.

Bowel gas is a serious problem and prevents adequate pancreatic examination in about 20 per cent of patients. Filling the stomach with large amounts of methyl cellulose can help overcome this. Rotation of the patient towards the left so that the common duct lies between the tranducer and the portal vein can give better ductal visualisation [7]. Pancreatic ultrasound compares poorly with computed tomography and endoscopic pancreatography in the diagnosis of chronic pancreatitis and carcinoma, although it is very effective in defining the size, nature, and location of pancreatic pseudocysts. Fine-needle aspiration biopsy using ultrasonic guidance is a method of obtaining pancreatic material for cytological diagnosis [19].

COMPUTED TOMOGRAPHY

Computed tomography (CT) has been established as a major advance in the visualisation of tissue structures. The examination of body sections can be performed with scan times of only a few seconds and views with good resolution of the tissues can be obtained.

Tomography of the liver and pancreas is still at an early stage of evaluation but does seem promising. It compares well with hepatic scintigraphy and ultrasound in the definition of intrahepatic neoplasm or abscess and can show dilated intrahepatic bile ducts. Unlike ultrasound examination it produces good results in obese patients [18, 31].

The pancreas is usually well shown except in emaciated subjects who have little delineating fat. Pancreatitis produces alterations in size or configuration of the pancreatic outline and dilatation of the pancreatic duct and cysts can be well shown. Calcifications may be evident when they cannot be visualised on plain films [27].

Pancreatic carcinomas give localised alterations of pancreatic contour or extend outside the gland to obscure the peripancreatic fat planes; they are usually slightly more dense than the surrounding normal pancreas. The major limitation to the use of the whole body computed tomography at the present time is the high capital and maintenance cost of the equipment.

Computed tomography of the gallbladder may be of help when conventional radiography and ultrasound have been non-contributory and can demonstrate gallbladder calculi in 80 per cent of patients [32].

INTRAVENOUS CHOLANGIOGRAPHY

Intravenous cholangiography has been the method of choice for demonstration of the bile ducts until recently, but now grey scale ultrasound examination is reducing the need for this investigation. The extrahepatic ducts and variable portion of the intrahepatic ducts can be visualised. Gallbladder opacification will also be achieved in patients who do not have cystic duct occlusion, but it is not as satisfactory as the oral method for demonstrating the gallbladder. Because intravenous cholangiography is more time-consuming and hazardous it is reserved for those situations where cholecystography and echography have proved or would be non-contributory.

INDICATIONS FOR INTRAVENOUS CHOLANGIOGRAPHY

1. Symptoms of biliary disease after cholecystectomy.
2. Non-opacifications of the gallbladder or bile ducts by oral cholecystography.
3. Investigation of biliary colic and mild jaundice.
4. Assessment of bile ducts prior to surgery [67].
5. Diagnosis of acute cholecystitis.
6. Suspected choledochal cyst [39].
7. Foreign bodies in the bile ducts [48].

Liver function must be reasonably good to obtain visualisation of the bile ducts, the serum bilirubin level should be less than 45 mmol/l and subsiding to normal levels rather than increasing. There is a correlation between the excretion of cholangiographic media and bromsulphalein (BSP). If retention of the latter exceeds 40 per cent the bile ducts are unlikely to be visualised (Fig. 3.4).

CONTRAINDICATIONS TO INTRAVENOUS CHOLANGIOGRAPHY

1. Combined liver and renal disease.
2. Severe jaundice.
3. Serum paraprotein abnormalities, e.g. Waldenstrom's macroglobulinaemia.
4. Known sensitivity to contrast medium.

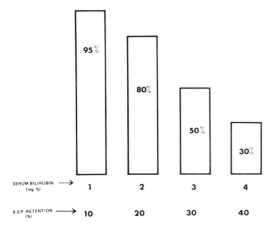

Fig. 3.4. Frequency of visualisation with IV cholangiography in relation to serum bilirubin and bromsulphalein retention. Modified from Wise: *Intravenous Cholangiography*, 1962; courtesy of Charles C. Thomas, Springfield, Ill.

5. Recent cholecystogram.
6. Ischaemic heart disease.
7. Pregnancy.

METHOD

Cholangiographic media are freely soluble in aqueous solution and are thus suitable for intravascular injection. They bind with serum protein before active transport through the liver which has a limited excretory capacity. Increasing the dose of contrast medium beyond the optimum fails to produce better bile duct opacification and increases renal excretion. Slow infusion over 30 minutes or longer produces higher bile concentrations than intravenous injection over 5–10 minutes [8] and is associated with fewer side-effects, such as nausea and retching [53].

Films are taken following infusion at intervals up to 2 hours. Once the bile ducts are visualised tomography should be performed to obtain better views of the common duct (Fig. 3.5). In hepatocellular failure or obstructive jaundice there is delayed visualisation and views after 8 hours may be necessary [13]. When the gallbladder opacifies it should be examined with erect views and after fat. Biliary-enteric fistulae allow the medium to drain rapidly from the bile ducts and thus prevent visualisation. The presence of gas in the bile ducts on the preliminary plain film is a strong indication that cholangiography is unlikely to be successful.

Pethidine or morphine have been used to delay bile duct emptying and so to improve visualisation but they may provoke painful spasm of the sphincter of Oddi. The use of short-acting duodenal relaxants during tomography is said to improve visualisation of the lower common bile duct.

Minor side-effects during injection are common and include retching, dizzy feelings, flushing, and urticaria. Severe reactions such as hypotensive collapse or bronchospasm occur much more commonly than following intravenous urography and a mortality rate of one in 5000 examinations has been reported [2]. Emergency drugs and equipment should always be available in the x-ray room.

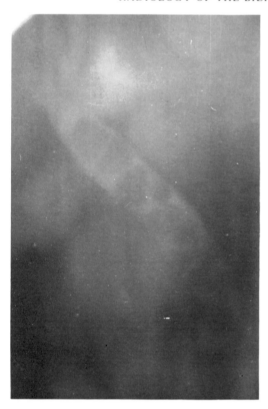

Fig. 3.5. Tomographic demonstration of multiple calculi in a dilated common bile duct during intravenous cholangiography.

Sudden death due to gel precipitation of the plasma has occurred in patients with abnormal serum proteins as in Waldenstrom's macroglobulinaemia [5]. Examination should also be avoided in patients with multiple myeloma. Hepatotoxic reactions and renal failure have been reported with higher doses of contrast medium and where there was hepatorenal disease. Acute renal failure has been described in a patient with the Dubin–Johnson syndrome [62].

Cholangiography should not be carried out within several days of oral cholecystography because both contrast media compete in protein binding and liver transport, biliary opacification is impaired and reactions occur more commonly [23].

NORMAL FINDINGS

The internal diameter of the common bile duct just above the level of the pancreas as measured on radiographs averaged 5–7 mm. There is variation in the agreed upper limit of normal from 10 to 15 mm [66, 45, 47]. A width of 14 mm or more should be considered abnormal even in a large person. The common hepatic duct is wider than the common bile duct giving a tapered configuration to the normal main bile duct. There is no evidence that the bile duct dilates following cholecystectomy [45, 47].

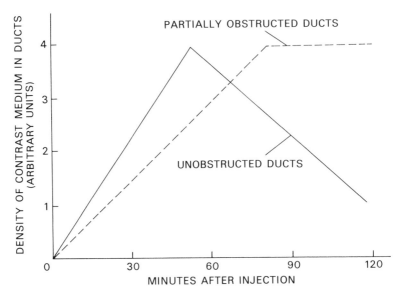

Fig. 3.6. Relative density of contrast during intravenous cholangiography in partially obstructed and unobstructed ducts. Redrawn from Wise: *Intravenous Cholangiography*, 1962; courtesy of Charles C. Thomas, Springfield, Ill.

In the normal unobstructed duct the radiodensity of the bile duct begins to decrease after 45–60 minutes and is gone at 2 hours (Fig. 3.6).

ABNORMAL FINDINGS

The most important application of intravenous cholangiography is in the demonstration of bile duct calculi. Strictures of the bile duct are not often shown, as these are usually associated with jaundice which impairs visualisation, but in the non-jaundiced patient it can be a valuable investigation (Fig. 6.8).

Dilatation of the bile duct and loss of its normal tapered configuration indicates obstruction of the lower common bile duct and gives indirect evidence of the presence of a lower bile duct calculus. Partial obstruction is often associated with increasing opacification after 1 hour, especially if the gallbladder has been removed [66, 67]. These features are also seen with papillary stenosis and bile duct tumours. Although the upper bile duct may be dilated in chronic pancreatitis the intrapancreatic bile duct usually shows a tapered configuration.

DIAGNOSTIC ACCURACY

When intravenous cholangiography is carefully performed the accuracy of diagnosis of bile duct calculi in a cholecystectomised patient is 90–95 per cent [6, 20]. Accuracy falls if the gallbladder and cystic duct are patent when the bile is usually not so well opacified.

The finding of a normal unobstructed duct following cholecystectomy is usually a good indication that it is not diseased, and is most helpful in the management of the patient who has persisting symptoms following cholecystectomy.

PERCUTANEOUS TRANSHEPATIC CHOLANGIOGRAPHY

Although percutaneous cholangiography has been in use for over 20 years it has recently become more diagnostically useful because of the development of the fine-needle technique, which is relatively easy to perform and which causes less patient discomfort and is safer than previously used techniques.

INDICATIONS

JAUNDICE OF OBSCURE AETIOLOGY
The major indication for percutaneous cholangiography is undiagnosed jaundice which is believed to be due to mechanical bile duct obstruction. Normal calibre intrahepatic ducts may be demonstrated with the fine needle technique so that jaundiced patients can be investigated before the intrahepatic ducts have become dilated and the duct anatomy in patients with primary biliary cirrhosis or sclerosing cholangitis may be defined. A normal duct system may be shown in patients with non-surgical jaundice (Fig. 3.7). The reader is referred to Chapter 4 which deals with obstructive jaundice.

KNOWN MECHANICAL BILE DUCT OBSTRUCTION
The method may be used to assess the proximal bile ducts where the cause of obstruction is already known and to localise the precise site of obstruction as a means of preparing for, and planning of, the operation and further management [35, 63]. This technique is, therefore, extremely useful in making diagnostic decisions in the management of both benign and malignant strictures and occlusions of the ductal system, as detailed in Chapters 4, 5, 6, and 7.

CONTRAINDICATIONS TO PERCUTANEOUS TRANSHEPATIC CHOLANGIOGRAPHY

1. Bleeding tendency.
2. Sensitivity to contrast media.
3. Cholangitis—acute or subacute.
4. Liver metastasis, if extensive.

TECHNIQUE

Puncture of the intrahepatic bile ducts and the injection of water-soluble contrast medium (hypaque 25 per cent, urografin 30 per cent) may be achieved by one of three methods, namely (a) catheter-sheathed needle, (b) fine (Chiba) needle, and (c) transjugular catheter.

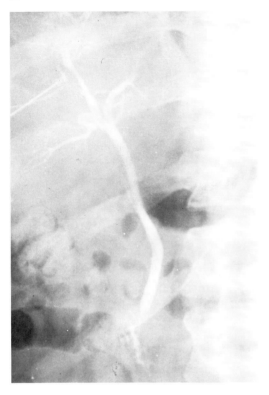

Fig. 3.7. Fine-needle percutaneous transhepatic cholangiogram in a patient with jaundice of obscure cause. Cholangiogram shows a normal biliary tree, thereby avoiding surgical intervention.

The examination is performed under local anaesthesia using image intensification. The patient's prothrombin time should be within 3 seconds of the control and facilities for the prompt surgical relief of biliary obstruction should be available. Antibiotic cover is indicated for all patients, but especially if the patient has been pyrexial.

Previous hepatic scintiscan or ultrasound is desirable to exclude intrahepatic masses and a preliminary plain film is necessary to plan the puncture site and exclude interposition of bowel.

SHEATHED NEEDLE
This technique was described by Shaldon in 1962. A polythene catheter sheathed over a steel needle is advanced into the liver from an anterior subcostal approach. The needle is removed and the catheter withdrawn gradually until bile is aspirated whereupon contrast medium is injected under screen control. The technique is usually only successful when the intrahepatic ducts are dilated because of the relatively large diameter of the catheter. If no duct is entered after six advances in separate directions the examination is terminated. Wide ducts are usually entered on the first or second attempt.

If an obstructed system is outlined radiographs are taken in several different projections so as to show the level of obstruction. The presence of sludge within the bile duct may prevent contrast medium reaching the level of obstruction, and the patient needs to be turned to the left or elevated so as to define the obstruction.

The catheter can be left *in situ* to drain bile until surgery is performed.

FINE NEEDLE

Okuda of the University of Chiba described this method in 1974. The flexible needle, which is 0.7 mm in outer diameter, is inserted laterally into the liver from a right intercostal space. Because of its small calibre bile cannot be aspirated and the needle tip is positioned within a bile duct using injected contrast medium. This needle is easier to advance into the liver than a sheathed needle, is relatively atraumatic, and up to ten advances may be made.

If an obstructed system is outlined prompt surgical decompression is desirable. In some centres a catheter is inserted using the sheathed-needle method so as to drain the obstructed system until operation [34].

TRANSJUGULAR CATHETER

The right internal jugular vein is catheterised and the catheter is advanced through the vena cava into the hepatic vein [28]. A modified transeptal needle is then used to puncture the liver parenchyma and adjacent bile duct. The quoted advantages of this technique are the avoidance of peritoneal bleeding and bile leakage. However, the procedure has not had extensive trials up to the present time.

COMPLICATIONS

Bile leakage, intraperitoneal bleeding, bacteraemia, and septicaemia are the important complications of this procedure, and these aspects have been recently reviewed by Sali and co-workers [56].

Although bile leakage and bleeding are less frequent and severe if the fine-needle technique is used these complications still occur, and immediate laparotomy and decompression may still be necessary. Acute cholangitis and septicaemia in the presence of obstruction may occur more often with the fine needle than a sheathed needle since biliary decompression is not possible, and the patient should be observed closely for evidence of septicaemia which may develop very rapidly. While septicaemia is more common in association with gallstones infective complications may occur with malignant obstruction as well. The routine use of broad-spectrum preventative antibiotics has significantly lowered the risk of septicaemia developing after this procedure.

ABNORMAL FINDINGS

In addition to defining the level of obstruction cholangiography may elucidate the cause. Calculi may be seen as lucent defects within the contrast-filled duct, or if impacted may show a crescentic upper border (Fig. 3.8). However, biliary calculi are common and may coexist with a malignant stricture. Carcinomatous narrowings due to bile duct or pancreatic neoplasm produce strictures with

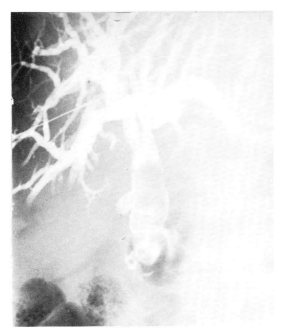

Fig. 3.8. Percutaneous transhepatic cholangiogram showing several lucent defects in the common bile duct caused by calculi.

abrupt or shouldered upper margins (Fig. 3.9). Post-traumatic strictures are usually short (Fig. 3.10). Dilatation of the gallbladder is a feature of malignant, common bile duct stricture. Strictures which follow previous bile duct-intestinal anastomoses, such as hepaticojejunostomy, are well detected by this procedure (Fig. 3.11).

Chronic pancreatitis gives a smoothly tapered narrowing of the lower common bile duct and sclerosing cholangitis affects both the intrahepatic, as well as the extrahepatic, bile ducts which assume a beaded appearance due to dilation of the ducts between the multiple short strictures (Chapter 6). The differentiation between sclerosing bile duct carcinoma and sclerosing cholangitis is often difficult, and this problem is dealt with in detail in Chapters 6 and 7 (Fig. 3.12). Congenital cystic dilation of the intrahepatic ducts (Caroli's disease) or choledochal cysts also produce characteristic appearances [3]. It is sometimes not possible to be sure of the nature of the obstructing lesion prior to laparotomy, and in these cases the major value of percutaneous cholangiography lies in confirming that there is an obstruction to the bile ducts which requires surgical relief.

DIAGNOSTIC ACCURACY

Using the older sheathed-needle technique a diagnostic cholangiogram was achieved in 80 per cent of patients with jaundice due to extrahepatic obstruction. If no cholangiogram was obtained there was still a 20–25 per cent chance that an obstructive lesion could be present. This unsatisfactory situation was greatly improved following the introduction of the fine needle which has a much higher

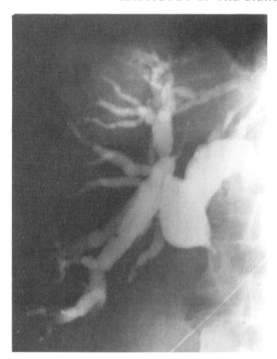

Fig. 3.9. Percutaneous transhepatic cholangiogram showing abrupt and complete bile duct obstruction caused by a cancer of the head of the pancreas. Bile ducts are markedly dilated.

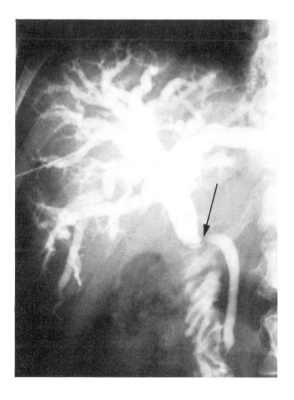

Fig. 3.10. Percutaneous transhepatic cholangiogram of a short post-traumatic stricture of the common bile duct which recurred after a previous end-to-end reconstruction of the duct.

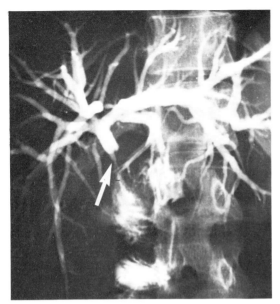

Fig. 3.11. Percutaneous transhepatic cholangiogram of a stricture which followed a previous hepaticojejunostomy performed for an operative bile duct injury.

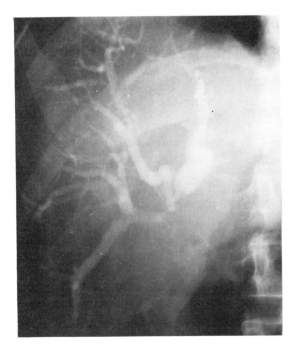

Fig. 3.12. Percutaneous transhepatic cholangiogram showing almost complete obstruction at the origin of the common hepatic duct with only a thin streak of contrast passing down the bile duct. Differentiation between sclerosing cholangitis and carcinoma was achieved by endocholedochal biopsy (Chapters 6 & 7).

success rate. Extrahepatic obstruction may be defined in 95–100 per cent of cases and a normal biliary system in 70 per cent [21]. The greatest difficulty is experienced with sclerosing conditions of the intrahepatic ducts.

The fine-needle method has removed much of the uncertainty associated with percutaneous transhepatic cholangiography, so that there has been a resurgence of interest in the method which is relatively easy to perform. Since the risk of bile leakage is so much less it is usually not necessary to perform a laparotomy on the day of the procedure, as was the custom with the wider-bore sheathed needle.

ENDOSCOPIC RETROGRADE CHOLANGIOGRAPHY AND PANCREATOGRAPHY (ERCP)

In 1968 McCune described endoscopic cannulation of the papilla of Vater, which was made possible for the first time by the development of side-viewing duodenoscopes. ERCP is now established as a safe and satisfactory method of diagnosing biliary and pancreatic disease. Although some lesions adjacent to the papilla may be evident endoscopically, ERCP is primarily a radiological procedure which requires close cooperation between the radiological and endoscopic teams if interpretable radiographs are to be achieved [57].

INDICATIONS FOR ERCP

In the presence of jaundice with serum bilirubin levels in excess of 45 mmol/l, or impaired hepatic function, intravenous cholangiography usually fails to demonstrate the bile ducts and retrograde cholangiography may be used in its place. Lesions of the pancreas causing jaundice can be delineated, the papilla can be inspected prior to cannulation, and there is less need for prompt surgery if biliary obstruction is shown, so that ERCP is often preferable to percutaneous cholangiography in the first instance. For further details please see Chapter 4 which deals with obstructive jaundice. Endoscopic cholangiography can be used to monitor the progress of lesions in patients with known biliary disease, such as biliary stricture or sclerosing cholangitis; it has proved especially valuable in showing abnormalities following biliary surgery, such as retained calculi and strictures. The cause of jaundice may be identified in 70–80 per cent of patients in whom simpler investigations have proved non-contributory, and laparotomy may be avoided in those with a normal biliary tree. Cholangiography is a necessary preliminary to endoscopic sphincterotomy.

ERCP is particularly valuable in those cases in which both pancreatic and biliary tract pathology may be present, such as chronic pancreatitis with cholestasis or pancreatic carcinoma with bile duct obstruction (Chapter 4). It is also of great value in the diagnosis of obscure abdominal pain, which may have a biliary or pancreatic origin especially postcholecystectomy (Chapter 5).

Supplementary techniques in relation to the pancreas, such as juice aspiration, ductal brushing, or controlled percutaneous needle aspiration, may be used to obtain material for cytological examination. Choledochoscopy with a fine choledoscope has recently been introduced but its place has not been evaluated. Endoscopic sphincterotomy is described in Chapter 13.

CONTRAINDICATIONS TO ERCP

1. Sensitivity to contrast medium.
2. Obstructive lesion of the upper gastrointestinal tract (occasionally ERCP is successful in this group).
3. Subtotal gastrectomy of the Polya type, or total gastrectomy.
4. Acute pancreatitis.
5. Pancreatic pseudocyst.
6. Hepatitis antigen present (a probable contraindication).
7. Suppurative cholangitis.

METHOD

The technique has been well described by Burwood and co-workers in 1973 and by Salmon in 1974. In order to demonstrate small pancreatic ducts and bile duct calculi it is necessary to have good fluoroscopic and radiographic facilities which are best provided in a main x-ray department. Most ERCP is performed on fluoroscopic tables of the conventional type that can be tilted so that the patient may be radiographed in the upright position when necessary.

The side-viewing duodenoscope is introduced into the descending duodenum with the patient sedated with intravenous diazepam or phenoperidine. The papilla of Vater is usually recognized on the posterolateral wall by the arrangement of transverse and longitudinal folds surrounding it. Duct cannulation is performed following the injection of intravenous buscopan. Antibiotic is probably best used as a preventative routinely (Chapter 9).

When the catheter tip is adequately positioned, so as to fill the duct of interest, contrast medium is injected under careful fluoroscopic control; the biliary system should be scrutinised for delayed filling, strictures, or small calculi, and a biliary enteric fistula may be missed if the possibility is not considered at this stage. Pancreatic duct filling should similarly be observed for strictures and holdup. The pancreatic parenchyma should be viewed frequently for contrast staining, which is a signal that injection is complete. Injection must be terminated the moment that filling of a pancreatic cavity is appreciated, to avoid contamination of a pancreatic cyst, and the amount of medium injected above a biliary stricture should be limited to that required to show its extent.

CONTRAST MEDIUM
The amount of contrast medium used varies greatly depending on the capacity of the biliary and pancreatic ducts and the amount of reflux into the duodenum. At the start of the injection the catheter is primed with contrast medium such as angiografin or conray 280 which can be used to demonstrate the pancreatic ducts, or normal calibre bile ducts. If the common duct is dilated, especially if calculi are suspected, the medium is changed to a more dilute solution such as 25 per cent hypaque.

ASSOCIATED CYTOLOGICAL TECHNIQUES
Material can be obtained for cytological examination in three main ways using

retrograde cannulation of the pancreatic duct, which may help in distinguishing between chronic pancreatitis and carcinoma:

1. Juice aspiration—this may be performed after ERCP, but is probably better done at a separate occasion following secretin/pancreozymin injection.

2. Brushing of the pancreatic duct.

3. Percutaneous fine-needle aspiration—this can be performed anteriorly or posteriorly, using a fine needle inserted to the appropriate depth to a position determined by preliminary ERCP.

FINDINGS

Cholangiographic appearances are similar for both the endoscopic and percutaneous methods. Examples of endoscopic cholangiograms are presented in Figs. 3.13–3.16. In the presence of completely obstructing lesions, which are only defined distally by the retrograde method, percutaneous cholangiography is indicated to show the proximal ducts and the upper limit of the lesion. In these cases retrograde cholangiography and percutaneous cholangiography are thus complementary (Fig. 3.16).

The normal pancreatic duct is smooth in outline and tapers gradually from the head of the gland, where it is normally 5 mm or less in diameter, towards the tail where it is usually 2–3 mm in diameter [17].

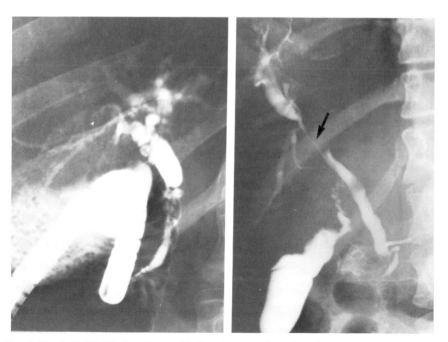

Fig. 3.13. (*left*) ERCP showing multiple strictures of the intrahepatic and extrahepatic bile ducts caused by sclerosing cholangitis in patient with chronic ulcerative proctocolitis. There are also many small calculi in the gallbladder.

Fig. 3.14. (*right*) ERCP of a carcinoma of the common hepatic duct.

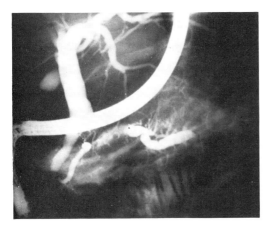

Fig. 3.15. ERCP of a patient with chronic relapsing pancreatitis and recurrent jaundice caused by strictures of the distal pancreatic and distal common bile duct. Courtesy of Dr. Ian Roberts-Thomson, Melbourne.

In chronic pancreatitis of mild degree the pancreatic ducts may appear normal. The earliest changes occur in the side ducts which show irregularity, dilatation, and short strictures. At a later stage the main duct becomes involved in a similar way and concrements may be shown within the ducts [40, 68]. Dilated side ducts form smooth-walled retention cysts, whereas pancreatic pseudocysts are more often a sequel to acute pancreatitis and have irregular walls. Pancreatic carcinoma can produce occlusion of the duct or strictures which may be tapered. The ducts upstream of obstruction are usually dilated whereas those downstream

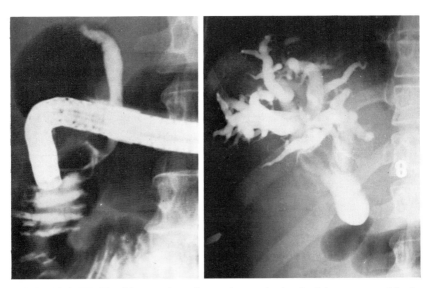

Fig. 3.16. (*left*) ERCP with complete obstruction at the level of the common bile duct. (*right*) Percutaneous transhepatic cholangiogram of same patient showing dilated proximal ducts and complete obstruction of the common hepatic duct, caused by a ligature accidentally tied around the bile duct during cholecystectomy. The two investigations were thus complementary.

are normal. In chronic pancreatitis the changes are more diffuse. Pancreatitis and carcinoma may both cause complete duct obstruction and distinction between them may be impossible [55]. Cytology or angiography may be useful in this situation [24].

RISKS

ERCP is a relatively safe procedure when performed by an experienced team; however, there are a number of hazards to be taken into account, which may result from pre-existing pathology, premedication, instrumentation, contrast-medium injection, and irradiation. A recent multicentre survey of 10 435 ERCP examinations in the United States reported complications in 3 per cent, and a mortality rate of 0.2 per cent [12].

Injection pancreatitis was the commonest complication and occurred in 1.0 per cent of patients, usually following overfilling of the pancreatic ducts. Careful fluoroscopic observation to avoid parenchymal opacification reduces the incidence of hyperamylasaemia which occurs in about 25 per cent of patients who have had ERCP, and some workers recommend careful manometry during pancreatic injection. ERCP should be avoided for 6 weeks after an attack of acute pancreatitis. Prophylactic aprotinin (trasylol) or glucagon have not been shown to have any definite advantages in this regard.

Although less frequent than injection pancreatitis, septic cholangitis (0.8 per cent) and abscess formation in a pancreatic pseudocyst (0.3 per cent) have a much more sinister prognosis and have been responsible for the majority of deaths, so that great care must be taken to avoid filling any pancreatic cyst with contrast medium. Ten per cent of patients with cholangitic sepsis and 20 per cent of patients with infected cyst died. In the presence of bile duct obstruction the minimum amount of medium should be used to outline the upper end of the obstruction. Prophylactic antibiotics, such as cephazolin or ampicillin and gentamicin, should be initiated immediately biliary obstruction is demonstrated, and probably their routine prophylactic use is the wisest policy (Chapter 9). Careful postinvestigative observation of all patients for 24 hours following ERCP is most important, and any evidence of infective complication should be regarded seriously. Instrumental injury occurred in 0.2 per cent of cases.

The radiation hazard to the patient and to the operators is really very small if experienced radiological personnel are supervising the procedure, and the dose levels to the skin and gonads are within the range used for barium studies and less than those of intravenous cholangiography.

OPERATIVE CHOLANGIOGRAPHY

Although cholangiographic demonstration of the bile ducts during operation has been in extensive use since 1932, a divergence of opinion still exists regarding its place in biliary tract surgery. The majority of surgeons employ it routinely [25], others occasionally, and a few do not use it at all.

TECHNIQUE

Operative cholangiography can be a valuable procedure only if the technique employed is meticulous in its attention to detail. Inexpert and haphazard methods are a hindrance rather than a help in the performance of a biliary operation [33, 43, 58].

A satisfactory technique includes a cassette tunnel and a high-powered x-ray unit. Although portable image intensifiers can be used to observe the flow of contrast medium during injection the image resolution is very poor and radiographs should always be taken to demonstrate duct calculi. Two films are exposed during the injection of contrast medium, the first after 4–5 ml and the second after 12–15 ml or more if the ducts are dilated. Dilute contrast agents such as hypaque 25 per cent, urografin 30 per cent, or retro conray are used to prevent obscuring a small stone [36]. It is important to prefill the catheter or needle with contrast medium before insertion into the duct so as to avoid the introduction of air bubbles which may simulate calculi. A portable lead screen draped with sterile towels is needed to give the operator radiation protection during the injection.

Oblique views with the patient turned about 15° towards the right project the lower bile duct away from the spine. The x-ray beam should be centred over the junction of the cystic and common hepatic duct and perpendicular to the plane of the gridded film cassette beneath the patient.

If the gallbladder is still present and a cholecystectomy is being performed anyway the cholangiogram is most conveniently done with a polyethylene catheter introduced into the bile duct through the cystic duct (Fig. 3.17). Recently, Berci has introduced an improved metal cannula (Fig. 3.19) [9].

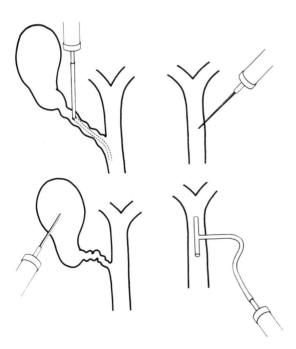

Fig. 3.17. Methods of performing operative cholangiography. (*top left*) Catheter in cystic duct (most common method). (*top right*) Direct needling of common bile duct. (*bottom left*) Through the gallbladder. (*bottom right*) Through common duct T tube.

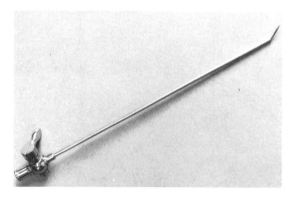

Fig. 3.18. Needle for operative cholangiography. From Kune [41].

In the postcholecystectomised patient, or in cases where the cystic duct cannot be cannulated for technical reasons, the cholangiogram is performed after needle puncture of the common bile duct. The angled needle with a guard and a two-way tap shown in Fig. 3.18 is most useful for the puncture of the bile duct [41]. It eliminates air bubbles from the system and prevents damage to the bile duct and surrounding structures. In order to minimise the risk of a bile leak through the puncture wound needle puncture is usually best reserved for cases in which the bile duct is likely to be explored. The contrast medium may also be introduced through a normal gallbladder, but the films obtained may not be satisfactory because the quantity of medium passing into the ducts is insufficient (Fig. 3.17).

If the common bile duct has been opened a postexploration operative T-tube cholangiogram may be taken before the abdomen is closed. However, the interpretation of these films is usually difficult because of the presence of air bubbles which can be difficult to eliminate and because of spasm of the sphincter of Oddi. For these reasons it is probably more accurate to rely on post-exploration fibreoptic choledochoscopy than on postexploration T-tube cholangiography (Chapter 5).

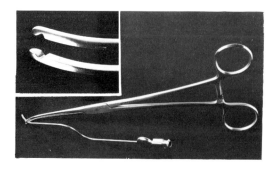

Fig. 3.19. S-shaped metal cholangiocatheter devised by Berci, introduced into the cystic duct and held in place by a modified Borge clamp (inset), which is clamped around the cystic duct. Courtesy of Dr. George Berci, Los Angeles.

INDICATIONS

Operative cholangiography has a universal application in biliary surgery.

GALLSTONE DISEASE AND POSTCHOLECYSTECTOMY CASES

Gallstone disease and postcholecystectomy cases are by far the most common and important indications for operative cholangiography. The usefulness of the investigation has been clearly shown in certain types of choledocholithiasis, such as the presence of multiple stones, small stones, intrahepatic stones, and stones in the distal end of the common bile duct [33, 43, 58]. However, the critical question is whether operative cholangiography should be used as a routine in the surgery of gallstones. If adequate facilities are available operative cholangiography should be routinely employed for the following reasons:

1. Only by doing operative cholangiography routinely will be operator's technique be perfected.

2. Cholangiograms through the cystic duct during cholecystectomy will avoid a number of needless bile duct explorations [1, 4, 16, 38, 58, 59].

3. Gallstones may be revealed in instances where no other indication is present for exploration of the bile duct and, therefore, the gallstones would have been otherwise overlooked [4, 58, 59].

4. Unsuspected aspects of the condition may be revealed, such as unsuspected intrahepatic gallstones, multiple gallstones, gallstones in diverticula of the distal bile duct, and unusual configuration and course of the bile ducts [33, 42, 58, 59].

5. The routine use of operative cholangiography has been shown to have reduced significantly the incidence of overlooked bile duct stones [1, 4, 38, 43, 58].

LAPAROTOMY FOR JAUNDICE

Operative cholangiography may be a valuable investigation when a laparotomy is performed for prolonged jaundice (Chapter 4). It may demonstrate the cause of the jaundice, such as gallstones or a stricture. It is equally valuable in confirming laparotomy findings which indicate that a mechanical obstruction is *not* present, for then the attending physicians may confidently manage the patient as a case of 'medical jaundice' after operation (Chapter 4).

TRAUMATIC BILIARY STRICTURES

Operative cholangiography can be helpful during the repair of strictures which follow operative injuries of the bile ducts; this is considered in the section on Traumatic Biliary Strictures in Chapter 6.

MISCELLANEOUS INDICATIONS

This investigation can provide valuable information in surgery for benign and malignant tumours which involve the biliary tract (Chapter 7), in surgery of biliary cysts (Chapter 8), in parasitic infestations of the liver, such as hydatids (Chapter 15), or when laparotomy is performed for such unusual conditions as haemobilia.

THE NORMAL OPERATIVE CHOLANGIOGRAM

An example of a normal operative cholangiogram is shown in Fig. 3.20. This shows filling of the common hepatic and common bile ducts and filling of the major intrahepatic radicles. The narrow distal bile duct is clearly seen. There are no filling defects present. There may or may not be reflux into the pancreatic

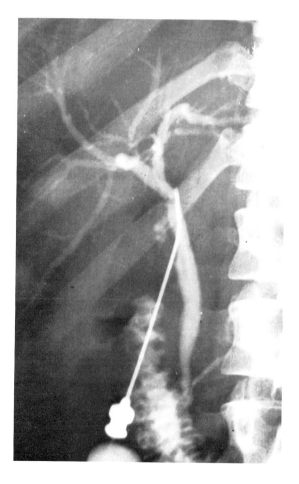

Fig. 3.20. Normal operative cholangiogram. The entire duct system, including the narrow distal portion, is clearly seen, the ducts are not dilated, there are no filling defects and the contrast passes freely into the duodenum.

duct. The dye passes freely into the duodenum. The significance of the width of the common bile duct has been discussed earlier (see Width of the Supraduodenal Common Bile Duct in Chapter 1); in a normal cholangiogram this is usually less than about 15 mm.

ABNORMAL FINDINGS

Gallstones may be identified as filling defects as seen in Fig. 3.21 and in the cholangiograms shown in Chapter 5, or they may produce complete obstruction of the dye, in which case only the crescentic upper border of the stone is visible.

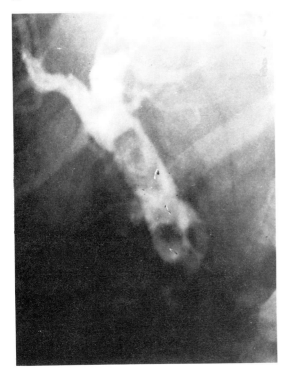

Fig. 3.21. Operative cholangiogram showing com-
plete obstruction of the
bile duct by several stones.
There are also stones in the
left hepatic duct.

Benign strictures may be demonstrated, such as seen in operative bile duct
injuries, in cases of sclerosing cholangitis, or in stenosis caused by chronic
pancreatitis or long-standing choledocholithiasis (see Chapter 6).

In the presence of stenosis of the sphincter of Oddi the operative cholangiogram is not characteristic, because this region is narrow normally. There is
considerable variation in the degree of narrowing in various subjects and during
various phases of sphincteric activity in the same subject. The refinement of
cinecholangiography combined with manometry shows the distal segment to be
unchanged, and there is abnormally high sphincteric resistance. This high resistance cannot be overcome by drugs that normally release the sphincteric
mechanism. As radiomanometry is not generally available the operative findings
are complemented by routine operative cholangiography, and by preliminary
ERCP if this is available. The cholangiographic finding that would support an
operative diagnosis of stenosis of the sphincter of Oddi shows a dilated common
bile duct and a narrow distal segment which remains unchanged in all the
exposures taken, together with other evidence of stenosis as outlined in Chapter
6.

Malignant tumours usually produce complete bile duct obstruction, with a
blunt or conical obstruction, and a marked dilatation of the proximal ducts (Fig.
3.22). Less commonly, malignant tumours produce incomplete obstruction
which resembles a benign stricture, and the cholangiographic differentiation of
these two conditions may be difficult (Chapter 7). In the presence of malignant

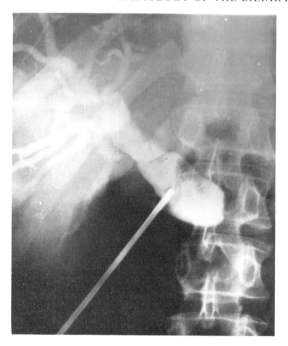

Fig. 3.22. Operative cholangiogram showing typical complete bile duct obstruction due to a malignant tumour. The obstruction is conical and the proximal bile duct is markedly dilated.

obstruction the cholangiogram may provide information regarding the site of insertion of the cystic duct in relation to the tumour. If a bypass is then contemplated the cholangiogram is helpful in deciding whether the gallbladder or the proximal bile duct should be employed for the bypass procedure.

Benign tumours of the bile ducts are most uncommon. The cholangiographic appearances of polyps closely resemble those of gallstones (Chapter 7).

In the presence of hydatids the hydatid elements may be seen in the bile ducts, or a bile duct is seen to communicate with the hydatid cyst in the liver (Chapter 15).

The operative cholangiogram can be useful during laparotomy for haemobilia in showing a cavity in the liver following trauma, or the presence of a liver abscess or tumour. Biliary cysts are clearly outlined by this procedure as shown in Chapter 8. It may also demonstrate unsuspected rare biliary conditions, such as multiple ectasia of the intrahepatic bile ducts (Caroli's disease) as shown in Fig. 3.23.

COMPLICATIONS

Operative cholangiography is a particularly safe procedure. Attacks of acute pancreatitis and a flare-up of cholangitis have been blamed on operative cholangiography, but a review of these reports indicates that these postoperative complications are equally common when cholangiography is not used. All recent large series of cases show the procedure to be particularly free from complications [4, 33, 58].

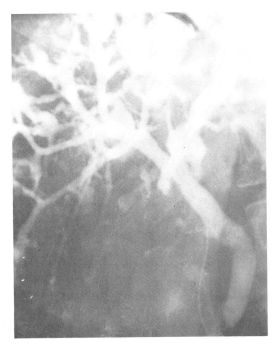

Fig. 3.23. Operative cholangiogram showing caver-
nous ectasia of the intrahepatic bile ducts, Caroli's
disease. Courtesy of Pro-
fessor Whitehouse.

DIAGNOSTIC ACCURACY

Operative cholangiography is used in the entire spectrum of biliary tract surgery but there is insufficient data to allow discussion of its diagnostic accuracy in each condition. From a review of the recent literature, in which a critical analysis was made, it appears that technical faults occur in about 1–2 per cent of cases, false positives in about 2–3 per cent, and false negatives in about 2 per cent [16, 38, 58, 22]. These figures are approximate and represent merely the order of error than can be reasonably expected with good technique. It indicates that in the usual type of biliary cases such as gallstone disease, postcholecystectomy cases, and cases where laparotomy is done for jaundice the diagnostic accuracy of the procedure is 92–95 per cent.

TECHNICAL FAULTS

Technical faults in operative cholangiography relate to failures in exposure and processing of the films and failure to cannulate or inject the bile duct adequately. The patient may be incorrectly positioned, so that the bile duct shadow overlies the spine shadow (Fig. 3.24). Equally, too much oblique tilt may cause the dye in the duodenum to overlie the bile duct shadow (Fig. 3.25). Radiopaque swabs, packs, instruments, intragastric tube, or residual barium from a recent barium enema may obscure the cholangiogram (Fig. 3.26); the incidence of these problems decreases with experience and with cooperation between surgeon and radiologist. Rarely, a satisfactory film cannot be obtained even after several

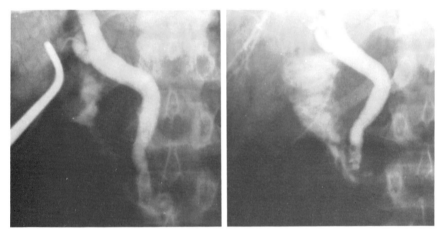

Fig. 3.24. Operative cholangiogram demonstrating the need for correct positioning of the patient. (*left*) Distal end of the common bile duct is obscured by vertebral column in the supine patient. (*right*) Patient is slightly tilted with right side up—bile duct stone now clear of vertebral column and demonstrates several filling defects due to gallstones.

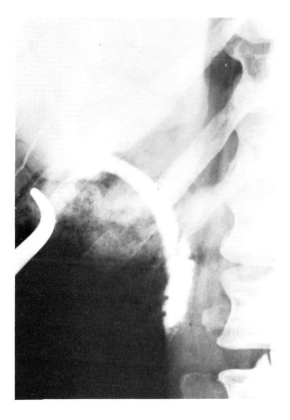

Fig. 3.25. Operative cholangiogram in which too much oblique tilt of the patient has caused the dye in the duodenum to obscure the cholangiogram of the distal end of the bile duct.

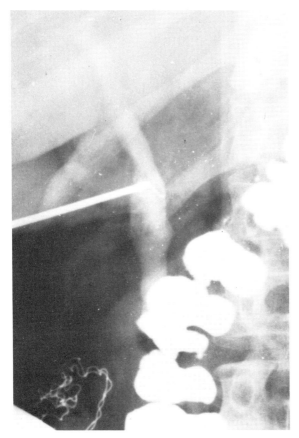

Fig. 3.26. Operative cho-langiogram in which the lower end of the common bile duct is obscured by a recent barium enema (solved by mobilisation of the hepatic flexure of the colon).

attempts; in such a case the procedure is best abandoned to avoid undue prolongation of the operating time.

FALSE POSITIVES
False positives are usually the commonest sources of error and may be due to the following factors:

Air bubbles. These may mimic gallstones, as seen in Fig. 3.27. Operative T-tube cholangiograms are particularly prone to this, and it may be most difficult to eliminate air from the system completely. Flushing with saline and the use of a Trendelenburg or anti-Trendelenburg position, or a lateral projection in which air bubbles rise to the top, may be helpful in differentiating gallstones from air bubbles but these procedures are often cumbersome and time-consuming. Postexploration T-tube cholangiography is now replaced in many centres by choledochoscopy (Chapter 5).

Sphincteric spasm. Spasm of the sphincter of Oddi may occur after exploration of the bile duct, particularly when instruments have been passed through the

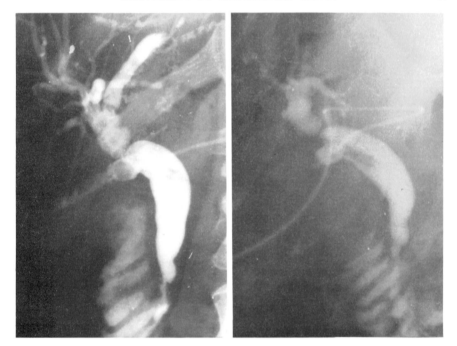

Fig. 3.27. (*left*) T-tube postexploration cholangiogram with air bubbles mimicking gall-stones. (*right*) Cholangiogram after air bubbles were cleared.

sphincter (Fig. 3.28). This may be mistaken for a gallstone occluding the distal bile duct. An important point is that there are no filling defects and that the spastic segment is crescentic downward, in contrast to a gallstone. Also, it is useful to compare this film with pre-exploration cholangiograms.

In general, cholangiographic interpretation is perplexing if the surgeon is unaware of the cyclic changes which occur in the region of the sphincter of Oddi (Chapter 2). Thus, the contractile phase may simulate a gallstone, spasm, or fibrosis. On occasion, if the film is taken at the very extreme of the contractile phase, a filling defect may be seen which is slightly crescentic upward, producing the 'pseudocalculus' sign as seen in Fig. 3.29 [9]. These diagnostic dilemmas are resolved by taking more than one film. Also, postexploration choledochoscopy is now replacing postexploration cholangiography, thus obviating the problem.

Overlying gas shadows. Gas in the colon may overlie the bile-duct shadow and can be mistaken for a gallstone (Fig. 3.30). This error is more likely in the interpretation of wet films, but careful inspection usually shows that the gas shadow is continuous with one outside the bile duct.

Others. Kinking of the common bile duct, compression by the adjacent hepatic artery, or pancreatic nodularity have all been described as uncommon causes of

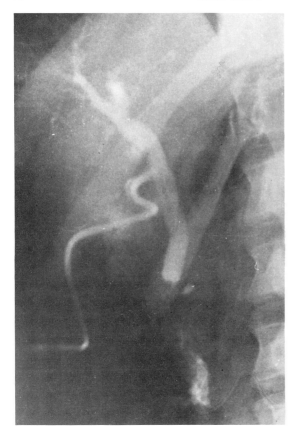

Fig. 3.28. Postexploration T-tube cholangiogram showing spasm of the sphincter of Oddi.

false positive cholangiograms. Sometimes the terminaton of a spiral cystic duct is seen 'end-on' and this appearance can mimic a gallstone (Fig. 3.31).

FALSE NEGATIVES
Gallstones may not be shown up in the bile ducts if too much dye is injected before the first film is taken and the dye in the duodenum obscures the distal bile duct. False negatives may also be obtained if too little dye is used and the hepatic ducts are not adequately filled, or if the dye is too concentrated.

SUMMARY

Operative cholangiography is a simple, safe, and highly accurate peroperative investigation. The technique of cholangiography must be meticulous in its attention to detail if accurate results are to be achieved. Its consistent use in gallstone surgery has reduced the incidence of unnecessary common bile duct explorations, has occasionally disclosed unsuspected gallstones, and has signifi-cantly reduced the incidence of overlooked stones. It will outline the anatomy of the bile ducts in a particular case. Operative cholangiography may be helpful in

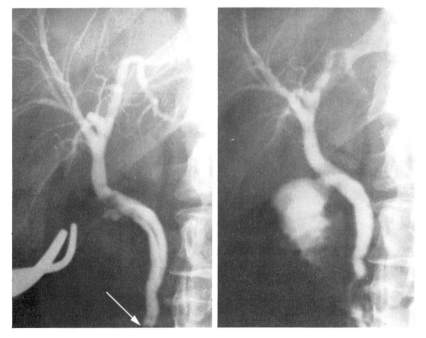

Fig. 3.29. (*left*) 'Pseudocalculus' sign in the lower end of the bile duct. Note there is no dye in the duodenum. (*right*) Extreme spasm relieved at a later film, which now shows a normal bile duct.

the operative diagnosis and management of jaundiced patients who are subjected to laparotomy, in biliary strictures, and in tumours of the biliary tract, as well as in less common conditions such as biliary cysts, hydatids, and haemobilia.

If adequate facilities are available the procedure is recommended as a routine part of all biliary tract operations.

POSTOPERATIVE T-TUBE CHOLANGIOGRAPHY

When the common bile duct has been explored a T-tube cholangiogram performed 7–14 days after surgery is advocated as a routine. This gives useful information before the T tube is removed concerning the state of the bile duct and whether any gallstones have been overlooked. For the management of this problem of the overlooked bile duct stone picked up on a postoperative T-tube cholangiogram the reader is referred to Chapter 5. It can be difficult to eliminate air bubbles from the system, but in case of doubt the cholangiograms can be repeated at leisure until satisfactory films are obtained. The cholangiographic technique and the interpretation of the films are otherwise similar to operative and preoperative cholangiography.

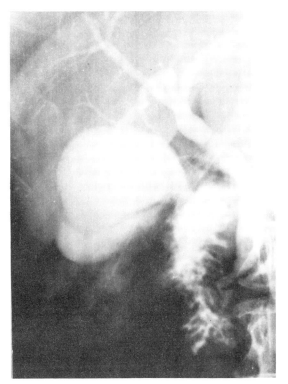

Fig. 3.30. Operative cholangiogram with gas in the colon overlying the distal bile duct and resembling a gallstone. Note that the gas shadow extends outside the bile duct shadow.

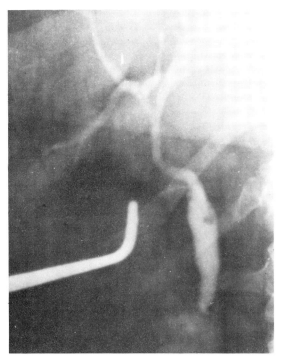

Fig. 3.31. The termination of a spiral cystic duct is seen 'end-on' in this operative cholangiogram and it mimics a gallstone.

REFERENCES

1. ALLEN K.L. Routine operative cholangiography. *Am. J. Surg.* **118:**573, 1969.
2. ANSELL G. *Complications in Diagnostic Radiology.* Blackwell, Oxford, 1976.
3. BADDELEY H., NOLAN D. & SALMON P.R. *Radiological Atlas of Biliary and Pancreatic Disease.* H.M. & M. Publishers, Aylesbury, 1978.
4. BARDENHEIER J.A. III, KAMINSKI D.L., WILLMAN V.L. & HANLON C.R. Ten years' experience with direct cholangiography. *Am. J. Surg.* **118:**900, 1969.
5. BAUER K., TRAGL K.H., BAUER G., VYEUDILIK W. & HOCKER P. Denaturierung von plasmoproteinen bei einer IgM paraproteinamie, ansgelöst durch ein intravenos verabreichtes a lebergangiges rontgenkontrastmittel. *Wein Klin. Wschr.* **86:**766, 1975.
6. BEARGIE R.J., HODGSON J.R., HUIZENGA K.A. & PRIESTLY J.T. Relation of cholangiographic findings after cholecystectomy to clinical and surgical findings. *Surg. Gynec. Obstet.* **115:**143, 1962.
7. BEHAN M. & KAZAM E. Sonography of the common bile duct: value of the right anterior oblique view. *Am. J. Roentgenol.* **130:**701, 1978.
8. BELL G.D., FAYADH M.H., FRANK J., SMITH P.L.C. & KELSEY-FRY I. Intravenous cholangiography, is technique important? *Gut* **16:**841, 1975.
9. BERCI G. & SHORE J.M. Improved cannula for operative (cystic duct) cholangiography. *Am. J. Surg.* **137:**826, 1979.
10. BERK R.N. Radiology of the gallbladder and bile ducts. *Surg. Clin. N. Amer.* **53:**973, 1973.
11. BERK R.N. Cholecystokinin cholecystography in the diagnosis of chronic acalculous cholecystitis and biliary dyskinesia. *Gastrointest. Radiol.* **1:**325, 1977.
12. BILBAO M.K., DOTTER C.T., LEE T.G. & KATON R.M. Complications of endoscopic retrograde cholangiopancreatography (ERCP). *Gastroenterology* **70:**314, 1976.
13. BURGENER F.A. & FISCHER H.W. Intravenous cholangiography in jaundice. *Lancet* **1:**274, 1975.
14. BURWOOD R.J., DAVIES G.T., LAWRIE B.W., BLUMGART L.H. & SALMON P.R. Endoscopic retrograde choledochopancreatography. A review with a report of a collaborative series. *Clin. Radiol.* **24:**397, 1973.
15. CANALES C.O., SMITH G.H., ROBINSON J.C., REMMERS A.R. & SARLES H.E. Acute renal failure after the administration of iopanoic acid as a cholecystographic agent. *New Eng. J. Med.* **281:**89, 1969.
16. CHAPMAN M., CURRY R.C. & LEQUESNE L.P. Operative cholangiography. An assessment of its reliability in the diagnosis of a normal, stone-free common bile duct. *Br. J. Surg.* **51:**600, 1964.
17. COTTON P.B. The normal endoscopic pancreatogram. *Endoscopy* **6:**65, 1974.
18. COTTON P.B., DENYER M.E., HUSBAND J., MEIRE H.B. & KREEL L. Clinical impact of pancreatography, EMI scanning and ultrasonography. *Gut* **18:**399, 1977.
19. CLOUSE M.E., GREGG J.A., MCDONALD D.G. & LEGG M.A. Percutaneous fine needle aspiration biopsy of pancreatic carcinoma. *Gastrointest. Radiol.* **2:**67, 1977.
20. EDHOLM P. & JONSSON G. Preoperative cholangiography. Its value in detecting common bile duct stones. *Acta Chir. Scand.* **122:**486, 1961.
21. ELIAS E. Progress report: cholangiography in the jaundiced patient. *Gut* **17:**801, 1976.
22. FARHA G.J. & PEARSON R.M. Transcystic duct operative cholangiography. Personal experience with 500 consecutive cases. *Am. J. Surg.* **131:**228, 1976.
23. FINBY N. & BLASBERG G. A note on the blocking of hepatic excretion during cholangiographic study. *Gastroenterology* **46:**276, 1964.
24. FREENY P.C. & BALL T.J. Evaluation of endoscopic retrograde cholangiopancreatography and angiography in the diagnosis of pancreatic carcinoma. *Am. J. Roentgenol.* **130:**683, 1978.
25. GEORGE P. Disorders of the extrahepatic bile ducts. *Clin. Gastroenterol.* **2:**127, 1973.
26. GRAINGER R.G. Renal toxicity of radiological contrast media. *Br. Med. Bull.* **28:**191, 1972.

27. HAAGA J.R., ALFIDI R.J., ZELCH M.G., MEANY T.F., BOLLER M., GONZALES L. &
    JELDEN G. Computed tomography of the pancreas. *Radiology* **120**:589, 1976.
28. HANAFEE W. & WEINER M. Transjugular percutaneous cholangiography. *Radiology*
    88:35, 1967.
29. HARNED R.K. & LEVEEN R. Preliminary abdominal films in oral cholecystography:
    are they necessary? *Am. J. Roentgenol.* **130**:477, 1978.
30. HARVEY I.C., THWE M. & LOW-BEER T.S. The value of the fatty meal in oral
    cholecystography. *Clin. Radiol.* **27**:117, 1976.
31. HAVRILLA T.R., HAAGA J.R., ALFIDI R.J. & REICH N.E. Computed tomography and
    obstructive biliary disease. *Am. J. Roentgenol.* **128**:765, 1977.
32. HAVRILLA T.R., REICH N.E., HAAGA J.R., SEIDELMANN F.E., COOPERMAN A.M. &
    ALFIDI R.J. Computed tomography of the gallbladder. *Am. J. Roentgenol.* **130**:1059,
    1978.
33. HESS W. *Surgery of the Biliary Passages and the Pancreas*. Van Nostrand, Princeton,
    N.J. 1965.
34. HOEVELS J., LUNDERQUIST A. & IHSE. Percutaneous transhepatic intubation of bile
    ducts form combined internal–external drainage in preoperative and palliative treat-
    ment of jaundice. *Gastrointest. Radiol* **3**:23, 1978.
35. HUGH T.B. Percutaneous cholangiography. *Med. J. Aust.* **1**:593, 1967.
36. HUTCHINSON W.B. & BLAKE T. Operative cholangiography. *Surgery* **41**:605, 1957.
37. JOHNSON H.C. JR., MINOR B.D., THOMPSON J.A. & WEENS H.S. Diagnostic value of
    intravenous cholangiography during acute cholecystitis and acute pancreatitis. *New
    Eng. J. Med.* **260**:158, 1959.
38. JOLLY P.C., BAKER J.W., SCHMIDT H.M., WALKER J.J. & HOLM J.C. Operative
    cholangiography: a case for its routine use. *Ann. Surg.* **168**:551, 1968.
39. JONES C.A. & OLBOURNE N.A. Choledochal cyst with associated cholelithiasis diag-
    nosed by infusion cholangiography and tomography. *Br. J. Radiol.* **46**:711, 1973.
40. KASUGAI T., KUNO N., KIZU M., KOBAYASHI S. & HATTORI K. Endoscopic pancreato-
    cholangiography: normal and abnormal. *Gastroenterology* **63**:217 and 227, 1972.
41. KUNE G.A. Needle for operative cholangiography. *Br. Med. J.* **2**:620, 1964.
42. KUNE G.A. Gallstones in diverticula of the lower common bile duct. *Gut* **6**:95, 1965.
43. KUNE G.A. The elusive common bile duct stone. *Med. J. Aust.* **1**:254, 1966.
44. LEOPOLD G.R., AMBERG J., GOSINK B.B. & MITTELSTAEDT C. Gray scale ultrasonic
    cholecystography—a comparison with conventional radiographic techniques.
    Radiol. **121**:445, 1976.
45. LEQUESNE L.P., WHITESIDE C.G. & HAND B.H. The common duct after cholecystec-
    tomy. *Br. Med. J.* **1**:329, 1959.
46. LOW-BEER T.S., HEATON K.W. & ROYLANCE J. Oral cholecystography in patients
    with small bowel disease. *Br. J. Radiol.* **45**:427, 1972.
47. MAHOUR G.H., WAKIM K.G., FERRIS D.O. & SOULE E.H. The common bile duct after
    cholecystectomy: comparison of common bile ducts in patients who have intact
    biliary systems with those in patients who have undergone cholecystectomy. *Ann.
    Surg.* **166**:964, 1967.
48. MARTINEZ L.O., VIAMONTE M., GASSMAN P. & BOUDET L. Present status of intra-
    venous cholangiography. *Am. J. Roentgen.* **113**:10, 1971.
49. MCCUNE W.S., SHORT P.E. & MOSCOVITZ H. Endoscopic cannulation of the ampulla
    of Vater: a preliminary report. *Ann. Surg.* **167**:752, 1968.
50. MCNULTY J.G. Oral cholecystography: a sign of gallbladder disease. *Br. Med. J.* **1**:38,
    1975.
51. MUDGE G.H. Uricosuric action of cholecystographic agents—a possible factor in
    nephrotoxicity. *New Eng. J. Med.* **284**:929, 1971.
52. MUJAHED Z. Factors interfering with the opacification of a normal gallbladder.
    Gastrointest. Radiol. **1**:183, 1976.
53. NOLAN D.J. & GIBSON M.J. Improvements in intravenous cholangiography. *Br. J.
    Radiol.* **43**:652, 1970.

54. OKUDA K., TARIKAWA K., EMURA T. *et al.* Non-surgical percutaneous transhepatic cholangiography—diagnostic significance in medical problems of the liver. *Am. J. Dig. Dis.* **19**:21, 1974.
55. ROHRMANN C.A., SILVIS S.E. & VENNES J.A. The significance of pancreatic ductal obstruction in the differential diagnosis of the abnormal endoscopic retrograde pancreatogram. *Radiology* **121**:311, 1976.
56. SALI A., YOUNG G., NAGESH A., JONES T., HARE W.S.C., HUNT P.S. & KUNE G.A. Percutaneous transhepatic cholangiography. A multicentre study of its diagnostic accuracy and complications. (In press).
57. SALMON P.R. Fibreoptic endoscopy. Pitman Medical, London, 1974.
58. SCHULENBURG C.A.R. Operative cholangiography. Butterworth, London, 1966.
59. SCHULENBURG C.A.R. Operative cholangiography: 1000 cases. *Surgery* **65**:723, 1969.
60. SHALDON S. The investigation of bile ducts by percutaneous cholangiography: investigations and technique. *Proc. Roy. Soc. Med.* **55**:587, 1962.
61. SMITH R. Discussion on percutaneous transhepatic cholangiography. *Med. J. Aust.* **1**:863, 1968.
62. SPRENT J., SPOONER R. & POWELL W. Acute renal failure complicating intravenous cholangiography in a patient with Dubin Johnson Syndrome. *Med. J. Aust.* **2**:446, 1969.
63. THORBJARNARSON B. The anatomical diagnosis of jaundice by percutaneous cholangiography and its influence on treatment. *Surgery* **61**:347, 1967.
64. WARREN K. & KUNE G.A. Trends in biliary surgery. *New Eng. J. Med.* **273**:1322, 1965.
65. WEILL F., EISENCHER A. & ZELTNER F. Ultrasonic study of the normal and dilated biliary tree. *Radiology* **127**:221, 1978.
66. WISE R.E. & O'BRIEN R.G. Interpretation of the intravenous cholangiogram. *J.A.M.A.* **160**:819, 1956.
67. WISE R.E. Intravenous cholangiography. Thomas, Springfield, Ill. 1962
68. ZIMMON D.S., FALKENSTEIN D.B., ABRAMS R.M., SELINGER G. & KESSLER R.E. Endoscopic retrograde cholangiopancreatography in the diagnosis of pancreatic inflammatory disease. *Radiology* **113**:287, 1974.

4. Obstructive Jaundice

The central problem in a case of prolonged jaundice is the diagnosis of the cause. In particular, the clinician must establish whether the jaundice is caused by major bile duct obstruction, which requires surgical relief, or whether the cause is medical, when surgery is clearly unnecessary and may even be harmful.

The diagnosis of mechanical bile duct obstruction may be difficult, because the clinical features and the results of laboratory investigations are frequently not totally characteristic. Also, non-mechanical causes of bile stasis in intrahepatic biliary radicles (intrahepatic cholestasis) presents clinical and laboratory findings which closely resemble those of mechanical bile duct obstruction. A further diagnostic problem is that hepatocellular and obstructive features may occur together, making the interpretation of laboratory tests difficult. Thus prolonged mechanical obstruction can produce both acute and chronic liver damage. Similarly, primary liver disease, such as acute or chronic hepatitis may have associated with it an intrahepatic cholestatic element which imitates the features of mechanical obstruction.

The clinician is well aware of these diagnostic problems. An understanding of the bilirubin metabolism and the pathophysiology of jaundice on which modern clinical classification of jaundice is based forms the background to sound diagnosis and appropriate management. The diagnosis is based on the clinical features and on the evaluation of the diagnostic significance of appropriate laboratory and radiological investigations. This should then answer the central question in prolonged jaundice, which is: operation or no operation!

BILIRUBIN METABOLISM

The metabolic pathways of bilirubin are represented in Fig. 4.1. Most of the bilirubin is produced by the breakdown of haemoglobin; approximately 300 mg is produced per day [75]. About 15–20 per cent of bilirubin is derived from immature erythrocytes in the bone marrow and from other haem-containing compounds, such as cytochromes and catalases, that are present in the liver and kidneys [4, 40].

Bilirubin is insoluble in water and it is bound to serum albumin in the bloodstream. Bilirubin enters the liver cells by a mechanism which is uncertain. It is then conjugated in the microsomes, almost entirely as a glucuronide, through the action of glucuronide transferase. This conjugation converts the lipid-soluble bilirubin into a water-soluble substance, bilirubin glucuronide.

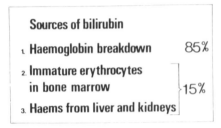

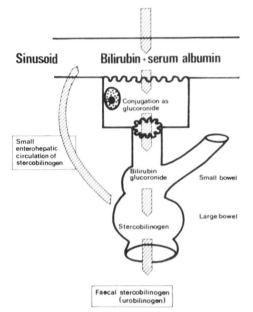

Fig. 4.1. Metabolic pathways of bilirubin.

The conjugated bilirubin is then excreted from the liver cell into the bile canaliculus. The microsomes may be concerned with this process, which is probably an active mechanism requiring energy [75].

From the bile canaliculus the conjugated bilirubin reaches the intestines where it is converted by bacteria in the colon into unconjugated bilirubin and urobilinogen (stercobilinogen). Most of the unconjugated bilirubin and urobilinogen is excreted in the faeces. Only a small amount of urobilinogen (stercobilinogen) is absorbed into the portal vein and this is then again excreted by the liver. A minimal amount of urobilinogen which has been absorbed cannot be excreted by the liver and this is excreted in the urine.

CLINICAL CLASSIFICATION OF JAUNDICE

Jaundice may arise when an abnormality of bilirubin metabolism occurs. In 1962 Sherlock made a substantial contribution when she proposed a clinical classification of jaundice, in which the various causes were related to the site of the abnormality in the bilirubin metabolic pathway [74].

Although this classification is very useful it must be remembered that most cases of prolonged jaundice will be shown to be due to one of the following causes: viral hepatitis A or B, drug jaundice, acute alcoholic hepatitis, chronic liver disease, choledocholithiasis, or malignant bile duct obstruction. Our knowledge regarding the causes of jaundice is incomplete in some conditions and in other instances, such as viral hepatitis, the disturbance in bilirubin metabolism may occur at more than one level [75]. Nevertheless, it is still useful to look at all the causes of jaundice in a systematic way, as shown in Fig. 4.2 and Table 4.1, which represents a modification of the Sherlock classification.

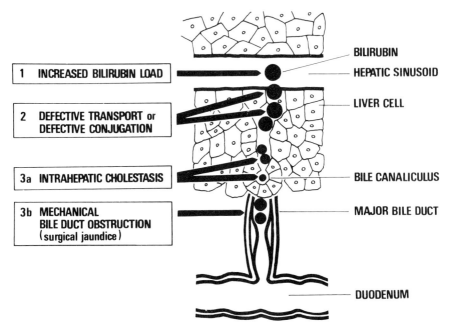

Fig. 4.2. Clinical classification of jaundice based on site of the block in bilirubin metabolism. Redrawn from Warren and Kune [91].

INCREASED BILIRUBIN LOAD

Increased bilirubin load is usually caused by excessive haemolysis, such as may be seen in congenital or acquired haemolytic anaemias and after incompatible blood transfusions. A very rare condition has been described in which there is an overproduction of bilirubin from the destruction of abnormal red cell precursors in the bone marrow [3]. This condition is probably familial; it is termed primary 'shunt' hyperbilirubinaemia.

In this group of conditions the level of serum bilirubin very rarely rises higher than 3 mg per 100 ml, unless there is an associated hepatocellular disturbance, and clinically it is a rarity for a patient to present with prolonged jaundice as their primary problem.

DEFECTIVE BILIRUBIN TRANSPORT OR CONJUGATION

In this group of cases the defect lies either in the transfer of bilirubin from the serum to its site of conjugation in the liver cell, or in an actual disturbance of bilirubin conjugation; jaundice results from unconjugated bilirubin.

Gilbert's syndrome is the commonest type of familial unconjugated hyperbilirubinaemia; it is probably inherited as a Mendelian dominant and probably caused by an inherent difficulty in taking up bilirubin into the liver cell. The jaundice is mild and intermittent and the prognosis is excellent [75].

The Crigler–Najjar syndrome is a rare familial disturbance of bilirubin conjugation, probably transmitted as a Mendelian recessive [19]. It is associated with very high serum levels of unconjugated bilirubin, resulting in damage to the central nervous system and, usually, early death.

Disturbances of bilirubin conjugation occur in neonatal jaundice. This may be due to a foetal deficiency of enzyme responsible for bilirubin conjugation, or to enzyme inhibition factors in maternal milk [6, 7].

Disturbances of bilirubin uptake and conjugation occur in acute viral hepatitis, in hepatitis caused by drugs and infections, and in the various forms of chronic hepatitis, but in most of these cases other factors, such as cholestasis and excessive haemolysis, contribute to the jaundice [75].

CHOLESTASIS

Cholestasis may be defined as the inability of conjugated bilirubin and other constituents of bile to reach the duodenum. This interruption of bile flow may occur at any level, from the hepatic cell to the major bile ducts. The term *cholestatic jaundice* has replaced *obstructive jaundice*, because mechanical obstruction forms only one group of causes responsible for the syndrome of cholestasis.

THE SYNDROME OF CHOLESTASIS

The syndrome comprises certain pathologic, clinical, and laboratory findings which are similar, irrespective of the cause. There may also be additional or different clinical and laboratory findings specific to the cause of the cholestatic syndrome in a particular instance.

Pathologic findings. The extent and rate of development of the pathologic changes depend on the duration and completeness of cholestasis. The changes are more extensive with the passage of time, but evidence of biliary cirrhosis is more common with incomplete, rather than complete, obstruction.

The liver slowly enlarges and becomes green. Bile accumulates in hepatic cells and in dilated bile canaliculi, forming bile thrombi which consist mainly of conjugated bilirubin [75]. With increased duration of cholestasis mononuclear cells accumulate in the periportal areas. This is followed by portal zone fibrosis which extends and eventually encloses the hepatic lobule. The full picture of biliary cirrhosis is seen with extensive fibrosis and nodular regeneration, at which

Table 4.1. Clinical classification of jaundice

---

1. INCREASED BILIRUBIN LOAD

Excessive haemolysis
   Congenital haemolytic anaemias
   Acquired haemolytic anaemias
   Haemolytic disease of the newborn
   Incompatible blood transfusion
   Haemolysis caused by drugs and infections
Primary 'shunt' hyperbilirubinaemia

2. DEFECTIVE BILIRUBIN TRANSPORT AND CONJUGATION

Gilbert's syndrome
Crigler–Najjar syndrome
Neonatal jaundice
Acute viral hepatitis   Frequently other factors involved
Chronic hepatitis   such as cholestasis and excessive
Hepatitis caused by drugs and infection   haemolysis

3. CHOLESTASIS

Intrahepatic cholestasis

Cholestatic form of acute viral hepatitis
Acute alcoholic hepatitis
Postnecrotic cirrhosis (sometimes)
Dubin–Johnson and Rotor syndromes
Drug-induced cholestasis
   Methyl testosterone
   Phenothiazine drugs—chlorpromazine, prochlorperazine,
                     trifluoperazine
   Oral hypoglycaemics—chlorpropamide, glibenclamide
   Erythromycin estolate
   Imipramine
   Methyl dopa
Cholestatic jaundice of pregnancy
Oral contraceptives
Postoperative cholestatic jaundice
Primary biliary cirrhosis
Benign recurrent idiopathic cholestasis

Mechanical bile obstruction—extrahepatic cholestasis

Choledocholithiasis
Malignant obstruction
   Bile duct
   Gallbladder
   Pancreas
   Papilla of Vater
   Duodenum
   Liver

Benign strictures
   Traumatic (postoperative)
   Stenosis of the papilla of Vater
   Primary sclerosing cholangitis
   Recurrent pyogenic cholangitis
Pancreatic inflammation
   Acute pancreatitis
   Chronic pancreatitis
   Pancreatic cysts
   Pancreatic abscesses
Parasitic infestation
   Hydatids
   Ascaris (roundworm)
Congenital biliary atresia

---

stage distinction from other forms of cirrhosis may be extremely difficult. The spleen eventually enlarges and portal hypertension may develop.

Clinical findings. Jaundice develops slowly and the patient feels relatively well. Pruritus is usually present. Xanthomas of the skin develop with a rise of serum lipids. With complete cholestasis there is no bilirubin in the faeces, which become pale, loose and bulky. With prolonged cholestasis steatorrhoea leads to failure of absorption of calcium and the fat-soluble vitamins A, D and K.

Laboratory findings. Serum bilirubin level is elevated: this is mainly conjugated bilirubin. The serum alkaline phosphatase is usually raised. Total serum cholesterol increases. With chronic cholestasis there is a considerable increase of serum lipids, particularly phospholipids [75]. The serum albumin is normal, but in the terminal stages of liver failure it falls. Serum globulins are increased, particularly the lipoprotein fraction, which travels electrophoretically with the beta globulins [75].

INTRAHEPATIC CHOLESTASIS
Intrahepatic cholestasis is one of the two broad classes of cholestatic jaundice; the other is cholestasis due to mechanical obstruction of major bile ducts. In the intrahepatic category the cause of cholestasis lies within the liver, distal to the site of bilirubin conjugation, in the liver cell, in the biliary canaliculi, or in the interlobar bile ducts.

In this group of patients the pathologic, clinical, and laboratory findings of cholestasis are all present. Thus, the clinical features of patients with intrahepatic cholestasis closely resemble those with mechanical bile duct obstruction. However, contrary to the latter instances, cholangitis and pain are usually absent and the liver is not usually enlarged. Histologically, there is no bile ductule dilatation, no multiplication of bile ducts, no 'bile lakes', nor any bile necrosis of liver cells, features which are seen in patients with mechanical obstruction. Intrahepatic cholestasis forms an important group, because the management of these patients is essentially medical.

A group of hepatocellular conditions is responsible for intrahepatic cholestasis due to difficulty in the excretion of conjugated bilirubin into the biliary canaliculi. Occasionally, acute viral hepatitis takes on the picture of cholestasis rather than that of helatocellular involvement, for reasons that are uncertain [24]. A similar type of hepatitis with cholestatic features has been seen in acute hepatitis of the alcoholic and in some cases of postnecrotic cirrhosis [69, 75].

There is a group of uncommon familial intermittent conjugated hyperbilirubinaemias of the Dubin–Johnson and Rotor types, which present as a cholestatic picture, although some features such as pruritus and raised serum alkaline phosphatase levels are lacking. The liver has a characteristic deep pigmentation [23, 65]. These lesions are probably due to difficulty of excretion of conjugated bilirubin from the hepatic cell. The prognosis is excellent [75].

Cholestatic jaundice may be seen following the administration of methyl testosterone and related steroids; the defect seems to involve the bile canaliculi [70, 75]. Drugs of the phenothiazine group such as chlorpromazine, prochlorperazine, or trifluoperazine may induce a cholestatic type of jaundice. The reaction appears to be of a sensitivity type and is therefore unrelated to dose [75]. The lesion probably involves the biliary ductules, but there is evidence of liver cell damage as well [62, 75]. Complete recovery is the rule, but very occasionally biliary cirrhosis develops and, rarely, death ensues from liver failure [75, 89]. Other drugs which have been reported to cause a cholestatic type of jaundice include the oral hypoglycaemic agents such as chlorpropramide and rarely, glibenclamide, erythromycin estolate, imipramine, and methyl dopa [75].

A type of cholestatic jaundice may appear in the last trimester of pregnancy. It may be caused by an unusual response to a steroid produced in pregnancy. Evidence has been presented that patients prone to cholestatic jaundice of pregnancy are also prone to the development of cholestatic jaundice following the administration of oral contraceptives [38, 61, 75, 85]. The prognosis is excellent.

Cases of cholestatic jaundice have been reported following surgery, but the mechanism is uncertain; full recovery is the rule [42, 56, 72].

Primary biliary cirrhosis produces a picture of intrahepatic cholestasis involving the interlobular bile ducts which are surrounded by an inflammatory reaction. There is evidence of damage to the involved ducts, and eventually periportal fibrosis and biliary cirrhosis result [9, 66]. A mitochondrial immunofluorescence test has been described which is positive in 85 per cent of patients with primary biliary cirrhosis and only uncommonly positive in jaundice due to mechanical obstruction of main bile ducts [22, 75]. The average duration of the illness is about 6 years; the condition is almost always fatal [30, 75].

MECHANICAL BILE DUCT OBSTRUCTION—EXTRAHEPATIC CHOLESTASIS
This refers to obstruction of major bile ducts and is occasionally also termed *obstructive jaundice* or *surgical jaundice*. The term *extrahepatic cholestasis* is not entirely accurate, because on occasion the mechanical obstruction involves major bile ducts within the liver.

Added to the general picture of cholestasis is dilatation of bile ducts proximal to the obstruction and not infrequently the presence of biliary tract infection.

Histologically, the bile ducts show dilatation and proliferation around the portal tracts associated with a periportal polymorphonuclear reaction. Discrete areas of liver cell necrosis may be seen with central bile staining, referred to as 'bile lakes', features which are not seen with intrahepatic cholestasis.

Bile duct gallstones (Chapter 5) and malignant obstruction of the ducts (Chapter 7) are the commonest causes of mechanical obstruction. The malignancy may arise in the biliary system, such as carcinoma of the bile ducts, may be an extension of gallbladder carcinoma, or may be due to a carcinoma of the pancreas, papilla of Vater, or duodenum occluding the bile ducts from outside. Carcinoma of the head of the pancreas is the commonest cause in this group. Obstruction of the bile ducts in the porta hepatis by malignant lymph nodes is a rare cause. Intrahepatic carcinoma, primary or secondary, may cause mechanical bile duct obstruction, but with these there is also a variable degree of hepatocellular disturbance.

Benign strictures of the bile ducts (Chapter 6) such as postoperative strictures, stenosis of the papilla of Vater, and primary sclerosing cholangitis, may be responsible for mechanical obstruction. Recurrent pyogenic cholangitis (Chapter 9) is associated with gallstones, strictures, and biliary infection and is a common cause of obstructive jaundice in certain parts of the Orient.

Periductal inflammation and compression of the bile duct caused by acute or chronic pancreatitis and by pancreatic cysts and abscesses may also be responsible for obstructive jaundice [2, 31, 44, 47, 49, 68, 90].

Parasitic infestations of the liver and biliary tract are occasional causes of obstructive jaundice in certain parts of the world. Intrabiliary rupture of hepatic hydatid cysts is followed by obstructive jaundice (Chapter 15). The roundworm, *Ascaris lumbricoides*, not uncommonly causes hepatic infestation in the Far East. It may be responsible for obstructive jaundice by lodging in the bile duct or by forming the nucleus of gallstones [1, 83].

DIAGNOSIS

The essential task in diagnosis is to decide whether the jaundice is caused by mechanical obstruction of a bile duct or not. To paraphrase the Bard: Operation or no operation, that is the question!

The diagnostic process in jaundice first involves obtaining a careful history of the symptoms and a thorough physical examination. Clinical examination is always followed by a number of basic and relatively simple non-invasive laboratory and radiologic investigations which include liver imaging, as described later in this chapter. In this regard ultrasound imaging of the liver and bile ducts has become a routine part of this basic workup as a screening test in all jaundiced patients [12, 55, 81, 88].

In many cases of prolonged jaundice the diagnosis is reached at this stage with reasonable certainty and further investigations are unnecessary and meddlesome.

In a significant proportion of patients the diagnosis remains uncertain after the clinical profile and the basic investigations. In the past, these patients were observed in hospital for 2 or 3 weeks and during this time a number of more sophisticated special investigations were performed and, if the diagnosis was still unclear, a diagnostic laparotomy was performed [45]. This policy has changed radically with the advent of new techniques outlining the biliary ductal system in the jaundiced patient and these include ultrasonography (US), percutaneous transhepatic cholangiography using the fine Chiba needle (PTC), and endoscopic retrograde cholangiography (ERCP) [12]. When doubt remains about diagnosis it is essential to outline precisely the biliary ductal system by one or more of the above techniques (Fig. 4.5). Ultrasonography of the bile ducts is the initial technique used. If the bile ducts are found to be dilated, and/or there is a point of duct obstruction demonstrated, an operation is usually required to relieve the obstruction. If the ducts are of normal calibre and also if no point of obstruction is shown the jaundice has a medical cause, the management is conservative, and it involves a liver biopsy, as well as other special serological and immunological investigations [12].

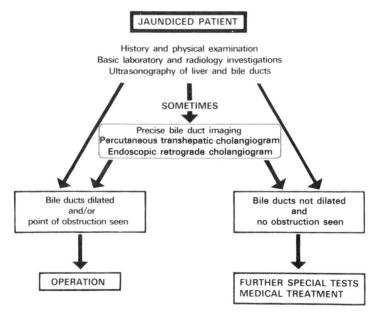

Fig. 4.3. Outline of the diagnostic process used in a case of prolonged jaundice.

The flow chart for the current approach to diagnosis in a case of prolonged jaundice is summarised in Fig. 4.3. Clearly, there will be exceptions and uncertainties of interpretation, or unavailability of certain investigative procedures and this flow chart is merely intended to show the guiding principles of diagnosis in a case of prolonged jaundice.

CLINICAL EXAMINATION

The relevant points of the history and physical examination will merely be summarised as, in the main, they are well known.

AGE

The incidence of viral hepatitis decreases with age, but up to the age of 30 about 90 per cent of patients who present with jaundice have viral hepatitis. In infancy and childhood the congenital and familial causes of jaundice mentioned earlier may be seen. The incidence of malignant obstruction and choledocholithiasis rises over the age of 40.

FAMILY HISTORY

Positive histories are helpful in the familial hyperbilirubinaemias, haemolytic jaundice, and gallstones.

CONTACT, INJECTIONS, TRANSFUSIONS

A positive history of these factors is of value in the diagnosis of viral hepatitis and homologous serum jaundice.

DRUGS AND ALCOHOL

Hepatotoxic drugs, such as chlorpromazine and others mentioned earlier or a history of alcoholism, may be an important diagnostic clue.

GENERAL HEALTH

Progressive deterioration may be caused by malignant obstruction, but is sometimes also seen with choledocholithiasis. With hepatocellular jaundice the patient feels ill, but with most forms of intrahepatic cholestasis he feels relatively well.

MODE OF ONSET

Anorexia and nausea followed by rapid onset of jaundice suggest a diagnosis of viral hepatitis. An abrupt onset is also seen with cholestatic drug jaundice or choledocholithiasis. Gradual onset may be seen with chronic hepatitis or malignant obstruction.

NATURE OF JAUNDICE

Fluctuating jaundice suggests choledocholithiasis, whereas progressive jaundice suggests malignancy. Persistent mild jaundice may mean haemolysis or chronic hepatitis.

PAIN

Pain of the biliary colic type suggests choledocholithiasis. Persistent pain, particularly with pain in the back, may mean carcinoma of the pancreas, but is also seen in chronic pancreatitis. Previous episodes of pain suggest gallstones or chronic relapsing pancreatitis. Pain is uncommon in viral hepatitis and intrahepatic cholestasis. Contrary to previous teaching, pain is the typical accompaniment of malignant obstruction.

RIGORS

A shaking chill and fever suggest gallstones or a benign biliary stricture. This picture is rare in viral and drug-induced hepatitis and uncommon with malignant obstruction.

PAST OPERATION

If the previous operation was on the biliary system or pancreas, recurrent or overlooked choledocholithiasis, traumatic stricture or recurrent malignancy may be suspected. If the operation was not related to the biliary area, postoperative cholestasis, serum hepatitis, or anaesthetic agent, hepatoxicity is suggested [35, 42, 75].

URINE AND STOOLS

Descriptions of the urine and faeces by patients are frequently unreliable. Pale stools and dark urine are seen in mechanical obstruction, but also with intrahepatic cholestasis and in some cases of hepatitis. In haemolytic jaundice the stools are coloured and the urine is not dark. The combination of bleeding and pale stools may produce the 'silver stools' of a patient with carcinoma of the papilla of Vater, but this is a most uncommon symptom.

PHYSICAL EXAMINATION

DEPTH OF JAUNDICE

Patients with haemolytic jaundice are described as pale yellow, with hepatocellular jaundice as orange, and with prolonged biliary obstruction as a deep greenish tint, but in practice this is not of great diagnostic value.

EVIDENCE OF HEPATOCELLULAR INSUFFICIENCY

There may be evidence of some intellectual deterioration and in more advanced cases hepatic foetor and a flapping tremor. Palmar erythema, spider naevi, gynaecomastia, testicular atrophy, and loss of hair also indicate cirrhosis. Easy bruising may mean a prothrombin deficiency.

ABDOMINAL EXAMINATION

Liver. A large, hard, nodular liver suggests hepatic malignancy. An enlarged, firm liver is seen in cirrhosis, but also in extrahepatic obstruction. The liver is usually slightly enlarged and may be tender in acute viral hepatitis. It is usually neither enlarged nor tender in intrahepatic cholestasis.

Gallbladder. A palpable non-tender gallbladder suggests malignant obstruction of the distal bile duct, such as in carcinoma of the pancreas, and this is a highly discriminatory sign. However, the gallbladder may be palpable in choledocho-lithiasis if there is simultaneous obstruction of the cystic duct by a gallstone, though in these cases the gallbladder is frequently tender to palpation. The gallbladder area may be tender in the presence of gallstones.

Spleen. Splenomegaly may suggest cirrhosis with portal hypertension, or hae-molysis, but it is also occasionally seen in acute viral hepatitis and in patients who have carcinoma of the pancreas with splenic vein thrombosis.

Ascites. This suggests cirrhosis or malignancy with peritoneal spread.

BASIC LABORATORY INVESTIGATIONS

URINE AND FAECES

Bile pigment in the urine is present in hepatitis and in cholestasis. Persistent absence of urobilinogen suggests a haemolytic type of jaundice. Persistently acholic stools suggest cholestasis, whereas an excess of stercobilin suggests haemolytic jaundice.

Persistently positive occult blood in the faeces suggests carcinoma of the papilla of Vater, carcinoma of the alimentary tract, or cirrhosis associated with portal hypertension.

BLOOD

Polymorphonuclear leucocytosis suggests choledocholithiasis or a benign stric-ture; it may occur with malignant obstruction, but is most uncommon in acute viral hepatitis. A normal or low leucocyte count with relative lymphocytosis suggests hepatocellular jaundice [75]. Eosinophilia is seen in some cases of drug-induced jaundice, such as that due to chlorpromazine [75].

If a haemolytic type of jaundice is suspected further help may be obtained from a reticulocyte count, tests of red cell fragility, Coombs' test, and bone marrow biopsy.

LIVER FUNCTION

A large number of tests may be performed to investigate various aspects of liver function, but in practice the following are useful in the diagnosis of the cause of jaundice:

SERUM BILIRUBIN

This establishes the severity of jaundice. Serial determinations may be useful in following the progress of the jaundice. Estimations of the ratio of conjugated to unconjugated bilirubins are rarely of diagnostic value.

SERUM ALKALINE PHOSPHATASE

The normal serum alkaline phosphatase level is less than 100 International Units or less than four Bodansky Units, or less than 13 King-Armstrong Units per 100 ml. In hepatocellular jaundice the level is usually raised, but in over 90 per cent it is less than three times the upper limit of normal [96].

In cholestatic jaundice the levels are usually above three times the upper limit of normal. In certain forms of incomplete cholestasis, such as primary biliary cirrhosis and biliary stricture, very high values may be obtained, quite out of proportion to the level of the serum bilirubin [75]. In the presence of complete mechanical obstruction, such as that due to carcinoma of the pancreas, the serum alkaline phosphatase level is usually extremely high. Elevated levels may be obtained in hepatic tumours, or other space-occupying lesions, even in the absence of jaundice [75]. Serum alkaline phosphatase may also be raised in primary bone disease, but this is rarely a diagnostic problem, as these patients are not jaundiced.

Thus the level of the serum alkaline phosphatase is useful in the diagnosis of jaundice, but it should be noted that overlap is common [94].

SERUM TRANSAMINASE

Aspartate transaminase (AST) and glutamic pyruvic transaminase (GPT) are present in the heart, kidney, skeletal muscle, and liver. They are released into the bloodstream when these tissues are acutely destroyed. GPT is said to be more specific for liver damage than is AST, but in practice only AST is measured in the investigation of the patient with jaundice, as the differentiation of myocardial infarction from hepatobiliary disease is not a problem, clinically.

High values above 300 units suggest hepatocellular jaundice, such as acute viral hepatitis, and the levels may rise to over 1000 units. Transaminase values may also be high in active chronic hepatitis [75].

In the presence of intrahepatic cholestasis AST values are usually elevated, but it is uncommon to have values greater than 300 units. In the various forms of extrahepatic obstruction slight elevations of AST, such as two or three times the upper limit of normal, are common but high values are unusual. However, in the presence of cholangitis, high values are occasionally seen, presumably due to liver damage caused by infection [96].

SERUM PROTEINS

Determination of serum protein levels and the electrophoretic pattern can be of value in the differential diagnosis of jaundice.

In acute forms of jaundice the serum protein levels may not be greatly altered. In jaundice associated with chronic hepatitis there is a rise in gamma globulins and a depression of serum albumin. In prolonged viral hepatitis there is some depression of albumin and an elevation of gamma and beta globulins. In prolonged cholestatic jaundice there is typically a rise in alpha-2 and beta globulins, but the albumin and gamma globulin levels are not greatly altered.

BASIC RADIOLOGY

Three routine radiologic investigations may be useful in diagnosis, namely a radiograph of the chest, a radiograph of the abdomen, and a barium meal examination.

A radiograph of the chest may show up a primary or secondary lung tumour or some other unusual lesion, such as sarcoidosis.

A plain radiograph of the abdomen may show a radiopaque gallstone (about 10 per cent of gallstones are radio-opaque), but it is important to note that this may not be the cause of the jaundice. Pancreatic calcification suggests chronic pancreatitis and one may see calcification in the wall of a hydatid cyst.

A barium meal examination may show oesophageal varices. A distortion of the duodenal wall or a lack of mobility of the duodenum may be seen with carcinoma of the pancreas, but also with chronic pancreatitis. A widening of the duodenal loop may be seen with pancreatic carcinoma or with a pancreatic cyst, but the range of normality has not been determined and, occasionally, a wide duodenal loop is seen in normal subjects.

LIVER IMAGING

Liver imaging can be a useful investigation in the jaundiced patient to diagnose certain of the causes, such as diffuse liver disease associated with jaundice (e.g. cirrhosis, liver infiltrations), or mass lesions of the liver associated with jaundice (e.g. liver hydatid, liver metastases).

Radionuclide scanning of the liver (RN) was the earlier and most useful screening test, but more recent evidence indicates that grey scale ultrasonography is probably as useful and as accurate as radionuclide scanning for both diffuse and localised lesions of the liver [10, 32, 80, 82]. Thus for the detection of mass lesions in the liver, in the presence of jaundice, either modality may be used as a screening test. Radionuclide scanning has an advantage in being able to produce dynamic scans which can be useful in the presence of diffuse liver disease, such as cirrhosis, and in detecting metastatic lesions in the liver which are associated with jaundice.

Ultrasonography is attractive because it is relatively cheap, non-invasive, without radiation hazard, and can be easily repeated. Ultrasound examination of the liver and bile ducts has, therefore, become the major initial screening investigation, but radionuclide scanning may be used as a complementary investigation to ultrasound.

Computerised tomography of the liver (CT) is probably best reserved for the more accurate topographic delineation of a mass lesion in the liver, which will aid operative tactics and it is not necessary to use CT scanning as a screening test [10, 15, 93]. Thus the large hepatic mass lesion shown in Fig. 4.4 is a CT scan associated with jaundice and first picked up equally well by both US and RN scanning. The CT scan was performed to accurately localise the mass lesion and

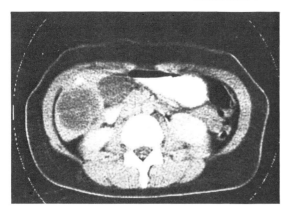

Fig. 4.4. CT scan clearly outlining a large mass lesion in the right lobe of the liver, which was associated with jaundice. This investigation was used as a refinement after a previous radionuclide scan had detected the lesion, in order to help the surgeon plan his incision and exposure.

to decide whether an abdominothoracic approach will or will not be necessary for its removal. For examples of liver imaging the reader is referred to Chapter 15 which deals with hepatobiliary hydatids, as these emphasise the principles of use of these various liver-imaging methods in our present state of knowledge.

BILE DUCT IMAGING

Ultrasonography of the intrahepatic and extrahepatic bile ducts has become the basic screening investigation in jaundice and, in cases of doubt, or where a more precise characterisation of the biliary ductal system is required, percutaneous transhepatic cholangiography, or endoscopic retrograde cholangiography, or both, will be used as well. Fig. 4.5 is the flow chart and decision tree of bile duct imaging in the jaundiced patient.

ULTRASONOGRAPHY (US)

Bile duct imaging by ultrasound is a highly accurate screening test for the presence or absence of bile duct dilatation in both the intrahepatic and extrahepatic bile ducts and which, in experienced hands, is able to distinguish 'surgical jaundice' from 'medical jaundice' in about 95 per cent of cases [10, 12, 55, 81, 88, 92, 97]. The test is cheap, non-invasive, and without complications. On the debit side is its frequent inability to detect the site and cause of bile duct obstruction when an abnormally dilated bile duct is encountered and if the cause is a mass lesion then computed tomography is useful as a complementary investigation [36, 57, 81]. Also, experience is required in the interpretation of the images. Bile duct obstruction sometimes occurs without significant ductal dilatation and, in these cases, ultrasound would give a false negative result [10, 12]. Fig. 4.6 is the ultrasound image of a normal bile duct, while Fig. 4.7 shows a dilated bile duct, the cause of which is not seen, and Fig. 4.8 shows a dilated duct due to a mass lesion of the pancreas which at operation was shown to be cancer of the pancreas. Fig. 4.9 shows multiple dilated intrahepatic ducts, which at operation were found to be caused by a cancer of the common hepatic duct.

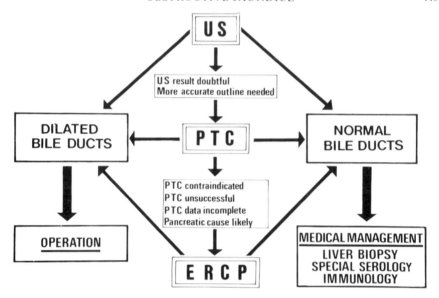

Fig. 4.5. Decision tree and flow chart for bile duct imaging in the jaundiced patient.

PERCUTANEOUS TRANSHEPATIC CHOLANGIOGRAPHY (PTC)

Percutaneous transhepatic cholangiography (PTC) was introduced over 50 years ago and it has been shown to be a most reliable and accurate technique to outline the bile ducts [52]. The procedure has also been made much safer with the introduction of a long, thin needle, developed by Okuda in the University of Chiba in 1969 [86]. The method is described in Chapter 3, and here only the specific indication for PTC and its accuracy in cases of prolonged jaundice will be discussed. Chapter 3 also has six illustrations which demonstrate various aspects of PTC, and especially when related to the investigation of jaundice (see Figs. 3.7–3.12 in Chapter 3).

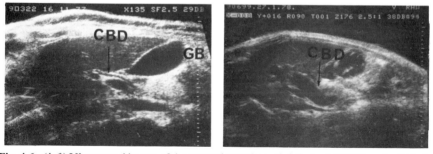

Fig. 4.6. (*left*) Ultrasound image of the normal extrahepatic bile duct (CBD) and gallbladder (GB). Courtesy of Dr. Peter Warren, Sydney.

Fig. 4.7. (*right*) Ultrasound of an abnormally dilated extrahepatic bile duct (CBD) in a jaundiced patient. Courtesy of Dr. Peter Warren, Sydney.

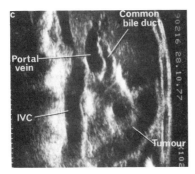 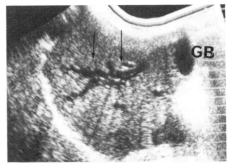

Fig. 4.8. (*left*) Ultrasound image of a dilated extrahepatic bile duct and a pancreatic mass lesion, causing obstructive jaundice. Courtesy of Dr. Peter Warren, Sydney.

Fig. 4.9. (*right*) Ultrasound showing multiple dilated intrahepatic bile ducts (arrows) in a jaundiced patient. Courtesy of Dr. Peter Warren, Sydney.

At present PTC is used after ultrasound of the bile ducts has indicated a dilated duct, but when more precise characterisation of the ductal system is needed when ultrasound results are inconclusive or when ultrasound facilities are not available. All recent reports indicate that dilated bile ducts can be successfully outlined by PTC in 95–100 per cent of cases, but the success rate with non-dilated ducts is extremely variable, ranging from 25 to 73 per cent in different series [11, 25, 60]. Fig. 4.10 is an example of a PTC demonstrating the site and cause of the jaundice in a patient with a cancer of the papilla of Vater growing into the bile duct and blocking it completely. Other examples of the use of PTC in jaundice can be seen in Chapters 3, 4, 5, 6, and 7.

The risks of the procedure are haemorrhage, bile leakage, and septicaemia. The risk of haemorrhage and bile leakage has been considerably decreased by the use of the fine needle. While it is now not necessary to operate on the patient the day of the procedure as with the previous techniques, the complications of haemorrhage and bile leakage still do occur and, when blocked ducts are demonstrated at PTC, operation is best done within the next day or two [41]. Septicaemia remains as a serious and potentially fatal complication, and patients need to have preventative antibiotics at the time of the PTC, and the antibiotics should have a broad range covering both aerobic and anaerobic organisms as outlined in Chapter 9 [11].

Recent work from Scandinavia points to therapeutic extensions of PTC [16, 17, 87]. The initial technique involved PTC followed by catheterisation of the bile ducts and external drainage which relieved the jaundice and improved the patient's general condition for a definitive operative procedure. This concept was extended by Burcharth in 1978 with the development of an endoprosthesis inserted under local anaesthetic during PTC as palliation of the jaundice caused by malignant bile duct obstruction [16]. The exact place of these ingenious extensions to PTC need further evaluation and the results are eagerly awaited. An example of this technique is shown in Fig. 7.8.

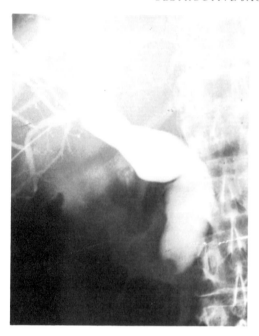

Fig. 4.10. Percutaneous transhepatic cholangiogram of a jaundiced patient showing complete occlusion of the bile duct by a cancer of the papilla of Vater which has grown into the duct.

ENDOSCOPIC RETROGRADE CHOLANGIOPANCREATOGRAPHY (ERCP)

The endoscopic cannulation of the papilla of Vater and retrograde cholangiography and pancreatography (ERCP) has been used since 1969 to outline the biliary ductal system and is a particularly useful method in the jaundiced patient [12, 13]. This technique is discussed in more detail in Chapter 3 dealing with the radiology of the biliary tract.

Endoscopic retrograde cholangiography is employed if precise delineation of the bile duct is required and when PTC has been unsuccessful, if PTC has not given enough information, or if PTC is contraindicated because of a severe bleeding diathesis. ERCP is also valuable if a pancreatic cause for the jaundice is suspected, such as cancer of the pancreas or chronic pancreatitis, because additional diagnostic information can be obtained by the use of pancreatography (Fig. 4.5). Also, the endoscopic procedure can give further diagnostic information by either biopsy or cytology in cases of neoplasms of the papilla of Vater, pancreas, or bile duct [11, 12, 13, 25, 64]. Examples of ERCPs in the diagnosis of jaundice are shown in Chapter 3, Fig. 3.13–3.16.

Septicaemia is a potential complication with bile duct obstruction and this can be minimised by the systemic use of broad-spectrum antibiotics administered just prior to the procedure as outlined in Chapter 9.

SURGICAL INTERVENTION

INDICATIONS FOR SURGERY

When the diagnosis of mechanical obstruction is made the need for surgical intervention is clear. Exploratory laparotomy in these cases should be performed without delay. The exception to this is the patient who has a mechanical obstruction of the bile ducts, but in whom the jaundice is rapidly resolving. In this group it is safest to allow the jaundice to subside completely before operation is undertaken.

With the recent advances in bile duct imaging diagnostic laparotomy to rule out mechanical bile duct obstruction is now rarely performed. In the past when a medical cause for jaundice was found operative mortality was high, particularly when laparotomy showed acute viral hepatitis or chronic liver disease and, therefore, modern techniques of bile duct imaging represent a major advance [33, 34].

THE OPERATION

The presence of mechanical obstruction of the major bile ducts can almost always be confirmed or refuted at operation, when a careful exploration is performed, particularly when laparotomy is complemented by operative cholangiography and tissue diagnosis or cytology.

The description that follows is an outline of the sequence of steps taken when laparotomy is performed on a jaundiced patient. This description is a guide only and not a rigid plan, because modifications are frequently necessary according to the circumstances of the particular case.

The abdomen is usually opened through a long right paramedian incision. A thorough laparotomy is performed, examining all the abdominal viscera. Special attention is given to the gallbladder, bile ducts, duodenum, pancreas, liver, and spleen.

The state of the gallbladder will give the operator the most important first clue regarding the presence and probable site of bile duct obstruction. The operative tactics will, therefore, be guided in the first instance by the appearance of the gallbladder (Table 4.2).

DISTENDED GALLBLADDER

If the gallbladder is distended, blue in colour, thin-walled, and contains no gallstones, it is likely that the obstruction is caused by a malignancy near the distal bile duct, such as a carcinoma of the head of the pancreas (Courvoisier's dictum). The bile duct is examined next, because it is usually also dilated, blue, and thin-walled. Attention is next directed to the head of the pancreas and the duodenum. These structures are mobilised by division of the peritoneum lateral to the second part of the duodenum. This area is felt for a hard mass.

Similar findings may be noted when obstruction is caused by chronic pancreatitis but, in a typical case, the gallbladder, although slightly distended, is usually thickened and opaque. With chronic pancreatitis causing jaundice the bile duct is usually dilated, but it is also thickened and opaque. A mass may be felt in the head of the pancreas.

Table 4.2. State of gallbladder and operative tactics in jaundice

State of gallbladder	Possible causes	Areas specifically focused on	Special peroperative tests used
Distended gallbladder	1. Malignant obstruction (usually pancreas cancer, but can be distal bile duct, papilla of Vater or duodenal cancer) 2. Acute cholecystitis ± choledocholithiasis Mucocoele ± choledocholithiasis 4. Chronic pancreatitis	1. Head of pancreas 2. Distal bile duct 3. Papilla of Vater 4. Duodenum	1. Operative cholangiogram 2. Lymph node biopsy 3. Endocholedochal biopsy or cytology 4. Fine-needle aspiration cytology of mass lesion
Collapsed gallbladder	1. Proximal bile duct cancer 2. Intrahepatic cancer 3. Sclerosing cholangitis	1. Porta hepatis 2. Proximal bile duct 3. Liver	1. Lymph node biopsy 2. External mass biopsy 3. Endohepatodochal biopsy or cytology
Gallbladder stones	1. Choledocholithiasis 2. Chronic pancreatitis	1. Common bile duct 2. Pancreas	Operative cholangiogram
Solid gallbladder lump	Gallbladder cancer	1. Gallbladder 2. Porta hepatis	Biopsy of mass lesion
Absent gallbladder	1. Choledocholithiasis 2. Bile duct stricture	Bile duct	Operative cholangiogram
Normal gallbladder	Intrahepatic 'medical' cause	Liver	Liver biopsy

If a mass is found in the region of the head of the pancreas, and the surgeon is uncertain whether it is malignant obstruction or chronic pancreatitis, it may be necessary to proceed to other measures such as biopsy of parapancreatic lymph glands, operative cholangiography, intracholedochal biopsy, or aspiration cytology with a fine needle. In recent years the use of fine-needle aspiration cytology in these doubtful cases has been of great value and the procedure is particularly accurate if the cytologist reports neoplastic cells [48, 67]. This form of tissue diagnosis is most appealing because it is almost without risk, while it is known that open-wedge biopsy of the pancreas is both inaccurate and dangerous [37, 67].

A distended gallbladder may also be due to acute or subacute cholecystitis, but the gallbladder wall in such cases is thickened, oedematous, and vascular. Transient jaundice is frequently seen with acute cholecystitis in the absence of bile duct stones, but prolonged jaundice of the type discussed in this chapter is usually due to associated choledocholithiasis. Rarely, acute cholecystitis is caused by a malignant bile duct tumour; then the jaundice is caused by the tumour blocking the bile duct (see Carcinoma of the Gallbladder in Chapter 7). If the gallbladder is distended but contains gallstones and a clear viscid fluid the patient has a mucocoele of the gallbladder, and the jaundice is also usually due to bile duct gallstones. With acute cholecystitis, subacute cholecystitis, or a mucocoele of the gallbladder, attention is next directed to the common bile duct and an operative cholangiogram is also performed.

Thus, if a distended gallbladder is found the surgeon moves his attention to the distal common bile duct and to the head of the pancreas and papillary area, because these are the areas where the obstruction is most likely to be found.

COLLAPSED GALLBLADDER
If the gallbladder is collapsed it is likely that the obstruction is above the point of entry of the cystic duct into the common hepatic duct. In such cases attention is directed next to the area of the common hepatic duct in the porta hepatis. This region is palpated and dissected for the presence of an obstructing bile duct tumour or, less commonly, for the presence of a non-malignant stricture. If a lesion is found in this area further steps are taken to establish its nature. This may mean biopsy and frozen section of part of the outside of the lesion, choledochotomy of the collapsed bile duct below the lesion, and intradochal manipulation and biopsy or cytology of the lesion.

GALLBLADDER STONES
If the gallbladder is thickened and contains gallstones, but is neither distended or collapsed, the most probable cause of the jaundice is choledocholithiasis. In such cases attention is directed next to the common bile duct and an operative cholangiogram is also performed. The duodenum and head of the pancreas are mobilised, the distal bile duct palpated, and the pancreas examined for the presence of chronic pancreatitis.

Chronic pancreatitis is sometimes responsible for bile duct obstruction and jaundice without associated gallstones. In a typical case the bile duct is slightly dilated but is thick-walled and opaque. The gallbladder may be of normal size or only slightly distended, but it is usually thickened, having the appearance of chronic cholecystitis. Chronic pancreatitis is sometimes difficult to distinguish from malignant obstruction; this is discussed shortly.

SOLID GALLBLADDER

A solid lump in the gallbladder usually means a primary gallbladder carcinoma. The jaundice is usually due to extension of the tumour to the bile ducts in the porta hepatis. In these cases there is usually other clear evidence of the malignant nature of the tumour, such as infiltration into the liver or the presence of lymph gland and liver metastases.

ABSENT GALLBLADDER

If the gallbladder has been removed previously the most likely cause of sub-sequent jaundice is choledocholithiasis or a non-malignant bile duct stricture. Less commonly, chronic pancreatitis or an overlooked malignant obstruction is found. In such cases the bile duct is exposed and examined, the duodenum and head of the pancreas mobilised, and an operative cholangiogram performed.

NORMAL GALLBLADDER

If the gallbladder is of normal size, not thickened, and without gallstones when emptied, it is likely that a mechanical obstruction of the bile duct is not present. This suspicion is confirmed by the examination of the bile duct, duodenum, and pancreas. An operative cholangiogram is then performed. The operation is concluded with a liver biopsy.

SUMMARY

The abdomen is thoroughly explored, with special attention to the gallbladder, bile ducts, pancreas, duodenum, and liver. An operative cholangiogram is usually performed. The state of the gallbladder gives the operator the first clue regarding the presence and probable site of bile duct obstruction. According to the gallbladder findings the surgeon then logically concentrates his attention on one of several regions—the area of the head of the pancreas and duodenum, the region of the porta hepatis, the bile duct itself, or the liver. By doing this he confirms the site of the obstruction and then proceeds to establish the cause of the obstruction by a number of described measures, such as operative cholangiography, lymph node biopsy, biopsy or cytology of a mass lesion, or liver biopsy as indicated in Table 4.2.

OPERATIVE FINDINGS

In the absence of mechanical bile duct obstruction the biliary tract and the pancreas are normal, and the operative cholangiogram will show a normal biliary system without obstruction. With such findings the patient can be confi-dently treated as a case of 'medical' jaundice.

Further details of the operative findings and surgical treatment of a number of biliary tract conditions causing jaundice may be found in appropriate sections of this book. These conditions include choledocholithiasis (Chapter 5), postoperative biliary strictures (Chapter 6), primary sclerosing cholangitis (Chapter 6), recurrent pyogenic cholangitis (Chapter 9), carcinoma of the gallbladder (Chapter 7), carcinoma of the bile ducts (Chapter 7), and hydatidosis of the hepatobiliary system (Chapter 15).

CANCER OR CHRONIC PANCREATITIS?

Carcinoma, causing obstruction of the distal common bile duct, may arise in the head of the pancreas, the bile duct, the papilla of Vater or the duodenum. The operative diagnosis is established by finding a hard mass in these areas which, in the case of a carcinoma of the papilla of Vater or the duodenum, may be ulcerated. There may be obvious peritoneal, lymph nodal, or hepatic metastases. A characteristic feature of all these malignant obstructions is the gross dilatation of the bile ducts and of the gallbladder proximal to the obstruction. The dilated biliary system is thin-walled and blue. In the presence of jaundice the operative cholangiogram shows a complete obstruction (Fig. 4.11).

In chronic pancreatitis which causes jaundice there is a firm-to-hard mass

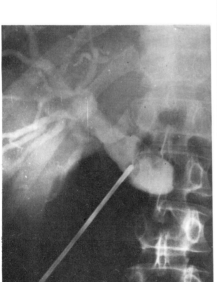
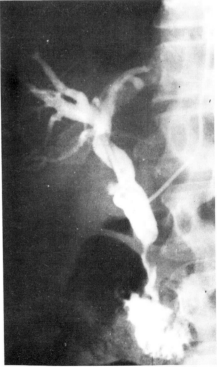

Fig. 4.11. Cancer or chronic pancreatitis? Both operative cholangiograms were in patients who were jaundiced, have had a previous cholecystectomy, and the preoperative differentiation between chronic pancreatitis and cancer was difficult. (*left*) Note conical complete block of the bile duct typical of pancreas cancer. (*right*) Note long stricture of the distal bile duct, but some dye is getting through into the duodenum and this signifies chronic pancreatitis.

involving the pancreas diffusely or, occasionally, it is localised to the head of the gland. The mass is nodular with areas of fibrosis. There may be small or large retention cysts present and calcification may be felt in the pancreas. The pancreatic duct may be dilated and one or more strictures may be seen if an operative pancreatogram is performed. In contrast to malignant obstruction the proximal bile duct is usually thick-walled and opaque. The bile duct is frequently slightly dilated and may contain gallstones. The gallbladder is usually thickened and slightly distended and may or may not contain gallstones. Even in the presence of jaundice the operative cholangiogram in chronic pancreatitis shows only a narrowing of the bile duct, and it is rare to get a complete block to the passage of dye (Fig. 4.11).

It has already been discussed that if the distinction between chronic pancreatitis and malignant obstruction is difficult then special preoperative tests can be helpful, such as operative cholangiography, lymph node biopsy, or fine-needle aspiration cytology (Table 4.2).

SPECIFIC PREOPERATIVE AND POSTOPERATIVE MANAGEMENT OF THE JAUNDICED PATIENT

The jaundiced patient is generally a poor subject for major surgery and must be brought to as good a condition as possible before operation. If anaemia is present then the blood picture is brought to normal by transfusion and vitamin K_1 is administered parenterally.

Malnutrition for protein, fat, and vitamins is common, especially in the presence of malignant bile duct obstruction. Our group and others have shown that one can argue for 'two-stage' operations in these malnourished patients in order to decrease the mortality and morbidity caused by major postoperative infections and healing disasters [12, 46]. The first stage consists of some simple form of biliary decompression and during this time total parenteral nutrition is administered over a 10 to 14-day period, before proceeding to the major definitive operative procedure, such as pancreaticoduodenectomy or bile duct reconstruction. This appears to be especially important in the jaundiced patient with malignant disease, as this group is especially prone to infection and wound-healing problems after surgery [39, 45].

Preventative antibiotics should also be used at the time of surgery, as septicaemia can be a serious problem in these compromised jaundiced patients [12, 46]. The antibiotics are best administered so that there is a high blood and tissue level achieved at the time of surgery and there should be a broad-spectrum antibiotic cover for both aerobic and anaerobic organisms. Postoperative oliguric renal failure is a real risk in patients with jaundice, especially with serum bilirubin levels exceeding 150 mmol/1 [12, 20, 21]. The reasons for this are not entirely clear, but there is evidence for decreased extracellular volume and dehydration in jaundice, endotoxaemia caused by poor reticuloendothelial function of the liver, as well as functional and structural changes in the kidneys and a special sensitivity to renal ischaemic damage, factors which all predispose the jaundiced patient to postoperative oliguric renal failure. Thus in the presence of prolonged jaundice the extracellular compartment needs to be corrected before surgery, and a mannitol infusion given preventatively during and after surgery with an adequate sodium intake [12, 21].

REFERENCES

1. AGGARWAL S.K., AGGARWAL S.P. & AGGARWAL D.C. Demonstration of a round worm in the common bile duct. *Am. J. Roentgen.* **91**:869, 1964.
2. ALTEMEIER W.A. & ALEXANDER J.W. Pancreas abscess. A study of 32 cases. *Arch. Surg. (Chicago)* **87**:80, 1963.
3. ARIAS I.M. Chronic unconjugated hyperbilirubinaemia (CUH) with increased production of bile pigment not derived from the haemoglobin of mature circulating erythrocytes. *J. Clin. Invest.* **41**:1341, 1962.
4. ARIAS I.M. Hepatic aspects of bilirubin metabolism. *Ann. Rev. Med.* **17**:257, 1966.
5. ARIAS I.M. & GARTNER L.M. Production of unconjugated hyperbilirubinaemia in full-term newborn infants. *Nature (London)* **203**:1292, 1964.
6. ARIAS I.M., GARTNER L.M., SEIFTER S. & FURMAN M. Prolonged neonatal unconjugated hyperbilirubinaemia associated with breast feeding and a steroid, pregnone-3 (alpha) 20 (beta) diol in maternal milk that inhibits glucuronide formation *in vitro. J. Clin. Invest.* **43**:2037, 1964.
7. ARIAS I.M., WOLFSON S., LUCEY J.F. & McKAY R.J. JR. Transient familial neonatal hyperbilirubinaemia. *J. Clin. Invest.* **44**:1442, 1965.
8. ARIEL I.M. & HOLANDER D. Hepatic gamma scanning. *Am. J. Surg.* **118**:5, 1969.
9. BAGGENSTOSS A.J., FOULK W.T., BUTT H.R. & BAHN R.C. The pathology of primary biliary cirrhosis with emphasis on histogenesis. *Am. J. Clin. Path.* **42**:259, 1964.
10. BAKER C. & WAY L.W. Clinical utility of CAT body scans. *Am. J. Surg.* **136**:37, 1978.
11. BENJAMIN I.S., ALLISON M.E.M., MOULE B., BLUMGART L.H. The early use of fine-needle percutaneous transhepatic cholangiography in an approach to the diagnosis of jaundice in a surgical unit. *Br. J. Surg.* **65**:92, 1978.
12. BLUMGART L.H. Biliary tract obstruction. New approaches to old problems. *Am. J. Surg.* **135**:19, 1978.
13. BLUMGART L.H., SALMON P.R. & COTTON P.B. Endoscopy and retrograde choledochopancreatography in the diagnosis of the patient with jaundice. *Surg. Gynec. Obstet.* **138**:565, 1974.
14. BOSNIACK M.A. & PHANTHUMACHINDA P. Value of arteriography in the study of hepatic disease. *Am. J. Surg.* **112**:348, 1966.
15. BRYAN P.J., DINN W.M., GROSSMAN Z.D., WISTOW B.W., McAFEE J.G., KIEFFER S.A. Correlation of computed tomography, gray scale ultrasonography and radionuclide imaging of the liver in detecting space-occupying processes. *Radiology* **124**:387, 1977.
16. BURCHARTH F. A new endoprosthesis for nonoperative intubation of the biliary tract in malignant obstructive jaundice. *Surg. Gynec. Obstet.* **146**:76, 1978.
17. BURCHARTH F., CHRISTIANSEN L., EFSEN F., NIELBO N. & STAGE P. Percutaneous transhepatic cholangiography in diagnostic evaluation of 160 jaundiced patients. Results of an improved technic. *Am. J. Surg.* **133**:559, 1977.
18. CHRISTIAN E.R. Behaviour of serum iron in various diseases of liver. *A.M.A. Arch. Intern. Med.* **94**:22, 1954.
19. CRIGLER J.R. JR. & NAJJAR V.A. Congenital familial non-hemolytic jaundice with kernicterus. *Pediatrics* **10**:169, 1952.
20. DAWSON J.L. Post-operative renal function in obstructive jaundice: Effect of a mannitol diuresis. *Br. Med. J.* **1**:82, 1965.

21. DAWSON J.L. Acute post-operative renal failure in obstructive jaundice. *Ann. R. Coll. Surg. Eng.* **42**:163, 1968.

22. DONIACH D., ROITT I.M., WALKER J.G. & SHERLOCK S. Tissue antibodies in primary biliary cirrhosis, active chronic (lupoid) hepatitis, cryptogenic cirrhosis and other liver diseases and their clinical implications. *Clin. Exp. Immun.* **1**:237, 1966.

23. DUBIN I.N. & JOHNSON F.B. Chronic idiopathic jaundice with unidentified pigment in the liver cells: A new clinicopathological entity with a report of twelve cases. *Medicine (Baltimore)* **33**:155, 1954.

24. DUBIN I.N., SULLIVAN B.H. JR., LEGOLVAN D.C. & MURPHY L.C. The cholestatic form of viral hepatitis: Experiences with viral hepatitis at Brooke Army Hospital during the years 1951 to 1953. *Am. J. Med.* **29**:55, 1960.

25. ELIAS E., NAMLYN A.N., JAIN S., LONG R.G., SUMMERFIELD J.A., DICK R. & SHERLOCK S. A randomised trial of percutaneous cholangiography with the Chiba needle versus endoscopic retrograde cholangiography for bile duct visualisation in jaundice. *Gastroenterology* **71**:439, 1976.

26. EYLER W.R., DUSAULT L.A., POZNANSKI A.K. & SCHUMAN B.M. Isotope scanning in the evaluation of the jaundiced patient. *Radiol. Clin. N. Amer.* **4**:589, 1966.

27. EYLER W.R., DUSAULT L.A., POZNANSKI A.K. & SCHUMAN B.M. Liver scanning with special reference to jaundiced patients. *Lahey Clin. Found. Bull.* **17**:13, 1968.

28. FAHEY J.L. Antibodies and immunoglobulins. I. Structure and function. II. Normal development and changes in disease. *J.A.M.A.* **194**:71, 255, 1965.

29. FARRELL W.J. Angiography of the liver: Practical applications and demonstration of color subtraction technique. *Radiol. Clin. N. Amer.* **4**:571, 1966.

30. FOULK W.T., BAGGENSTOSS A.H. & BUTT, H.R. Primary biliary cirrhosis: Reevaluation by clinical and histologic study of 49 cases. *Gastroenterology* **47**:354, 1964.

31. GONZALES L.L., JAFFE M.S., WIOT J.F. & ALTEMEIER W.A. Pancreatic pseudocyst: A cause of obstructive jaundice. *Ann. Surg.* **161**:569, 1965.

32. GROSSMAN Z.G., WISTOW B.W., BRYAN P.J., DINN W.M., McAFEE J.G. & KIEFFER S.A. Radionuclide imaging, computed tomography and gray-scale ultrasonography of the liver: A comparative study. *J. Nuclear. Med.* **18**:327, 1977.

33. HARDY K.J. & HUGHES E.S.R. Laparotomy in viral hepatitis. *Med. J. Aust.* **1**:170, 1968.

34. HARVILLE D.D. & SUMMERSKILL W.H.J. Surgery in acute hepatitis: Cause and effects. *J.A.M.A.* **184**:257, 1963.

35. HAUBRICH W.S. Adverse hepatic reactions to halothane: Risks and safeguards. *Chicago Med. Sch. Quart.* **26**:95, 1966.

36. HAVRILLA T.R., HAAGA J.R., ALFIDI R.J. & REICH N.E. Computed tomography and obstructive biliary disease. *Am. J. Roentgenol.* **128**:765, 1977.

37. HESS W. Surgery of the biliary passages and the pancreas. Van Nostrand, Princeton, N.J., 1965.

38. HOLZBACH R.T. & SANDERS J.H. Recurrent intrahepatic cholestasis of pregnancy. Observations on pathogenesis. *J.A.M.A.* **193**:542, 1965.

39. IRVIN T.T., VASSILAKIS J.S., CHATTOPADHYAY & GREANEY M.G. Abdominal wound healing in jaundiced patients. *Br. J. Surg.* **65**:521, 1978.

40. ISRAELS L.G., LEVITT M., NOVAR W., FOERSTER J. & ZIPURSKY A. The 'early' bilirubin. In I.A.D. Bouchier & B.H. Billing (eds.), *Bilirubin Metabolism.* Blackwell, Oxford, 1967.

41. JULER, G.L., CONROY R.M. & FUELLEMAN R.W. Bile leakage following percutaneous transhepatic cholangiography with the Chiba needle. *Arch. Surg.* **112**:954, 1977.

42. KANTROWITZ P.A., JONES W.A., GREENBERGER N.J. & ISSELBACHER K.J. Severe postoperative hyperbilirubinemia simulating obstructive jaundice. *New Eng. J. Med.* **276**:591, 1967.

43. KAWAGUCHI J., BERK E. & SOBLE A.R. Studies with I[131] labelled rose bengal. *Am. J. Dig. Dis.* **7**:300, 1962.

44. KUNE G.A. Abscesses of the pancreas. *Aust. New Zeal. J. Surg.* **38**:125, 1968.

45. KUNE G.A. The management of obstructive jaundice. *Med. J. Aust.* **1:**320, 1968.
46. KUNE G.A. Life-threatening surgical infection: Its development and prediction. Hunterian Lecture. *Ann. R. Coll. Surg. Eng.* **60:**92, 1978.
47. KUNE G.A. Indications for surgical intervention in acute pancreatitis. In Keynes & Keith (eds.), *The Pancreas.* Heinemann, London (to be published).
48. KUNE G.A., HOBBS J.B., BUTTERFIELD D. & SALI A. Cancer of the pancreas in young adults. *Med. J. Aust.* **2:**626, 1978.
49. KUNE G.A. & KING R. The late complications of acute pancreatitis. *Med. J. Aust.* **1:**1241, 1973.
50. LEGER L. Splenoportography: Diagnostic phlebography of the portal venous system. Thomas, Springfield III, 1966.
51. LOUTFI G.I. & GROGAN R.H. Failure of corticosteroid test in the differential diagnosis of jaundice. *J.A.M.A.* **197:**48, 1966.
52. MACHADO A.L. Percutaneous transhepatic cholangiography. *Br. J. Surg.* **58:**616, 1971.
53. MADDEN R.E. Complications of needle biopsy of the liver. *Arch. Surg. (Chicago)* **83:**778, 1961.
54. MAN E.B., KARTIN B.L., DURLACHER S.H. & PETERS J.P. The lipids of serum and liver in patients with hepatic disease. *J. Clin. Invest.* **24:**623, 1945.
55. MCKAY A.J., DUNCAN J.G., LAM P., HUNT D.R. & BLUMGART L.H. The role of grey scale ultrasonography in the investigation of jaundice. *Br. J. Surg.* **66:**162, 1979.
56. MILLER D.F. & IRVINE R.W. Jaundice in acute appendicitis. *Lancet* **1:**321, 1969.
57. MORRIS A.I., FAWCITT R.A., FORBES W.S.C., ISHERWOOD I. & MARSH M.N. Computed tomography, ultrasound and cholestatic jaundice. *Gut* **19:**685, 1978.
58. NEBESAR R.A., POLLARD J.J. & STONE D.L. Angiographic diagnosis of malignant diseases of the liver. *Radiology* **86:**284, 1966.
59. NORDYKE R.A. Surgical vs nonsurgical jaundice. Differentiation by a combination of rose bengal I[131] and standard liver function tests. *J.A.M.A.* **194:**949, 1965.
60. OKUDA K., TANIKAWA K., EMURA T., KURATOMI S., JINNOUCHI S., URABE K., SUMIKOSHI H., KANDA Y., FUKUYAMA Y., MUSHA H., MORI H., SHIMOKAWA Y., YAKUSHIJI F. & MATSUURA Y. Nonsurgical percutaneous transhepatic cholangiography—diagnostic significance in medical problems of the liver. *Am. J. Dig. Dis.* **19:**21, 1974.
61. ORELLANA-ALCALDE J.M. & DOMINGUEZ F.P. Jaundice and oral contraceptive drugs. *Lancet* **2:**1278, 1966.
62. POPPER H., RUBIN E., GARDIOL D., SCHAFFNER F. & PARONETTO F. Drug-induced liver disease. A penalty for progress. *Arch. Intern. Med. (Chicago)* **115:**128, 1965.
63. QUINN J.L. Scintillation scanning in clinical medicine. Saunders, Philadelphia, 1964.
64. ROBERTS-THOMSON I.C. Endoscopic retrograde cholangiography. *Aust. New Zeal. J. Surg.* **48:**247, 1978.
65. ROTOR A.B., MANAHAN L. & FLORENTIN A. Familial nonhemolytic jaundice with direct van den Bergh reaction. *Acta Med. Philipp.* **5:**37, 1948.
66. RUBIN E., SCHAFFNER F. & POPPER H. Primary biliary cirrhosis. Chronic non-suppurative destructive cholangitis. *Am. J. Path.* **46:**387, 1965.
67. REUBEN A. & COTTON P.B. Operative pancreatic biopsy. *Ann. R. Coll. Surg. Eng.* **35:**34, 1978.
68. SARLES H. & SAHEL J. Cholestasis and lesions of the biliary tract in chronic pancreatitis. *Gut* **19:**851, 1978.
69. SCHAFFNER E., LOEBEL A., WEINER H.A. & BARKA T. Hepatocellular cytoplasmic changes in acute alcoholic hepatitis. *J.A.M.A.* **183:**343, 1963.
70. SCHAFFNER F., POPPER H. & PEREZ V. Changes in bile caniculi produced by norethandrolone: Electron microscopic study of human and rat liver. *J. Lab. Clin. Med.* **56:**623, 1960.
71. SCHAMROTH L., EDELSTEIN W., POLITZER W.M. & STEVENS W. Serum iron in the diagnosis of hepatobiliary disease. *Brit. Med. J.* **1:**960, 1956.

72. SCHMID M., HEFTI M.L., GATTIKER R., KISTLER H.J. & SENNING A. Benign post-operative intrahepatic cholestasis. *New Eng. J. Med.* **272**:546, 1965.
73. SEDGWICK C.E. & POULANTZAS J.K. Portal hypertension. Little Brown, Boston, 1967.
74. SHERLOCK S. Jaundice. *Br. Med. J.* **1**:1359, 1962.
75. SHERLOCK S. *Diseases of the Liver and Biliary System* (5 e). Blackwell, Oxford, 1975.
76. SIBER F.J. Colloidal gold (^{198}Au) and the diagnosis of hepatic tumours. *Radiol. Clin. N. Amer.* **4**:583, 1966.
77. SMITH R. *Pers. Commun.*, 1965.
78. SUMMERSKILL W.H.J., CLOWDUS D.F. II, BOLLMAN J.L. & FLEISCHER G.A. Clinical and experimental studies on the effect of corticotrophin and steroid drugs on bilirubinemia. *Am. J. Med. Sci.* **241**:555, 1961.
79. SUMMERSKILL W.H.J. & JONES F.A. Corticotrophin and steroids in the diagnosis and management of 'obstructive jaundice'. *Br. Med. J.* **2**:1499, 1958.
80. TAYLOR K.J.W., CARPENTER D.A., HILL C.R. & MCREADY V.R. Gray scale ultrasound imaging. The anatomy and pathology of the liver. *Radiology* **119**:415, 1976.
81. TAYLOR K.J.W. & ROSENFIELD A.T. Gray-scale ultrasonography in the differential diagnosis of jaundice. *Arch. Surg.* **112**:820, 1977.
82. TAYLOR K.J.W., SULLIVAN D., ROSENFIELD A.T. & GOTTSCHALK A. Gray scale ultrasound and isotope scanning: complementary techniques for imaging the liver. *Amer. J. Roentgenol.* **128**:277, 1977.
83. TEOH T.B. A study of gallstones and included worms in recurrent pyogenic cholangitis. *J. Path. Bact.* **86**:123, 1963.
84. THALER H. Uber Vorteil und Risiko der Leberbiopsie Methode nach Menghini. *Wien. Klin. Wschr.* **29**:533, 1964.
85. THULIN K.E. & NERMARK J. Seven cases of jaundice in women taking an oral contraceptive, Anovlar. *Br. Med. J.* **1**:584, 1966.
86. TSUCHIYA Y. A new safer method of percutaneous cholangiography. *Jap. J. Gastroenterol.* **66**:438, 1969.
87. TYLEN U., HOEVELS J. & VANG J. Percutaneous transhepatic cholangiography with external drainage of obstructive biliary lesions. *Surg. Gynec. Obstet.* **144**:13, 1977.
88. VALLON A.G., LEES W.R. & COTTON P. Grey-scale ultrasonography in cholestatic jaundice. *Gut* **20**:51, 1979.
89. WALKER C.O. & COMBES B. Biliary cirrhosis induced by chlorpromazine. *Gastroenterology* **51**:631, 1966.
90 WARREN K.W. Surgical management of chronic relapsing pancreatitis. *Am. J. Surg.* **117**:24, 1969.
91. WARREN K.W. & KUNE G.A. Surgical approach to jaundice. *Hosp. Med.* **2**:46, 1966.
92. WHEELER P.G., THEODOSSI A., PICKFORD R., LAWS J., KNILL-JONES R.P. & WILLIAMS R. Non-invasive techniques in the diagnosis of jaundice—ultrasound and computer. *Gut* **20**:196, 1979.
93. WITKOWSKI R., ECONOMOU S.G., MATEGRANO V., PETASNICK J.P. & SOUTHWICK H.W. Computed tomography of the abdomen as an aid to preoperative diagnosis. *Am. J. Surg.* **135**:776, 1978.
94. SAMCHEK N. & KLAUSENSTOCK O. Liver biopsy: II. The risk of needle biopsy. *New Eng. J. Med.* **249**:1062, 1963.
95. ZIMMERMAN H.J. Serum enzymes in the diagnosis of hepatic disease. *Gastroenterology* **46**:613, 1964.
96. ZIMMERMAN H.J. The differential diagnosis of jaundice. *Med. Clin. N. Amer.* **52**:1417, 1968.
97. ZUSMER N.R., HARWOOD S.R., PEVSNER N.H., JANOWITZ W.R. & SERAFINI A.N. Gray scale ultrasonography and rose bengal scintigraphy in the evaluation of the patient with jaundice. *Surg. Gynec. Obstet.* **147**:321, 1978.

5. Gallstones

Gallstones are by far the commonest disorder of the biliary system, and a paraphrase of the old dictum would be close to the truth—'Know gallstones, and all else will come to you in biliary surgery'.

The last decade has seen rapid advances in our understanding of the changes in bile composition which lead to the formation of cholesterol gallstones. Dissolution of gallbladder stones has now become possible. Various non-surgical techniques are now available for the treatment of bile duct stones. Exciting advances in diagnostic techniques have also been made with the introduction of grey scale ultrasonography, endoscopic retrograde cholangiopancreatography (ERCP), percutaneous transhepatic cholangiography (PTC), using the Chiba needle, and computed tomography (CT).

GALLBLADDER STONES

FORMATION

Gallstone disease occurs in epidemic proportions and there is conflicting evidence whether it is or is not becoming more frequent [21, 164]. Approximately 16 000 000 Americans have gallstones and 800 000 new cases develop each year. A recent study in Wales has shown that 10 per cent of the population over 40 years of age have gallstones [14]. An autopsy study in Prague and Malmo has shown gallstones to be present in 33 per cent of males and 50 per cent of females [380].

Gallstones are classified as pure cholesterol, mixed cholesterol, and pigment stones. However, chemical analysis shows that there is no sharp division, but rather a continuous spectrum of stone formation. Pure cholesterol stones and pigment stones each make up to 10 per cent of gallstones. Mixed cholesterol stones contain at least 70 per cent cholesterol by weight, and it is estimated that they account for 80 per cent of gallstones in Westernised countries [344]. Cholesterol stones are light brown, smooth or faceted, and on cross-section show a laminated and/or crystalline appearance.

For many years obstruction and bile stasis have been cited as important mechanisms of gallstone formation. This may certainly be a factor in 'primary' bile duct stones (see Choledocholithiasis in this chapter). However, stasis and obstruction are not seen in the normal gallbladder and these factors cannot explain gallstone formation in that organ. The only type of gallbladder stone in which stasis may play a part is that which follows gastric surgery, especially vagotomy, but also gastrectomy, because in these cases gallbladder emptying becomes sluggish (see Gallbladder Function in Chapter 2). If this is true, we may expect a crop of gallstones in the future as a result of the large number of vagotomies performed for peptic ulceration.

Enormous progress has been made in the elucidation of the mechanisms responsible for the formation of cholesterol gallstones. Bile contains three major components. Bile acids conjugated to either glycine or taurine, phospholipids (principally lecithin), and cholesterol. Bile acid conjugates are water-soluble detergent-like molecules which in aqueous solution form small aliquots called micelles. Lecithin is insoluble in aqueous systems but can be dissolved by bile acids. Cholesterol is a water-insoluble lipid which is kept in solution by mixed micelles of bile acids and phospholipids in which cholesterol can be solubilised [1, 77]. It is the relative proportions of these three substances in bile which determines whether the cholesterol is maintained in a micellar solution, or whether it is likely to precipitate as microcrystals as shown in Fig. 5.1 [1, 166]. It is believed that these microcrystals can aggregate to form stones [1, 135, 352].

Normally, excess bile acid and phospholipid are present in bile so that all the cholesterol excreted from the liver can be solubilised [1, 163]. Bile is unsaturated for cholesterol most of the time in subjects who do not have gallstones [6, 328, 345, 361]. Studies of the relative composition of bile at the time of cholecystectomy have shown that while many patients with cholesterol gallstones secrete supersaturated hepatic bile, this is not always the case [150, 224, 329]. There are many possible mechanisms involved in the formation of supersaturated bile, e.g. excessive cholesterol secretion due to increased synthesis or mobilisation of

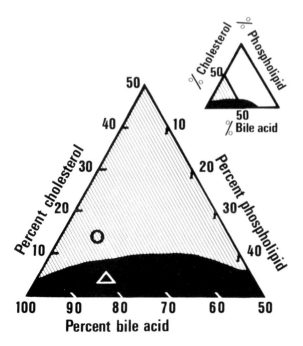

Fig. 5.1. Triangular coordinates illustrating gallbladder bile composition. The larger triangle is an expanded section of the phase diagram. △ represents bile in the micellar zone and ○ represents bile in the supersaturated zone.

cholesterol pools, disturbances in the enterohepatic circulation of bile acids, and increased and uncompensated loss of bile acids [9, 11, 25, 64, 86, 109, 132, 147, 148, 149, 156, 311]. In most patients there is no obvious reason for biochemical abnormalities in bile. Sarles and co-workers in 1970 showed a correlation between gallstones, biliary cholesterol content, and the total amount of calories ingested [312]. This finding has been supported by Murray and others [267]. An Australian survey did not show any difference in calorie intake between gallstone patients and a control group, although the patients with stones ate less fat [372]. Obesity is associated with an excessive secretion of cholesterol in bile [9, 25, 109, 311]. It is thought that highly refined diets as consumed in developed countries could increase the frequency of gallstones by increasing biliary cholesterol [78, 146]. Oral contraceptive drugs and clofibrate increase the risk of gallstone development [25, 38, 39, 71, 74, 96, 135]. Clofibrate may induce gallstones by increasing cholesterol in bile. Truncal vagotomy is alleged to predispose to subsequent gallstone formation [63, 353]. However, it has been shown that vagotomy does not alter bile composition from the normal micellar zone to the abnormal lithogenic zone [304, 331, 339]. If gallstones do form after vagotomy they apparently do so by mechanisms not presently understood.

Pigment stones are rare, but have been described frequently in the Orient. They account for 60 per cent of radio-opaque stones. It is thought that haemolysis is mainly responsible for the formation of these stones. Stagnation, infection of bile, and dietary deficiencies have also been implicated [242, 244, 333, 356, 369].

SYMPTOMLESS GALLSTONES

A considerable body of information has become available regarding the natural history of symptomless gallstones. Thus, in a large series, approximately half of all subjects with symptomless gallstones eventually develop symptoms and approximately a quarter develop serious complications, such as acute cholecystitis and choledocholithiasis [72, 93, 222, 288, 370].

The risk of carcinoma of the gallbladder developing in a patient who has gallstones is difficult to estimate, but is probably 1–2 per cent [222, 290, 370].

The risk of mortality in patients with unoperated gallstones is also difficult to compute, but at least in one large series mortality was about 3 per cent, although even in this series a possible fatal course was prevented by surgery in a number of cases [222]. Cooke, Jones, and Keech in 1953 found, in a necropsy series of 231 patients in whom gallstones were present, that 12 per cent had died of complications arising from the gallstones [73]. It will be seen in the latter part of this chapter that the risk of operative mortality, when cholecystectomy is performed for uncomplicated gallstones, is less than 1 per cent and probably approaches 0.5 per cent.

The preceding data have been presented in order to give a perspective regarding the advisability of prophylactic cholecystectomy or medical dissolution for symptomless gallstones. The figures indicate that the risk associated with untreated gallstones in the fit patient, even if symptomless, are greater than the risk of prophylactic cholecystectomy or medical dissolution.

The authors recommend prophylactic cholecystectomy or medical dissolution to patients with symptomless gallstones, but allow the patients to make the final decision after they are made aware of the risks of cholecystectomy, the efficacy of medical dissolution, and of no treatment. It is this group of patients that are generally most suitable for medical dissolution.

SYMPTOMATIC GALLSTONES

Patients with symptomatic gallstones suffer from recurrent attacks of 'biliary colic'. Cholecystectomy and medical dissolution are the two types of treatment available. Medical dissolution can be considered if the patient's general condition is not satisfactory, if he fears operation and the pain is not severe or occurring frequently. The results of cholecystectomy in this group are likely to be uniformly good. At operation, the entire biliary tract is carefully examined to be sure that additional disease, such as gallstones in the common bile duct, is not overlooked. The rest of the abdominal viscera, especially the liver, pancreas, oesophageal hiatus, stomach, and duodenum, are also examined in order not to miss coincidental conditions, such as hiatus hernia or peptic ulcer.

Flatulence and dyspepsia for fatty and fried foods have always been regarded as the minor symptoms of gallbladder stones. These symptoms are more common in those with a normal cholecystogram and cholecystectomy may not relieve the symptoms [152, 298, 330].

DISSOLUTION OF GALLBLADDER STONES

Cholesterol comprises more than 70 per cent of the total crystalline material in most of the gallstones found in patients in the Western world [344]. The possible mechanisms of the development of cholesterol gallstones have already been discussed. Many patients with cholesterol gallstones have a reduced bile acid pool which is associated with a relative increase in biliary cholesterol [80, 360]. To increase the bile acid pool, Thistle and Schoenfield in 1971 gave the bile acid chenodeoxycholic acid, orally, to women with gallstones and in addition to restoring the bile acid pool there was a significant decrease in the relative proportion of cholesterol in bile [349]. Later, this group went on to show that with this medication it was possible to dissolve gallstones [79]. Since then several groups throughout the world have confirmed and extended these original findings [113, 179, 341]. The non-operative management of gallstones has recently been reviewed by Sali and Iser in 1978, who believe that the following criteria must be satisfied before patients are accepted for treatment [307]:
1. The patient must have a functioning gallbladder.
2. The stones must be radiolucent, that is, they should consist mainly of cholesterol. Calcified stones or stones with a calcium shell do not respond, presumably

because calcium prevents bile from gaining access to the cholesterol. Citrate, which is a strong calcium-binding agent, has recently been shown to be present in bile after ingestion [306]. It is possible that the combination of oral citrate and bile acid therapy may make it possible to dissolve calcium-containing stones.

3. Stones should be small. It has been shown that only patients with small stones which are less than 22 mm in diameter respond well to treatment.

4. Women capable of bearing children and not using adequate contraception should not be included.

5. Patients with liver disease are not suitable.

6. Patients must not have severe or frequent episodes of pain.

METHOD OF TREATMENT

Dosage. Iser and others have shown that 13–15 mg per kg of chenodeoxycholic acid per day produces unsaturated bile [179]. More recently this group have suggested that obese patients require larger than normal doses (18–20 mg per kg per day) [180]. The duration of chenodeoxycholic acid therapy varies, depending on stone size. Small stones of less than 10 mm in diameter dissolve in 6 months in 70–80 per cent of patients, but larger stones of up to 22 mm in diameter may require up to 2 years' treatment.

Assessment. To ensure that bile has become unsaturated in cholesterol suitable patients have duodenal bile collected and analysed before and during treatment. Oral cholecystogram is performed at 3–6-monthly intervals depending on stone size. Success of treatment is demonstrated in the cholecystograms shown in Fig. 5.2.

Side effects. Chenodeoxycholic acid may cause dose-related diarrhoea but this usually remits spontaneously. However, it may be necessary to decrease the dose transiently or add simple antidiarrhoeal agents. Hypertransaminaseaemia has been reported but based on hundreds of liver biopsies throughout the world there has been no evidence of structural liver damage [23, 76, 179, 182, 348].

The possibility of an underlying carcinoma of the gallbladder in association with gallstones exists but gallbladder cancer is a rare condition and until now there has been no report of this condition being present in patients receiving chenodeoxycholic acid therapy.

Ursodeoxycholic acid. Attempts have been made to utilise other agents for gallstone dissolution. Phenobarbitone which is a microsomal enzyme inducer can affect bile acid synthesis but its long-term treatment in epileptics has failed to protect them from gallstone formation [41, 46, 193, 320, 371].

The most promising of the alternative gallstone-dissolving agents is ursodesoxycholic acid, which is structurally related to chenodeoxycholic acid [309]. Recent studies suggest that ursodesoxycholic acid produces unsaturated bile in smaller doses than chenodeoxycholic acid, without producing the diarrhoea or hypertransaminaseaemia [92, 243, 309, 340].

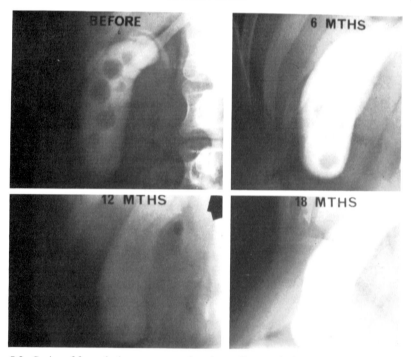

Fig. 5.2. Series of four cholecystograms showing gallstones before treatment with cheno-deoxycholic acid, and then at 6-monthly intervals until 18 months when gallstones completely dissolved.

FAILURE OF TREATMENT AND RECURRENCE

Surgery is indicated if patients develop severe symptoms while on chenodeoxy-cholic acid therapy. Results show, however, that the need for surgical interven-tion is low at about 8 per cent [179]. Patients with radiolucent stones may have pigment stones which would prove resistant to treatment. Iser and co-workers in 1978 found that six of 120 patients with radiolucent stones and functioning gallbladders were ultimately found at operation to have typical pigment stones or debris [180]. A summary of the overall results in this series is presented in Fig. 5.3. It may be possible to prevent stone recurrence with either low dose chenodeoxy-cholic acid, weight control, or dietary manipulation, especially by increasing the dietary fibre content of the patient, as has been originally proposed by Sali in 1977 [305]. Medical treatment of gallstones can now offer an alternative to surgery for suitable patients.

ACUTE CHOLECYSTITIS

AETIOLOGY

The commonest precipitating cause of acute cholecystitis is occlusion of the cystic duct or of Hartmann's pouch by one or more gallstones [171, 202, 330].

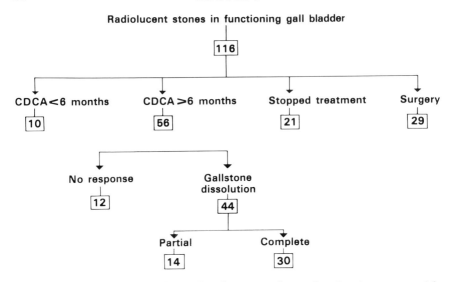

Fig. 5.3. Flow chart showing the results of treatment in a series of patients accepted for medical dissolution of gallstones. Courtesy of Dr. John H. Iser, Melbourne.

Acute acalculous cholecystitis has been described following trauma and burns [3, 195, 330, 323]. Acalculous cholecystitis has also been reported in Nigerians without any obvious cause implicated [277]. The subject of acute acalculous cholecystitis is covered in more detail in Chapter 12. Very occasionally, a carcinoma of the bile duct or the gallbladder occludes the cystic duct and presents with acute cholecystitis [255, 287, 350].

Bacterial contamination and infection are probably secondary in most cases. Bacteriological studies in most series have shown that infection is uncommon in patients whose symptoms are of less than 48 hours' duration, but after that time the incidence of infection in the gallbladder bile rises sharply [130, 131, 194, 202, 204, 273]. In one series, however, the incidence of infection was about 50 per cent and this was true, irrespective of the duration of symptoms [98].

PATHOLOGY

The gallbladder becomes tense, swollen, oedematous, and vascular. As the condition progresses this inflammatory process spreads to the gastrohepatic omentum, involving the area of the common bile duct and porta hepatis.

A fleeting jaundice is not uncommonly seen with an attack of acute cholecystitis, but the pathologic basis of this is uncertain, because bile duct stones are not found subsequently in the majority of these cases [60, 188]. The various hypotheses to explain this jaundice include pressure of the oedematous gallbladder on the common bile duct, a functional disturbance of bile transit in the common duct due to the oedema, as described in Chapter 2, and a secondary cholangitis [49, 152]. Ostrow has shown that inflammation of the gallbladder allows the absorption of conjugated bilirubin from gallbladder bile through the normally impermeable epithelium of the gallbladder [282].

Inflammation of the gallbladder may be initiated by the release of lysosomal enzymes from cells, as a result of damage to the gallbladder epithelium by a gallstone, lysolecithin is produced from the lecithin in gallbladder bile. Lysolecithin may act as a mediator of acute cholecystitis by causing additional cell damage [327]. An increase of lysolecithin in gallbladder bile has been shown in patients with acutely inflamed gallbladders [134, 327]. The importance of bacterial contamination and the direct toxic effects of bile salts as aetiological factors is unclear [314].

Spontaneous resolution of the acute inflammatory process takes place in about 85 per cent of cases [75, 152, 159, 251]. In approximately 15 per cent of cases the acute inflammatory process does not settle down, but progresses to the localised complications of empyema formation, or gangrene and perforation with formation of a pericholecystic or subphrenic abscess. A recent study indicates that a high proportion of patients older than 60 years of age require an operation during their initial hospitalisation because of increased mortality with delayed operation [262]. The reported incidence of localised complications varies considerably in different series, depending on a number of factors, such as the actual selection for operation, the proportion being operated on, and the accuracy of recording and defining in medical histories precisely what constitutes such a local complication [43, 75, 89, 159, 202, 252, 291].

Acute free perforation of the gallbladder with general biliary peritonitis is an uncommon sequel of acute cholecystitis, occurring in about 2 per cent of reported cases [52, 159, 202, 219, 262, 263, 291, 292].

CLINICAL FEATURES

The diagnosis of acute cholecystitis is usually made on clinical grounds alone. The illness begins with an attack of 'biliary colic' type of pain, but the pain does not settle down and remains unabated for one or more days. The pain is associated with varying degrees of nausea and vomiting [137].

There is guarding and tenderness localised to the right upper quadrant of the abdomen. As the inflammatory process progresses the patients develop pyrexia and in some the gallbladder becomes palpable and tender. In a series of over 300 cases reported by one of the authors the gallbladder was palpable in 40 per cent and similar figures have been found by others [49, 202]. A fleeting and relatively mild jaundice is not uncommonly seen during an attack of acute cholecystitis. The authors found this in 10 per cent of cases, Burnett and Robinson noted jaundice in 13 per cent, and Braasch, Wheeler, and Colcock in 14 per cent [43, 49, 202].

A polymorphonuclear leucocytosis of over 10 000 per cubic millimetre is present in approximately two-thirds of cases [49].

At present, ultrasonography would appear to be the best screening investigation for the detection of gallstones during the acute episode (Fig. 5.4). However, gallstones may be present in the absence of acute cholecystitis [20, 83, 192, 253,

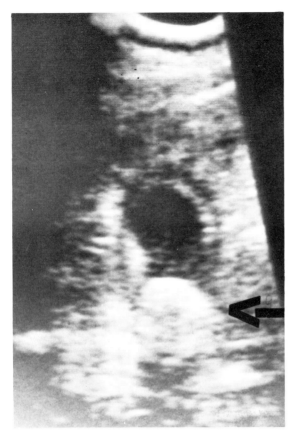

Fig. 5.4. Ultrasound examination of the gallbladder in a case of acute cholecystitis, showing a gallstone blocking the gallbladder outlet (arrow).

294, 347, 359]. Intravenous cholangiography should also be performed if the diagnosis remains uncertain. In acute cholecystitis the cystic duct is obstructed and the gallbladder does not opacify. The cystic duct, however, may be occluded by gallstones in the absence of acute cholecystitis, and this detracts from the diagnostic value of the investigation. In addition, the success of intravenous cholangiography depends on efficient hepatic excretion of the contrast agent. If the gallbladder is opacified acute cholecystitis can be excluded and this may have diagnostic value in some cases.

A clinical diagnosis of acute cholecystitis can be made with reasonable certainty in about 90 per cent of cases [138, 202].

De Dombal's group have shown that diagnostic accuracy is improved by utilizing the computer to assess accurate clinical findings [82, 168, 335, 375]. In some cases acute cholecystitis must be differentiated from a perforated peptic ulcer, acute pancreatitis, acute appendicitis, acute bowel obstruction, and rarely, acute myocardial infarction.

The local complications of empyema formation, gangrene, and pericholecystic abscess can usually be discerned from the clinical course, as both the general condition of the patient and the local abdominal signs persist and progressively deteriorate. Thus, pyrexia and tachycardia persist and the local signs show a progression of abdominal guarding, rigidity, and tenderness. The abdominal mass may increase in size. However, in some elderly patients a local complication, such as a pericholecystic abscess, is unexpectedly found at operation, because it was unsuspected from the clinical course.

A clinical diagnosis of free perforation is only uncommonly made, preoperatively. These patients usually present with the features of general peritonitis and the cause of this peritonitis is discovered only at laparotomy.

TREATMENT

Surgery is the current form of treatment advocated, and medical dissolution is contraindicated in acute cholecystitis.

It is generally conceded that when these patients are first seen, and if the clinical diagnosis is reasonably certain, they require a number of medical measures to bring them into the best possible condition as soon as practicable. Adequate analgesia for pain is given. The fluid and electrolyte balance is restored, if this has been disturbed. Broad-spectrum antibiotics, such as tetracycline, ampicillin, chloramphenicol, or cephazolin are given if the possibility of septicaemia exists, but they will not alter the outcome of the local disease (see Chapter 9). Antibiotics are usually given prior to cholecystectomy to decrease postoperative infection (see Chapter 9). Cardiac and respiratory disease, commonly coexistent with acute cholecystitis in elderly patients, is corrected.

During this period of resuscitation frequent observations are made of both the general condition of the patient and of the local abdominal signs in order to ascertain that a complication such as local perforation has not occurred. Should the patient continue to be treated conservatively for one or another reason these observations are continued during the whole of the patient's stay in hospital.

Most authorities agree that a small group of patients with acute cholecystitis require surgical intervention as soon as practicable after hospital admission. This group includes patients in whom a serious complication, such as pericholecystic abscess or free perforation with general biliary peritonitis, is suspected. Early operation is also necessary when the diagnosis of acute cholecystitis is uncertain and when another acute abdominal condition which requires urgent surgery, such as a perforated peptic ulcer, cannot be excluded with certainty, because of the severity of the abdominal signs.

There is the occasional patient in whom the diagnosis is uncertain, but the clinical findings do not indicate the presence of an acute abdominal condition requiring urgent laparotomy. These patients are treated medically and, subsequently, a cholecystogram with or without ultrasonography is performed in order to confirm the presence of gallbladder disease. Finally, there is a very small proportion of patients in whom surgery is contraindicated because they have serious associated medical conditions, such as decompensated heart failure, respiratory failure, or severe chronic renal failure.

There is almost universal agreement on the principles of management so far suggested for the above groups of patients, but these form only a minority of all cases. One contentious question remains: When should we operate on the usual type of patient with acute cholecystitis, namely, the patient in whom the diagnosis is clear, who is a reasonable risk for operation, and in whom a complication is not suspected? Should the operation be performed during the attack of acute cholecystitis, or should it be done when the acute episode has settled down?

TIMING OF SURGICAL INTERVENTION

We are now discussing the timing of surgery in a patient in whom the diagnosis of uncomplicated acute cholecystitis is reasonably certain, who has been resuscitated, and whose general medical condition is satisfactory. In the past the acute attack was allowed to settle and surgery undertaken at a later time of election, usually 2–3 months after the acute attack. In the past 20 years a large volume of evidence has been collected from all over the world which shows that the surgeon may proceed to operation during the attack of acute cholecystitis and, in practice, this usually means that the operation is carried out within the first few days of hospital admission. Gagic and his colleagues in 1975 reported no particular difficulty in performing the operation between 5 and 7 days after the onset of symptoms [110]. Thus, an emergency operation is not necessary and the procedure can be done as a semi-elective case during that hospital admission.

Mortality and morbidity. The reported mortality rates in large series of cases indicate that early operation has the same mortality as operation performed when the acute attack has resolved [22, 94, 98, 111, 126, 159, 171, 196, 202, 206, 219, 223, 249, 254, 289, 357]. There has been no mortality reported in the early surgery group in three controlled series [206, 249, 357]. In the large series treated by early operation on 441 patients reported by Hinchey, Elias, and Hampson in 1965, there were two deaths, or a mortality rate of 0.5 per cent [159]. In one of the author's own series of 83 consecutive cases of acute cholecystitis 77 were treated by early operation, without a single death [202]. In McKenzie's series of 132 consecutive patients 131 had early operation with two postoperative deaths [254].

Morbidity due to respiratory and wound infections has not increased by early operation in the present author's series, but others have shown an increase [43, 101, 126, 202, 206, 283, 289, 295].

Injury to the bile ducts during early operation for acute cholecystitis is frequently cited as an argument against early surgery, yet it has not been reported in any of the recent series [22, 43, 101, 111, 126, 202, 206, 249, 283, 289, 357].

Ease of operation. Frequently, the operation is no more difficult than it is for elective cholecystectomy. It is a fallacy to believe that cholecystectomy is easier once the attack has settled down. Indeed, patients who have had attacks of acute cholecystitis managed conservatively are a group who provide the greatest operative difficulties when an elective cholecystectomy is undertaken later, because of induration and fibrosis in the porta hepatis [202, 206, 289, 330, 357].

Sometimes the area of the porta hepatis and gastrohepatic omentum is oedematous and vascular. Nevertheless, dissection and identification of the ducts is still usually possible without hazard, although the time taken for this may be longer than in an average case. Very occasionally, the dissection needs to be abandoned in favour of cholecystostomy, particularly if the gallbladder has become gangrenous and there is an extensive pericholecystic abscess. However, experienced surgeons record a very infrequent need for cholecystostomy even under these circumstances [22, 43, 126, 159, 171, 196, 202, 206, 254, 283, 289].

Exploration of the bile ducts. It is sometimes stated that if exploration of the bile duct is necessary in the presence of acute cholecystitis this procedure may be difficult or dangerous, or both. A review of the vast literature now available on large series of cholecystectomies performed during the attack of acute cholecystitis show that, in the majority of cases, bile duct exploration is neither more difficult nor more dangerous than when this is performed for an elective case. Also, there is no evidence from these series that the incidence of overlooked stones is greater than when cholecystectomy is performed after the acute attack has settled down [22, 43, 126, 159, 171, 196, 202, 206, 254, 283, 289].

Hospital stay. The duration of hospitalisation has been decreased by early surgical treatment [111, 206]. One of the authors reviewed 302 patients who had treatment for acute cholecystitis at the Royal Melbourne Hospital and found that the average hospital stay was considerably reduced with early surgical intervention [202].

Thus in the typical patient with acute cholecystitis, who has been adequately resuscitated, and in whom the diagnosis is clear, we recommend cholecystectomy during that hospital admission.

CHOLECYSTECTOMY

Cholecystectomy is by far the commonest biliary tract operation.

INDICATIONS

GALLBLADDER STONES
This indication has been discussed in the sections on Symptomless Gallstones and Symptomatic Gallstones in this chapter.

ACUTE CHOLECYSTITIS
Cholecystectomy for acute cholecystitis has been discussed in the section dealing with treatment of Acute Cholecystitis in this chapter.

'CHRONIC CHOLECYSTITIS' WITHOUT GALLSTONES
Surgeons are cautious in recommending cholecystectomy to patients who do not have radiologically demonstrable gallstones, even in the presence of symptoms

suggestive of gallbladder disease [139, 330, 364]. Similarly, a poorly functioning gallbladder on cholecystectomy should not be taken in itself as evidence of gallbladder disease. The incidence of postcholecystectomy symptoms is high in patients who had their gallbladder removed for 'chronic cholecystitis' in the absence of gallstones [34, 152, 330].

Rarely, chronic cholecystitis is present in typhoid carriers; in these, cholecystectomy will minimise the typhoid carrier state considerably [152].

The readers are referred to Chapter 12 which deals with acalculous benign biliary disease for a planned approach to the difficult management of this group of patients, who have no gallstones.

TUMOURS OF THE GALLBLADDER
The need for cholecystectomy in the presence of benign and malignant gallbladder tumours is described in Chapter 7.

MISCELLANEOUS INDICATIONS
These indications include trauma to the gallbladder, part of another operation, such as pancreaticoduodenectomy or right hemihepactomy, volvulus of the gallbladder, and external or internal biliary fistula involving the gallbladder.

SURGICAL TECHNIQUE

'We should publicise the fact that cholecystectomy is a dangerous operation . . . .' So spoke the late Dr. Frank L. Lahey, and these words are no less true now. There are few operations where so much damage can be done with one cut of the scissors!

The operation is performed under general anaesthesia with endotracheal intubation and a muscle relaxant.

INCISION AND LAPAROTOMY
The choice of incision is usually one of personal preference; a median right, paramedian or a right subcostal incision is equally suitable. If a subcostal incision is used it should be generous, extending to the left of the midline and slightly more transverse than the classic Kocher incision. A paramedian incision should extend from the right of the xiphoid process to just below the umbilicus.

When the abdomen is opened the diagnosis is confirmed and a careful laparotomy is performed in order to examine the whole of the biliary-pancreatic area as well as the other intra-abdominal viscera. It may not be possible to palpate the gallstones, especially if the gallbladder is distended and the stones are small.

EXPOSURE OF THE OPERATIVE FIELD
Exposure of the operative area can now begin. This is meticulously performed, because it is essential to the ease and safety of the operation. A hand is introduced below the right diaphragm and the right lobe of the liver is pushed downward. It

is usually unnecessary to empty the gallbladder, except when it is excessively distended, such as in the presence of acute cholecystitis.

A clamp is now placed on the fundus of the gallbladder. At this stage it may be necessary to pull down the hepatic flexure of the colon, or the duodenum or both, and divide adhesions that have formed between these organs and the undersurface of the gallbladder.

Abdominal packs and retractors are now placed in position (Fig. 5.5). A large abdominal pack is used to pack away the colon. A Deaver-type retractor pulls this down and to the left, so that the upper margin of the duodenum is just exposed. A second pack may have to be placed to displace the stomach to the left. A Deaver retractor may, if necessary, be placed to retract the stomach to the left and slightly upward. A long rectangular type of retractor is placed medial to the gallbladder in relation to the undersurface of the liver, in order to rotate the liver

Fig. 5.5. Position of abdominal packs and retractors during cholecystectomy.

slightly upward and thus obtain a better view of the porta hepatis. Retractors are generally more useful than the assistant using his hand in place of the retractor. This way the retractor can be handed to the nurse if the assistant is required to assist in another way during the operation. For an adequate exposure of this type two assistants are necessary, one of whom may be a nurse.

The adequacy of illumination is checked. Hartmann's pouch is grasped with forceps and pulled slightly outward and upward. Excessive traction on this clamp may lead to damage to the cystic duct or even the bile duct.

DIVISION OF THE VISCERAL PERITONEUM

The peritoneum over the free edge of the gastrohepatic omentum is carefully incised with fine scissors in the area of the cystic duct and porta hepatis, over a distance of about 2–3 cm (Fig. 5.6). The two peritoneal flaps so created are carefully pushed to either side, using small gauze pledgets mounted on long artery forceps. This blunt dissection is continued until the cystic artery, cystic duct, and bile ducts are accurately identified. The Lahey type of fine, right-angled clamps is a most useful instrument for carrying out this dissection, as are small

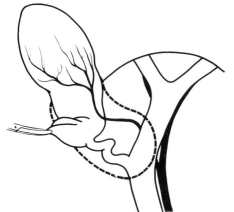

Fig. 5.6. Dotted line indicates incision of the visceral peritoneum, which exposes the cystic artery, cystic duct, and common bile duct.

Lahey swabs, mounted on Moynihan, or other similar forceps. Another useful dictum is that of Professor James Watts of Adelaide, who said that the scissors should never by 'closed' during the dissection and identification of these structures.

DISSECTION OF THE CYSTIC ARTERY

Ligation and division of the cystic artery is best performed before the cystic duct is divided, because this diminishes the risk of subsequent haemorrhage and also because division of the cystic artery helps to 'uncoil' the cystic duct and allow a more precise delineation of it from the bile ducts (Figs. 5.7 & 5.8). The cystic artery is a relatively fine vessel and it is best divided in continuity with an aneurysm needle. Some surgeons prefer to divide this vessel between haemostats, but if this is done, light long haemostats with fine points should be employed. The cystic artery is closely related to the 'cystic' lymph gland, which may serve as an aid in identification (Fig. 1.10). The vessel must be carefully dissected out in order

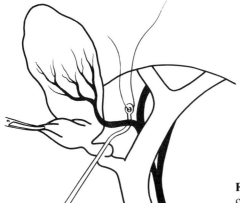

Fig. 5.7. Identification, double ligation in continuity, and division of the cystic artery with the use of an aneurysm needle.

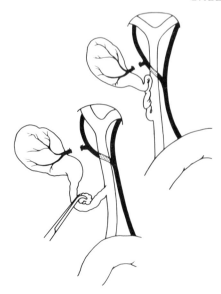

Fig. 5.8. Cystic artery divided. Note how it helps to 'uncoil' the cystic duct. Re-drawn from Warren, McDonald, and Kune [365].

to be sure that it is actually passing to the gallbladder and that it is not the right hepatic artery which occasionally forms a 'loop' in Calot's triangle (Figs. 5.9 & 1.11). In some cases there are two cystic arteries. On occasions the cystic artery has an unusual site of origin, or it may pass in front of the bile duct (Chapter 1).

DISSECTION OF THE CYSTIC DUCT

The junction of the cystic duct with the common hepatic duct is then precisely identified (Fig. 5.10). This is a critical step in the operation because accurate identification will prevent operative injury of the bile ducts. The junction of the ducts must be clearly seen, and the right lateral border of the common hepatic

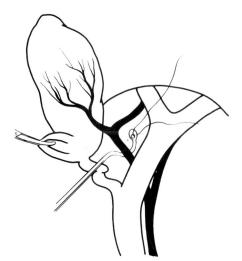

Fig. 5.9. When the right hepatic artery makes a 'loop' close to the gallbladder it may be inadvertently ligated. This mistake is avoided by careful dissection and identification of the vessels.

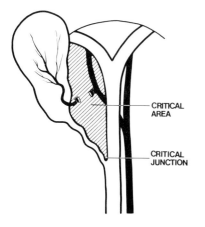

CRITICAL
AREA

CRITICAL
JUNCTION

Fig. 5.10. The critical area must be carefully dissected, and the critical junction
must be precisely identified before the
cystic duct may be divided during cholecystectomy.

duct must be identified. At this stage a dissection is also made of the triangle
bounded by the right border of the common hepatic and the right hepatic ducts,
by the cystic duct, and by the liver, to make sure that there is not another bile duct
in that area, because it might be damaged after division of the cystic duct. As
noted in Chapter 1 the right hepatic duct or the right anterior bile duct may run
close to the cystic duct in this area. If this area is clear the cystic duct is divided
and ligated close to its junction with the common hepatic duct. Sometimes the
cystic duct has a long parallel or spiral course alongside the bile duct, joining the
common duct in its retropancreatic portion. In such cases it is unnecessary to
remove the whole of the cystic duct provided it contains no gallstones, because a
normal cystic duct remnant is not responsible for postoperative symptoms (see
Postcholecystectomy Syndrome in this chapter). Operative cholangiography
through the cystic duct is usually performed before its division (Chapter 3).
Unless the bile ducts are clearly identified in the manner described there is a risk
of injury to the duct system [201]. It is again emphasised that *the usual cause of a
bile duct injury during cholecystectomy is inadequate identification of the ducts with
the common hepatic duct often being mistaken for the cystic duct*, as seen in Fig.
5.11 (Chapter 6).

There are certain anatomical configurations, which can lead to difficulties in
identification, but these are uncommon and in practice most unusual causes of
ductal injury. They are described in Chapter 6 and illustrated in Fig. 6.2.

REMOVAL OF THE GALLBLADDER
The peritoneal reflection on either side of the gallbladder is divided and the
gallbladder is separated from its fossa, usually with finger dissection. The two
peritoneal folds may be sutured together or left open after bleeding sites within
the fossa are controlled.

The operative area is checked for haemostasis. At this stage the abdominal
packs are removed and the common bile duct palpated again, but this will be
described later in this chapter. A drain tube is inserted to the gallbladder fossa in

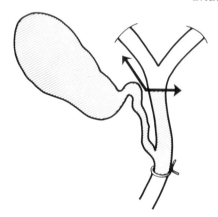

Fig. 5.11. The most common cause of bile duct injury during cholecystectomy. The common hepatic duct is mistaken for the cystic duct because of inadequate operation dissection of the area. From Kune [201].

order to drain an unexpected leakage of bile and thus minimise the dangers of an intraperitoneal bile collection.

Recently, there have been a number of groups advocating no drainage of the gallbladder fossa [55, 129, 189, 238, 374]. It has been shown that drainage may not prevent subhepatic abscesses or collection of blood or bile [374]. It has also been considered that drains can be a source of postoperative fever [268]. There may be a group of cholecystectomy patients in whom drainage is unnecessary. However, present knowledge does not allow us to identify this group accurately and, therefore, the authors continue to advocate routine drainage following cholecystectomy.

MANAGEMENT OF OPERATIVE DIFFICULTIES

Unexpected haemorrhage. Venous haemorrhage is not usually a serious problem; it is generally due to inadvertent division of a cystic vein or one of the veins forming a plexus over the common bile duct. Pressure to the bleeding area will usually control this type of haemorrhage.

Unexpected arterial haemorrhage is usually caused by inadvertent division of the cystic artery; rarely, it is due to an injury of the right hepatic or the common hepatic artery.

Brisk arterial haemorrhage can be most alarming. The inexpert management of such bleeding may be responsible for a bile duct injury, because it is tempting to apply large clamps to the area, blindly and impulsively. The correct management involves reassessment of the adequacy of the exposure and of the illumination. An assistant gently sucks out the blood and the surgeon accurately identifies the bleeding point. If the bleeding is coming from the cystic artery the vessel may be clamped with a fine haemostat or underrun with fine silk on a needle. If the bleeding is due to an injury of the right hepatic or common hepatic artery this should be repaired with fine arterial suture, or, if this is not available, with fine silk on a small needle. Repair of the hepatic artery may prove to be a most difficult and time-consuming procedure.

If the bleeding is so severe that it cannot be sucked away adequately the common hepatic artery should be temporarily occluded by the pressure of the thumb over the index and middle fingers of the left hand of the surgeon, inserted well into the foramen of Winslow (Pringle's method). The blood can then be aspirated and the bleeding point identified by gradually releasing the pressure on the hepatic artery. Compression of the coeliac axis by an assistant has been advocated as an alternative under these circumstances, because this leaves the surgeon free to deal with the bleeding point [365]. If the hepatic artery has to be ligated because of the inability to repair it, it is unlikely that there will be significant consequences, particularly when the patient has not had previous hepatocellular dysfunction [245].

Difficulties in identifying the duct system. This problem arises in patients who have had numerous attacks of acute cholecystitis in the past, and the region of the common bile duct and porta hepatis has become fibrotic and indurated. The problem is also seen in patients who have had a relatively recent episode of acute cholecystitis treated conservatively, the acute inflammatory process has apparently settled down clinically, but the region of the porta hepatis is still oedematous and brawny [330, 364, 365].

Under these circumstances it is usually relatively easy to identify the common bile duct just above the duodenum, because this region is not commonly involved in the inflammatory process. The bile duct should be opened between stay sutures and a small Bakes dilator inserted upward toward the porta hepatis (Fig. 5.12). This will be a considerable help in delineation of the common hepatic and right hepatic ducts and in the subsequent dissection of the cystic artery and cystic duct [364, 365].

If the induration in the porta hepatis is excessive and the ducts cannot be adequately demonstrated even after a prolonged dissection, it is wisest to per-

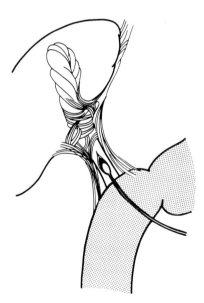

Fig. 5.12. Choledochotomy and insertion of a probe to delineate duct system when excessive fibrosis makes identification of the ducts difficult. Redrawn from Warren, McDonald, and Kune [365].

form a cholecystostomy only and removal of the stones from the gallbladder [231, 364, 365].

'Fundus-down' cholecystectomy. This method of cholecystectomy is sometimes advocated as a means of aiding the identification of the duct system in more difficult cases, such as in the presence of acute cholecystitis.

The authors do not favour this method for a number of reasons. First, the cystic duct and cystic artery will still need to be identified accurately, irrespective of the method of cholecystectomy. Second, initial dissection of the gallbladder from its fossa will inevitably lead to bleeding. This blood collects in the porta hepatis, the very thing one is trying to avoid, because this makes the dissection more difficult. Third, excessive traction, which is facilitated by the already dissected-out gallbladder, may lead to avulsion of the cystic artery or the cystic duct, or both [152]. Fourth, 'fundus-down' cholecystectomy has been shown to be responsible on occasion for operative injuries to the bile ducts, probably because excessive traction on the gallbladder has distorted the anatomy of the duct system [203].

However, once the cystic artery and cystic duct have been identified and divided, it is of no moment whether the gallbladder is removed in the orthograde or the retrograde manner.

Duct injury recognised at operation. This is dealt with in detail in Chapter 6.

RESULTS OF CHOLECYSTECTOMY

MORTALITY

In large series of cases reported in recent years the postoperative mortality of elective cholecystectomy performed for cholelithiasis is about 1 per cent [12, 16, 37, 65, 66, 118, 171, 230, 289, 319, 351, 363]. However, in patients over 60 years of age the mortality is 2–3 per cent [37, 66, 110, 115, 119, 175, 268, 337, 378]. Hollender has recently reviewed the special risks of biliary surgery in the elderly [165]. Coexistent factors, such as cardiac and respiratory disease, particularly in aged people, increase the risk of the operation [85]. The mortality of early cholecystectomy in acute cholecystitis was discussed earlier in this chapter and the evidence indicates that the mortality rate is not influenced by early cholecystectomy.

MORBIDITY

It is difficult to compute the incidence of non-fatal complications from a review of the literature, because of differences in definition and differences in the extent to which these complications are looked for and recorded. However, about 10–25 per cent of patients suffer some type of non-fatal complication following cholecystectomy [37, 65, 66, 85, 123, 133, 171, 289].

Pulmonary complications are the commonest. Wound infection, intra-abdominal infection, deep vein thrombosis, and cardiovascular complications are responsible for most of the others.

The incidence of bile duct injury during cholecystectomy is difficult to estimate (see Operative Injuries of the Bile Ducts—Traumatic Biliary Strictures in Chapter 6). In the hands of an experienced surgeon it may happen only once in a surgical career. Operative injuries are more likely when the operation is performed in a careless, haphazard, or inexperienced fashion. Diarrhoea may be present for a short period after surgery, but it rarely persists [174, 346]. It is thought that this diarrhoea is due to an excess of bile acid entering the colon and cholecystectomy carried out in combination with vagotomy and pyloroplasty increases the incidence of diarrhoea [174, 346].

POSTCHOLECYSTECTOMY SYNDROME

This term has been overglamorised, and is by now so much part of the surgical vocabulary that we have to accept it and discuss the various postcholecystectomy symptoms under this heading. A number of patients complain of persistent abdominal symptoms, or they develop abdominal symptoms following cholecystectomy, and the term postcholecystectomy syndrome has been invented to place all these patients into this one group. It is categorically stated that there is no evidence whatever that this is a solitary condition which can be clinically characterised as a syndrome, nor is there anything specific about the operation of cholecystectomy which should produce such symptoms and such a syndrome [30, 33, 34, 50, 91, 120]. Indeed, the 'postcholecystectomy syndrome' is a surgical myth. Instead, we can discuss the incidence, causes, and management of persistent or recurrent symptoms in patients who have had a cholecystectomy.

DEFINITION

Pain or discomfort in the upper abdomen of the same distribution as biliary colic is the most usual postcholecystectomy symptom. Some clinicians also include under this heading flatulence, dyspepsia of any type, alteration of bowel habit, sweats and shivers suggestive of cholangitis, and a history of jaundice. Jaundice, or cholangitis, at the time of presentation are excluded from this category by us because in these a mechanical bile duct obstruction is clearly present.

INCIDENCE

Of the patients who have had a cholecystectomy about 70 per cent become and remain free of symptoms after operation [5, 33, 34, 36, 50, 211, 301, 315]. The actual percentage of symptomless patients varies from 60 to 86 per cent in different series, but the definition of postoperative distress is very variable.

Approximately 30 per cent of patients have some persistent symptoms or occurrence of new symptoms following cholecystectomy. In the majority of cases these symptoms are mild, cause little disability, and are nothing more than a nuisance to the patient. In only about 2–5 per cent of cases are the symptoms of a severe and disabling nature [5, 33, 34, 36, 50, 301].

CAUSES

Causes may be related to the biliary tract or they may be extrabiliary, having no connection whatever to the previous cholecystectomy. The actual proportion of these causes varies in different reports according to definition and modes of selection of the series [30, 50, 68, 122, 152, 209, 324].

EXTRABILIARY CAUSES

Sometimes symptoms develop or persist following cholecystectomy due to conditions entirely unrelated to the biliary system. The following four conditions are relatively common: *hiatus hernia, chronic peptic ulceration, chronic pancreatitis, chronic hepatitis.*

These four conditions may coexist with cholelithiasis and may cause dyspepsia, flatulence, upper abdominal pain, and upper abdominal discomfort. These symptoms can therefore be easily attributed, in error, to a disorder of the biliary system. There is evidence for an association between cholelithiasis and hiatus hernia [54].

Irritable bowel syndrome. This condition is something of an enigma in itself. A number of patients have episodes of abdominal discomfort, passage of excessive flatus, and alteration of bowel habit attributed to 'the irritable bowel syndrome' [87, 152, 239]. These symptoms are usually present before operation [152].

Neurosis. Some patients with anxiety or depressive states focus a great deal of attention on minimal gastrointestinal symptoms which may be described almost as physiological, such as a feeling of postprandial fullness and flatulence. Many of these patients also have other symptoms of a functional type such as migraine and the irritable bowel syndrome [33, 34, 152]. A number have had other abdominal organs removed in the past, such as the appendix and the uterus, for what seem to be meagre indications. Some have had their gallbladder removed for 'acalculous cholecystitis'.

This is an important and common group of patients in whom the fundamental problem is a neurosis and *not* a disorder of the biliary tract. The attending surgeons frequently miss this diagnosis, and instead blame the symptoms on 'stenosis of the papilla of Vater', 'biliary dyskinesia', 'amputation neuroma', 'cystic duct stump syndrome', 'cholecystectomy for acalculous cholecystitis', or anything else that happens to be medically fashionable at the time.

BILIARY CAUSES

The following conditions may be causes of postcholecystectomy symptoms arising from disorders of the biliary tract:

Choledocholithiasis. Gallstones overlooked in the bile ducts during cholecystectomy will be responsible for postcholecystectomy symptoms. Choledocholithiasis is an important cause of persistent symptoms and it is discussed in detail later in this chapter.

Cystic duct stump. During the past 30 years numerous reports have appeared of patients with postcholecystectomy symptoms associated with incomplete removal of the cystic duct at the original operation [62, 112, 120, 127, 155, 177, 208, 209, 264]. It was believed that the symptoms were caused by inflammation and infection in the stump, as well as by gallstones which have been left there or which have formed there since cholecystectomy. Removal of the cystic duct stump was reported to have relieved the symptoms in most cases.

Most of these reports were not critical evaluations. They were not compared to the state of the cystic stump in asymptomatic cases, nor was the effect of associated disease and treatment, especially associated choledocholithotomy, taken into account in the assessment of the final results. Indeed, critical clinical and post-mortem studies have shown that a cystic duct stump is as common in asymptomatic cases as in patients who have postcholecystectomy symptoms [29, 33, 34, 35, 258].

There is in fact no real evidence to show that the cystic duct stump can in itself be responsible for postcholecystectomy symptoms unless it contains gallstones, or unless there is associated bile duct pathology, which is also dealt with at operation [29, 33, 34, 35, 167, 211, 258].

Amputation neuroma. A number of cases have been described of postcholecystectomy amputation neuroma of the biliary tract causing bile duct obstruction [17, 58, 338]. Most were associated with marked fibrosis and chronic inflammatory changes in the bile ducts. It is thus possible that many of these cases were, in fact, postoperative bile duct strictures with an associated neuroma formation at the site of the bile duct injury. It was suggested that amputation neuromas are responsible for postcholecystectomy pain and discomfort, and that their removal would relieve these symptoms [172, 355, 376]. Subsequent critical evaluations have shown that these neuromas are not the cause of postcholecystectomy symptoms and that their excision is not followed by the relief of these symptoms unless some other cause for the pain, such as choledocholithiasis, is found and corrected [29, 33, 34, 58, 211].

Strictures of the biliary tract. Non-malignant strictures of the bile ducts may be responsible for postcholecystectomy symptoms. Stenosis of the papilla of Vater is usually cited as a relatively common cause [122, 152, 232, 324]. It will be seen in Chapter 6 that this condition is uncommon and has probably been invoked too often as a cause of postcholecystectomy pain.

Postoperative strictures of the bile duct usually present in a dramatic way, such as obstructive jaundice or severe cholangitis or both and, therefore, do not fall into the category of postcholecystectomy symptoms (see earlier section on Definition). On occasion, however, a relatively mild stricture is seen with episodes of pain or discomfort only.

Cholecystectomy for 'acalculous cholecystitis'. A very high proportion of patients who have a cholecystectomy for 'acalculous cholecystitis' have persistent postcholecystectomy symptoms [33, 34, 36, 330]. The diagnosis of acalculous cholecystitis is often suspect. The symptoms probably persist not because a functioning gallbladder has been removed, but because most of these patients remain neurotic.

Investigation begins with a careful clinical history which ascertains the events leading up to cholecystectomy. Frequently, one finds that the symptoms for which the operation was performed were not due to gallstones and clearly they would persist after operation. The presence of other symptoms suggestive of a neurosis is looked for.

The operative findings are important. Were there gallstones in the gallbladder or just 'cholecystitis'? Was the bile duct explored? A stormy postoperative course is suggestive of a traumatic stricture.

The nature of the postcholecystectomy symptoms is also important. Attention is paid to whether these symptoms are persistent ones or whether they differ from the preoperative symptoms.

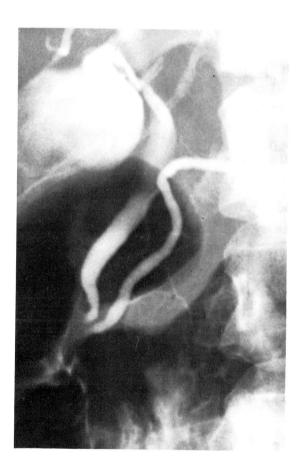

Fig. 5.13. A normal endoscopic retrograde cholangiopancreatogram. Useful to exclude a biliary and a pancreatic cause for postcholecystectomy pain. Courtesy of Dr. Ian Roberts-Thomson, Melbourne.

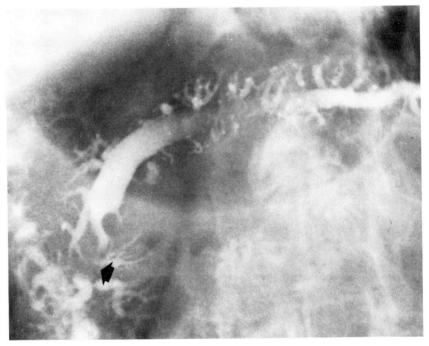

Fig. 5.14. Endoscopic retrograde pancreatogram in a postcholecystectomy patient with attacks of pain. The symptoms were due to chronic relapsing pancreatitis, as seen in this radiograph. Courtesy of Dr. Ian Roberts-Thomson, Melbourne.

A thorough physical examination is performed, although this usually gives little diagnostic return.

The nature of the special investigations depends on the symptoms. An intravenous cholangiogram (see Chapter 3) is almost always necessary. This may show up stones overlooked in the bile duct or in the cystic duct stump. Postoperative strictures are only occasionally shown, because these patients do not usually excrete the dye due to jaundice and poor liver function. A normal intravenous cholangiogram is also important, because it almost always means that the biliary system is *not* responsible for symptoms. If it is not possible to obtain a satisfactory intravenous cholangiogram, ultrasonography, percutaneous transhepatic cholangiography, or endoscopic retrograde cholangiography may be required in order to show gallstones or bile duct strictures as outlined in the chapter dealing with obstructive jaundice (Figs. 5.13 & 5.14).

In the search for extrabiliary causes a barium meal is the most frequently used investigation. It may show a peptic ulcer or oesophageal hiatal hernia. Other investigations which may be helpful include gastrointestinal fibroscopy, barium enema examination, tests of liver and pancreatic function, and liver biopsy. Organ imaging such as ultrasonography, computed tomography, or radio-isotope scanning may be helpful for either diffuse disease of the liver or pancreas or a mass lesion (Fig. 5.15).

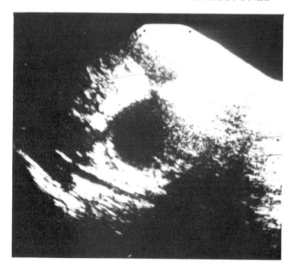

Fig. 5.15. Ultrasonogram in a postcholecystectomy patient, whose pain was caused by this large pancreatic cyst, associated with chronic pancreatitis.

Endoscopic retrograde cholangiopancreatography as been shown to be an important advance in the elucidation of biliary and pancreatic problems in the postcholecystectomy patient [301].

TREATMENT

If the underlying cause of the symptoms is clear treatment is directed to the cause. If the cause is extrabiliary this may mean treatment for hiatal hernia, peptic ulceration, irritable bowel, chronic pancreatitis, or neurosis. If the cause of the symptoms is in the biliary tract re-operation is usually necessary. This may involve removal of overlooked stones in the bile duct or in the cystic duct stump, correction of a traumatic biliary stricture, or augmentation of biliary drainage for stenosis of the papilla of Vater. With the advent of modern investigational techniques laparotomy is very infrequently required.

The authors believe that consultation and management, in conjunction with a gastroenterologic physician and a psychiatrist, is required to deal with a small group of patients with persistent symptoms.

CHOLEDOCHOLITHIASIS

The incidence of concomitant choledocholithiasis in patients who have gallbladder stones has been estimated as between 8 and 16 per cent [10, 18, 33, 66, 116, 170, 171, 188, 226, 227]. The incidence of choledocholithiasis increases with age and reaches a high figure (about 25 per cent) in patients over 60 years [90, 116, 119]. The increased incidence of bile duct stones with age is a reflection of the natural history of gallstone disease, in that gallbladder calculi eventually migrate into the bile duct with the passage of time. It is notable that the overall incidence of choledocholithiasis has been gradually declining during the past 30 years, possibly because more patients with gallbladder stones are being operated on earlier than in previous years.

SURGICAL PATHOLOGY

The majority of bile duct calculi have migrated there from the gallbladder. Common duct calculi are frequently bigger than the lumen of the cystic duct; this implies that the original gallstone has grown since the time of its passage from the gallbladder.

PRIMARY STONES

Clinical and experimental evidence shows that sometimes gallstones are formed primarily in the bile ducts [104, 117, 143, 176, 226, 227, 302, 336]. Primary choledocholithiasis is often associated with bile duct obstruction and biliary stasis. It is seen in association with non-malignant biliary strictures, such as stenosis of the papilla of Vater, postoperative traumatic strictures, the uncommon condition of primary sclerosing cholangitis (all discussed in Chapter 6), and in the condition named recurrent pyogenic cholangitis encountered in the Orient (see Chapter 9).

Rarely, a silk ligature which was used to ligate the cystic duct at a previous cholecystectomy forms the nidus for gallstone formation in the bile duct, presumably after it had sloughed off and ulcerated into the duct [2, 108, 258, 326].

Very occasionally, primary bile duct stones form in the absence of a demonstrable obstructive factor (Fig. 5.26) [226, 227]. Some of these patients have a thickened bile duct, and it is possible that there is a disturbance of bile transit resulting in gallstone formation. The hepatic secretion of lithogenic bile may be an important factor in the development of primary duct stones in some patients [308].

Primary bile duct stones are generally single and usually ovoid, conforming to the shape of the bile duct in which they are formed. They are usually very soft and disintegrate easily at operation [226, 227]. These primary or stasis stones assume special significance in their management, because not only must they be removed but if there is an underlying obstructive cause this must also be corrected to prevent recurrence, as described further in this chapter.

LOCATION OF STONES

Most gallstones are situated in the supraduodenal and retropancreatic portions of the common bile duct. Gallstones in the distal end of the bile duct usually arrest just above the narrow distal segment and only occasionally do they become impacted in the thick narrow segment (Fig. 5.16). Sometimes they are located in shallow pouches situated just proximal to the thickened distal portion of the terminal common bile duct [198, 199]. Outside the Orient the incidence of intrahepatic stones in all cases of cholelithiasis is about 5 per cent [32, 151]. However, the incidence in the patient with choledocholithiasis has been found to be much higher, 24 per cent by Norman in 1951 and 16 per cent by Hess in 1955 [151, 274].

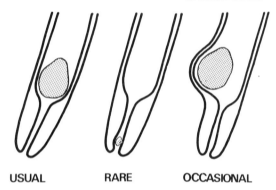

USUAL   **RARE**   **OCCASIONAL**

Fig. 5.16 Location of gall-stones in the lower end of the common bile duct.

PATHOLOGICAL ASPECTS

The pathological changes which are secondarily produced as a result of bile duct stones vary enormously according to the length of time the stone was in the duct, the degree of obstruction it produced, and the extent of biliary tract infection that resulted. A stone not associated with obstruction or infection may have very little effect on the biliary tract or the liver. In the presence of biliary tract obstruction the bile duct proximal to the obstruction is usually dilated, and the bile often contains Gram-negative enteric organisms. Prolonged obstruction and cholangitis will lead to biliary cirrhosis, although this only rarely goes on to extensive liver damage and extensive fibrosis [106, 145, 212]. Very rarely does a bile duct gallstone produce biliary cirrhosis of such severity as to result in significant portal hypertension.

DIAGNOSIS

SYMPTOMS

The classic symptoms of choledocholithiasis are pain of the biliary colic type, associated with obstructive jaundice. Fever with shaking chills suggests cholangitis, and this is the third classic symptom usually quoted. It is clear that there is an enormous variation in the clinical features of patients with bile duct stones and that the classic symptoms are often absent or modified [137].

Pain is of the biliary colic type and, contrary to what was thought in the past, has exactly the same qualities as pain arising in the gallbladder (see Biliary Tract Pain in Chapter 2). In a small proportion of cases pain is entirely absent. In some, abdominal discomfort is the only symptom.

Jaundice is of the obstructive type, not particularly deep, and characteristically fluctuant. In some, jaundice is entirely absent. In others, it is not fluctuant, but static or even progressive. In some, the jaundice is not accompanied by pain. The patient may have noted that the colour of the urine is dark and that the stools are pale.

The symptoms of cholangitis are seen in a small proportion of patients only. Rarely, an episode of pain, jaundice, fever and shaking chills is associated with a rapid deterioration in the general condition of the patient and with hypovolaemic shock. This syndrome has been named acute obstructive cholangitis [84, 125, 158, 281, 297, 303]. The recognition, prompt resuscitation, and surgical decompression of the bile duct is essential in these cases, as delay in treatment is associated with an extremely high mortality.

PHYSICAL EXAMINATION

The physical examination of a patient with choledocholithiasis may be completely negative. An area of tenderness may be present in the right upper quadrant of the abdomen. The patient may be clinically jaundiced and have an elevated temperature.

INVESTIGATIONS

In the jaundiced patient the urine contains bile. Serum bilirubin and serum alkaline phosphatase levels will be elevated, but the serum proteins and serum transaminase levels will usually be normal, unless there has been an associated biliary cirrhosis or liver cell damage due to cholangitis as discussed in Chapter 4. Intravenous cholangiography is usually used in the non-jaundiced patient, if choledocholithiasis is suspected (Fig. 3.5). In the jaundiced patient the recently introduced investigations of ultrasonography, percutaneous transhepatic cholangiography, and endoscopic retrograde cholangiography can now accurately diagnose and locate bile duct gallstones, as outlined in Chapter 3 and 4 (Fig. 3.8).

DIFFERENTIAL DIAGNOSIS

From a clinical viewpoint the differential diagnosis of choledocholithiasis may be entertained under one of three contexts:

Obstructive jaundice. The diagnostic process used and the management undertaken is discussed in detail in Chapter 4.

Postcholecystectomy symptoms. Choledocholithiasis was mentioned earlier in this chapter as the commonest biliary cause of postcholecystectomy symptoms and the reader is referred to that section for a detailed discussion.

Gallbladder stones and choledocholithiasis. In the absence of jaundice, the preoperative diagnosis of bile duct stones in a patient who has gallbladder stones is not of great practical importance, because the bile duct stones will be discovered and dealt with at operation. However, preoperative clues to associated choledocholithiasis are a history of jaundice in the past and a positive intravenous cholangiogram.

EXPLORATION OF THE BILE DUCTS

Exploration of the bile ducts is the second commonest biliary tract procedure, cholecystectomy being the commonest. Exploration of the bile ducts is almost always performed for choledocholithiasis and only this aspect will be discussed.

There are, however, indications other than calculi for choledochotomy. These include bile duct exploration for a hydatid cyst when the cyst ruptures into the bile ducts and produces obstructive jaundice (Chapter 15), bile duct exploration as a preliminary to the operative diagnosis of bile duct tumours (Chapter 7), and choledochotomy to delineate the bile ducts during a difficult cholecystectomy or difficult duodenal operation.

INDICATIONS

The indications for exploration of the bile ducts fall into two main categories:
1. Preoperative indications, when the surgeon operates with the specific plan of exploring the bile ducts, usually based on positive preoperative cholangiography or ultrasonography.
2. Operative indications, when during cholecystectomy for gallstones the operative findings lead the surgeon to believe that there may be stones in the duct.

PREOPERATIVE INDICATIONS
Positive cholangiography. Clearly, positive preoperative intravenous, endoscopic retrograde, or percutaneous transhepatic cholangiograms are definite indications for bile duct exploration.

Jaundice. Jaundice at the time of admission is clearly an indication for exploration of the bile ducts if, indeed, at operation the cause is found to be due to gallstones.

A clear history of jaundice in a patient who is being operated on for gallbladder stones has long been regarded as an indication for exploration. However, if this indication is consistently practised, gallstones will be found in only about half the bile ducts explored [19, 65, 67, 265, 367]. There is now strong evidence that, if at operation gallstones are not palpable in the bile duct and the operative cholangiogram is negative, it is unnecessary to explore the bile ducts, in spite of a clear history of jaundice. However, if operative cholangiography is not available, it is probably best to explore the bile duct in these cases.

Postcholecystectomy symptoms. In the postcholecystectomy patient, either an intravenous cholangiogram or other investigations discussed previously showing a gallstone are an important indication for bile duct exploration. If investigations reveal a normal unobstructed duct the bile duct need not be explored, and the cause of the patient's symptoms should be sought elsewhere.

OPERATIVE INDICATIONS
During operation, direct evidence of bile duct calculi is the most important indication for exploration. This direct evidence consists of palpable calculi, a positive operative cholangiogram, or both. Other indications for exploration consist of indirect evidence of choledocholithiasis; this evidence is less important and certainly much less reliable.

Palpable stones. The presence of a palpable stone along the course of the bile duct is clearly an important indication for exploration. The actual technique of palpation is described later in this chapter. The reliability of recovering what appears to be a palpable stone has been examined by a number of workers; it was uniformly found that false positives were most uncommon [45, 65, 200, 265, 367].

In spite of the most meticulous palpation of the bile ducts some stones will remain unpalpable [19, 145, 199, 200, 265, 367]. Intrahepatic gallstones obviously cannot be palpated. Similarly, soft stones and small stones, particularly when situated in the lower end of the common bile duct, may be overlooked by palpation alone. Associated chronic pancreatitis also increases the difficulty in palpating stones.

Thus, false positives on palpation are most uncommon, but false negatives do occur and, therefore, palpation alone is not completely reliable in all cases.

Positive operative cholangiogram. We pointed out in Chapter 3 that meticulous technique in operative cholangiography results in only a small number of false negatives and false positives. Therefore, a positive operative cholangiogram is a most important indication for exploration of the duct as seen in Fig. 5.17 [152, 170, 188, 200, 212, 265, 318, 367].

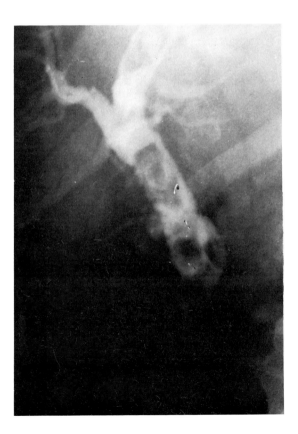

Fig. 5.17. Operative cholangiogram showing multiple stones in both extrahepatic and intrahepatic bile ducts. Clearly an indication for duct exploration.

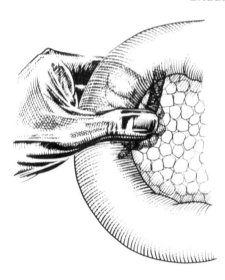

Fig. 5.18. Method of preoperative palpation of the common bile duct groove of the pancreas.

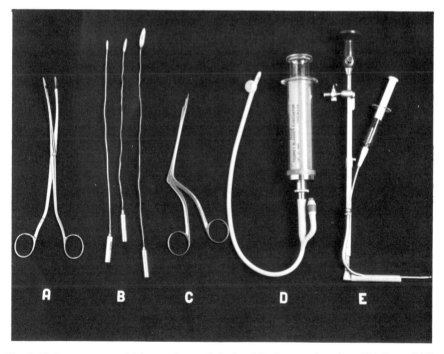

Fig. 5.19. Instruments which may be used during bile duct exploration. (A) Curved bile duct forceps. (B) Graduated dilators of the sphincter of Oddi. (C) Spincterotomy scissors (Rodney Smith type). (D) Toomey syringe and Foley catheter. (E) Choledochoscope and Fogarty biliary catheter.

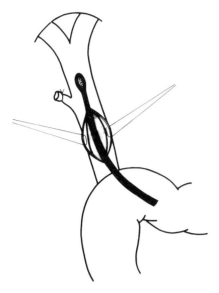

Fig. 5.20. Technique of instrumental exploration of the bile duct.

sufficient evidence for patency, and that the passage of graduated dilators is unnecessary and may even be traumatic. It is important to be sure that the dilator has in fact passed into the duodenum. With experience one can usually feel a 'give' of the instrument as it passes into the duodenum. Probably, the surest method is actually to see the metal tips of the dilator 'shine' through the duodenal wall (Fig. 5.21). On a number of occasions the authors tested this method prior to duodenotomy, and no false positives were encountered.

Following bile duct exploration and demonstration of patency of the sphincter of Oddi, the bile ducts are irrigated in both a proximal and distal

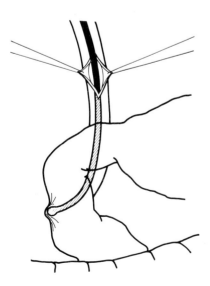

Fig. 5.21. Testing the patency of the sphincter of Oddi. One must see the metal tip of the dilator 'shine' through the duodenum when it is pushed against the anterior duodenal wall (Julian Orm Smith's method).

direction with a Foley catheter inserted into the bile ducts and connected to a Toomey syringe filled with saline. To confirm that gallstones are flushed out, choledochoscopy is repeated.

CHOLEDOCHOSCOPY

The development of the choledochoscope by Wildegans in 1953 provided a new means of visualising the interior of the bile ducts at operation [373]. The instrument resembles the cystoscope in construction, optical design, and use. In recent years both rigid and flexible fibreoptic choledochoscopes have been designed which have marked advantages on the original instruments (Fig. 5.22) [13, 325].

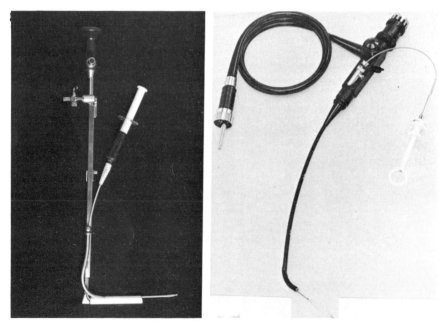

Fig. 5.22. Photographs of choledochoscopes. (*left*) The rigid Storz type. (*right*) Flexible Fujinon type with a Dormia type basket in position.

The instrument is introduced into the bile ducts after a thorough exploration of the ductal system is thought to have cleared the ducts of gallstones. With the use of this technique overlooked gallstones have been discovered in a surprisingly high proportion of cases [26, 27, 105, 191, 214, 215, 216, 221, 316, 325].

Many surgeons have felt in the past that the routine use of both operative cholangiography and choledochoscopy would unduly prolong the operating time in an average uncomplicated case of choledocholithiasis. However, we are now prepared to spend less time on conventional 'blind' exploration before using the choledochoscope to locate remaining stones. With less time for conventional exploration choledochoscopy does not greatly increase the overall operating time. The choledochoscope is a particularly useful instrument in complicated cases in which multiple bile duct calculi are found or intrahepatic gallstones are present. Its use has replaced peroperative postexploration T-type cholangiograms because of difficulties with the interpretation of these cholangiograms caused by air bubbles and sphincter spasm.

MODIFIED FOGARTY CATHETER

The balloon-tipped catheter developed by Fogarty for the removal of arterial emboli has been modified for the extraction of calculi in the bile ducts (Fig. 5.23). The catheter is passed beyond the gallstone, the balloon is blown up, and the

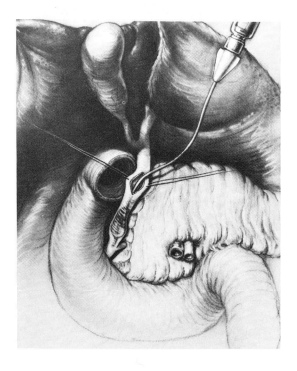

Fig. 5.23. The Fogarty biliary balloon catheter in use. It has a particularly useful function in the retrieval of intrahepatic stones.

catheter and gallstone pulled through. A number of reports have demonstrated the successful use of this technique [7, 31, 107]. The principal value appears to be the extraction of intrahepatic calculi. However, it has also been used for the extraction of calculi from the distal common duct, for the extraction of free-floating common duct stones and debris, and for peroperative cholangiography [7]. The catheter can be more accurately directed in the bile duct through a choledochoscope.

DORMIA BASKET

Dormia and other similar baskets may be directed into the bile duct through the choledochoscope to retrieve bile duct stones (Fig. 5.22). This can be a particularly useful technique in the extraction of intrahepatic stones.

INSERTION OF T TUBE

Most surgeons employ intraductal drainage, usually in the form of a T tube, over which the choledochotomy incision is closed. This acts as a safety valve to prevent extravasation of bile through the choledochotomy incision. Spasm will occur in the postoperative period with the use of morphine-like drugs. This spasm and oedema increases the risk of biliary extravasation and a T tube is an effective safety device. It is valuable for a postoperative T-tube cholangiogram before the tube is removed. The T tube can also be useful later for the management of retained calculi (see Treatment of retained bile duct stones, p. 172).

From time to time surgeons have advocated primary closure of the common bile duct without drainage, reasoning that the T tube may be responsible for stricture formation and also that continuous loss of bile will delay recovery [69, 70, 299, 313]. Perusal of any large series of choledochotomies in which a T tube has been used shows that these two supposed complications are not a problem in actual practice.

TRANSDUODENAL EXPLORATION OF THE BILE DUCTS

In the course of exploration of the bile ducts for calculi it may be necessary to perform a transduodenal sphincterotomy or sphincteroplasty for one of a number of reasons:

1. When a gallstone is known to be present in the lower end of the bile duct, but technical difficulties are encountered in its removal through a choledochotomy incision. This almost always applies to a gallstone impacted in the distal end of the bile duct.

2. When numerous calculi and a large amount of biliary debris are present in the bile ducts, or when soft stones crumble during their removal. In such cases the surgeon wants to be sure that all particles of stone and biliary sediment have been removed and that adequate biliary drainage has been established.

3. During exploration of the bile ducts when a dilator cannot be passed through the sphincter of Oddi after an adequate trial. This can be caused by a number of conditions. It may be due to a calculus, to the uncommon condition of stenosis of the papilla of Vater, or to extramural narrowing of the distal bile duct by chronic pancreatitis in case of pain. Not uncommonly, the sphincteric region cannot be negotiated merely for anatomic reasons, because the lumen of the narrow distal segment of the bile duct has an eccentric position in relation to the wide proximal portion (Fig. 1.23).

These three groups of indications for transduodenal exploration are agreed on by most authorities [200, 212, 364]. In reports of several series of cases the indications for transduodenal sphincterotomy have been made quite liberal, or even routine, or transduodenal exploration is advocated as the sole means of exploration without a preliminary choledochotomy [8, 56, 87, 128, 142, 173, 185, 240, 285, 377]. It is of interest that in one series of 41 consecutive cases the addition of transduodenal exploration did not decrease the incidence of retained stones when compared with 307 cases of conventional supraduodenal exploration, but did increase the mortality and morbidity [322]. An adequate trial comparing routine and selective indications for transduodenal exploration has not so far been made, and it is difficult to evaluate the extra benefit gained from liberalisation of indications for transduodenal exploration and sphincterotomy. On the other hand, it is known that this procedure carries an increased hazard to the patient (see Sphincterotomy and Sphincteroplasty in Chapter 14). For these reasons the authors believe that the indications for transduodenal exploration should remain selective at present.

The techniques of transduodenal sphincterotomy and transduodenal sphincteroplasty are described in Chapter 14, which deals with biliary drainage procedures.

MANAGEMENT OF PROBLEM CASES

Under certain circumstances problems are encountered in the removal or management of bile duct calculi, due to their situation, their number, or associated pathologic changes.

INTRAHEPATIC CALCULI

Aetiology. Most intrahepatic calculi arise in the gallbladder and migrate to the hepatic ducts. However, there is evidence that occasionally intrahepatic stones will migrate back into the extrahepatic bile ducts with the passage of time [358].

However, primary intrahepatic bile duct calculi can form in a way similar to those in the extrahepatic ducts. These calculi may be associated with an underlying obstruction or stasis in the ducts, or due to the production of lithogenic bile by the liver [252, 308]. If the obstruction is in the extrahepatic bile ducts there will almost always be extrahepatic calculi present as well. Very occasionally, the stasis or obstruction is intrahepatic, and then the extrahepatic ducts may be entirely normal. Thus, instances in which a dilated stagnant segment of an intrahepatic bile duct was associated with gallstones have been described; presumably these are congenital in origin [40, 124, 274].

A peculiar form of recurrent pyogenic cholangitis, also called oriental cholangiohepatitis, is found in the Far East, mostly in Chinese people. This condition is characterised by recurrent bouts of cholangitis, multiple bile duct strictures, intrahepatic gallstones, and liver abscesses. It is fully discussed by Ong and Chou in Chapter 9, which deals with biliary infections.

There is a high incidence of intrahepatic gallstones in Japan. The gallstones contain a large quantity of calcium and are almost always found in association with calculi in the common duct [234, 235].

There has been a change in the composition of gallstones in Japan over the last 30 years. Gallstones in the past were mainly calcium bilirubinate and related to a high prevalence of infections of the biliary tract, but gallstones at present appear to be predominantly cholesterol [233, 243, 256, 269, 270]. The cause of this change is unknown, but it is most probably related to dietary changes following World War II [233, 270].

Diagnosis. The clinical features of intrahepatic calculi are similar to those produced by extrahepatic ones, but with multiple intrahepatic calculi the history is frequently long, the incidence of cholangitis is high, and the patient usually has had one or more previous bile duct explorations. It is of interest that cases of obstructive jaundice have been reported that were caused by gallstones obstructing one hepatic duct only [42, 334]. The probable explanation of this is the lack of adequate biliary anastomosis between the two lobes of the liver, coupled with the inability of unobstructed lobe to deal with the bilirubin regurgitated into the bloodstream.

A firm diagnosis of intrahepatic calculi can usually be made by percutaneous transhepatic cholangiography, or endoscopic retrograde cholangiography [187, 369]. The stones may be overlooked at operation as they are not palpable and there may be no abnormalities seen in the extrahepatic bile ducts. During instrumental exploration an intrahepatic stone may be 'felt' at the end of the instrument, but by exploration alone these gallstones may be overlooked [152, 153, 200, 256]. Operative cholangiography is a most valuable method of operative diagnosis [40, 151, 187, 200, 274, 334]. Gallstones may be directly outlined as filling defects (Fig. 5.17), or their presence is deduced indirectly from non-filling of a main hepatic duct (Fig. 5.24). Finally, those who use choledochoscopy regularly have reported that they discovered intrahepatic gallstones that would otherwise have been overlooked [27, 105, 152, 217, 325].

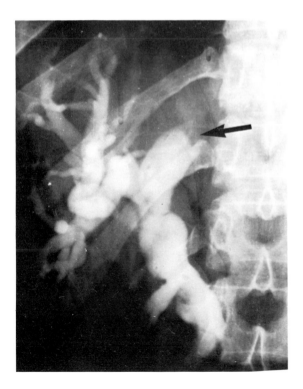

Fig. 5.24. Operative cholangiogram of an intrahepatic gallstone in the left hepatic duct. Diagnosis was made by the crescentic filling defect produced by a gallstone, as there is non-filling of the bile duct beyond and the actual stone is not outlined.

Treatment. Removal of intrahepatic stones has been described previously in this chapter.

If an underlying obstructive process is also present this needs to be corrected; otherwise the stones are likely to recur. Patients with multiple intrahepatic stones frequently have an associated non-malignant stricture of the intrahepatic bile duct, possibly secondary to the prolonged presence of the gallstone and cholangitis. The stricture must be forcibly dilated, the gallstone removed, and the strictured area splinted with an internal splint, such as a transhepatic tube, as described in Chapter 6. In the presence of multiple stones and strictures transhepatic removal of stones and dilatation of strictures have been done [235].

Surgeons with considerable experience with cases of multiple intrahepatic calculi, with or without associated intrahepatic strictures, have found a very high incidence of overlooked gallstones and recurrent stone formation [15, 40, 235, 369]. In the recurrent cases the addition of a choledochojejunostomy has been of great benefit in reducing the incidence of further recurrences and of subsequent reoperations [234]. This was also noted by Ong [1962] in patients with recurrent pyogenic cholangitis [276]. The reason for this is uncertain, because the biliary-intestinal anastomosis is distal to the underlying disease process, but the procedure possibly ameliorates the course of the disease by providing biliary drainage that is even better than normal.

Hepatic lobectomy is reserved for the most severe type of case with multiple gallstones, strictures, abscesses, and destruction of liver parenchyma, but only when the disease is localised to one lobe [15, 154, 169, 234, 235, 276, 342]. When this situation is present in both lobes of the liver the prognosis is extremely poor.

GALLSTONES IN DISTAL END OF THE COMMON BILE DUCT
If gallstones are impacted in the lower end of the common bile duct it is usually not possible to remove them adequately through a cholechotomy incision and, usually, a transduodenal sphincterotomy is necessary for their removal [200, 212, 364]. Only uncommonly can one manipulate such a stone up the bile duct. Not uncommonly, the stone breaks during its removal and a transduodenal exploration may still have to be performed, to be sure of complete removal.

Sometimes gallstones lodge in shallow diverticular of the distal bile duct, just above the thickened narrow terminal segment [199, 200]. These are easily missed at operation, unless an operative cholangiogram and then postexploration choledochoscopy is performed, because the instruments used for bile duct exploration may slip past the stone (Figs. 1.25 & 5.25). Removal of these stones also requires a transduodenal sphincterotomy [199].

MULTIPLE GALLSTONES, PREVIOUS CHOLEDOCHOLITHOTOMIES, PRIMARY CHOLEDOCHOLITHIASIS
The addition of a biliary drainage procedure. Cases in which numerous bile duct stones are found, cases in which one or more previous choledocholithotomies have been performed, and cases in which a 'primary' bile duct stone is present have a particularly high risk of having one or more gallstones overlooked at operation. There is also a high risk of recurrent stone formation, particularly in

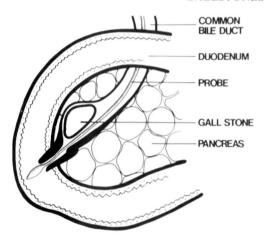

COMMON
BILE DUCT

DUODENUM

PROBE

GALL STONE

PANCREAS

Fig. 5.25. Instrument slipping past a gallstone which is in a diverticulum of the distal common bile duct. Redrawn from Kune [200].

the group with 'primary' choledocholithiasis, because in these cases an underlying obstructive factor, such as stenosis of the papilla of Vater, is usually present and the hepatic bile composition may also be abnormal.

Cases of multiple gallstones, previous choledocholithotomies, and primary choledocholithiasis who have been shown to have an obstructive factor, require removal of the gallstones combined with a biliary drainage procedure. Expert opinion is divided regarding the most suitable drainage procedure, some advocating transduodenal sphincteroplasty, others side-to-side choledochoduodenostomy [53, 87, 95, 100, 162, 183, 184, 185, 186, 190, 227, 236, 240, 284]. The advantages, disadvantages, mortality, morbidity, and functional results following these procedures are fully discussed in Chapter 14. The authors prefer transduodenal sphincteroplasty, particularly in a young patient, because the long-term results are probably somewhat better than with choledochoduodenostomy. However, for elderly poor-risk patients a choledochoduodenostomy is probably the safer operation (see Chapter 14).

Fig. 5.26 shows the cholangiograms of a 67-year-old woman who produced huge recurrent bile duct gallstones 18 months after choledocholithotomy. At her last operation the bile duct was dilated and thickened and contained two large gallstones. An underlying obstruction in the distal duct was not present. Choledocholithotomy and a choledochoduodenostomy relieved her symptoms.

MANAGEMENT OF T TUBE

In the postoperative period the T tube is allowed to drain freely into a drainage bag. A T-tube cholangiogram is performed about 8–10 days postoperatively, and if this is satisfactory the T tube is pulled out. It is unnecessary to clamp the T tube temporarily before its removal if a cholangiogram has been done and shows that the bile ducts are clear.

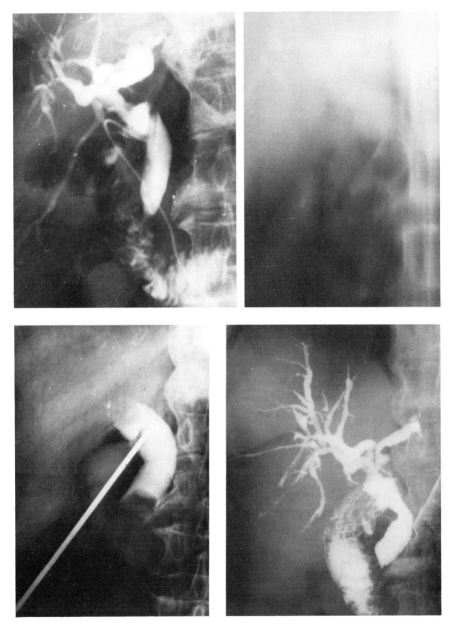

Fig. 5.26. Sequence of cholangiograms demonstrating primary bile duct gallstones and their management. (*top left*) Postoperative T-tube cholangiogram 10 days after choledocholithotomy, showing bile ducts clear of stones. (*top right*) Intravenous cholangiography 15 months later showing two large gallstones. (*bottom left*) Operative cholangiogram at second operation, confirming the two gallstones which were removed and choledochoduodenostomy also performed. (*bottom right*) Barium meal 12 months after second operation showing good function of the choledochoduodenostomy and normal biliary ductal system.

An illustration of the management of a patient with choledocholithiasis is seen in Fig. 5.27. With this type of management the surgeon is absolutely certain that a gallstone has not been overlooked.

RESULTS OF BILE DUCT EXPLORATION

MORTALITY

In recent large series the operative mortality in bile duct exploration has been 2–4 per cent [19, 67, 85, 116, 145, 284, 367]. The majority of deaths occur in jaundiced patients, in those 60 years or older, and in those who have associated pre-existing diseases. Exploration of the common bile duct in itself does not increase the mortality rate significantly in patients undergoing cholecystectomy, as judged from the mortality in those who have a 'negative' exploration [65, 67].

MORBIDITY

If we exclude the problems of the overlooked and the recurrent stone the non-fatal complications following bile duct exploration are similar to, though slightly more common than, those following cholecystectomy [65, 85, 123, 171]. Thus, pulmonary complications are the commonest and wound and abdominal infections, deep vein thrombosis, and cardiovascular complications cause most of the other non-fatal complications.

Retained T tubes are occasionally seen. The incidence of postoperative pancreatitis is higher than after cholecystectomy, particularly if transduodenal sphincterotomy has been performed (see Sphincterotomy and Sphincteroplasty in Chapter 14).

OVERLOOKED AND RECURRENT GALLSTONES

These two conditions are the most important causes of persistent or recurrent symptoms following bile duct exploration.

EXTENT OF THE PROBLEM

A review of the vast literature over the past two decades clearly shows that gallstones are more likely to be overlooked under certain circumstances [28, 51, 114, 140, 145, 171, 200, 266, 279, 332, 367]. Thus, when no indications are present during cholecystectomy for exploration of the ducts, stones are overlooked in only about 1 per cent of cases. A much higher incidence of overlooked stones, about 5 per cent, occurs in those cases in which there was an indication for exploration of the bile ducts. Further analysis of this latter group shows a high incidence of overlooked stones, about 10 per cent, in those in which a stone was actually removed at the first exploration. This rises to 20 per cent in those who have had two previous explorations in which gallstones were removed. Fig. 5.28 is a histogram which summarises the situation of overlooked gallstones. These figures show that current indications for exploration are valid, but our means of being sure that all gallstones have been removed are inadequate.

The precise incidence of overlooked gallstones is in fact difficult to ascertain.

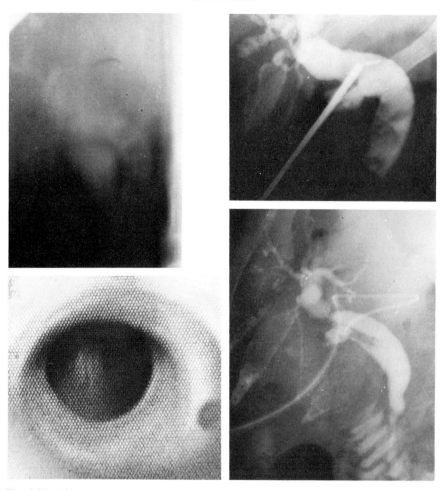

Fig. 5.27. The operative sequence to illustrate modern management of choledocholithiasis in a patient who had gallstones overlooked at a previous cholecystectomy. (*top left*)
Intravenous cholangiogram showing multiple bile duct stones. (*top right*) Operative
cholangiogram confirming gallstones. (*bottom left*) Postexploration check choledochoscopy shows ductal system is clear. (*bottom right*) Postoperative T-tube cholangiogram
confirms ducts are clear of stones.

It was shown earlier that gallstones can form in the bile ducts per primum, so that
there is a group which is really recurrent rather than overlooked. The likelihood
of this being the case increases with the number of previous explorations.
Opposing these cases are an equally uncertain number in which stones were
overlooked, but are never detected, because they cause no further symptoms, or
pass spontaneously.

FACTORS RESPONSIBLE
It is apparent from the data presented earlier that one or more factors may be

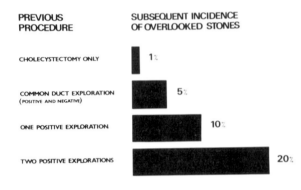

PREVIOUS PROCEDURE

SUBSEQUENT INCIDENCE OF OVERLOOKED STONES

CHOLECYSTECTOMY ONLY — 1%

COMMON DUCT EXPLORATION (POSITIVE AND NEGATIVE) — 5%

ONE POSITIVE EXPLORATION — 10%

TWO POSITIVE EXPLORATIONS — 20%

Fig. 5.28. Incidence of overlooked bile duct gallstones after various previous procedures. Note that in the most recent series the incidence of overlooked stones is significantly lower.

responsible for overlooked and recurrent choledocholithiasis. These factors may be summarised as follows:

Problems of operative diagnosis. The means of operative diagnosis of choledocholithiasis are imperfect. Palpation, operative cholangiography, and choledochoscopy all have their shortcomings.

Problems of removal of gallstones. A wide variety of probes, sounds, catheters, dilators, and forceps are available for the instrumental exploration of the bile ducts. Even if full advantage is taken of these one cannot be absolutely certain that all gallstones have been removed. Also, a fragment is left behind sometimes and this may be the nidus for further stone formation.

Situation and number of gallstones. The intrahepatic bile ducts and, to a lesser degree, the distal common bile duct are relatively inaccessible for accurate exploration. Thus, gallstones in these locations are more likely to be overlooked. Gallstones lodged in diverticular of the distal common duct are particularly prone to be missed, because the instruments used for exploration may slip past the diverticulum. Finally, in the presence of a large number of stones, such as a hundred stones or more, one or two can be easily overlooked.

Underlying obstruction or stasis. If an underlying obstructive factor, such as stenosis of the papilla of Vater is missed, or there is abnormal hepatic bile composition, it is very likely that further 'primary' gallstones will form in the bile ducts if gallstones are removed without treatment of the cause.

SOLUTION OF THE PROBLEM

How can the problem of overlooked and recurrent gallstones be solved or minimised? It is clear that this type of surgery should be undertaken by experienced surgeons only. Careful palpation of the bile ducts and operative cholangiography of a good standard are most important. A thorough exploration of the ducts in the conventional way is essential. Choledochoscopy enables a more thorough exploration of the bile ducts to be carried out and it can also be used to direct the modified Fogarty catheter or Dormia basket. For example, Leslie in 1979 found that in 124 explorations using the choledochoscope no bile duct stones were overlooked [217]. The indications for transduodenal exploration should be clearly understood. In some patients with recurrent gallstone formation the surgeon should realise the need for a biliary drainage procedure in addition to the removal of gallstones. With an increasing understanding of the factors regulating hepatic bile composition it may be possible to prevent stone recurrence in some patients.

Reports from centres where these principles of operative management are consistently followed show that the incidence of overlooked and recurrent gallstone formation, after a previous choledocholithotomy, has been reduced from 10 per cent to about 2 per cent [152, 153, 185, 197, 200, 217, 318, 366].

MANAGEMENT OF THE POSTCHOLEDOCHOTOMY RETAINED STONE

Should one or several stones be shown to be retained in the postoperative T-tube cholangiogram there are now several alternative non-operative modes of treatment available to clear the bile duct. Thus, retained stones may be flushed through the bile duct into the duodenum or they may be dissolved by T-tube infusion. Also, it is now possible to remove these stones with mechanical instruments introduced through the track of the T tube under x-ray control and, finally, endoscopic papillotomy is now also available to enlarge the papillary orifice and allow the passage or removal of retained bile duct gallstones. Sali and Iser in 1978, as well as others, have recently reviewed progress in this important area [278, 307]. Fig. 5.29 is a flow chart which indicates a general guide to the management and the indications, advantages, and problems associated with each of these non-operative techniques. We are most grateful to Professor H. Joachim

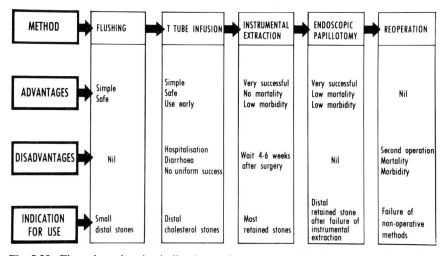

Fig. 5.29. Flow-chart showing indications, advantages, and disadvantages of the various methods available for treating postcholedochotomy retained gallstones.

Burhenne, Professor of Diagnostic Radiology at the University of British Columbia, for providing us with his current results of the non-operative instrumental extraction of retained bile duct stones, and we are reproducing his technique as well as his latest results.

FLUSHING THROUGH T TUBE

It is possible to flush stones through the bile duct after relaxation of the sphincter of Oddi by local anaesthetic and glucagon. Success is likely with this method only if the stones are less than 10 mm in diameter, and probably also the method is likely to be more successful if the stones are distal to the T tube [57, 343]. This technique should be tried before T-tube cholate or other forms of T-tube infusion are performed. Adequate antibiotic cover is essential.

DISSOLUTION BY T-TUBE INFUSION

Organic solvents have been used as early as the last century in attempts to dissolve bile duct gallstones, using ether and chloroform [272, 362]. The potential risks of these two substances, however, prevented their widespread subsequent use. Although in 1937 Rewbridge successfully dissolved bile duct stones by long-term treatment with oral bile acids the importance of cholesterol saturation and its relationship to bile acids was not understood [296]. However, Way and co-workers in 1972 utilised this latter principle when they treated retained bile duct stones with T-tube sodium cholate infusion and this treatment was successful in 12 out of 22 patients [367]. Others have reported similar successes with sodium cholate and also with the use of heparin [4, 61, 181, 207, 354, 371]. While results from *in vitro* experiments are conflicting it seems clear that a significant proportion of stones can be dissolved chemically by infusion through a T tube [59, 102, 141, 205].

Treatment takes from 1 to 2 weeks, during which time the complications of diarrhoea, impaction of the stone in the region of the papilla of Vater, pancreatitis, and cholangitis have been reported [44, 181, 259, 354, 367]. At times, pain during infusion can also be a problem. Diarrhoea, which occurs because of the action of bile salts on the large bowel, can usually be controlled with simultaneous oral cholestyramine or, as recently described by Sali, with the use of aluminium hydroxide which is free of the problems usually associated with cholestyramine treatment [61, 181, 310, 354, 367].

It is not possible to dissolve intrahepatic stones nor those lying in the hepatic bile ducts above the limb of the T tube, unless a catheter is inserted through the lumen of the T tube and the bile acid infusion is directed towards the calculous. The useful aspect of this treatment is that one may be able to dissolve these stones early after surgery, as with mechanical extraction one needs to wait for 4–6 weeks after surgery so that a satisfactory track is established for safe instrumental manipulation. Prolonged hospitalisation is, however, required and its use is associated with side-effects as described.

MECHANICAL EXTRACTION THROUGH T-TUBE TRACK
DATA FROM H. JOACHIM BURHENNE

Following the first report of successful extraction of retained common duct stones through the sinus track of the T tube by Mondet, other successful methods of stone removal have been described in recent years [47, 48, 103, 144, 161, 210, 228, 229, 246, 247, 248, 260, 293, 350].

Thus, retained common duct stones may be removed by instrumentation under x-ray control, either through the T tube or down the track, after the T tube had been *in situ* for at least 6 weeks. Although the stone may be extracted by a variety of different instruments Dormia-type baskets are the ones most frequently used. Also, a flexible and steerable catheter has been developed by Burhenne in 1973, which can be angulated to 90° to facilitate entry into the bile duct, as shown in Fig. 5.30 [47]. A Dormia or other type of stone removing basket, as shown in Fig. 5.31, is then inserted through this flexible catheter in order to remove the stone or stones.

The success of this technique relies heavily on adequate radiological fluoroscopy, but more importantly on the experience of the operator. The size of the gallstone that can be removed is determined by the diameter of the T-tube tract, and stones which are greater than 10 mm usually require fragmentation before

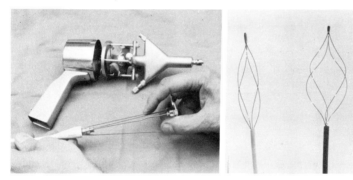

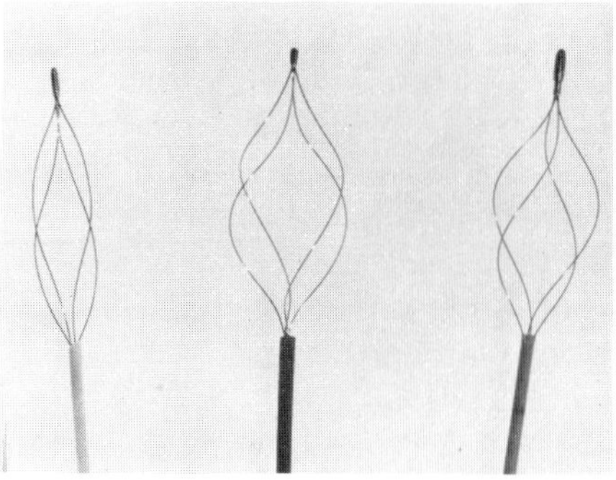

Fig. 5.30. (*left*). Instrument and steerable catheter used by Burhenne and made by Meditech Inc. Mass. USA. By courtesy of Professor H. Joachim Burhenne, Vancouver, Canada.

Fig. 5.31. (*right*). Various types of stone baskets used in the instrumental extraction of retained stones, Dormia, Cook, Meditech from left to right. By courtesy of Professor H. Joachim Burhenne, Vancouver, Canada.

they are removed or flushed through the bile duct into the duodenum. Extraction procedures are more likely to be successful when a large-bore T tube, such as No. 14 to No. 16 F, is employed, and when this has been brought out subcostally to make the shortest possible direct connection from the common bile duct to the skin.

Thus, in an analysis of 661 personal cases of Professor Burhenne, extrahepatic stones were present in 80 per cent, intrahepatic stones in 15 per cent, and at both sites in 5 per cent. Single stones were present in three-quarters of the patients and multiple stones present in one-quarter of the cases. The success rate in this series of 661 patients was 95 per cent, and in only 33 patients was there a failure to remove these retained stones. The commonest reason for failure was an inability to engage the hepatic stones, and less common reasons were inability to catheterise or recatheterise the track and the bile duct. In two cases the stones could not be removed because they were impacted in the lower end of the common bile duct at the level of the papilla of Vater. It is important to note that there was no mortality associated with this large series of cases and the complications associated with it were seen in only 4 per cent of cases. The commonest complication was fever and sepsis, followed by leakage from the sinus track, whereas peritoneal spillage and bile collection as well as pancreatitis were seen in a total of only six of the 661 patients. Multiple sessions of extractions can be performed and the reasons for multiple sessions are to fragment stones for the removal of multiple stones, intrahepatic stones, impacted stones as well as for associated strictures or stones located in the cystic duct stump. Thus the type of retained stone shown in a postoperative T-tube cholangiogram in Fig. 5.32 is an ideal type of case for this form of non-operative stone extraction and a high degree of success can be guaranteed for removal of such stones especially in expert hands.

Recently, a number of interesting modifications of non-operative instrumental extractions have been described, including the use of small-calibre fibroscopes which enable the extraction of bile duct stones under direct vision, as well as a

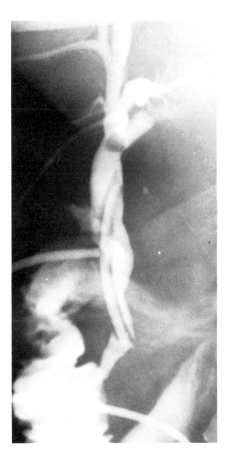

Fig. 5.32. A 12-mm stone retained at the origin of the common hepatic duct, which was later successfully removed through the T-tube track, as described in the text.

preliminary report which has described the fragmentation of a large, hard bile duct stone with an ultrasonic drill inserted through the T-tube track [81, 321, 379]. Also, recently the removal of a distal common bile duct stone through percutaneous transhepatic catheterisation has been described, and this may provide yet another alternative to removal of stones in the common bile duct of patients who no longer have a T tube in place [286].

ENDOSCOPIC PAPILLOTOMY STONE REMOVAL

The development of endoscopic retrograde cannulation of the common bile duct through the papilla of Vater has been the basis of endoscopic papillotomy, a technique which is described in detail by Dr. Claude Liguory in Chapter 13. In certain cases instrumental removal through the T-tube track and endoscopic papillotomy can be complementary in that some of the stones can be removed through the T-tube track, but if there is a stone impacted in the lower end of the common bile duct then this may be removed later by endoscopic papillotomy. A case of this type is shown in Fig. 5.33.

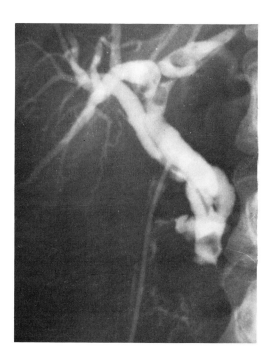

Fig. 5.33. Postoperative T-tube cholangiogram showing multiple retained intrahepatic and extrahepatic stones, including a stone impacted at the level of the sphincter of Oddi. This type of case needs multiple sessions of instrumental removal through the T-tube track and this may need to be complemented by endoscopic papillotomy for the distally impacted stone.

REOPERATION

Reoperation is now only uncommonly required for stones which have been retained in the bile ducts after a recent choledochotomy. The non-operative techniques have, therefore, been a major advance because re-operation carries with it a reasonable mortality, and this has been significantly reduced by the non-operative methods of treatment.

However, reoperation may be necessary if the non-operative methods of treatment have been unsuccessful and significant-sized stones are still known to be present in the biliary ductal system. The type of case that may require reoperation is the patient who has very many retained stones including intrahepatic stones, patients who have stones still impacted in the distal end of the common bile duct, and patients who have residual large stones in the cystic duct stump, as shown in Fig. 5.34.

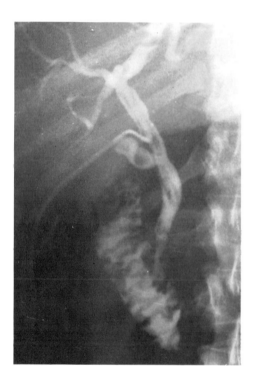

Fig. 5.34. Postoperative T-tube cholangiogram showing multiple retained intrahepatic and extrahepatic stones, including two stones impacted in the distal duct and two stones in the cystic duct stump. In such a case, non-operative methods of removal should be attempted, but reoperation is likely to be required.

REFERENCES

1. ADMIRAND W.H. & SMALL D.M. Physicochemical basis of cholesterol gallstone formation in man. *J. Clin. Invest.* **47**:1043, 1968.
2. AHLBERG A. Silk ligature as a cause of choledocholithiasis after cholecystectomy. *Acta Chir. Scand.* **118**:22, 1959.
3. ALAWNEH I. Acute non calculous cholecystitis in burns. *Br. J. Surg.* **65**:243, 1978.
4. ALLEN B.L., DEVENY C.W. & WAY L.W. Chemical dissolution of bile duct stones. *World J. Surg.* **2**:429, 1978.
5. ANDERSON I., ANDERSON P.T., POULSEN T. & RASMUSSEN T. Surgical treatment of cholelithiasis. II. Late results. *Danish Med. Bull.* **7**:161, 1960.
6. ANDERSON F. & BOUCHIER I.A.D. Phospholipids in human lithogenic gallbladder bile. *Nature* **221**:372, 1969.
7. ANDERSON R.P., LEAND P.L. & ZUIDEMA G.D. Uses of the balloon-tipped catheter in biliary tract surgery. *Am. J. Surg.* **117**:55, 1969.

8. ANDREASSON M. Combined supra and transduodenal choledocholithotomy. *Acta Chir. Scand.* **125:**129, 1963.

9. ANGEL, A. Pathophysiologic changes in obesity. *Canad. Med. Ass. J.* **119:**1401, 1978.

10. APPLEMAN R.M., PRIESTLEY J.T. & GAGE R.P. Cholelithiasis and choledocholithiasis; factors that influence relative incidence. *Mayo Clin. Proc.* **39:**473, 1964.

11. ARNESJÖ B., STÅHL E., SÖRBRIS R. & KOCK N.G. Taurocholate metabolism in patients with small intestinal stagnant loops. *Scan. J. Gastroenterol.* **9:**579, 1974.

12. ARNOLD D.J. 28 621 cholecystectomies in Ohio: Results of a survey in Ohio Hospitals by the Gallbladder Survey Committee, Ohio Chapter American College of Surgeons, *Am. J. Surg.* **119:**714, 1970.

13. ASHBY B.S. Choledochoscopy. *Clin. Gastroenterol.* **7:**685, 1978.

14. BAINTON D., DAVIES G.T., EVANS K.T. & GRAVELLE I.H. Gallbladder Disease Prevalence in a South Wales industrial town. *New Eng. J. Med.* **294:**1147, 1976.

15. BALASEGARAM M. Hepatic calculi. *Ann. Surg.* **175:**149, 1972.

16. BARTAK L. Value of telecholangioscopy in operations on the biliary tract. *Rozhl. Chir.* **52:**538, 1973.

17. BARTLETT M.K. & MCDERMOTT W.V. JR. Amputation neuroma of the bile ducts with obstructive jaundice. *New Eng. J. Med.* **251:**213, 1954.

18. BARTLETT M.K. & QUINBY W.C. Surgery of the biliary tract. *New Eng. J. Med.* **254:**154, 1956.

19. BARTLETT M.K. & WADDELL W.R. Indications for common duct exploration. Evaluation in 1000 cases. *New Eng. J. Med.* **258:**164, 1958.

20. BARTRUM R.J., CROWE H.C. & FOOTE S.R. Ultrasonic and radiographic cholecystography. *New Eng. J. Med.* **296:**538, 1977.

21. BATESON M.C. & BOUCHIER I.A.D. Prevalence of gallstones in Dundee: a necropsy study. *Br. Med. J.* **4:**427, 1975.

22. BECKER W.F., POWELL J.L. & TURNER R.J. Clinical study of 1060 patients with acute cholecystitis. *Surg. Gynec. Obstet.* **104:**491, 1957.

23. BELL G.D., MOK H.Y.I., THWE M., MURPHY G.M., HENRY K. & DOWLING R.H. Liver structure and function in cholelithiasis: effect of chenodeoxycholic acid. *Gut* **15:**165, 1974.

24. BENNION L.J., GINSBERG R.J., GARNICK M.B. & BENNETT P.H. Effects of oral contraceptives on the gallbladder bile of normal women. *New Eng. J. Med.* **294:**189, 1976.

25. BENNION L.J. & GRUNDY S.M. Effects of obesity and caloric intake on biliary lipid metabolism in man. *J. Clin. Invest.* **56:**996, 1975.

26. BERCI G. Choledochoscopy. The exploration of the extrahepatic biliary system under visual control. *Med. J. Aust.* **2:**860, 1961.

27. BERCI G., SHORE J.M., MORGENSTERN L. & HAMLIN J.A. Choledochoscopy and operative fluorocholangiography in the prevention of retained bile duct stones. *World J. Surg.* **2:**411, 1978.

28. BERGDAHL L. & HOLMLUND D.F.W. Retained bile duct stones. *Acta Chir. Scand.* **142:**145, 1976.

29. BERGE T. & HAEGER K. Clinical significance of amputation neuroma and length of cystic duct remnant. *Acta Chir. Scand.* **166:**83, 1967.

30. BERK J.E. Post-cholecystectomy syndrome. *Am. J. Dig. Dis.* **6:**1002, 1961.

31. BERMAN I.R. & PFEFFER R.B. Technic of extraction of hepatic duct calculi with modified Fogarty catheter and report of case. *Am. J. Surg.* **114:**969, 1968.

32. BEST R.R. The incidence of liver stones associated with cholelithiasis and its clinical significance. *Surg. Gynec. Obstet.* **78:**425, 1944.

33. BODVALL B. Late results following cholecystectomy in 1930 cases and special studies on postoperative biliary distress. *Acta Chir. Scand.* (Suppl. 329), 1964.

34. BODVALL B. The post cholecystectomy syndromes. *Clin. Gastroenterology* **2:**103, 1973.

35. Bodvall B. & Overgaard B. Cystic duct remnant after cholecystectomy; incidence studied by cholegraphy in 500 cases, and significance in 103 reoperations. *Ann. Surg.* **163:**382, 1966.

36. Bodvall B. & Overgaard B. Computer analysis of postcholecystectomy biliary tract symptoms. *Surg. Gynec. Obstet.* **124:**723, 1967.

37. Boquist L., Bergdahl L. & Andersson A. Mortality following gallbladder surgery. A study of 3,257 cholecystectomies. *Surgery* **71:**616, 1972.

38. Boston Collaborative Drug Surveillance Programme. Oral contraceptives and venous thrombo-embolic disease, surgically confirmed gallbladder disease, and breast tumours. *Lancet* **1:**1399, 1973.

39. Boston Collaborative Drug Surveillance Programme. Surgically confirmed gallbladder disease, venous thrombo-embolism and breast tumours in relation to post-menopausal estrogen therapy. *New Eng. J. Med.* **290:**15, 1974.

40. Bove P., de Oliveira M.R. & Speranzini M. Intrahepatic lithiasis. *Gastroenterology* **44:**251, 1963.

41. Boyd G.S. & Percy-Robb I.W. Enzymatic regulation of bile acid synthesis. *Am. J. Med.* **51:**580, 1971.

42. Braasch J.W. & Preble H.E. Unilateral hepatic duct obstruction. *Ann. Surg.* **158:**17, 1963.

43. Braasch J.W., Wheeler W.M. & Colcock B.P. Acute cholecystitis. *Surg. Clin. N. Amer.* **44:**707, 1964.

44. Britton D.C., Gill B.F., Taylor R.M.R. & James O. Removal of retained gallstones from the common bile duct: experience with sodium cholate infusion and the Burhenne catheter. *Br. J. Surg.* **62:**520, 1975.

45. Brown R.W. & Osborne D.P. The reliability of palpation for common duct stones. *A.M.A. Arch Surg.* **78:**310, 1959.

46. Bucher N.L.R., Overath P. & Lynen F. β-hydroxy-β methyl glutaryl co-enzyme A reductase, cleavage and condensing enzymes in relation to cholesterol formation in rat liver. *Biochim. Biophys. Acta* **40:**491, 1960.

47. Burhenne H.J. Non-operative retained biliary tract stone extraction: A new roentgenologic technique. *Am. J. Roentgen.* **117:**388, 1973.

48. Burhenne H.J. Non-operative instrument extraction of retained bile duct stones. *World J. Surg.* **2:**439, 1979.

49. Burnett W. & Robinson P. The management of acute cholecystitis. *Med. J. Aust.* **1:**770, 1966.

50. Burnett W. & Shields R. Symptoms after cholecystectomy. *Lancet* **1:**923, 1958.

51. Buxton R.W. & Burk L.B. Jr. Choledochotomy. *Surgery* **23:**760, 1948.

52. Byrne J.J. Acute cholecystitis. *Am. J. Surg.* **97:**156, 1959.

53. Capper W.M. External choledochoduodenostomy. An evaluation of 125 cases. *Br. J. Surg.* **49:**292, 1961.

54. Capron J.P., Payenneville H., Dumont M., Dupas J.L. & Lorriaux A. Evidence for an association between cholelithiasis and hiatus hernia. *Lancet* **2:**329, 1978.

55. Carpenter W.S., Kambouris A.A. & Allaben R.D. Review of 555 cholecystectomies without drainage. *Am. J. Surg.* **44:**200, 1978.

56. Carter A.E. Kocher's perampullary approach for common bile duct calculi. *Br. J. Surg.* **60:**117, 1973.

57. Catt P.B., Hogg D.F., Clunie G.J.A. & Hardie I.R. Retained biliary calculi: removal by a simple non operative technique. *Ann. Surg.* **180:**247, 1974.

58. Cattell R.B. & St. Ville J. Amputation neuromas of the biliary tract. *Arch. Surg. (Chicago)* **83:**242, 1961.

59. Cheung L.Y., Englert E., Moody F.G. & Wales E.E. Dissolution of gallstones with bile salts, lecithin and heparin. *Surgery* **76:**500, 1974.

60. Cheung L.Y. & Maxwell J.G. Jaundice in patients with acute cholecystitis. Its validity as an indication for common bile duct exploration. *Am. J. Surg.* **130:**746, 1975.

61. CHRISTIANSEN L.A., NIELSEN O.V. & EFSEN F. Non-operative treatment of retained bile duct calculi in patients with an indwelling t-tube. *Br. J. Surg.* **65**:581, 1978.
62. CINTI G. & LUCCI G. La sindrome del moncone colecistico. *Arch. Ital. Chir.* **87**:435, 1961.
63. CLAVE R.A. & GASPAR M.R. Incidence of gallbladder disease after vagotomy. *Am. J. Surg.* **118**:169, 1969.
64. COHEN S., KAPLAN M., GOTTLIEB L. & PATTERSON J. Liver disease and gallstones in regional enteritis. *Gastroenterology* **60**:237, 1971.
65. COLCOCK B.P. & MCMANUS J.E. Experiences with 1356 cases of cholecystitis and cholelithiasis. *Surg. Gynec. Obstet.* **101**:161, 1955.
66. COLCOCK B.P. & PEREY B. The treatment of cholelithiasis. *Surg. Gynec. Obstet.* **117**:529, 1963.
67. COLCOCK B.P. & PEREY B. Exploration of the common bile duct. *Surg. Gynec. Obstet.* **118**:20, 1964.
68. COLE W.H. & GROVE W.J. Persistence of symptoms following cholecystectomy with special reference to anomalies of the ampulla of Vater. *Ann. Surg.* **136**:73, 1952.
69. COLLINS P.G. Further experience with common bile duct suture without intraductal drainage following choledochotomy. *Br. J. Surg.* **54**:854, 1967.
70. COLLINS P.G., REDWOOD C.R.M. & WYNNE-JONES G. Common bile duct suture without intraductal drainage following choledochotomy. *Br. J. Surg.* **47**:661, 1960.
71. COOPER J., GEIZEROVA H. & OLIVER M.H. Clofibrate and gallstones. *Lancet* **1**:1083, 1975.
72. COMFORT M.W., GRAY H.K. & WILSON J.M. The silent gallstone: A 10–20 year follow-up study of 112 cases. *Ann. Surg.* **128**:931, 1948.
73. COOKE L., JONES F.A. & KEECH M.K. Carcinoma of the gallbladder. A statistical study. *Lancet* **2**:585, 1953.
74. CORONARY Drug Project Research Group. Gallbladder disease: as a side effect of drugs influencing lipid metabolism. Experience in the coronary drug project research group. *New Eng. J. Med.* **296**:1185, 1977.
75. COX K.R. Cholecystectomy for acute cholecystitis. *Aust. New Zeal. J. Surg.* **28**:128, 1958.
76. COYNE M.J., BONORRIS G.C., CHUNG A., GOLDSTEIN L.I., LAHANA D. & SCHOEN-FIELD L.J. Treatment of gallstones with chenodeoxycholic acid and phenobarbital. *New Eng. J. Med.* **292**:604, 1975.
77. COYNE M.J., MARKS J. & SCHOENFIELD L.J. Mechanism of cholesterol gallstone formation. *Clin. Gastroenterol.* **6**:129, 1977.
78. CUMMINGS J.H. Dietary fibre. *Gut* **14**:69, 1973.
79. DANZINGER R.G., HOFMANN A.F., SCHOENFIELD L.J. & THISTLE J.L. Dissolution of cholesterol gallstones by chenodeoxycholic acid. *New Eng. J. Med.* **286**:1, 1972.
80. DANZINGER R.G., HOFMANN A.F., THISTLE J.L. & SCHOENFIELD L.J. Effects of oral chenodeoxycholic acid on bile acid kinetics and biliary lipid composition in women with cholelithiasis. *J. Clin. Invest.* **52**:2809, 1973.
81. DAVIES H., BEAN W.J. & BARNES F.S. Breaking up residual gallstones with an ultrasonic drill. *Lancet* **2**:278, 1977.
82. DE DOMBAL F.T., LEAPER D.J., HORROCKS J.C., STANILAND, J.R. & MCCANN, A.P. Human and computer aided diagnosis of abdominal pain: Further report with emphasis of performance of clinicians. *Br. Med. J.* **1**:376, 1974.
83. DEMPSEY P.J., PHILIPS J.F., WARREN D.L. & DONOVAN A.J. Cholecystosonography for the diagnosis of cholecystolithiasis. *Ann. Surg.* **187**:465, 1978.
84. DOW R.W. & LINDENAUER S.M. Acute obstructive suppurative cholangitis. *Ann. Surg.* **169**:272, 1969.
85. DOWDY G.S., JR & WALDRON G.W. Importance of coexistent factors in biliary tract surgery. (An analysis of 2,285 operations.) *Arch. Surg. (Chicago)* **88**:314, 1964.
86. DOWLING R.H., BELL G.D. & WHITE J. Lithogenic bile in patients with ileal dysfunction. *Gut* **13**:415, 1972.

87. DROUIN J.P. Cholecystectomy with routine sphincteroplasty. *Canad. J. Surg.* **7**:367, 1964.

88. DUMONT A.E. Significance of hyperbilirubinaemia in acute cholecystitis. *Surg. Gynec. Obstet.* **142**:855, 1976.

89. EDDEY H.H. Acute obstruction cholecystitis. *Roy. Melbourne Hosp. Clin. Rep.* **21**:16, 1950.

90. EDHOLM P. & JONSSON G. Bile duct stones related to age and duct width. *Acta Chir. Scand.* **124**:75, 1962.

91. EDITORIAL. 'Post cholecystectomy syndrome'. *Med. J. Aust.* **2**:955, 1973.

92. EDITORIAL. 'Cheno and Urso': What the goose and the bear have in common. *New Eng. J. Med.* **293**:1255, 1975.

93. EDITORIAL. 'Dangers of silent gallstones' *Br. Med. J.* **1**:415, 1975.

94. EDITORIAL. 'Treatment of acute cholecystitis'. *Lancet* **1**:182, 1976.

95. EDITORIAL. 'Bigger outlet for the bile duct' *Br. Med. J.* **1**:130, 1978.

96. EDITORIAL. 'Clofibrate': A final verdict? *Lancet* **2**:1131, 1978.

97. EDITORIAL. 'Leave no stone unturned'. *Br. Med. J.* **1**:771, 1979.

98. EDLUND Y. & OLSSON O. Acute cholecystitis: Its aetiology and course with special reference to the timing of cholecystectomy. *Acta Chir. Scand.* **120**:479, 1961.

99. ELMSLIE R.G. The Kocher manoeuvre. *Aust. New Zeal. J. Surg.* **42**:345, 1973.

100. ENGIN A., HABERAL M. & SANAC Y. Side to side choledochoduodenostomy in the management of choledocholithiasis. *Br. J. Surg.* **65**:99, 1978.

101. ESSENHIGH D.M. Management of acute cholecystitis. *Brit. J. Surg.* **53**:1032, 1966.

102. FARRELL K.E., SMITH D.C. & MACKAY C. Gallstone dissolution in vitro. *Br. J. Surg.* **60**:900, 1973.

103. FENNESSY J.J. & YOU K.D. A method for the expulsion of stones retained in the common bile duct. *Am. J. Roent. Rad. Ther. Nucl. Med.* **110**:256, 1970.

104. FERRIS D.O., THOMFORD N.R. & CAIN J.C. Recurrent common bile duct stones. *Arch. Surg. (Chicago)*, **88**:486, 1964.

105. FINNIS D. & ROWNTREE T. Choledochoscopy in exploration of the common bile duct. *Br. J. Surg.* **64**:661, 1977.

106. FLINN W.R., OLSEN D.F., OYASU R. & BEAL J.M. Biliary bacteria and hepatic histopathologic changes in gallstone disease. *Ann. Surg.* **185**:593, 1977.

107. FOGARTY T.J., KRIPPAEHNE W.W., DENNIS D.L. & FLETCHER W.S. Evaluation of an improved operative technic in common duct surgery. *Am. J. Surg.* **116**:177, 1968.

108. FOX B.W. Non-absorbable ligature as a cause of obstructive jaundice. *Aust. New Zeal. J. Surg.* **32**:85, 1962.

109. FRIEDMAN G.D., KANNEL W.B. & DAWBER T.R. The epidemiology of gallbladder disease: Observations in the Framingham Study. *J. Chronic Dis.* **19**:273, 1966.

110. GAGIC N., FREY C.F. & GAINES, R. Acute cholecystitis. *Surg. Gynec. Obstet.* **140**:868, 1975.

111. GARDNER B., MASUR R. & FUJIMOTO J. Factors influencing the timing of cholecystectomy in acute cholecystitis. *Am. J. Surg.* **125**:730, 1973.

112. GARLOCK J.H. & HURWITT E.S. The cystic duct syndrome. *Surgery* **29**:833, 1951.

113. GEROLAMI A., SARLES H., BRETTE R., PARAF A., RAUTUREAU J., DEBRAY C., BERMANN C., ETIENNE J.P., CHAPUT J.C. & PETITE J.P. Controlled trial of chenodeoxycholic therapy for radiolucent gallstones. A multi-centre study. *Digestion* **16**:299, 1977.

114. GLENN F. Common duct exploration for stones. *Surg. Gynec. Obstet.* **95**:431, 1952.

115. GLENN A. A 26-year experience in the surgical treatment of 5037 patients with non-malignant biliary tract disease. *Surg. Gynec. Obstet.* **109**:591, 1959.

116. GLENN F. Choledochotomy in nonmalignant disease of the biliary tract. *Surg. Gynec. Obstet.* **124**:974, 1967.

117. GLENN F. Postcholecystectomy choledocholithiasis. *Surg. Gynec. Obstet.* **134**:249, 1972.

118. GLENN F. Trends in surgical treatment of calculous disease of the biliary tract. *Surg. Gynec. Obstet.* **140:**877, 1975.

119. GLENN F. Acute cholecystitis. *Surg. Gynec. Obstet.* **143:**56, 1976.

120. GLENN F. & JOHNSON G. JR. Cystic duct remnant, a sequela of incomplete cholecystectomy. *Surg. Gynec. Obstet.* **101:**331, 1955.

122. GLENN F. & MCSHERRY C.K. Secondary abdominal operations for symptoms following biliary tract surgery. *Surg. Gynec. Obstet.* **121:**979, 1965.

123. GLENN F., MCSHERRY C.K. & DINEEN P. Morbidity of surgical treatment for non-malignant biliary tract disease. *Surg. Gynec. Obstet.* **126:**15, 1968.

124. GLENN F. & MOODY F.G. Intrahepatic calculi. *Ann. Surg.* **153:**711, 1961.

125. GLENN F. & MOODY F.G. Acute obstructive suppurative cholangitis. *Surg. Gynec. Obstet.* **113:**265, 1961.

126. GLENN F. & THORBJARNARSON B. The surgical treatment of acute cholecystitis. *Surg. Gynec. Obstet.* **116:**61, 1963.

127. GLENN F. & WHITSELL J.C. II. The surgical treatment of cystic duct remnants. *Surg. Gynec. Obstet.* **113:**711, 1961.

128. GOINARD P. & PELISSIER G. Total sphincteroplasty without drainage of the common bile duct in the treatment of biliary tract disease. *Surg. Gynec. Obstet.* **111:**339, 1960.

129. GOLDBERG I.M., GOLDBERG J.P., LIECHTY R.D., BUERK C., EISEMAN B. & NORTON L. Cholecystectomy with and without surgical drainage. *Am. J. Surg.* **130:**29, 1975.

130. GOLDMAN L. Discussion of paper: Cholecystostomy in acute cholecystitis, by R.A. Gingrich, W.C. Awe, A.M. Boydon & C.G. Peterson. *Am. J. Surg.* **116:**310, 1968.

131. GOLDMAN L., MORGAN J. & KAY J. Acute cholecystitis. Correlation of bacteriology and mortality. *Gastroenterology* **11:**318, 1948.

132. GORBACH S.L. & TABAQCHALI S. Bacteria, bile and the small bowel. *Gut* **10:**963, 1969.

133. GORDON A.B., BATES, T. & FIDDIAN R.V. A controlled trial of drainage after cholecystectomy. *Br. J. Surg.* **63:**278, 1976.

134. GOTTFRIES A. Studies on acute cholecystitis. *Acta Chir. Scand.* (Suppl. 393), 1968.

135. GRUNDY S.M., AHRENS E.H. JR., SALEN G., SCHREIBMAN P.H. & NESTEL T.J. Mechanism of action of clofibrate on cholesterol metabolism in patients with hyperlipidaemia. *J. Lipid Research* **13:**531, 1972.

136. GRUNDY S.M., METZGER A.L. & ADLER R.D. mechanisms of lithogenic bile formation in American Indian women with cholesterol gallstones. *J. Clin. Invest.* **51:**3026, 1972.

137. GUNN A. & KEDDIE N. Some clinical observations on patients with gallstones. *Lancet* **2:**239, 1972.

138. HALASZ N.A. Counterfeit cholecystitis. A common diagnostic dilemma. *Am. J. Surg.* **130:**189, 1975.

139. HAM J.M., BOLIN T.D., WILTON N., STEVENSON D. & JEFFERIES S. Diagnosis and treatment of functional disorders of the biliary tract. *Aust. New Zeal. J. Surg.* **48:**494, 1978.

140. HAMPSON L.G. & PETRIE E.A. The problem of stones in the common bile duct with particular reference to retained stones. *Canad. J. Surg.* **7:**361, 1964.

141. HARDIE I.R., GREEN M.K., BURNETT W., WALL D.R. & HALL-BROWN A. *In vitro* studies of gallstone dissolution using bile salt solutions and heparinized saline. *Br. J. Surg.* **64:**572, 1977.

142. HARDY E.G. & DAVENPORT T.J. The transduodenal approach to the common bile duct. *Br. J. Surg.* **56:**667, 1969.

143. HARDY J.D. Some lesions of the biliary tract. Idiopathic retroperitoneal fibrosis and other problems. *Am. J. Surg.* **103:**457, 1962.

144. HARE W.S.C. Treatment of retained stones in common bile duct. *Aust. New Zeal. J. Med.* **8:**563, 1978.

145. HAVARD C. Non-malignant bile duct obstruction. *Ann. R. Coll. Surg. Eng.* **26:**88, 1960.

146. HEATON K.W. The aetioloty of human gallstones: The refining of dietary carbo-
hydrate? In: K.W. Heaton (ed.), *Bile Salts in Health and Disease*. Churchill Livingstone, Edinburgh, 1972.

147. HEATON K.W. Disturbances of bile acid metabolism in intestinal disease. *Clin.
Gastroenterol.* **6**:69, 1977.

148. HEATON K.W., AUSTAD W.I., LACK L. & TYOR M.P. Enterohepatic circulation of
C14-labelled bile salts in disorders of the distal small bowel. *Gastroenterology* **55**:5,
1968.

149. HEATON K.W. & READ A.E. Gallstones in patients with disorders of the terminal
ileum and disturbed bile salt metabolism. *Br. Med. J.* **3**:494, 1969.

150. HELLER F. & BOUCHIER I.A.D. Cholesterol and bile salt studies on the bile of patients
with cholesterol gallstones. *Gut* **14**:83, 1973.

151. HESS W. *Operativ Cholangiographie*. Thieme, Stuttgart, 1955.

152. HESS W. *Surgery of the Biliary Passages and the Pancreas*. Van Nostrand, Princeton,
N.J., 1965.

153. HICKEN N.F. & MCALLISTER A.J. Operative cholangiography as an aid in reducing
the incidence of 'overlooked' common bile duct stones. A study of 1293 choledocholithotomies. *Surgery* **55**:753, 1964.

154. HICKEN N.F., MCALLISTER A.J. & NILLSSEN J. Resection of entire left lobe of liver:
Intrahepatic abscesses, stones, and foreign bodies. *Am. J. Surg.* **105**:278, 1963.

155. HICKEN N.F., WHITE L.B. & CORAY Q.B. Incomplete removal of the cystic duct as a
factor in producing postcholecystectomy complications. *Surgery* **21**:309, 1947.

156. HILL G.L., MAIR W.J.S. & GOLIGHER J.C. Gallstones after ileostomy and ileal
resection. *Gut* **16**:932, 1975.

157. HILTON H.D. & GRIFFIN W.T. Common duct exploration in acute cholecystitis:
Review of 100 consecutive cases. *Surgery* **65**:269, 1969.

158. HINCHEY E.J. & COUPER, C.E. Acute obstructive suppurative cholangitis. *Am. J.
Surg.* **117**:62, 1969.

159. HINCHEY E.J., ELIAS G.L. & HAMPSON L.G. Acute cholecystitis. *Surg. Gynec. Obstet.*
120:475, 1965.

160. HINSHAW D.B. & CARTER R. Acute obstructive cholecystitis—pathogenesis and
surgical aspects. *Am. J. Surg.* **104**:216, 1962.

161. HO C.S. Non-operative removal of retained common bile duct stones. *Canad. J.
Surg.* **21**:244, 1978.

162. HOERR S.O. & HERMANN R.E. Side to side choledochoduodenostomy. *Surg. Clin.
North Amer.* **53**:1115, 1973.

163. HOFMANN A.F. & SMALL D.M. Detergent properties of bile salts: correlation with
physiological function. *Annual Rev. Med.* **18**:333, 1967.

164. HOLLAND C. & HEATON K.W. Increasing frequency of gallbladder operations in the
Bristol clinical area. *Br. Med. J.* **3**:672, 1972.

165. HOLLENDER L.F., MEYER CH., JAMART T. & ALEXIOU D. Particularités et risques de
la chirurgie biliaire au-delà de 75 ans. *Bulletin De L'Academie Nationale De Méde-
cine.* **161**:543, 1977.

166. HOLZBACH R.T., MARSH M., OLSZEWSKI M. & HOLAN, K. Cholesterol solubility in
bile. Evidence that supersaturated bile is frequent in healthy man. *J. Clin. Invest.*
52:1467, 1973.

167. HOPKINS S.F., BIVINS B.A. & GRIFFEN W.O. JR. The problem of the cystic duct
remnant. *Surg. Gynec. Obstet.* **148**:531, 1979.

168. HORROCKS J.C. & DE DOMBAL F.T. Clinical presentation of patients with 'dyspepsia'.
Detailed symptomatic study of 360 patients. *Gut* **19**:19, 1978.

169. HUANG CHIH-CH'IANG. Partial resection of the liver in treatment of intrahepatic
stones. *Chin. Med. J.* **79**:40, 1959.

170. HUGH T.B. Suggested new rules for exploration of the common bile duct at cholecystectomy. *Aust. New Zeal. J. Surg.* **45**:380, 1975.

171. HUGHES E.S.R. Surgery for gall-stones. *Med. J. Aust.* **1**:255, 1957.

172. HUME R.H. & BUXTON R.W. Postcholecystectomy amputation neuroma. *Am. Surg.* **20**:198, 1954.

173. HUNTER R.R. Choledochotomy and transduodenal sphincterotomy. *Ann. Roy. Coll. Surg. Eng.* **51**:250, 1972.

174. HUTCHEON D.F., BAYLESS T.M. & GADACZ T.R. Post cholecystectomy diarrhoea. *J.A.M.A.* **241**:823, 1979.

175. IBACH J.R., HUME A.H. & ERB W.H. Cholecystectomy in the aged. *Surg. Gynec. Obstet.* **126**:523, 1968.

176. IMAMOGLU K., PERRY J.F. JR. & WANGENSTEEN O.H. Experimental production of gallstones by incomplete stricture of the terminal common bile duct. *Surgery* **42**:623, 1957.

177. INGRAM D. & KERMODE D.G. Recurrent biliary calculi due to non absorbable cystic duct ligatures. *Aust. New Zeal. J. Surg.* **48**:509, 1978.

178. ISER J.H. Medical treatment of gallstones. *Aust. New Zeal. J. Med.* **8**:562, 1978.

179. ISER J.H., DOWLING R.H., MOK H.Y.I. & BELL G.D. Chenodeoxycholic acid treatment of gallstones. A follow-up report and analysis of factors influencing response to therapy. *New Eng. J. Med.* **293**:378, 1975.

180. ISER J.H., MATON P.N., MURPHY G.M. & DOWLING R.H. Resistance to cheno-deoxycholic acid (CDCA) treatment in obese patients with gallstones. *Br. Med. J.* **1**:1509, 1978.

181 ISER J.H., SAXTON H., WIEGALD J. & DOWLING R.H. Efficacy and complications of T-tube cholate infusion in the treatment of retained common bile duct (CBD) stones. *Gut* **17**:815, 1976.

182. JAMES O.W.F., SCHEUER P.J. & BOUCHIER I.A.D. The effect of chenodeoxycholic acid on liver function and histology in man. *Digestion* **8**:432, 1973.

183. JONES S.A. Sphincteroplasty (not sphincterotomy) in the treatment of biliary tract disease. *Surg. Clin. North Amer.* **53**:1123, 1973.

184. JONES S.A. The prevention and treatment of recurrent bile duct stones by transduo-denal sphincteroplasty. *World J. Surg.* **2**:473, 1978.

185. JONES S.A., SMITH L.L., KELLER T.B. & JOERGENSON E.J. Choledochoduodenostomy to prevent residual stones. *Arch. Surg. (Chicago)* **86**:1014, 1963.

186. JOHNSON A.G. & HARDING-RAINS A.J. Prevention and treatment of recurrent bile duct stones by choledochoduodenostomy. *World J. Surg.* **2**:487, 1978.

187. JOHNSON L.F. & WALTA D.C. Intrahepatic pigment stones. An Asian disease diag-nosed with retrograde cholangiography. *Digestive Diseases* **23**, (Suppl.) 13S 1978.

188. KAKOS G.S., TOMPKINS R.K., TURNIPSEED W. & ZOLLINGER R.M. Operative cholan-giography during routine cholecystectomy: A review of 3012 cases. *Arch. Surg.* **104**:484, 1972.

189. KAMBOURIS A.A., CARPENTER W.S. ALLABEN R.D. Cholecystectomy without drainage. *Surg. Gynec. Obstet.* **137**:613, 1973.

190. KAMINSKI D.L., BARNER H.B., COOD J.E. & WOLFE B.M. Evaluation of the results of external choledochoduodenostomy for retained, recurrent or primary common duct stones. *Am. J. Surg.* **137**:162, 1979.

191. KAPPAS A., ALEXANDER-WILLIAMS J., KEIGHLEY M.R.B. & WATTS G.T. Operative choledoschoscopy. *Br. J. Surg.* **66**:177, 1979.

192. KAPPELMAN N. & SANDERS R.C. Ultrasound in the investigation of gallbladder disease. *J.A.M.A.* **239**:1426, 1978.

193. KATO R., ONODA K. & OMORI Y. Effect of phenobarbital on biosynthesis and elimination of cholesterol in rats. *Jap. J. Pharmacol.* **18**:514, 1968.

194. KEIGHLEY M.R.B. Micro-organisms in the bile. A preventable cause of sepsis after biliary surgery. *Ann. R. Coll. Surg. Eng.* **59**:328, 1977.

195. KITCHEN, P.R.B. Post traumatic cholecystitis without gallstones. *Med. J. Aust.* **2**:595, 1973.

196. KLINGENSMITH W., WATKINS W. & OLES P. Cholecystectomy in acute cholecystitis. *Arch. Surg. (Chicago)* **92**:689, 1966.

197. KOURIAS B. Pre- and post-operative cholangiography. An evaluation of 2000 cho-langiograms. In *Second World Congress of Gastroenterology*, vol 3, p. 626. Karger, Basel, 1962.
198. KUNE G.A. Surgical anatomy of common bile duct. *Arch. Surg. (Chicago)* **89**:995, 1964.
199. KUNE G.A. Gallstones in diverticula of the lower common bile duct. *Gut* **6**:95, 1965.
200. KUNE G.A. The elusive common bile duct stone. *Med. J. Aust.* **1**:254, 1966.
201. KUNE G.A. Bile duct injury during cholecystectomy. Causes, prevention and surgical repair in 1979. *Aust. New Zeal. J. Surg.* **49**:35, 1979.
202. KUNE G.A. & BIRKS D. Acute cholecystitis. An appraisal of current methods of treatment. *Med. J. Aust.* **2**:218, 1970.
203. KUNE G.A., HARDY K.J., BROWN G. & McKENZIE G. Operative injuries of the bile ducts. *Med. J. Aust.* **2**:233, 1962.
204. KUNE G.A. & SCHUTZ E. Bacteria in the biliary tract. A study of their frequency and type. *Med. J. Aust.* **1**:255, 1974.
205. LAHANA D.A., BONORRIS G.G. & SCHOENFIELD L.J. Gallstone dissolution in vitro by bile acids, heparin, and quaternary amines. *Surg. Gynec. Obstet.* **138**:683, 1974.
206. LAHTINEN J., ALHAVA E.M. & AUKEE S. Acute cholecystitis treated by early and delayed surgery. A controlled clinical trial. *Scand. J. Gastroenterol.* **13**:673, 1978.
207. LANSFORD C., MEHTA S. & KERN F. JR. The treatment of retained stones in the common bile duct with sodium cholate infusion. *Gut* **15**:48, 1974.
208. LARMI T.K.I. & FOCK G. Cystic duct remnant: A cause of biliary distress following cholecystectomy. *Acta Chir. Scand.* **114**:361, 1957.
209. LARMI T.K.I., MOKKA R., KEMPPAINEN P. & SEPPÄLÄ A. A critical analysis of the cystic duct remnant. *Surg. Gynec. Obstet.* **141**:48, 1975.
210. LEARY J.B. & PARSHALL W.A. Percutaneous common duct stone extraction. *Radiology* **105**:452, 1972.
211. LEQUESNE L.P. Post-cholecystectomy Symptoms. In R. Smith & S. Sherlock (eds.), *Surgery of the Gallbladder and Bile Ducts*. Butterworth, London, 1964.
212. LEQUESNE L.P. Choledocholithiasis. In R. Smith & S. Sherlock (eds.), *Surgery of the Gallbladder and Bile Ducts*. Butterworth, London, 1964.
213. LEQUESNE, L.P., WHITESIDE C.G. & HAND B.H. The common duct after cholecystectomy. *Br. Med. J.* **1**:329, 1959.
214. LESLIE D.R. The use of the choledochoscope; or leaving no stone unturned. *Med. J. Aust.* **1**:235, 1962.
215. LESLIE D.R. The width of the common bile duct. *Surg. Gynec. Obstet.* **126**:761, 1968.
216. LESLIE D.R. Endoscopy of the bile duct: An evaluation. *Aust. New Zeal. J. Surg.* **44**:340, 1974.
217. LESLIE D.R. *Pers. Commun.* 1979.
218. LESTER R. Why is conjugation necessary for bilirubin excretion in the biliary system? In W. Taylor (ed.), *Symposium of the NATO Advanced Study Institute*. Blackwell, Oxford, 1965.
219. LINDAHL F. & CEDERQVIST C.S. The treatment of acute cholecystitis. *Acta Chir. Scand.* (Suppl. 396) 9, 1969.
220. LONG T.M., HEINBACH D.M. & CARRICO C.J. Acalculous cholecystitis in critically ill patients. *Am. J. Surg.* **136**:31, 1978.
221. LONGLAND C.J. Choledochoscopy in choledocholithiasis. *Br. J. Surg.* **60**:626, 1973.
222. LUND J. Surgical indications in cholelithiasis: Prophylactic cholecystectomy elucidated on the basis of long-term follow-up of 526 non-operated cases. *Ann. Surg.* **151**:153, 1960.
223. MACDONALD J.A. Early cholecystectomy for acute cholecystitis. *Canad. Med. Assoc. J.* **65**:797, 1974.
224. MACKAY C., CROOK J.N., SMITH D.C. & MACALLISTER R.A. The composition of hepatic and gallbladder bile in patients with gallstones. *Gut* **13**:759, 1972.
225. MACLEISH D.G. *Pers. Commun.* 1969.

226. MADDEN J.L. Common duct stones. Their origin and surgical management. *Surg. Clin. North Amer.* **53**:1095, 1973.

227. MADDEN J.L., VANDERHEYDEN L. & KANDALAFT S. The nature and surgical significance of common duct stones. *Surg. Gynec. Obstet.* **126**:3, 1968.

228. MAGAREY C.J. Removal of retained bile duct calculous without operation. *Br. J. Surg.* **56**:312, 1969.

229. MAGAREY C.J. Non-surgical removal of retained biliary calculi. *Lancet* **1**:1044, 1971.

230. MAGEE R.B. & MACDUFFEE R.D. One thousand consecutive cholecystectomies. *Arch. Surg. (Chicago)* **96**:858, 1968.

231. MAINGOT R. Cholecystostomy. In R. Smith & S. Sherlock (eds.), *Surgery of the Gall Bladder and Bile Ducts.* Butterworth, London, 1964.

232. MAINGOT R. Stenosis of the Sphincter of Oddi. In R. Smith & S. Sherlock (eds.), *Surgery of the Gall Bladder and Bile Ducts.* Butterworth, London, 1964.

233. MAKI T. Cholelithiasis in the Japanese. *Arch. Surg.* **82**:599, 1961.

234. MAKI T., SATO T. & MATSUSHIRO T. A re-appraisal of surgical treatment for intraheptic gallstones. *Ann. Surg.* **175**:155, 1972.

235. MAKI T., SATO T., YAMAGUCHI I. & SATO T. Treatment of intrahepatic gallstones. *Arch. Surg. (Chicago)* **88**:260, 1964.

236. MALLET-GUY P. Re-operations for 'missed' or recurrent stones secondary to an initial choledochotomy for lithiasis. *Lyon Chir.* **74**:25, 1978.

237. MALLET-GUY P. & DESCOTES J. Indications et résultats, des opérations de vagotomie dans les syndrome d'hypertonie du sphincter d'Oddi. *Lyon Chir.* **48**:55, 1953.

238. MAN B., KRAUS L. & MOTOVIC A. Cholecystectomy without drainage, nasogastric suction and intravenous fluids. *Am. J. Surg.* **133**:312, 1977.

239. MANNING A.P., THOMPSON W.G., HEATON K.W. & MORRIS A.F. Towards positive diagnosis of the irritable bowel. *Br. Med. J.* **2**:653, 1978.

240. MARSHALL R.D. Transduodenal ampulloplasty in the surgery of the common bile duct. *Aust. New Zeal. J. Surg.* **32**:160, 1962.

241. MASSIE J.R., COXE J.W. III, PARKER C. & DIETRICK R. Gall bladder perforations in acute cholecystitis. *Ann. Surg.* **145**:825, 1957.

242. MASUDA H. & NAKAYAMA F. Composition of bile pigment in gallstones and bile and their aetiological significance. *J. Lab. Clin. Med.* **93**:353, 1979.

243. MATON P.N., MURPHY G.M. & DOWLING R.H. Ursodeoxycholic acid treatment of gallstones. Dose response study and possible mechanism of action. *Lancet* **2**:1297, 1977.

244. MATSUSHIRO T., SUZUKI N., SATO T. & MAKI T. Effects of diet on glucaric acid concentration in bile and the formation of calcium bilirubinate gallstones. *Gastroenterology* **72**:630, 1977.

245. MAYS E.T. Vascular occlusion. *Surg. Clin. North Amer.* **57**:291, 1977.

246. MAZZARIELLO R. Removal of residual biliary tract calculi without re-operation. *Surgery* **67**:566, 1970.

247. MAZZARIELLO R. Review of 220 cases of residual biliary tract calculi treated without re-operation: An 8 year study. *Surgery* **73**:299, 1973.

248. MAZZARIELLO R.M. A 14 year experience with non-operative instrument extraction of retained bile duct stones. *World J. Surg.* **2**:447, 1978.

249. MCARTHUR P., CUSCHIERE A., SELLS R.A. & SHIELDS R. Controlled clinical trial comparing early with interval cholecystectomy for acute cholecystitis. *Br. J. Surg.* **62**:850, 1975.

250. MCBURNEY R.P. & GARDNER H.C. Non-surgical removal of retained common duct stones: Case report. *Ann. Surg.* **173**:298, 1971.

251. MCCUBBREY D. & THIEME T. In defense of the conservative treatment for acute cholecystitis with an evaluation of the risk. *Surgery* **45**:930, 1959.

252. MCDOUGALL R.M., WALKER R. & THURSTON O.G. Prolonged secretion of lithogenic bile after cholecystectomy. *Ann. Surg.* **182**:150, 1975.

253. MCKAY A.J., DUNCAN J.G., IMRIE C.W., JOFFE S.N. & BLUMGART L.H. A prospec-

tive study of the clinical value and accuracy of Grey scale ultrasound in detecting gallstones. *Br. J. Surg.* **65**:330, 1978.

254. McKenzie G.G.C. Pers. commun. 1970.

255. McLaughlin C.W. Jr. Carcinoma of the gallbladder. An added hazard in untreated calculous cholecystitis in older patients. *Surgery* **56**:757, 1964.

256. Millbourn E.W. *Overlooked Calculi in the Deep Biliary Ducts as the Cause of Postoperative Biliary Distress.* Imp. Med. et. Sci., Brussels, 1950.

257. Millbourn E. On reoperation for choledocholithiasis. Experience from and comments on 34 operated cases. *Acta Chir. Scand.* **99**:285, 1950.

258. Millbourn E. On the importance of the remnant cystic duct in the development of post-operative biliary distress following cholecystectomy. A study partly based on a cholangiography series. *Acta Chir. Scand.* **100**:448, 1951.

259. Mok H.Y.I., Bell G.D., Whitney B. & Dowling R.H. Stones in the common bile duct: Non operative management. *Proc. Roy. Soc. Med.* **67**:658, 1974.

260. Mondet A. Tecnica de la extraccion incruenta de los calculos on la litiasis residual del coledoco. *Bol. Soc. Circ. Bs. Aires* **14**:278, 1962.

261. Moore A.R. An instrument for the accurate measurement of the common bile duct. *Surg. Gynec. Obstet.* **70**:323, 1973.

262. Morrow D.J., Thompson J. & Wilson S.E. Acute cholecystitis in the elderly. A surgical emergency. *Arch. Surg.* **113**:1149, 1978.

263. Morse L., Krynski B. & Wright A.R. Acute perforation of the gallbladder. *Am. J. Surg.* **94**:772, 1957.

264. Morton C.B. II. Post-cholecystectomy symptoms from cystic duct remnants. *Ann. Surg.* **139**:679, 1954.

265. Mullen J.T., Carr R.E., Rupnik E.J. & Knapp R.W. 1000 cholecystectomies, extra ductal palpation and operative cholangiography. *Am. J. Surg.* **131**:672, 1976.

266. Mullen J.L., Rosato F.E., Rosato E.F., Miller W.T. & Sullivan, M. The diagnosis of choledocholithiasis. *Surg. Gynec. Obstet.* **133**:774, 1971.

267. Murray W.R., Agnew M. & MacKay C. Diet and bile composition in gallstone patients. *Br. J. Surg.* **61**:917, 1974.

268. Myers M.B. Drain fever: A complication of drainage after cholecystectomy. *Surgery* **52**:314, 1962.

269. Nagase M., Tanimura H., Setoyama M. & Hikasa Y. Present features of gallstones in Japan. A collective review of 2144 cases. *Am. J. Surg.* **135**:788, 1978.

270. Nakayama F. & Miyake H. Changing state of gallstone disease in Japan. *Am. J. Surg.* **120**:794, 1970.

271. Nakgawa S., Makino L., Ishizaki T. & Dohi L. Dissolution of cholesterol gallstones by ursodeoxycholic acid. *Lancet* **2**:367, 1977.

272. Narat J.K. & Cipolla A.F. Fragmentation and dissolution of gallstones by chloroform. *Arch. Surg.* **51**:51, 1945.

273. Nielsen M.L. & Justesen T. Anaerobic and aerobic bacteriologic studies in biliary tract disease. *Scand. J. Gastroenterol.* **11**:437, 1976.

274. Norman O. Studies on the hepatic ducts in cholangiography. *Acta Radiol.* (Suppl. 84), 1951.

275. Northfield T.C. & Hofmann A.F. Relationship between bile acid pool size, bile acid output and production of lithogenic bile. *Gastroenterology* **64**:164, 1973.

276. Ong G.B. A study of recurrent pyogenic cholangitis. *Arch. Surg. (Chicago)* **84**:199, 1962.

277. Onuigbo W.I.B. Acalculous cholecystitis in Nigerian Igbos. *Am. J. Surg.* **134**:564, 1977.

278. Orloff M.J. Retained and recurrent bile duct stones—Introduction. *World. J. Surg.* **2**:401, 1978.

279. Orloff M.J. Importance of surgical technique in prevention of retained and recurrent bile duct stones. *World J. Surg.* **2**:403, 1978.

280. Orr K.B. External choledochoduodenostomy for retained common duct stone: Reappraisal of an old technique. *Med. J. Aust.* **2**:1027, 1966.

281. Ostermiller W. Jr. Thompson R.J. Jr., Carter R. & Hinshaw D.B. Acute obstructive cholangitis. *Arch. Surg. (Chicago)* **90**:392, 1965.

282. Ostrow J.D. Absorption of organic compounds by the injured gallbladder. *J. Lab. Clin. Med.* **78**:255, 1971.

283. Payne R.A. Evaluation of the management of acute cholecystitis. *Br. J. Surg.* **56**:200, 1969.

284. Peel A.L.G., Bourke J.B., Herman-Taylor J., MacLean A.D.W., Mann C.V. & Ritchie H.D. How should common bile duct be explored? *Ann. R. Coll. Surg. Eng.* **56**:124, 1975.

285. Peel A.L.G., Hermon-Taylor J. & Ritchie H.D. Technique of transduodenal exploration of the common bile duct. Duodenoscopic appearances after biliary sphincterotomy. *Ann. R. Coll. Surg. Eng.* **55**:236, 1974.

286. Perez M.R., Oleaga J.A., Freiman D.B., McLean G.L. & Ring E.J. Removal of a distal common bile duct stone through percutaneous transhepatic catheterization. *Arch. Surg.* **114**:107, 1979.

287. Person D.A. Carcinoma of the gallbladder presenting as acute cholecystitis and leading to a missed clinical and pathologic diagnosis. *Am. J. Surg.* **108**:95, 1964.

288. Peskin G.W. The treatment of silent gallstones. *Surg. Clin. North Amer.* **53**:1063, 1973.

289. Pheils M.T., Andersen P.T., Silverton R.P. & Duraiappah B. Acute cholecystitis: the question of early or late operation. *Aust. New Zeal. J. Surg.* **43**:24, 1973.

290. Piehler J.M. & Crichlow R.W. Primary carcinoma of the gallbladder. *Surg. Gynec. Obstet.* **147**:929, 1978.

291. Pines B. & Rabinovitch J. Perforation of the gallbladder in acute cholecystitis. *Ann. Surg.* **140**:170, 1954.

292. Plessis D.J. du & Jersky J. The management of acute cholecystitis. *Surg. Clin. North Amer.* **53**:1071, 1973.

293. Pohlenz O. & Weber J. Unblutige Entfernung von intraoperativ Zurückgelassenen Steinen aus den Gallenwegen Chirurg. **45**:425, 1974.

294. Prian G.W., Norton L.W., Eule J. Jr & Eiseman B. Clinical indications and accuracy of Grey scale ultrasonography in the patient suspected of biliary tract disease. *Am. J. Surg.* **134**:705, 1977.

295. Raine P.A.M. & Gunn A.A. Acute cholecystitis. *Br. J. Surg.* **62**:697, 1975.

296. Rewbridge A.G. The disappearance of gallstone shadows following the prolonged administration of bile salts. *Surgery* **1**:395, 1937.

297. Reynolds B.M. & Dargan E.L. Acute obstructive cholangitis. *Ann. Surg.* **150**:299, 1959.

298. Rhind J.A. & Watson L. Gallstone dyspepsia. *Br. Med. J.* **1**:32, 1968.

299. Rienhoff W.F. Primary closure of the common duct. *Ann. Surg.* **151**:255, 1960.

300. Rose J.D. Serial cholecystography. A means of preoperative diagnosis of biliary dyskinesia. *A.M.A. Arch. Surg.* **78**:56, 1959.

301. Ruddell W.S.J., Lintott D.J., Ashton, M.G. & Axon A.T.R. Endoscopic retrograde cholangiography and pancreatography in investigation of post-cholecystectomy patients. *Lancet* **1**:444, 1980.

302. Saharia P.C., Zuidema G.D. & Cameron J.L. Primary common duct stones. *Ann. Surg.* **185**:598, 1977.

303. Saik R.P., Greenburg A.G., Farris J.M. & Peskin G.W. Spectrum of cholangitis. *Am. J. Surg.* **130**:143, 1975.

304. Sali A. *Neurohumoral control of hepatic bile secretion.* PhD Thesis, Monash University, Melbourne, 1977.

305. Sali A. Unpublished data, 1977.

306. Sali A., Crowe C., Iser J., Donohue W. & Kune G.A. Biliary citrate secretion. *Aust. New Zeal. J. Med.* **10**:114, 1980.

307. SALI A. & ISER J. The non-operative management of gallstones. *Aust. New Zeal. J. Surg.* **48**:484, 1978.

308. SALI A., ISER J.H. & KUNE G.A. Bile composition in patients with recurrent bile duct calculi. (In preparation.)

309. SALI A., MACKAY C. & ADAMS F.G. Phenobarbitone and gallstone disease. (In press.)

310. SALI A., MURRAY W.R. & MACKAY C. Aluminium hydroxide in bile salt diarrhoea. *Lancet* **2**:1051, 1977.

311. SALMON P.A. Intestinal by-pass: Clinical experience and experimental results. In G.A. Bray (ed.), *Obesity in Perspective,* (Publ. Number (NIH) Vol. 2), D.H.E.W., Washington,

312. SARLES H., CHABERT C., POMMEAU Y., SAVE E., MOURET H. & GÉROLAMI A. Diet in cholesterol gallstones. A study of 101 patients with cholelithiasis compared to 101 matched controls. *Am. J. Dig. Diseases* **14**:531, 1969.

313. SAWYERS J.L., HERRINGTON J.L. JR. & EDWARDS W.H. Primary closure of the common bile duct. *Am. J. Surg.* **109**:107, 1965.

314. SCHEIN C.J. *Acute cholecystitis.* Evanston, Illinois, 1972.

315. SCHEIN C.J. *Post cholecystectomy syndrome. A clinical Approach to Aetiology, Diagnosis and Management.* Harper and Row, New York, 1978.

316. SCHEIN C.J., HURWITT E.S. & HERSKOVITZ A. Endoscopy of the major bile ducts. *N.Y. J. Med.* **62**:3412, 1962.

317. SCHULENBURG C.A.R. *Operative Cholangiography.* Butterwortth, London 1966.

318. SCHULENBURG C.A.R. Operative cholangiography: 1000 cases. *Surgery* **65**:723, 1969.

319. SELTZER M.H., STEIGER E. & ROSATO F.E. Mortality following cholecystectomy. *Surg. Gynec. Obstet.* **130**:64, 1970.

320. SHEFER S., HAUSER S. & MOSBACH E.H. 7α-hydroxylation of cholestanol by rat liver microsomes. *J. Lipid. Res.* **9**:328, 1968.

321. SHERMAN H.I., MARGESON R.C. & DAVIS R.C. Postoperative retained choledocho-lithiasis. Percutaneous endoscopic extraction. *Gastroenterology* **68**:1024, 1975.

322. SHIEBER W. Duodenotomy with common duct exploration. *Arch. Surg. (Chicago)* **85**:944, 1962.

323. SHIELDS M.A. Acute acalculous cholecystitis: An important complication of trauma. *Ann. R. Coll. Surg. Edinb.* **18**:83, 1973.

324. SHINGLETON W.W. & PEETE W.P.J. The postcholecystectomy syndrome. *Am. Surg.* **28**:29, 1962.

325. SHORE J.M. & SHORE E. Operative biliary endoscopy: Experience with the flexible choledochoscope in 100 consecutive choledocholithotomies. *Ann. Surg.* **171**:269, 1970.

326. SIGLER L. & SAHLER C.O. Silk: the nidus of a common duct calculus. *Surgery* **65**:276, 1969.

327. SJÖDAHL R., TAGESSON, C. & WETTERFORS J. On the pathogenesis of acute cholecys-titis. *Surg. Gynec. Obstet.* **146**:199, 1978.

328. SMALL D.M. & RAPO S. Source of abnormal bile in patients with cholesterol gallstones. *New Eng. J. Med.* **283**:53, 1970.

329. SMALLWOOD R.A., JABLONSKI P. & WATTS J. McK. Intermittent secretion of abnor-mal bile in patients with cholesterol gallstones. *Br. Med. J.* **4**:263, 1972.

330. SMITH R. Cholecystitis and Gallstones. In R. Smith & S. Sherlock (eds.), *Surgery of the Gall Bladder and Bile Ducts.* Butterworth, London, 1964.

331. SMITH D.C., CROOK J.N., MCALLISTER R.A. & MACKAY C. The comparison of gallbladder bile in patients with gallstones and in patients with duodenal ulcer before and after vagotomy. *Br. J. Surg.* **59**:306, 1972.

332. SMITH S.W., ENGEL C., AVERBROOK B. & LONGMIRE W.P. JR. Problems of retained and recurrent common bile duct stones. *J.A.M.A.* **164**:231, 1957.

333. SOLLOWAY R.D., TROTMAN B.W. & OSTROW J.D. Pigment gallstones. *Gastroentero-logy* **72**:167, 1977.
334. STAFFORD E.S. & ISAACS J.P. Stone in the left hepatic duct causing jaundice. *Ann. Surg.* **147**:812, 1958.
335. STANILAND J.R., DITCHBURN J. & DE DOMBAL F.T. Clinical presentation of acute abdomen: A study of 600 patients. *Br. Med. J.* **3**:393, 1972.
336. STARR K.W. Recurrent choledocholithiasis and obstructive and pancreatic prob-lems after choledochotomy. *Aust. New. Zeal. J. Surg.* **23**:206, 1954.
337. STEIGER E., SELTZER M.H. & ROSATO F.E. Cholecystectomy in the aged. *Ann. Surg.* **174**:142, 1971.
338. STEMBRIDGE V.A. Amputation neuroma following cholecystectomy. *Ann. Surg.* **132**:1048, 1951.
339. STEMPEL J.M. & DUANE W.C. Biliary lipids and bile acid pool size after vagotomy in man. Evidence against the predisposition to gallstones. *Gastroenterology* **75**:608, 1978.
340. STIEHL A., CZYGAN P., KOMMERELL B., WEIS H.J. & HOLTERMÜLLER K.H. Urso-deoxycholic acid versus chenodeoxycholic acid. Comparison of their effects on bile acid and bile lipid composition in patients with cholesterol gallstones. *Gastroentero-logy* **75**:1016, 1978.
341. STIEHL A., RAEDSCH R. & KOMMERELL B. Increased sulphation of lithocholate in patients with cholesterol gallstones during chenodeoxycholate treatment. *Digestion* **12**:105, 1975.
342. STOCK F.E. & FUNG J.H.T. Oriental Cholangiohepatitis: In R. Smith & S. Sherlock (eds.), *Surgery of the Gall Bladder and Bile Ducts.* Butterworth, London, 1964.
343. STRICKLER J.H., MULLER J.J., RICE C.O. & BARONOFSKY I.D. Non operative treat-ment of retained postoperative common duct stones. *Ann. Surg.* **133**:174, 1951.
344. SUTOR D.H. & WOOLEY S.E. A statistical survey of the composition of gallstones in 8 countries. *Gut* **12**:55, 1971.
345. TAMESUE N. & JUNIPER K. JR. Concentrations of bile salts at the critical micellar concentration of human gall bladder bile. *Gastroenterology* **52**:473, 1967.
346. TAYLOR T.V., LAMBERT M.E., QURESHI S. & TORRANCE B. Should cholecystectomy be combined with vagotomy and pyloroplasty? *Lancet* **1**:295, 1978.
347. THAL E.R., WEIGELT J., LANDAY M. & CONRAD M. Evaluation of ultrasound in the diagnosis of acute and chronic biliary tract disease. *Arch. Surg.* **113**:500, 1978.
348. THISTLE J.L. & HOFMANN A.F. Efficacy and specificity of chenodeoxycholic acid therapy for dissolving gallstones. *New Eng. J. Med.* **289**:655, 1973.
349. THISTLE J.L. & SCHOENFIELD L.J. Induced alterations in composition of bile of persons having cholelithiasis. *Gastroenterology* **61**:488, 1971.
350. THORBJARNARSON B. Carcinoma of the gallbladder and acute cholecystitis. *Ann. Surg.* **151**:241, 1960.
351. TODD G.J. & REEMTSMA K. Cholecystectomy with drainage. Factors influencing wound infection in 1000 elective cases. *Am. J. Surg.* **135**:622, 1978.
352. TOMPKINS R.K., BURKE L.G., ZOLLINGER R.M. & CORNWELL D.G. Relationship of biliary phospholipid and cholesterol concentrations to the occurrence and dissolu-tion of human gallstones. *Ann. Surg.* **172**:936, 1970.
353. TOMPKINS R.K., CRAFT A.R., ZIMMERMAN E., LICHTENSTEIN J.E. & ZOLLINGER R.M. Clinical and biochemical evidence of increased gallstone inflammation after com-plete vagotomy. *Surgery* **71**:196, 1972.
354. TOOULI J., JABLONSKI P. & WATTS J. MCK. Dissolution of stones in the common bile duct with bile salt solutions. *Aust. New Zeal. J. Surg.* **44**:336, 1974.
355. TROPOLLI D.V. & CELLA L.J. JR. Postcholecystectomy syndrome. *Ann Surg.* **137**:250, 1953.
356. TROTMAN B.W. Insights into pigment stone disease. *J. Lab. Clin. Med.* **93**:349, 1979.
357. VAN DER LINDEN W. & SUNZEL H. Early versus delayed operation for acute cholecys-titis: A controlled clinical trial. *Am. J. Surg.* **120**:7, 1970.

358. VENNET K.V. & COLE W.H. Stones in the intrahepatic ducts. *Arch. Surg. (Chicago)* **91**:474, 1965.

359. VICARY F.R. Ultrasound and gastroenterology. *Gut* **18**:386, 1977.

360. VLAHCEVIC Z.R., BELL C.C., BUHAC I., FARRAR J.T. & SWELL, L. Diminished bile acid pool size in patients with gallstones. *Gastroenterology* **59**:165, 1970.

361. VLAHCEVIC Z.R., BELL C.C. & SWELL L. Significance of the liver in the production of lithogenic bile in man. *Gastroenterology* **59**:62, 1970.

362. WALKER J.W. The removal of gallstones by ether solution. *Lancet* **1**:874, 1891.

363. WARD-MCQUAID J.N. Early postoperative abdominal complications and re-operations after gallbladder, colonic and gastric surgery. *Proc. Roy. Soc. Med.* **70**:384, 1977.

364. WARREN K.W. Choledochostomy and cholecystectomy. *Surg. Clin. N. Amer.* **40**:681, 1960.

365. WARREN K.W., McDONALD W.M. & KUNE G.A. Bile Duct Strictures. New Concepts in the Management of an Old Problem. In W.T. Irvine (ed.), *Modern Trends in Surgery* (2e). Butterworth, London, 1966.

366. WAY L.W. Retained common duct stones. *Surg. Clin. N. Amer.* **53**:1139, 1973.

367. WAY L.W., ADMIRAND W.H. & DUNPHY J.E. Management of choledocholithiasis. *Ann. Surg.* **347**:176, 1972.

368. WAYNE R., CEGIELSKI M., BLEICHER J. & SAPORTA J. Operative cholangiography in uncomplicated biliary tract surgery. Review of 354 cholangiography studies in patients without indication of common duct pathology. *Am. J. Surg.* **131**:324, 1976.

369. WEN C.C. & LEE H.C. Intrahepatic stones: a clinical study. *Ann. Surg.* **175**:166, 1972.

370. WENCKERT A. & ROBERTSON B. The natural course of gallstone disease. Eleven-year review of 781 non-operated cases. *Gastroenterology* **50**:376, 1966.

371. WHEELER M.H. Dissolution of retained choledochal calculi. *Ann. R. Coll. Surg. Eng.* **59**:153, 1977.

372. WHEELER M., HILLS L.L. & LABY B. Cholelithiasis: A clinical and dietary survey. *Gut* **11**:430, 1970.

373. WILDEGANS H. Endoscopy of the biliary tract. *German Med. Monthly.* **12**:377, 1958.

374. WILLIAMS C.B., HALPIN D.S. & KNOX J.S. Drainage following cholecystectomy. *Br. J. Surg.* **59**:293, 1972.

375. WILSON P.D., HORROCKS J.C., LYNDON P.J., YEUNG C.K. PAGE R.E. & DE DOMBAL F.T. Simplified computer-aided diagnosis of acute abdominal pain. *Br. Med. J.* **2**:73, 1975.

376. WOMACK N.A. & CRIDER R.L. The persistence of symptoms following cholecystectomy. *Ann. Surg.* **126**:31, 1947.

377. WRIGHT A.D. Surgery of the biliary tract. *Ann. R. Coll. Surg. Eng.* **27**:373, 1960.

378. WRIGHT H.K., HOLDEN W.D. & CLARK J.H. Age as a factor in the mortality rate for biliary tract operations. *J. Am. Geriatr. Soc.* **11**:422, 1963.

379. YAMAKAWA T., MIENO K. & SHIKATA J. Improved choledocho fiberscopes and non surgical removal of retained biliary calculi under direct visual control. *Gastroenterology* **68**:1051, 1975.

380. ZAHOR Z., STERNBY N.H., KAGAN A., UEMERA K., VANECEKT R. & VICHERT A.M. Frequency of cholelithiasis in Prague and Malmö: An autopsy study. *Scand. J. Gastroenterol.* **9**:3, 1974.

6. Benign Biliary Strictures

Benign strictures of the bile ducts are uncommon. The clinical course of some types, if untreated, can progress to a fatal outcome, thus their correct management is important. In this chapter the following conditions are discussed:
1. Operative bile duct injuries—post-traumatic biliary stricture.
2. Postinflammatory strictures
   (a) associated with choledocholithiasis;
   (b) associated with chronic pancreatitis.
3. Primary sclerosing cholangitis.
4. Stenosis of the papilla of Vater (including papillitis).

There are also a number of other rare causes of non-malignant biliary strictures, such as strictures which follow inflammation or suppuration near the bile ducts, extrenal trauma, and congenital strictures as a result of hypoplasia [9, 24, 130, 141]. These are not discussed in detail, but their management follows principles similar to the conditions described in this chapter. Sometimes, strictures follow biliary intestinal anastomosis of normal bile ducts, such as choledochoduodenostomy, and the management of these is covered in Chapter 14.

OPERATIVE BILE DUCT INJURIES
POST-TRAUMATIC BILIARY STRICTURES

Operative injuries of the bile ducts usually have serious consequences in terms of morbidity and ultimate mortality. The life of these patients is usually one of considerable distress unless correct treatment is instituted. The magnitude of the tragedy is made greater by the knowledge that most of these operative accidents are preventable.

INCIDENCE

The incidence of operative injuries is difficult to compute with accuracy. Standards of surgery vary widely; many cases are not reported, others escape attention under various disguises and 'non de plumes', such as sclerosing cholangitis. A review of the literature, from centres in which the surgery is usually performed by qualified surgeons, shows that the incidence of bile duct injury is about one in 300–500 gallstone operations [13, 71, 78, 102, 129].

Almost all injuries of the bile ducts occur during cholecystectomy. Some occur after exploration of the common bile duct and a few are secondary to gastrectomy or operations on the pancreas [141].

AETIOLOGY

The usual cause of a bile duct injury is inadequate dissection and demonstration of the bile ducts during cholecystectomy. A less common cause is inadvertent haemorrhage followed by blind clamping of the bleeding area while removing the gallbladder.

INADEQUATE DISSECTION OF THE BILE DUCTS

The usual cause for this is poor surgical technique. In a few cases certain anatomical and pathological factors predispose to inaccurate identification of the duct system.

Poor surgical technique. Lack of adequate training in surgery is a frequent reason for bile duct injury. In some countries, such as the United States and Australia, doctors are permitted to perform a cholecystectomy even if they have had no surgical training, provided they are registered medical practitioners. In view of the advanced nature of these countries this situation is deplorable. Adequately trained surgeons occasionally damage the bile duct during an 'easy' cholecystectomy. These injuries are generally caused by hurry or carelessness, or by a momentary loss of concentration [63].

The usual error is that the common hepatic duct is mistaken for the cystic duct and it is partially excised and in a number, the proximal common hepatic duct is also ligated (Fig. 6.1). This mechanism of injury also explains why almost all of these injuries sustained during cholecystectomy are very high injuries of the

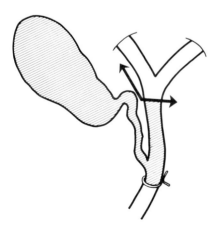

Fig. 6.1. Typical bile duct injury. A segment of the common hepatic duct is mistaken for the cystic duct and is excised with the gallbladder.

194   CHAPTER 6

common hepatic duct, and only a tiny stump remains for subsequent reconstruction (Figs. 6.8–6.12) [63, 115].

Anatomical factors. There are a number of anatomical predispositions to bile duct injury during cholecystectomy, and the manner of arrangement of the ducts tricks the unaware surgeon into a mistaken identification of the duct system. A frequent associated feature is a narrow-calibre bile duct, which even further encourages the surgeon to believe that this duct 'must be the cystic duct'. It is emphasised that these anatomical reasons for duct injury are uncommon (Fig. 6.2).

In approximately a quarter of subjects the right hepatic duct is absent and then the right anterior and right posterior bile ducts join the left hepatic duct directly. In some of these cases the right anterior duct has a long course running close to the cystic duct, and is very prone to injury (Fig. 6.2a). In some cases the right hepatic duct passes close to the cystic duct and may be injured (Fig. 6.2b). Duct injury may also occur when the cystic duct joins the right hepatic duct (Fig. 6.2c), or when the cystic duct is absent (Fig. 6.2d).

Evidence has been presented that bile duct injury may occur when the cystic duct is adherent to the common hepatic duct before it joins it (parallel mode of union) [61, 129, 136]. The common hepatic duct is injured when a clamp is applied to the incompletely mobilised cystic duct (Fig. 6.2e).

Excessive traction on the cystic duct, leading to tenting of the junction of the bile ducts with the cystic duct and their inclusion in a clamp or ligature, has been quoted as a frequent cause of injury (Fig. 6.2f). In fact, there is little evidence that this is a common mode of injury, and most strictures are proximal to this junction. However, this type of injury may be important if a fundus-down cholecystectomy is performed, or when the cystic duct is short or absent [61,64].

Pathological factors. The pathological conditions which may contribute to incomplete demonstration of the bile ducts during cholecystectomy are oedema and friability of the ducts in the presence of acute cholecystitis, or extensive fibrosis in the region of the porta hepatis in a patient who has had numerous attacks of cholecystitis in the past. In fact, these are uncommon causes of bile duct injury, probably because the surgeon approaches the operation with special caution when encountering these pathological states [129].

INADVERTENT HAEMORRHAGE
During cholecystectomy, severe unexpected arterial haemorrhage in the porta hepatis may be the cause of injury to the bile ducts if haemostats are blindly and impulsively applied in the region [24, 64, 129, 136]. The bleeding usually arises from a divided cystic artery or, less commonly, from a right hepatic artery. The resultant duct injuries are proximal injuries, involving the common hepatic duct or one of the hepatic ducts.

OTHER CAUSES
A difficult gastrectomy for a chronic duodenal ulcer in the second part of the

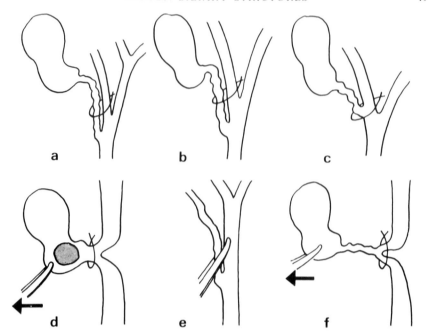

Fig. 6.2. Anatomical predispositions to bile duct injury. For details see text. It is emphasised that these are uncommon causes of duct injury.

duodenum may be associated with injury of the lower end of the common bile duct and, occasionally, also with injury of the pancreatic duct [24, 53, 64].

Rarely, the bile ducts are injured when an operation is performed to excise a diverticulum of the duodenum which lies close to the papilla of Vater, or during an operation on the pancreas.

PREVENTION

Almost all operative injuries of the bile ducts are preventable. The complete prevention of these tragedies would be a great advance in biliary tract surgery.

Inadequate demonstration of the bile ducts and the haphazard management of accidental haemorrhage are the two principal causes of bile duct injury during cholecystectomy; correct surgical technique aims at overcoming these problems.

The incision must be of adequate length and location. Paramedian incisions are frequently made too low and too short. Subcostal incisions are frequently too short and too oblique.

The cystic artery should be identified and dissected to show that it enters the gallbladder. It should be ligated close to the gallbladder wall, in order to avoid damage to the common hepatic duct, the right hepatic duct, and the right hepatic artery.

Excessive traction on the gallbladder should be avoided to prevent avulsion of the cystic artery and to prevent tenting of the common bile duct.

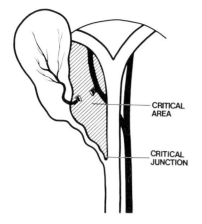

Fig. 6.3. The critical area is carefully dissected and the critical junction is identified.

The triangular area bounded by the right borders of the common hepatic duct and right hepatic duct, by the upper surface of the gallbladder and cystic duct, and by the liver is critical (Fig. 6.3). This is the region where large unexpected bile ducts, such as the right anterior bile duct, may be present.

The precise point of junction of the cystic duct with the common hepatic duct must be clearly demonstrated in all cases. In this regard it is important to separate the cystic duct when it is adherent to the common hepatic duct and thereby locate its termination (Fig. 6.4). With a spiral type of cystic duct it is quite unnecessary, however, to trace this to its termination, provided its junction with the bile duct is clearly seen [115].

When dense fibrosis prevents the precise dissection of the anatomic structures

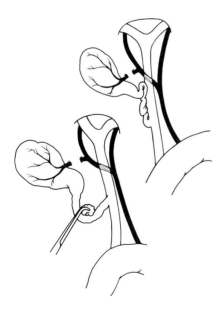

Fig. 6.4. Method of separation of the cystic duct, which is adherent to the common hepatic duct. Redrawn from Warren, McDonald, and Kune [136].

in the porta hepatis, a valuable procedure is a deliberate choledochotomy in the supraduodenal part of the common bile duct and insertion of a probe or dilator in the proximal direction. This will provide a satisfactory delineation of the common hepatic and right hepatic ducts. If there are still problems with bile duct identification the surgeon had best content himself by performing a cholecystos-tomy only.

The management of accidental bleeding during cholecystectomy must be deliberate and precise. The exposure is reassessed and the illumination, if unsatis-factory, is improved. The blood is best removed by gentle suction. Venous bleeding will stop with pressure. Torrential arterial haemorrhage can be tempor-arily controlled with finger and thumb pressure on the hepatic artery in the free edge of the gastrohepatic omentum. Digital compression of the coeliac axis by an assistant is a suitable alternative which leaves the surgeon free to deal with the haemorrhage [136].

In the performance of the Polya-type gastrectomy, for a low chronic duo-denal ulcer, if the surgeon feels that the bile duct may be injured a deliberate choledochotomy and insertion of a Bakes dilator through the sphincter of Oddi will protect the duct from injury [136].

PATHOLOGY

The pathological changes which follow a bile duct injury have not been studied extensively, yet an understanding of them is essential in management. These changes vary in extent, depending on the nature of the original injury and on the length of time partial or complete biliary obstruction has been present.

The area of injury, if not attended to immediately, becomes the seat of inflammation and fibrosis, and a biliary stricture results. There is some evidence that this inflammatory response is contributed to by the irritant properties of the extravasated bile in the area [33, 36, 78].

The bile ducts proximal to the stricture may be dilated and are frequently thick-walled and fibrotic. Biopsy of the bile duct, proximal to an established traumatic biliary stricture, shows extensive mucosal changes of atrophy, nec-rosis, or squamous metaplasia, as well as subepithelial fibrosis and inflammatory infiltration (Figs. 6.5 & 6.6). Similar changes may be encountered in the bile ducts distal to the stricture, and sometimes the distal bile duct is completely obliterated by fibrous tissue (Fig. 6.7). There is some recent evidence that atrophy and fibrosis of the distal bile duct is the result of operative interference with bile duct blood supply [88]. The bile in the proximal ducts is almost always infected, usually with enteric organisms.

Surgical reconstruction of established postoperative biliary strictures is fre-quently followed by restenosis of the anastomotic area. This tendency for restenosis is probably due to the presence of infected bile, in association with the epithelial, subepithelial, and peridochal changes described above. Healing of the anastomosis will occur with fibrosis, and the subsequent contraction of this fibrous tissue will result in restenosis. Restenosis is probably also contributed to

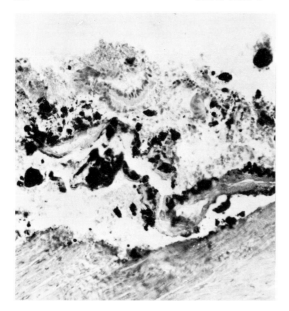

Fig. 6.5. Biopsy of bile duct proximal to an established traumatic biliary stricture. Note epithelial necrosis, desquamation of epithelium, biliary debris, and subepithelial fibrosis.

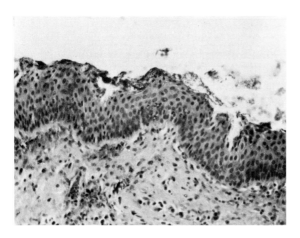

Fig. 6.6. Biopsy of bile duct proximal to an established traumatic biliary stricture. Note squamous metaplasia of epithelium and subepithelial fibrosis.

by the technical difficulties of achieving accurate mucosa-to-mucosa apposition during the construction of the anastomosis.

Because of these pathological processes the methods and techniques of biliary reconstruction of traumatic strictures follow principles which are different from the suturing and anastomosis of normal bile ducts. Thus, the bile duct distal to the stricture cannot be used for an anastomosis if it has become fibrotic. Also, in all established strictures, an internal splint of some type is recommended. This splint it left *in situ* for a long time and removed only when it is expected that all the fibrosis, which inevitably takes place around the anastomosis, has already developed.

External biliary fistulas are common after bile duct injuries. Internal biliary

Fig. 6.7. Biopsy of bile duct distal to an established traumatic biliary stricture. Note epithelial atrophy and subepithelial fibrosis. Could some of these changes be due to operative interference with bile duct blood supply?

fistulas are also sometimes found; these usually connect the bile ducts proximal to the stricture with the duodenum. Some degree of biliary decompression is undoubtedly obtained in this way, but biliary obstruction is never completely relieved, and cholangitis usually persists [24, 64].

Liver changes of periportal inflammation, periportal fibrosis, and established biliary cirrhosis are regularly seen in patients with traumatic biliary strictures. These changes are progressive if the biliary obstruction is not adequately relieved, and this progression usually determines the ultimate prognosis [24, 48].

The incidence of portal hypertension in patients with established biliary strictures is about 20 per cent [113]. However, when the bile duct stricture has been effectively treated, complications of this portal hypertension are uncommonly seen. When the stricture has not been adequately treated biliary cirrhosis is progressive and a number of patients develop bleeding oesophageal varices as a consequence of their portal hypertension [113].

DIAGNOSIS

CLINICAL FEATURES

The presence of an operative injury of the bile ducts is painfully obvious in most cases. In a few instances the diagnosis is made during the initial operation; in the rest it is made either in the early postoperative period or some months later.

The occurrence of obstructive jaundice or of excessive bile drainage from the wound, or both, in the early postoperative period, usually indicates injury to the bile ducts. In some cases an intra-abdominal collection of bile is drained at a second operation, and this is the signal of a bile duct injury.

In a number of patients symptoms are noted only some months after the injury. These symptoms usually consist of recurring bouts of fever, rigors, and transient jaundice. In some the onset of obstructive jaundice some months after operation is the first evidence that a duct injury occurred. Close questioning of patients who first present some time after their operation frequently brings to light a history of prolonged biliary drainage, or a postoperative septic course after the initial operative procedure [64, 136].

Physical examination will reveal a variable depth of jaundice, its intensity depending on whether the bile duct obstruction is complete or partial and whether an external or an internal biliary fistula is also present. For these reasons it should be noted that pale stools are not always present. The general appearance of the patient depends on the nature and duration of the symptoms. Thus, patients will look ill and debilitated when they have had many episodes of cholangitis or when they have had a large external biliary fistula for some time. Hepatomegaly and splenomegaly are usually present in those who have a long-standing obstruction and portal hypertension.

LABORATORY TESTS

In most patients there is bile pigment in the urine. As most of these patients are jaundiced the liver function tests will show an obstructive (cholestatic) pattern (Chapter 4). Thus, the serum bilirubin level is elevated and the serum alkaline phosphatase activity increased. The serum transaminase level may be within normal limits but may be elevated in the presence of cholangitis. The serum prothrombin activity is frequently depressed. Changes in the serum protein levels are noted only when obstruction and cholangitis have been longstanding.

RADIOLOGY

Intravenous cholangiography. This technique is not usually of value, because most of the patients are jaundiced and visualisation of the bile ducts cannot be obtained. The investigation can, however, be of value in the non-jaundiced patient who has recurrent symptoms after repair of a bile duct injury (Fig. 6.8).

Fistulography. On occasion, contrast medium can be introduced through an external biliary fistula. This may outline the duct system proximal to the injury and may show its level (Figs. 6.9 & 6.10).

Percutaneous transhepatic cholangiography (PTC). This technique has been used with increasing frequency in patients who have biliary obstruction due to a bile duct injury, especially since the procedure has become safer and more reliable with the introduction of the fine needle devised at the Chiba University in Japan (Chapters 3 & 4). A successful cholangiogram will show the level and degree of obstruction as seen in Fig. 6.11, which is the PTC of a typical high, bile duct injury. PTC is also most valuable in the diagnosis of a recurrent stricture after previous reconstruction, especially in the jaundiced patient in whom intravenous cholangiography cannot be performed, or is unsuccessful (Figs. 6.12, 3.10 & 3.11). Endoscopic retrograde cholangiography is rarely of value in these cases, because the contrast will not usually get into the bile ducts above the stricture or injury.

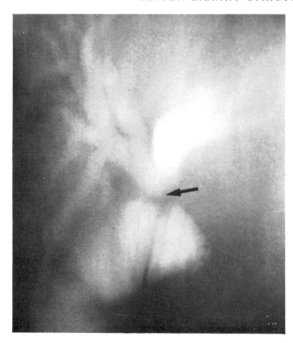

Fig. 6.8. Intravenous cholangiogram in a patient
with recurrent symptoms
of cholangitis following a
previous hepaticojejunos-
tomy repair. Note stricture
at the level of the anastomosis and bile dilatation.

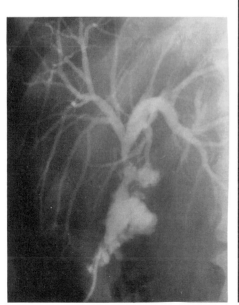

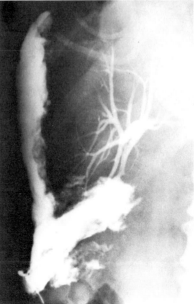

Fig. 6.9. (*left*). Fistulogram through a postoperative external biliary fistula, which shows a typical high injury of the common hepatic duct.

Fig. 6.10. (*right*). Fistulogram through a postoperative external biliary fistula, again showing a typical duct injury, as well as outlining a subphrenic and subhepatic abscess cavity.

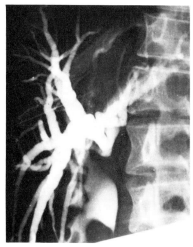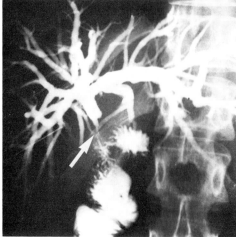

Fig. 6.11. (*left*). Percutaneous transhepatic cholangiogram of a typical high injury of the common hepatic duct. In this case the common hepatic duct was excised and there was also a ligature around the proximal common hepatic duct.

Fig. 6.12. (*right*). Percutaneous transhepatic cholangiogram of a bile duct stricture, which had recurred after a previous hepaticojejunostomy Roux-en-Y. The patient had rigors and jaundice.

PREOPERATIVE MANAGEMENT

Patients who have sustained a bile duct injury should rapidly be brought into the most favourable condition possible, before surgical reconstruction is undertaken. They may require a blood transfusion if they are particularly anaemic. In the presence of cholangitis the administration of a broad-spectrum antibiotic is a valuable temporary adjunct to treatment. Ultimately, the only sure way of dealing with cholangitis is to provide surgical decompression of the obstructed bile duct. Preoperative preventative antibiotics which cover both aerobes and anaerobes is recommended as a routine method of prophylaxis. Vitamin K is necessary to improve the depressed prothrombin activity.

In the presence of a longstanding external biliary fistula these patients lose large amounts of sodium, potassium, and chloride ions. They develop an electrolyte imbalance—termed the choledochostomy acidotic syndrome—and this requires correction preoperatively (see External biliary fistula, Chapter 11) [21, 59].

The nutritional state of some of the more debilitated patients may need to be improved. Success has been achieved by forced artificial feeding through a transnasal tube, in which up to 6000 calories is administered per day with significant weight gains [134]. More recently, preoperative and postoperative total parenteral nutrition has also been found to be of great value in the debilitated, malnourished patient [62].

Patients whose biliary strictures have been left uncorrected for some time will develop biliary cirrhosis and portal hypertension; the management of this is discussed later in this chapter. Very occasionally, the patient's immediate major problem is one of bleeding oesophageal varices; then the correction of the biliary stricture may be delayed in favour of a splenorenal shunt as the first procedure [113].

TREATMENT

Surgical correction of the injured or strictured bile duct holds the only prospect of cure. One can obtain a satisfactory ultimate result even after several reconstructive operations [137]. It is therefore the surgeon's responsibility to impress on the patient the need for this surgery, even though many of these patients have become dejected and lost hope as a consequence of past failures.

INJURIES RECOGNISED AT OPERATION

The initial consideration is the competence and experience of the surgeon. If the surgeon does not feel experienced enough to undertake immediate repair of the injury it is best to provide adequate external biliary drainage of the proximal bile duct and then refer the patient immediately to a centre where further surgery can be carried out.

When the surgeon feels sufficiently experienced to proceed to immediate repair his first objective is to ascertain precisely the extent of the injury. This is best performed by a combination of careful dissection, instrumental exploration of the injured bile duct, and operative cholangiography. When this is completed the surgeon may be faced with one of two situations.

Defect not circumferential. These minimal injuries are, unfortunately, rare. When only a small side hole has been made in the bile duct, and the injury is not circumferential, it is sufficient to mobilise the duodenum and the head of the pancreas and suture the defect transversely (Fig. 6.13a). The bile duct is drained with a T tube.

If the defect is larger, but the injury is not circumferential, so that no loss of length has occurred, the defect can still be sutured transversely after mobilisation of the duodenum, or a venous patch graft may be performed (Fig. 6.13b). This latter method has been reported in the literature, and there is experimental and clinical evidence that epithelialisation of the venous patch graft takes place fairly rapidly, though the present writers have had no personal experience with this technique [11, 78].

Circumferential defect with loss of length. Almost invariably the injury is circumferential and involves the loss of a variable length of the bile duct. These are the instances in which the common hepatic duct or the common bile duct, or both, was mistaken for the cystic duct, the duct was ligated and a portion excised before the injury was discovered.

A further technical problem is that many of these injured bile ducts are of a narrow calibre; this is one of the reasons for their being mistaken for the cystic

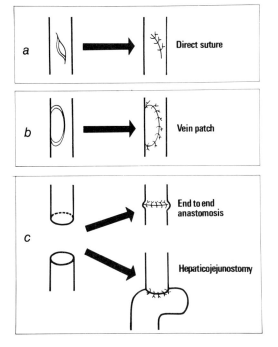

Fig. 6.13. Methods of repair of injuries recognised during the initial operation. (a) Direct suture. (b) Venous patch graft. (c) End-to-end anastomosis, or hepaticojejunostomy Roux-en-Y. For further details see text.

duct. The reconstruction is thus frequently a difficult technical exercise, and precise mucosa-to-mucosa apposition may not be obtained, and healing may occur with eventual fibrosis and stricture formation.

If the two ends of the bile duct can be apposed fairly accurately, and without obvious tension on the anastomosis, an end-to-end ductal anastomosis may be considered (Fig. 6.13c). If this is done the duodenum and head of the pancreas should be fully mobilised. The anastomosis may be done with one layer of interrupted silk or fine chromic catgut sutures.

If the two ends cannot be apposed without tension an immediate biliary intestinal anastomosis is necessary. In these cases, it is unlikely that the duodenum can be brought up to the proximal bile duct and anastomosed to it without tension. A hepaticojejunostomy Roux-en-Y is the most suitable anastomosis in such a case (Fig. 6.13c).

The anastomosis in both types of repair should be made over a splint, such as a T tube, which is brought out from the bile duct at a site away from the anastomotic line. The length of time this splint should remain is not certain. If the anastomosis seems accurate, and there is not postoperative bile leakage, the splint can probably be removed after about 6 weeks. If the anastomosis is not thought to be an accurate mucosa-to-mucosa apposition then the splint should remain in place for several months. Restricturing of these anastomoses is of the order of 50 per cent. This high rate of stenosis is attributed to technical difficulties at obtaining accurate mucosal apposition, tension on the anastomosis, and frequently bile leakage and infection, all contributing to postoperative scarring.

The principles of surgical treatment of established traumatic biliary strictures involve the provision of adequate biliary drainage without obstruction, and the prevention of recurrent stricture formation.

General considerations. Healing of these anastomoses will be frequently associated with fibrosis, because of the pathological changes previously described and because accurate mucosa-to-mucosa apposition may not be obtained at the time of the reconstruction. For these reasons recurrent stricture formation is likely to follow unless measures are taken to prevent it. This state of affairs cannot be compared with an anastomosis performed on a cleanly cut normal duct, such as after pancreaticoduodenectomy, or in the experimental animal, because in these the risk of anastomotic stricture formation is low. Principles of management, based on results obtained in the experimental animal or in normal bile ducts, are not applicable to a traumatic biliary stricture, nor to an area of recent operation with perioperative infection and bile extravasation, and should be largely ignored.

Selection of an effective surgical procedure. No one operation is suitable for all biliary strictures; each case is evaluated according to the conditions found at operation [136]. Based on a review of 900 traumatic biliary strictures treated at the Lahey Clinic in Boston, Warren, McDonald, and Kune, 1966, described the following factors that are important in the choice of operation.

Site and extent of stricture. Minimal and localised strictures may be dealt with by simple transverse closure of a vertical incision through the stricture. Proximal strictures with substantial loss of length usually mean that an end-to-end ductal anastomosis cannot be performed without tension and some type of biliary intestinal anastomosis is usually necessary.

Quality and calibre of proximal and distal ducts. If the duct proximal to the stricture is much wider than the distal one an end-to-end anastomosis is not recommended. Also, if the distal duct is fibrotic, non-distensible, or obliterated, it should not be used in an end-to-end ductal anastomosis.

Presence of complicating local factors. A staged procedure may be required because of large abscesses or because of infected bile or severe portal hypertension.

General condition of the patient. Poor general condition at the time of surgery may again lead to a staged operation.

Effective operative procedures. The available effective operative procedures are:
1. A staged operation in which the first stage is simple, external drainage of the proximal bile duct.

2. Plastic reconstruction based on the Heineke–Mikulicz repair.

3. End-to-end anastomosis.

4. Biliary intestinal anastomosis, such as hepaticojejunostomy or hepaticoduo-denostomy.

It is again emphasised that the usual lesion, or subsequent stricture, involves a significant loss of length of the common hepatic duct and common bile duct. Thus, the *usual* operative procedure at present is a hepaticojejunostomy Roux-en-Y, and this is described in detail shortly [63, 81, 141].

External hepaticostomy drainage only. Some patients, when first seen, are extremely debilitated and jaundiced, with evidence of liver failure. In others, an abscess or a localised biliary extravasation in the region of the injured duct produces extensive oedema and friability of the tissues, which make a corrective procedure inadvisable. In still others, severe haemorrhage is encountered in the porta hepatis due to portal hypertension. In a few instances a repair procedure is planned, but the patient's condition dramatically deteriorates during the operation.

In these patients a staged procedure is advocated, consisting of external hepaticostomy drainage of the bile duct proximal to the stricture as the first stage. This external biliary fistula is maintained until the clinical condition has improved, the biliary system is adequately decompressed, local infection is controlled, and the patient's nutritional and metabolic state is improved [26, 136]. The management of the patient, in whom hepaticostomy is done for severe bleeding due to portal hypertension, is discussed shortly.

Plastic repair. When a localised minimal stricture is found in a relatively low and accessible part of the biliary tract a plastic reconstructive procedure is advocated. This consists of a vertical incision made across the strictured area, and then the horizontal closure of this incision, to widen the lumen of the duct. In order to relieve the tension on the suture line the duodenum is mobilised completely by Kocher's method. This type of minimal structure is, unfortunately, only rarely encountered.

End-to-end ductal anastomosis. Excision of the stricture and end-to-end anastomosis of the bile ducts is theoretically the ideal mode of reconstruction, because this re-establishes the normal physiologic state. This procedure is recommended only when the two ends of the bile duct are of approximately the same calibre, and when the anastomosis can be performed without tension following complete mobilisation of the duodenum and the head of the pancreas. A single layer of accurate interrupted, fine, through-and-through sutures are used (Fig. 6.14). If these conditions cannot be satisfied a biliary intestinal anastomosis is recommended.

Biliary intestinal anastomosis. This type of reconstruction is indicated with loss of bile duct length and when conditions are not suitable for end-to-end anasto-

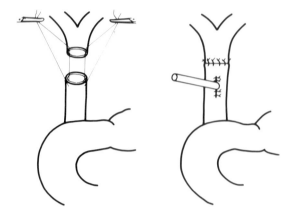

Fig. 6.14. Technique of end-to-end ductal anastomosis. Note that T tube does *not* come through the anastomosis. Duodenum and pancreas must be fully mobilised for this procedure.

mosis. Evidence from large series clearly shows that end-to-end anastomosis is not superior to biliary intestinal anastomosis, so the surgeon should have no qualms about constructing the latter, if it is necessary [64, 136, 137]. Indeed, biliary intestinal reconstruction, usually in the form of a hepaticojejunostomy Roux-en-Y, is the commonest method of repair used in bile duct injuries and in postoperative strictures.

Often there is a discrepancy between the sizes of the proximal and distal bile ducts, or the distal duct is fibrotic and non-distensible, or even obliterated. On other occasions an end-to-end anastomosis cannot be performed without tension, even with full mobilisation of the duodenum and the head of the pancreas. This last situation is almost always present with extensive proximal strictures involving the common hepatic duct. Finally, a biliary intestinal anastomosis should be performed for strictures which involve the retropancreatic portion of the bile duct, such as those that result from injury during gastrectomy. In these, excision of the stricture and end-to-end anastomosis are technically difficult and dangerous.

Strictures that involve the distal common bile duct are suitably dealt with by choledochoduodenostomy, either side-to-side as described in Chapter 14, or end-to-side as shown in Fig. 6.15 [64, 123].

Strictures and injuries involving the hepatic duct are best dealt with by hepaticojejunostomy rather than hepaticoduodenostomy [63, 64, 81, 117, 119, 136, 141]. Hepaticoduodenostomy, as shown in Fig. 6.15, has been advocated in the past for these high injuries, but in many series a high incidence of restenosis followed [25, 64, 72]. The probable reasons are that it is frequently not possible to perform a hepaticoduodenostomy without tension, and also because the hepaticoduodenostomy becomes stretched by the continuous peristaltic activity of the duodenum. The interposition of an isolated segment of isoperistaltic jejunum between the stricture and the duodenum was first described by Grassi in 1973, but this operation has not so far been given an extensive trial [42, 143].

When a hepaticojejunostomy is performed the Roux-en-Y technique is preferred to a loop jejunostomy [64, 117]. A Roux-en-Y anastomosis eliminates

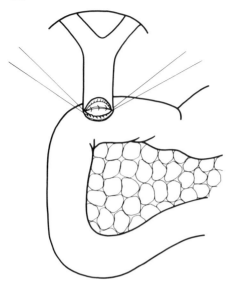

Fig. 6.15. Technique of end-to-side chole-dochoduodenostomy in the presence of a biliary stricture. The duodenum and head of the pancreas must be fully mobilised.

intestinal reflux, makes reoperations easier with regard to localisation of the anastomosis, and minimises the problems associated with a postoperative anastomotic fistula. This method will be described in detail shortly.

INTERNAL SPLINT

Following the reconstruction of an established biliary stricture an internal splint is regarded as essential by most authorities [25, 49, 63, 64, 81, 115, 136, 137]. As noted in the section on pathology earlier in this chapter most of these anastomoses will heal with fibrosis and subsequent contraction of the fibrous tissue. The splint maintains an adequate stoma during this process and should not be removed until the fibrous tissue has matured and contracted.

Two large series of cases clearly showed that the longer the internal splint remained in place, the more likely was the patient to obtain a satisfactory final result [64, 137]. Fig. 6.16 relates the final result to the length of time the tube was in place, in a series of 50 cases studied by the author and his co-workers, and it lends support to the use of these internal splints. Thus, the splint should remain in place for about 6 to 9 months in relatively simple cases, and for 12 months or even longer in more difficult cases, in which a considerable amount of fibrosis is expected to take place [25, 64, 136, 137].

Some experimental and clinical work opposes the use of an internal splint [47, 66, 68]. Work in dogs can be discounted because in these animals the bile ducts are of relatively good quality and healing of the anastomosis is expected to take place without much fibrosis. Healing of relatively normal quality human bile ducts also takes place without significant fibrosis, and the risk of anastomotic strictures is low. The number of cases in humans with established strictures in whom a splint was not used is small and the follow-up period is frequently less

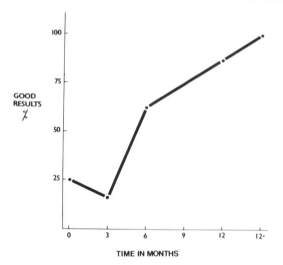

Fig. 6.16. Frequency of satisfactory results of surgery for traumatic biliary stricture related to the length of time the internal splint was retained.

than 3 years, so that adequate conclusions cannot be drawn, and the present authors continue to advocate the use of these internal splints.

There is insufficient information regarding the length of time internal splints should be retained following the repair of injuries recognised at operation and in which secondary changes have not occurred in the bile ducts. If a relatively accurate anastomosis is obtained it seems reasonable to use the splint merely as an external vent which prevents bile extravasation through the anastomosis. It can be removed when the anastomosis has healed, that is, after about 6–12 weeks. If local complications of suppuration or bile extravasation occur the tube should be left *in situ* for a longer period, probably 6 months.

Three types of internal splints are currently in use, the rubber T tube, the rubber Y tube, now uncommonly used, and transhepatic splinting with a straight tube which is probably the most commonly used splint at present. The long-armed rubber T tube is a satisfactory splint for end-to-end ductal anastomosis, but it can also be used for a choledochoduodenostomy, or a hepaticojejunos-tomy. The external arm of a T tube must never be brought out through the anastomosis [25]. It is led to the exterior through the bile duct above or below the anastomosis, or through a hole in the jejunum or duodenum in a biliary intestinal anastomosis. The authors do not recommend a T tube for difficult anastomoses high up in the porta hepatis, because these tubes have to be in place for about a year and they are liable to be dislodged accidentally or by the peristaltic activity of the bowel, so for these high strictures and injuries a transhepatic tube is advocated (Figs. 6.22, 6.23 & 6.25).

HEPATICOJEJUNOSTOMY ROUX-EN-Y
SURGICAL TECHNIQUE OF THE TYPICAL CASE

Exposure. The most satisfactory exposure is usually obtained through a long, right paramedian incision. It is unnecessary to do a thoracoabdominal exposure. The abdomen is opened in the lowest part of the incision, because this is least likely to be involved with adhesions. The adhesions are dissected from the parietal peritoneum and from the under-surface of the liver. This is usually a tedious procedure, because of previous operations and possibly because bile extravasation creates a large number of adhesions, which obliterate the usual cleavage planes.

The strictured area, as well as the proximal and distal bile duct, is best exposed after mobilisation of the hepatic flexure and duodenum. Both the hepatic flexure and the duodenum are best mobilised from below upward, starting in an area in which there are few adhesions (Figs. 6.17 & 6.18).

The method of mobilisation of the hepatic flexure and duodenum is similar to that used for exploration of the bile ducts, but it is more difficult owing to the adhesions.

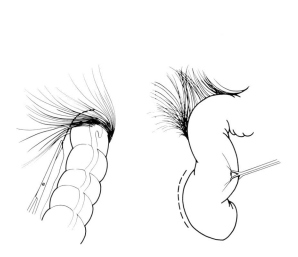

Fig. 6.17. (*far left*) Mobilisation of hepatic flexure from below up to gain access to the biliary tract. Redrawn from Warren, McDonald, and Kune [136].

Fig. 6.18. Mobilisation of the duodenum and head of pancreas from below up in the presence of adhesions, to gain access to the biliary tract. Dotted line indicates beginning of the incision in the visceral peritoneum. Redrawn from Warren, McDonald, and Kune [136].

Finding the distal bile duct. Following the mobilisation of the duodenum a search is made for the bile duct distal to the stricture. Useful landmarks are the common duct gland (see Common Bile Duct in Chapter 1) and the gastroduodenal artery. The distal common bile duct is situated in the anterior aspect of the gastrohepatic ligament and is almost always superiormedial to the common duct gland (Fig. 6.19).

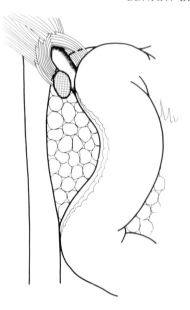

Fig. 6.19. Method of finding the bile duct distal to the stricture. Note 'common duct' lymph gland and fibrosis of the area. For further details see text.

Extensive dissection and sectioning of the pancreas to find the intrapancreatic portion of the common bile duct is inadvisable, because the morbidity associated with this is greater than the benefit gained from end-to-end ductal anastomosis [136].

When the bile duct distal to the stricture has been found its proximal end is trimmed and the duct is examined. If the distal duct is partially or completely obliterated by fibrosis, or if it cannot be made to distend to an adequate lumen (about 10 mm), it is not deemed suitable for anastomosis. If it is found suitable it should be explored with probes and forceps in the usual way, to make sure that no calculi or other forms of obstruction are present.

Finding the proximal duct. Obviously, the most important step of the operation is to find the bile duct proximal to the stricture or proximal to the site of injury in a recent case. This part of the operation can be most difficult and requires of the surgeon, a patient, systematic approach. The bile duct proximal to the stricture is usually found anterolateral to the pulsation of the hepatic artery at the liver hilum. Thus the dissection, which is usually a combination of sharp and blunt dissection, is best commenced about 2 or 3 cm to the right lateral side of the pulsation of the hepatic artery in the region of the porta. To the right of this arterial pulsation the occluded common hepatic duct may be identified by inspection, by feeling a soft distended bulging structure, by finding the cleavage plane between the anterior wall of the duct and the liver substance, by aspiration of bile with a needle and syringe, by identifying a ligature on the common hepatic duct, by identifying the track of an external biliary fistula, or by a combination of all these techniques (Fig. 6.20). Sometimes the fibrotic track of an internal fistula between the proximal bile duct and the duodenum is demonstrated at a stage

Fig. 6.20. Method of finding the bile duct proximal to the stricture. Note bulbous proximal end and fibrosis of the area. For further details see text.

when the adherent duodenal loop is being dissected off from the hilum of the liver. The fistulous track is usually cut across during this dissection. It is frequently narrow, fibrotic, and tortuous, and it oozes a little bile after it has been cut across, and a fine probe inserted upwards helps in the subsequent identification of the proximal bile duct.

When the proximal duct is found it is carefully dissected and trimmed by a combination of sharp and blunt dissection, until a rim of bile duct is obtained which is as free from fibrosis as possible. Operative surgery texts and articles on this subject tend to idealise the size and quality of this stump. The majority of these injuries are high injuries of the common hepatic duct made worse by subsequent retraction of the stump as well as by fibrosis, so that the reality confronting the surgeon is a few millimetres of fibrotic rim leading to a fibrous tunnel in the porta hepatis, oozing bile. Often it is not possible to be sure where fibrosis ends and bile duct mucosa begins. When the proximal duct has been so prepared it is explored carefully with probes, dilators, and forceps, to establish its patency and freedom from calculi and biliary debris. The proximal ducts are then carefully and repeatedly irrigated with warm saline. The most difficult cases are those in which the proximal end of the stricture is at the level of the union of the hepatic ducts, or when it involves individual hepatic ducts. There have been two reports of exposure of the intrahepatic ducts by separation of the functional lobes of the liver through the plane of the lobar fissure [126, 131]. This enabled the correction of intrahepatic biliary strictures and has also been used by the authors for injuries involving individual hepatic ducts.

Operative cholangiography. The needling of the proximal bile duct and the performance of an operative cholangiogram before the bile duct has been formally dissected is not often of great value, because the cholangiogram does not indicate the exact location of the ducts at the hilum of the liver [136]. The ducts still need to be dissected in the same manner, irrespective of an operative cholangiogram.

Once the proximal ducts have been dissected, however, an operative cholangiogram using a needle or a small catheter is most valuable in verifying the duct anatomy (Fig. 6.21). If the opening in the proximal duct has already been enlarged to its full width undue leakage of the contrast can be prevented by using a balloon catheter inflated in the lumen of the bile duct stump. By this method the surgeon can be sure that the whole of the strictured area has been dealt with and that the anastomosis which is to follow will achieve complete and adequate biliary decompression.

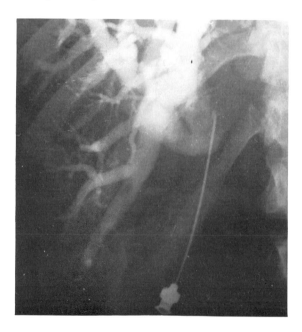

Fig. 6.21. Operative cholangiogram of a typical high stricture, which verifies the duct anatomy showing that the stricture is at the commencement of the common hepatic duct.

Biopsy. In some cases an underlying carcinoma of the bile ducts is overlooked, because it is assumed that the cause of the symptoms after the first operation is due to the development of a traumatic stricture. Biopsy of tissue in the strictured area and of adjacent lymph glands is advisable when the strictured area has been dissected out.

Construction of the hepaticojejunostomy The general principles of biliary intestinal anastomosis require a meticulous surgical technique aimed at mucosa-to-mucosa apposition, a stoma as wide as possible, and lack of tension on the anastomosis [117, 118]. Unfortunately, these principles cannot always be satisfied in practice, although in recent years with certain advances in surgical technique as described below, we are getting closer to these ideals. The techniques of plastic repair of minimal strictures, end-to-end anastomosis, and choledocho-duodenostomy, have already been described. The description which follows refers to the most common procedure, hepaticojejunostomy.

Transhepatic tube. It has been noted that the present authors regard the use of an internal splint as an essential part of bile duct reconstruction. For the usual type of high injury involving the common hepatic duct the use of a transhepatic tube, widely advocated by Paul Praderi in Uruguay and by Rodney Smith in London (now Lord Smith of Marlow), has been an important advance in surgical management [94, 95, 115, 117]. This involves the passage of curved bile duct forceps through the proximal duct and up one of the main hepatic ducts. Then perforating the surface of the liver, a long straight rubber tube, appropriately fenestrated, is pulled down and placed across the anastomosis (Fig. 6.22). This technique is also eminently suitable for the splinting of anastomoses involving individual hepatic ducts (Fig. 6.23). Also, if the distal limb of this tube is brought out through the jejunum to the surface, it is possible to replace a plugged tube at a later date without reoperation, and this is called a U tube (Fig. 6.23) [10, 94, 107, 125].

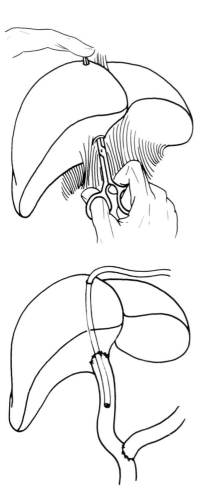

Fig. 6.22. Method of insertion of a transhepatic tube. (*top*) Liver perforated from below with angled bile duct forceps. (bottom) Transhepatic tube in place. Redrawn from Smith [117].

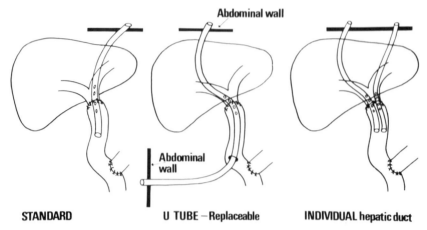

Fig. 6.23. Various methods of transhepatic intubation. (*left*) The standard fenestrated transhepatic tube. (*middle*) The fenestrated U tube, which is replaceable. (*right*) Transhepatic tubes into each individual hepatic duct.

Preparation of Roux-en-Y jejunal segment. A defunctionalised segment of jejunum is constructed in the usual way and this should be at least 40 cm long in order to prevent gastrointestinal reflux (Figs. 6.22–6.25). The end of the jejunum is closed and a new opening is made in the side of the jejunum close to the end. The jejunal segment is brought to the porta hepatis anterior to the colon, because this situation facilitates subsequent procedures with it, should reoperation be necessary later.

Mucosal apposition or 'mucosal graft'. In the uncommon situation when an adequate margin of relatively healthy proximal bile duct with normal mucosa is present, a conventional mucosa-to-mucosa anastomosis is constructed using a single row of fine interrupted through-and-through sutures (Fig. 6.24). If the bile duct is thick-walled it is possible to use two layers with a posterior interrupted layer of seromuscular on the jejunal side and peridochal adventitia on the bile duct side, followed by a continuous all-coats layer of chromic catgut or Dexon. A two-layer anastomosis has the advantage over the one-layer anastomosis in that it is usually completely bile tight. In the one-layer anastomosis it makes no difference to the end result whether absorbable or non-absorbable sutures are used [16]. After the anastomosis has been completed a few sutures are used to suspend the jejunum to the under-surface of the liver, to decrease drag on the anastomosis.

In the usual case it is not possible to perform an accurate mucosa-to-mucosa anastomosis with confidence, because the proximal bile duct, even after meticulous dissection, is merely a fibrous rim leading to a fibrous tunnel in the porta hepatis. For this type of case a modification of hepaticojejunostomy, the 'mucosal graft' procedure, was introduced by Lord Smith of Marlow, which in the authors' experience represents an important advance in surgical technique for these difficult problems [63, 115, 119]. A Roux-en-Y jejunal segment is prepared

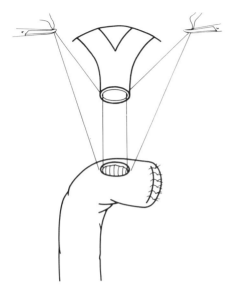

Fig. 6.24. Technique of end-to-side hepaticojejunostomy Roux-en-Y using mucosa-
to-mucosa apposition.

in the usual way, the end closed, and a seromuscular disc about 1.5 cm in
diameter is excised from the side of the jejunum, but the mucosa is left intact. The
margins are slightly undermined and by gently squeezing the air in the jejunal
segment this 'mucosal graft' balloons out (Fig. 6.25). The straight transhepatic
tube is now in place, coming through the common hepatic duct stump, and this
end is now placed into the jejunal segment through a small opening created at the
top of the ballooned-out mucosa. The tube is positioned so that two fenestrations
are in the hepatic duct in order to allow bile to trickle through from either hepatic
duct. The ballooned mucosa is then 'hitched up' to the tube by two or three
absorbable sutures which are passed through the mucosa and the tube. The
transhepatic tube, to which is now attached the mucosal graft and therefore the

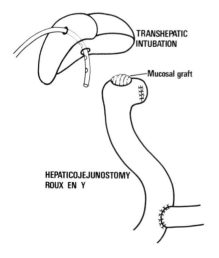

Fig. 6.25. Diagram illustrating the essential aspects of biliary reconstruction of a
typical bile duct injury. This involves a
hepaticojejunostomy Roux-en-Y, transhepatic intubation, and a 'mucosal graft'
type of anastomosis.

jejunal segment, is pulled gently into the fibrous tunnel stump of the common hepatic duct until it feels snug and there is a firm elastic resistance to pull. The intended effect of this manoeuvre is to place a ring of jejunal mucosa high up in the common hepatic duct and thereby facilitate mucosa-to-mucosa apposition and healing without undue fibrosis, thus lowering the risk of recurrent stricture formation. It is emphasised that, with careful attention to detail, this is techni-cally an easier operation than a formal anastomosis, as no sutures are inserted. When the 'mucosal graft' is in place the jejunal segment is suspended to the under-surface of the liver by a few sutures in order to decrease drag on the mucosal graft.

External drainage. External drainage of the operative area is necessary to drain serous fluid or blood, but more especially, any bile which had leaked through the anastomosis. Suction drainage, particularly of the sump type, is most useful in reducing local postoperative septic complications, such as subhepatic and sub-phrenic collections.

Management of the transhepatic tube. The tube is allowed to drain freely for the first 2 weeks after surgery. A cholangiogram is then performed and here the patient needs to be positioned with a slight head-down tilt and the contrast medium injected slowly in order to fill the hepatic ducts. Subsequently, one or two repeat cholangiograms are useful to check the position of the tube and also to confirm that the hepatic ducts are adequately decompressed (Fig. 6.26). Irriga-tion of the tube once or twice per week by the patient with about 50 ml of water is usually advised, but its value is probably only as 'occupational therapy' as the tubes tend to slowly silt up with biliary mud over a period of a few months. The length of time the tube is kept in place has already been discussed in the previous section dealing with internal splints, but as a guideline the time is about 6 months if the anastomosis or mucosal graft was felt to be accurately done, and about 12 months for the very difficult cases in which the surgeon was unhappy about adequate mucosal apposition. In the really severe cases it may be decided to leave the tube in place for several years, but in such cases, the tubes need to be replaced every 6–12 months by using a U-tube arrangement as shown in Fig. 6.23, because they inevitably block up with biliary debris. Blocking of the tube is usually heralded by bouts of cholangitis with fever and rigors.

MANAGEMENT OF PORTAL HYPERTENSION

In a review of 900 patients treated for an established biliary stricture at the Lahey Clinic in Boston, Sedgwick, Poulantzas, and Kune, 1966, found that portal hypertension of some degree was present in about 20 per cent. When the bile duct stricture had been effectively treated significant complications of portal hyper-tension were uncommon. Bleeding oesophageal varices are the commonest complication, whereas hypersplenism or the development of ascites is much less common, and when these complications occur the prognosis becomes much graver [113, 141].

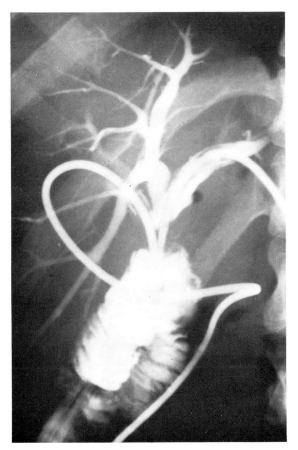

Fig. 6.26. Transhepatic tube cholangiogram to check state of anastomosis and bile ducts before removal of the tube. (In this case, each hepatic duct was joined individually to the jejunum using two transhepatic tubes.)

The usual type of patient who develops complications of portal hypertension is one whose biliary stricture had been neglected for some time, and frequently one or more successful attempts at repair had been made. In the Lahey Clinic series portal hypertension appeared on the average 4–5 years after the onset of the stricture, but in neglected strictures it appeared within 2 years. Bleeding varices were first noted from 1–9 years after onset of the stricture, the average being 5 years [113].

The management of these difficult cases has received relatively little attention in the literature [4, 38, 113, 141]. Four aspects of this problem require discussion.

Torrential haemorrhage during stricture repair. If profuse haemorrhage due to portal hypertension is encountered during the course of stricture repair a hepaticostomy drainage is performed as the first procedure. A splenorenal shunt can be established after about 3 weeks, when improvement of liver function has taken place. A shunt is not usually possible at the first procedure, because of a high degree of biliary obstruction and poor liver function. Reconstruction of the bile ducts is performed at a third operation when liver function is at an optimum level. This third operation can be carried out with a minimum of bleeding [113, 136].

Bleeding oesophageal varices and uncorrected strictures. Patients may present with severe bleeding oesophageal varices in the presence of uncorrected biliary strictures. These patients usually have lesser degrees of biliary obstruction than the first group, possibly because those with severe biliary tract symptoms come to operation sooner. If the bleeding does not stop with conservative measures a two-stage operation is recommended. An immediate splenorenal shunt is the first stage and bile duct reconstruction is the second, performed a few weeks later [113, 141].

Bleeding oesophageal varices and corrected strictures. These are usually patients who had severe biliary cirrhosis at the time of stricture correction. Irreversible changes have probably occurred in the liver, and the onset of bleeding varices may be expected to occur with the same frequency as in cirrhosis from any cause. A splenorenal shunt is indicated, sometimes as an emergency measure, or as an interval operation after a severe bleed, if the patient satisfies the accepted preoperative criteria for the performance of a shunt [77, 113, 114].

Hypersplenism. Patients sometimes present with hypersplenism; these are recommended to have a splenectomy and a splenorenal shunt. A satisfactory result may be expected, particularly if liver function is not grossly impaired [113].

Surgical treatment. A splenorenal, rather than a portacaval, shunt is advised. The latter type is technically difficult or impossible, because of the previous surgery in the area, and also subsequent reconstructive work on the bile ducts may jeopardise the patency of the shunt [113]. In patients with uncorrected strictures a shunt may be performed with relatively poor liver function, if the surgeon anticipates that hepatic function will improve following repair of the stricture [113, 114].

This group of patients are usually poor surgical risks. Their morale is low and they have usually lost all hope of being restored to normal health. In practise their management is much more difficult than this relatively facile description would suggest [4, 113].

PROGNOSIS AND RESULTS

FACTORS INFLUENCING PROGNOSIS
The following factors are obviously interrelated and are important in determining the prognosis of traumatic biliary strictures:
1. Location of the stricture.
2. Quality of the proximal bile duct.
3. Extent of irreversible liver damage.
4. Adequacy of surgical reconstruction.

The proximal limit of the stricture has a considerable influence on the final result, probably because the more proximal the stricture the more difficult it is to perform an adequate reconstruction. When the proximal limit is intrahepatic, or just at the porta hepatis, the ultimate result is significantly worse than when the proximal limit is more distally situated [27, 63, 136].

The quality of the proximal bile duct in terms of scarring and pericholedo-chitis is important. The more scarred the area the more difficult it is to repair, and the more likely that restenosis will follow. The number of previous repair procedures adversely influences the final result although, ultimately, a good result can still be obtained after several repairs [24, 64, 137].

Irreversible liver damage with biliary cirrhosis and the presence of portal hypertension with bleeding oesophageal varices clearly militate against a satis-factory outcome, as has just been described in the preceding section. The sequel of prolonged unrelieved biliary obstruction is progression of liver damage with its attendant complications, which ultimately determines the prognosis. Patients die from liver failure or from the complications of portal hypertension. The latter can sometimes be favourably influenced by the performance of portal systemic shunts.

The adequacy of surgical reconstruction is paramount in determining the prognosis. Untreated cases have a uniformly fatal termination. Surgical treat-ment which offers only partial relief of biliary obstruction also leads to progres-sive liver damage and ultimately a fatal outcome. Clearly, the surgeon perform-ing the reconstructive operation must have the ability and the experience to choose the most appropriate procedure in order to give the patient the best possible chance to be restored to normal health. The authors believe that the increasing use of the transhepatic tube, of a Roux-en-Y hepaticojejunostomy, and a 'mucosal graft', have been major recent advances in surgical technique, all contributing to a better prognosis [63, 115, 141].

OPERATIVE MORTALITY AND MORBIDITY
The operative mortality is 5–8 per cent [24, 63, 64, 141]. The common causes of mortality are hepatorenal failure, uncontrollable haemorrhage, or both. Severe infections, external fistulas, and pulmonary complications, are the causes of most of the remaining operative deaths.

The postoperative morbidity following reconstructive surgery is high. At least one patient in ten is likely to have one or more major non-fatal complica-tions [24]. The common non-fatal complications are major infections (sub-phrenic, subhepatic, pelvic, wound, cholangitis, septicaemia), major haemor-rhage, external fistulas, and pulmonary complications.

The incidence of restenosis is difficult to compute accurately, but in most large series in the past it has been about 30 per cent [25, 64]. When restenosis occurs the patient must be subjected to a further operation, because an ultimately good result can still be obtained even after several failures. Restenosis usually occurs within the first 3 years after repair and is uncommon after that time [25]. In more recent series the incidence of restenosis after 3 years is much lower, and it is of the order of 10–15 per cent [63, 141].

At present, approximately 85 per cent of patients who have sustained an operative injury of the bile ducts are restored to normal health if surgical reconstruction is undertaken by those experienced in this type of surgery [25, 63, 64, 102, 129, 141]. The ultimate mortality has been about 30 per cent in the past, now reduced to about 15 per cent in more recent series. About 5–8 per cent die in the early postoperative period and the rest die from liver failure and from the complications of portal hypertension, especially bleeding oesophageal varices, months or years later.

POSTINFLAMMATORY STRICTURES

These are uncommon bile duct strictures, usually seen in association with either chronic pancreatitis or with choledocholithiasis.

STRICTURES AND CHRONIC PANCREATITIS

Transient or persistent cholestasis with jaundice is seen in about one-third of patients who have chronic pancreatitis [106]. One of the less common causes of cholestasis in this group of patients is a biliary stricture.

PATHOLOGICAL FEATURES
The usual type of stricture is a long, narrow stricture of the retropancreatic part of the common bile duct, and it is thought to be due to peripancreatic sclerosis as seen in Fig. 6.27 [105]. These strictures are usually seen only in advanced cases of chronic calcific pancreatitis, usually of the alcoholic type. However, the authors have also seen shorter strictures in the distal end of the common bile duct with chronic non-alcoholic pancreatitis, as shown in Fig. 6.28, as well as examples of definite stenosis of the sphincter of Oddi in association with definite chronic pancreatitis.

CLINICAL FEATURES
The usual clinical signal is transient jaundice with or without pain and only very occasionally is it associated with persistent jaundice [106]. Sarles and his colleagues in Marseille have found cholangitis with fever and rigors to be exceptional in these cases, while Warshaw from Boston and the present writers have found it to be present in a significant number [106, 140]. In our cases, cholangitis was seen especially in advanced alcoholic cases, who were also debilitated and malnourished.

RADIOLOGICAL FEATURES
The usual type of stricture seen at endoscopic retrograde, percutaneous transhepatic, or operative cholangiography, is a long stenosis of variable length involving the retropancreatic portion of the common bile duct and shown in Fig. 6.27. The common bile duct above the stricture is usually dilated and in a few cases also contains biliary debris, or 'primary' soft gallstones (Chapter 5). An important

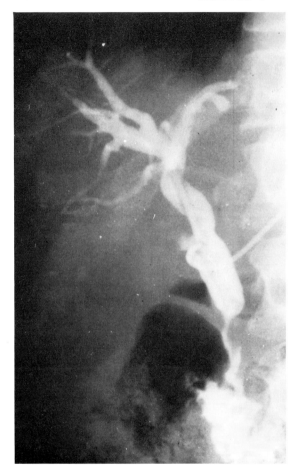

Fig. 6.27. Long, narrow stricture of the retropancreatic bile duct, characteristic of a postinflammatory stricture of chronic pancreatitis.

radiological feature which distinguishes this type of stricture from a malignant stricture is that some contrast gets through the stricture, outlining the entire bile duct and the duodenum, whereas in a malignant obstruction there is usually a complete block to the passage of the contrast medium (Chapter 4 and Fig. 4.11).

Less commonly, one sees a short stricture in the distal end of the bile duct in association with chronic pancreatitis as seen in Fig. 6.28 and, rarely, the stenosis is at the level of the papilla of Vater only.

TREATMENT
Surgical treatment is reserved for marked strictures, whatever their length, which have caused cholestasis or cholangitis, or both [106, 140]. Biliary bypass procedures sometimes need to be combined with pancreatic ductal decompression, such as pancreaticojejunostomy, as was performed on the patient whose cholangiogram is shown in Fig. 6.28.

The most suitable biliary bypass procedure in these cases employs the common bile duct, and choledochojejunostomy Roux-en-Y is superior to side-to-side

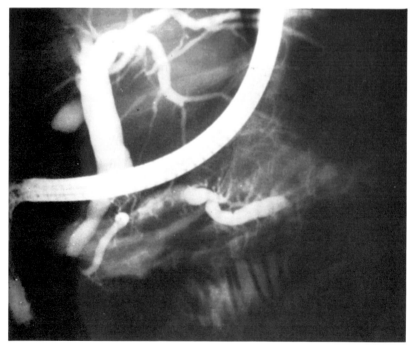

Fig. 6.28. Short stricture of distal common bile duct and distal pancreatic duct in a patient with chronic pancreatitis and gallstones, as revealed on an ERCP.

choledochoduodenostomy, although the latter operation is simpler and is preferable in the poor-risk patient (Chapter 14). Cholecystojejunostomy is a poor long-term bypass operation, while transduodenal sphincterotomy or sphincteroplasty will not deal with these strictures and these procedures are, therefore, not advocated in this situation. Properly constructed biliary bypass operations deal very well with these strictures, affording long-term relief of cholestasis and cholangitis [65].

STRICTURES AND CHOLEDOCHOLITHIASIS

This is a rare complication of choledocholithiasis. For example, Cattell and Braasch in 1959 only had three such cases in a series of 501 biliary strictures. Intrahepatic strictures in association with intrahepatic gallstones are frequently seen in advanced cases of recurrent pyogenic cholangitis seen in South-east Asia, and this is discussed in Chapter 9. Intrahepatic gallstones, consisting mainly of calcium bilirubinate, appear to be relatively commonly present in Japan and these can be associated with intrahepatic strictures, but will not be further discussed here [73, 128]. Patients who, in the past, have had biliary tract surgery for gallstones and later develop a stricture are also excluded, because the stricture is likely to be the result of operative injury.

The authors are indebted to Professor John M. Ham of Sydney, Australia, who has had personal experience with 12 strictures of the bile duct associated with choledocholithiasis, and has helped us to crytallise our ideas on diagnosis and management.

RADIOLOGY

Strictures in this group typically involve a short segment of the bile duct and may occur in any part of the bile duct (Fig. 6.29).

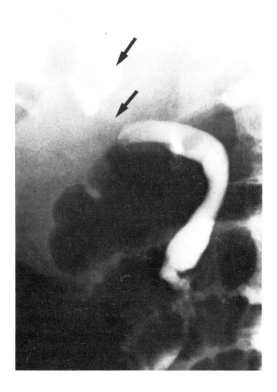

Fig. 6.29. Endoscopic retrograde cholangiogram showing a localised bile duct stricture of the common hepatic duct, in association with choledocholithiasis.

DIAGNOSIS

Diagnosis is based on cholangiography and on the operative findings. Differentiation of these localised strictures from carcinoma of the bile duct may be difficult in some cases when direct visualisation of the mucosa by choledochoscopy, aided by intraluminal biopsy or cytology, can be diagnostic. It is important to emphasise that only positive biopsy or cytology for carcinoma is diagnostic, and a negative biopsy does *not* exclude cancer. In doubtful cases only a long period of follow-up extending over several years will prove the benign nature of the stricture, as some localised sclerosing carcinomas of the bile duct can be very slow-growing.

TREATMENT

A suitably constructed biliary bypass usually relieves the symptoms very effect-ively. The nature of the bypass depends on the site and extent of the stricture and follows the principles which are described in the other sections of this chapter. Thus, for a short stricture of the distal common bile duct, a side-to-side choledo-choduodenostomy is usually satisfactory, while for more proximal or more extensive strictures a choledochojejunostomy, or a hepaticojejunostomy Roux-en-Y is most suitable. Associated bile duct gallstones are naturally also removed. Cholecystojejunostomy is not advocated because it frequently fails in the long-term.

PRIMARY SCLEROSING CHOLANGITIS

Progressive inflammatory obliteration of the bile ducts—primary sclerosing cholangitis—is an uncommon but distinct entity of uncertain cause. This condi-tion has been described under various names, such as obliterative cholangitis, sclerostenosing cholangitis, stenosing cholangitis, and chronic fibrosing choledo-chitis [40, 58, 67, 101].

In some cases an obliterative process is secondary to severe peridochal infection, such as a subhepatic abscess; in others it follows biliary surgery with bile extravasation, or it follows cholecystitis or cholangitis due to gallstones [135]. In these cases the process is secondary to the underlying cause. Such cases are excluded from this discussion. Probably not more than 100 genuine cases have so far been described [30].

AETIOLOGY

The cause of primary sclerosing cholangitis is uncertain. There are a number of aetiologic associations.

ULCERATIVE COLITIS

The most commonly associated disease of primary sclerosing cholangitis is ulcerative colitis, present or past [40, 52, 96, 116, 127, 130, 135]. The chronic ulcerative colitis is frequently longstanding or entirely quiescent when the condi-tion of sclerosing cholangitis makes its appearance.

Some workers have tried to fit sclerosing cholangitis into the spectrum of cholestatic liver disease, which is known to be associated with chronic ulcerative colitis. Others have used the colitis as evidence for an infective or autoimmune basis of the condition.

INFECTION

Evidence exists from both clinical and experimental studies that a low-grade portal bacteraemia is frequently present in patients with ulcerative colitis and, occasionally, also present in normal subjects, and that some of these organisms are excreted into the bile [17, 108, 112].

It is of interest that there is only one report in the literature of the association of primary sclerosing cholangitis and Crohn's disease [7]. The possible reason for this, if the infective theory is pursued, is that the small bowel is sterile or has only a low bacterial content and ulceration is less frequent in Crohn's disease than in ulcerative colitis.

Some patients have apparently improved with the use of antibiotics, and after colectomy, and this may be taken as further evidence of an infective origin.

Most of the evidence of the infective theory is circumstantial, and it is not known how the organisms set up an inflammatory process in the absence of underlying biliary stasis.

AUTOIMMUNITY
An autoimmune basis for the association of primary sclerosing cholangitis and ulcerative colitis is a theoretical possibility, but direct evidence is not available and there are few reports of immunological studies in these patients [127, 144].

CARCINOMA
Some hold the view that these cases are in fact examples of slowly growing sclerosing carcinoma of the bile ducts [6]. Certainly, most of the cases presented to the writers as examples of primary sclerosing cholangitis turned out to be bile duct carcinomas. Others believe this to be entirely a non-malignant clinical entity and undoubtedly there are now sufficient well-documented reports to justify this view [135]. In recent years evidence has accumulated which weds these opposing views. Patients with chronic ulcerative colitis may develop not only an inflammatory condition of the liver and bile ducts, but also subsequently a carcinoma of the liver and biliary tract [8, 45, 46, 90, 97].

PATHOLOGY

EXTENT OF INVOLVEMENT
The condition is usually a diffuse process involving both extrahepatic and intrahepatic ducts with the changes more marked in the extrahepatic and hilar ducts. A number of segmental cases have also been described, but it is debatable whether these represent the same entity [110, 135]. They are, however, included here and referred to as cases with 'segmental involvement'. Bhathal and Powell in 1969 described a variant of primary sclerosing cholangitis, which affected intrahepatic ducts only, and which would be difficult to differentiate from primary biliary cirrhosis, but in these cases mitochondrial antibodies are absent [12]. Patients with chronic ulcerative colitis usually have diffuse bile duct involvement, including liver changes of cholestasis, pericholangitis, and periductal fibrosis.

HISTOLOGICAL APPEARANCE
The histological appearance of the involved bile ducts is similar, irrespective of whether it is diffusely or segmentally involved. The mucosa is damaged, showing atrophy and patchy necrosis, and there is a variable degree of subepithelial and peridochal chronic inflammatory reaction with fibrosis. Giant cell formation and

lymph follicles have not been reported. Amyloid was seen in some cases, sugges-tive of a chronic septic process [135].

ASSOCIATED PATHOLOGICAL CHANGES
Fleshy, hyperplastic lymph nodes are frequently present in the porta hepatis and these probably mirror the extent of the chronic inflammatory process in the bile ducts [52, 135].

The liver changes of cholestasis, pericholangitis, and pericholedochal fibrosis, have already been mentioned. The appearance of biliary cirrhosis and portal hypertension is secondary to the chronic obliterative process and cholan-gitis. The rapidity with which liver damage and portal hypertension develop and progress is the most important determinant of the prognosis in an individual case [116, 135].

Associated chronic ulcerative colitis is frequent. In some cases associated chronic pancreatitis has also been noted [89, 101, 111, 116].

DIAGNOSIS

CRITERIA FOR DIAGNOSIS
The essential criterion is diffuse (or rarely segmental) thickening and stenosis mainly involving the extrahepatic bile ducts, the absence of previous biliary surgery, biliary calculi, previous intra-abdominal sepsis and the exclusion of sclerosing carcinoma of the bile ducts by long follow-up or post-mortem exam-ination.

CLINICAL AND LABORATORY FEATURES
The clinical features are those of chronic progressive biliary tract obstruction and cholangitis. Nothing in the clinical features is typical of primary sclerosing cholangitis. Indeed, the inability to make a preoperative diagnosis is the charac-teristic feature of the condition.

The length of history is variable, ranging from months to years. Almost all the patients are jaundiced, they are in poor health, and many have a history of chills and fever. Some have biliary tract pain. Hepatomegaly and splenomegaly are common [135].

Although chronic ulcerative colitis is commonly associated with primary sclerosing cholangitis the reverse does not hold. Thus, jaundiced patients with ulcerative colitis are more likely to have other causes for their jaundice, such as purely hepatic involvement.

Laboratory tests indicate a cholestatic type of jaundice, frequently with a particularly high level of serum alkaline phosphatase [87, 135, 144].

RADIOLOGICAL FEATURES
Cholecystography and intravenous cholangiography cannot be done, because almost all the patients are jaundiced. Percutaneous transhepatic cholangiogra-phy, endoscopic retrograde cholangiography and operative cholangiography will add important evidence to the diagnosis and should be performed in every

suspected case. This will show a diffuse, or rarely, a localised smooth or irregular narrowing of the bile ducts, at times with a spider-leg appearance. In some cases a beaded appearance is seen indicating that the process is not uniform along the length of the bile duct, but this appearance is not specific to sclerosing cholangitis [144]. In segmentally involved cases there is often bile duct dilatation proximal to the stenotic portion. Clearly, these cholangiographic appearances may be impossible to distinguish from bile duct carcinoma. Figs. 6.30–6.32 are five cholangiograms which show the spectrum of radiological appearances that may be encountered in primary sclerosing cholangitis.

OPERATIVE FINDINGS

The definite diagnosis of primary sclerosing cholangitis can be made only at operation. There is a diffuse or localised thickening of the bile ducts. The involved ducts have a particularly narrow lumen. Operative cholangiography is important to perform and the various possible findings have already been described.

There may be biliary debris proximal to the stricture, and usually there is evidence of biliary cirrhosis and portal hypertension. Fleshy peridochal lymph glands are frequently seen; biopsy of these merely shows hyperplasia [135].

It is particularly important to exclude at operation carcinoma of the bile ducts [6, 135]. In the absence of obvious local spread and of lymph-nodal, peritoneal, or liver metastases this distinction may be difficult, because the two conditions appear similar, and also because a carcinoma may develop in primary sclerosing cholangitis. Biopsy and frozen section examination of peridochal lymph nodes may be helpful, but only if this is positive of a secondary carcinoma.

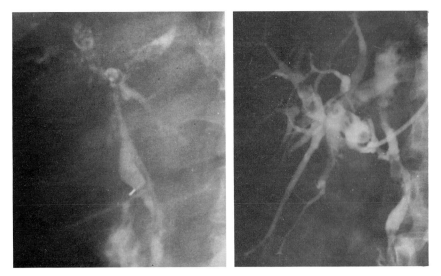

Fig. 6.30. (*left*) Cholangiogram of diffuse primary sclerosing cholangitis showing 'the spider leg' appearance of the intrahepatic bile ducts. (*right*) Cholangiogram of diffuse primary sclerosing cholangitis showing 'the beaded' appearance.

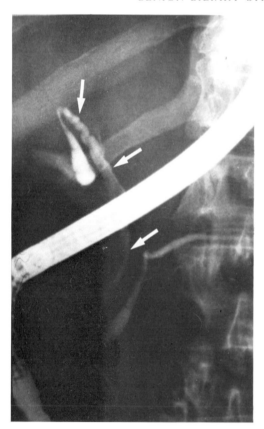

Fig. 6.31. T-tube cholangiogram of primary sclerosing cholangitis involving mainly the extrahepatic ducts. Note irregular narrowing of the bile duct.

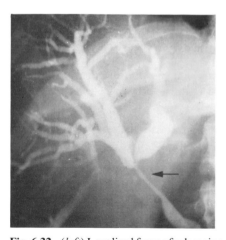
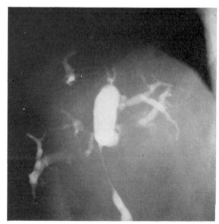

Fig. 6.32. (*left*) Localised form of sclerosing cholangitis mainly involving the distal half of the common hepatic duct and proximal common bile duct (arrow). (*right*) Localised form of sclerosing cholangitis involving the common hepatic duct; courtesy of Dr. K. W. Warren, Boston. Differentiation from bile duct cancer may be difficult in these cases.

Choledochostomy and intracholedochal mucosal biopsy using a scoop or a spoon, and frozen section examination of the specimen or cytology, have proved a most valuable mode of peroperative differentiation of the two conditions [135].

TREATMENT

DIFFUSE INVOLVEMENT
The treatment of patients with diffuse involvement is usually unsatisfactory.

Surgical decompression. The aim of biliary decompression is the relief of obstructive symptoms and the protection of the liver from further damage. Because of the diffuse nature of the condition, and because of some involvement of the intrahepatic bile ducts, adequate decompression cannot usually be achieved.

Some reports have appeared showing improvement following prolonged external drainage with a T tube or following hepaticojejunostomy over an indwelling Y tube [52, 116, 135]. It is difficult to understand why a T tube or a Y tube in the middle of a thickened duct, which often has multiple sites of narrowing proximally, should improve biliary drainage. Perhaps these tubes are occasionally beneficial by decreasing the total 'obstructive load'. They are certainly of value in performing serial T-tube cholangiograms to assess changes in bile duct calibre.

Antibiotics. Broad-spectrum antibiotics have been used in a number of cases after an operative diagnosis had been made. In some, improvement of the jaundice and control of cholangitis have been reported [96, 110, 111, 144]. Antibiotics should only be used to control cholangitis and not on a long-term basis [144].

Cortisone. There is considerable evidence that long-term corticosteroid therapy is valuable [110,144]. Initial treatment with prednisolone 30–50 mg daily is advised until jaundice is controlled and then reduced to a maintenance level of 10–15 mg daily. Treatment is continued for at least 6 months.

Colectomy. Patients with diffuse primary sclerosing cholangitis, seen in association with chronic ulcerative colitis, have shown improvement following total colectomy [96, 135]. Colectomy was also beneficial in some patients who had ulcerative colitis with liver involvement of cholestasis and pericholangitis in the absence of major bile duct involvement. However, there is insufficient evidence at present to advocate colectomy routinely.

SEGMENTAL INVOLVEMENT
The place of surgical decompression is logical in the presence of localised disease. It follows principles which are similar to the surgical treatment of traumatic biliary strictures. Thus, if the involvement is of the distal common bile duct,

choledochojejunostomy or choledochoduodenostomy may be done. If the segment involves the proximal part of the common duct, hepaticojejunostomy is performed. When the stenotic segment involves the intrahepatic portions of the hepatic ducts the mode of surgical decompression is more difficult. The bile duct may be divided at the level of the common hepatic duct, followed by the forcible dilatation of the involved segments and the construction of a hepaticojejunostomy over a Y tube, a transhepatic tube or a U tube as described earlier in this chapter in the section dealing with traumatic strictures.

PROGNOSIS

The outlook for patients with diffuse primary sclerosing cholangitis is gloomy. A review of the literature of thoroughly documented cases shows that about 90 per cent are dead or else live with evidence of progressive liver damage and jaundice, and only about 10 per cent are apparently well [116, 127, 135]. In the majority of cases a fatal outcome can be expected between 3 and 8 years after the onset of symptoms. Death is usually due to liver failure, or to bleeding oesophageal varices. There is little evidence at present that medical or surgical treatment influences the ultimate prognosis to a great extent, but it does provide temporary improvement of symptoms.

The prognosis of the less common type of case with localised involvement can be favourably influenced by adequate surgical decompression of the biliary tract [135]. When surgical relief of the obstruction is not obtained the ultimate prognosis is similar to that seen in diffuse primary sclerosing cholangitis [116].

STENOSIS OF THE PAPILLA OF VATER

BY IAN C. ROBERTS-THOMSON

Stenosis of the papilla of Vater implies partial obstruction to the outflow of biliary or pancreatic secretions, because of an inflammatory stricture in the region of the papilla. The pathogenesis of the disorder remains unclear and there is a continuing controversy regarding its frequency and mode of diagnosis. The current status of this disorder is here reviewed, knowing that at present the disease cannot be clearly defined on clinical, investigational, pathological, or operative criteria.

ANATOMICAL CONSIDERATIONS

The musculature of the papilla is a complex system consisting of a spiral longitudinal muscle, a sphincter at the orifice of the papilla, and separate sphincters located at the distal ends of the common bile duct and main pancreatic duct [15, 124]. Theoretically, an inflammatory process might only involve one of the three sphincters, but radiological evidence of narrowing of both ducts exists in many patients. However, differences in the degree of narrowing of one or other duct might account for variation in the clinical presentation between individual patients.

The frequency of stenosis of the papilla in patients subjected to biliary surgery has varied widely in several studies. The major reason appears to be due to differences in the criteria for diagnosis. Cholangiography with manometry was advocated by Mallet-Guy and led to a diagnosis of stenosis in 10–30 per cent of all biliary operations [50, 74]. With experience, the diagnostic rate decreased in some centres, in part because alternative techniques such as fluoroscopy and 'flowmetry' were adopted [51]. In general, the frequency of stenosis of the papilla has been lower in centres in which the diagnosis was based on operative findings. Thus, Colcock and Perey found organic stenosis in only 4 per cent of 503 explorations of the common bile duct, while Paulino and Roselli had a diagnostic rate of 2.5 per cent in 511 biliary operations [28, 93]. However, a higher frequency was noted by Madden in patients with bile duct stones, many of whom were considered to have 'primary stasis stones' (Chapter 5) [69]. In the absence of firm criteria for diagnosis the frequency of stenosis remains unclear although concern has been expressed that the disorder has been overdiagnosed [134],

AETIOLOGY

The factors leading to the development of stenosis of the papilla remain unknown in most patients. The hypothesis that sphincteric spasm ultimately results in stenosis cannot be tested at the present time. Chronic papillitis may precede the development of stenosis and may arise from a number of disorders.

GALLSTONES
In most studies the majority of patients have calculi in the gallbladder or bile duct at the time of diagnosis, or have had previous surgery for gallstone disease [2, 23, 41, 93]. In some patients bile duct stones may be secondary to the stenotic process and may not be of aetiological importance. Inflammation of the papilla is observed at duodenoscopy in about 50 per cent of patients with choledocholithiasis, but endoscopic studies have not been reported following surgery and endoscopic biopsies, being relatively superficial, do not permit an assessment of inflammation in the region of the ducts.

PANCREATITIS
Papillitis frequently accompanies overt clinical episodes of pancreatitis. However, at present, there is no evidence that relapsing pancreatitis results in stenosis of the papilla. Spasm of the sphincter of Oddi followed by reflux of bile into pancreatic ducts was postulated as a cause of recurrent pancreatitis by Doubilet and Mulholland [35]. They performed sphincterotomy and cholecystectomy in 319 patients with recurrent pancreatitis with satisfactory relief from symptoms in

the majority of patients. However, 44 per cent of patients had a 'diseased' gallbladder and the additional benefit from sphincterotomy remains unclear.

DAMAGE TO BILIARY EPITHELIUM
In some series substantial numbers of patients with stenosis of the papilla had prior exploration of the common bile duct. Visual and histological studies suggest that instrumental dilatation of the papilla results in significant trauma if performed with a Bakes dilator larger than number 3 [99]. However, there is no evidence that instrumental dilatation of the papilla increases the likelihood of subsequent stenosis [5, 18]. Stenosis may also occur following operative or endoscopic sphincterotomy, perhaps because of scar formation related to the incision or to subsequent low-grade infection in the region of the papilla [50].

IDIOPATHIC PAPILLITIS
Papillitis may rarely occur in the absence of one of the above disorders. The aetiology of this syndrome remains unclear, but one possible explanation is a bacterial infection in the mucous glands of the papilla [1].

PATHOLOGY

A variety of pathological changes have been described in association with stenosis of the papilla. These include fibrosis, muscle hypertrophy, mucosal proliferation, glandular abnormalities, and cellular infiltration. Marked fibrosis was noted in biopsies from ten of 38 patients studied by Acosta and Nardi, but in only three of 23 patients studied by Paulino and Cavalcanti [1, 92]. Muscle hypertrophy was the predominant abnormality in patients described by Paulino and Cavalcanti, but was recognised less frequently by other authors [2, 84, 92]. Mucosal proliferation, variably described as hyperplasia or pseudopolyp formation, appeared to occur in 10–20 per cent of patients. Cystic dilatation of submucosal glands was noted in some patients and was usually associated with severe chronic inflammation.

Histological evidence of inflammation was observed in most patients, although variation was noted in the site and severity of inflammation and in the type of inflammatory cell. For example, Paulino and Cavalcanti found that the degree of inflammation was usually mild, was usually localised to the mucosa, and was largely composed of lymphocytes, plasma cells, and eosinophils [92]. In contrast, Acosta and Nardi found some patients with focal erosions and large numbers of polymorphs, and others with a dense chronic inflammatory infiltrate through all layers of the papilla [2].

Despite variation in the histological findings it would appear that the diagnosis of stenosis of the papilla is unacceptable in the presence of a normal biopsy. Whether variation between studies can be attributed to patient selection, histological interpretation, phases in the evolution of disease, or to distinct disease entities, remains to be determined.

ASSOCIATED PATHOLOGICAL CHANGES

Common bile duct. Dilatation and thickening of the common bile duct occurs in most patients with stenosis of the papilla [2, 23]. Indeed, the diagnosis of stenosis must be suspect in the absence of this finding. Stenosis restricted to the main pancreatic duct is a theoretical possibility, but appears to be unusual in clinical practice [1]. Gallstones and debris are found in the common bile duct in some patients and may be secondary to stasis of bile [23]. Cholangitis is uncommon in the absence of biliary calculi.

Pancreas. In two reported series 7 per cent and 15 per cent of patients with stenosis of the papilla had evidence of chronic pancreatitis at the time of surgery [23, 41]. Conversely, stenosis appears to be an uncommon finding in patients with known chronic pancreatitis, although fibrosis secondary to pancreatitis might obscure the initiating event [139].

Liver. Biliary cirrhosis due to extrahepatic obstruction appears to be rare in the absence of co-existing biliary calculi.

DIAGNOSIS

CLINICAL SYNDROMES

Abdominal pain. Almost all patients with stenosis of the papilla describe abdominal pain [23, 83]. Pain is usually episodic with features which strongly suggest biliary disease. Occasionally, persistent pain occurs punctuated by episodes during which symptoms increase in severity [43]. The typical patient has had a previous cholecystectomy followed by a symptom-free period and subsequently develops pain which is similar to that prior to the operation. About 20 per cent of patients show a minor elevation of serum amylase or lipase following episodes of pain [3, 43]. In the absence of choledocholithiasis abnormalities of liver function tests appear to be less common, although some patients show a mild elevation of serum alkaline phosphatase [23].

Papillitis. Papillitis of unknown aetiology appears to be a distinct clinical entity with an uncertain relationship to stenosis of the papilla. The disorder is rare in the United States, Great Britain, and Australia, but is diagnosed more frequently in European centres [14]. The typical patient has biliary-type pain, a fever of 37°C to 39°C, and develops abnormalities of liver function tests which gradually revert to normal as the attack subsides. Cholangitis may be present in some patients, but the fever settles spontaneously in others. Jaundice may develop. Many of these patients are treated by operative sphincteroplasty or endoscopic sphincterotomy, but the author has seen two patients with this entity who have been managed without surgery and have continued to have episodes of pain and jaundice about once per year.

INVESTIGATIONS

Choledochography. Following cholecystectomy an intravenous or oral choledochogram will be necessary to exclude retained or recurrent biliary calculi. In patients with stenosis of the papilla without gallstones, the common bile duct will usually be dilated and the density of contrast may be greater at 120 minutes than at 60 minutes (Chapter 3).

Morphine–neostigmine test. The ability of injections of morphine to induce abdominal pain in some individuals has been recognised for many years. Nardi and Acosta induced abdominal pain and an elevation of serum amylase in 14 of 15 patients with idiopathic pancreatitis by an intramuscular injection of morphine (10 mg) and neostigmine (1 mg) [84]. Similar positive responses also occurred in patients with pancreatitis associated with biliary calculi. Interest in this investigation was rekindled by Gregg and co-workers, who studied 23 patients with a positive morphine–neostigmine test and found that 16 had features of stenosis of the papilla at endoscopic retrograde cholangiopancreatography [43]. Eleven of these 16 patients subsequently had biliary exploration with confirmation of stenosis and an operative sphincteroplasty. Despite these studies the sensitivity and specificity of this investigation remains unclear, and positive responses in the absence of biliary and pancreatic disease have been noted [82]. Unfortunately, studies are not directly comparable as different criteria for positivity of the test have been used.

Endoscopic retrograde cholangiopancreatography (ERCP). Preliminary studies suggest that endoscopic and radiological findings at ERCP are helpful for the preoperative diagnosis of stenosis of the papilla. Gregg and co-workers noted that in patients with stenosis it was only possible to impact the catheter in the papilla (severe stenosis), or to cannulate the main pancreatic duct with difficulty (moderate stenosis) [43]. Some patients clearly showed stenosis of the distal main pancreatic duct with prestenotic dilatation in the head of the pancreas and delayed ductal emptying (Fig. 6.33). Retrograde cholangiography may be technically difficult but will usually show dilatation of the common bile duct, delayed ductal emptying, and absence of peristalsis in the region of the papilla (Fig. 6.34). In addition, retrograde cholangiography may identify biliary calculi not shown by intravenous or oral choledochograms. Manometric studies of the papilla by endoscopic means have so far not been of diagnostic benefit.

OPERATIVE FINDINGS

In most studies the diagnosis of stenosis of the papilla has been established at the time of operation [23, 28, 93]. Most surgeons have followed the lead of Cattell, who advocated the use of various-sized probes to establish the degree of patency of the sphincter of Oddi [23]. Cattell considered that the diagnosis is made by the inability of the surgeon to pass without undue force, a 3-mm Bakes dilator through the sphincter of Oddi and into the duodenum, after an adequate trial. An adequate trial implies a careful exploration of the common bile duct, mobilisation of the duodenum by Kocher's method, and duodenotomy if necessary.

However, the passage of a dilator through the papilla will depend not only on the aperture of the sphincteric region, but also on the course and anatomic

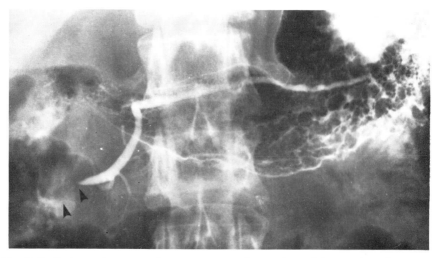

Fig. 6.33. Endoscopic retrograde pancreatogram in a patient with stenosis of the papilla of Vater showing a persistent stricture of the main pancreatic duct in the region of the papilla (arrows) and mild dilatation of the duct in the head of the pancreas.

features of the distal common bile duct. A narrow or long distal segment or an eccentric opening to the distal segment will increase the degree of operative difficulty, and under these circumstances failure to pass a dilator is not diagnostic of stenosis.

Examination of the papilla for induration, and the presence of a fibrotic feel when the region is divided, are important corroborative features of organic stenosis. The bile duct should also be dilated and thickened and may contain gallstones or debris.

Operative cholangiography and manometry. The use of operative cholangiogra-

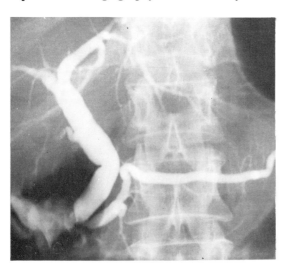

Fig. 6.34. Endoscopic retrograde cholangiopancreatogram in a patient with stenosis of the papilla of Vater, showing dilatation of the common bile duct and pancreatic duct. Emptying from both ducts was delayed and peristalsis was absent in the region of the papilla during fluoroscopy.

phy to detect diseases of the papilla was first described by Mirizzi in 1932 [79]. Subsequently, Mallet-Guy advocated the use of cholangiography combined with biliary manometry [74]. Stenosis of the papilla was diagnosed by dilatation of the common bile duct, delayed ductal emptying, absence of peristalsis in the region of the papilla, and an elevated pressure for passage of saline through the papilla. These criteria appeared to be widely adopted in Europe, although it was recognised that false positive results could result from sphincter spasm induced by surgical manipulation, premedication, or high pressures of injection. Subsequently, Hess described 'flowmetry' accompanied by fluoroscopy [51]. When the biliary pressure was maintained at 30 cm of water patients with stenosis showed flow rates of less than 10 ml per minute, whereas flow rates of greater than 10 ml per minute were found in all control subjects. Increasing surgical experience, together with the use of 'flowmetry' in his Department, resulted in a reduction from 21 to 8 per cent in the frequency of the diagnosis of papillitis in patients undergoing cholecystectomy.

The use of pharmacological agents, such as local anaesthetics and antispasmodic drugs, does not appear to have facilitated the differentiation of organic stenosis from spasm. Nevertheless, the diagnosis of organic stenosis is largely excluded if the bile duct is of normal calibre and shows changes in the appearance of the sphincter region on serial x-ray as shown in Fig. 6.35.

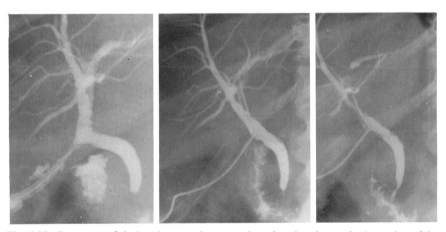

Fig. 6.35. Sequence of cholangiograms in one patient showing the gradual opening of the sphincteric region, thereby disproving that the patient has stenosis of the sphincter of Oddi. (*left*) Sphincter closed and adjacent duodenum contracted. (*middle*) Sphincter slightly open. (*right*) Sphincter open and duodenum relaxed.

Biopsy. Biopsy of the papilla is not widely practised, but pathological changes are present in most patients as described above.

TREATMENT

The aim of therapy is to facilitate drainage from the biliary and/or pancreatic system in the belief that pain develops following distension of ducts (Chapter 2).

The best method of achieving this aim has not yet been determined. There have been no trials of medical therapy and no comparative studies of the various surgical procedures. Furthermore, the natural history of this disorder is uncertain. In the author's opinion most patients with severe stenosis will benefit from a surgical procedure, but some patients with moderate stenosis and infrequent episodes of pain can be managed by the intermittent use of analgesics and antispasmodic drugs.

SURGICAL PROCEDURES

A number of surgical procedures have been used to facilitate drainage from ducts and the techniques are described in detail in Chapter 14. The procedure currently advocated by most workers is transduodenal sphincteroplasty, despite a significant morbidity and mortality, largely related to postoperative pancreatitis [43, 57, 83]. This operation permits a longer incision than transduodenal sphincterotomy and appears to result in a greater impairment of sphincter mechanisms and a lower incidence of restenosis [57, 61]. However, the sphincter surrounding the main pancreatic duct is usually spared and symptoms may continue in patients in whom pain is of pancreatic origin. This small group of patients may benefit from the additional procedure of dilatation of the main pancreatic duct or excision of the septum between the two ducts (transampullary septectomy) [3, 80, 133].

Side-to-side choledochoduodenostomy is favoured by some surgeons, because it is relatively simple and is associated with a low morbidity and mortality [19, 109, 121]. Furthermore, the frequency of long-term complications such as cholangitis, pain and obstruction of the anastomosis, appears to be low [70]. However, the procedure should not be performed unless the common bile duct is dilated and this operation clearly cannot be expected to facilitate drainage from the main pancreatic duct [70].

Forcible transcholedochal dilatation of the sphincter of Oddi was an early form of therapy, now largely abandoned because of unsatisfactory results [50]. Choledochojejunostomy may rarely be indicated in patients with stenosis associated with a stricture of the distal bile duct [93]. Endoscopic sphincterotomy, using a high frequency diathermy papillotome, has been performed in some patients with stenosis, although selective cannulation of the common bile duct (a necessary prerequisite for sphincterotomy) is frequently difficult and the long-term results have not been reported [104]. Endoscopic papillotomy is discussed in detail by Dr. Claude Liguory in Chapter 13.

CONCLUSION

Stenosis of the papilla of Vater involves pathological changes in the region of the papilla, causing delay in drainage from the biliary and probably, also, the pancreatic ducts. The most common presentation is with episodes of biliary type pain, sometimes accompanied by a mild elevation of the serum level of amylase or alkaline phosphatase. Intravenous cholangiography almost always reveals dilatation of the common bile duct and a morphine–neostigmine test may reproduce pain and elevate the serum level of amylase or lipase. Preliminary studies suggest that endoscopic assessment of the papilla and retrograde pancreatography are also helpful. At operation the sphincter is difficult to negotiate with a fine probe and, at operative cholangiography, the common bile duct is dilated with delayed emptying and absence of peristalsis in the region of the papilla. Manometric and flow studies have been helpful in some centres, but have not been widely adopted. Biopsy of the papilla has revealed a variety of pathological changes which might be related to different phases in the evolution of stenosis, or to distinct disease syndromes. In many patients stenosis appears to involve both ductal systems, although variation in the degree of narrowing of one or other duct might explain differences in the clinical presentation in individual patients. Transduodenal sphincteroplasty appears to be the most popular form of therapy in patients with substantial pain, followed by choledochoduodenostomy, but comparative studies of the various surgical procedures have not been reported. Future studies may identify a subgroup of patients who may benefit from transduodenal septectomy to facilitate drainage from the main pancreatic duct. Endoscopic papillotomy may, in the future, find an increasing place in the treatment of this condition.

REFERENCES

1. ACOSTA J.M. & NARDI G.L. Papillitis. Inflammatory disease of the ampulla of Vater. *Arch. Surg. (Chicago)* **92**:354, 1966.
2. ACOSTA J.M., CIVANTOS F., NARDI G.L. & CASTLEMAN B. Fibrosis of the papilla of Vater. *Surg. Gynec. Obstet.* **124**:787, 1967.
3. ACOSTA J.M., NARDI G.L. & CIVANTOS F. Distal pancreatic duct inflammation. *Ann. Surg.* **172**:256, 1970.
4. ADSON M.A. & WYCHULIS A.R. Portal hypertension in secondary biliary cirrhosis. *Arch. Surg. (Chicago)* **96**:604, 1968.
5. ALLEN A.W. & WALLACE R.H. Surgical management of stone in the common bile duct: follow-up studies with special reference to graded dilatation of the sphincter of Oddi. *Ann. Surg.* **111**:838, 1940.
6. ALTEMEIER W.A., GALL E.A., CULBERTSON W.R. & INGE W.W. Sclerosing carcinoma of the intrahepatic bile ducts. *Surgery* **60**:191, 1966.
7. ATKINSON A.J. & CARROLL W.W. Sclerosing cholangitis. Association with regional enteritis. *J.A.M.A.* **188**:175, 1964.
8. BABB R.R., LEE R.H. & PECK O.C. Cancer of the bile duct and chronic ulcerative colitis. *Am. J. Surg.* **119**:337, 1970.
9. BADDELEY R.M. & STAMMERS F.A.R. Benign, non-traumatic stricture of the extrahepatic bile ducts. *Br. J. Surg.* **51**:25, 1964.
10. BEART R.W. JR., PUTNAM C.W. & STARZL T. Use of a U tube in the treatment of biliary disease. *Surg. Gynec. Obstet.* **124**:912, 1976.
11. BELZER F.O., WATTS J.McK., ROSS H.B. & DUNPHY J.E. Autoreconstruction of the common bile duct after venous patch graft. Ann. 125 cases, *Br. J. Surg.* **49**:292, 1961.
12. BHATHAL P.S. & POWELL L.W. Primary intrahepatic obliterating cholangitis: a possible variant of 'sclerosing cholangitis'. *Gut* **10**:886, 1969.
13. BORGSTROM S. Operative injury of the choledochus. *Acta. Chir. Scand.* **118**:25, 1959.
14. BOVE P. Inflammation de la papille de Vater. Son diagnostic et son traitment par la papillotomie transduodenale. *Arch. Mal. App. Dig.* **45**:147, 1956.
15. BOYDEN E.A. & BERGH L. The anatomy of the choledochal junction in man. *Surg. Gynec. Obstet.* **104**:641, 1957.

16. BRAASCH J.W. *Pers. Commun.* 1965.

17. BROOKE B.N. & SLANEY G. Portal bacteraemia in ulcerative colitis. *Lancet* **1**:1206, 1958.

18. BRUSH B.E., PONKA J.L., DAMAZO F. & WHITCOMB J. Evaluation of dilatation of the sphincter of Oddi. *Arch. Surg.* **70**:766, 1955.

19. CAPPER W.M. External choledochoduodenostomy. An evaluation of 125 cases. *Br. J. Surg.* **49**:292, 1961.

20. CAROLI J. *Les Papillites Primitives Icterigenes.* Vigot, Paris, 1950.

21. CASS M.H., ROBSON B. & RUNDLE F.F. Electrolyte losses with biliary fistula: post-choledochotomy acidotic syndrome. *Med. J. Aust.* **1**:165, 1955.

22. CATTELL R.B. & COLCOCK B.P. Fibrosis of the sphincter of Oddi. *Ann. Surg.* **137**:797, 1953.

23. CATTELL R.B., COLCOCK B.P. & POLLACK J.L. Stenosis of the sphincter of Oddi. *New Eng. J. Med.* **256**:429, 1957.

24. CATTELL R.B. & BRAASCH J.W. General considerations in the management of benign strictures of the bile duct. *New Eng. J. Med.* **261**:929, 1959.

25. CATTELL R.B. & BRAASCH J.W. Primary repair of benign strictures of the bile duct. *Surg. Gynec. Obstet.* **109**:531, 1959.

26. CATTELL R.B. & BRAASCH J.W. Two-stage repairs of benign strictures of the bile duct. *Surg. Gynec. Obstet.* **109**:691, 1959.

27. CATTELL R.B. & BRAASCH J.W. Repair of benign strictures of the bile duct involving both or single hepatic ducts. *Surg. Gynec. Obstet.* **110**:55, 1960.

28. COLCOCK B.P. & PEREY B. Exploration of the common bile duct. *Surg. Gynec. Obstet.* **118**:20, 1964.

29. COLCOCK B.P. & BRAASCH J.W. Surgery of the small intestine in the adult. Saunders, Philadelphia, 1968.

30. CUTLER B. & DONALDSON G.A. Primary sclerosing cholangitis and obliterative cholangitis. *Am. J. Surg.* **177**:502, 1969.

31. DAHL-IVERSEN E., SORENSON A.H. & WESTENGAARD E. Pressure measurement in the biliary tract in patients after cholecystolithotomy and in patients with dyskinesia. *Acta. Chir. Scand.* **114**:181, 1957.

32. DINEEN P. The importance of the route of infection in experimental biliary tract obstruction. *Surg. Gynec. Obstet.* **119**:1001, 1964.

33. DONALDSON G.A., ALLEN A.W. & BARTLETT M.K. Postoperative bile duct strictures. Their etiology and treatment. *New Eng. J. Med.* **254**:50, 1956.

34. DOUBILET H. & MULHOLLAND J.H. Surgical treatment of recurrent pancreatitis by endocholedochal sphincterotomy. *Surg. Gynec. Obstet.* **86**:295, 1948.

35. DOUBILET H. & MULHOLLAND J.H. Eight-year study of pancreatitis and sphincterotomy. *J.A.M.A.* **160**:521, 1956.

36. DRAGSTEDT L.R. & WOODWARD E.R. Transduodenal reconstruction of the bile ducts. *Surg. Gynec. Obstet.* **94**:53, 1952.

37. DROUIN J.P. Cholecystectomy with routine sphincteroplasty. *Canad. J. Surg.* **7**:367, 1964.

38. EKMAN C.A. & SANDBLOM P. Bilio-intestinal anastomosis as a cause of liver cirrhosis with portal hypertension. *Acta. Chir. Scand.* **123**:383, 1962.

39. FAHRLANDER A. Uber die Klinik der Erkrankungen der extrahepatischen Gallenwege. *Gastroenterologia (Basel)* **87**:248, 1957.

40. GOLDGRABER M.B. & KIRSNER J.B. Chronic granulomatous cholecystitis and chronic fibrosing choledochitis associated with chronic ulcerative colitis. *Gastroenterology* **38**:821, 1960.

41. GRAGE T.B., LOBER P.H., IMAMOGLU K. & WANGENSTEEN O.H. Stenosis of the sphincter of Oddi. A clinicopathologic review of 50 cases. *Surgery* **48**:304, 1960.

42. GRASSI G., BROGLIA S. & DELL'OSSO A. Hepaticojejunoduodenoplasty in reoperation of the bile ducts. First World Congress, Coll. Int. Clin. Dig. 1973, Proceedings.

43. GREGG J.A., TADDEO A.E., MILANO A.F., McCARTNEY A.J., SANTORO B.T., FRAGER

S.H. & CAPOBIANCO A.G. Duodenoscopy and endoscopic pancreatography in patients with positive Morphine Prostimine tests. *Am. J. Surg.* **134**:318, 1977.

44. GRUA O.E. & McMURRIN J.A. Sclerosing cholangitis. Review and presentation of an unusual pathologic variant. *Am. J. Surg.* **116**:659, 1968.

45. HAM J.M. Tumours of biliary epithelium and ulcerative colitis. *Ann. Surg.* **168**:1088, 1961.

46. HAM J.M. & McKENZIE D.C. Primary carcinoma of the extrahepatic bile ducts. *Surg. Gynec. Obstet.* **118**:977, 1964.

47. HARRIDGE W.H. Alterations in common bile duct strictures. *Surg. Forum* **3**:411, 1953.

48. HAVARD C. Non-malignant bile duct obstruction. *Ann. Roy. Coll. Surg. Eng.* **26**:88, 1960.

49. HERTZER N.R., GRAY H.W., HOERR S.O. & HERMANN R.E. The use of T tube splints in bile duct repairs. *Surg. Gynec. Obstet.* **137**:413, 1973.

50. HESS W. *Surgery of the Biliary Passage and the Pancreas.* Van Nostrand, Princeton, N.J., 1965.

51. HESS W. Manometry and radiography in the biliary system during surgery. In L. Demling & M. Classen (ed.), *Endoscopic Sphincterotomy of the Papilla of Vater.* Georg Thieme Publishers, Stuttgart, 1978.

52. HOLUBITSKY I.B. & McKENZIE A.D. Primary sclerosing cholangitis of the extra-hepatic bile ducts. *Canad. J. Surg.* **7**:277, 1964.

53. HUGHES E.S.R. & SYME G.A. Combined common bile duct and pancreatic duct injury occurring during gastrectomy. Successful repair. *Aust. New Zeal. J. Surg.* **29**:340, 1960.

54. IMAMOGLU K., PERRY J.F. JR. & WANGENSTEEN O.H. Experimental production of gallstones by incomplete stricture of the terminal common bile duct. *Surgery* **42**:623, 1957.

55. JONES S.A., SMITH L.L., KELLER T.B. & JOERGENSON, E.J. Choledochoduodenos-tomy to prevent residual stones. *Arch. Surg. (Chicago)* **86**:104, 1963.

56. JONES S.A., STEEDMAN R.A., KELLER T.B. & SMITH L.L. Transduodenal sphincter-oplasty (not sphincterotomy) for biliary and pancreatic disease. Indications, con-traindications and results. *Amer. J. Surg.* **118**:292, 1969.

57. JONES S.A. & SMITH L.L. A reappraisal of sphincteroplasty (not sphincterotomy). *Surgery* **71**:565, 1972.

58. JUDD E.S. Stricture of common bile duct. *Ann. Surg.* **84**:404, 1926.

59. KNOCHEL J.P., COOPER E.B. & BARRY K.G. External biliary fistula; a study of electrolyte derangements and secondary cardiovascular and renal abnormalities. *Surgery* **51**:746, 1962.

60. KUNE G.A. Surgical anatomy of common bile duct. *Arch. Surg. (Chicago)* **87**:995, 1964.

61. KUNE G.A. The influence of structure and function in the surgery of the biliary tract. *Ann. R. Coll. Surg. Eng.* **47**:78, 1970.

62. KUNE G.A. Life-threatening surgical infection: its development and prediction. *Ann. R. Coll. Surg. Eng.* **60**:92, 1978.

63. KUNE G.A. Bile duct injury during cholecystectomy. Causes, prevention and surgi-cal repair in 1979. *Aust. New Zeal. J. Surg.* **49**:35, 1979.

64. KUNE G.A., HARDY K.J., BROWN G. & McKENZIE G. Operative injuries of the bile ducts. *Med. J. Aust.* **2**:233, 1969.

65. KUNE G.A. & McKENZIE G.G.C. The surgeon's role in chronic pancreatitis. Pro-ceedings, First Australian Pancreas Congress, University of Melbourne, 1978.

66. LARY B.C. & SCHEIBE J.R. The effect of rubber tubing on the healing of common duct anastomoses. *Surgery* **32**:789, 1952.

67. MACLEISH D.G. Sclerostenosing cholangitis. *Roy. Melbourne Hosp. Clin. Rep.* **24**:95, 1954.

68. MADDEN J.L. & McCANN W.J. Reconstruction of the common bile duct by end-to-

end anastomosis without the use of an internal splint or stent support. *Surg. Gynec. Obstet.* **112**:305, 1961.

69. MADDEN J.L., VANDERHEYDEN L. & KANDALAFT S. The nature and surgical significance of common duct stones. *Surg. Gynec. Obstet.* **126**:3, 1968.

70. MADDEN J.L., CHUN J.Y., KANDALAFT S. & PAREKH M. Choledochoduodenostomy. An unjustly maligned surgical procedure. *Am. J. Surg.* **119**:45, 1970.

71. MADSEN C.M., SORENSEN H,R. & TRUELSEN F. The frequency of operative bile duct injuries illustrated by a Danish county survey. *Acta. Chir. Scand.* **119**:110, 1960.

72. MAINGOT R. Injuries of the biliary tract, including operative and postoperative complications. In R. Smith & S. Sherlock (eds.), *Surgery of the Gallbladder and Bile Ducts,* Butterworth, London, 1964.

73. MAKI T., SATO T. & MATSUSHIRO T. A reappraisal of surgical treatment for intrahepatic gallstones. *Ann. Surg.* **175**:155, 1972.

74. MALLET-GUY P. Value of peroperative manometric and roentgenographic examination in the diagnosis of pathologic changes and functional disturbances of the biliary tract. *Surg. Gynec. Obstet.* **94**:385, 1952.

75. MALLET-GUY P. & ROSE J.D. Peroperative manometry and radiology in biliary tract disorders. *Br. J. Surg.* **44**:55, 1956.

76. MARSHALL R.D. Transduodenal ampulloplasty in the surgery of the common bile duct. *Aust. New Zeal. J. Surg.* **32**:160, 1962.

77. MCDERMOTT B.W. JR., PALAZZI H., NARDI G.L. & MONDET A. Elective portal systemic shunt. An analysis of 237 cases. *New Eng J. Med.* **264**:419, 1961.

78. MICHIE W. & GUNN A. Bile duct injuries. A new suggestion for their repair. *Br. J. Surg.* **51**:96, 1964.

79. MIRIZZI P.L. La colangiografia durante las operationes de la vias biliares. *Bol. Soc. cir. B. Aires.* **16**:1325, 1932.

80. MOODY F.G., BERENSON M.M. & MCCLOSKEY D. Transampullary septectomy for post-cholecystectomy pain. *Ann. Surg.* **186**:415, 1977.

81. MOOSSA A.R., BLOCK G.E., SKINNER D.B. & HALL A.W. Reconstruction of high biliary tract strictures employing transhepatic intubation. *Surg. Clin. N. Amer.* **56**:73, 1976.

82. MYRHE J., NESBITT S. & HURLY J.T. Response of serum amylase and lipase to pancreatic stimulation as a test of pancreatic function; mecholyl-secretin and morphine-secretin tests. *Gastroenterology* **13**:127, 1949.

83. NARDI G.L. Papillitis and stenosis of the sphincter of Oddi. *Surg. Clin. N. Amer.* **53**:1149, 1973.

84. NARDI G.L. & ACOSTA J.M. Papillitis as a cause of pancreatitis and abdominal pain: role of evocative test, operative pancreatography and histologic evaluation. *Ann. Surg.* **164**:611, 1966.

85. NASH T.P. The behaviour of the sphincter of Oddi in health and disease. *Aust. New Zeal. J. Surg.* **31**:40, 1961.

86. NEGRI A. *Histofisiopatologia de las Vias Biliares.* Aniceto Lopez, Buenos Aires, 1941.

87. NEIBLING H.A. Sclerosing obliterative cholangitis. *Am. Surg.* **31**:245, 1965.

88. NORTHOVER J.M.A. & TERBLANCHE I. A new look at the arterial blood supply of the bile duct in man and its surgical implications. *Br. J. Surg.* **66**:379, 1979.

89. OLSON O.C. & SCHNUG E. Primary sclerosing cholangitis. *Northwest Med.* **64**:26, 1965.

90. PALMER W.L., KIRSNER J.B., GOLDGRABER M.B. & FUENTES S.S. Disease of the liver in chronic ulcerative colitis. *Am. J. Med.* **36**:856, 1964.

91. PAULINO F. & CAVALCANTI A. Anatomy and pathology of the distal common duct. Special reference to stenosing odditis. *Am. J. Dig. Dis.* **5**:697, 1960.

92. PAULINO F. & CAVALCANTI A. Biopsy of the ampulla of Vater for demonstration of organic stenosis. *Surgery* **48**:698, 1960.

93. PAULINO F. & ROSELLI A. Stenosis of sphincter of Oddi. *Surgery* **54**:865, 1963.

Indirect evidence of choledocholithiasis. For many years a number of operative findings were regarded as indications for bile duct exploration, in the absence of direct evidence of choledocholithiasis. With modern anaesthesia the bile duct can now be leisurely palpated, and an adequate operative cholangiogram can be performed in most centres, so that these indirect indications for exploration are losing their significance and becoming antiquated.

Dilated common bile duct. The width of the supraduodenal common bile duct varies enormously in different individuals, with a range of 4–15 mm. Most surgeons do not actually measure the diameter of the bile duct at operation, so that the term, dilated duct, is merely an educated guess in most reports! A ruler has been devised that allows rapid and accurate measurement of the diameter of the common bile duct during operation [261]. If a dilated duct is present gallstones are removed from the duct in less than half of the cases [19, 65, 152, 200, 226, 265, 367]. Leslie in 1968 found that if the duct was less than 9 mm, it never contained gallstones, if between 9 and 17 mm it might or might not contain gallstones, and if over 17 mm it always contained gallstones or some other disease state [215]. It is clear, therefore, that gallstones may be present in ducts which are within the normal range of diameters and of normal external appearance [19, 65, 153, 200, 215, 265, 367, 368].

Miscellaneous indirect indications. When the gallstones in the gallbladder are smaller than the diameter of the cystic duct it has been held that the bile duct should be explored [67, 114, 364]. It certainly should alert you to the x-ray findings. However, recovery of stones from the common duct occurs in only about 10 per cent or less of such cases [67, 265, 266]. The other indications usually mentioned are a history of pancreatitis, chronic pancreatitis at the time of surgery, a shrunken fibrotic gallbladder without gallstones, and the presence of biliary sediment aspirated from the bile duct (if the surgeon is in the habit of aspirating the bile duct).

If palpation and operative cholangiography are positive these indirect indications for exploration are superfluous. If palpation and operative cholangiography are clearly negative these indirect indications only very rarely will yield gallstones on exploration of the bile ducts. It is conceded, however, that if the findings on palpation are doubtful, or if operative cholangiography is unavailable, or the result of cholangiography is technically unsatisfactory or doubtful, these indirect indications assume importance and should be considered in deciding the need for choledochotomy.

TECHNIQUE

The choice of incision is similar to that for cholecystectomy. If the gallbladder is still intact this organ is removed and an operative cholangiogram is performed.

EXPOSURE OF THE COMMON BILE DUCT
It may be necessary to mobilise the hepatic flexure of the colon downward,

particularly if the patient has had a previous cholecystectomy. The duodenum and head of the pancreas are mobilised by Kocher's method. The peritoneum and areolar tissue overlying the front of the supraduodenal common bile duct is cleared.

PALPATION OF THE BILE DUCTS

Careful palpation of the common bile duct is an important preliminary to exploration [171, 200]. The key to reliable palpation lies in a knowledge of the exact anatomy of the common bile duct. No doubt more stones are felt as the experience of the surgeon increases.

Palpation of the bile duct is facilitated if the surgeon moves to the left side of the operating table, as in this position he can feel the duct more comfortably with his left hand. The supraduodenal portion of the common bile duct and the common hepatic duct may be palpated between the fingers and thumb, with the fingers located in the foramen of Winslow, and the thumb in front of the bile duct.

The common bile duct groove of the pancreas, described in Chapter 1, is the important landmark for the palpation of the retropancreatic portion of the common bile duct. The retropancreatic portion of the common bile duct itself cannot be palpated. However, the groove in which the bile duct lies and any gallstones situated in the duct may be palpated. The fingers are insinuated behind the second part of the duodenum and slowly moved medially with the thumb in front of the duodenum in order to feel the groove (Fig. 5.18). The groove is usually much closer to the second part of the duodenum than the surgeon anticipates. Mobilisation of the duodenum by Kocher's method will allow a more precise palpation of the groove [99].

EXPLORATION OF THE BILE DUCTS

Following adequate exposure and palpation, if there is any doubt about the identity of the bile duct, it should be aspirated with a fine needle on a syringe. After suitable arrangement of packs and retractors, in a way similar to that described for cholecystectomy, two fine, stay sutures are placed through the anterior wall of the bile duct, which is then incised. The type of equipment used for bile duct exploration is shown in Fig. 5.19.

The bile ducts are gently explored in proximal and distal directions with bile duct forceps (Fig. 5.20). When the exploration is performed in the proximal direction slightly curved bile duct forceps are usually the most suitable. It is important to pass the forceps into both hepatic ducts, or into three hepatic ducts in those cases in which the right hepatic duct is absent and the two principal right-sided bile ducts open directly into the left hepatic duct. When the exploration is performed in the distal direction the right-angled forceps, or even the more curved bile duct forceps, are the most suitable to use.

When the bile ducts appear to have been cleared of gallstones and biliary debris the patency of the sphincter of Oddi is tested. For this purpose Bakes dilators are the most suitable. The authors feel that if a small Bakes dilator (3 or 4 mm) can be readily passed through the sphincter into the duodenum, this is

94. PRADERI R. Twelve years experience with transhepatic intubation. *Ann. Surg.* **179**:937, 1974.
95. PRADERI R., PARODI H. & DELGADO B. Tratamiento de las obstrucciones neoplasicas de la via biliar suprapancreatico. *An. Fac. Med. Montevideo* **49**:221, 1964.
96. RANKIN J.G., BODEN R.W., GAULSTON S.T. & MORROW W. The liver in ulcerative colitis. Treatment of pericholangitis with tetracycline. *Lancet* **2**:1110, 1959.
97. RANKIN J.G., SKYRING A.P. & GOULSTON S.J.M. Liver in ulcerative colitis. Obstructive jaundice due to bile duct carcinoma. *Gut* **7**:433, 1966.
98. RATHCKE L. *Die Nachoperationen an den Gallenwegen.* Enke, Stuttgart, 1949.
99. REYNOLDS B.M. Immediate effects of instrumental dilatation of the ampulla of Vater. *Ann. Surg.* **164**:271, 1966.
100. RIDDELL D.H. & KIRTLEY J.A. JR. Stenosis of the sphincter of Oddi. Transduodenal sphincterotomy and some other surgical aspects. *Ann. Surg.* **149**:773, 1959.
101. ROBERTS J.M. Stenosing cholangitis. *Western J. Surg.* **62**:253, 1955.
102. ROSENQVIST H. & MYRIN S.O. Operative injuries to the bile ducts. *Acta Chir. Scand.* **119**:92, 1960.
103. ROTHWELL-JACKSON R.L. Sphincteroplasty in the treatment of biliary and pancreatic disease. *Br. J. Surg.* **55**:616, 1968.
104. SAFRANY L. Duodenoscopic sphincterotomy and gallstone removal. *Gastroenterology* **72**:338, 1977.
105. SARLES H., PAYAN N., TASSO, F. & SAHEL J. Chronic pancreatitis, relapsing pancreatitis, calcifications of pancreas. In H.L. Bockus (ed.), *Gastroenterology* Chap. 138, p. 1040. Saunders, Philadelphia, 1976.
106. SARLES H. & SAHEL J. Cholestasis and lesions of the biliary tract in chronic pancreatitis. *Gut* **19**:851, 1978.
107. SAYPOL G.M. & KURIAN G. A technique of repair of stricture of the bile duct. *Surg. Gynec. Obstet.* **128**:1971, 1969.
108. SCHATTEN W.E., DESPRES, J.D. & HOLDEN W.D. Bacteriological study of portal vein blood in man. *A.M.A. Arch. Surg.* **71**:404, 1955.
109. SCHWARTZ F., BENSHIMOL A. & HURWITZ A. Choledochoduodenostomy in the treatment of stenosis of the lower portion of the common bile duct. *Surgery* **46**:1020, 1959.
110. SCHWARTZ S.I. Primary sclerosing cholangitis: a disease revisited. *Surg. Clin. N. Amer.* **53**:1161, 1973.
111. SCHWARTZ S.I. & DALE W.A. Primary sclerosing cholangitis. Review and report of six cases. *A.M.A. Arch. Surg.* **77**:439, 1958.
112. SCOTT A.J. & KHAN G.A. Origin of bacteria in bile duct bile. *Lancet* **2**:790, 1967.
113. SEDGWICK C.E., POULANTZAS J.K. & KUNE G.A. Management of portal hypertension secondary to bile duct strictures: review of 18 cases with splenorenal shunt. *Ann. Surg.* **163**:949, 1966.
114. SEDGWICK C.E. & POULANTZAS J.K. Portal hypertension. Little Brown, Boston, 1967.
115. SMITH (Lord of Marlow). Obstructions of the bile duct. *Br. J. Surg.* **66**:69, 1979.
116. SMITH M.P. & LOE R.H. Sclerosing cholangitis. Review of recent case reports and associated diseases in four new cases. *Am. J. Surg.* **110**:239, 1965.
117. SMITH R. Hepaticojejunostomy with transhepatic intubation. A technique for very high strictures of the hepatic ducts. *Br. J. Surg.* **51**:186, 1964.
118. SMITH R. Hepaticojejunostomy: choledochojejunostomy. A method of intrajejunal anastomosis. *Br. J. Surg.* **51**:183, 1964.
119. SMITH R. Strictures of the bile ducts. *Proc. Roy. Soc. Med.* **62**:131, 1969.
120. SODERLAND G. On fibrotic, non-traumatic stenosis of the common duct. *Acta Chir. Scand.* **106**:77, 1953.
121. STARR K.W. Choledochoduodenostomy. *Med. J. Aust.* **2**:37, 1953.
122. STARR K.W. Recurrent choledocholithiasis and obstructive and pancreatic problems after choledochotomy. *Aust. New Zeal. J. Surg.* **23**:206, 1954.

123. STEPHENS F.O. Benign bile duct strictures; methods of repair. *Med. J. Aust.* **2**:57, 1968.

124. STOLTE M., BECKER K.D., TROMMSDORFF A. & TROMMSDORFF L. Pathological anatomy of the papilla of Vater. In L. Demling & M. Classen (eds.), *Endoscopic Sphincterotomy of the Papilla of Vater*. Georg Thieme Publishers, Stuttgart, 1978.

125. STONE R., COHEN Z., TAYLOR B., LANGER B. & TOUEE E. Bile duct injury. Results of repair using a changeable stent. *Am. J. Surg.* **125**:253, 1973.

126. TEMPLETON J.Y. & DODD G.D. Anatomical separation of the right and left lobes of the liver for intrahepatic anastomosis of the biliary ducts. *Ann. Surg.* **157**:287, 1963.

127. THORPE M.E.C., SCHEUER P.J. & SHERLOCK S. Primary sclerosing cholangitis, the biliary tree and ulcerative colitis. *Gut* **8**:435, 1967.

128. TSUCHIYA R., TANAKA N., TSUNODA T. & HARADA N. Extended hepaticocholedochojejunostomy for treatment of intrahepatic cholestasis. *Proceedings Fifth World Congress, Coll. Int. Chir. Dig. Sao Paulo*, 1978, abst. 166.

129. VIIKARI S.J. Operative injuries of the bile ducts. *Acta Chir. Scand.* **119**:83, 1960.

130. VINNIK I.A. & KERN F. JR. Biliary cirrhosis in a patient with chronic ulcerative colitis. *Gastroenterology* **45**:529, 1963.

131. WADDELL W.R. Exposure of intrahepatic bile ducts through interlobar fissure. *Surg. Gynec. Obstet.* **124**:491, 1967.

132. WALTERS W., NIXON J.W. JR & HODGINS F.E. Strictures of the common bile duct. Five to 25 year follow-up of 217 operations. *Ann. Surg.* **149**:781, 1959.

133. WARREN K.W. & VEIDENHEIMER M. Pathological considerations in the choice of operation for chronic relapsing pancreatitis. *New Eng. J. Med.* **262**:323, 1962.

134. WARREN K.W. & KUNE G.A. Trends in biliary surgery. *New Eng. J. Med.* **273**:1322, 1965.

135. WARREN K.W., ATHANASSIADES S. & MONGE J.L. Primary sclerosing cholangitis. A study of 42 cases. *Am. J. Surg.* **111**:23, 1966.

136. WARREN K.W., MCDONALD W.M. & KUNE G.A. Bile duct strictures. New concepts in the management of an old problem. In W.T. Irvine (ed.), *Modern Trends in Surgery* (2e). Butterworth, London, 1966.

137. WARREN K.W., POULANTZAS J.K. & KUNE G.A. Use of a Y tube splint in the repair of biliary strictures. *Surg. Gynec. Obstet.* **122**:785, 1966.

138. WARREN K.W. & HARDY K.H. The damaged bile duct. *Surg. Clin. N. Amer.* **47**:1077, 1967.

139. WARREN K.W. & KUNE G.A. Surgical treatment of chronic relapsing pancreatitis. In H.R. Hawthorne, A.S. Frobese & J.A. Sterling (eds.), *The Acute Abdomen and Emergent Lesions of the Gastrointestinal Tract*. Thomas, Springfield, Ill., 1967.

140. WARSHAW A.L., SCHAPIRO R.H., FERRUCCI J.T. JR. & GALDABINI J.J. Persistent obstructive jaundice, cholangitis and biliary cirrhosis due to common bile duct stenosis in chronic pancreatitis. *Gastroenterology* **70**:562, 1976.

141. WAY L.W. & DUNPHY J.E. Biliary stricture. *Am. J. Surg.* **124**:287, 1972.

142. WESTPHAL K. Muskelfunktion, Nervensystem and Pathologie der Gallenwege. *Z. Klin. Med.* **96**:22, 1923.

143. WHEELER E.S. & LONGMIRE W.P. JR. Repair of benign stricture of the common bile duct by jejunal interposition choledochoduodenostomy. *Surg. Gynec. Obstet.* **146**:260, 1978.

144. WHELTON M.J. Sclerosing cholangitis. *Clin. Gastroenterol.* **2**:163, 1973.

7. Biliary Tumours

Benign tumours, hyperplasias, and malformations of the biliary tract, are most interesting conditions from a theoretical angle but are uncommon and easily treatable. In contrast, malignant tumours are relatively common, but their surgical treatment is unsatisfactory and the prognosis usually poor.

GALLBLADDER TUMOURS

BENIGN TUMOURS AND HYPERPLASIAS

CLINICOPATHOLOGICAL CLASSIFICATION

A clinicopathological classification of benign tumours and hyperplasias of the gallbladder that has been adapted from Ochsner [110] is presented here. This classification into adenomyomatosis, polyps, and sessile mucosal tumours, is based on cholecystographic appearances, so a single pathological lesion may be found in more than one category.

Adenomyomatosis. These lesions have also been called cholecystitis glandularis proliferans, cholecystitis cystica, epitheliomyoma, Rokitansky–Aschoff sinuses, adenomyoma, gallbladder dysplasia, and hamartoma [83]. The lesion may be diffuse, segmental, or localised (Fig. 7.1). The localised form is almost always at the fundus of the gallbladder. The lesions consist of a variable admixture of smooth muscle, stoma, and glandular elements. The glands are frequently compressed or appear cystic or diverticular. Both macroscopically and radiologically the lesions have a variety of appearances, according to the extent of gallbladder involvement, the relative proportion of the various elements, and the degree of distension of the gallbladder [83].

Polyps. Polyps refer merely to a circumscribed lesion on a stalk. Gallbladder polyps include a variety of pathological lesions—inflammatory or hyperplastic polyps, such as the polypoid variety of adenomyomatosis, cholesterol polyps which consist of cholesterol-laden macrophages, polypoid adenomas, and papillomas. Polypoid carcinoma *in situ* has also been described, but the invasive nature of the lesions has been questioned [110, 111, 141, 156].

Sessile mucosal tumours. These include sessile adenomas and papillomas and other unusual benign tumours, such as fibroadenomas or neurinomas [110].

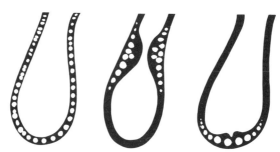

Fig. 7.1. Various types of adenomyomatosis. (*left*) Diffuse. (*centre*) Segmental. (*right*) Localised. Redrawn from Gutras and Levesque, 1966.

Sessile or polypoid carcinomas are most uncommon. Even if they do occur they cannot usually be picked up on cholecystography, because they are almost always associated with diseased gallbladders and with gallstones [110].

DIAGNOSIS

The diagnosis of benign tumours and hyperplasias of the gallbladder is entirely dependent on cholecystography.

Adenomyomas are variable lesions, but they usually have a diagnostic triad of a filling defect, an opaque central speck of dye corresponding to the umbilication of the lesion, and opaque peripheral dots due to the diverticula (Fig. 7.2) [83].

Polypoid lesions are differentiated from gallstones in that the former maintain a constant position in reference to the gallbladder when films are taken with the patient in various positions (Fig. 7.3). Similarly, sessile mucosal lesions also maintain a constant position in relation to the gallbladder. A sessile lesion may

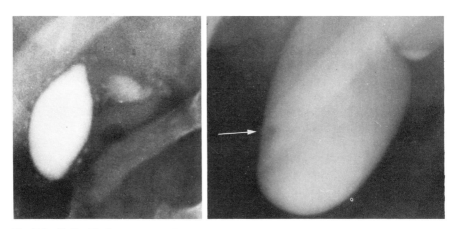

Fig. 7.2. (*left*). Cholecystogram showing diffuse adenomyomatosis.

Fig. 7.3. (*right*). Cholecystogram of a gallbladder polyp. Note that polyps do *not* move in reference to the gallbladder when films are taken with the patient in various positions.

be differentiated from a polyp by a tangential projection in which the profile of the lesion produces a notch in the opacified lumen of the gallbladder [110].

TREATMENT

It is uncertain whether adenomyomatosis produces symptoms, but most clinicians feel that the condition is asymptomatic. Good results were reported in some cases following cholecystectomy for adenomyomatosis in patients who had biliary colic or digestive disturbances [65, 83]. In the present state of our ignorance we should not entirely deny the clinical significance of this condition. A logical approach to the management of this condition is presented in Chapter 12, which deals with various aspects of acalculous benign biliary disease. It is certain, however, that adenomyomatosis is not a premalignant condition [83, 110].

Whether the intramural diverticula are prone to perforation and biliary extravasation is also uncertain, but some surgeons recommend cholecystectomy as a prophylaxis against this complication [74].

Polyps and sessile mucosal lesions are not usually responsible for symptoms and require no special treatment [49, 110]. However, if symptoms are present for which no other cause can be found, it is reasonable to recommend cholecystectomy [23]. Malignant change of these lesions is very unlikely, especially if the lesions occur without gallstones [49, 110, 119, 144]. If the lesions are associated with gallstones, malignancy may develop, but then the polyps or sessile mucosal lesions are merely coincidental.

CARCINOMA OF THE GALLBLADDER

Cancer of the gallbladder is a most depressing condition because of the hopeless outlook in the majority of cases.

INCIDENCE

carcinoma of the gallbladder is an uncommon neoplasm that is found in about 0.5 per cent of all autopsies performed in adult hospitals and in about 2 per cent of all operations on the gallbladder. It also constitutes about 4 per cent of all carcinomas found at necropsy [10, 69, 103, 148, 154]. This carcinoma is the most common malignant lesion of the biliary tract and the fifth most common of the digestive tract [163].

There is some evidence that the condition is commoner in North America and Australia than in England and this may be related to the high incidence of gallstones in the former regions [16, 38, 154]. A study of 24 countres has found that Japan has the highest mortality from gallbladder and liver cancer [44, 143]. A high incidence of gallbladder cancer has been reported in Japanese immigrants to the United States and also in American Indians [66, 86, 87, 107, 131, 147, 175]. It is most commonly seen in patients over 65 years of age with a female predominance of about 3:1. It is hoped that the incidence of cancer of the gallbladder will decrease because stone-ridden gallbladders are now treated at an earlier stage than in the past. Results from the United States show that there has been a decrease in the incidence and death from this condition [86].

AETIOLOGY

The cause of gallbladder cancer is unknown. As noted earlier malignant change in benign tumours of the gallbladder is rare.

All series show that gallbladder stones are present in about 70–80 per cent of cases. The precise incidence of associated gallstones is uncertain, because not all cases come to removal of the gallbladder or to autopsy [10, 66, 73, 86, 113, 122, 148, 154, 173]. Removal of the gallstones by cholecystostomy does not necessarily protect the patient from the development of a gallbladder carcinoma at a later date [88]. Clinical data does not establish a causative role for gallstones in the development of carcinoma of the gallbladder. However, the association is frequent enough to suggest common antecedents or at least a facilitative role.

Looked at from another angle the risk of gallbladder cancer developing in a patient with gallstones is small, probably about 1–2 per cent [3, 18, 38, 66, 73, 100, 122, 179]. This risk appears to increase, however, the longer the patient has had gallstones. Of the patients who have gallstones and who are older than 50 about 6–10 per cent will, ultimately, develop carcinoma of the gallbladder [63, 80]. Porcelain gallbladder, which is due to calcification of the gallbladder wall, has a high risk of developing carcinoma [17, 123].

On the experimental side, Fortner and co-workers have induced carcinoma of the gallbladder in cats and dogs following the introduction of methylcholanthrene into the gallbladder [60, 62, 64]. Methyl cholanthrene is a highly potent carcinogen and its chemical composition is related to bile acids. Bile acids have been shown to influence the growth and morphology of cultured fibroblasts [166] and *in vivo* experiments have shown that bile acids promote large bowel cancer [130].

Anaerobic organisms can be cultured from gallbladder bile of patients with calculi [51, 146]. Clostridial organisms, which are suspected of producing carcinogens from bile salts in the stool, account for about 40 per cent of all anaerobe isolates from the gallbladder [51]. It is possible that carcinogens are produced in a similar way in the gallbladder by anaerobes.

Occupation and lifestyle may be an important aetiological factor. Gallbladder cancer has been shown to be statistically more prevalent in automotive and rubber-plant workers [101]. An association between gallbladder cancer and typhoid carrier state has been shown but there is no known mechanism for this association [11, 170, 198].

PATHOLOGY

Most gallbladder malignancies are adenocarcinomas or anaplastic carcinomas; less commonly, the histological type is squamous cell carcinoma, carcinoid, melanoma, or even a sarcoma [1, 45, 121, 122, 127, 145, 173].

The common modes of spread are important because of their surgical implications. Direct spread to adjacent organs is common, with involvement of the liver, common bile duct, duodenum, colon, stomach, omentum, pancreas, and anterior abdominal wall [45, 54, 127, 128, 148, 169, 173, 184].

Lymphatic spread is to the 'cystic' lymph gland (see Blood supply and lymphatics, Chapter 1), the glands along the common bile duct, the pancreatico-duodenal glands, and then the coeliac or superior mesenteric glands. It is of interest that retrograde lymphatic spread up to the hilum of the liver probably does not occur [3, 45, 54, 105, 127, 128, 148, 164]. Lymph node metastases were present in at least 50 per cent of reported cases, with the exception of the observations of Smith in 1964 who found this in only 25 per cent [54, 173, 184].

Vaittinen, in an extensive review of cancer of the gallbladder, found carcinoma confined in the gallbladder to 6 per cent of cases, infiltrating the liver in 83 per cent, metastasised to regional nodes in 38 per cent, adhering or infiltrating other organs in 42 per cent, and metastasised to distant sites in 38 per cent [169].

Vascular spread is through the cholecystic vein, if one is present, but mainly through the plexus of veins surrounding the gallbladder wall and draining either directly into the liver substance or into the plexus of veins around the common bile duct. This type of invasion is less common than direct or lymphatic spread and is likely to involve only the adjacent portions of the liver and common bile duct. Blood-borne multiple liver metastases do occur, but are uncommon [54, 148].

The incidence of distant metastases is uncertain, but is probably infrequent [54, 148, 165, 184]. Perineural spread is relatively common and intraductal spread uncommon [54].

MODES OF PRESENTATION

Cholecystectomy for gallstones. In a number of cases the gallbladder is removed for gallstones, and the pathologist reports the presence of an associated carcinoma which was not suspected.

Biliary tract pain. In these cases laparotomy is performed for biliary tract pain believed to be caused by gallstones, but at operation it is clear that a cancer of the gallbladder is present.

Acute cholecystitis. Very occasionally, acute cholecystitis is caused by a carcinoma occluding the cystic duct [89, 118, 162]. Carcinoma may be a coincidental finding when the inflammatory response is presumably due to obstruction of the cystic duct by a stone. About one-sixth of patients with carcinoma of the gallbladder have been reported to present with acute cholecystitis [122, 164].

Obstructive jaundice. This is the mode of presentation in about half the cases; it almost always implies considerable spread and a hopeless prognosis.

Distant spread. This is an uncommon mode of presentation, but rarely patients present with ascites, an internal fistula into the gastrointestinal tract, or obstructive symptoms in the gastrointestinal tract [67, 148, 157].

DIAGNOSIS

The preoperative diagnosis of carcinoma of the gallbladder may be suspected, but a definite diagnosis is usually made only at operation.

Clinical features. Unfortunately, cancer of the gallbladder has no characteristic features to distinguish it from gallstone disease. Pain is the commonest symptom; obstructive jaundice or a hard mass under the right costal margin is present in about half the cases [16, 45, 63, 121, 122, 127, 148, 173]. In a patient with obstructive jaundice and a palpable gallbladder the mistaken diagnosis of carcinoma of the pancreas is usually made. The diagnosis of carcinoma of the gallbladder may be suggested in patients who have had intermittent attacks of pain in the past and whose pain has now become constant.

Laboratory tests. If the patient is not jaundiced the liver function tests will usually be normal. In the jaundiced patient the liver function tests will show an obstructive (cholestatic) pattern, but they will give no clue to the cause of the obstruction.

Occasionally, serum alkaline phosphatase is elevated without elevation of bilirubin, and this can indicate tumour involvement of the liver or obstruction to portion of the biliary tree. A patient with an elevated serum alkaline phosphatase, in conjunction with normal serum bilirubin and transaminases, should be suspected of hepatic malignancy in the absence of bone disease [45].

Radiology. In the non-jaundiced patient oral cholecystography will show a non-functioning gallbladder and intravenous cholangiography will show a blockage of the cystic duct. These findings are also seen in gallstone disease and are therefore not of diagnostic value. In the jaundiced patient oral cholecystography and intravenous cholangiography are of no value, because the dye will not be excreted by the liver.

Percutaneous transhepatic cholangiography or endoscopic retrograde choleangiopancreatography in the jaundiced patient will show the site of bile duct obstruction caused by the spread of the carcinoma, but they will not distinguish from obstruction caused by a primary bile duct carcinoma.

A liver scan may show the extent of hepatic metastases. If these are localised to the right lobe extensive resection may be contemplated; if both lobes are involved radical surgery is fruitless.

Operative diagnosis. In most cases the operative diagnosis is clear, because the gallbladder is replaced by a hard mass which invades the adjacent liver. There may also be obvious spread into the area of the bile duct and into adjacent organs. Obvious lymph gland, peritoneal, or hepatic metastases may be present. If the lesion is localised to the gallbladder the associated gallstones may be palpated, but unless the removed gallbladder is opened the carcinoma may be missed. For this reason it is advisable to open at the time of surgery all gallbladders removed for cholelithiasis and to inspect the mucosa.

TREATMENT

Excisional surgery holds the only prospect of survival. Unfortunately, the extent of the malignant process is such that in the majority of cases potentially curative excision is not possible at the time of surgery.

In an individual case the nature of the surgery depends on assessment of the following factors:

1. Extent of the malignant process.
2. Age and general condition of the patient.
3. Ability and experience of the surgeon to perform major excisional surgery.

In practical terms one of three situations may be encountered, namely, an unexpected finding after cholecystectomy, a resectable and potentially curable lesion, or an extensive, incurable lesion.

Unexpected finding after cholecystectomy. In this type of case probably nothing further needs to be done. In the relatively fit patient, in whom histological studies showed invasion of the gallbladder wall, Smith [1964] argues for reoperation and right hepatic lobectomy. At present no figures are available to support or deny this proposition. A review of recent series shows that most surgeons have not in fact reoperated on such cases [3, 9, 16, 35, 69, 169, 173].

Resectable carcinoma with or without local spread. This is the type of case in which the tumour is confined to the gallbladder without macroscopic extension into the bile duct and without more distant spread. In this category is also placed the lesion which has spread only locally into the liver and has not involved the bile duct. If the diagnosis can be made at the time of laparotomy, cholecystectomy alone has a virtually hopeless prognosis [3, 16, 19, 20, 21, 69, 148, 173].

In the relatively fit patient more radical surgery has been advocated [3, 18, 26, 53, 70, 115, 121, 148, 169]. Earlier workers advocated resection of the tumour with a wide, local excision of the surrounding liver tissue, together with excision of the lymph nodes in the area of the gallbladder and gastrohepatic omentum. Other surgeons have argued that even this is inadequate and advocated extended right hepatic lobectomy or 'middle' hepatic lobectomy [26, 53, 115, 116, 148]. Not enough surgery of this type has been performed to know whether such radical surgery does influence the prognosis. However, there is doubt that radical treatment can influence prognosis [128]. The immediate operative mortality is still reasonably high. On the other hand the prognosis of this group is appalling, and radical surgery may lead to an occasional long-term survival. If the patient is relatively fit, and the surgeon is experienced at major hepatic resection, radical treatment is advised.

Extensive and unresectable involvement. In this type of case the malignant process has extended to the bile duct or to numerous other surrounding organs, or there are multiple hepatic metastases. In many of these cases it is not possible to perform a definite procedure of any type.

In some who have bile duct obstruction it may be possible to establish biliary drainage by dilatation of the malignant stricture and insertion of a T tube [148,

173]. This does not alter the ultimate prognosis but may give temporary relief of pruritus, which can be an intolerable symptom.

Continuous prolonged chemotherapeutic infusion through the hepatic artery has been used for patients with hepatic involvement, and at least temporary objective palliation has been obtained in a number of cases [176, 177]. Others have had less optimistic results [41].

PROGNOSIS

The prognosis of cancer of the gallbladder is poor. In any series about 80 per cent are dead within 1 year of diagnosis and only about 2–5 per cent are alive after 5 years [3, 16, 21, 35, 42, 78, 86, 122, 127, 135, 154, 169, 173].

Long-term survival does occur in the patient whose gallbladder is removed for gallstones and in whom a coexistent carcinoma is discovered by the pathologist [9, 16, 35, 45, 69, 135]. This group has been reported to have a 5-year survival of about 5 to 10 per cent [105, 169]. The only long-term survivor that one of the authors has seen was a case of this type. Only a handful of long-term survivors have been reported after radical surgery [26, 63, 148].

PREVENTION

Prevention is placed last in this section, in order to contrast it with the prognosis of an actual carcinoma of the gallbladder.

It has been stated that the risk of cancers developing in a patient with gallstones is significant, but not high. It was also shown in Chapter 5 that the risk of non-malignant complications supervening in patients with gallstones is very high, and that when surgery is performed in these complicated cases the mortality is higher than in an elective case. The risks of mortality from these non-malignant complications, together with the hopeless prognosis if a malignancy supervenes, should make us advise early operation or medical dissolution for both symptomatic and asymptomatic cases, particularly in the patient who is otherwise fit [3, 16, 69, 80, 109, 122, 127].

BILE DUCT TUMOURS

BENIGN TUMOURS AND HYPERPLASIAS

Non-malignant epithelial proliferations of the bile ducts are most uncommon. To the present time about 150 such cases have been reported [30, 33, 36, 37, 46, 82, 90, 97]. The exact incidence of these lesions is uncertain, because some are asymptomatic and others are unreported.

CLINICOPATHOLOGICAL CLASSIFICATION

The following clinicopathological classification takes into consideration the histological appearances and the behaviour of these non-malignant epithelial lesions. (Non-epithelial tumours are rare, and are not included.) There are four categories (Fig. 7.4):

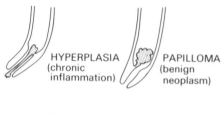

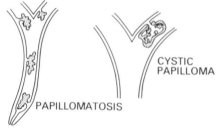

Fig. 7.4. Various types of bile duct hyperplasias and benign tumours.

1. Hyperplasia.
2. Papilloma.
3. Multiple papillomas and papillomatosis.
4. Cystic papilloma.

Hyperplasia. Clearly, hyperplastic lesions of the bile duct are not tumours, but
they are included here because they resemble papillomas clinically and histologically. Differentiation from a papilloma may be difficult, but in a typical case the
hyperplastic epithelium is associated with subepithelial chronic inflammatory
change. The hyperplastic lesions are probably the result of a chronic inflammatory process of the distal bile duct, or the duodenum; they are almost always
found in the region of the papilla of Vater [2, 14, 40]. The mucosa of this region is
normally thrown into papillary folds and is, therefore, predisposed to a polypoid
hyperplasia as a response to an inflammatory process. Some hyperplastic lesions
may progress to fibrotic stenosis of the papilla of Vater [2].

Rarely, a hyperplastic lesion is encountered as a result of persistent irritation,
such as that due to unabsorbable ligatures, gallstones, or a T tube [37].

Papilloma. These are the commonest benign tumours, and are usually situated in
the region of the papilla of Vater. The lesions are usually of a polypoid type,
rarely bigger than 2–3 cm in diameter, and have regular, tall columnar cells,
sometimes mixed with goblet cells; there is a minimum of subepithelial inflammatory change. Distinction from a hyperplasia may be difficult microscopically. The
malignant potentialities of these lesions have been emphasised by some workers
[30, 33, 34].

Multiple papillomas and papillomatosis. These are most uncommon; only seven
have been reported in the literature [32, 33, 46, 50]. These lesions have a structure
similar to that of a papilloma but have enormous proliferative potential. They
are prone to recurrence and malignant change.

Cystic papilloma. These are also most uncommon, only four having been reported [15, 33, 68, 136]. They are cystic lesions with intracystic papillary projections. In all four cases the lesion was proximally situated in the common hepatic duct or in one of the hepatic ducts.

DIAGNOSIS

Clinical features. Hyperplasias and benign tumours of the bile ducts may be symptomless and may be discovered only at autopsy [14, 36]. If symptoms do occur they are due to biliary tract obstruction. No clinical features are characteristic of this condition. From a review of the literature, Dowdy and co-workers in 1962 found that the order of frequency of symptoms were: jaundice, pain, weight loss, and cholangitis [64]. The incidence of associated gallstones is very high, and in any one case it may be difficult to decide to what degree each condition contributes to the symptoms.

Radiology. If the patient is not jaundiced an intravenous cholangiogram may show a filling defect, or it may show partial biliary obstruction as evidenced by the time-density-retention concept (Chapter 3) [112, 185]. The jaundiced patient may be investigated by either percutaneous transhepatic cholangiography or endoscopic retrograde cholangiopancreatography [39, 140]. With endoscopic retrograde cholangiopancreatography it is possible to do cytological examination of bile, intraduct brushing cytology, and even biopsy [12, 55, 134]. Sometimes a barium meal examination will show up a papilloma of the papilla of Vater as a filling defect [72, 112].

   In most instances a preoperative diagnosis is not made; in some the diagnosis is missed even at operation [30, 46, 112].

Operative Diagnosis. At operation the lesion may be palpable, particularly if it is large and situated in the region of the papilla of Vater. However, not all papillomas are palpable. The bile duct proximal to the lesion is usually dilated, but it may be of normal size. With lesions of the distal bile duct instrumentation will reveal an obstruction, but sometimes the instruments slip past the tumour and the lesion escapes detection.

   Operative cholangiography is most valuable in confirming the presence of a filling defect and excluding other associated pathology, as noted in Fig. 7.5.

   A thorough exploration of the entire biliary tract is important, because of the high incidence of associated biliary tract disease. Choledochoscopy can be most helpful in detecting intrahepatic lesions and also to ensure that their removal has been complete [160].

TREATMENT

The treatment of hyperplastic lesions and papillomas of the bile ducts is local excision. Frozen section of the specimen is a useful measure, because if a malignant focus is found in the lesion the surgeon is advised to proceed to a more radical operation [30, 33, 112]. Uniformly good results have been obtained with

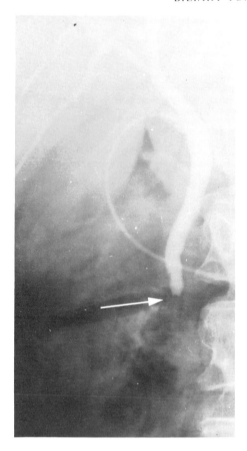

Fig. 7.5. Operative cholangiogram showing a filling defect in the lower end of the
common bile duct, which turned out to be
a benign papilloma. Note that cholangio-
graphically the condition cannot be differentiated from a gallstone.

local excision, particularly if the associated pathological condition, such as
choledocholithiasis, has also been dealt with adequately [33, 37, 46, 112].

Local excision and histological examination of frozen sections are advised for
multiple papillomas and for papillomatosis. Technical difficulties may be
encountered in removing all the papillomas, particularly when these are situated
in the intrahepatic bile ducts. In such cases curettage of the bile ducts may be a
helpful adjunct. The prognosis of this group is ultimately poor, because of the
tendency for recurrence and malignant change [25, 30, 33, 50].

Local excision of the cystic papilloma was a satisfactory mode of treatment in
three of the four reported cases. In the fourth case a local recurrence was treated
by further excision, and a satisfactory final result was achieved [15].

CARCINOMA OF THE BILE DUCTS

Cancer arising in the major bile ducts is less common than cancer of the
gallbladder. The outlook in most cases is poor, though a significant number of
long-term survivals have now been recorded following excisional surgery and

even following palliative biliary decompression. Carcinoma of the papilla of Vater has been excluded from this discussion.

INCIDENCE

Bile duct carcinoma is found in about 0.2 per cent of autopsies and in about 0.5 per cent of biliary tract operations; it also constitutes about 2 per cent of all cancers coming to autopsy [85, 86, 91, 108, 139].

In 1957, Sako and co-workers made an exhaustive review of the literature and collected 570 documented cases of bile duct carcinoma [139]. Since then a number of other series of cases as well as many individual reports have appeared in the literature, so that up to the present time about 1500 cases have been reported [4, 5, 8, 25, 58, 61, 81, 91, 95, 134, 155, 159, 162, 167, 186]. The largest consecutive series comes from the Lahey Clinic in Boston from where Braasch, Warren, and Kune reported the experience of the Clinic with 173 cases of malignant bile duct tumours [25].

AETIOLOGY

The cause of carcinoma of the bile ducts is unknown. A number of aetiological factors have been noted.

Gallstones. Gallstones have been found in association with cancer of the bile ducts, but less frequently than with cancer of the gallbladder. Incidence of the association with bile duct cancer varies from 20 to 57 per cent in different reports [5, 8, 24, 25, 108, 139, 153, 155]. It is possible that some of these gallstones are secondary to an obstructing carcinoma.

The mechanism by which gallstones produce bile duct cancer is unknown. It is possible that gallstones or the change in the chemical composition of bile associated with gallstone formation may be important. Willis in 1942 theorised that there may be a conversion of bile acids into methylcholanthrene, which may have a carcinogenic action in susceptible subjects [183]. The development of cancer of the bile ducts has been reported in experimental animals after injection of bile from humans with bile duct cancer [60, 151].

Choledochal cysts. The incidence of bile duct cancer is high in patients with these cysts. The early onset of cancer (mean age 32 years) reinforces the argument that stasis of bile may be a significant risk factor for bile duct cancer [57, 99].

Papillomas and papillomatosis. Carcinoma developing in papillomas and in patients with papillomatosis has been reported, but this association must be most uncommon [25, 33, 43, 141]. At any rate, papillary carcinoma of the bile ducts is uncommon.

Primary sclerosing cholangitis and ulcerative colitis. An increasing body of evidence shows that patients with primary sclerosing cholangitis, following chronic ulcerative colitis, are prone to develop cancer of the biliary epithelium (see Primary sclerosing cholangitis, Chapter 6).

PATHOLOGY

The macroscopic and microscopic appearances as well as the modes of spread of these tumours have been extensively studied [24, 25, 91, 139, 155, 162]. No segment of the bile duct is immune to cancer. However, cancers in the hilum of the liver and in the distal common duct are more frequent than those in the central part of the duct system.

The tumour is usually a solid, nodular type, less commonly a scirrhous, infiltrating type, and least commonly a papillary type. The nodular and infiltrating types produce varying degrees of bile duct obstruction; eventually the papillary type produces obstruction also. The bile ducts proximal to these tumours are almost always dilated.

The microscopic appearances are usually those of adenocarcinoma or anaplastic carcinoma and, rarely, papillary carcinoma. Mucinous and scirrhous types are classed as occasional variants of adenocarcinoma. Squamous cell carcinomas, carcinoids, and sarcomas, are rare lesions [25, 79, 96, 162].

The mode of spread of bile duct cancer is of practical importance. A frequent feature is considerable subepithelial spread of the tumour within the wall of the bile duct, both in a proximal and distal direction [25, 91, 155, 162]. This fact alone may militate against successful radical surgery.

The extent of local spread to adjacent organs and the incidence of metastases vary in different reports, according to the proportion of autopsy and operative cases in the series. The relatively frequent invasion of nerves has been reported, and this may be at least one of the causes of pain that is so commonly seen [91, 108]. Direct spread or metastasis is present in about one-half to two-thirds of cases [4, 91, 153, 155, 162]. Direct spread may involve the portal vein, hepatic artery, pancreas, duodenum, and gallbladder. The regional peridochal glands are involved first, then the pancreaticoduodenal, the coeliac, and the superior mesenteric glands. Hepatic metastases are relatively common, but distant metastases are uncommon.

A number of workers state that in some cases neither local spread nor metastasis can be demonstrated at operation or at post mortem, so that an optimistic and aggressive surgical attack on these lesions is worth while.

DIAGNOSIS

Clinical features. There is nothing characteristic about the clinical features of bile duct cancer. A preoperative diagnosis is frequently suspected but rarely made with certainty.

There is a wide range in the age distribution, the average age being in the sixth and seventh decades. In contrast to the situation with cancer of the gallbladder males are somewhat more commonly affected than females [8, 25, 81, 86, 91, 139, 155, 162, 186].

A rapid onset of symptoms with progressive obstructive jaundice is characteristic. Fluctuation of the jaundice both clinical and biochemically has been reported. This may tie in with the observations that in some cases bile is present in the duodenum and that at operation complete obstruction to probing is not always present, but the patient is jaundiced [8, 91, 108, 162]. It is possible that in such cases there is associated oedema, or that subepithelial spread has converted the bile duct into a rigid tube, interfering with bile transit (see Discharge of bile into the duodenum, Chapter 2). Intraluminal sequestration and the passage of this slough through the bile duct may also be a reason for intermittent jaundice.

Upper abdominal pain, pruritus, and considerable weight loss are frequent associated findings. Less commonly, patients have chills and fever or other symptoms such as anorexia, vomiting, and diarrhoea [4, 5, 25, 137, 139]. Very occasionally, patients present with typical acute cholecystitis if there is obstruction of the cystic duct [138]. Occasionally, patients without jaundice present with biliary colic-type pain as their only symptom, as was seen in the patient whose cholangiogram appears in Fig. 7.7.

Hepatomegaly is frequent and a palpable gallbladder may be present in tumours which are distal to the point of insertion of the cystic duct. Ascites or splenomegaly is occasionally seen [25, 139, 161].

Laboratory findings. Liver function tests show jaundice of the cholestatic type (Chapter 4). Thus, there is a variable elevation of the serum bilirubin level and the serum alkaline phosphatase level is consistently high, but flocculation tests, serum proteins, and transaminase, are frequently within normal limits. This indicates a rapid onset of obstruction without significant parenchymal liver damage at the time of presentation [91, 161]. Patients may also be found to be anaemic [81].

A number of workers reported enthusiastically on cytological examination of duodenal and biliary aspirate, noting that positive findings were confirmed at operation [47, 92, 93, 133, 134, 180].

Radiology. Intravenous cholangiography is usually not helpful as obstructive jaundice prevents the excretion of dye in the bile ducts. Percutaneous transhepatic cholangiography will demonstrate the site of obstruction in the jaundiced patient but will usually not reveal the cause of the obstruction (Fig. 7.6). Endoscopic retrograde cholangiopancreatography in the jaundiced patient will merely show the distal bile duct, but it can be complementary to percutaneous cholangiography to outline the extent of the lesion and one may also be able to obtain fluid for cytology [133]. In the non-jaundiced patient ERCP can be valuable in outlining the bile duct and the actual tumour, as may be seen in Fig. 7.7.

Recent work indicates therapeutic extensions to percutaneous transhepatic cholangiography in bile duct cancer [29, 117]. Following percutaneous cholangiography an endoprosthesis is inserted through the constricting tumour over a guide wire. An example of this useful technique is shown in Fig. 7.8, and this was performed for a cancer of the common hepatic duct in a very poor-risk patient. Barium meal examination may show a distortion of the duodenum, but this may be seen in all masses which occur in the head of the pancreas [25, 71, 77].

Operative diagnosis. The definitive diagnosis of bile duct cancer is established at

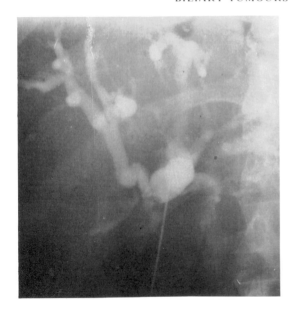

Fig. 7.6. Percutaneous transhepatic cholangiogram showing complete bile duct obstruction at the origin of the common hepatic duct caused by a bile duct cancer.

operation. The diagnosis is established on the macroscopic appearance and feel of the tumour, the presence of local extension, or the presence of metastases.

An operative cholangiogram is most helpful in showing narrowing or a complete block of the bile duct, but no special features distinguish a carcinoma from other forms of ductal or periductal obstruction, such as that due to carcinoma of the head of the pancreas or a non-malignant stricture [52, 76, 155, 183]. Complete occlusion usually means a cancer, but partial occlusion may have a benign or a malignant cause (Fig. 7.9).

The diffusely infiltrating scirrhous type of tumour may be difficult to distinguish from a non-malignant stricture, and especially from primary sclerosing cholangitis. These difficulties are accentuated if the lesion is high up in the hepatic ducts [6, 162].

In doubtful cases biopsy and frozen section examination of regional lymph nodes may be most helpful, but this is of diagnostic value only if positive for secondary carcinoma. Another useful preoperative procedure is a choledochotomy incision proximal or distal to the tumour, the scooping out of tissue from within the lumen of the bile duct, and the frozen-section examination of the specimen [25, 164]. Choledochoscopy can be useful for examining intrahepatic bile duct lesions and taking biopsies [94, 160].

TREATMENT

When the tumour does not involve vital strictures and when there are no obvious metastases, radical excision of the tumour provides the only hope of survival. Unfortunately, there are only a few instances in which radical excisional surgery is possible. If excision is not possible some type of palliative biliary decompression is attempted. In a number of cases no definitive surgical procedure is

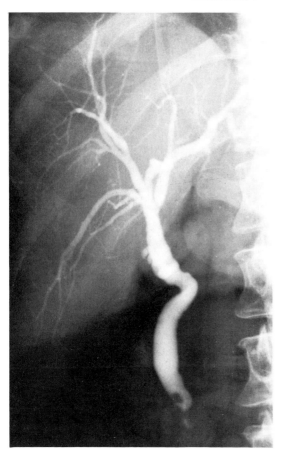

Fig. 7.7. Endoscopic retro-grade cholangiogram of a patient with a filling defect in the lower end of the bile duct caused by a papillary carcinoma. The pictures resembles a gallstone, but sphincterotomy revealed the true nature of the lesion.

possible. In some cases prolonged chemotherapeutic infusion of cytotoxic agents through the hepatic artery has achieved a measure of palliation, but only if bile duct decompression has also been obtained [25, 174].

The actual nature of the surgery, whether it be radical excision or decompression, depends on the site of the tumour. The exception is the type of tumour which has involved the entire extrahepatic system and has infiltrated the vital structures in the area. Usually, in such cases very little can be done. For practical purposes bile duct tumours can be divided into three groups—proximal, central, and distal.

Proximal tumours

Resection. These involve either the common hepatic duct at its bifurcation, or the individual hepatic ducts. If only one hepatic duct is involved it may be excised in continuity with the lobe of liver it supplies [25, 31]. This is an extensive procedure, advocated only when the surgeon has experience with major hepatic resections and when he can be reasonably certain that the tumour can be removed completely with a margin of apparently uninvolved tissue. When the

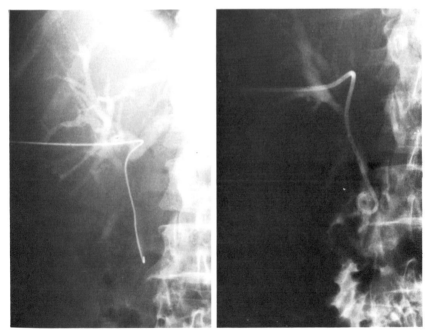

Fig. 7.8. Percutaneous transhepatic cholangiogram showing a cancer of the common hepatic duct. A guide wire passes through the cancer into the common bile duct (left). An endoprosthesis catheter was inserted over the guide wire, which transtubated the tumour allowing internal drainage of bile (right).

tumour involves the bifurcation of the hepatic ducts, and it is resectable, resection of the tumour together with resection of portions of the three confluent ducts is advocated [4, 61, 76, 81, 129, 148, 167]. A successful resection involving the tumour *en bloc* with left-sided hepatic lobectomy has been described [84]. With anterior extension into the liver, excision of the lesion and quadrate lobectomy *en bloc* has also been advocated [126, 152]. These various modes of radical resection are illustrated in Fig. 7.10.

Palliative biliary decompression. When the tumour is not resectable palliative biliary decompression should be attempted. Because of the proximal position of these tumours even palliative decompression is usually technically difficult, and the provision of adequate drainage has exercised the ingenuity of many surgeons.

   The different methods of palliative biliary decompression of proximal tumours are shown in Figs. 7.11 and 7.12. With involvement of an individual hepatic duct, or of the confluence of the hepatic ducts, forcible dilatation and transtumour intubation with a T, Y, or U tube may be done [25, 95, 129, 155, 158, 159]. Retrograde biliary decompression of the left and right hepatic ducts using transhepatic tubes as external hepaticostomies has also been described [13, 102, 126]. Retrograde drainage of the left hepatic duct with amputation of part of the left liver lobe and cholangiojejunostomy (Longmire procedure) has been used by a number of surgeons [7, 95, 98, 171]. Choledochocholecystostomy has also been

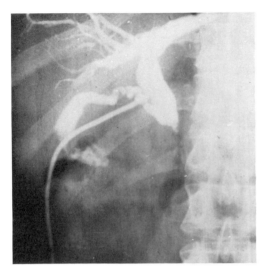

Fig. 7.9. Operative cholangiogram showing a complete block of the proximal part of the common bile duct, shown to be due to a bile duct cancer by endocholedochal biopsy.

described [149]. It is appreciated that if there is tumour involvement of the bifurcation of the hepatic duct the opposite lobe of the liver will remain obstructed after this procedure. For this reason retrograde drainage of both left and right hepatic ducts, using bilateral cholangiojejunostomy in a way similar to the Longmire procedure, has been described [76, 142].

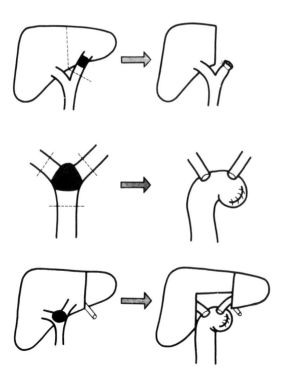

Fig. 7.10. Methods of radical resection of proximal bile duct tumours. (*top*) Left hemihepatectomy. (*centre*) Excision of the origin of the common hepatic duct and reconstruction with bilateral hepaticojejunostomy. (*bottom*) Excision of tumour and quadrate lobectomy. Reconstruction with bilateral hepaticojejunostomy.

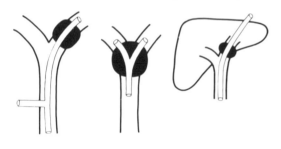

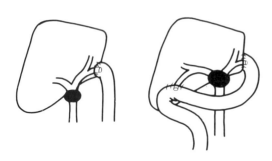

Fig. 7.11. Methods of palliative decompression of proximal bile duct tumours. (*top*) Transtumour intubation using T tube, Y tube, or transhepatic tube. (*bottom left*) Longmire procedure. (*bottom right*) Bilateral retrograde hepaticojejunostomy.

Of all of these palliative decompressions the most useful and most universally applicable is transhepatic intubation, advocated by Praderi of Uruguay and Lord Smith of Marlow [124, 125, 149]. This is a most useful procedure, particularly when a U tube is inserted, as this is replaceable and the technique is shown in Fig. 7.12. The actual technique of transhepatic intubation is described in Chapter 6.

Recently, it has been shown that bile duct decompression can be achieved without operation by using the percutaneous transhepatic cholangiogram of

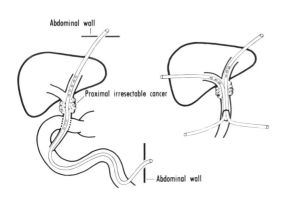

Fig. 7.12. Transhepatic intubation of non-resectable proximal bile duct tumours using a U tube (If two ends are connected it is called an O tube.) This is the most useful and most adaptable of the palliative decompressive procedures. (*left*) Tube through the duodenum and out through jejunum. (*right*) Transhepatic tubes (two in this case) brought out through bile duct below the tumour. (After Raul Praderi of Uruquay.)

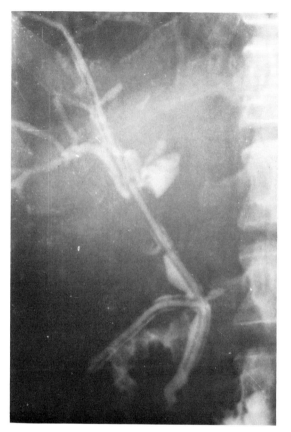

Fig. 7.13. Cholangiogram following transtumour intubation of a common hepatic duct cancer (arrow). The T tube acts as a splint and will be clipped off so that the bile can flow normally into the gut.

Okuda which employs the Chiba needle [114]. Percutaneous insertion of a transhepatic catheter through the Chiba needle with external drainage as a combination of internal–external drainage has been successful [104, 106, 168]. Also, after percutaneous cannulation of the bile duct the malignant duct stricture can be dilated under local anaesthesia by a series of catheters passed over a guide wire, the largest catheter then left *in situ* as an end prosthesis (Fig. 7.8) [29, 48, 75, 117]. These percutaneous techniques may be used for tumours at various sites, and at present are mainly used in the poor-risk patient who cannot withstand an operation, but with increasing experience and evaluation this method may find a wider use.

In all these palliative decompressive measures it is preferable if some type of internal rather than external drainage is provided. A corollary to this is that in all transtumour intubations the external limb of the tube should be clipped off if possible and used merely for irrigation, so that the bile will still flow into the gastrointestinal tract, as shown in Fig. 7.13.

Hepatic transplantation has been suggested as a form of treatment and an auxiliary liver allograft has also been described in the treatment of this tumour [61, 150, 181, 182]. With more successful immunosuppressive measures, and

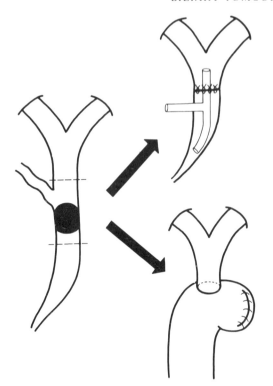

Fig. 7.14. Methods of resection of central bile duct tumour. Reconstruction can be either end-to-end or, more usually, hepaticojejunostomy Roux-en-Y.

more success with the technical aspects, orthotopic liver transplanatation could be the treatment of choice in selected cases.

Central tumours

Resection. These involve the distal common hepatic duct or the supraduodenal portion of the common bile duct and it may be possible to resect the lesion. Continuity may then be restored by end-to-end ductal anastomosis, although usually a hepaticojejunostomy is necessary because an end-to-end anastomosis cannot often be performed without tension [Fig. 7.14].

Palliative biliary decompression. Palliative decompression of these tumours may be obtained by forcible dilatation and transtumour intubation with various tubes as for proximal tumours, or a biliary-intestinal short circuit (as seen in Fig. 7.15). These tubes occasionally become blocked but it is possible to flush them or even change them without reoperation. A technique of non-operative T-tube replacement has also been described [132]. As with proximal tumours it is more desirable to obtain some type of internal biliary-intestinal drainage rather than external drainage. Again, if a T tube is used, the external limb of it should be used merely for daily irrigation, so that most of the bile still passes into the duodenum Cholecystojejunostomy may be done when the lesion is distal to the point of insertion of the cystic duct. However, hepaticojejunostomy rather than cholecys-

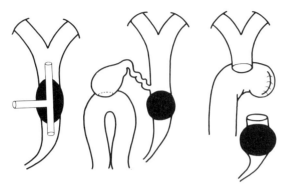

Fig. 7.15. Methods of palliative decompression of a central bile duct tumour. (*left*) Transtumour intubation with a T tube. (*centre*) Cholecystojejunostomy. (*right*) Hepaticojejunostomy Roux-en-Y.

tojejunostomy is preferred, because the tumour is frequently close to or actually occluding the cystic duct, and also because hepaticojejunostomy provides a more satisfactory and reliable mode of biliary drainage [25, 95, 155]. Cholecystojejunostomy is, however, a relatively simple procedure and may be used for palliation if the prognosis is poor (see Cholecystojejunostomy, Chapter 14).

Distal tumours
Resection. If the lesion involves the retropancreatic or distal portion of the common bile duct, and if it is resectable and no metastases are evident, a pancreaticoduodenal resection is advocated (Fig. 7.16) [24, 25, 56, 81, 95, 155]. In patients with deep or prolonged jaundice, and whose general medical condition is poor, resection may be done in two stages, usually with a loop cholecystojejunostomy as the first stage.

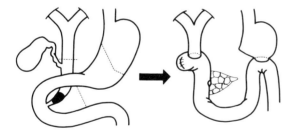

Fig. 7.16. Radical resection of a distal bile duct tumour by pancreaticoduodenectomy.

Palliative biliary decompression. Palliative bypass of these lesions is usually possible. Choledochojejunostomy is again preferred to cholecystojejunostomy, because the former provides more reliable decompression (Fig. 7.17). Cholecystojejunostomy and gastrojejunostomy are done for the patient with a bad prognosis, particularly if his general condition is poor at the time of surgery [25, 81, 95, 155].

PROGNOSIS
The outlook in the majority of cases of carcinoma of the bile ducts is poor. Thus, in two large consecutive series of cases reported by Thorbjarnarson in 1959 and

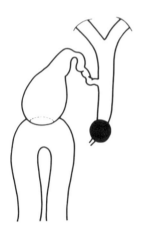 

Fig. 7.17. Methods of palliative decompression of distal bile duct tumours. (*left*) Cholecystojejunostomy. (*right*) Division of bile duct above tumour and choledochojejunostomy Roux-en-Y.

Braasch, Warren, and Kune in 1967, amounting to just over 200 cases, only eight patients were alive and well after 3 years. The average survival time is 3–6 months [8, 25, 81, 139, 161]. This gloomy picture is not generally appreciated, because many reports deal only with the description of relatively long-term survivals.

Untreated cases run a particularly short course and the majority are dead within about 3 months of diagnosis [25, 27, 91, 161]. Palliative decompression appears to prolong survival for a variable period, but even in this group the majority of patients are dead within 6 months of diagnosis. However, even if survival is not prolonged by more than 2–3 months, decompression does, at least for a short time, relieve the patient's misery caused by the pruritus and the jaundice. There is some evidence that an internal decompression, which allows the bile to get into the gut, prolongs life for a longer period than does an external drainage, possibly because of the problems associated with prolonged loss of fluids and electrolytes in the bile with external drainage only [6, 25, 71, 124, 125, 126, 142, 155, 158, 159].

Although palliative decompression does not alter the outlook significantly in the majority of cases very occasional long-term survivals of 3 years or more have been reported, and palliation should therefore be attempted in every case [6, 25, 71, 124, 125, 126, 142, 155, 158, 159]. Prolonged survival after palliative decompression is more frequent in patients with a sclerosing scirrhous type of carcinoma of the bile ducts [6].

Radical resection of the tumour in the apparent absence of metastases is occasionally followed by a long-term survival of 5 years or more [8, 22, 25, 27, 42, 81, 95, 120, 126]. The opportunities to perform a radical resection are few, and every such opportunity should be taken, because this is the only hope the patient has of a long-term survival.

REFERENCES

1. ABELL M.R. Diseases of the gallbladder: Their nature and classification. *Canad. Med. Ass. J.* **72**:565, 1955.

2. ACOSTA J.M. & NARDI G.L. Papillitis. Inflammatory disease of the ampulla of Vater. *Arch. Surg. (Chicago)* **92:**354, 1966.

3. ADSON M.A. Carcinoma of the gallbladder. *Surg. Clin. N. Amer.* **53:**1203, 1973.

4. AKWARI O.E. & KELLY K.A. Surgical treatment of adenocarcinoma. Location: junction of the right, left and common hepatic biliary ducts. *Arch. Surg.* **114:**22, 1979.

5. ALTEMEIER, W.A. & CULBERTSON W.R. Sclerosing carcinoma of the hepatic bile ducts. *Surg. Clin. N. Amer.* **53:**1229, 1973.

6. ALTEMEIER W.A., GALL E.A., ZINNINGER M.M. & HOXWORTH P.I. Sclerosing carcinoma of the major intrahepatic ducts. *A.M.A. Arch. Surg.* **75:**450, 1957.

7. ALVAREZ A.F. Carcinoma of the main hepatic ducts within the liver: A report of two cases treated by intrahepatic cholangiojejunostomy. *Ann. Surg.* **148:**773, 1958.

8. ANDERSSON A., BERGDAHL L., VAN DER LINDEN W. Malignant tumours of the extrahepatic bile ducts. *Surgery* **81:**198, 1977.

9. APPLEMAN R.M., MORLOCK C.G., DAHLIN D.C. & ADSON M.A. Long-term survival in carcinoma of the gallbladder. *Surg. Gynec. Obstet.* **117:**459, 1963.

10. ARMINSKI T.C. Primary carcinoma of the gallbladder: A collective review with the addition of 25 cases from the Grace Hospital, Detroit, Michigan. *Cancer* **2:**379, 1949.

11. AXELROD L., MUNSTER A.M. & O'BRIEN T.F. Typhoid cholecystitis and gallbladder carcinoma after interval of 67 years. *J.A.M.A.* **217:**83, 1971.

12. AYOOLA A., VENNES J.A., SILVIS J.E., ROHRMANN C.A. & ANSEL M.J. Endoscopic retrograde intrahepatic cholangiography in liver disease. *Gastrointest. Endoscopy* **22:**156, 1976.

13. BABCOCK W.W. Drainage of the exteriorized liver (external hepaticostomy): A palliative operation for jaundice. *Surgery* **12:**925, 1942.

14. BAGGENSTOSS A.H. Major duodenal papilla. Variations of pathologic interest and lesions of the mucosa. *Arch. Path.* **26:**853, 1938.

15. BARBER K.W. JR., REMINE W.H., HARRISON E.G. JR & PRIESTLEY U.T. Benign neoplasms of the extrahepatic bile ducts, including papilla of Vater. *Arch. Surg. (Chicago)* **81:**479, 1960.

16. BENNETT R.C. & JEPSON R.P. Carcinoma of the gallbladder. *Aust. New Zeal. J. Surg.* **34:**278, 1965.

17. BERK R.N., ARMBUSTER C.G. & SALTZSTEIN S.L. Carcinoma of the porcelain gallbladder. *Radiology* **106:**29, 1973.

18. BEVAN G. Tumours of the gallbladder. *Clin. Gastroenterology* **2:**175, 1973.

19. BIVINS B.A., MEEKER W.R. & GRIFFIN W.O. Importance of histologic classification of carcinoma of the gallbladder. *Am. Surg.* **41:**121, 1975.

20. BIVINS B.A., MEEKER W.R., WEISS D.L. & GRIFFIN W.O. Carcinoma in situ of the gallbladder; a dilemma. *South Med. J.* **68:**297, 1975.

21. BOOHER R.J. & PACK G.T. Cancer of the gallbladder. Report of a 5-year cure of anaplastic carcinoma with metastases. *Am. J. Surg.* **78:**175, 1949.

22. BOOHER R.J. & PACK G.T. Recurrent cancer of the common bile duct and periampullary region. *A.M.A. Arch. Surg.* **64:**224, 1952.

23. BORGERSON R.J., DELBECCARO E.J. & CALLAGHAN P.J. Polypoid lesions of the gallbladder. *Arch. Surg. (Chicago)* **85:**234, 1962.

24. BRAASCH J.W. Carcinoma of the bile duct. *Surg. Clin. N. Amer.* **53:**1217, 1973.

25. BRASSCH J.W., WARREN K.W. & KUNE G.A. Malignant neoplasms of the bile duct. *Surg. Clin. N. Amer.* **47:**627, 1967.

26. BRASFIELD R.D. Right hepatic lobectomy for carcinoma of the gallbladder: A five-year cure. *Ann. Surg.* **153:**563, 1961.

27. BROWN D.B., STRANG R., GORDON J. & HENDRY E.B. Primary carcinoma of the extrahepatic bile ducts. *Br. J. Surg.* **49:**22, 1961.

28. BROWN G. Surgical removal of tumours of the hepatic ducts. *Postgrad. Med. J.* **16:**79, 1954.

29. BURCHARTH F. A new endoprosthesis for nonoperative intubation of the biliary tract in malignant obstructive jaundice. *Surg. Gynec. Obstet.* **146**:76, 1978.

30. BURHANS R. & MYERS R.T. Benign neoplasms of the extrahepatic biliary ducts. *Am. Surg.* **37**:161, 1971.

31. CADY B. & FORTNER J.G. Surgical resection of intrahepatic bile duct cancer. *Am. J. Surg.* **118**:104, 1969.

32. CATTELL R.B., BRAASCH J.W. & KAHN F. Polypoid epithelial tumors of the bile ducts. *New Eng. J. Med.* **266**:57, 1962.

33. CAROLI J. Diseases of the intrahepatic biliary tree. *Clin. Gastroenterol.* **2**:147, 1973.

34. CATTELL R.B. & PYRTEK L.J. Premalignant lesions of the ampulla of Vater. *Surg. Gynec. Obstet.* **90**:21, 1950.

35. CHANDLER J.J. & FLETCHER W.S. A clinical study of primary carcinoma of the gallbladder. *Surg. Gynec. Obstet.* **117**:297, 1963.

36. CHO C., RULLIS I. & ROGERS L.S. Bile duct adenomas as liver nodules. *Arch. Surg.* **113**:272, 1978.

37. CHU P.T. Benign neoplasms of the extrahepatic biliary ducts. Review of the literature and report of a case of fibroma. *A.M.A. Arch. Path.* **50**:84, 1950.

38. COOKE L., JONES F.A. & KEECH M.K. Carcinoma of the gallbladder; a statistical study. *Lancet* **2**:585, 1953.

39. COTTON P.B. Progress report ERCP. *Gut* **18**:316, 1977.

40. DARDINSKI V.J. Inflammatory adenomatoid hyperplasia of major duodenal papilla in man. *Am. J. Path.* **7**:519, 1931.

41. DAVIS H.L., RAMIREZ G. & ANSFIELD F.J. Adenocarcinomas of stomach, pancreas, liver and biliary tracts: survival of 328 patients treated with fluoropyrimidine therapy. *Cancer* **33**:193, 1974.

42. DENDESTEN L. & LIECHTY R.D. Cancer of the biliary tree. *Am. J. Surg.* **109**:587, 1965.

43. DICK J.C. Carcinoma of the lower end of the bile duct. *Br. J. Surg.* **26**:757, 1939.

44. DOLL R., PAYNE P. & WATERHOUSE J. Cancer incidence in 5 continents. A Technical report. *Geneve Int. Union Against Cancer*, 1966.

45. DONALDSON L.A. & BUSUTTIL A. A clinico-pathological review of 68 carcinomas of the gallbladder. *Brit. J. Surg.* **62**:26, 1975.

46. DOWDY G.S. JR., OLIN W.G. JR., SHELTON E.L. JR. & WALDRON G.W. Benign tumors of the extrahepatic bile ducts. *Arch. Surg. (Chicago)* **85**:503, 1962.

47. DREILING D.A., NIEBURGS H.E. & JANOWITZ H.D. The combined secretin and cytology test in the diagnosis of pancreatic and biliary tract cancer. *Med. Clin. N. Amer.* **44**:801, 1960.

48. EDITORIAL: Tubal relief of malignant bile duct obstruction. *Lancet* **1**:419, 1979.

49. EELKEMA H.H., HODGSON J.R. & STAUFFER M.H. Fifteen-year follow-up of polypoid lesions of the gallbladder diagnosed by cholecystography. *Gastroenterology* **42**:145, 1962.

50. EISS S., DIMAIO D. & CAEDO J.P. Multiple papillomas of the entire biliary tract. Case report. *Ann. Surg.* **152**:320, 1960.

51. ENGLAND D.M. & ROSENBLATT J.E. Anaerobes in human biliary tracts. *J. Clin. Microbiol.* **6**:494, 1977.

52. EVANS J.A. & MUJAHED Z. Roentgenographic aids in the diagnosis of neoplasms of liver and extrahepatic ducts. *J.A.M.A.* **171**:7, 1959.

53. FAHIM R.B., FERRIS D.O. & MCDONALD J.R. Carcinoma of the gallbladder. An appraisal of its surgical treatment. *Arch. Surg. (Chicago)* **86**:334, 1963.

54. FAHIM R.B., MCDONALD J.R., RICHARDS J.C. & FERRIS D.O. Carcinoma of the gallbladder: a study of its modes of spread. *Ann. Surg.* **156**:114, 1962.

55. FALKENSTEIN D.B., RICCOBONI C., SIDHU G., ABRAMS R.M., SELIGER G. & ZIMMON D.S. The endoscopic intrahepatic cholangiogram. Clinico-pathologic correlation with postmortem cholangiograms. *Invest. Radiol.* **10**:358, 1975.

56. FETHERS J. Carcinoma of the common duct. *Aust. New Zeal. J. Surg.* **32**:311, 1963.

57. FLANIGAN D.P. Biliary carcinoma associated with biliary cysts. *Cancer* **40**:880, 1977.

58. FLEMING W.B. Carcinoma of the extrahepatic bile ducts. *Aust. New Zeal. J. Surg.* **23:**148, 1953.

59. FORTNER J.G. Experimental induction of primary carcinoma of gallbladder. *Cancer* **8:**689, 1955.

60. FORTNER J.G. Experimental bile duct cancer possibly induced by bile of humans with bile duct cancer. *Cancer* **8:**683, 1955.

61. FORTNER J.G., KALLUM B.O. & KIM D.K. Surgical management of carcinoma of the junction of the main hepatic ducts. *Ann. Surg.* **184:**68, 1976.

62. FORTNER J.G. & LEFFALL L.D. Carcinoma of the gallbladder in dogs. *Cancer* **14:**1127, 1961.

63. FORTNER J.G. & PACK G.T. Clinical aspects of primary carcinoma of the gallbladder. *A.M.A. Arch. Surg.* **77:**742, 1958.

64. FORTNER J.G. & RANDALL H.T. On the carcinogenicity of human gallstones. *Surg. Forum* **12:**155, 1961.

65. FOTOPOULOS J.P. & CRAMPTON A.R. Adenomyomatosis of the gallbladder. *Med. Clin. N. Amer.* **48:**9, 1964.

66. FRAUMENI J.F. Cancers of the pancreas and biliary tracts: epidemiological considerations. *Cancer Res.* **35:**3437, 1975.

67. FREIDMAN I.H., MEHLER G. & GINZBURG L. Pyloroduodenal obstruction due to carcinoma of the gallbladder. *Am. J. Gastroenterol.* **52:**224, 1969.

68. GERBER A. Retention cyst of the liver due to a bile duct polyp. *Ann. Surg.* **140:**906, 1954.

69. GERST P.H. Primary carcinoma of the gallbladder. A thirty-year summary. *Ann. Surg.* **153:**369, 1961.

70. GLENN F. & HAYS D.M. The scope of radical surgery in the treatment of malignant tumors of the extrahepatic biliary tract. *Surg. Gynec. Obstet.* **99:**529, 1954.

71. GOLDENBERG I.S. Carcinoma of the biliary tract. *Am. J. Surg.* **86:**292, 1953.

72. GOLDSTEIN H.S. & DAVIGLUS G.F. Benign adenomatous polyp of the papilla of Vater with partial obstruction. *Ann. Surg.* **160:**844, 1964.

73. HART J., MODAN B. & SHARNI M. Cholelithiasis in the aetiology of gallbladder neoplasms. *Lancet* **1:**1151, 1971.

74. HEPP J. Vésicule fraîse et cholecystite avec Sinus de Rokitansky. *Actualités hépato-gastroentérologiques de l'Hôtel-Dieu.* Masson, Paris, 1958.

75. HERLINGER H. & RING E. Palliative transhepatic catheter management of common bile duct obstruction by tumour. *Gut* **19:**A450, 1978.

76. HESS W. *Surgery of the Biliary Passages and the Pancreas.* Van Nostrand, Princeton, N.J., 1965.

77. HODES P.J., PENDERGRASS E.P. & WINSTON N.J. Pancreatic ductal and vaterian neoplasms: Their roentgen manifestations. *Radiology* **62:**1, 1954.

78. HOLMES S.L. & MARK J.B.D. Carcinoma of the gallbladder. *Surg. Gynec. Obstet.* **133:**561, 1971.

79. HORN R.C. JR., YAKOVAC W.C., KAYE R. & KOOP C.E. Rhabdomyosarcoma of the common bile duct: Report of a case. *Cancer* **8:**469, 1955.

80. HORWITZ A. & ROSENSWEIG J. Carcinoma of the gallbladder—a real hazard. *J.A.M.A.* **173:**234, 1960.

81. INOUYE A.A. & WHELAN T.J. Carcinoma of the extrahepatic bile ducts: A 10 year experience in Hawai. *Am. J. Surg.* **136:**90, 1978.

82. ISHAK K.G., WILLIS G.W., CUMMINS S.D. & BULLOCK A.A. Biliary cystadenoma and cystadenocarcinoma: a report of 14 cases and review of the literature. *Cancer* **39:**322, 1977.

83. JUTRAS J.A. & LEVESQUE H.P. Adenomyoma and adenomyomatosis of the gallbladder. Radiologic and pathologic correlations. *Radiol. Clin. N. Amer.* **4:**483, 1966.

84. KELLY K.A. Successful resection of adenocarcinoma of junction of right, left and common hepatic biliary ducts. Report of a case. *Mayo Clin. Proc.* **47:**48, 1972.

85. KIRSCHBAUM J.D. & KOZOLL D.C. Carcinoma of the gallbladder and extrahepatic bile ducts. *Surg. Gynec. Obstet.* **73**:740, 1941.

86. KRAIN L.S. Gallbladder and extrahepatic bile duct carcinoma; Analysis of 1808 cases. *Geriatrics* **27**:111, 1972.

87. KRAIN L.S. Carcinoma of the gallbladder in California 1955–1969. *J. Chronic Dis.* **25**:65, 1972.

88. KUNE G.A. Carcinoma of the gallbladder 24 years after cholecystostomy. *Med. J. Aust.* **1**:544, 1971.

89. KUNE G.A. & BIRKS D. The management of acute cholecystitis. An appraisal of current methods of treatment. *Med. J. Aust.* **2**:218, 1970.

90. KUNE G.A. & POLGAR V. Leiomyoma of the common bile duct causing obstructive jaundice. *Med. J. Aust.* **1**:698, 1976.

91. KUWAYTI K., BAGGENSTOSS A.H., STAUFFER M.H. & PRIESTLEY J.T. Carcinoma of the major intrahepatic and the extrahepatic bile ducts exclusive of the papilla of Vater. *Surg. Gynec. Obstet.* **104**:357, 1957.

92. LEMON H.M. The application of cytologic diagnosis to cancers of the stomach, pancreas and biliary system. *Ann. Intern. Med.* **37**:523, 1952.

93. LEMON H.M. & BYRNES W.W. Cancer of the biliary tract and pancreas; diagnosis from cytology of duodenal aspirations. *J.A.M.A.* **141**:254, 1949.

94. LESLEY D. Endoscopy of the bile duct: An evaluation. *Aust. New Zeal. Surg.* **44**:340, 1974.

95. LIPPMAN H.N., MCDONALD L.C. & LONGMIRE W.P. JR. Carcinoma of the extrahepatic bile ducts. *Am. J. Surg.* **25**:819, 1959.

96. LITTLE J.M., GIBSON A.A.M. & KAY A.W. Primary common bile duct carcinoid. *Br. J. Surg.* **55**:147, 1968.

97. LIVOLSI V.A., PERZIN K.H., BADDER E.M., PRICE J.B. JR. & PORTER M. Granular cell tumours of biliary tract. *Arch. Path.* **95**:13, 1973.

98. LONGMIRE W.P. JR. & LIPPMANN H.N. Intrahepatic cholangiojejunostomy—an operation for biliary obstruction. *Surg. Clin. N. Amer.* **36**:849, 1956.

99. LOWENFELS A.B. Does bile promote extracolonic cancer? *Lancet* **2**:239, 1978.

100. LUND J. Surgical indications in cholelithiasis: Prophylactic cholecystectomy elucidated on the basis of long-term follow-up on 526 nonoperated cases. *Ann. Surg.* **151**:153, 1960.

101. MARCUSO T.F. & BRENNAN M.S. Epidemiological considerations of cancer of the gallbladder bile ducts and salivary glands in the rubber industry. *J. Occupational Med.* **12**:333, 1970.

102. MEYEROWITZ B.R. & AIRD I. Carcinoma of the hepatic ducts within the liver. *Br. J. Surg.* **50**:178, 1962.

103. MOHARDT J.H. Carcinoma of the gallbladder: Collective review. *Int. Abstr. Surg.* **69**:440, 1939.

104. MOLNAR W. & STOCKUM A.E. Relief of obstructive jaundice through percutaneous transhepatic catheter—a new therapeutic method. *Am. J. Roentgenol. Radium Ther. Nucl. Med.* **122**:356, 1974.

105. MOOSA A.R., ANAGNOST M., HALL A.W., MORALDI A. & SKINNER D.B. The continuing challenge of gallbladder cancer. *Am. J. Surg.* **130**:57, 1975.

106. MORI K., MISUMI A., SUGIYAMA M., OKABE M., MATSUOKA T. ISHII J. & AKAGI M. Percutaneous transhepatic bile drainage. *Ann. Surg.* **185**:111, 1977.

107. MOORIS D.L., BUECHLEY R.W., KEY C.R. & MORGAN M.V. Gallbladder disease and gallbladder cancer among American Indians in tricultural New Mexico. *Cancer* **42**:2472, 1978.

108. NEIBLING H.A., DOCKERTY M.B. & WAUGH J.M. Carcinoma of the extrahepatic bile ducts. *Surg. Gynec. Obstet.* **89**:429, 1949.

109. NIELD J.M. Primary carcinoma of the gallbladder. *Aust. New Zeal. J. Surg.* **34**:43, 1964.

110. OCHSNER S.F. Solitary polypoid lesions of the gallbladder. *Radiol. Clin. N. Amer.* **4**:501, 1966.

111. OCHSNER S.F. & GAGE M. Papilloma of the gallbladder with carcinoma-in-situ. *Ochsner Clin. Rep.* **2**:27, 1956.

112. OH C. & JEMERIN E.E. Benign adenomatous polyps of the papilla of Vater. *Surgery* **57**:495, 1965.

113. OHLSSON E.G. & ARONSEN K.F. Carcinoma of the gallbladder; a study of 181 cases. *Acta Chir. Scand.* **140**:475, 1974.

114. OKUDA K., TANIKAWA K., EMURA T., KURATOMI S., JINNOUCHI S., URABE K., SUMIKOSHI T., KANDA Y., FUKUYAMA Y., MUSH H., MOIR H., SHIMOKAWA Y., YAKUSHI I.F. & MATSUVRA Y. Nonsurgical, percutaneous transhepatic cholangiography—diagnostic significance in medical problems of the liver. *Am. J. Dig. Dis.* **19**:21, 1974.

115. PACK G.T. & MILLER T.R. Middle hepatic lobectomy for cancer. *Cancer* **14**:1295, 1961.

116. PACK G.T., MILLER T.R. & BRASFIELD R.D. Total right hepatic lobectomy for cancer of the gallbladder. Report of three cases. *Ann. Surg.* **142**:6, 1955.

117. PEREIRAS R.V., RHEINGOLD O.J., HUTSON D., MEJIA J., VIAMONTE M., CHIPRUT R.O. & SCHIFF E.R. Relief of malignant obstructive jaundice by percutaneous insertion of a permanent prosthesis in the biliary tree. *Ann. Intern. Med.* **89**:589, 1978.

118. PERSON D.A. Carcinoma of the gallbladder presenting as acute cholecystitis and leading to a missed clinical and pathologic diagnosis. *Am. J. Surg.* **108**:95, 1964.

119. PHILLIPS J.B. Papilloma of the gallbladder. *Am. J. Surg.* **21**:38, 1933.

120. PICKRELL K.L. & BLALOCK A. The surgical treatment of carcinoma of the common bile duct. *Surgery* **15**:923, 1944.

121. PIEHLER J.M. & CRICHLOW R.W. Primary carcinoma of the gallbladder. *Arch. Surg.* **112**:26, 1977.

122. PIEHLER J.M. & CRICHLOW R.W. Primary carcinoma of the gallbladder. *Surg. Gynec. Obstet.* **147**:929, 1978.

123. POLK H.C. Carcinoma and the calcified gallbladder. *Gastroenterology* **50**:582, 1966.

124. PRADERI R.C. Twelve years experience with transhepatic intubation. *Ann. Surg.* **179**:937, 1974.

125. PRADERI R., ESTEFAN A. & DAVIDENKO N. Drainage transhépatiques en double 'O' *Nouv. Presse med.,* **6**:2515, 1977.

126. PRADERI R., PARODI H. & DELGADO B. Tratamiento de las obstrucciones neoplasticas de la via biliar suprapancreatica. *Ann. Fac. Med. Montevideo* **49**:221, 1964.

127. PRAKASH A.T.M., SHARMA L.K. & PANDIT P.N. Primary carcinoma of the gallbladder. *Br. J. Surg.* **62**:33, 1975.

128. PREADWELL T.A. & HARDIN W.J. Primary carcinoma of the gallbladder. The role of adjuvant therapy in its treatment. *Am. J. Surg.* **132**:703, 1976.

129. QUATTLEBAUM J.K. & QUATTLEBAUM J.K. JR. Malignant obstruction of the major hepatic ducts. *Ann. Surg.* **161**:876, 1965.

130. REDDY B.S., NARASAWA R., WEISBURGER J.H. & WYNDER E.L. Promoting effect of sodium deoxycholate on colon adenocarcinomas in germ-free rats. *J. Natl. Cancer Inst.* **56**:441, 1976.

131. RICHENBACH B. Autopsy incidence of disease among South-Western American Indians. *Arch. Pathol.* **84**:81, 1967.

132. RING E.J., FREIMAN D.B., OLEAGA J.A., MACKIE J.A., PEREZ M.R. & SCHIFF D.P. Clinical applications of non-operative T-tube replacement. *Surg. Gynec. Obstet.* **148**:213, 1979.

133. ROBERTS-THOMSON I.C. & HOBBS J.C. Cytodiagnosis of pancreatic and biliary cancer by endoscopic duct aspiration. *Med. J. Aust.* **1**:370, 1979.

134. ROBERTS-THOMSON I.C., STRICKLAND R.G. & MACKAY I.R. Bile duct carcinoma in chronic ulcerative colitis. *Aust. New Zeal. J. Surg.* **3**:264, 1973.

135. ROBERTSON W.A. & CARLISLE B.B. Primary carcinoma of the gallbladder. Review of 52 cases. *Am. J. Surg.* **113**:738, 1967.

136. ROGERS K.E. A papillary cystadenoma of the common hepatic duct. *Canad. Med. Ass. J.* **55**:597, 1946.

137. ROSS A.P., BRAASCH J.W. & WARREN K.W. Carcinoma of the proximal bile ducts. Report of 103 cases. *Surg. Gynec. Obstet.* **136**:923, 1973.

138. ROTHENBERG R.E. & ARONSON S.G. Acute cholecystitis preceding neoplastic bile duct obstruction. *Ann. Surg.* **112**:400, 1940.

139. SAKO S., SEITZINGER G.L. & GARSIDE E. Carcinoma of the extrahepatic bile ducts. Review of the literature and report of six cases. *Surgery* **41**:416, 1957.

140. SALMON P.R. Endoscopic Retrograde Choledochopancreatography (ERCP). In A.E. Read, *Modern trends in Gastroenterology 5*, Butterworth, London, 1975.

141. SCHNUG G.E. So-called papillomas of the gallbladder. *Amer. J. Surg.* **96**:296, 1958.

142. SCHUTT R.P. Bilateral intrahepatic cholangiojejunostomy. *Amer. J. Surg.* **107**:777, 1964.

143. SEGI M. & KURIHARA M. *Cancer mortality for selected sites in 24 countries.* No. 4 Sendai Japan, Dept. of Public Health, University School of Medicine, Tohoku, 1966.

144. SELZER D.W., DOCKERTY M.B., STAUFFER M.H. & PRIESTLY J.T. Papillomas (so-called) in the non-calculous gallbladder. *Am. J. Surg.* 103–472, 1962.

145. SHIFFMAN M.A. & JULER G. Carcinoid of the biliary tract. *Arch. Surg. (Chicago)* **89**:1113, 1964.

146. SHIMADA K., INAMATSU T. & YAMASHIRO M. Anaerobic bacteria in biliary disease in elderly patients. *J. Infect. Dis.* **135**:850, 1977.

147. SIEVERS M. & MARQUIS J. The South-Western American Indians' Burden; biliary disease. *J.A.M.A.* **182**:570, 1962.

148. SMITH R. Carcinoma of the Gall Bladder and of the Common Hepatic Duct. In R. Smith and S. Sherlock (eds.), *Surgery of the Gall Bladder and Bile Ducts.* Butterworth, London, 1964.

149. SMITH, LORD OF MARLOW. Obstructions of the bile duct. *Br. J. Surg.* **66**:69, 1979.

150. STARZL T.E., PORTER K.A., PUTMAN C.W., SCHROTER G.P.J., HALGRIMSON C.G., WEIL R., HOELSCNER M. & REID H.A.S. Ortho topic liver transplantation in 93 patients. *Surg. Gynec. Obstet.* **142**:487, 1976.

151. STEINER P.E. A carcinogenic extract from human bile and gallbladders. *Proc. Soc. Exp. Biol. Med.* **51**:352, 1942.

152. STEPHEN J.L. Quadrate lobectomy. *Proc. R. Soc. Med.* **57**:551, 1964.

153. STEWART H.L., LIEVER M.M. & MORGAN D.R. Carcinoma of the extrahepatic bile ducts. *Arch. Surg.* **4**:662, 1940.

154. STRAUCH G.O. Primary carcinoma of the gallbladder; presentation of seventy cases from the Rhode Island Hospital and a cumulative review of the last ten years of the American literature. *Surgery* **47**:368, 1960.

155. STROHL E.L., REED W.H., DIFFENBAUCH W.G. & ANDERSON R.E. Carcinoma of the bile ducts. *Arch. Surg. (Chicago)* **87**:567, 1963.

156. TABAH E.J. & MCNEER G. Papilloma of the gallbladder with in-situ carcinoma. *Surgery* **34**:57, 1953.

157. TANGA M.R. & EWING J.B. Unusual manifestations of carcinoma of the gallbladder. *Int. Surg.* **53**:44, 1970.

158. TERBLANCHE J. Is carcinoma of the main hepatic duct junction an indication for liver transplantation or palliative surgery? A plea for the U-tube palliative procedure. *Surgery* **79**:127, 1976.

159. TERBLANCHE J. & LOUW J.H. U-tube drainage in the palliative therapy of carcinoma of the main hepatic duct junction. *Surg. Clin. N. Amer.* **53**:1245, 1973.

160. THOMPKINS R.K., JOHNSON J., STORM F.K. & LONGMIRE W.P. Operative endoscopy in the management of biliary tract neoplasms. *Am. J. Surg.* **132**:174, 1976.

161. THORBJARNARSON B. Carcinoma of the bile ducts. *Cancer* **12**:708, 1959.

162. THORBJARNARSON B. Carcinoma of the gallbladder and acute cholecystitis. *Ann. Surg.* **151**:241, 1960.
163. THORBJARNARSON B. Carcinoma of biliary tree—1 Carcinoma of gallbladder. *N.Y. State J. Med.* **75**:550, 1975.
164. THORBJARNARSON B. & Glenn F. Carcinoma of the gallbladder. *Cancer* **12**:1009, 1959.
165. TONGCO R.C. Unusual skin metastases from carcinoma of the gallbladder. *Amer. J. Surg.* **102**:90, 1961.
166. TRIAS X., STREBEL H.M., PAUMGARTNER G. & WIESMANN U.N. Effects of bile and bile acids on cultural human fibroblasts. *Eur. J. Clin. Invest.* **7**:189, 1977.
167. TSUZUKI T. & UEKUSA M. Carcinoma of the proximal bile ducts. *Surg. Gynec. Obstet.* **146**:933, 1978.
168. TYLEN U., HOEVELS J. & VANG J. Percutaneous transhepatic cholangiography with external drainage of obstructive biliary lesions. *Surg Gynec. Obstet.* **144**:13, 1977.
169. VAITTINEN E. Carcinoma of the gallbladder: a study of 390 cases diagnosed in Finland 1953–67. *Ann. Chir. Gynec. Finn.* **59** (Suppl. 168), 7, 1970.
170. VOGELSANG T.M. Typhoid and paratyphoid carriers and their treatment. *Universitet I Bergen. Arbok 1950, Medisinskrekke Nr 1, A. S.* John Griegs, Boktrykkeri, Bergen, Norway, 1950.
171. WADDELL W.R. & BURBANK C.B. Cholangiojejunostomy (Longmire operation) for relief of biliary obstruction due to carcinoma. *New Eng. J. Med.* **247**:929, 1952.
172. WARREN K.W. Personal communication, 1965.
173. WARREN K.W., HARDY K.J. & O'ROURKE M.G.E. Primary neoplasia of the gall-bladder. *Surg. Gynec. Obstet.* **126**:1036, 1968.
174. WARREN K.W., MOUNTAIN J.C. & LLOYD-JONES W. Malignant tumours of the bile ducts. *Br. J. Surg.***59**:501, 1972.
175. WATERHOUSE J., MUIR C., CORREA P. & POWELL J. (eds.), *Cancer Incidence in Five Continents*, vol. 3. Lyon International Agency for Research on Cancer, 1976.
176. WATKINS E. JR. & KHAZEI A.M. Arterial infusion chemotherapy of liver cancer. *Bull. Soc. Int. Chir.* **3**:279, 1966.
177. WATKINS E. JR. & SULLIVAN R.D. Cancer chemotherapy by prolonged arterial infusion. *Surg. Gynec. Obstet.* **118**:3, 1964.
178. WELTON J.C., MARR J.S. & FRIEDMAN S.M. Association between hepatobiliary cancer and typhoid carrier state. *Lancet* **1**:791, 1979.
179. WENCKERT A. & ROBERTSON B. The natural course of gallstone disease. Eleven-year review of 781 nonoperated cases. *Gastroenterology* **50**:376, 1966.
180. WENGER J. & RASKIN H.F. Diagnosis of cancer of pancreas, biliary tract and duodenum by combined cytologic and secretory methods. II. Secretin test. *Gastroenterology* **34**:1009, 1958.
181. WILLIAMS R. Current position of liver transplantation. Liver, Proceedings of an International Liver Conference, Pitman Medical, London, 1973.
182. WILLIAMS R., SMITH M., SHOLKIN K.B., HERBERTSON B., JOSEY V. & CALNE R. Liver transplantation in man: the frequency of rejection, biliary tract complications, and recurrence of malignancy based on an analysis of 26 cases. *Gastroenterology* **64**:1026, 1973.
183. WILLIS R.A. Some aspects of the carcinomata of the biliary tract. *Med. J. Aust.* **2**:340, 1942.
184. WILLIS R.A. *Pathology of Tumours* (3e). Butterworth, London, 1960.
185. WISE R.E. *Intravenous Cholangiography*. Thomas, Springfield, Ill. 1962.
186. WONG J., LIM S.T.K., LAM K.H. & ONG G.B. Unresectable malignant obstruction of the bile ducts. *Aust. New Zeal. J. Surg.* **48**:503, 1978.

8. Biliary Cysts

BY TREVOR JONES

Biliary cysts are uncommon and most of them tend to gravitate to centres with a special interest in the problem, hence the personal experience of any one surgeon will be limited.

If untreated the condition almost invariably leads to death and therefore correct diagnosis and treatment of this condition is critical.

INCIDENCE

The condition is uncommon and reported cases number only about 1000 [10], although many more cases obviously go unreported.

There appears to be a racial difference in incidence, as approximately 30 per cent of cases involve Japanese, and females predominate over males in the ratio 4:1.

Most cases present in youth, although no age is exempt [12, 24, 31].

CLASSIFICATION

The clinicopathological classification of biliary cysts has been adapted from Alonso-Lej and co-workers and is represented in a diagrammatic form in Fig. 8.1 [1]. It does not include intrahepatic cysts which have no communication with the biliary tract, even though they have a lining which resembles biliary epithelium. Also excluded from this classification are those dilatations of the biliary system which may have a cystic appearance on radiology, but which are secondary to some underlying obstructive lesion, such as gallstones, tumours, or benign strictures. Peripapillary duodenal diverticula are also excluded.

CHOLEDOCHAL CYST
Choledochal cyst is by far the commonest type encountered. It is also referred to as congenital cystic dilatation of the common bile duct. The lesion is well localised, but shows considerable variation in volume. It is usually associated with narrowing of the terminal common bile duct and a varying degree of proximal dilatation (Figs. 8.1, 8.3, 8.4, 8.5 & 8.9).

CONGENITAL DIVERTICULUM OF THE BILE DUCT
This condition is very uncommon and arises laterally from the bile duct (Figs. 8.1, 8.8 & 8.10) [1]. The rest of the biliary tree is either normal or slightly dilated. Acquired diverticula of the distal bile duct are described in Chapters 1 and 5.

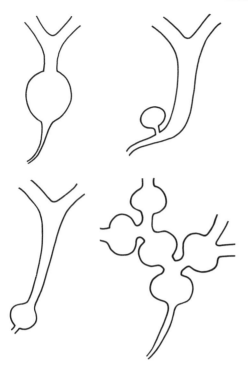

Fig. 8.1. Clinicopathological classification of biliary cysts. (*top left*) Choledochal cyst. (*top right*) Congenital diverticulum of the bile duct. (*bottom left*) Choledochocoele. (*bottom right*) Multiple biliary cysts.

CHOLEDOCHOCOELE

This again is an uncommon lesion, analogous to a ureterocoele [37]. It is characterised by cystic dilatation of the intraduodenal part of the terminal common bile duct (Figs. 8.1 & 8.14).

MULTIPLE BILIARY CYSTS

This condition, again rare, was described by Caroli in 1958, and features multiple, usually intrahepatic, biliary cysts (Figs. 8.1 & 3.23).

AETIOLOGY

The aetiology of biliary cysts is unknown, although a number of causes have been postulated. These hypotheses fall into two main groups—congenital and acquired. The congenital hypothesis suggests that the cause is a weakness or hypoplasia of a segment of the developing bile duct, obstruction to the bile flow with resultant raised intraluminal pressure, or a combination of these two factors [21, 27, 28].

The hypotheses supporting an acquired cause presume that the primary defect is obstruction to the outflow of bile such as due to gallstone, stricture, or tumour [20, 36].

A combined theory involving features of the congenital and acquired hypotheses is probably the most acceptable [1, 39]. This presupposes a congenital weakness of a segment of the duct system on which is imposed distal obstruction. This latter factor may be congenital or acquired (Fig. 8.2).

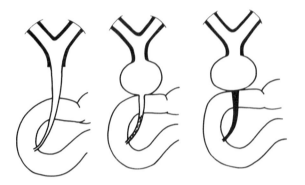

Fig. 8.2. Pathogenesis of choledochal cysts. (*left*) Developmental hypoplastic segment of bile duct shown by thin line. (*Middle*) Progressive dilatation of supraduodenal portion with progression of distal obstructive factor. (*right*) Complete obstruction of distal segment and onset of symptoms.

PATHOLOGY

PATHOLOGICAL FEATURES OF THE CYST

The wall of the cyst varies in thickness up to 1 cm [11]. Biliary cysts do not usually have a complete epithelial lining [20, 26, 36]. The lining may be completely absent, or islands of epithelial cells may be present.

The bile within the cyst is usually infected, the common organisms being *E. coli* and other intestinal bacteria [20, 36]. Biliary sediment and gallstones may be seen in these biliary cysts [17, 20, 29, 36].

COMPLICATIONS

Rupture, either spontaneous or associated with abdominal trauma, has been reported [4, 5, 34]. Pregnancy appears to have some predisposing effect in this regard [25]. The diagnosis, even at laparotomy, in these cases may be quite difficult as the cyst tends to collapse when ruptured.

Malignant change within the cyst has also been reported [10, 13]. The incidence of carcinoma within a cyst is significantly higher than in a normal biliary tree [23]. The age incidence is also lower than in carcinoma of the biliary tree generally. The tumour is usually an adenocarcinoma.

Other complications include biliary cirrhosis, following long-standing biliary obstruction, and this may in turn lead to portal hypertension and its complications [14]. Cholangitis due to stasis, and pancreatitis have also been reported [18].

DIAGNOSIS

CLINICAL FEATURES

The classical triad of a biliary cyst is abdominal pain, jaundice, and an abdominal mass. With a greater awareness of the condition and consequent earlier diagnosis the triad is now infrequently seen, and only one or two features may be present [1,

9, 36]. The pain is generally in the right upper quadrant and may radiate anteriorly or posteriorly. The jaundice is of the obstructive type, and is frequently intermittent in the early stages. The mass is usually in the right upper quandrant, smooth and discreet, and it may vary in size from time to time.

SPECIAL INVESTIGATIONS
Haematological and liver function tests are of limited diagnostic value, but give an assessment of the degree of jaundice and secondary liver damage.

Ultrasonography is a valuable non-invasive investigation in this condition and an example is shown in Fig. 8.3 [32].

Conventional biliary tract radiography, that is, oral cholecystography and intravenous cholangiography, is of no value in the jaundiced patient. In the

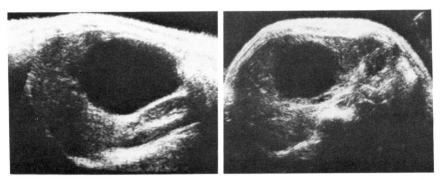

Fig. 8.3. Ultrasonographic findings in a large choledochal cyst. (*left*) Vertical section. (*right*) Transverse section.

non-icteric patient intravenous cholangiography can be useful in outlining the cyst, as seen in Fig. 8.4, and in these cases an oral cholecystogram may show displacement of the gallbladder away from the cyst.

Endoscopic retrograde cholangiography and percutaneous transhepatic cholangiography are now the usual methods of making a preoperative diagnosis, especially in the jaundiced patient (Fig. 8.5). Operative cholangiography will confirm the diagnosis as described shortly.

Acquired dilatations are also excluded by cholangiography, as well as other rare conditions which may mimic a cyst, such as an intrahepatic gallbladder (Figs. 8.6 & 8.7). Hydatid disease is excluded on serology (Chapter 15).

Percutaneous cyst puncture and cystography is contraindicated, because of the likelihood of leakage of the cyst contents into the peritoneal cavity resulting in biliary peritonitis [6, 38].

OPERATIVE DIAGNOSIS
The definitive diagnosis of a biliary cyst is confirmed at operation. The relationship of the cyst to the rest of the biliary tract and to the adjacent structures is thoroughly evaluated. Other biliary tract abnormalities are frequently associated with this condition and should be looked for.

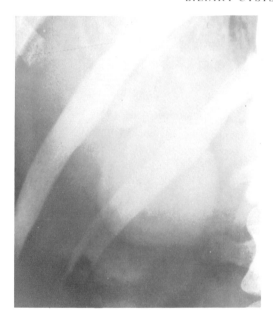

Fig. 8.4. Intravenous cho-langiogram of a choledo-chal cyst in a non-jaun-diced patient. Courtesy of Professor Hiram Beddeley.

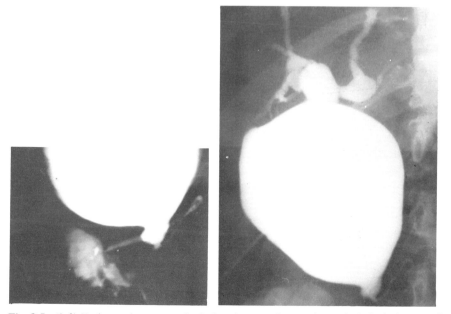

Fig. 8.5. (*left*) Endoscopic retrograde cholangiogram shows a large choledochal cyst and a dilated bile duct, which joins the pancreatic duct well proximal to the papilla. (*right*) The choledochal cyst confirmed by an operative cholangiogram, which also shows some dilatation of the intrahepatic ducts. Courtesy of Professor Hiram Baddeley.

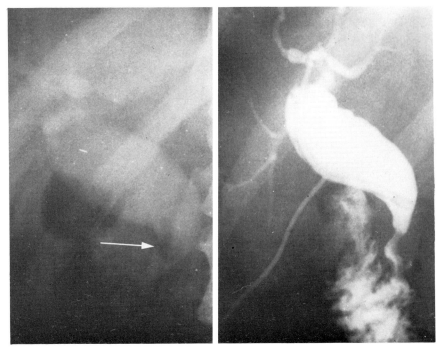

Fig. 8.6. Differential diagnosis of biliary cysts. (*left*) Intravenous cholangiogram showing marked choledochal dilatation resembling a cyst but caused by a gallstone (arrow). (*right*) Post-exploration T-tube cholangiogram after removal of single, large stone.

The most important single investigation is an operative cholangiogram, and this may be done through the cystic duct, gallbladder, the bile duct below, or through the biliary cyst itself (Figs. 8.5, 8.8, 8.9 & 8.10).

TREATMENT

The treatment of choledochal cysts is surgical, as untreated cases have a fatal outcome.

The nature of surgical treatment of choledochal cysts has been more aggressive in recent years and a number of procedures must be condemned as they are unsatisfactory or dangerous. Thus, aspiration of the cyst should never be done, because this predisposes to biliary peritonitis and does not deal with the underlying condition. External drainage should never be used except as a first-stage temporary procedure in very ill patients with prolonged jaundice [15]. Dilatation of the distal common bile duct has proved valueless, probably because of the subsequent restenosis of the hypoplastic distal segment. Another reason may be that adequate drainage of the stagnant cyst may need a stoma which is even larger than that provided by the normal distal common bile duct. Cholecystenterostomy is now not used because it does not usually provide adequate decompression of the cyst. Subtotal resection and reconstruction of the cyst is not

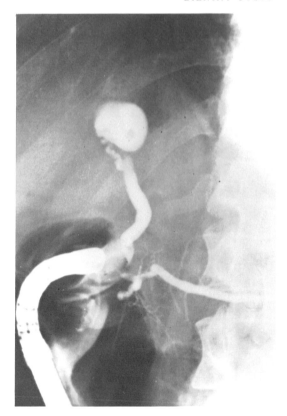

Fig. 8.7. Differential diagnosis of biliary cysts—endoscopic retrograde cholangiogram of an intrahepatic gallbladder containing a lucent calculus. Courtesy of Professor Hiram Baddeley.

advocated, because this does not deal with the underlying pathology, and because it is very likely to lead to subsequent stricture formation.

Successful surgical treatment of choledochal cysts is provided by either cyst resection and hepatic duct-intestinal anastomosis, or some form of cyst enterostomy, such as cystoduodenostomy or cystojejunostomy.

Cystoduodenostomy is a quick and relatively simple procedure with a low operative mortality and the surgical technique is illustrated in Fig. 8.11 [12, 15, 25, 30, 33]. However, a review of the literature suggests that cystoduodenostomy is followed by a fairly high incidence of stricture formation, cholangitis, or both [1, 20, 25, 36]. All advocates of this procedure mention that the anastomosis should be in the lowest possible part of the cyst for dependant drainage.

Cystojejunostomy Roux-en-Y is probably the most widely used method of drainage of choledochal cysts, and the technique is illustrated in Fig. 8.12 [2, 17, 20, 25, 26]. The operative mortality of reported cases is not higher than that for cystoduodenostomy, and the incidence of subsequent anastomotic stricture formation and of cholangitis is much lower than that following cystoduodenostomy [17, 20, 36].

Cyst excision and hepaticojejunostomy Roux-en-Y, as shown in Fig. 8.13, has been advocated by recent writers [1, 8, 20, 36]. The advantages of this

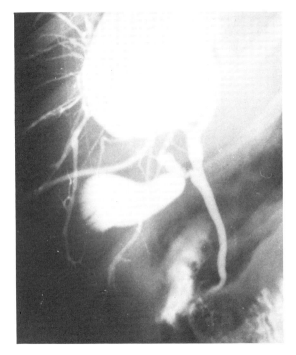

Fig. 8.8. Operative cholangiogram of a large cyst arising from the left hepatic duct and protruding into the porta hepatis from the liver. From Kune and McKenzie [20].

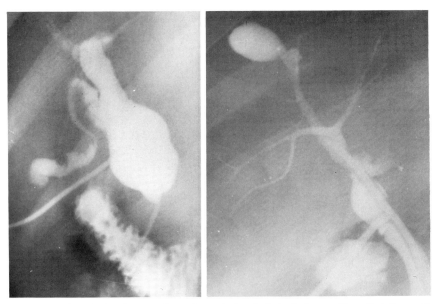

Fig. 8.9. (*left*). Cholangiogram done through the choledochal cyst. Note that the cystic duct opens into the cyst. From Kune and McKenzie [20].

Fig. 8.10. (*right*). T-tube cholangiogram outlining a localised cystic dilatation of a branch of the right hepatic duct—this cyst can probably be classified as a congenital diverticulum. Courtesy of Professor Hiram Baddeley.

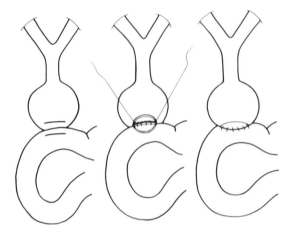

Fig. 8.11. Surgical technique of cystoduodenostomy.

procedure compared with cyst intestinal anatomosis are that the stagnant cyst is excised, and that the anastomosis is epithelium to epithelium, rather than epithelium to fibrous tissue. The risk of subsequent stricture formation is low and the late results are good. Excision of the biliary cyst also prevents the development of carcinoma in the cyst, which is an unusual but real complication. The operative risk associated with cyst excision has been higher than with cyst intestinal anastomosis [1, 3, 25]. The reason for this higher mortality probably lies in the increased complexity of the operation, especially in the presence of other biliary and vascular abnormalities. Cyst excision cannot be performed with safety in some cases because the cyst is attached to surrounding structures by dense adhesions, usually due to previous surgery. In these cases, cystojejunostomy Roux-en-Y is advocated.

The treatment of a congenital diverticulum of the bile duct is excision of the cyst and reconstitution of the bile duct, if this is technically possible. If this

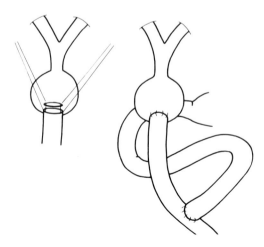

Fig. 8.12. Surgical technique of cystojejunostomy Roux-en-Y.

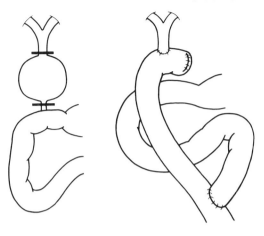

Fig. 8.13. Surgical technique of cyst excision and hepaticojejunostomy Roux-en-Y.

cannot be done for technical reasons, the diverticulum should be drained into the duodenum or the jejunum.

Two successful approaches have been used in the treatment of a cholecochocoele; either cyst excision to allow free biliary drainage or cyst excision and reconstruction with possible pancreatic duct reimplantation (Fig. 8.14).

Surgical treatment of the rare multiple biliary cysts is most difficult, and it aims to provide adequate biliary drainage for stagnant cysts, usually by some

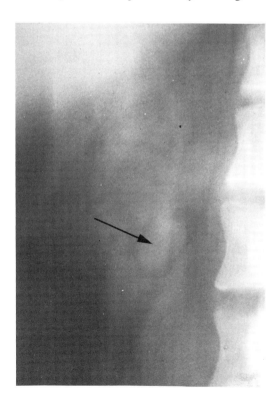

Fig. 8.14. Intravenous cholangiogram showing a normal bile duct and a choledochocoele of the intra-duodenal part of the common duct. Transduodenal cyst excision would be the surgical treatment of choice in this case. Courtesy of Dr. Terry Tydd, Bendigo, Australia.

type of cystojejunostomy Roux-en-Y, perhaps combined with partial excision of the cysts [2, 20].

It has been suggested by some authors that cholecystectomy should be performed for all types of cysts for a number of reasons [11, 35]. First, reflux and cholangitis are less when there is a continuous free bile flow. Secondly, in patients in whom a secondary operation has been necessary, the gallbladder has shown clinical and histological evidence of cholecystitis. Thirdly, there is evidence that when the biliary tree is decompressed with an intestinal anastomosis, reflux is well tolerated without infection in those patients in whom the gallbladder has been removed.

PROGNOSIS

The prognosis of untreated choledochal cysts is uniformly poor. The mortality associated with surgical intervention has dropped from 60 per cent reported by Gross in 1933, to the region of 10 per cent in more recent reports [1, 36]. In these latter, the procedure of cyst excision and hepaticojejunostomy has a higher mortality than cyst intestinal anastomosis, although in expert hands the mortality of cyst excision is not higher. The long-term results of cyst excision are superior to cyst intestinal anastomosis. The long-term results appear to be better with cystojejunostomy than with cystoduodenostomy.

The fate of the actual choledochal cysts after cyst intestinal anastomosis is uncertain; a gradual decrease in size has been noted by some and no change in size by others [3, 16, 19, 24, 36, 40].

REFERENCES

1. ALONSO-LEJ F., REVER W.B. & PESSAGNO D.J. Congenital choledochal cyst, with a report of 2 and an analysis of 94 cases. *Int. Abstr. Surg.* **108**:1, 1959.
2. ARTHUR G.W. & STEWART J.O.R. Biliary cysts. *Br. J. Surg.* **51**:671, 1964.
3. ATTAR S. & OBEID S. Congenital cyst of the common bile duct. A review of the literature and a report of 2 cases. *Ann. Surg.* **142**:289, 1955.
4. BATTERSBY C. Ruptured choledochal cyst: Recognition and management. *Aust. N.Z. J. Surg.* **48**:515, 1978.
5. BLEGER H.M. & BOYER E.L. Perforation of a choledochus cyst with biliary peritonitis. *Lancet* **66**:177, 1946.
6. BYRNE J.J. & BOTTOMLEY G.T. Bile peritonitis in infants. *Am. J. Dis. Child.* **6**:694, 1953.
7. CAROLI J., SOUPALT R., KASSABOWSKI J. & OTHERS. La dilatation polykystique congenitale des voies biliares intrahepatiques; essay de classification. *Sem. Hop. Paris* **34**:488, 1958.
8. ELGAR D.E. & GUDGEON D.H. Choledochus cyst complicating pregnancy. *Br. J. Surg.* **56**:868, 1969.
9. FERRIS D.O. & YaDEAU R.E. Choledochal cysts. *Proc. Mayo Clinic* **39**:332, 1964.
10. FLANIGAN D.P. Biliary Cysts. *Ann. Surg.* **182**:635, 1975.
11. FONKALSRUD E.W. Choledochal Cysts. *Surg. Clin. N. Amer.* **58**:1275, 1973.

12. Fonkalsrud E.W. & Boles E.T. Choledochal cysts in infancy and childhood. *Surg. Gynaec. Obstet.* **121:**733, 1965.

13. Fujiwara Y., Ohizumi T., Kazikaki G. & Ishidate T. A case of congenital choledochal cyst associated with carcinoma. *J. Paediat. Surg.* **11:**587, 1976.

14. Gillis D.W. & Sergeant C.K. Prolonged biliary obstruction and massive gastrointestinal bleeding secondary to choledochal cyst. *Surgery* **52:**391, 1962.

15. Gross R.E. Idiopathic dilatation of the common bile duct in children. *J. Paediat.* **3:**730, 1933.

16. Hertzler J.H. & Maguire C.E. Congenital dilatation of the common bile duct. Report of 2 cases in children. *A.M.A. Arch. Surg.* **62:**275, 1951.

17. Jackson F.C. & Maxwell J.W. Jr. Intrahepatic diverticulum—common hepatic bile duct. *Arch. Surg. (Chicago)* **89:**706, 1964.

18. Karjoo M., Bishop H., Barns P. & Hatzapple P.G. Choledochal cyst presenting as recurrent pancreatitis. *Paediatrics* **51:**289, 1973.

19. Keith L.M. Jr., Rini J.M. & Martin L.H. Cystic dilatation of the common bile duct (choledochal cyst). *A.M.A. Arch. Surg.* **75:**143, 1957.

20. Kune G.A. & McKenzie G. The management of biliary cysts. *Aust. N.Z. J. Surg.* **39:**132, 1969.

21. Landing B.H. Consideration of the pathogenesis of neonatal hepatitis, biliary atresia and choledochal cyst; the concept of infantile obstructive cholangiopathy. *Progs. Paediat. Surg.* **6:**113, 1974.

22. Liebner E.J. Roentgenographic study of congenital choledochal cysts. Pre and postoperative analysis of 5 cases. *Am. J. Roent.* **80:**950, 1958.

23. Longmire W.P. Jr., McArthur M.S., Bastounis E.A. & others. Carcinoma of the extrahepatic biliary tree. *Ann. Surg.* **178:**333, 1973.

24. Madding G.F. Congenital cystic dilatation of the common bile duct. *Ann. Surg.* **154:**288, 1961.

25. Maingot R. Congenital abnormalities of the bile ducts. In R. Smith & S. Sherlock (eds.), *Surgery of the Gallbladder and Bile Ducts,* pp. 52–60. Butterworth & Co., London, 1964.

26. McWhorter G.L. Congenital cystic dilatation of the common bile duct; report of a case. *Arch. Surg.* **8:**604, 1924.

27. Ravitch M.M. & Synder G.B. Congenital cystic dilatation of the common bile duct. *Surgery* **44:**752, 1958.

28. Saltz N.J. & Glaser K. Congenital cystic dilatation of the common bile duct. *Am. J. Surg.* **91:**56, 1956.

29. Serfas L.S. & Lyter C.S. Choledochal cyst. With a report of an intraduodenal choledochal cyst. *Am. J. Surg.* **93:**979, 1957.

30. Shields A.B. Congenital cystic dilatation of the common bile duct. Follow up of 3 cases and discussion of pertinent features. *Am. J. Surg.* **108:**142, 1964.

31. Shockett E., Hallenbeck G.A. & Hayles A.B. Choledochal cyst. Report of cases. *Proc. Mayo Clinic* **30:**83, 1955.

32. Suruga K., Hiron Y., Nagashima K. & others. Ultrasonic echo examination as an aid in diagnosis of congenital bile duct lesions. *J. Paediat. Surg.* **4:**452, 1969.

33. Swenson O. *Paediatric Surgery.* Appleton-Century-Crofts, New York, 1958.

34. Tagart R.E. Perforation of a congenital cyst of the common bile duct. *Br. J. Surg.* **44:**18, 1956.

35. Trout H.H. & Longmire W.F. Long term follow-up study of patients with congenital cystic dilatation of the common bile duct. *Am. J. Surg.* **121:**68, 1971.

36. Warren K.W., Kune G.A. & Hardy K.J. Biliary duct cysts. *Surg. Clin. N. Amer.* **48:**567, 1968.

37. Wheeler W.I. DeCourcey. An unusual case of obstruction to the common duct (choledochocoele). *Br. J. Surg.* **27:**446, 1940.

38. Wrightson P. Congenital cystic dilatation of the common bile duct; case occurring in infancy. *Aust. New Zeal. J. Surg.* **23:**110, 1953.

39. Yotuyanagi S. Contribution to the aetiology and pathology of idiopathic cystic dilatation of the common bile duct with report of 3 cases; a new aetiological theory based on supposed unequal epithelial proliferation at the stage of the physiological epithelial occlusion of the primary choledochus. *Jpn. J. Cancer Res.* **30:**601, 1936.
40. Zezulin W., Kanter J.R., Maldonado A. & Wilson R.E. Choledochal cyst visualized by oral cholecystography. *Lahey Clin. Found. Bull.* **18:**65, 1969.

9. Biliary Infections

Biliary tract infections have been mentioned in various parts of this book, because they have numerous causes and clinical presentations. The purpose of this chapter is to summarise present knowledge regarding the causes, pathogenesis, diagnosis, and principles of treatment, to give the reader a perspective on biliary infections. The following aspects will be described:
1. Preventative antibiotics in biliary tract surgery.
2. Antibiotic use in acute cholecystitis.
3. Anaerobic infections.
4. Cholangitis.
5. Recurrent pyogenic cholangitis—this common type of biliary infection in certain parts of the Orient is discussed by Professor G. B. Ong and Dr. S. T. Chou.

BACTERIOLOGICAL ASPECTS

NORMAL BILE

Bile cultures from a normal gallbladder or normal bile duct do not usually grow organisms, unless culture methods are extremely sophisticated, when occasional isolates can be obtained [19, 23, 29, 42, 65]. Thus, infection of the bile is usually secondary to some type of biliary tract disease, such as cholelithiasis, or various forms of bile duct obstruction.

BILIARY TRACT DISEASE

In the presence of biliary tract disease the rate with which positive cultures are obtained is related to a number of factors. Thus, the rate appears to increase with the age of the patient, especially with gallbladder stones, the incidence becoming appreciable in patients 60 years or older [25, 56, 74].

The nature of the biliary pathology is also important. Thus, with gallbladder stones the incidence ranges from 13 to 50 per cent, while in acute cholecystitis in corresponding series the incidence is usually higher, ranging from 25 to 75 per cent [19, 20, 21, 23, 25, 42, 51, 56, 65, 74]. There is also some evidence that in acute cholecystitis the incidence of positive cultures rises steeply 48 hours after the onset of symptoms, but this is probably only a reflection of the proliferation of the organisms in the blocked gallbladder, making a positive culture easier to obtain with standard bacteriological methods [20, 21]. In the presence of bile duct pathology the rate of recovery of microorganisms is related to the nature of the obstruction. Thus, with cholelithiasis positive cultures are obtained in 59–87 per cent in different reports, in benign biliary strictures the incidence is usually 100 per cent, but in malignant obstruction the rate is much lower, zero to 36 per cent in different reports [19, 36, 42, 65].

The last factor which influences the rate of recovery of organisms is dependent on the degree of sophistication of the bacteriological techniques used, and in recent years this has become a specially important factor in the isolation of anaerobic organisms from the bile [19, 21, 36, 65].

NATURE OF MICROORGANISMS IN BILE

The rate of culture and the types of organisms recovered can be increased with meticulous bacteriological techniques, especially for anaerobic organisms [19, 21, 65]. The usual type of organisms cultured are enterobacteria, and mixed growths are extremely common. The commonest organism is *Escherichia coli* with other enteric organisms following, such as klebsiella, proteus, pseudomonas, *Streptococcus faecalis*, etc. Gram-positive organisms, such as *Staphyloccus pyogenes* and streptococci are uncommonly seen [19, 20, 21, 25, 42, 52, 65]. Anaerobes are uncommon and were seen only in 13 per cent of infected cases by Keighley in 1977 and in 39 per cent by Nielsen and Justasen, who were using sophisticated culture methods. Clostridia are the commonest anaerobes followed by anaerobic streptococci, while bacteroides are uncommon. Anaerobes usually, but not always, are found as mixed growths with aerobes.

PREVENTATIVE ANTIBIOTICS IN BILIARY SURGERY

RATIONALE

The general concept of preventative antibiotic use during surgery is now on a sound experimental and clinical base, following the pioneering work of Dr. John Burke of Boston [6, 7, 40]. He, and many others subsequently, have repeatedly shown that if an antibiotic is to be of value in *preventing* infections it must be present in the tissues in high concentrations at the time of contamination, that is, at the time of surgery. Antibiotics are of little value in preventing postoperative infection if administered some hours after contamination had occurred. The question, which so far is not entirely answered, is whether preventative antibiotics should be used routinely in all contaminated operations, or whether antibiotic use should be reserved for certain groups, who are deemed to be at high risk of developing a postoperative infection. Also, the benefits of preventative antibiotics versus the risks of antibiotic use under these circumstances has not been entirely documented.

INDICATIONS IN BILIARY SURGERY

There is now sufficient clinical evidence to recommend the use of preventative antibiotics for biliary surgery in certain high-risk groups. The factors of importance are: over 70 years of age, lowered general resistance to infection, the presence of acute cholecystitis or other emergency cause for surgery, known choledocholithiasis, previous biliary tract surgery, or a recent history suggestive of cholangitis [7, 9, 36, 44]. Other groups at risk are those with general problems of lowered resistance, such as malnutrition, diabetes, alcoholism, steroid administration, etc. [40]. Further groups at risk during surgery are those with massive contamination, such as a pericholecystic abscess. Keighley's group believes that operative Gram's staining of bile is also effective in identifying groups at risk [36, 37, 60].

More recently it has been suggested that preventative antibiotics should be used routinely in biliary surgery, particularly because in a significant number of patients postoperative infection develops in the so-called 'low risk' group, who cannot be identified preoperatively [3, 63, 70, 72]. Evidence so far indicates that preventive antibiotics will be used in biliary surgery routinely in the future, particularly if it can be shown that a 'single dose' preoperative treatment is accompanied by minimal risk, and that it is effective in lowering the rate of postoperative infections.

It has already been noted, in the chapters dealing with cholangiography and obstructive jaundice, that the routine use of preventative antibiotics is most valuable in reducing septicaemias occurring after biliary tract investigational procedures, such as percutaneous transhepatic cholangiography and endoscopic retrograde cholangiography.

METHOD OF ADMINISTRATION AND ANTIBIOTICS USED

It is now clear that the antibiotic needs to be in the tissues in a high concentration at the time of surgery and this usually means systemic administration just prior to, or during, operation. The duration of preventative antibiotic treatment has seen a radical change from the 5-day course of 20 years ago, to the 24-hour routine, to the 'single dose' method used at present [3, 9, 63, 70, 72].

Antibiotics used for prophylaxis need to satisfy certain criteria which are different from those that apply to the use of antibiotics in established infections. Thus, it must be safe, it should not encourage the production of resistant organisms, and it should be effective against the majority of the known spectrum of organisms likely to be encountered during this type of surgery in a particular environment and in a particular part of the world. This means that one cannot provide categorical rules, though certain practical guidelines can be laid down.

At present cephalosporins such as cephazolin, or cephamandole, given as an intramuscular injection 1 g 1 hour before surgery, or as a simple intravenous bolus immediately before operation, is most used as it is non-toxic and widely effective against enteric organisms, as well as against *Staphylococcus aureus* [3, 9,

13, 36, 46, 60, 63, 70, 72, 83]. Lincomycin, kanamycin, and chloramphenicol have not been commonly used for prophylaxis in biliary surgery, probably because of fear of side-effects.

With increasing sophistication in anaerobic culture in recent years a significant yield of anaerobes has been obtained from the bile of patients with gallstone disease [25, 65]. Antibiotics which are active against anaerobes have not been used in biliary surgery prophylaxis. At present neither metronidazole nor tinidizole is widely available for systemic use and, therefore, these antibiotics need to be given in high doses orally some hours before surgery.

Thus, at present, cephazolin or cephamandole appears to be most suitable, and this may in the future be used with metronidazole or tinidizole for anaerobic cover. The antibiotics used may well change in future years with new antibiotics and with changes in microorganism sensitivities.

ACUTE CHOLECYSTITIS

It has already been mentioned, in the section dealing with bacteriology, that in acute cholecystitis a high proportion of patients have infected gallbladder bile containing organisms similar to those seen in gallstone disease in general. The proliferation of microorganisms in acute cholecystitis is regarded as a secondary phenomenon to cystic duct obstruction by a gallstone.

The administration of antibiotics should, therefore, have no effect on the outcome of the attack, nor on the rate of development of local infective complications such as gangrene, empyaema, or pericholecystic abscess and this has in fact been shown to be the case [26, 44]. The rate of septicaemia developing during acute cholecystitis perhaps could be lowered with the routine use of the appropriate antibiotics, but the evidence for this is inconclusive at present [44]. However, there is now strong evidence that the preventive use of antibiotics during surgery for acute cholecystitis will lower the rate of postoperative septic complications [9, 36, 44].

On present evidence we advocate the *routine* use of antibiotics *during* surgery for acute cholecystitis, in order to lower the rate of postoperative infections. We advocate the *selective* use of antibiotics in patients who are considered at '*high risk*' for the development of systemic infections when their acute cholecystitis is being managed conservatively. The usual antibiotic used is cephazolin, perhaps with the addition of metronidazole or tinidizole for anaerobic cover, as dicussed in detail earlier in the previous section dealing with preventative antibiotics.

ANAEROBIC INFECTIONS

Severe anaerobic infections, especially clostridial infections, have been reported over the years in association with acute cholecystitis and following biliary tract surgery, but these infections are most uncommon [55, 71, 73, 74, 86, 87]. Anaerobes have been cultured in infected cases usually in association with gallstones, with a frequency varying from 10 to 39 per cent [25, 36, 56, 65]. Clostridia are the commonest, anaerobic streptococci less common, and bacteroides are uncommon. Anaerobes are usually, but not exclusively, present as mixed isolates with aerobic organisms.

PATHOGENESIS

While contamination with anaerobic organisms is relatively common it is clear that for an actual infection to develop certain predisposing factors need to be present, because actual anaerobic biliary infections are in fact rare.

A review of the literature indicates that the predisposing conditions which put patients in high-risk groups of developing anaerobic sepsis include an obstruction to bile flow, such as acute cholecystitis or obstructive jaundice, together with general causes of debility and lowered resistance, such as malnutrition, diabetes, alcoholism, the presence of diffuse malignant disease, and the continued use of immunosuppressive drugs, such as steroids. Operations, such as bile duct surgery, can also lead to postoperative systemic anaerobic infections, in susceptible patients, presumably by the opening up of vascular channels in the presence of contaminated bile.

The principal modes of presentation of clinical anaerobic infection related to the biliary tract are two, namely acute pneumocholecystitis and anaerobic septicaemia.

ACUTE PNEUMOCHOLECYSTITIS

These patients present with the features of acute cholecystitis, but their general clinical condition shows rapid deterioration. Many of the patients are males and many are diabetic. A preoperative diagnosis can be made with a plain x-ray of the abdomen which shows gas in the gallbladder, as seen in Fig. 9.1 [55, 61, 71, 73, 86]. Gangrene and perforation are common.

Early cholecystectomy is essential, because there is a high mortality with delay in treatment. Preoperative and postoperative chloramphenicol is recommended, but with the advent of injectable metronidazole the latter antibiotic may in the future replace chloramphenicol [73].

ANAEROBIC SEPTICAEMIA

Systemic anaerobic infections have been described in association with acute cholecystitis or choledocholithiasis with jaundice, especially in elderly or debilitated subjects. Severe clostridial infections have also been described after both cholecystectomy and bile duct exploration [71, 73]. These patients develop a high temperature and tachycardia, and pass rapidly into a state of shock with renal failure [71, 73].

In dogs the ligation of the hepatic artery is followed by clostridial hepatitis

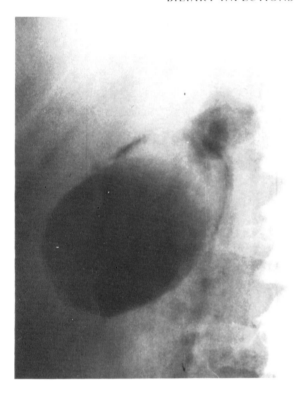

Fig. 9.1. Plain radiograph of the abdomen in a case of acute pneumocholecystitis. Note gas outlining the gallbladder.

and septicaemia, which can be prevented by antibiotics [8]. Although this has never been shown to occur in humans, should the hepatic or right hepatic artery be ligated inadvertently during cholecystectomy, large doses of penicillin and chloramphenicaol are advised postoperatively.

If a case of postoperative clostridial infection is suspected high doses of intravenous penicillin and chloramphenicol should be given [74]. In the future, injectable metronidazole may replace chloramphenicol. These cases also require urgent treatment of their hypovolaemic shock and of oliguric renal failure (described in the next section). The outlook in the postoperative cases is poor, unless the clinician has a high index of suspicion and commences treatment early.

At present there is insufficient evidence regarding the value of routine anaerobic antibiotic prophylaxis before biliary surgery, but the authors do advocate the use of anaerobic cover, such as tinidizole or metronidazole in very high-risk groups as described earlier.

CHOLANGITIS

The term *cholangitis* refers to a bacterial infection of the bile ducts. Recent advances in understanding the pathogenesis of this condition have radically influenced treatment.

PATHOGENESIS

There is clinical and experimental evidence to show a continuous passage of bacteria from the gastrointestinal tract up the portal vein and into the liver [17, 43, 76]. There is also evidence that the portal blood frequently carries bacterial endoxin into the liver from the gut [33, 85]. It is assumed that almost all of these organisms are destroyed by the extensive network of reticuloendothelial cells, the Kupffer cells that line the liver sinusoids (Fig. 9.2) [66]. In normal livers the

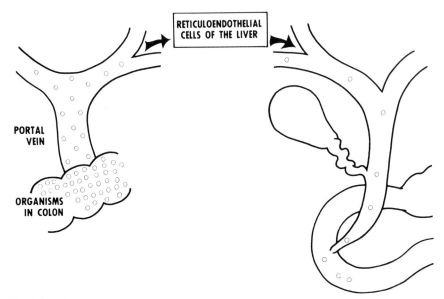

Fig. 9.2. Diagrammatic representation of enterobiliary passage of organisms in a normal subject. For further details see text.

organisms are not passed into the hepatic vein and thence into the systemic circulation, unless the clearance mechanism is defective, as occasionally seen in cirrhotic patients who can develop a spontaneous bacteraemia or septicaemia, presumably of gut origin [66]. Thus, an important function of the liver is to act as a barrier to intestinal microorganisms and their toxins against systemic invasion [32].

A very small number of these organisms are excreted into the bile from the liver and are returned to the gut (Fig. 9.2). Thus, culturing normal liver and normal bile will only occasionally yield organisms and, even then, only by using very meticulous culture techniques [19, 33, 65, 85].

The theory of bile contamination by the systemic haematogenous route has some support [65, 79]. Anatomically, this would need to assume bacteria passing from the gut into a main lymphatic trunk and entering the jugular vein and then into the arterial circulation, or that bacteria pass directly into a systemic vein at the two ends of the gastrointestinal tract, that is, the oesophagus and the anus. At present there is no direct evidence for this hypothesis. There is also no good evidence that ascent of bacteria from the duodenum up the bile duct is a likely mode of contamination, and indeed, bile duct obstruction itself would appear to militate against this [17, 43]. This last mechanism of contamination up the bile duct from the duodenum may, however, occur in the patient who also has a juxtapapillary duodenal diverticulum, but not otherwise [45, 49].

Under certain abnormal circumstances of the gastrointestinal tract an abnormally large seeding of organisms passes up the portal vein to the liver (Fig. 9.3).

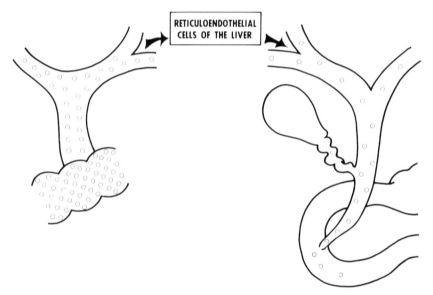

RETICULOENDOTHELIAL CELLS OF THE LIVER

Fig. 9.3. Abnormally large seeding of gut organisms into the portal vein seen in chronic ulcerative colitis and in recurrent pyogenic cholangitis.

This situation occurs in patients with chronic ulcerative colitis and in recurrent pyogenic cholangitis (Oriental cholangiohepatitis) [5, 67]. It is likely that this large seeding of organisms is responsible for the initiation of the condition of recurrent pyogenic cholangitis. There is also some evidence that the liver changes and the condition of primary sclerosing cholangitis seen in chronic ulcerative colitis may be related to this abnormally high transit of organisms from the colon (see Primary sclerosing cholangitis, Chapter 6). There is some evidence that associated poor liver function, or poor reticuloendothelial function often seen associated with this condition, lowers the ability of the liver to filter bacteria, and further encourages bile contamination [33, 66, 85].

Bile duct obstruction and stasis of bile flow give rise to multiplication of the

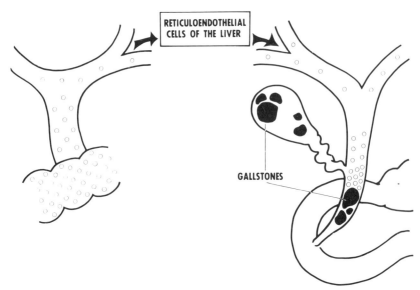

Fig. 9.4. Normal seeding of gut organisms in portal vein, but multiplication of these organisms occurring in the bile duct due to partial obstruction and stasis caused by gallstones.

organisms in the bile, which would otherwise have been excreted into the duodenum (Fig. 9.4). This converts bacterial contamination of the bile duct into bacterial infection or cholangitis. The nature of the obstruction influences the frequency with which cholangitis develops. It is very commonly seen with gallstones and with strictures, but much less so with malignant obstruction. Thus, a positive culture has been found in 64–90 per cent of cases with choledocholithiasis and in 100 per cent with non-malignant strictures, but only in about 10 per cent with malignant obstruction [20, 21, 23, 42, 56, 65, 78]. This probably indicated that gallstones and the biliary sediments seen in biliary strictures give rise to stasis of the bile at an early stage, allowing a much longer time for cholangitis to develop. Also, this may indicate that in the presence of certain forms of biliary disease, such as gallstones, there are complex physicochemical changes, which affect the chances of survival and multiplication of microorganisms in the bile. It is important to appreciate that bacteria can be present in the bile in high concentration without obvious clinical symptoms [23].

The final phase in the pathogenesis of cholangitis occurs with the onset of the clinical symptoms of fever and shaking chills or rigors (Fig. 9.5). These symptoms are due to a systemic bacteraemia, probably produced by cholangiovenous reflux of organisms (bile duct to hepatic vein sinusoid), as a result of a rise in intrabiliary pressure, perhaps aided by trauma to the mucosa [31, 34, 62]. Thus, in patients who have fever and rigors, organisms similar to those found in their bile can be recovered on blood culture [23, 35, 42, 75].

If this cholangiovenous reflux of intestinal organisms is not controlled, septicaemia may ensue. This has a serious outlook and can be ultimately fatal if it remains untreated [1, 90]. Two important aspects in the pathogenesis of this type

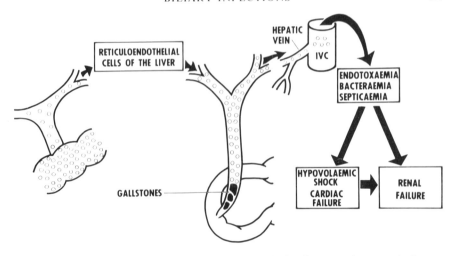

Fig. 9.5. Progression in the pathogenesis of cholangitis, leading to endotoxaemia, bacteraemia, septicaemia, hypovolaemic shock, and oliguric renal failure. For details see text.

of septicaemia are of importance in treatment. First, patients develop a profound alteration of haemodynamics, with either hypovolaemic shock or a low cardiac output, or both [50, 90]. Second, the stage is set for oliguric renal failure due to a reduction of renal blood flow and consequent decrease of glomerular filtration rate in a kidney which has been made more vulnerable to renal shutdown by the retained pigments of obstructive jaundice, and perhaps also by bacterial endotoxaemia [14, 15, 29, 84, 89, 90].

Prolonged biliary tract obstruction which is associated with cholangitis will eventually lead to biliary cirrhosis and portal hypertension. This complication of cholangitis is usually encountered only in patients with neglected traumatic bile duct strictures, as was noted by Sedwick, Poulantzas, and Kune in 1966. Of interest is the evidence produced by Scott and Khan in 1968, that in patients with partial biliary obstruction and cholangitis organisms accumulate in the stagnant segment of the bile duct and lead to significant soiling of the small intestine with bacteria, which probably produce the abnormalities of tryptophan and bile acid metabolism, and a disturbance of vitamin B_{12} absorption. This situation is, therefore, similar to the 'blind loop' syndrome of the gastrointestinal tract.

SO-CALLED ASCENDING CHOLANGITIS

There is no evidence to show that cholangitis is due to the reflux of organisms from the gastrointestinal tract through the sphincter of Oddi. The only possible exception to this may be patients who have juxtapapillary duodenal diverticula [45, 49]. There is also no evidence for the assumption that reflux of gastrointestinal contents, through the stomas of surgically created biliary intestinal anastomoses, is responsible for cholangitis. The onset of cholangitis in these instances of biliary intestinal anastomoses has been shown to be due to a stricture of the stoma and a resultant biliary obstruction (Chapter 14). Material containing organisms refluxes into the bile ducts owing to the pressure exerted by the peristaltic activity of the gut, and such reflux is known to take place even through narrowed and strictured openings. These refluxed organisms can then proliferate in the bile ducts because there is an outflow obstruction.

The concept of cholangitis 'ascending' from the gastrointestinal tract to the biliary system may be safely discarded in patients who have no biliary obstruction or stasis. However, once cholangitis is present due to biliary stasis or obstruction, there is in fact a spread of infection proximally in the bile ducts, resulting in cholangiovenous reflux and a systemic bacteraemia or septicaemia.

AETIOLOGY

The causes of cholangitis in clinical practice can be summarised as follows.

CHOLEDOCHOLITHIASIS
This is the commonest cause of cholangitis because of the frequency of bile duct gallstones, but rigors and fever are relatively uncommon symptoms of choledocholithiasis.

BILIARY STRICTURES
Non-malignant strictures of the bile duct (Chapter 6), such as postoperative traumatic strictures, stenosis of the sphincter of Oddi, primary sclerosing cholangitis and strictures which follow biliary intestinal anastomoses, almost always have infection of choledochal bile, and the frequency of rigors and fever is high. Strictures associated with chronic pancreatitis can also occasionally present with cholangitis, especially in the alcoholic patient.

BILE STASIS
Stasis of bile, such as may be seen in choledochal cysts, particularly if associated with an element of obstruction, is frequently responsible for bile duct infection and cholangitis.

In this regard biliary intestinal anastomoses, such as choledochoduodenostomy, may also be responsible for bile duct infection and the clinical features of cholangitis, even when the anastomotic stoma is widely patent. In these cases it is very likely that the organisms multiply in the distal 'blind' segment of the bile duct.

MALIGNANT OBSTRUCTION
Malignant obstruction of the bile duct is only occasionally associated with the growth of organisms in the bile duct.

DIAGNOSTIC PROCEDURES
Percutaneous transhepatic cholangiography or endoscopic retrograde cholangiography may be followed by a bacteraemic or septicaemic picture, especially in the presence of choledocholithiasis, or a benign biliary stricture (Chapter 3).

In many patients bile duct infection is present without obvious clinical manifestations. In others pyrexia and leucocytosis are the only features which suggest cholangitis.

The onset of fever and rigors is regarded as the classic sign of cholangitis and, as noted earlier, this really means a bacteraemia or a septicaemia.

The most serious clinical form of bile duct infection has been termed acute obstructive cholangitis [4, 18, 22, 28, 29, 75]. These patients develop pain, jaundice, fever, and shaking chills, associated with a rapid deterioration of their general condition, leading to hypovolaemic shock and oliguric renal failure. The underlying cause is usually choledocholithiasis. It is clear from the discussion on pathogenesis that these patients have the most serious form of cholangitis because septicaemia has developed. The serious nature of this condition must be recognised early, as delay in treatment is associated with a very high mortality.

PRINCIPLES OF TREATMENT

The treatment of cholangitis depends on the severity and the underlying cause. The principles of treatment can be summarised thus:
1. Prevention.
2. Surgical decompression and drainage of the obstructed and infected bile duct.
3. Administration of antibiotics to deal with bacteraemia or septicaemia.
4. Correction of hypovolaemic shock or of low output cardiac failure, if these are present.
5. Prevention or treatment of oliguric renal failure.

PREVENTION
It has already been shown in this chapter that the preventative use of antibiotics in certain groups of patients can often prevent bacteraemia or septicaemia in a patient who has an infected bile duct. There is now sufficient evidence to advocate the use of prophylactic antibodies in all patients who are about to have invasive diagnostic procedures performed on the bile duct, such as percutaneous transhepatic cholangiography, as well as on all patients who require bile duct surgery.

SURGICAL DECOMPRESSION
The appearance of rigors and fever indicates that intrabiliary pressure is high and that the surgeon should relieve bile duct obstruction and establish adequate biliary drainage as soon as the patient has been adequately resuscitated. This may mean bile duct exploration and choledocholithotomy, or the repair, reconstruction, or bypass of a stricture. The actual nature of the surgery performed has been described in the relevant sections.

With acute obstructive cholangitis, surgical decompression must also be carried out early. Recent work indicates that correction of hypovolaemic shock, antibiotics, and management of renal failure are first priorities before surgery [4, 22]. However, operation must not be unduly delayed, and in cases which are refractory to medical management operation may need to be done while resuscitation or dialysis is in progress [22]. In these, choledochotomy and the insertion of a T tube may be all that the patient can withstand. It may then be necessary to return at a later date in order to deal with the underlying cause.

ANTIBIOTICS

When cholangitis is suspected the administration of antibiotics is essential and is continued until after surgical drainage. There is little hope that antibiotics will sterilise an obstructed, infected, bile duct, but the systemic manifestations can usually be controlled until surgical decompression is achieved [4, 29, 75, 90]. It is, therefore, necessary to obtain a high blood concentration of the antibiotic. If possible, blood cultures should be taken before antibiotic therapy is begun.

Before a positive blood or bile culture is obtained, and the sensitivities of the organisms determined, the choice of an antibiotic depends on a knowledge of probabilities, and especially a knowledge of the local situation in a hospital or a community with respect to likely antibiotic sensitivities.

Cholangitis, especially with a positive blood culture, is a most serious threat to the patient's life, and before antibiotic sensitivities are available it is best to cover the patient for both gram positive and gram negative organisms, as well as for anaerobes. This usually means a combination of antibiotics. Gentamicin and ampicillin are often used. For the most serious cases, gentamicin, a cephalosporin and anaerobic cover with chloramphenicol is often used. In the future, systemic metronidazole or tinidizole may provide good anaerobic cover, but adequate data are not yet available on these latter antibiotics in severe cholangitis.

TREATMENT OF SEPTIC SHOCK

It was noted earlier that in septicaemia either hypovolaemic shock or low cardiac output failure, or both, may occur. This demands the monitoring of central venous pressure and the insertion of a urethral catheter which measures hourly urine output. If the central venous pressure is low, then fluid replacement is necessary, including plasma or plasma expanders. If the central venous pressure is high, attempts should be made to improve cardiac output with the use of digitalis or drugs with a positive inotropic action [84, 90].

PREVENTION AND TREATMENT OF RENAL FAILURE

Patients who are jaundiced and septicaemic are at a considerable risk of developing oliguric renal failure [14, 16, 29, 90]. If the kidneys are producing dilute urine, particularly in the presence of circulating blood pigment, they are less likely to develop ischaemic damage [16, 64, 90].

The urethral catheter measures hourly urine output, which should be maintained at more than 30 ml per hour. Adequate correction of hypovolaemia will usually achieve such urine flow, but if it does not, 5 per cent mannitol is given intravenously, its rate dependent on the urine output [90].

If an operation is undertaken, mannitol should be given prophylactically, prior to, during, and for the first 48 hours after surgery [15, 16]. One hour before the operation 500 ml of a 10 per cent solution of mannitol is given. During and after surgery a high urine flow is maintained with the use of a 5 per cent solution [16].

Some patients are first seen after they have developed renal shutdown. A mannitol diuresis may also be attempted in these, but dialysis is usually necessary. If the sepsis can be adequately controlled by antibiotics then dialysis is the first priority in management before surgical decompression of the bile duct is undertaken [4].

RECURRENT PYOGENIC CHOLANGITIS

BY G. B. ONG & S. T. CHOU

Recurrent pyogenic cholangitis (RPC) is a form of cholangitis characterised by recurrent infections of the biliary tract by enteric organisms, chiefly *E. coli*, frequent occurrence of intrahepatic stones, and the association of multiple liver abscesses; gallbladders are either normal or inflamed and only a few of them contain stones. The term, coined by Cook and his associates, is the most appropriate, though Oriental cholangitis and Asiatic cholangiohepatitis have also been used to describe this condition [12, 39, 83].

INCIDENCE

RPC is common in the Chinese population of Hong Kong, being one of the common causes of abdominal emergencies admitted to hospitals [67]. It also occurs with great frequency in Korea, Vietnam, Malaysia and Singapore, less frequently in Japan, and occasionally in Chinese migrants in North America and Australia [11, 30, 53]. In Hong Kong both sexes are equally affected and the peak incidence is found between the age of 30 and 40 years; children may also be affected [11, 12, 67, 91].

PATHOGENESIS

The pathogenesis is as yet not fully understood. Like any hollow tube in the body, obstruction, partial or complete, of the biliary tract predisposes to infection. It has been suggested that parasites inhabiting the biliary tract may initiate varying degrees of bile stasis. While this may be true in some cases, statistically it is not convincing. The association of liver fluke infestation with RPC reported from Hong Kong is probably coincidental. The incidence is comparable to that of a control group matched for age and sex [12, 27, 67]. Furthermore, the liver fluke can stay in the human bile ducts for a long time without evidence of biliary infection, and intrahepatic stones are also common in some Asiatic regions where liver fluke infestation is rare or unknown [2, 39, 88]. Adult *Ascaris lumbricoides* is discovered in the biliary tract of some patients with RPC during surgery, but is not seen in patients who die in the chronic stage of the disease, suggesting that the presence of parasite in the bile ducts brings about symptoms rather than causes the disease.

There is little doubt that bile infection is caused by enteric bacteria, mostly *E. coli*. Unlike bacterial cholangitis in Western countries in which the infection is usually the result of pre-existing cholecystitis, many patients with RPC have macroscopically normal gallbladders [11, 24, 48, 78]. It has been suggested that in RPC, bacteria in the gastrointestinal tract spreads to the biliary tract via the portal circulation [67]. While this has gained support from animal experiments bacteriologic studies in humans are far from conclusive [10]. In RPC the bile is usually positive for enteric organisms, but portal bacteraemia is not unduly common [67, 76]. The fact that intrahepatic bile sludges or stones were found at necropsy in all cases of RPC in Hong Kong suggests that biliary sludge may be the initial factor which produces bile stasis that converts transient innocuous bacteria into a pathogenic phenomenon in the biliary system [11]. This view is shared by endoscopic retrograde cholangiographic studies, which demonstrate that in RPC early cholangitic changes are detectable in intrahepatic ducts which already harbour stones [48]. The stones in RPC consist mainly of calcium bilirubinate. The prevalence of this type of stone in the Orient is said to be related to the low protein diet which causes a deficiency of glucaro 1:4 lactone in the bile that normally inhibits B-glucuronidase [54]. B-glucuronidase hydrolyses bilirubin glucuronide into free bilirubin and glucuronic acid. The liberated bilirubin combines with calcium to form calcium bilirubinate. This hypothesis has been tested by animal experiment and substantiated by observations that most patients with RPC belong to the lower socioeconomic class, and that the incidence of calcium bilirubinate stones among Japanese has decreased remarkably since World War II, due to increased consumption of food rich in protein and fat [57].

The sequence of events in RPC is proposed and summarised in Fig. 9.6. Both glucuronidase and glucaro 1:4 lactone are normal components of the bile and their activities are in balance in the normal state. However, low protein diet causes a deficiency of glucaro 1:4 lactone which is the main inhibitor of B-glucuronidase. A net increase in glucuronidase in the bile results in sludge or stone formation in the intrahepatic ducts which favours biliary infection [19, 77]. Portal bacteraemia is probably an important source of organisms because the pathology of the early lesion in RPC is marked by thrombophlebitis and pericholangitis in the portal tracts [11]. Once infection is established in the biliary tract the concentration of glucuronidase of bacterial origin in the bile is increased. This results in further hydrolysis of bilirubin glucuronide, more stone formation, and recurrent infection, thus forming a continuous cycle.

PATHOLOGY

The primary pathology is in the intrahepatic bile ducts which often contain bile sludges or stones; the liver is involved secondarily and its appearance is dictated by the development and evolution of portal tract inflammation and abscess formation in different parts. In the acute stage the liver is enlarged due to

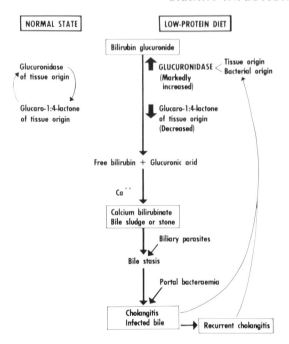

| NORMAL STATE | | LOW-PROTEIN DIET |

Bilirubin glucuronide

Glucuronidase of tissue origin

GLUCURONIDASE (Markedly increased) ‹ Tissue origin / Bacterial origin

Glucaro-1:4-lactone of tissue origin

Glucaro-1:4-lactone of tissue origin (Decreased)

Free bilirubin + Glucuronic acid

Ca⁺⁺

Calcium bilirubinate Bile sludge or stone

Biliary parasites

Bile stasis

Portal bacteraemia

Cholangitis Infected bile → Recurrent cholangitis

Fig. 9.6. Proposed mechanism in the pathogenesis of recurrent pyogenic cholangitis. Modified from Matsushiro *et al* [57].

congestion, oedema, and abscesses of varying sizes. If there have been several previous attacks the liver may be shrunken and the surface scarred. Fibrous adhesions are present between the liver surface and the diaphragm. The left hepatic duct and its branches are more frequently affected and the left lobe of the liver may become atrophic and scarred. Occasionally, the intrahepatic portal veins are seen to be fibrous cords. Microscopically, the main changes are in the portal tracts. In the early stages there is pericholangitis with polymorph infiltration and thrombophlebitis of the portal veins (Fig. 9.7). With recurrent attacks the bile ducts become thickened and stenosed, being ensheathed by collars of fibrous tissue and chronic inflammatory infiltrate. Biliary proliferation may occur but is never marked (Fig. 9.8). In the advanced stage the periductal fibrous tissue becomes dense and acellular and the ducts stenosed with proximal dilatation. The portal veins are reduced in number or totally absent due to intimal fibrosis and organisation of thrombi. Fibrous scars in the portal tracts often extend to the liver substance and the liver may appear like postnecrotic macronodular cirrhosis. True cirrhosis is, however, not a complication of RPC.

CHANGES IN THE BILE DUCTS
The larger bile ducts in the liver may undergo stenosis, most commonly at the confluence of two ducts. The duct proximal to this stenosis becomes dilated and contains stones or biliary mud (Fig. 9.9). When these changes involve the larger ducts a whole segment or lobe of the liver may be converted to a fibrous sac, in which mucopus with myriads of stones may be found.

The extrahepatic ducts do not undergo stenosis. On the contrary, they may be

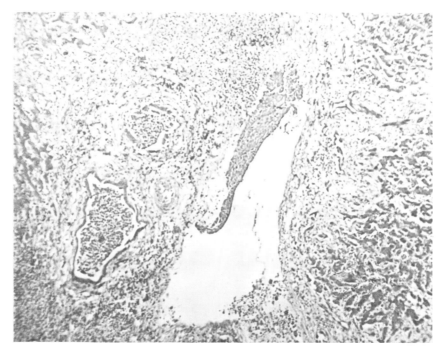

Fig. 9.7. Microscopic findings in the liver of a patient seen in the early stages of recurrent pyogenic cholangitis. For details see text.

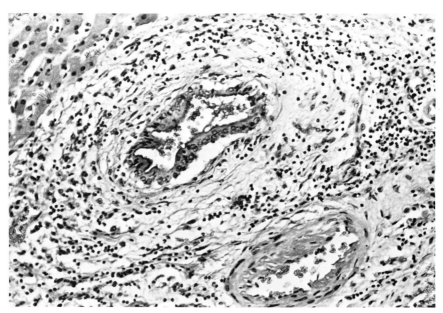

Fig. 9.8. Microscopic features in the liver of a patient with established recurrent pyogenic cholangitis. For details see text. (Reproduced with kind permission of Editor of *Pathology*.)

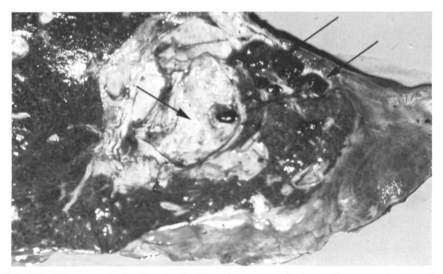

Fig. 9.9. Macroscopic findings in the liver in a case of advanced recurrent pyogenic cholangitis. Note liver abscess and multiple intrahepatic gallstones situated in dilated bile ducts (arrows). (Courtesy of Dr. V. N. Niteckis, Melbourne.)

grossly dilated, usually as the result of obstruction either by a stone or by inflammatory changes in the sphincter of Oddi. In the early stage of dilatation the bile ducts are thin-walled and quickly regain their original calibre. However, with prolonged obstruction and infection a state of chronic cholangitis is set up. This leads to a loss of elasticity of the ducts which, together with an increase of fibrous tissue, converts the extrahepatic biliary ducts into rigid tubes. The duct will not collapse even when the obstruction is removed. The dilatation may terminate at two levels, one just above the first part of the duodenum and the other at the sphincter of Oddi.

CHANGES IN THE GALLBALDDER
The gallbladder may be markedly distended and oedematous due to obstruction in the extrahepatic ducts. Adhesions do not form around the gallbladder and consequently it is often felt as a pear-shaped swelling which moves freely with respiration. The mucosa may ulcerate, and in severe cases it may be completely denuded of epithelium. Extreme distension with infection will end in empyema of the gallbladder. If this obstruction is not relieved gangrene with multiple per-forations may take place. Occasionally, stones are found in the gallbladder. With repeated infection the organ becomes thickened and contracted.

CHANGES IN THE SPHINCTER OF ODDI
Papillitis is a common feature and may occur as the result of stone impaction. The sphincter may show varying changes, including acute inflammation, stric-ture, pseudopolyp, and adenoma formation [67]. On plain x-ray, air may be seen in the biliary tract. In over 90 per cent of these cases a fistula between the lower

end of the common bile duct and the second part of the duodenum can be demonstrated [67]. The fistula is usually just above the sphincter of Oddi and is the result of erosion by an impacted stone.

STONES

The stones in RPC are earthy and friable and consist mainly of calcium bilirubinate. Pure pigment or cholesterol stones are not seen (Fig. 9.9). They can occur at any level of the biliary tract. At operation about 26 per cent are found in the intrahepatic ducts, 50 per cent in the common bile duct, and 15–25 per cent in the gallbladder. Intrahepatic biliary mud or stones are much more common in post-mortem cases and in one study were found in all 46 cases [11]. Biochemical analysis shows that all stones in RPC, irrespective of their location, contain about 22 per cent of cholesterol and 42 per cent of bile pigments, and that more bile pigments are present in intrahepatic stones than the stones in the gallbladder [11].

CHANGES IN OTHER ORGANS

Acute pancreatitis complicating RPC occurs in 12.2 per cent of cases. The pancreatitis is usually mild and the pancreas is marked by oedema and fat necrosis [69]. Splenomegaly, due either to septic reaction or to portal vein thrombosis, is seen in about one-quarter of the cases.

COMPLICATIONS

Liver abscess. Single or multiple liver abscesses are common. The abscesses are not those of the cholangitic type and some of them are probably the result of portal bacteraemia (Fig. 9.9). The abscess may rupture into the subdiaphragmatic space and, at times, through the diaphragm into the pericardium or the pleural cavity. Empyema thoracis or lung abscess may develop as the result of the subphrenic abscess. At times the lung abscess is discharged into the bronchus and may be coughed up.

Rupture of the gallbladder. This is a serious complication. The bile is almost invariably infected. As there are few fibrous adhesions around the gallbladder extensive flooding of the highly infectious bile will give rise to severe peritonitis with shock and often death. This is often associated with an impacted stone in the lower end of the common bile duct, or at the cystic duct.

Biliary enteric fistula. The development of a biliary enteric fistula is more commonly found at the lower end of the common bile duct. Shui reported a patient who not only had a fistula between the lower end of the common bile duct and the duodenum but also had a second one between the gallbladder and the first part of the duodenum [81].

Gram-negative Septicaemia. This is a serious condition and may end fatally unless active treatment is instituted. Besides supportive treatment and antibiotics decompression of the biliary tract should be performed. In desperate cases decompression with a T tube without removal of the obstruction may tide the patient over an otherwise fatal outcome. Positive blood cultures can usually be obtained in such cases. According to Flemma and co-workers the organism gains entry into the bloodstream through a break in the biliary epithelium [23]. This proposition is supported by the fact that the organism obtained from blood culture is similar to the one found in the bile (see previous section dealing with cholangitis).

Pancreatitis. Acute pancreatitis is found in 12.2 per cent of patients. The pancreatitis is usually mild and is diagnosed mainly at operation. Unlike pancreatitis of other aetiology surgical exploration of the biliary tract with adequate toilet and T-tube drainage of the common bile duct is essential. If obstruction and infection of the biliary tract is relieved recovery from pancreatitis usually follows [69].

Thrombophlebitis of the hepatic veins. On rare occasions this has been known to give rise to septic emboli which lodge in the pulmonary arterioles, resulting in pulmonary hypertension [47].

CLINICAL FEATURES

HISTORY

A typical history in recurrent pyogenic cholangitis is a recurrent attack of chill, fever, pain, and jaundice. The fever is usually ushered in by a chill or rigor. There may be no previous feeling of dyspepsia or biliousness. The fever is low grade and is seldom higher than 38°C (100°F). The pain is mild and distending in character; it is localised to the right upper quadrant and does not radiate to the back, nor is it referred to the shoulder. Jaundice is hardly noticeable. This initial attack may be followed by spontaneous remission.

After a varying interval, sometimes up to 2 years or more, a second episode may take place, and the whole process is repeated. Now the jaundice is deeper and the pain is often described as sharp, stabbing, or lancinating. It may extend to the xiphisternum or may be referred to the shoulders. Spontaneous remission may occur, but more usually remission results from the administration of antibiotics.

With each subsequent attack the period of remission is shortened and, ultimately, the patient becomes incapacitated once every 2–3 months. At any time during this acute illness there may be hyperpyrexia of 39° to 40°C; this must be treated promptly to avoid a fatal outcome. Vomiting occurs in over 80 per cent of cases but it is never very severe.

The dark-coloured urine is always noticed by the patient and is invariably described as tea-coloured. In an occasional case the stool is clay-coloured; then the jaundice is usually very deep.

PHYSICAL EXAMINATION

Jaundice is often noticed only in the sclera. The general condition of the patient is good during remission, but may be poor during the acute phase of the disease. Anaemia may be noticeable.

The upper abdomen, as a rule, is spastic, and it is not always possible to palpate the liver, which is enlarged in more than half the cases. The spleen is palpable in one-quarter of cases [67, 68]. The gallbladder may at times appear as a mass which moves with respiration—this may disappear suddenly with relief of pain.

LABORATORY FINDINGS

Blood. A varying degree of anaemia may be encountered, but cases with a very low haemoglobin can be seen in cases of ancylostomiasis [67].

A rise in leucocyte count is usual, but not to a marked degree. Very high polymorphonuclear leucocyte counts are found in those with very severe infection. A similar response is seen in fulminating secondary infection of the biliary tract infested by *Clonorchis sinensis* [59].

Alkaline phosphatase level is raised to a varying degree and does not always revert to normal, even as long as 6 months after successful treatment. Serum glutamic oxalacetic transaminase (SGOT) and serum glutamic pyruvic transminase (SGPT) levels are not raised, unless there is marked obstruction with severe infection. Liver necrosis is found in many patients. Serum amylase was raised in 13 of 101 patients examined [67].

Urine and stools. The urine shows an increase in urobilinogen and the presence of bile pigment. Examination of the stool may yield a 25 per cent recovery of *Clonorchis* ova. *Ascaris* ova can be demonstrated in 13 per cent [68].

Bacteriology. Bile is usually infected by enteric organisms. A positive culture was found in 88 per cent. The commonest organism was *E. coli*; *Salmonella* was demonstrated in 4 per cent [58]. The bile will probably never be sterile despite treatment with antibiotics. Instead, there may be a change of the bacterial flora; repeated cultures may yield *Proteus vulgaris* on one occasion, *E. coli* on another, *Pseudomonas aeruginosa* on a third.

In one series these organisms could be demonstrated in the portal blood in 40 per cent of cases during the acute phase and in 6 per cent during remission [67].

Radiology. Plain x-ray of the abdomen seldom helps, as almost all the stones found in recurrent pyogenic cholangitis are radiolucent. Air may be present in the biliary tract in about 2 per cent of cases. An oral cholecystogram does not help in the visualisation of the stones, because the gallbladder does not concentrate the bile to the extent necessary to show up the outline. However, in a small percentage of cases, a combined oral and intravenous cholangiogram may visualise the biliary tract and the stones in them.

Percutaneous transhepatic cholangiograms (PTC) can demonstrate the dilated biliary tract with stones (Fig. 9.10). PTC should be used with caution, because it may induce a septicaemic shock and prophylactic antibiotics need to be used in these cases. There is also danger that the infected bile may leak into the

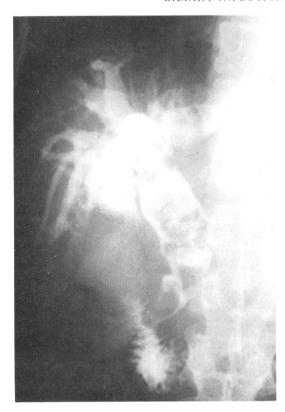

Fig. 9.10. Typical cholangiogram in a case of recurrent pyogenic cholangitis. (Courtesy of Dr. K. P. Wong, Hong Kong.)

general peritoneal cavity, especially if there is acute obstruction of the biliary tract.

Endoscopic retrograde cholangiography (ERC) has certain advantages over other cholangiograms. It gives a clear delineation of the biliary tract and can demonstrate early ductal changes. ERC is performed when the acute attack is over. It may flare up the infection, hence prophylactic antibiotics should be given [48].

DIAGNOSIS

The diagnosis of RPC in endemic areas is usually not difficult. There is a history of chills and fever, followed by jaundice. Physical examination may reveal an enlarged liver and sometimes a palpable gallbladder. The urine will show the presence of bile with or without increase of urobilinogen. Raised alkaline phosphatase level is usually associated with this condition.

During the stage of remission, when jaundice has subsided, ERC may show a stricture or dilatation of intrahepatic ducts with radiolucent stones, and thus establish the diagnosis.

When there is chronic partial obstruction of the bile ducts the condition may simulate carcinoma of the bile duct or of the head of the pancreas. Here, an ERC or a percutaneous cholangiogram may be used to establish the diagnosis. In a borderline case needle biopsy of the liver may show fibrous tissue ensheathing the bile ducts in portal tracts with little bile duct proliferation, a feature quite characteristic of RPC, but is unusual in extrahepatic obstruction.

Viral hepatitis is commonly mistaken for RPC. This is particularly so when there is jaundice with mild pain. In certain cases examination of the blood does not help in differentiating the two diseases; then liver biopsy will be useful.

The obstructive jaundice present in carcinoma of the large bile ducts may be mistaken for stones obstructing the lower end of the common bile duct. A history of progressive jaundice with a loss of body weight should alert the physician to the malignant nature of the condition. This can be confirmed by ERC or operative cholangiogram.

Ruptured liver abscess may set up peritonitis, which in its initial stage may be confined to the upper abdomen. The spasm in the upper abdomen and the tender hypochondrium have been mistaken for RPC. However, as a rule, there is no jaundice. There may or may not be a history of amoebiasis. X-ray may show an elevated diaphragm. In such cases the diagnosis is made at operation, but the inexperienced surgeon may miss a ruptured liver abscess. It is a good practice to explore the superior surface of the liver whenever peritonitis is found and no pathology in the abdomen can account for it.

Ruptured primary carcinoma of the liver, usually the hepatocellular type, may be the cause of upper abdominal pain. In contrast to RPC the onset is sudden and usually there is no fever. The liver may be felt to be nodular, and paracentesis abdominis will demonstrate the presence in the carcinoma patients of free blood in the abdomen.

When the jaundice is mild a diagnosis of perforated peptic ulcer is frequently made. The demonstration of free air in the peritoneal cavity and the clinical findings will allow differentiation between the ulcer and RPC.

The diagnosis of ruptured appendix with general peritonitis is often found to be erroneous at laparotomy. This is especially likely to be so when RPC is complicated by empyaema of the gallbladder or by pancreatitis. A detailed history with careful examination can usually prevent a wrong diagnosis from being made. However, if there is any doubt, exploratory laparotomy should be carried out.

TREATMENT

CONSERVATIVE TREATMENT

As most cases of recurrent pyogenic cholangitis will undergo remission, when treated conservatively, this regimen should be undertaken in the first instance. It is advantageous to operate on these patients as elective cases, because stones are often found in the intrahepatic ducts. Removal of these stones is difficult and often involves extensive manipulation. An hourly chart of pulse rate, temperature, and blood pressure is kept. Vomiting can be relieved by gastric decompression through a nasogastric tube. Intravenous fluids are given, and pain is controlled by small doses of meperidine (demerol, pethidine). A 30-mg dose of intravenous vitamin K is given daily. Broad-spectrum antibiotics, such as terra-mycin or chloramphenicol, are given.

INDICATIONS FOR SURGICAL INTERVENTION
Conservative treatment must be abandoned under any of the following condi-tions:
1. Severe colic that is not relieved by administration of analgesics.
2. Rising pulse with elevation of blood pressure. This indicates severe obstruc-tion of the common bile duct and may be a prelude to septicaemia. Unless biliary decompression with energetic supportive treatment is now carried out the patient will quickly develop septicaemic shock.
3. Signs of general peritonitis, which may be due to the development of pancrea-titis secondary to an impacted stone or rupture of gallbladder empyema. At times biliary peritonitis may occur without empyema of the gallbladder. This may be due to rupture of the distended hepatic ducts near the surface of the liver.

OPERATIVE TREATMENT
Operative treatment is directed to the relief of obstruction by stones and to the establishment of adequate drainage of the biliary tract.

External drainage. Temporary external drainage can be acomplished by chole-dochostomy and insertion of a T tube. When the obstruction to the biliary tract is acute, and of short duration, the common bile duct is thin-walled and elastic. When the obstructing stone is removed the duct will regain its former size. In such cases T-tube drainage is all that is necessary. In desperately ill patients with septicaemic shock this operation may have to be carried out under local anaes-thesia. When such an operation is done as a last resort the impacted stone is left *in situ* and removed only when the patient has completely recovered.

Internal drainage. With repeated infection of the biliary tract the common bile duct tends to become dilated and thickened and it loses its elasticity. Under such circumstances a permanent internal drainage has to be established. The follow-ing methods are available:

Transduodenal choleochoduodenostomy (sphincteroplasty). This operation is carried out for recurrent pyogenic cholangitis when the common bile duct is permanently dilated and this dilatation extends down to the retroduodenal portion. After a thorough exploration of the abdomen the hepatic flexure is mobilised. This exposes the second part of the duodenum. A longitudinal incision is made along its anterior border and the duodenal papilla is identified. A lateral incision is made in the sphincter of Oddi. This is best done with a pair of scissors. With each cut the walls of the common bile duct and duodenum are brought together with thread stitches. This is continued until the largest diameter of the duct is reached. Stones and sludge can now be removed. Stones high up in the biliary tract will require separate incision in the common bile duct for their removal. The duodenal incision is closed in two layers. After a T tube has been inserted the abdomen is closed.

The extraperitoneal approach is employed when, despite repeated operations, stones are still left in the lower end of the common bile duct. This avoids dissecting through the dense and often vascular adhesions. A transverse incision is made midway between the xiphisternum and the umbilicus. The muscles are cut in line with the incision and the peritoneum is stripped from the right kidney. On further dissection the second part of the duodenum is reached. Care must be exercised before opening the duodenum, because the hepatic flexure of the colon may be closely adherent and thus mistaken for it. The rest of the procedure is the same as in the transperitoneal choledochoduodenostomy. The incision is closed with drainage of the extraperitoneal space.

Supraduodenal choledochoduodenostomy. This may be done with an end-to-side anastomosis. The common bile duct is transected and the distal end closed. The proximal end is then implanted into the first part of the duodenum. A side-to-side anastomosis has also been done by Stock and Tinckler (see Choledochoduodenostomy in Chapter 14) [82]. Success can be expected in a proportion of cases in which the dilatation ends at the upper border of the duodenum. When the dilatation extends to the retroduodenal portion of the bile duct, however, drainage will occur only as a spillover. Stasis below the anastomosis will continue to be present; consequently more stones will form and cause further obstruction and cholangitis.

Choledochojejunostomy. This is by far the best procedure for recurrent pyogenic cholangitis. In the selection of cases for such treatment the common bile duct must be enlarged and rigid. When the duct is temporarily dilated, as a result of acute obstruction, it will shrink to its original size when the offending stone is removed. Under such circumstances, when choledochojejunostomy is carried out, subsequent shrinkage of the duct will reduce the stoma to such an extent that there may be further obstruction. In order to prevent reflux the vertical limit of the Roux loop should be about 40 cm. A one-layer anastomosis between the intestine and divided common bile duct is performed. The common bile duct can be temporarily drained by inserting either a transhepatic tube or a T tube (see Choledochojejunostomy, Chapter 14).

Cholecystectomy. The gallbladder is not the primary seat of the disease and, although its absorbing function is impaired, it still serves as a safety valve when there is obstruction to the common duct. Hence it is not removed, except under one or more of the following circumstances:
1. When the gallbladder is contracted.
2. When empyema has developed or when the gallbladder has ruptured.
3. When there are multiple stones in the gallbladder.

Segmental resection of the liver. Intrahepatic stones may be confined to one lobe or one segment of the liver. At times the whole lobe is destroyed. In other cases the duct distal to the stones may be strictured. Removal of these stones may be difficult. Hepatolithotomy will often be followed by a fistula or a recurrence. Segmental resection of the liver will be the only form of treatment possible in such cases. This is usually performed in combination with one of the drainage procedures described.

PROGNOSIS

As the name implies this is a recurrent disease and may continue to be so for many years. It is most unpredictable in its outcome. However, the prognosis is good if all the stones in the intrahepatic ducts are completely removed and the ducts themselves are not irreparably damaged.

The prognosis is grave when the complications set in. Septicaemic shock carries a very high mortality. When it is complicated by liver abscess, especially when multiple, recovery can seldom be expected.

REFERENCES

1. ALTEMEIER W.A., TODD J.C. & INGE W.W. Gram-negative septicaemia: a growing threat. *Ann. Surg.* **166**:530, 1967.
2. ATTWOOD H.D. & CHOU S.T. The longevity of Clonorchis sinensis. *Pathology* **10**:153, 1978.
3. BATCH A., AMERY A.H., LALEMAND R.C. & SOLAN M.J. Biliary surgery. Routine prophylactic with antibiotics? Fifth World Congress, Collegium Internationale Chirugiae Digestive, Sao Paulo, Brazil, 1978. Abst. 19.
4. BISMUTH H., KUNTZIGER H. & CORLETTE M.B. Cholangitis with acute renal failure. Priorities in therapeutics. *Ann. Surg.* **181**:881, 1975.
5. BROOKE B.N. & SLANEY G. Portal bacteraemia in ulcerative colitis. *Lancet* **1**:1206, 1958.
6. BURKE J.F. The effective period of preventive antibiotic action in experimental incisions and dermal lesions. *Surgery* **50**:161, 1961.
7. BURKE J.F. Preventive antibiotic management in surgery. *Ann. Rev. Med.* **24**:289, 1973.
8. CHAN A.Y.S., GOLDBLOOM V.C. & GURD F.N. Clostridial infection as a cause of death after ligation of the hepatic artery. *A.M.A. Arch. Surg.* **63**:390, 1951.
9. CHETLIN S.H. & ELLIOT D.W. Preoperative antibiotics in biliary surgery. *Arch. Surg.* **107**:319, 1973.
10. CHOU S.T. & GIBSON J.B. Experimental cholangitis and cholelithiasis. *Br. J. Exp. Path.* **49**:565, 1968.
11. CHOU S.T. & CHAN C.W. Recurrent pyogenic cholangitis: a necropsy study. (To be published in *Pathology*, 1980.)
12. COOK J., HOU P.C., HO H.C. & MCFADZEAN A.J.S. Recurrent pyogenic cholangitis. *Br. J. Surg.* **42**:188, 1954.
13. CUNHA B.A., PYRTEK L.J. & QUINTILIANI R. Prophylactic antibiotics in cholecystectomy. *Lancet (letter to Editor)* **1**:207, 1978.
14. DAWSON J.L. The incidence of postoperative renal failure in obstructive jaundice. *Br. J. Surg.* **52**:663, 1965.
15. DAWSON J.L. Postoperative renal failure in obstructive jaundice: effect of a mannitol diuresis. *Br. Med. J.* **1**:82, 1965.

16. DAWSON J.L. Acute postoperative renal failure in obstructive jaundice. *Ann. R. Coll. Surg. Eng.* **42:**163, 1968.

17. DINEEN P. The importance of the route of infection in experimental biliary tract obstruction. *Surg. Gynec. Obstet.* **119:**1001, 1964.

18. DOW R.W. & LINDENAUER S.M. Acute obstructive suppurative cholangitis. *Ann. Surg.* **169:**272, 1969.

19. DYE M., MACDONALD A. & SMITH G. The bacterial flora of the biliary tract and liver in man. *Br. J. Surg.* **65:**285, 1978.

20. EDLUND Y., MOLLSTEDT B. & OUCHTERLONY O. Bacteriologic examination of operation cases of biliary tract disease. *Acta Chir. Scand.* **113:**473, 1957.

21. EDLUND Y., MOLLSTEDT B. & OUCHTERLONY O. Bacteriological investigation of the biliary system and liver in biliary tract disease correlated to clinical data and micro-structure of the gallbladder and liver. *Acta Chir. Scand.* **116:**461, 1958.

22. FABER R.G., IBRAHIM S.Z., THOMAS D.M., BEYNON G.P.J. & LEQUESNE L.P. Gall-stone disease presenting as septicaemic shock. *Br. J. Surg.* **65:**101, 1978.

23. FLEMMA R.J., FLINT L.M., OSTERHOUT S. & SHINGLETON W. Bacteriologic studies of biliary tract infection. *Ann. Surg.* **166:**563, 1967.

24. FLINN W.R., OLSON D.F., OYASU R. & BEAL J.M. Biliary bacteria and hepatic histologic changes in gallstone disease. *Ann. Surg.* **185:**593, 1977.

25. FUKUNAGA F.H. Gallbladder bacteriology, histology and gallstones. *Arch. Surg.* **106:**169, 1973.

26. GARDNER B., MASUR R. & FUJIMOTO J. Factors influencing the timing of cholecystec-tomy in acute cholecystitis. *Am. J. Surg.* **125:**730, 1973.

27. GIBSON J.B. Cholelithiasis and recurrent pyogenic cholangitis in the Far East. In H. Spencer (ed.), *Tropical Pathology*. Springer-Verlag, Berlin, 1973.

28. GLENN F. & MOODY F.C. Acute obstructive suppurative cholangitis. *Surg. Gynec. Obstet.* **113:**265, 1961.

29. HINCHEY E.J. & COUPER C.E. Acute obstructive suppurative cholangitis. *Am. J. Surg.* **117:**62, 1969.

30. HO C.S. & WESSON D.E. Recurrent pyogenic cholangitis in Chinese immigrants. *Am. J. Roentgenol. Radium Ther. Nucl. Med.* **122:**368, 1974.

31. HULTBORN A., JACOBSON B. & ROSENGREN B. Cholangiovenous reflux during cholan-giography. An experimental and clinical study. *Acta Chir. Scand.* **123:**111, 1962.

32. HUNT D.R. Pers. Commun. 1979.

33. JACOB A.I., GOLDBERG P.K., BLOOM N., DEGENSHEIN G.A. & KOZINN P.J. Endotoxin and bacteria in portal blood. *Gastroenterology* **72:**1268, 1977.

34. JACOBSSON B., KJELLANDER J. & ROSENGREN B. Cholangiovenous reflux. An experi-mental study. *Acta Chir. Scand.* **123:**316, 1962.

35. JONES E.A., CROWLEY N. & SHERLOCK S. Bacteraemia in association with hepatocel-lular and hepatobiliary disease. *Postgrad. Med. J.* **43** (Suppl 7), 1967.

36. KEIGHLEY M.R.B. Microorganisms in the bile. A preventable cause of sepsis after biliary surgery. *Ann. Roy. Coll. Surg. Eng.* **59:**328, 1977.

37. KEIGHLEY M.R.B., McLEISH A.R., BISHOP H.M., BURDON D.W., QUORAISHI P.H., OATES G.D., DORRICOTT M.J. & ALEXANDER-WILLIAMS J. Identification of the pre-sence and type of biliary microflora by immediate gram stains. *Surgery* **81:**469, 1977.

38. KHAN G.A. & SCOTT A.J. The place of rifamycin-B-diethylamide in the treatment of cholangitis complicating biliary obstruction. *Br. J. Pharmacol.* **31:**506, 1967.

39. KING M.S. Biliary tract disease in Malaya. *Br. J. Surg.* **58:**829, 1971.

40. KUNE G.A. Life-threatening surgical infection. Its development and prediction. *Ann. R. Coll. Surg. Eng.* **60:**92, 1978.

41. KUNE G.A. & BIRKS, D. Acute cholecystitis. An appraisal of current methods of treatment. *Med. J. Aust.* **2:**218, 1970.

42. KUNE G.A. & SCHUTZ E. Bacteria in the biliary tract. A study of their frequency and type. *Med. J. Aust.* **1:**255, 1974.

43. KUNE G.A., HIBBERD J. & MORAHAN R. The development of biliary infection. An experimental study. *Med. J. Aust.* **1**:301, 1974.

44. KUNE G.A. & BURDON J.G.W. Are antibiotics necessary in acute cholecystitis? *Med. J. Aust.* **2**:627, 1975.

45. KUNE G.A., LEINKRAM C. & ROBERTS-THOMSON I.C. Juxtapapillary duodenal diverticula. Association with gallstones and pancreatitis. *Med. J. Aust.* **1**: 209, 1980.

46. KUNE G.A., LEINKRAM C. & SALI A. (Unpublished data, 1980.)

47. LAI K.S., MCFADZEAN A.J.S. & YOUNG R.T.T. Microemboli pulmonary hypertension in pyogenic cholangitis. *Br. Med. J.* **1**:22, 1968.

48. LAM S.K., WONG K.P., CHAN P.K.W., NGAN H. & ONG G.B. Recurrent pyogenic cholangitis: a study by endoscopic retrograde cholangiography. *Gastroenterology* **74**:1196, 1978.

49. LOTVEIT T., OSMES M. & AUNE S. Bacteriological studies of common bile duct bile in patients with gallstone disease and juxta-papillary duodenal diverticula. *Scand. J. Gastroenterol.* **13**:93, 1978.

50. MACLEAN L.D., MULLIGAN W.G., MCLEAN A.P.H. & DUFF J.H. Patterns of septic shock in man—a detailed study of 56 patients. *Ann. Surg.* **166**:543, 1967.

51. MACLEISH D.G. *Pers. Commun.*, 1969.

52. MADDOCKS A.C., HILSON G.R.F. & TAYLOR R. The bacteriology of the obstructed biliary tree. *Ann. R. Coll. Surg. Eng.* **52**:316, 1973.

53. MAGE S. & MOREL A.S. Surgical experience with cholangiohepatitis (Hong Kong disease) in Canton Chinese. *Ann. Surg.* **162**:187, 1965.

54. MAKI T. Pathogenesis of calcium bilirubinate gallstones: role of *E. coli* B-glucuronidase and coagulation by inorganic ions polyelectrolytes and agitation. *Ann. Surg.* **164**:90, 1966.

55. MARSHALL J.F. & HARZOG D.C. JR. Acute emphysematous cholecystitis. *Ann. Surg.* **159**:1011, 1964.

56. MASON G.R. Bacteriology and antibiotic selection in biliary tract surgery. *Arch. Surg. (Chicago)* **97**:533, 1968.

57. MATSUSHIRO T., SUSUKI N., SATO T. & MAKI T. Effects of diet on glucaric acid concentration in bile and the formation of calcium bilirubinate gallstones. *Gastroenterology* **72**:630, 1977.

58. MCFADZEAN A.J.S. & ONG G.B. Intrahepatic typhoid carriers. *Br. Med. J.* **1**:1567, 1966.

59. MCFADZEAN A.J.S. & YEUNG R.T.T. Hypoglycaemia in suppurative pancholangitis due to Clonorchis sinensis. *Trans. Roy. Soc. Trop. Med. Hyg.* **59**:179, 1965.

60. MCLEISH A.R., KEIGHLEY M.R.B., BISHOP H.M., BURDON D.W., QUORAISHI A.H., DORRICOTT H.J., OATES G.D. & ALEXANDER-WILLIAMS J. Selecting patients requiring antibiotics in biliary surgery by immediate Gram's stains of bile at operation. *Surgery* **81**:473, 1977.

61. MCSHERRY C.K., STUBENBORD W.T. & GLENN F. The significance of air in the biliary system and liver. *Surg. Gynec. Obstet.* **128**:49, 1969.

62. MIXER H.W., RIGLER L.G. & ODDONE M.G. Experimental studies on biliary regurgitation during cholangiography. *Gastroenterology* **9**:64, 1947.

63. MORRAN C., MCNAUGHT W. & MCARDLE C.S. Prophylactic co-trimoxazole in biliary surgery. *Br. Med. J.* **2**:462, 1978.

64. MUELLER C.B. The mechanism of acute renal failure after injury and transfusion and its prevention by solute diuresis. *Surg. Clin. N. Amer.* **45**:499, 1965.

65. NIELSEN M.L. & JUSTASEN T. Anaerobic and aerobic bacteriological studies in biliary tract disease. *Scand J. Gastroenterol.* **11**:437, 1976.

66. NOLAN J.P. Bacteria and the liver. *New Eng. J. Med.* (editorial) **299**:1069, 1978.

67. ONG G.B. A study of recurrent pyogenic cholangitis. *Arch. Surg. (Chicago)* **84**:199, 1962.

68. ONG G.B. Recurrent pyogenic cholangitis. *Med. Ann.* **25**, 1968.

69. ONG G.B., ADISESHIAH M. & LEONG C.H. Acute pancreatitis associated with recurrent pyogenic cholangitis. *Br. J. Surg.* **58**:891, 1971.

70. PAPACHRISTODOULOU A.J., MACKENZIE A., NORMAN J. & KARRAN S.J. Single dose cephazolin prophylaxis in biliary tract surgery. *J. R. Coll. Surg. Edin.* **178**:23, 1978.

71. PLIMPTON N.C. Clostridium perfringes infection: a complication of gallbladder surgery. *Arch. Surg. (Chicago)* **89**:499, 1964.

72. POWIS S.J.A. & SEVERN M. *Prophylactic antibiotics in biliary surgery.* Fifth World Congress, Collegium Internationale Chirurgiae Digestive, Sao Paulo, Brazil, 1978. Abst. 20.

73. PYRTEK L.J. & BARTUS S.A. Clostridium welchii infection complicating biliary tract surgery. *New Eng. J. Med.* **266**:689, 1962.

74. PYRTEK L.J. & BARTUS S.A. An evaluation of antibiotics in biliary tract surgery. *Surg. Gynec. Obstet.* **125**:101, 1967.

75. SAIK R.P., GREENBURG A.G., FARRIS J.M. & PESKIN G.W. Spectrum of cholangitis. *Am. J. Surg.* **130**:145, 1975.

76. SCHETTEN W.E., DESPREZ J.D. & HOLDEN W.E. A bacteriological study of portal vein in man. *Arch. Surg.* **71**:404, 1955.

77. SCOTT A.J. Bacteria and disease of the biliary tract. *Gut* **12**:487, 1971.

78. SCOTT A.J. & KHAN G.A. Origin of bacteria in bile duct bile. *Lancet* **2**:790, 1967.

79. SCOTT A.J. & KHAN G.A. Partial biliary obstruction with cholangitis producing a blind loop syndrome. *Gut* **9**:187, 1968.

80. SEDGWICK C.E., POULANTZAS J.K. & KUNE G.A. Management of portal hypertension, secondary to biliary strictures. *Ann. Surg.* **163**:949, 1966.

81. SHUI M.H. An unusual case of spontaneous internal biliary fistula. *Br. J. Surg.* **54**:969, 1967.

82. STOCK F.E. & TINCKLER L. Choledochoduodentostomy in the treatment of cholangiohepatitis. *Surg. Gynec. Obstet.* **101**:499, 1955.

83. STRACHAN, C.J.L., BLACK J., POWIS S.J.A., WATERWORTH T.A., WISE R., WILKINSON A.R., BURDON D.W., SEVERN M., MITRA B. & NORCOTT H. Prophylactic use of cephazolin against wound sepsis after cholecystectomy. *Br. Med. J.* **1**: 1254, 1977.

84. STRAUCH M., McLAUGHLIN J.S., MANSBERGER A., YOUNG J., MEDONCA P., GRAY K. & COWLEY R.A. Effects of septic shock on renal function in humans. *Ann. Surg.* **165**:536, 1967.

85. TRIGER D.R., BOYER T.D. & LEVIN J. Portal and systemic bacteraemia and endotoxaemia in liver disease. *Gut* **19**:935, 1977.

86. TRINCA G.W. Acute emphysematous cholecystitis. *Aust. New Zeal. J. Surg.* **30**:217, 1961.

87. TURNER F.P. Fetal clostridium welchii septicaemia following cholecystectomy. *Am. J. Surg.* **108**:3, 1964.

88. WEN C.C. & LEE H.L. Intrahepatic stones: a clinical study. *Ann. Surg.* **175**:166, 1972.

89. WILKINSON S.P., ARROYO V., GAZZARD B.G., MOODIE H. & WILLIAMS R. Relation of renal impairment and haemorrhagic diathesis to endotoxaemia in fulminant hepatic failure. *Lancet* **1**:521, 1974.

90. WILLIAMS R. & DAWSON J.L. The management of ascending cholangitis. *Proc. R. Soc. Med.* **62**:243, 1969.

91. YUE P.C.K. Recurrent pyogenic cholangitis in children. *Aust. New Zeal. J. Surg.* **44**:53, 1974.

10. Biliary Peritonitis

Extravasation of bile into the peritoneal cavity is an uncommon condition that has a number of widely different causes. It assumes importance in biliary surgery because, in some cases, diagnosis is difficult and because adequate surgical treatment will forestall an otherwise fatal outcome. It is curious that a detailed consideration of biliary peritonitis has been neglected in the surgical literature and in current texts dealing with biliary surgery.

CAUSES

The causes of biliary peritonitis are summarised in Table 10.1.

ACUTE CHOLECYSTITIS

Perforation of the acutely inflamed gallbladder is the commonest cause of biliary peritonitis. The incidence of free perforation in acute cholecystitis resulting in biliary peritonitis has been variously estimated, but is probably of the order of 2 per cent.

Occasionally, a gangrenous gallbladder is present without perforation, but the gallbladder wall must have become permeable to bile, because there is an associated bile-stained peritoneal exudate [5, 6, 16].

POSTOPERATIVE BILE LEAKAGE

Biliary tract surgery is sometimes followed by biliary extravasation. This complication of surgery is important because it may have an insidious clinical course and diagnosis may therefore be delayed [20, 30]. In some cases the cause is not found even at autopsy. The following can cause postoperative biliary extravasation:

Bile duct injury. Unrecognised injury to a bile duct during cholecystectomy may result in biliary peritonitis [17]. This subject is fully discussed in Chapter 6. The injured duct may be the common hepatic duct or common bile duct, the right hepatic duct, or a segmental bile duct. Occasionally, a subvesical bile duct is present in the gallbladder bed, which can be inadvertently damaged during cholecystectomy (see Subvesical ducts, Chapter 1).

Table 10.1. Causes of biliary peritonitis

Acute cholecystitis
Rupture of gallbladder
Transudation of bile

Postoperative bile leakage
Bile duct injury
Slipped cystic duct stump ligature
Choledochotomy with primary closure of duct
Removal or dislodgement of T tube

Percutaneous liver puncture
Needle liver biopsy
Percutaneous transhepatic cholangiography

Uncommon causes
Traumatic rupture of gallbladder or bile ducts
Rupture of pathological gallbladder, bile duct, or cholangitic liver abscess
Spontaneous perforation of gallbladder or bile duct
Idiopathic-biliary peritonitis without apparent perforation

Slipped or sloughed ligature of cystic duct stump. This has been described as a cause, but is extremely rare [20, 26].

Bile duct exploration and suture without T-tube drainage. A number of such cases have also been described, but they must be most uncommon—otherwise experienced surgeons would not persist with primary closure of the bile duct [4, 20, 32].

Removal or dislodgement of T tube. Rarely, a T tube becomes dislodged following bile duct exploration in the first 2 or 3 days after operation, resulting in biliary peritonitis [20]. In some other cases the T tube is removed at the customary period, but for some reason a track had not formed to the exterior, and intraperitoneal biliary extravasation occurs [6, 20].

Attention has been drawn to the high risk of development of biliary peritonitis following the removal of T tubes which are made of plastic material, polyvinyl chloride (PVC) [37]. The authors have also encountered two such cases. The probable reason for this is the minimal peritoneal reaction which occurs with the use of PVC tubes. Their use must be discontinued.

Cause uncertain. In a number of instances a postoperative biliary peritonitis develops but, at the time of the second operation for its drainage, a cause cannot be found. In these cases it is assumed that the bile leak occurred from a small subvesical duct injured during cholecystectomy, or from other small bile ducts in the gallbladder fossa (Chapter 1).

PERCUTANEOUS LIVER PUNCTURE

In the presence of jaundice, due to mechanical bile duct obstruction, percutaneous needle liver biopsy or percutaneous transhepatic cholangiography may be followed by extravasation of bile into the peritoneal cavity [9, 18] (Chapters 3 & 4). The biliary extravasation is usually caused by the leakage of bile through the puncture wound in the liver, because bile duct pressure is high as a consequence of the mechanical obstruction. Bile extravasation, in these cases, can also be due to inadvertent puncture of the gallbladder or of a large bile duct in the porta hepatis.

The risk of bile leakage has been considerably decreased after percutaneous transhepatic cholangiography, by the use of the fine Chiba needle, but occasional cases still occur. Similarly, with fine-needle liver biopsy the risk of bile leakage has been minimised, but not eliminated completely [23].

UNCOMMON CAUSES

TRAUMATIC PERFORATION OF GALLBLADDER OR BILE DUCTS
Injury of the gallbladder or bile ducts due to blunt or penetrating trauma has been reported but is most uncommon [10, 12, 14, 36]. Avulsion of the papilla of Vater, or transection of the common bile duct following car accidents, or blunt trauma, usually present as a slowly developing biliary peritonitis [27, 33].

RUPTURE OF PATHOLOGICAL GALLBLADDER, BILE DUCT, OR CHOLANGITIC LIVER ABSCESS
Rupture of the bile duct above a stricture, rupture of the duct obstructed by gallstones, and rupture of a cholangitic liver abscess secondary to bile duct obstruction, have all been described [6, 22]. Other causes of rupture have been steroid therapy, typhoid fever, and acute pancreatitis [2, 15, 25, 29].

SPONTANEOUS PERFORATION OF GALLBLADDER OR BILE DUCTS
Spontaneous perforation of the gallbladder has been reported in a patient with thrombocytopenic purpura, and in others who may have had an infarct of the gallbladder wall due to cystic artery occlusion [6, 19]. Apparently, spontaneous rupture of the extrahepatic bile ducts has also been reported in about 15 cases [6, 13, 22, 35]. The cause in these cases may be infarction of the bile duct wall following arterial occlusion, or an unrecognised bile duct infection.

IDIOPATHIC-BILIARY PERITONITIS WITHOUT APPARENT PERFORATION
These are rare, but fascinating, cases, because the biliary system is apparently intact and macroscopically normal [6, 34]. Excluded from this group are cases in which bile permeates through an inflamed wall, such as is sometimes seen in acute cholecystitis.

It is difficult to believe that bile can leak through a normal gallbladder or bile duct. It is more likely that a minute perforation occurs—perhaps due to a small calculus, rupture of a small gallbladder diverticulum, or rupture of a mucous gland—which allows bile to exude, causing decompression of the biliary system, followed by sealing of the hole with fibrin [6, 34].

DIAGNOSIS

Little is known about the pathogenesis of the symptoms and signs seen in biliary extravasations. It is presumed that the clinical picture is caused by the combination of a number of factors [6, 21].

1. Chemical peritonitis produced by the irritating effect of bile.

2. Bacterial peritonitis if the bile is infected, resulting in septic shock and septicaemia.

3. Fluid loss into the peritoneal cavity.

4. Toxic effects of bile absorbed into the circulation.

The surgical literature is lacking in useful data on the clinical features and diagnosis of biliary peritonitis. In this regard the paper of McKenzie may be cited as a masterpiece of clinical observation [20].

The modes of presentation of biliary peritonitis can be divided into three relatively distinct groups, according to the severity of the clinical manifestations and the rapidity with which these features progress.

ACUTE AND DRAMATIC PRESENTATION

Fortunately, the majority of patients belong to this group. It is obvious from clinical examination that an abdominal catastrophe of some type has occurred. There is usually severe abdominal pain and tenderness. Abdominal distension is frequent, but rigidity may be absent. The features of shock with marked tachycardia are almost always present [6, 20].

The patient who has a free perforation of the gallbladder in association with acute cholecystitis usually presents with the picture of general peritonitis, the cause of which is not clear preoperatively, the diagnosis being made at operation.

In the postoperative patient the diagnosis of biliary peritonitis may be missed even if it has a dramatic onset, because the pain may be masked by the administration of analgesics and because the significance of abdominal tenderness is difficult to assess in a patient with a recent abdominal wound. These masked cases were probably the target of a well-known and astute Australian surgeon who had the following sign in his ward: 'No patient in my ward develops a coronary occlusion after cholecystectomy!' implying that a catastrophic occurrence after biliary surgery should mean a biliary leak rather than a 'medical' complication, until proven otherwise.

SUBACUTE AND INSIDIOUS PRESENTATION

In a number of cases the clinical features develop slowly and insidiously over a number of days. This group causes the greatest diagnostic problem and may be missed, unless the surgeon maintains a high index of suspicion in potential cases. The disease is seen in some postoperative bile leaks, or following percutaneous liver puncture, but the authors have also encountered it in a case of acute cholecystitis which was managed conservatively [20, 30].

In some of these cases a history of sudden onset of dramatic symptoms is in fact present, but is glossed over because of an equally rapid, though temporary, improvement.

Abdominal pain is frequently present, but is not usually severe. Vomiting and jaundice are uncommon. The abdominal signs are equally indefinite, but some degree of abdominal distension is common. Abdominal tenderness is occasionally present, but rigidity is uncommon.

The features of hypovolaemic shock are usually absent. However, a tachycardia of 110–140 beats per minute, which is out of keeping with the rest of the clinical picture, is so common that it must be regarded as the most important single clinical finding [20]. Fig. 10.1 represents the pulse rate of a patient referred to the authors after a needle liver biopsy had been performed in the presence of

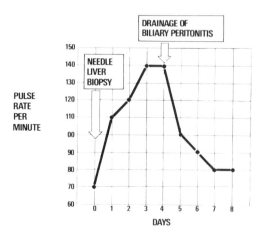

Fig.10.1. Daily pulse rate of a patient who developed peritonitis after needle liver biopsy in the presence of complete mechanical bile duct obstruction. The bile was drained at operation as indicated.

complete mechanical bile duct obstruction. If free fluid is present in the abdomen, on clinical examination, paracentesis may be diagnostic [30].

A number of cases show clinical and radiologic signs in the right base of the lung due to an elevation of the right hemidiaphragm caused by a collection of bile, and a liver–lung radionuclide scan will show a filling defect as seen in Fig. 10.2.

Added to these clinical features are those related to the underlying cause, such as acute cholecystitis, a recent biliary tract operation, or the condition for which a percutaneous liver puncture was performed.

Modern organ-imaging techniques, such as computed tomography and ultrasound, can now accurately localise diffuse or loculated intra-abdominal fluid collections, including collections of bile, as seen in Fig. 10.3 [1, 8]. The problem is that with these insidiously presenting cases of biliary peritonitis the clinical suspicion may not be there and, therefore, an abdominal scan is not performed.

CHRONIC PRESENTATION

Rarely, the clinical picture of biliary extravasation is seen with very mild symptoms and it is very slow in development [6, 7, 11, 28, 30, 31]. Most cases have occurred in infants, but a number have also been reported in adults. The causes of

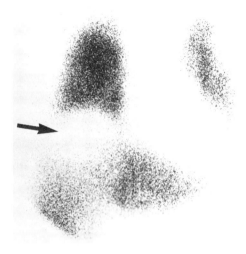

Fig. 10.2. Radionuclide liver–lung scan in a patient with a loculated subphrenic collection of bile (arrow).

biliary extravasation are similar to those seen with acute or subacute presentation. Perhaps a very slow rate of bile leakage, coupled with the absence of bacterial contamination, accounts for this unusual mode of presentation.

The clinical picture is characterised by gradual development of abdominal distension due to ascites in a patient who appears to be relatively well. This distension is associated with a variety of other symptoms, such as jaundice, anorexia, nausea, or diarrhoea, but without evidence of either peritonitis or shock. Abdominal paracentesis usually provides the diagnosis in these cases [31]. The condition may be confused with bile-stained ascites, but these ascitic patients also have evidence of liver cirrhosis and portal hypertension.

TREATMENT

In biliary peritonitis the following principles of treatment must be applied:
1. Drainage of biliary extravasation.
2. Correction of underlying cause.
3. Treatment of shock or infection, if present.

DRAINAGE OF BILIARY EXTRAVASATION
This almost always means operation, sucking out of the bile, and insertion of drainage tubes to the most appropriate region. In a number of cases of chronic bile collection repeated paracentesis was the only type of treatment required [31].

CORRECTION OF UNDERLYING CAUSE
If an underlying cause, or site of leakage, is found this is usually corrected at the same time as the biliary extravasation is drained.

Cholecystectomy is performed if the extravasation is due to acute cholecystitis. In postoperative cases the site and cause cannot be found in a significant

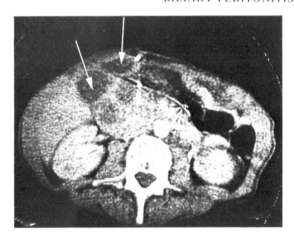

Fig. 10.3. Computed tomography in a patient with a large loculated intra-abdominal collection of bile presenting insidiously postoperatively (arrows).

number [20]. If the extravasation is due to a bile duct injury the injured duct is repaired (see Operative Bile Duct Injuries in Chapter 6). If biliary peritonitis follows accidental dislodgement of a T tube re-exploration is undertaken and the T tube is reinserted. Looked at from another angle, if a T tube becomes accidentally dislodged in the first 2 or 3 days after operation, it is best to reoperate and reinsert the T tube rather than wait for biliary peritonitis to develop. If a T tube is dislodged more than 3 days after surgery and there is no reason to suspect distal bile duct obstruction it is reasonable merely to observe the patient, because by this stage one would expect localisation and adhesion formation to be occurring [20]. However, if during this period of observation the clinical features suggest a biliary extravasation the patient should be reoperated without delay.

Biliary extravasation which follows percutaneous needle puncture of the liver almost always occurs only in a patient who has a mechanical bile duct obstruction of some type. The actual needle track requires no special treatment, but the underlying cause must be relieved, whether this be done by choledocholithotomy, correction of biliary stricture, or excision or bypass of a malignant tumour.

Traumatic perforation of the gallbladder is treated by cholecystectomy; traumatic injuries of the bile duct are reconstructed along lines similar to those of operative injuries. Clearly, rupture of a diseased gallbladder requires cholecystectomy, and that of an involved bile duct requires correction of the cause, such as choledocholithotomy or stricture repair. Spontaneous perforation of the gallbladder is treated by cholecystectomy, whereas that of the bile duct requires merely choledochotomy, and insertion of a T tube. In idiopathic biliary peritonitis it is probably safest to perform a choledochotomy and insertion of a T tube.

TREATMENT OF SHOCK AND INFECTION
If biliary tract infection or hypovolaemic shock, or both, is present the treatment is along similar lines to that described for cholangitis in Chapter 9. Following drainage of a biliary extravasation it is probably wisest to administer broad-spectrum aerobic and anaerobic antibiotic cover in the postoperative period, even if

the clinical features of a systemic infection, such as bacteraemia or septicaemia, are absent. The precise nature and mode of antibiotic cover follows similar principles to antibiotic use in biliary disease and is discussed in detail in Chapter 9.

PROGNOSIS

Undrained biliary extravasations are uniformly fatal [3, 6, 20, 24]. Even if the biliary extravasation is drained the mortality rate is appreciable [6, 20]. Deaths in these cases can be correlated to delay in diagnosis and, therefore, delay in institution of adequate treatment. Awareness of the possibility of biliary peritonitis, particularly in the insidious type of presentation, will clearly lower the mortality rate. The age of the patient also influences the mortality—the older the patient, the worse the outlook. The prognosis in infants who have biliary peritonitis is uniformly good [6, 7, 11, 28].

REFERENCES

1. ABRAMS H.L. & McNEIL B.J. Medical implications of computed tomography (CAT Scanning). *New Eng. J. Med.* **298:**310, 1978.
2. BUTLER D.B. & EICHHORN R. Acute pancreatitis with necrosis and perforation of common bile duct: case report. *Am. Surg.* **22:**512, 1956.
3. BUTLER R.M. & HARKINS H.N. Perforation of the gallbladder with special reference to cholecystenteric fistulas. *Am. J. Surg.* **101:**717, 1961.
4. COLLINS P.G. Further experience with common bile duct suture without intraductal drainage following choledochotomy. *Br. J. Surg.* **54:**854, 1967.
5. DALE G. & SOLHEIM K. Bile peritonitis in acute cholecystitis. *Acta Clin. Scand.* **141:**746, 1975.
6. ELLIS H. & CRONIN K. Bile peritonitis. *Br. J. Surg.* **48:**166, 1960.
7. ERICSSON N.O. & RUDHE U. Spontaneous perforation of the bile ducts in infants: presentation of a case and review of the literature. *Acta Chir. Scand.* **118:**439, 1960.
8. FERRUCCI J.T. JR. Medical progress—body ultrasonography. *New Eng. J. Med.* **300:**590, 1979.
9. FLEMMA R.J., CAPP M.P. & SHINGLETON W.W. Percutaneous transhepatic cholangiography. *Arch. Surg. (Chicago)* **90:**5, 1965.
10. FLETCHER W.S., MAHNKE D.E. & DUNPHY J.E. Complete division of the common bile duct due to blunt trauma: report of a case and review of the literature. *J. Trauma* **1:**87, 1961.
11. GERTZ T.C. Spontaneous perforation of the common bile duct: report of a case. *A.M.A. Arch. Surg.* **78:**7, 1959.
12. HALL E.R. JR., HOWARD J.M., JORDAN G.L. & MIKESKY W.E. Traumatic injuries of the gallbladder. *A.M.A. Arch. Surg.* **72:**520, 1956.
13. HARRIS W.G. & SHOESMITH J.H. Spontaneous perforation of the bile ducts. *Br. J. Surg.* **50:**426, 1963.
14. HINSHAW D.B., TURNER G.R. & CARTER R. Transection of the common bile duct caused by nonpenetrating trauma. *Am. J. Surg.* **104:**104, 1962.
15. KOLISCH P. DE R. Rupture of the gallbladder associated with steroid therapy: report of a case. *J. Med. Soc. New Jersey* **57:**81, 1960.
16. KUNE G.A. & BIRKS D. Acute cholecystitis. An appraisal of current methods of treatment. *Med. J. Aust.* **2:**218, 1970.

17. KUNE G.A., HARDY K.J., BROWN G. & MCKENZIE G. Operative injuries of the bile
    ducts. *Med. J. Aust.* **2**:233, 1969.
18. MADDEN R.E. Complications of needle biopsy of the liver. *Arch. Surg. (Chicago)*
    83:778, 1961.
19. MAINGOT R. *The Management of Abdominal Operations*, p. 827. Lewis, London, 1959.
20. MCKENZIE G. Extravasation of bile after operations on the biliary tract. *Aust. New
    Zeal. J. Surg.* **24**:181, 1955.
21. MILES R.M. & JECK H.S. Observations on experimental bile peritonitis. *Surgery*
    34:445, 1953.
22. MOORE H.D. Some unusual but instructive surgical emergencies. *Br. Med. J.* **2**:756,
    1950.
23. MORRIS J.S., GALLO A., SCHEVER P.J. & SHERLOCK S. Percutaneous liver biopsy in
    patients with large bile duct obstruction. *Gastroenterology* **68**:750, 1975.
24. MORSE L., KRYNSKI B. & WRIGHT A.R. Acute perforation of the gallbladder. *Am. J.
    Surg.* **94**:772, 1957.
25. MOUZAS G.L. & BRIGGS J.H. Perforation of the gallbladder during prednisone
    treatment. *Br. Med. J.* **2**:450, 1957.
26. NEWBURGER B. Spontaneous postoperative rupture of the bile ducts. *Ann. Surg.*
    107:558, 1938.
27. PARKINSON S.W. & WISNIEWSKI Z.S. Avulstion of the ampulla of Vater: an isolated
    injury following blunt abdominal trauma. *Aust. New Zeal. J. Surg.* **48**:562, 1978.
28. PETTERSSON G. Spontaneous perforation of the common bile duct in infants. *Acta
    Chir. Scand.* **110**:192, 1955.
29. PROTIC M.F. & GOLDBERGER A. Gallbladder perforation as a complication of typhoid
    fever. *Med. Arch.* **10**:81, 1956.
30. ROSATO E.F., BERKOWITZ H.D. & ROBERTS B. Bile ascites. *Surg. Gynec. Obstet.*
    130:494, 1970.
31. SANTSCHI D.R., HUIZENGA K.A., SCUDAMORE H.D., DEARING W.H. & WAUGH J.M.
    Bile ascites. *Arch. Surg. (Chicago)* **87**:85, 1963.
32. SAWYERS J.L., HERRINGTON J.L. JR. & EDWARDS W.H. Primary closure of the
    common bile duct. *Am. J. Surg.* **109**:017, 1965.
33. SHORTHOUSE A.J., SINGH M.P., TREASURE T. & FRANKLIN R.H. Isolated complete
    transection of the common bile duct by blunt abdominal trauma. *Br. J. Surg.* **65**:543,
    1978.
34. SMALL W.P. A case of biliary peritonitis. *Br. J. Surg.* **41**:552, 1954.
35. SNYDER R.E. Spontaneous rupture of the hepatic duct. *Ann. Surg.* **146**:246, 1957.
36. STEWART R. & SILEN W. Traumatic rupture of the bile duct. Review of the literature
    and report of a case of rupture following cholecystectomy and choledochotomy.
    Arch. Surg. (Chicago) **82**:387, 1961.
37. WINSTONE N.E., GOLBY M.G.S., LAWSON L.J. & WINDSOR C.W.O. Biliary peritonitis:
    a hazard of polyvinyl chloride T tubes. *Lancet* **1**:843, 1965.

11. Biliary Fistulas and Gallstone Ileus

Fistulas of the biliary tract are uncommon and have a wide variety of causes. A number of these fistulas have already been mentioned in other sections of this book.

TYPES OF FISTULA

There are two main types of biliary fistula:

1. External, in which the communication is between the skin and the biliary tract.

2. Internal, in which the biliary tract usually communicates with a portion of the gastrointestinal tract, such as the duodenum or colon. Less commonly there is a communication with the pleural cavity or a bronchus.

CAUSES

The causes of biliary fistulas, whether external or internal, can be divided for clinical purposes into three main groups, namely, intentional, postoperative, and pathological.

Intentional. These are intentionally created by the surgeon. Examples are cholecystostomy, choledochostomy, choledochoduodenostomy, and choledochojejunostomy.

Postoperative. These are fistulas which follow biliary surgery and are usually due to a surgical error of some type. Examples are fistulas that result from operative bile duct injuries or from gallstones overlooked in the common bile duct after choledochotomy.

Pathological. Examples are a choledochoduodenal fistula resulting from gallstone perforation into the duodenum, and a bronchobiliary fistula caused by rupture of a hepatic hydatid into the lungs.

EXTERNAL BILIARY FISTULA

CAUSES

INTENTIONAL

These surgically created fistulas are the commonest types and have been described previously.

326

Cholecystostomy. This is occasionally performed in acute cholecystitis when cholecystectomy is deemed difficult or dangerous, or when the general condition of the patient is poor (see Acute cholecystitis, Chapter 5). Rarely, it is performed during elective cholecystectomy for gallstones, if the anatomy of the ductal system cannot be adequately demonstrated owing to extreme fibrosis of the area (see Cholecystectomy, Chapter 5). If cholecystostomy is performed for gallstones it is important that all the stones are removed and to be sure that the cystic duct is patent; otherwise a persistent mucous fistula may result when the cholecystostomy tube is removed.

It is unwise to perform cholecystostomy as a decompressive procedure in malignant obstruction of the distal bile duct, unless resection is definitely contemplated within 10–14 days and unless correction of the water and electrolyte loss caused by the total external biliary fistula can be undertaken. Even in such cases most surgeons prefer a loop cholecystenterostomy as the first stage.

The procedure is usually performed under general anaesthesia, but it can be done under local anaesthesia if the condition of the patient is poor. Fig. 11.1 illustrates the surgical technique. First the gallbladder contents are emptied with

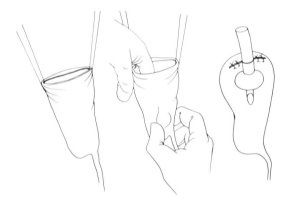

Fig. 11.1 The operative technique of cholecystostomy in the presence of gallstones.

a trocar-sucker. The fundus of the gallbladder is then opened between stay sutures, and the bile is sucked out. If cholecystostomy is done for gallstones then the gallbladder is explored with scoops and forceps, and then bimanually with fingers. It is essential to be sure that stones in the neck of the gallbladder are removed. The cholecystostomy tube should be retained for approximately 2 weeks, after which it is usually removed. A Foley-type catheter is useful as a tube (Fig. 11.1).

Choledochostomy. Choledochostomy, exploration of the bile ducts, and T-tube drainage is most commonly performed for choledocholithiasis (see Exploration of the bile ducts, Chapter 5). Much less common indications are for a hydatid cyst rupturing into the bile ducts (Chapter 15), as a preliminary to operative diagnosis of bile duct tumours and palliative decompression of bile duct tumours (Chapter 7), and as a method of delineating the hepatic ducts during a difficult cholecystectomy (see Cholecystectomy, Chapter 5). The surgical technique and management of the T tube have also been covered in Chapter 5.

Hepaticostomy. External hepaticostomy drainage is employed, occasionally, following operative injuries to the bile ducts, as a first-stage procedure when local conditions in the porta hepatis or the general condition of the patient do not allow repair (Chapter 6).

POSTOPERATIVE

These are usually due to an error of surgical technique or to an inadequate operation in which the surgeon has not dealt with the underlying pathology completely.

After cholecystostomy. A persistent biliary fistula or mucous fistula remaining after the cholecystostomy tube has been removed usually indicates unrecognised distal bile duct obstruction, usually due to gallstones as seen in Fig. 11.2, but occasionally due to an unrecognised malignant obstruction.

After cholecystectomy. A fistula persisting through the drainage tube track after cholecystectomy usually indicates a bile duct injury (Chapter 6, Ref. 45). Sometimes it is due to inadvertent damage of the small subvesical duct in the gallbladder fossa (Chapter 17), or to a slipped or sloughed ligature on the cystic duct

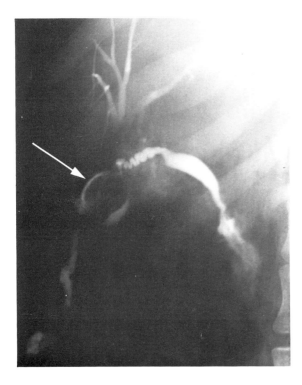

Fig. 11.2. Postcholecystostomy persistant mucous fistula due to large retained gallstone in Hartmann's pouch.

stump. One of the authors has removed two completely gangrenous and necrotic gallbladders which were in the middle of a pericholecystic abscess and the operations were performed more or less 'with the sucker'. The cystic duct was not ligated and all that could be done was to insert a drainage tube to the area. Both patients developed an external biliary fistula which discharged infected bile for some time, but which closed spontaneously after 3 and 5 weeks respectively (Fig. 11.3).

After choledochostomy. A biliary fistula persisting after removal of the T tube is usually due to overlooked choledocholithiasis, or to an overlooked malignant obstruction of the distal bile duct. T-tube cholangiography prior to the removal of the tube should be a routine procedure so that such a condition can be anticipated.

After biliary-intestinal drainage operations. An external biliary fistula persisting after a procedure such as transduodenal sphincteroplasty or choledochoduo-denostomy is usually due to a disruption of the suture line for one or another reason, such as ischaemic necrosis, abscess formation, postoperative pancrea-titis, or faulty surgical technique. In these cases it is important to establish whether the fistula is purely biliary, or whether is also contains duodenal or pancreatic juice.

PATHOLOGICAL
Spontaneous external biliary fistula as a result of some pathological process is extremely rare. It is usually due to neglected acute cholecystitis with a perichole-cystic abscess, or to a late stage of carcinoma of the gallbladder [57, 59, 61].

CONSEQUENCES

An external biliary fistula has a number of physiological and pathological consequences, the severity of which depends on the degree of biliary diversion present, the underlying cause of the fistula, and the length of time the fistula has been present. The important consequences are due to fluid and electrolyte depletion, the absence of bile from the gut, and sometimes the presence of biliary infection.

FLUID AND ELECTROLYTE DEPLETION
Bile is secreted at a rate of 500–1000 ml per day; it contains the ions of sodium, potassium, chloride, and calcium in concentrations equal to those in serum [6, 11, 33, 69, 70, 76, 77]. If the fluid loss is much more than 1000 ml daily it is very likely that an associated pancreatic, duodenal, or jejunal fistula is also present.

Patients who have a prolonged external biliary fistula will develop a fluid and electrolyte disturbance if replacement is not adequate. This disturbance is characterised by a decrease of sodium, potassium, and chloride. The sodium loss is in excess of the chloride loss, leading to an acidosis. This fluid and electrolyte upset has been called the choledochostomy acidotic syndrome [11, 32, 41, 60].

The serum potassium is lowered at first but, with the decrease in plasma volume due to dehydration, oliguria and azotaemia occur, followed by potassium retention and hyperkalaemia.

Patients who have this upset to any degree feel generally unwell, weak, and apathetic. In very severe cases stupor and sudden vasomotor collapse may occur.

ABSENCE OF BILE FROM THE GUT

Clearly, in a total biliary fistula bile is absent from the gastrointestinal tract and patients will have clay-coloured stools. There is also interference with the emulsification of fats and, therefore, with the absorption of fats and fat-soluble vitamins (A, D, and K). Bile salts are not essential for fat absorption but they are necessary for the absorption of sterols such as cholesterol and also the fat-soluble vitamins. In practice total biliary fistulas are not present long enough for significant clinical effects to follow, with the exception of vitamin-K deficiency. Calorie and protein malnutrition can also accompany longstanding cases.

INFECTION

Intentional external biliary fistulas are not usually associated with biliary tract infection. Indeed, they are sometimes performed in order to decompress obstructed and infected bile ducts. However, when the fistula is associated with an element of stasis or obstruction to bile flow, such as in postoperative bile duct injuries, biliary infection is usually also present.

SKIN DIGESTION

Bile does not cause excoriation or digestion of the skin. If skin digestion is evident then the external biliary fistula must also contain pancreatic, duodenal, or jejunal juice.

DIAGNOSIS

CLINICAL FEATURES

Only the diagnosis of postoperative external biliary fistulas will be discussed here, because pathological types are extremely rare. When presented with an established postoperative biliary fistula the diagnostic process begins with a history of the events leading up to the operation, followed by a consideration of the operative findings, the procedure performed, and the postoperative course. This is frequently sufficient to make a strong presumptive diagnosis that a bile duct gallstone or a malignant obstruction was overlooked, or that an operative bile duct injury occurred.

Clinical examination will confirm the presence of an external biliary fistula. It may show that the patient is jaundiced, languid, and dehydrated. There may be clinical evidence of metastatic malignancy, but usually there is little to learn from clinical examination regarding the cause of the fistula.

RADIOLOGY

When an intentional choledochostomy or cholecystostomy is created a cholangiogram through the tube is performed before the tube is removed. If this shows the presence of complete distal bile duct obstruction an external biliary fistula can be anticipated before it occurs.

Radiology may be helpful in locating the site or the cause of the fistula, either with a sinugram, a percutaneous transhepatic cholangiogram, or an endoscopic retrograde cholangiogram. A sinugram may delineate the bile ducts, show whether obstruction is present, and even give a clue to the cause. Instructive sinugrams of this type are seen in cases in which an external biliary fistula followed an operative bile duct injury (Figs. 6.9 & 6.10). Fig. 11.3 is the sinugram of a patient who had a gangrenous gallbladder removed and a large pericholecystic abscess drained and who developed an external biliary fistula postoperatively. This sinugram shows a large subhepatic cavity which communicates with the bile

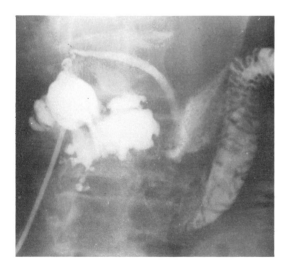

Fig. 11.3. Contrast medium introduced through an external biliary fistula, outlines an irregular cavity which communicates with the common bile duct. The fistula followed cholecystectomy of a gangrenous gallbladder lying in a pericholecystic abscess cavity, and it closed spontaneously after 5 weeks.

duct, but there is no bile duct obstruction. Because of the sinugraphic appearances spontaneous closure of the fistula was anticipated, and this, in fact, occurred 5 weeks postoperatively.

In the jaundiced patient help in diagnosis may be obtained from percutaneous transhepatic cholangiography, or an endoscopic retrograde cholangiogram, which may show the site of bile duct obstruction (see Percutaneous Transhepatic Cholangiography in Chapter 3).

PRINCIPLES OF TREATMENT

The treatment of external biliary fistulas may be considered under the following headings:
1. Correction of fluid and electrolyte imbalance.
2. Treatment of infection and skin excoriation, if these are present.
3. Treatment of the underlying cause of the fistula.

Prevention of fluid and electrolyte depletion can be achieved by intravenous administration of isotonic saline. With average losses of bile (300–500 ml per day), if the patient is able to take fluids orally, the volume lost is replaced by oral fluids and by the addition of 3–4 g of salt daily [11].

The treatment of an established case requires rehydration with intravenous saline according to the estimated extent of loss. With a persisting fistula, potassium chloride is added daily, but only if the urinary output is satisfactory. If a duodenal or pancreatic fistula is also present fluid and electrolyte replacement therapy becomes more complex and parenteral nutrition is usually required. Total parenteral nutrition is also a valuable preliminary to surgery in the patient who has a longstanding biliary fistula and who has developed a malnutrition state [44].

TREATMENT OF INFECTION AND SKIN EXCORIATION
The bile is cultured and if it contains organisms an appropriate antibiotic is administered, depending on the antibiotic sensitivity (Chapter 9).

Skin excoriation means a duodenal, pancreatic, or jejunal component to the fistula. The skin must be protected by some type of 'barrier' cream, such as aluminium paste. Insertion of a catheter and low-pressure suction in the fistula will prevent the fluid from reaching the skin and is most valuable in the treatment of skin digestion.

TREATMENT OF THE CAUSE
Medical. With most external biliary fistulas conservative management is the first line of treatment. The fluid and electrolyte loss is corrected, bile is cultured, antibiotics are given if necessary, and the daily bile flow is accurately measured. Total parenteral nutrition is also often employed. During this time special investigations, such as a sinugram, are undertaken.

Within a few days it usually becomes apparent if conservative management should be continued or further surgical intervention is necessary. Conservative treatment is continued if the bile drainage is decreasing and the general condition of the patient remains good. If, in such cases, the fistula closes, it is necessary to perform an intravenous cholangiogram at a later date, and check the patient regularly for evidence of recurrent symptoms of biliary obstruction over the next few years. Conservative treatment is also continued in the patient whose fistula is not due to a distal obstruction or bile duct damage, but to some localised infection that is in communication with the biliary system (Fig. 11.3). If an underlying obstruction is not suspected, leaking biliary-intestinal anastomosis, such as choledochoduodenostomy, is also managed conservatively.

Operative. Reoperation is necessary with persistent fistulas in which an underlying biliary obstruction or bile duct injury is thought to be present. These operations are frequently difficult, because of adhesion formation and the presence of intra-abdominal collections of bile, pus, or haematoma, in many cases.

Surgeons who are inexperienced with complicated biliary problems should not undertake reoperation on such cases.

The exposure is similar to all reoperations on the biliary tract, as described previously (see Operative bile duct injuries, Chapter 6). An accurate demonstration of the biliary system is obtained, and the underlying cause of the external biliary fistula is determined. The actual surgical treatment depends on the cause. Thus, the procedure may be bile duct exploration and choledocholithotomy (Chapter 5), repair of bile duct injuries (Chapter 6), or bypass or excision of a malignant obstruction (Chapter 7).

INTERNAL BILIARY FISTULA

CAUSES

INTENTIONAL

These include cholecystenterostomy, choledochoduodenostomy, choledochojejunostomy, or hepatodochojejunostomy. These operations are discussed fully in Chapter 14, which deals with biliary drainage procedures.

POSTOPERATIVE

Internal biliary fistulas are uncommon postoperatively. Following an operative injury to the bile ducts an internal fistula may develop, and it usually connects the hepatic duct with the duodenum. Occasionally, there is a postoperative fistula connecting the bile duct to the colon, and rarely a pleurobiliary or bronchobiliary fistula is present [1, 2]. It is most unusual for such a hepaticoduodenal fistula to provide adequate and complete biliary drainage and almost all these patients eventually develop cholangitis, obstructive jaundice, or both (Chapter 6).

PATHOLOGICAL

Fistulas of this type are relatively uncommon, so that any one surgeon has a small personal experience. A number of excellent reviews help to summarise current knowledge on this subject [4, 16, 20, 30, 34, 35, 51, 52, 62, 73, 78]. The pathological processes responsible include gallstones, duodenal ulcer, and malignancy.

Gallstones. Gallstones are by far the commonest cause of an internal biliary fistula. The process of fistula formation is uncertain. It is probably secondary to acute cholecystitis, with gangrene and abscess formation followed by the adherence of the gallbladder to an adjacent viscus and the subsequent erosion and perforation of the duodenum. The gallstones are usually large and barrel-shaped. The gallbladder may contain only one gallstone, or there may be multiple stones.

Perforation is usually from the gallbladder into the duodenum, but it may be into the colon. Much less commonly, the fistula opens into the stomach or the small bowel (Fig. 11.4). Rarely, a combined cholecystoduodenocolic fistula is present [19, 22, 62, 72].

Fistula formation between the bile duct and the duodenum, or the bile duct

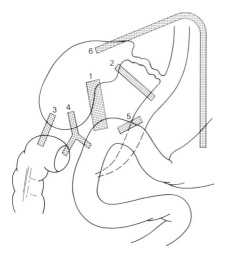

Fig. 11.4. Various types of pathological internal fistulas: (1) cholecystoduodenal (commonest type), (2) cholecystocholedochal (absent cystic duct as in Fig. 1.16), (3) cholecystocolic, (4) cholecystoduodenocolic, (5) choledochoduodenal, (6) cholecystogastric.

and the colon, is particularly uncommon. Occasionally, fistulisation occurs from Hartmann's pouch into the common bile duct. These are the cases in which the cystic duct has become occluded and fibrotic [43, 62, 73]. At operation the surgeon finds 'an absent cystic duct' as depicted in Fig. 1.16, Chapter 1).

Cholecystoduodenal fistula and gallstone obstruction of the ileum, known as gallstone ileus, constitute a distinct and characteristic entity that is discussed in a separate section later in this chapter.

Duodenal ulcer. Rarely, a penetrating chronic duodenal ulcer produces a choledochoduodenal or even a cholecystoduodenal fistula [39, 42, 46, 62].

Malignancy. Primary malignant tumours of the stomach, colon, or biliary tract can be responsible for an internal biliary fistula as noted in Fig. 11.5 [20, 49, 52].

Others. Very rarely, a liver hydatid or an amoebic abscess ruptures into the chest and, if it is in connection with a large bile duct, a pleurobiliary or a bronchobiliary fistula results [52].

DIAGNOSIS

CLINICAL FEATURES

There are no symptoms and signs specific to an internal biliary fistula and the diagnosis is usually not suspected on clinical examination. Most of the symptoms are due to the underlying cause of the fistula. Thus, many patients will have a long history of gallstone disease, others a long history of chronic duodenal ulceration and in some, clinical features may suggest an underlying malignancy.

The symptoms of cholangitis have been recorded in some cholecystenteric fistulas, although even this symptom is usually due to the underlying disease rather than to the infection ascending from the gastrointestinal tract by reflux.

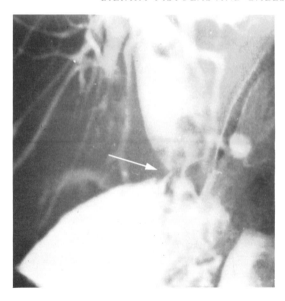

Fig. 11.5. A pathological choledochoduodenal fistula caused by an obstructing carcinoma of the bile duct which had spread into the first part of the duodenum (arrow). Note reflux of barium into a markedly dilated bile duct.

However, the proliferation of organisms in the bile ducts could occur as a result of reflux if there is stasis or obstruction to the outflow of the material refluxed from the gastrointestinal tract (see Cholangitis, Chapter 9). Similarly, jaundice may occur but this is not due to the fistula itself.

Diarrhoea is a feature of fistulas which communicate with the colon; this is marked in a cholecystoduodenocolic fistula [19, 20, 22, 52]. The clinical features of bowel obstruction may be seen in a patient with gallstone ileus (see later section in this chapter).

RADIOLOGY

Radiology may be most helpful in the diagnosis of an internal biliary fistula [4, 16, 20, 49, 52, 62, 63, 73, 78]. The investigations which may be valuable are a straight radiograph of the area, a gas choledochogram, endoscopic retrograde and transhepatic cholangiography, or a barium meal examination. A cholecystogram and an intravenous cholangiogram are rarely helpful in these cases.

Plain abdominal radiograph. This may show gas in the biliary tract, the presence of a gallstone in the small bowel in gallstone ileus, and the presence of small bowel obstruction with dilated small bowel (Figs. 11.6, 11.7 & 11.8).

Percutaneous transhepatic cholangiogram and endoscopic retrograde cholangiogram. Both of these techniques may be helpful in diagnosis, as outlined in Chapter 3. It may be possible to see dye flowing through the fistula and also to determine if there is obstruction to bile flow.

Gas choledochogram. This may be helpful if gas is suspected in the biliary tract on a plain film. The patient is given an effervescent drink and is then placed in the

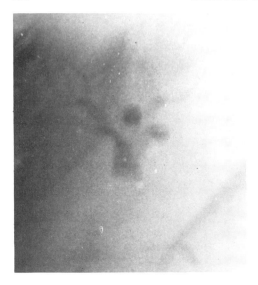

Fig. 11.6. Gas in the biliary tree on a plain x-ray, indicating in this case the presence of an internal biliary fistula, which at operation was shown to be a choledochoduodenal fistula.

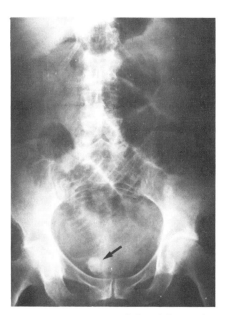

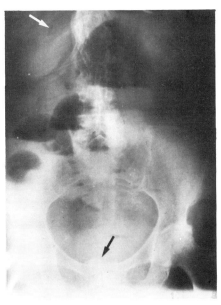

Fig. 11.7. Plain x-ray of the abdomen in the supine position in a patient with gallstone ileus. Note dilated small bowel. Radio-opaque gallstone in the pelvis is shown by the arrow.

Fig. 11.8. Plain x-ray of the abdomen in the erect position in the patient shown in Fig. 11.7. Note dilated small bowel with fluid levels and radio-opaque gallstone in the pelvis (arrow). Gas in the biliary tract is shown by the arrow.

supine position with his right side uppermost, to allow the gas to enter the biliary tract. This test is also valuable in checking the patency of an intentional fistula, such as a choledochoduodenostomy, as seen in Fig. 14.9.

Barium meal radiograph. Fistulas connecting the duodenum or the stomach with the gallbladder or the bile duct will show a reflux of barium into the biliary tract (Figs. 5.26, 11.5 & 14.8). This is also sometimes seen after transduodenal division of the sphincter of Oddi. The barium may also show the cause of the fistula, such as a chronic duodenal ulcer.

In the absence of outflow stasis or obstruction the barium is not retained in the biliary tract for longer than a few hours. Abnormally long retention indicates outflow obstruction or stasis. Thus, a barium meal may be used in investigating the patency of intentional fistulas, especially choledochoduodenostomy (Chapter 14).

Barium enema. In the presence of a fistula, connecting the biliary tree with the colon, a barium enema radiography may show reflux into the biliary tract. Simultaneous reflux of barium into the duodenum indicates the presence of a cholecystoduodenocolic fistula. If the underlying cause of the fistula is a carcinoma of the colon, this may also be shown.

TREATMENT

The principles of treatment of an internal biliary fistula may be summarised as follows:
1. Treatment of the underlying cause.
2. Disconnection of the fistula and closure of the gut.
3. Provision of satisfactory biliary drainage.

Management of bile duct injuries with an internal fistula is discussed elsewhere (Chapter 6). Treatment of gallstone ileus and the associated internal biliary fistula is described later in this chapter. Treatment of the remaining types of fistula is considered in this section according to underlying cause.

GALLSTONES

Most of these fistulas require operative treatment. These operations are frequently difficult because of adhesions and because of the presence of chronic fibrotic cholecystitis in most cases. Facilities should be available for operative cholangiography.

After disconnection of the internal biliary fistula the gut can usually be sutured with ease, because it is not narrowed. Cholecystectomy is always performed. The common bile duct frequently needs to be explored because of associated choledocholithiasis. An operative cholangiogram is a valuable aid in the diagnosis of choledocholithiasis and in determining whether there is obstruction to bile flow [23, 49, 62].

The uncommon choledochoduodenal fistula due to erosion by gallstones also requires surgical treatment. This usually involves cholecystectomy, exploration of the bile ducts, and choledocholithotomy. It is probably unnecessary to deal with the actual fistula. If a distal obstructive factor is present, such as stenosis of the papilla of Vater, a biliary-intestinal drainage procedure should be added, such as sphincteroplasty or choledochoduodenostomy [49].

DUODENAL ULCER

A duodenal ulcer that is responsible for a choledochoduodenal fistula requires surgical treatment. Good results have been obtained with a Polya type gastrec-tomy and antral exclusion [35, 46, 49, 51, 52, 62, 73]. It is usually unnecessary to separate the bile duct from the duodenum. It is, however, necessary to explore the bile duct with the aid of operative cholangiography, in order to be sure that it is not obliterated distally by fibrosis [35]. If distal obstruction is present the proximal duct should be anastomosed to the duodenal stump. If this is not possible because of inflammatory swelling a choledochojejunostomy is probably a better alternative than cholecystenterostomy. Unless the gallbladder is used for a bypass it is best to perform a cholecystectomy at the primary operation.

MALIGNANCY

The procedure employed in these cases depends on the origin of the tumour and extent of its spread. It may be possible to excise the primary tumour in continuity with the biliary fistula, and then obtain gastrointestinal continuity as well as some type of biliary reconstruction. If the primary tumour is unresectable a palliative bypass or decompression of the gastrointestinal and biliary tracts is all that can be done.

GALLSTONE ILEUS

Gallstone ileus refers to gallstone obstruction of the small bowel or, much less commonly, of the large bowel.

INCIDENCE

Gallstone ileus is responsible for about 2 per cent of all mechanical intestinal obstructions, but this incidence rises with age [8, 14, 31, 37, 62, 65, 78]. Most of the patients are between 60 and 80 years of age, and the majority are females.

PATHOLOGY

For a gallstone to be able to cause intestinal obstruction of the normal small bowel it must be at least 2.5 cm in diameter [26, 49, 67]. Impaction in the large bowel usually occurs only if a pre-existent pathological narrowing is present, such as diverticulitis of the pelvic colon [64]. Almost always the gallstone enters the gastrointestinal tract through an internal fistula, usually of the cholecysto-duodenal type. Very rarely, gallstone ileus is present without an internal biliary fistula [7, 13, 38, 58, 74]. Gallstones have been found impacted at any level, but the usual site is the low ileum, while the duodenum, jejunum, pylorus, and large bowel are much less common sites [3, 8, 13, 23, 27, 40, 48, 53, 62, 64, 68].

DIAGNOSIS

CLINICAL FEATURES

The clinical features of gallstone ileus are those of intestinal obstruction—colicky abdominal pain, vomiting, and abdominal distension.

In many cases the symptoms are intermittent, initially, probably because the gallstone is held up temporarily in several places and is then propelled onward with peristalsis, until its final point of impaction. The intermittent and incomplete nature of this obstruction in the initial stages is primarily responsible for the delay in diagnosis so commonly noted [9, 13, 18, 29, 62, 65, 67, 73].

The signs are those of intestinal obstruction, although obesity frequently makes difficult the assessment of abdominal distension. Only rarely can the calculus be felt in the abdomen, or per rectum.

RADIOLOGY

A plain radiograph of the abdomen in the erect and supine position is of considerable diagnostic value [4, 49, 62, 63, 66, 71, 73]. It is of interest that even when the diagnostic radiological features are present, the preoperative diagnosis of gallstone ileus is frequently missed, probably because of the rarity and lack of awareness of this condition.

Four radiological signs are characteristic:
1. Gas in the biliary tract.
2. Dilated loops of small bowel with fluid levels in the erect position.
3. Presence of the gallstone in the intestine (about one-third of these stones are radio-opaque) [66]; rarely, the gallstone is shown up by administration of barium [21].
4. Comparison with previous x-rays, if available, which show change in position of previously noted radio-opaque gallbladder stones [25, 63].

Figs. 11.7 and 11.8 are radiographs of a patient with gallstone ileus.

CONCLUSION

The diagnosis of gallstone ileus should be suspected in an elderly female who presents with small bowel obstruction in the absence of an obvious cause. This diagnostic suspicion is strengthened by a past history of biliary tract symptoms and by the intermittent nature of the obstruction. Plain radiographs of the abdomen are frequently diagnostic. The condition may be missed even with positive radiological evidence, particularly if the clinician does not suspect a gallstone ileus.

TREATMENT

The principles of treatment of gallstone ileus are:
1. Resuscitation of the patient.

2. Enterotomy and removal of the gallstone.
3. Disconnection of the fistula and cholecystectomy.

RESUSCITATION

Most patients have a fluid and electrolyte loss due to the small bowel obstruction, and the loss is frequently accentuated by the delay in diagnosis. This should be corrected by intravenous therapy and nasogastric suction. However, operation should not be unduly delayed, and it is rarely necessary for resuscitation to be prolonged more than 12–18 hours.

REMOVAL OF OBSTRUCTING GALLSTONES

Laparotomy is performed and it is usually a simple matter to find and remove the gallstone after an enterotomy. It is generally advocated that the gallstone be milked proximally and the enterotomy made over a non-impacted part of the bowel.

In neglected cases the small bowel may be necrotic over the site of impaction, and it is then necessary to resect the involved segment of bowel.

Before the abdomen is closed a careful search is made for further gallstones in the small bowel proximal to the obstruction and in the duodenum, because recurrent gallstone ileus may be caused by such a gallstone [10, 12, 24, 50, 62]. This is particularly important if the gallstone that was causing the obstruction was faceted. Only rarely does an obstructing gallstone pass spontaneously or after a barium enema [55].

DISCONNECTION OF FISTULA AND CHOLECYSTECTOMY

In most instances it is unwise to deal with the fistula at the same time as enterotomy is performed for gallstone ileus, because many of these patients are elderly and poor surgical risks. Cholecystectomy and disconnection of the fistula may be performed together with enterotomy, if the patient's general condition is satisfactory [5, 15, 16, 28, 49]. This will deal with the underlying condition, prevent further biliary symptoms arising from the gallbladder, and prevent recurrent gallstone ileus.

Patients who are too ill to have a cholecystectomy and disconnection of the fistula at the primary operation should be observed postoperatively at regular intervals. Further radiological studies of the gastrointestinal and biliary tract should be undertaken. If biliary tract symptoms recur, and if further gallstones are demonstrated in the gallbladder or in the bile ducts, reoperation is advised [13, 15, 49]. It may be possible to treat selected patients medically for gallstone dissolution.

PROGNOSIS

Mortality from gallstone ileus has declined progressively over the years. Thus, in 1925, Moore reported a mortality of 73 per cent, whereas in the period of 1940–1960 the mortality rates were 33–50 per cent [8, 17, 47, 54]. In more recent reports the mortality is down to 5–10 per cent [15, 29, 75]. This decline is attributed to a better understanding of resuscitation and to earlier diagnosis.

The risk of recurrent gallstone ileus has been estimated to be about 5–10 per cent [10, 12, 15, 40]. Recurrence is due to gallstones missed in the small bowel or duodenum at the initial operation, or to more gallstones passing into the gut through the cholecystenteric fistula. Recurrent biliary symptoms without recurrent gallstone ileus are not uncommon, particularly when the gallbladder is still intact, because a number of these patients have residual gallbladder and bile duct stones [15, 51].

REFERENCES

1. ADAMS H.D. A study of pleurobiliary and bronchobiliary fistulas. *J. Thorac. Cardiovasc. Surg.* **30:**255, 1955.
2. ADAMS H.D. Hepaticobiliary involvement of the thorax. *Surg. Clin. N. Amer.* **38:**611, 1958.
3. ARGYROPOULOS G.D., VELMACHOS G. & AXENIDIS P. Gallstone perforation and obstruction of the duodenal bulb. *Arch. Surg.* **114:**333, 1979.
4. BEACHLEY M.C., GHAHREMANI G.C., SOUTHWORTH L.E. & SICONOLFI E.P. Clinical and roentgen manifestations of cholecystoduodenal fistula. *Dig. Dis.* **21:**482, 1976.
5. BERLINER S.D. & BURSON L.C. One-stage repair for cholecystduodenal fistula and gallstone ileus. *Arch. Surg. (Chicago)* **90:**313, 1965.
6. BRAUER R.W. Mechanisms of bile secretion. *J.A.M.A.* **169:**1462, 1959.
7. BREWER M.S. Gallstone ileus produced by stone passed through ampulla of Vater. *Am. Surg.* **21:**508, 1955.
8. BROCKIS J.G. & GILBERT M.C. Intestinal obstruction by gallstones: A review of 179 cases. *Br. J. Surg.* **44:**461, 1957.
9. BUETOW G.W. & CRAMPTON R.S. Gallstone ileus. A report of 23 cases. *Arch. Surg. (Chicago)* **86:**504, 1963.
10. BUETOW G.W., GLAUBITZ J.P. & CRAMPTON R.S. Recurrent gallstone ileus. *Surgery* **54:**716, 1963.
11. CASS M.H., ROBSON B. & RUNDLE F.F. Electrolyte losses with biliary fistula: Post-choledochostomy acidotic syndrome. *Med. J. Aust.* **1:**165, 1955.
12. CLARIDGE M. Recurrent gallstone ileus. *Brit. J. Surg.* **49:**134, 1961.
13. COLLINS G.M. & CLAXTON R.C. Gall-stone intestinal obstruction: a review of the literature and presentation of new cases. *Med. J. Aust.* **1:**578, 1966.
14. COLLINS P.G. Further experience with common bile duct suture without intraductal drainage following choledochotomy. *Br. J. Surg.* **54:**854, 1967.
15. COOPERMAN A.M., DICKSON E.R. & REMINE W.H. Changing concepts in the surgical treatment of gallstone ileus. *Ann. Surg.* **167:**377, 1968.
16. DAY E.A. & MARKS C. Gallstone ileus: Review of literature and presentation of 34 new cases. *Am. J. Surg.* **129:**552, 1975.
17. DECKOFF S.L. Gallstone ileus: A report of 12 cases. *Ann. Surg.* **142:**52, 1955.
18. DONE H.J., GOULD L.V. & BROZIN I.H. Gall-stone ileus. *Br. J. Surg.* **49:**660, 1962.
19. DOWSE J.L.A. Cholecysto-duodenocolic fistulae due to gall-stones. *Br. J. Surg.* **50:**776, 1963.
20. DOWSE J.L.A. Spontaneous internal biliary fistulae. *Gut* **5:**249, 1964.
21. DRUCHER V. Small intestinal gallstone ileus and use of barium sulphate per os in its diagnosis. *A.M.A. Arch. Surg.* **79:**22, 1959.
22. EDMUNDS P.K.D. & HAVARD C. Duodeno-colic fistula due to gallstones. *Br. J. Surg.* **49:**253, 1961.
23. FELDMAN M. Choledocho-duodenal fistula associated with large gall-stone in stomach. *Am. J. Gastroent.* **28:**466, 1957.
24. FIDDIAN R.V. Gall-stone ileus. Recurrences and multiple stones. *Postgrad. Med. J.* **35:**673, 1959.

25. FIGIEL L.S., FIGIEL S.J., WIETERSEN F.K. & DRANGINIS E.J. Gall-stone obstruction. Clinical and roentgenographic considerations. *Am. J. Roentgen.* **74**:22, 1955.

26. FOX P.F. Planning the operation for cholecystoenteric fistula with gallstone ileus. *Surg. Clin. N. Amer.* **50**:93, 1970.

27. FRANCOIS M. & HUGUIER M. Obstruction duodenele par calcul biliare. *J. Chir.* **109**:473, 1975.

28. FRASER W.J. Intestinal obstruction by gallstones. *Br. J. Surg.* **42**:210, 1954.

29. GIBSON J.M. JR. Gallstone ileus. *Arch. Surg. (Chicago)* **88**:297, 1964.

30. GLENN F. & MANNIX H. JR. Biliary enteric fistula. *Surg. Gynec. Obstet.* **105**:693, 1957.

31. GREENE W.W. Bowel obstruction in the aged patient. A review of 300 cases. *Am. J. Surg.* **118**:541, 1969.

32. HARDY J.D. Some lesions of the biliary tract. Idiopathic retroperitoneal fibrosis and other problems. *Am. J. Surg.* **103**:457, 1962.

33. HEATON K.W. *Bile Salts in Health and Disease.* Churchill Livingstone, Edinburgh and London, 1972.

34. HICKEN N.F. & CORAY C.B. Spontaneous gastrointestinal biliary fistulas. *Surg. Gynec. Obstet.* **82**:723, 1946.

35. HUTCHINGS V.Z., WHEELER J.R. & PUESTOW C.B. Choledochoduodenal fistula complicating duodenal ulcer: A report of 5 cases and a review of the literature. *A.M.A. Arch. Surg.* **73**:598, 1956.

36. ISAACSON S., APPLEBY L.W. & HAMILTON E.L. A report upon choledochoduodenal fistula secondary to duodenal peptic ulcer. *J.A.M.A.* **179**:969, 1962.

37. JEKLER J. Intestinal obstruction caused by impacted gallstones. *Surgery* **46**:858, 1959.

38. JENKINS H.P., EVANS R. & KOLLERT W. Gallstone ileus. *Surg. Clin. N. Amer.* **41**:71, 1961.

39. JORDAN P.H. & STIRRETT L.A. Treatment of spontaneous internal biliary fistula caused by duodenal ulcer. *Am. J. Surg.* **91**:307, 1956.

40. KIRKLAND K.C. & CROCHE E.J. Gallstone intestinal obstruction. A review of the literature and presentation of 12 cases, including 3 recurrences. *J.A.M.A.* **176**:494, 1961.

41. KNOCHEL J.P., COOPER E.B. & BARRY K.G. External biliary fistula: A study of electrolyte derangements and secondary cardiovascular and renal abnormalities. *Surgery* **51**:746, 1962.

42. KOURIAS B.G. & CHOULIAROS A. Spontaneous gastrointestinal biliary fistula complicating duodenal ulcer. *Surg. Gynec. Obstet.* **119**:1013, 1964.

43. KUNE G.A. The influence of structure and function in the surgery of the biliary tract. *Ann. R. Coll. Surg. Eng.* **47**:78, 1970.

44. KUNE G.A. Life-threatening surgical infection: its development and prediction. *Ann. R. Coll. Surg. Eng.* **60**:92, 1978.

45. KUNE G.A., HARDY K.J., BROWN G. & McKENZIE G. Operative injuries of the bile ducts. *Med. J. Aust.* **2**:233, 1969.

46. KYLE J. Choledochoduodenal fistula due to duodenal ulceration. *Br. J. Surg.* **46**:124, 1958.

47. LEVOWITZ B.S. Spontaneous internal biliary fistulas. *Ann. Surg.* **154**:241, 1961.

48. LLOYD-THOMAS T., JAQUES P.F. & WEAVER P.C. Gallstone obstruction and perforation of the duodenal bulb. *Br. J. Surg.* **63**:131, 1976.

49. MAINGOT, R. Biliary Fistulae and Gallstone Ileus. In R. Smith & S. Sherlock (eds.), *Surgery of the Gall Bladder and Bile Ducts.* Butterworth, London, 1964.

50. MALT R.A. Experience with recurrent gallstone ileus applied to management of the first attack. *Am. J. Surg.* **108**:92, 1964.

51. MARSHALL S.F. & POLK, R.C. Spontaneous internal biliary fistulas. *Surg. Clin. N. Amer.* **38**:679, 1958.

52. McSHERRY C.K., STUBENBORD W.T. & GLENN F. The significance of air in the biliary system and liver. *Surg. Gynec. Obstet.* **128**:49, 1969.

53. MILSTOC M., BERGER A.R. & FINKEL J. Gallstone obstruction of the second portion of the duodenum. *Amer. J. Dig. Dis.* **14**:143, 1969.
54. MOORE G.A. Gallstone ileus. *Boston Med. Surg. J.* **192**:1051, 1925.
55. MOORE T.C. & BAKER W.H. Operative and radiologic relief of gallstone intestinal obstruction. *Surg. Gynec. Obstet.* **116**:189, 1963.
56. MORLOCK C.G., SHOCKETT E. & REMINE W.H. Intestinal obstruction due to gallstones. *Gastroenterology* **30**:462, 1956.
57. MOVSAS S. Spontaneous external biliary fistula. *S. Afr. Med. J.* **35**:800, 1961.
58. MULDER D.C. & FLYNN P.J. Gallstone ileus in the absence of biliary fistula. *Arch. Surg. (Chicago)* **76**:530, 1964.
59. NAYMAN J. Empyema necessitatis of the gallbladder. *Med. J. Aust.* **1**:429, 1963.
60. NORCROSS J.W. & DADEY J.L. Medical complications of operative bile duct injuries. *New Eng. J. Med.* **257**:1216, 1957.
61. O'REILLY K. Spontaneous external biliary fistulas. *Med. J. Aust.* **1**:63, 1970.
62. PIEDAD O.H. & WELS P.B. Spontaneous internal biliary fistula—obstructive and non-obstructive types. *Ann. Surg.* **175**:75, 1972.
63. PITMAN R.G. & DAVIES A. The clinical and radiological features of spontaneous internal biliary fistulae. *Br. J. Surg.* **50**:414, 1963.
64. PRYOR J.H. Gall-stone obstruction of the sigmoid colon with particular reference to aetiology. *Br. J. Surg.* **47**:259, 1959.
65. RAIFORD T.S. Intestinal obstruction caused by gallstones. *Am. J. Surg.* **104**:383, 1962.
66. RIGLER L.G., BORMAN C.N. & NOBLE J.F. Gallstone obstruction: Pathogenesis and roentgen manifestations. *J.A.M.A.* **117**:1753, 1941.
67. ROGERS F.A. & CARTER R. Gallstone intestinal obstruction: A review and presentation of 40 new cases. *Calif. Med.* **88**:140, 1958.
68. ROSE T.F. Gallstone obstruction of the second part of the duodenum. *Med. J. Aust.* **1**:384, 1970.
69. RUNDLE F.F., CASS M.H., ROBSON B. & MIDDLETON M. Bile drainage after choledochostomy in man, with some observations on biliary fistula. *Surgery* **37**:903, 1955.
70. SALI A. Neuro-humeral control of hepatic bile secretion. PhD Thesis, Melbourne, Monash University, 1977.
71. SCOTT M.G., PYGOTT F. & MURPHY L. The significance of gas or barium in the biliary tract. *Br. J. Radiol.* **27**:253, 1954.
72. SHARTSIS J.M. & DINAN J.T. JR. Benign cholecystogastroduodenocolic fistula. *Am. J. Dig. Dis.* **14**:424, 1969.
73. SHIRAZI S.S., ZIKE W.L. & PRINTEN K.J. Spontaneous enterobiliary fistulas. *Surg. Gynec. Obstet.* **137**:769, 1973.
74. TAYLOR P.J. & LIMBACHER H.P. The vomiting of gallstones: report of a case. *Am. J. Dig. Dis.* **15**:73, 1970.
75. THOMAS H.S., CHERRY J.K. & AVERBROOK B.D. Gallstone ileus. *J.A.M.A.* **179**:625, 1962.
76. THUREBORNE E. Human hepatic bile—composition changes due to altered enterohepatic circulation. *Acta Chir. Scand.* **303** (Suppl. 1), 1962.
77. WAITMAN A.M., DYCK W.P. & JANOWITZ H.D. Effect of secretin and acetazolamide on the volume and electrolyte composition of hepatic bile in man. *Gastroenterology* **56**:286, 1969.
78. WOLLOCH Y., GLANZ I. & DINTSMAN M. Spontaneous biliary-enteric fistulas—some considerations on the management of gallstones. *Am. J. Surg.* **131**:680, 1976.

12. Acalculous Benign Biliary Disease

BY JOHN M. HAM

This chapter deals with three distinct groups of conditions affecting the biliary tract. The first is under the general heading of acute acalculous cholecystitis; this is an uncommon, but well-established condition, both clinically and pathologically. The second group includes chronic acalculous cholecystitis and adenomyomatosis (or cholecystitis glandularis proliferans). These are clear-cut entities pathologically, but there is considerable dispute about the relationship between the pathological findings and patient symptoms. The final group is that of functional disorders of the gallbladder and distal bile duct sphincter, and this is the most controversial subject of the three. Many clinicians doubt the existence of such disorders [10, 11, 57].

Thus much of the discussion will be concerned with the clinical problem of the patient who has what appears to be typical biliary pain, but who does not have demonstrable gallstones.

ACUTE ACALCULOUS CHOLECYSTITIS

Acute acalculous cholecystitis may be defined as an acute inflammatory condition of the gallbladder which occurs in the absence of calculi in the gallbladder or common bile duct. This definition does not exclude that group of patients in whom stones were responsible for the inflammation and were then spontaneously passed into the bowel [4].

The condition is recognised as occurring in a variety of clinical settings; and there is a broad spectrum of pathological findings in the gallbladder, ranging from mild, acute inflammation to gangrene and perforation. It is an uncommon condition, although its exact incidence is unknown. It is probable that in most hospitals less than 1 per cent of cholecystectomies are carried out for this indication.

PATHOGENESIS

It is well recognised that acute acalculous cholecystitis may occur after operation, after severe burns, or other major injury, and as a complication of other serious illnesses in childhood [2, 8, 30, 49, 60, 61, 68, 74, 90]. It may also be associated with certain specific infections, such as typhoid fever and brucellosis, and with acute pancreatitis, and there are a variety of rare causes [4, 8].

It is likely that the pathogenesis is multifactorial [25]. As with acute calculous cholecystitis, cystic duct obstruction may be important, but the evidence for this is inconclusive. Possible factors include stasis of bile accompanying prolonged intravenous feeding, altered bile composition with perhaps deconjugation of bile salts due to infection, and vascular disease affecting the cystic artery especially in diabetic and elderly patients [8, 68]. It has also been suggested that the decreased tissue perfusion and hypoxia which occur in acutely ill patients may be important [49]. Thus the hypotheses of aetiology have much in common with those relating to stress ulceration of the stomach and duodenum. Perhaps the principal factor in the aetiology of acute acalculous cholecystitis is damage to the gallbladder 'mucosal barrier'.

DIAGNOSIS

Because of the types of patient in whom acute acalculous cholecystitis occurs (the young, the old, and the very sick) there may be considerable delay in establishing a firm diagnosis [74, 90]. The key features are right upper quadrant pain and tenderness, together with a mass produced by the distended gallbladder, and features of an inflammatory illness. Unfortunately, one or more of these features may be absent. Ultrasonic examination may confirm considerable distension of the gallbladder [17].

TREATMENT AND PROGNOSIS

The condition has a substantial mortality; partly because of delayed diagnosis, partly because gangrene and perforation of the gallbladder are common, and partly because of the patient's pre-existing disease [49, 74].

In both children and adults the alternatives in treatment are cholecystostomy and cholecystectomy [20, 49, 60, 61, 74]. The choice depends on the general condition of the patient, and the state of the gallbladder. In general, cholecystectomy is probably the best treatment, though cholecystostomy is very satisfactory in children [61, 90]. Cholangiography is desirable, first to exclude a duct stone and second, because jaundice is a common associated feature due to hepatic dysfunction as a consequence of the primary illness.

CHRONIC ACALCULOUS CHOLECYSTITIS

This is a pathological diagnosis, and one which cannot be disputed when the chronic inflammatory changes are marked. However, the diagnosis may be made when there is a minimal chronic inflammatory cell infiltrate in the gallbladder wall, and the significance of this finding is quite uncertain [36]. There is, indeed, a need for more objective pathological criteria for the diagnosis.

Apart from unusual causes, such as a typhoid infection, there are two main theories of aetiology. Andersson and co-workers have suggested that the chronic inflammatory changes in the gallbladder follow previous cystic duct obstruction by a stone, and the latter has been subsequently passed spontaneously. On the other hand, Siffert summarises evidence that the condition is secondary to a functional disorder of the biliary tract [4, 85]. A third possibility is that the chronic inflammation is due to primary bacterial infection of the gallbladder.

There is no conclusive evidence in favour of any one of these hypotheses. However, chronic cholecystitis has been reported in a number of patients thought to have functional disorders of the gallbladder [41, 55]. In these patients the chronic inflammation may be secondary to the functional disorders, as suggested by Siffert [85], or the latter may have been produced by the chronic inflammation.

In the author's view this condition should be grouped with functional disorders of the biliary tract, and the same diagnostic criteria should be used. This means that the diagnosis will only be made in retrospect, that is, after the gallbladder has been examined histologically.

ADENOMYOMATOSIS

The group of conditions included under the general heading of adenomyomatosis are also discussed in Chapter 7, but mainly in a pathology sense. It is intended in this section to concentrate on those aspects which are important in relation to functional disorders of the biliary tract.

There are numerous papers on the subject of adenomyomatosis, or cholecystitis glandularis proliferans, with the paper by King and MacCallum providing the first clear description of its pathology [56]. Subsequently, LeQuesne and Ranger related the clinical presentation to the pathological findings, and suggested that the condition resulted from a disturbance in the normal contraction of the gallbladder [59]. It is unfortunate that the work of Beilby, from the same hospital, has been largely ignored in the recent literature on this subject. He made a number of important observations on the pathology which may be summarised as follows [5, 6].

First, examination of 40 gallbladder strictures in adults showed that all contained muscle. Similar strictures were found in neonatal gallbladders and he concluded that these strictures may be congenital in origin. In the adult specimens the gallbladder wall distal to the stricture showed epithelial sinuses and cyst formation with muscular hypertrophy, progressing to cholecystitis glandularis proliferans when the stricture was narrow. These changes in the gallbladder wall distal to the stricture were never seen in the neonates. Beilby suggested that the changes were the result of raised intracystic pressure [5]. In a subsequent study of fundal adenomata he demonstrated marked narrowing in the region of the gallbladder neck due to muscular hypertrophy, and concluded that the pathogenesis of these lesions was similar to that of the more diffuse forms of adenomyomatosis [6].

These findings strongly suggest that at least some cases of cholecystitis glandularis proliferans have a congenital basis. Probably, the acquired lesions are also produced by excessive intraluminal pressure, although the cause of the latter is uncertain [54].

The combination of cholecystitis glandularis proliferans and gallstones is seen quite frequently. In a prospective study of the histopathology of 222 consecutive gallbladders, excised at this hospital, 19 (8.5 per cent) showed the features of cholecystitis glandularis proliferans [82]. Fifteen of these 19 cases had gallstones as well. It is possible that the gallstones preceded the cholecystitis glandularis proliferans in these patients, and may have produced the latter lesions by intermittent cystic duct obstruction. However, in some cases, the stones were found only in that part of the gallbladder distal to a stricture (Fig. 12.1), suggesting that the stones formed as a consequence of the stricture.

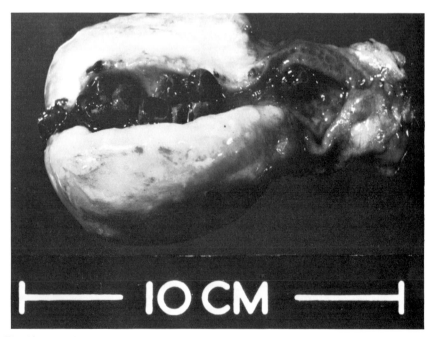

Fig. 12.1. Excised gallbladder in a patient with adenomyomatosis and gallstones. There is a stricture in the mid-body and gross muscle hypertrophy in the distal loculus. At the time of operation all the stones were confined to the distal loculus.

Adenomyomatosis is known to be associated with excessive gallbladder contraction, sometimes with incomplete emptying of a loculus distal to a stricture [25, 54, 59]. Thus, some of these patients have a true disorder of function of the gallbladder. The real problem is in deciding whether this may cause symptoms. There is no doubt that the changes of adenomyomatosis may be found incidentally in previously asymptomatic patients, and there are also patients who present with typical biliary pain and who have long-term relief after cholecystectomy [9, 12, 54, 55, 59, 81]. It is also of interest that the gallbladders of some patients diagnosed as having a functional biliary disorder, with apparently normal cholecystograms, have shown the changes of adenomyomatosis on histological examination [41, 92].

In view of the difficulty in relating these pathological and radiological features to clinical symptoms, we have chosen to evaluate these patients in the same way as patients with presumed functional biliary disorders who have negative radiological investigations. This approach is outlined below.

FUNCTIONAL BILIARY DISORDERS

A major problem in any discussion of this subject is the lack of a clear definition of these disorders. A variety of diagnostic terms has been used by previous authors, including biliary dyskinesia, acalculous cholecystitis, biliary pain without stones, and the postcholecystectomy syndrome [15, 16, 62, 79, 84]. In some studies the diagnostic criteria have been clinical, in others pathological, and in still others the diagnosis has depended on operative biliary manometry. Thus, it is extremely difficult to compare the results of treatment obtained by different authors.

The whole concept of biliary dyskinesia has been largely popularised by Caroli and by Mallet-Guy, and more recently by Siffert [15, 16, 62, 63, 84]. These authors have suggested that there are hypertonic and hypotonic disorders affecting the gallbladder and distal bile duct sphincter, and that the diagnosis may be made on the basis of the clinical features, radiological investigations, and operative biliary manometry. Siffert also discusses what he terms dyskinetic and dyssynergic abnormalities [84].

However, it must be stressed that many of the early papers on this subject were written before the recognition of the irritable bowel syndrome as a distinct clinical entity. The latter condition is now recognised as a common cause of abdominal pain, and it may mimic biliary pain. It is of considerable interest that Collins in 1977 has suggested that functional disorders following cholecystectomy may fall into one of three groups:

1. Continuation of 'irritable bowel syndrome' symptoms which were present before operation.

2. The emergence of 'irritable bowel syndrome' symptoms.

3. Symptoms emanating from the musculature in the region of the lower end of the common bile duct and the periampullary region of the duodenum.

He postulated that all three groups, and particularly the latter two, might be related to altered cholecystokinin levels [19]. The latter have been shown to be elevated following cholecystectomy [51].

It is unfortunate that there is as yet no reliable method of measuring cholecystokinin levels in routine clinical practice. Such measurements may be extremely valuable in the future.

Despite all these difficulties surgeons and gastroenterologists frequently see patients who appear to have typical biliary pain, and who do not have demonstrable gallstones or other organic disease. They may or may not have had a cholecystectomy and the majority have been extensively investigated. There is, therefore, a clinical problem and it was with this in mind that the following working definition of functional biliary disorders was developed in the author's department:

1. Pain compatible with biliary pain as assessed independently by a physician, surgeon, and psychiatrist.

2. Absence of clinical evidence of organic gastrointestinal disease, or other disorder which might produce abdominal pain.

3. Reproduction of the patient's symptoms by the administration of cholecystokinin (CCK) or morphine, or both.

It was recognised that gallstones or other gastrointestinal disease could only be excluded with reasonable certainty at operation. Thus, the diagnosis in patients treated conservatively was provisional. In addition, the experience outlined below has indicated certain ways in which the definition may have to be modified in the future.

CLINICAL DIAGNOSIS

By far the most important symptom is pain, and for the diagnosis to be seriously considered it should be indistinguishable from that due to gallstones. Thus the first clue to the possibility of a functional biliary disorder will usually be one or more normal cholecystograms in a patient who was confidently diagnosed as having gallstones. Other dyspeptic symptoms and fat intolerance may also be present, but in themselves are not significant.

The various factors which may induce pain have been discussed in detail elsewhere [11, 28, 41, 50, 70]. A detailed history of drug and alcohol intake is essential, since considerable improvement may be achieved by removal of a precipitating cause, such as codeine-containing mixtures or alcohol. The latter have been shown to produce contraction of the distal bile duct sphincter [7, 76]. The effects of a variety of other drugs have been assessed [7, 31, 43, 47].

It is important that the patient is independently assessed by a physician, surgeon, and psychiatrist, especially if operation is a serious possibility. Many of these patients are regarded as neurotic. However, it may be difficult to determine whether this is a primary psychiatric problem with abdominal pain as a manifestation, or whether any emotional symptoms are secondary to chronic pain. The resolution of this difficulty often requires expert psychiatric assessment [41].

There are, of course, a variety of disorders which present with upper abdominal pain, but the most important differential diagnoses are gallstones and the irritable bowel syndrome. As indicated earlier it is probable that many patients, thought to have a functional biliary disorder, in fact have the latter syndrome [19, 41, 44].

Most of these patients have had many previous investigations. Those which should be done—or repeated if there is any doubt about the previous ones—are tests of liver function, estimation of serum and urine amylase during an attack, liver scintiscan, echography, and upper gastrointestinal endoscopy [26]. The results of all of these should, of course, be normal. If the patient has had a previous cholecystectomy then endoscopic retrograde cholangiopancreatogra-

phy may be indicated, since it often detects abnormalities not previously suspected [10].

Cholecystokinin cholecystography. The first part of this investigation is the same
as the standard cholecystogram. It must be emphasised that views of the gallbladder should be obtained with the patient prone and erect, together with tomo-
grams. In some patients, stones which were not shown previously will be seen on
these films. Cholecystokinin is then administered intravenously, the patient being
unaware of the time of commencement of the injection. The dose in some studies
has been 75 Ivy units, but we have used 1.5 Ivy units per kg body weight [41].
Further films of the gallbladder are taken at intervals, and any effect on the
patient noted. The latter may be reproduction of the patient's pain, and it is
important to distinguish this from the lower abdominal discomfort, feeling of
fullness, and nausea which may also follow the injection.

This test has received enthusiastic support from a number of groups who
claim that abnormal gallbladder emptying, or reproduction of the patient's pain,
or both, are reliable indicators of a functional disorder of the gallbladder [37, 71,
72, 73, 77, 92]. The author has considerable reservations about the value of the
test, especially in the assessment of gallbladder emptying, since there seems to be
considerable overlap in the rate of emptying between patients with presumed
functional disorders and those in whom the biliary system is supposedly normal.
Production of severe 'biliary' pain by cholecystokinin may be more reliable, since
we have not seen such severe pain in control subjects. This has also been the
experience of Valberg and co-workers [92].

The controlled study of Dunn and co-workers is of great importance in
evaluating this test [29]. These authors demonstrated that 'abnormal' gallbladder
emptying and 'biliary' pain occurred in control subjects after cholecystokinin;
unfortunately, they did not attempt to assess the severity of this pain. They also
found that the test did not predict which patients would be cured by cholecystectomy, nor did it help predict the histological findings in the gallbladder. Finally,
they noted considerable observer disagreement in the radiological assessment.

It must be concluded that the test is not as reliable as originally suggested,
although reproduction of severe biliary pain by cholecystokinin may be of some
diagnostic assistance.

Other tests of gallbladder function. Freeman and co-workers have combined the
cholecystokinin cholecystogram with analysis of duodenal bile for cholesterol
crystals and bacteria, and suggest that this combination is more reliable than the
cholecystokinin cholangiogram alone [35].

Another approach has been to obtain gallbladder films 24 hours after the
administration of telepaque. Persistent visualisation of the gallbladder is said to
indicate that it is abnormal pathologically [1].

Moncada and co-workers have studied infusion tomography of the gallbladder in both acute and chronic cholecystitis [65]. Visualisation of the gallbladder

wall was seen in a considerable proportion of inflamed gallbladders, but not in those which were histologically normal. Unfortunately, a separate study has shown that gallbladder wall opacification does occur in some normal subjects [66].

It seems clear that all the currently available tests are insufficiently accurate to be used as reliable objective tests of acalculous gallbladder disease and, therefore, must be regarded as ancillary evidence.

Intravenous cholangiography. Intravenous cholangiography should be performed in all patients unless the common bile duct has been well demonstrated on the cholecystogram. Tomographic films are essential. We have combined this investigation with the administration of morphine 0.04 mg per kg body weight intravenously after the first series of films. In normal subjects this dose produces contraction of the distal bile duct sphincter, cessation of the flow of dye into the duodenum, and dilatation of the common bile duct. Similar, and sometimes more marked, changes are seen in patients with presumed functional disorders of the distal bile duct sphincter. However, this aspect of the test does not reliably distinguish between the former and latter groups. Production of severe pain occurs in some of the latter patients, and we have used this to confirm the results of the morphine provocation test (see below).

It is stressed that the main value of this test is in the exclusion of previously unrecognised bile duct disease.

Morphine provocation test. It has been recognised for many years that morphine or morphine-like drugs may induce pain resembling biliary pain, and that in some subjects elevation of serum amylase and liver enzymes occurs [13, 14, 40, 45, 58, 67, 91]. These observations prompted its introduction as a test for biliary dyskinesia, and it was claimed that it would distinguish reliably between normal controls and such patients [86, 88, 89]. It has also been used to detect the presence of papillitis and, therefore, as an indication for sphincteroplasty [69].

In the author's department the test is performed as follows: it is carried out in the early morning after an overnight fast. An intravenous cannula is inserted and 5 ml of saline injected and any effect on the patient noted. Approximately 10 minutes later morphine, 0.04 mg per kg body weight diluted in 5 ml of saline, is injected slowly. Again, any effect on the patient is noted, and he/she is asked to describe any symptoms. If pain occurs the patient rates this on an analogue scale in relation to the pain previously experienced. Blood samples are taken at 0, 6, and 24 hours for estimation of serum levels of amylase, alkaline phosphatase, gamma glutamyl transferase, and alanine aminotransferase.

The test has been performed in 23 asymptomatic control subjects of similar age and sex distribution as patients with presumed functional biliary disorders. Pain did not occur in any subject, and there were no changes in serum enzyme levels except in one in whom the serum amylase level rose from 270 U/l (normal value less than 300 U/l) to 710 U/l 6 hours after the injection [41].

In 24 of 32 patients being investigated for a possible functional biliary disorder pain was induced by the morphine injection, and in six of these there was also significant elevation (at least 100 per cent above control values) of the serum amylase and one or more of the liver enzymes 6 hours afterwards. These results are encouraging, but it is important to note that the assessment of the pain response is subjective, that not all patients who appear to have a functional biliary disorder have pain induced by morphine, and that enzyme elevations after morphine are relatively uncommon. On the other hand pain production by morphine is much more common in patients than controls, and it is of considerable interest that enzyme elevations occur at all.

The mechanism involved is uncertain, but it is usually suggested that enzyme elevation is due to abnormally elevated pressures in the bile ducts in the case of the liver enzymes [45, 67]. A direct effect of the morphine on the liver cell cannot be discounted, although the enzyme response is abolished, at least in some patients, by sphincteroplasty [41, 86].

Other authors have reported a higher frequency of postmorphine enzyme elevations than that summarised here [45]. This may be because the dose of morphine (usually 10 mg intramuscularly) has been higher than the 0.04 mg per kg body weight we have used. The latter dose was selected as sufficient to induce sustained contraction of the distal bile duct sphincter, but insufficient to mask any pain response by its cerebral effects.

In summary, the morphine provocation test may have value as a screening test for these disorders, but further controlled studies of its results in different groups of patients are required.

Operative biliary manometry. This technique is accepted as a useful adjunct to operative cholangiography in the detection of bile duct stones, or other causes of organic biliary obstruction [3, 46, 48, 62, 63, 80, 94]. It is also claimed to be a reliable method of detecting functional disorders of the distal bile duct sphincter [3, 63].

A variety of different methods of measuring biliary pressures have been described. These include those of Caroli and Daniel which measure resting and opening pressures, and that of Cushieri and co-workers which measures resting pressure and the response of the distal sphincter to a constant infusion into the bile duct [16, 22, 23, 24, 43, 48, 57]. Hopton has used common bile duct perfusion with saline at a constant pressure [46]. The methods of Caroli, Daniel, and Cushieri have been compared experimentally and it was concluded that either the Caroli or Daniel technique is suitable for the measurement of resting and opening pressures [64]. More complicated methods combined with image intensification are available; that described by Ribeiro and co-workers is an attractive one in that the possible effects of fluctuation in intraduodenal pressure are eliminated by an indwelling duodenal tube [78].

There is no clearcut evidence that any of these methods are capable of distinguishing that group of patients who might require a sphincteroplasty from control subjects, except possibly a small group who have fibrosis of the distal sphincter [48, 78, 80, 94]. Even the latter possibility has not been confirmed in a recent study [46].

It is likely that further advances in this field will depend on the development of methods of assessing biliary pressure responses using retrograde biliary cannulation (see below).

TREATMENT

Because of the lack of objective non-invasive diagnostic methods it must be concluded that the basic approach to the management of these patients should be conservative. Surgical treatment is only considered after a careful and complete evaluation, and a period of observation.

MEDICAL TREATMENT

The objectives of medical treatment are: first, withdrawal of factors which may aggravate the symptoms, such as drugs, alcohol or certain foods; second, trial of antispasmodic drugs especially in the treatment of acute attacks of pain. A trial of treatment for the irritable colon syndrome is worth while. Bodvall has claimed good results with the use of progestational steroids in patients with recurrent symptoms after cholecystectomy [11].

SURGICAL TREATMENT

In the author's opinion surgical treatment deserves serious consideration if at least the first five, and preferably all, of the following criteria are satisfied:

1. History of recurrent attacks of pain of biliary type, confirmed by independent consultants. Previously undiagnosed gallstones are a serious possibility.
2. No evidence of other causes of abdominal pain.
3. No evidence of a psychiatric disorder.
4. Evidence of adenomyomatosis on a cholecystogram.
5. Reproduction of the pain by cholecystokinin or morphine, or both.
6. Elevation of liver enzymes after morphine administration.
7. No response to treatment for the irritable bowel syndrome.

These criteria are strict, but it may be that even more strict criteria will need to be developed in the future.

Exploratory laparotomy alone is unwise; it is unlikely to relieve the patient's symptoms except temporarily, and the future management of the patient is compounded by the recent abdominal scar. If the clinical diagnosis is strong enough to justify operation then a definitive biliary operation should also be justifiable. In some patients stones or other previously undetected cause of the pain will be found, and operative treatment is then straightforward.

Cholecystectomy. The gallbladder should always be opened prior to its removal, since small gallstones are often impalpable. An operative cholangiogram is also an essential part of this procedure. The gallbladder should be carefully examined grossly and microscopically for evidence of stones, adenomyomatosis, or chronic cholecystitis [32, 33, 54].

Sphincteroplasty. This operation is the only option in patients who have had a previous cholecystectomy. It should not be performed until cholangiography and a careful exploration have excluded abnormalities in the duct proximal to the sphincter. The duodenum is then opened and the distal bile duct sphincter and ampulla assessed for evidence of stenosis or inflammatory changes (Chapter 6). It is essential that the sphincteric division extends well up the bile duct so as to ensure complete division of the smooth muscle of the distal bile duct sphincter (Chapter 14) [27, 52, 53].

Cholecystectomy and sphincteroplasty. This combination of operations should only be performed if there is clear evidence of abnormality of the distal bile duct sphincter. It should be avoided if the patient has adenomyomatosis of the gallbladder, or if he/she is young.

Operative liver biopsy. An operative liver biopsy should be performed in all patients immediately after the abdomen has been opened, as outlined in Chapter 17 [42]. In a few patients unsuspected primary liver disease will be found, and in a proportion of patients with functional biliary disorders there will be changes similar to those seen in extrahepatic obstruction (see results below).

RESULTS OF SURGICAL TREATMENT
It is extremely difficult to analyse the results reported by different authors because of variations in diagnostic criteria. The follow-up periods have frequently been short, and the assessment of results has usually not been carried out by independent observers. There have been no controlled studies of different methods of treatment.

Histological examination of the gallbladder of patients having cholecystectomy has frequently shown adenomyomatosis, chronic cholecystitis, or cholesterolosis [41, 55, 92]. The results of operation in these patients, particularly those with adenomyomatosis, are surprisingly good; 70–80 per cent are reported to have relief of their symptoms [9, 38, 55, 59, 72, 73]. However, the periods of follow-up in some studies have been relatively short. The results in those patients whose gallbladders are reported as normal are uncertain. One of the major problems in assessing this group is the fact that pathological changes of the type described by Beilby in the gallbladder neck may have been missed [6, 32, 33]. Any assessment of the results of cholecystectomy in those patients with functional biliary disorders must include a careful histological examination of the gallbladder with objective criteria for the diagnosis of adenomyomatosis, chronic cholecystitis, and cholesterolosis [32, 33, 55].

The results of sphincteroplasty are also difficult to interpret. First, the results of sphincteroplasty for functional biliary disorders are often presented in conjunction with those for sphincteroplasty for stone disease, or other organic problems [52, 53, 83, 93]. Second, in earlier reports the distinction between sphincteroplasty and sphincterotomy was not always appreciated, and so some patients did not have complete division of the distal bile duct sphincter. With these reservations there is evidence that with careful selection approximately two-thirds to three-quarters of patients will have complete, or near complete, relief of their symptoms [18, 41, 75, 83, 87, 89]. It has been suggested that the operation should only be performed in patients who have biopsy evidence of fibrosis of the distal sphincter and ampulla. This policy is difficult to accept, first because of the difficulties of pathological assessment in this region, especially on frozen section, and second because there is considerable dispute about the significance of such changes in the sphincter [27]. Grage and co-workers, for example, compared the histological changes in ampullary biopsies with those in autopsy material and were unable to demonstrate consistent histological changes in patients with presumed ampullary stenosis [39]. Problems of diagnosis of suspected stenosis of the papilla of Vater are discussed in detail in Chapter 6.

In the author's department 94 patients have been evaluated *prospectively* for possible functional disorders of the biliary tract over the past 6 years [41, 42]. Sixteen of the 94 were found to have gallstones, either on repeat radiological investigation, or at operation. Thirty-three patients were not thought to have biliary pain, and were diagnosed as having other organic gastrointestinal disease, the irritable bowel syndrome, a psychiatric disorder, or spinal disease.

Thus, 45 patients remained and 38 of these were treated surgically. It should be emphasised that these operations represented a very small proportion of the biliary surgery carried out in the Department during the same period—less than 3 per cent of all biliary operations.

Five patients early in the series did not have definitive biliary operations, and the results in this group have been poor. Fourteen patients had a cholecystectomy, four had cholecystectomy plus sphincteroplasty, and 15 had a sphincteroplasty alone. There was no mortality and no major morbidity. The results in each group, with follow-up periods of at least 1 year, have been similar. Approximately two-thirds of the patients have had complete or near-complete relief of their symptoms.

Pathological examination of the 18 excised gallbladders revealed adenomyomatosis in six, mild chronic cholecystitis in six, and cholesterolosis in three. The remainder showed no obvious abnormality. In only two patients was there any evidence of fibrosis of the distal bile duct sphincter.

One important aspect of this study is the assessment of the operative liver biopsies which were obtained in 32 patients [42]. Twenty-four of these showed some abnormality. Twenty biopsies were compared in a blind fashion with 77 biopsies which included control groups and groups with extrahepatic biliary obstruction. The results showed that the biopsies from the patients with functional biliary disorders resembled those from patients with partial or intermittent biliary obstruction. Thus, the findings were compatible with the hypothesis that they were due to intermittent increases in biliary pressure.

There have been no previous similar studies and it is obviously important that the results are confirmed in other centres. These abnormalities in the liver may provide an objective basis for the diagnosis of functional biliary disorders. Unfortunately, the changes are not necessarily apparent on a needle biopsy because of poor sampling of portal tracts.

It is of considerable interest that 15 of 17 biopsies carried out in patients who had their pain induced by morphine were abnormal. The biopsies in the six patients with enzyme elevations after morphine were all abnormal. The results suggest that it may be possible to correlate the liver biopsy abnormalities with the results of morphine provocation tests and thus provide a firm basis for the latter. The crucial question will then be whether both are correlated with a good response to treatment. At present we have inadequate data to confirm or deny this hypothesis.

At least 20 per cent of the patients treated surgically for functional biliary disorders have a bad result, and it is likely that this figure will be higher with longer periods of follow-up [11, 41]. It must be concluded that current diagnostic criteria are not sufficiently objective, and that many patients diagnosed as having a functional biliary disorder in fact have another cause for their pain. On the other hand a significant number of patients do obtain long-term relief of their symptoms, and this is unlikely to be simply a placebo effect since the latter is usually short lived. Future advances will therefore depend on better diagnostic criteria.

FUTURE RESEARCH

There are a number of avenues of research which may provide answers to these problems. More sophisticated methods of bile analysis may detect groups of patients who have microcalculi, or who have primary inflammation of the gallbladder or biliary tract. Accurate assays for cholecystokinin may provide evidence for abnormalities in cholecystokinin metabolism or responses before and after cholecystectomy. Techniques using radionuclides to measure gallbladder emptying are now being developed and these are likely to be much more accurate than previous methods. It is now possible to measure pressures in the bile duct and across the distal bile duct sphincter by retrograde cannulation, and this technique may well replace operative biliary manometry [21]. More objective methods need to be developed for the histological assessment of gallbladder and sphincteric disease [34].

The liver biopsy abnormalities noted in some patients suggests the possibility that these might be predicted by a preoperative test for mild 'cholestasis', perhaps performed in conjunction with morphine or other stimulus to contract the distal bile duct sphincter [42].

Finally, it is essential that these patients are carefully followed up. This is the only way in which preoperative and peroperative 'abnormalities' may be correlated with pathological findings and long-term results. Better diagnostic criteria may then be defined.

REFERENCES

1. ADAMS T.W. & FOXLEY E.G. JR. A diagnostic technique for acalculous cholecystitis. *Surg. Gynec. Obstet.* **142:**168, 1976.
2. ALAWNEH I. Acute non-calculous cholecystitis in burns. *Br. J. Surg.* **65:**243, 1978.
3. ALBOT G., OLIVIER C. & LIBAUDE H. Radiomanometric examination of the biliary ducts: experience with 418 cases. *Gastroenterology* **24:**242, 1953.
4. ANDERSSON A., BERGDAHL L. & BOQUIST L. Acalculous cholecystitis. *Am. J. Surg.* **122:**3, 1971.

5. BEILBY J.O.W. Stricture of the gallbladder. *J. Path. Bact.* **93**:175, 1967.
6. BEILBY J.O.W. Diverticulosis of the gallbladder. The fundal adenoma. *Br. J. Expt. Path.* **48**:455, 1967.
7. BERGH G.S. The sphincter mechanism of the common bile duct in human subjects. Its reaction to certain types of stimulation. *Surgery* **11**:299, 1942.
8. BERK J.E. & MONROE L.S. Acute cholecystitis. In H.L. Bockus (ed.), *Gastroenterology* (3e), vol 3, p. 790. Saunders, Philadelphia, 1976.
9. BEVAN G. Acalculous adenomyomatosis of the gallbladder. *Gut* **11**:1029, 1970.
10. BLUMGART L.H., CARACHI R., IMRIE C.W., BENJAMIN I.S. & DUNCAN J.G. Diagnosis and management of postcholecystectomy symptoms: the place of endoscopy and retrograde choledochopancreatography. *Br. J. Surg.* **64**:809, 1977.
11. BODVALL B. The postcholecystectomy syndromes. *Clin. Gastroenterol.* **2**:103, 1973.
12. BRICKER D.L. & HALPERT B. Adenomyoma of the gallbladder. *Surgery* **53**:615, 1963.
13. BURKE J.O., PLUMMER K. & BRADFORD S. Serum amylase response to morphine, mecholyl and secretin as a test of pancreatic function. *Gastroenterology* **15**:699, 1950.
14. BUTSCH W.L., McGOWAN J.M. & WALTERS W. Clinical studies on the influence of certain drugs in relation to biliary pain and to the variations in intrabiliary pressure. *Surg. Gynec. Obstet.* **11**:451, 1936.
15. CAROLI J. & MERCADIER M. Dyskinesies Biliaires. Vigot, Paris, 1949.
16. CAROLI J. Les Maladies du voies biliaires. In J. Caroli (ed.), *Traite des Maladies der Foie, des Voies Biliaires et du Pancreas.* Vigot, Paris, 1951.
17. CHEN P.S. Acute acalculous cholecystitis. *Arch. Surg.* **113**:1461, 1978.
18. CHRISTIANSEN J. & SCHMIDT A. The postcholecystectomy syndrome. *Acta Chir Scand.* **137**:789, 1971.
19. COLLINS P.G. Postsurgical disorders. *Clin. Gastroenterol.* **6**:689, 1977.
20. CONDON R.E. & NYHUS L.M. Cholecystectomy in the aged. *Amer. J. Surg.* **100**:544, 1960.
21. COTTON P.B. Research techniques in endoscopic retrograde cholangiopancreatography (ERCP). *Clin. Gastroenterol.* **7**:667, 1978.
22. CUSHIERI A., HOWELL HUGHES J. & COHEN M. Biliary-pressure studies during cholecystectomy. *Br. J. Surg.* **59**:267, 1972.
23. DANIEL O. A simple method of measuring intra-visceral pressure, of value in uretero-colic anastomosis and study of pressure and flow in the common bile duct. *Irish J. Med. Sci.* **6**:415, 1965.
24. DANIEL O. The value of radiomanometry in bile duct surgery. *Ann. R. Coll. Surg. Eng.* **51**:357, 1972.
25. DAWSON J.L. Cholecystitis and cholecystectomy. *Clin. Gastroenterol.* **2**:85, 1973.
26. DEGRAAFF C.S., DEMBNER A.G. & TAYLOR K.J.W. Ultrasound and false normal oral cholecystogram. *Arch. Surg.* **113**:877, 1976.
27. DELMONT J. In J. Delmont (ed.), *The Sphincter of Oddi.* p. 240. Basel, Karger, 1977.
28. DORAN F.S.A. The sites to which pain is referred from the common bile duct in man and its implication for the theory of referred pain. *Br. J. Surg.* **54**:599, 1967.
29. DUNN F.H., CHRISTENSEN E.C., REYNOLDS J., JONES V. & FORDTRAN J.S. Cholecystokinin cholecystography. Controlled evaluation in the diagnosis and management of patients with possible acalculous gallbladder disease. *J.A.M.A.* **228**:997, 1974.
30. DUPRIEST R.W. JR., KHANAEJA S.C. & COWLEY R.A. Acute cholecystitis complicating trauma. *Ann. Surg.* **189**:84, 1979.
31. ECONOMOU G. & WARD-McQUAID J.N. A cross-over comparison of the effect of morphine, pethidine, pentazocine and phenazocine on biliary pressure. *Gut* **12**:218, 1971.
32. ELFVING G. Crypts and ducts in the gallbladder wall. *Acta Path. Et Microb. Scand. Suppl.* **49**:135, 1960.
33. ELFVING G., PALMU A. & ASP K. Regional distribution of hyperplastic cholecystoses in the gallbladder wall. *Ann. Chir. Gynaec. Fenniae* **58**:204, 1969.
34. FERNANDEZ-CRUS L., PALACIN A. & PERA C. Benign strictures of the terminal

common bile duct. In J. Delmont (ed.), *The Sphincter of Oddi*, p. 137. Basel, Karger, 1977.

35. FREEMAN J.B., COHEN W.N. & DENBESTEN L. Cholecystokinin cholangiography and analysis of duodenal bile in the investigation of pain in the right upper quadrant of the abdomen without gallstones. *Surg. Gynec. Obstet.* **140**:371, 1975.

36. GLENN F. & MANNIX H. JR. The acalculous gallbladder. *Ann. Surg.* **144**:670, 1956.

37. GOLDSTEIN F., GRUNT R. & MARGULIES M. Cholecystokinin cholecystography in the differential diagnosis of acalculous gallbladder disease. *Am. J. Dig. Dis.* **19**:835, 1974.

38. GOUGH M.H. The cholecystogram is normal . . . but . . . *Br. Med. J.* **1**:960, 1977.

39. GRAGE T.B., LOBER P.H., IMAMOGLU K. & WANGENSTEEN O.H. Stenosis of the sphincter of Oddi. A clinicopathologic review of 50 cases. *Surgery* **48**:304, 1960.

40. GROSS J.B., COMFORT M.W., MATHIESON D.R. & POWER M.H. Elevated values for serum amylase and lipase following the administration of opiates: a preliminary report. *Proceedings of the Staff Meetings of the Mayo Clinic* **26**:81, 1951.

41. HAM J.M., BOLIN T.D., WILTON N., STEVENSON D. & JEFFERIES S. The diagnosis and treatment of functional disorders of the biliary tract. *Aust. New Zeal. J. Surg.* **48**:494, 1978.

42. HAM J.M., BOLIN T.D., STEVENSON D., JEFFERIES S. & LIDDELOW A. Operative liver biopsy abnormalities in patients with functional disorders of the biliary tract. *Aust. New Zeal. J. Surg.* **48**:499, 1978.

43. HAND B.H. Anatomy and function of the extrahepatic biliary system. *Clin. Gastroenterol.* **2**:3, 1973.

44. HARVEY R.F. Hormonal control of gastrointestinal motility. *Am. J. Dig. Dis.* **20**:523, 1975.

45. HOLTZER J.D. & HULST S.G. TH. Confirmation of postcholecystectomy biliary dyskinesia by elevation of serum transaminase (GOT and GPT) after injection of morphine? *Acta Med. Scand.* **194**:221, 1973.

46. HOPTON D. Common bile duct perfusion combined with operative cholangiography. *Br. J. Surg.* **65**:852, 1978.

47. HOPTON D.S. & TORRANCE H.B. Action of various new analgesic drugs on the human common bile duct. *Gut* **8**:296, 1967.

48. HOPTON D. & WHITE T.T. An evaluation of manometric operative cholangiography in 100 patients with biliary disease. *Surg. Gynec. Obstet.* **133**:949, 1971.

49. HOWARD R.J. & DELANEY J.P. Postoperative cholecystitis. *Am. J. Dig. Dis.* **17**:213, 1972.

50. IVY A.C. Motor dysfunction of the biliary tract. An analytical and critical consideration. *Am. J. Roentgenol. Rad. Therapy* **57**:1, 1947.

51. JOHNSON A.G. & MARSHALL C.E. The effect of cholecystectomy on serum cholecystokinin levels. *Br. J. Surg.* **63**:153, 1976.

52. JONES S.A., STEEDMAN R.A., KELLER T.B. & SMITH L.L. Transduodenal sphincteroplasty (not sphincterotomy) for biliary and pancreatic disease. *Am. J. Surg.* **118**:282, 1969.

53. JONES S.A. & SMITH L.L. A reappraisal of sphincteroplasty (not sphincterotomy). *Surgery* **71**:565, 1972.

54. JUTRAS A.J. The cholecystoses (adenomyomatosis, cholesterolosis, neuromatosis). In H.L. Bockus (ed.), *Gastroenterology* (3e) vol 3, p. 816. Saunders, Philadelphia, 1976.

55. KEDDIE N.C., GOUGH A.L. & GALLAND R.B. Acalculous gallbladder disease: a prospective study. *Br. J. Surg.* **63**:797, 1976.

56. KING E.S.J. & MACCALLUM P. Cholecystitis glandularis proliferans (cystica). *Br. J. Surg.* **18**:310, 1931.

57. KJELLGREN K. Persistence of symptoms following biliary surgery. *Ann. Surg.* **152**:1026, 1960.

58. LAURSEN T. & SCHMIDT A. Increase in serum-GPT and serum-LDH after administration of morphine to patients suffering from bile duct dyskinesia. *Scand. J. Clin. Lab. Invest. Suppl.* **92**:175, 1966.

59. LeQuesne L.P. & Ranger I. Cholecystitis glandularis proliferans. *Brit. J. Surg.* **44:**447, 1957.
60. Lindberg E.F., Grinnan G.L.B. & Smith L. Acalculous cholecystitis in Vietnam casualties. *Ann. Surg.* **171:**152, 1970.
61. Long T.N., Heimbach D.M. & Carrico C.J. Acalculous cholecystitis in critically ill patients. *Am. J. Surg.* **136:**31, 1978.
62. Mallet-Guy P. Value of peroperative manometric and roentgenographic examination in the diagnosis of pathologic changes and functional disturbance of the biliary tract. *Surgery* **94:**385, 1952.
63. Mallet-Guy P. & Rose J.D. Peroperative manometry and radiology in biliary tract disorders. *Br. J. Surg.* **44:**55, 1956.
64. McGlynn M., Jefferies S., Rose M. & Ham J.M. Experimental assessment of techniques of measuring biliary pressure. *Aust. New Zeal. J. Surg.* **48:**581, 1978.
65. Moncada R., Cardoso M. & Danley R. *et al.* Acute cholecystitis: 137 patients studied by infusion tomography of the gallbladder. *Am. J. Roentgenol.* **129:**583, 1977.
66. Morin M.E., Baker D.A. & Marsan R.E. Visualisation of the gallbladder at excretory urography. *Radiology* **125:**35, 1977.
67. Mossberg S.M., Bloom A., Berkowitz J. & Ross G. Serum enzyme activities following morphine. *Arch. Intern. Med.* **109:**105, 1962.
68. Munster A.M., Goodwin M.N. & Pruitt B.A. Jr. Acalculous cholecystitis in burned patients. *Am. J. Surg.* **122:**591, 1971.
69. Nardi G.L. & Acosta J.M. Papillitis as a cause of pancreatitis and abdominal pain: role of evocative test, operative pancreatography and histologic evaluation. *Ann. Surg.* **164:**611, 1966.
70. Nash T.P. The behaviour of the sphincter of Oddi in health and disease. *Aust. New Zeal. J. Surg.* **31:**40, 1961.
71. Nathan M.H., Newman A., McFarland J. & Murray D.J. Cholecystokinin cholecystography. *Radiology* **93:**1, 1969.
72. Nathan M.H., Newman A., Murray D.J. & Camponovo R. Cholecystokinin cholecystography. A four year evaluation. *Am. J. Roentgenol. Rad. Ther. Nucl. Med.* **110:**240, 1970.
73. Nora P.F. & McCarthy W. Cholecystokinin cholecystography in acalculous gallbladder disease. *Arch. Surg.* **108:**507, 1974.
74. Ottinger L.W. Acute cholecystitis as a postoperative complication. *Ann. Surg.* **184:**162, 1976.
75. Patterson D.R., O'Leary J.P. & Nelson E.W. Value of preoperative evaluation in predicting patient response to sphincteroplasty. *Gastroenterology* **75:**1075, 1978.
76. Pirola R.C. & Davis A.E. Effects of ethyl alcohol on sphincteric resistance at the choledocho-duodenal junction in man. *Gut* **9:**557, 1968.
77. Reid D.R.K., Rogers I.M. & Calder J.F. The cholecystokinin test: an assessment. *Br. J. Surg.* **62:**317, 1975.
78. Ribeiro B., Williams J.T.W., Lees W., Roberts M. & LeQuesne L.P. Synchronous cholangiomanometry during cholecystectomy. *Br. J. Surg.* **65:**814, 1978.
79. Roth J.L.A. & Berk J.E. Symptoms after cholecystectomy (postcholecystectomy syndrome). In H.L. Bockus (ed.), *Gastroenterology* (3e), vol 3, p. 900. Saunders, Philadelphia, 1976.
80. Schein C.J. & Beneventano T.C. Choledochoduodenal junction stenosis in the postcholecystectomy syndrome. *Surgery* **64:**1039, 1968.
81. Shapiro R. Fixed defects of the gallbladder wall and adenomyomatosis. *Surg. Gynec. Obstet.* **136:**745, 1973.
82. Sharp P. & Ham J.M. Unpublished observations.
83. Shingleton W.W. & Gamburg D. Stenosis of the sphincter of Oddi. *Am. J. Surg.* **119:**35, 1970.
84. Siffert G. Motor disorders of the biliary tract. Dyskinesia, dystonia, dyssynergia. In H.L. Bockus (ed.), *Gastroenterology* (3e), vol 3. p. 726. Saunders, Philadelphia, 1976.

85. SIFFERT G. Chronic noncalculous cholecystitis. In H.L. Bockus (ed.), *Gastroentero-logy* (3e), vol. 3, p. 811. Saunders, Philadelphia, 1976.
86. SØRENSEN A.B. Morfintransaminaseprøven ved dyskinesia biliaris. *Ugeskr. Laeg.* **126:**1393, 1964.
87. STEFANINI P., CARBONI M., BERNADINIS G. DE. & NEGRO P. Longterm results of papillostomy. In J. Delmont (ed.), *The Sphincter of Oddi*, p. 206. Basel, Karger, 1977.
88. STRODE J.E. Biliary dyskinesia from the surgical viewpoint. *Ann. Surg.* **117:**198, 1943.
89. TAFT D.A. & WREGGIT G.R. Sphincteroplasty for postcholecystectomy syndrome. *Am. Surg.* **40:**527, 1974.
90. TERNBERG J.L. & KEATING J.P. Acute acalculous cholecystitis. Complication of other illnesses in childhood. *Arch. Surg.* **110:**543, 1975.
91. TORSOLI A. The function of biliary 'sphincters'. *Ann. R. Coll. Surg. Edin.* **16:**270, 1971.
92. VALBERG L.S., JABBARI M., KERR J.W., CURTIS A.C., RAMCHAND S. & PRENTICE R.S.A. Biliary pain in young women in the absence of gallstones. *Gastroenterology* **60:**1020, 1971.
93. WHITE T.T. Indications for sphincteroplasty as opposed to choledochoduodenos-tomy. *Am. J. Surg.* **126:**165, 1973.
94. WHITE T.T., WAISMAN H., HOPTON D. & KAVLIE H. Radiomanometry, flow rates and cholangiography in the evaluation of common bile duct disease. A study of 220 cases. *Am. J. Surg.* **123:**73, 1972.

13. Endoscopic Sphincterotomy

BY CLAUDE LIGUORY

The advent of fibreoptic endoscopy has allowed a study of the detailed anatomy of the region of the papilla of Vater under ideal conditions [2]. The diagnosis of duodenal, biliary, and pancreatic affections has been greatly improved by the introduction of duodenoscopy and retrograde endoscopic cholangiography and pancreatography. It is now possible to treat these affections through the endoscope due to the development of endoscopic surgery of the papilla. Endoscopic sphincterotomy has been practised since 1973 [7, 19]. In this chapter the author will examine the indications, the contraindications, the technique, and the results of endoscopic sphincterotomy based on a personal experience of 467 cases.

INDICATIONS AND CONTRAINDICATIONS

Endoscopic sphincterotomy was performed in 467 cases and the indications for this have been summarised in Table 13.1.

It is emphasised that the patients are informed that they will be treated with a new technique which is intended to avoid surgical intervention, but they are also told of the possibility that if the technique fails, surgery may be required, either immediately as an emergency measure, or at a later date.

Endoscopic sphincterotomy was performed in 152 cases in order to treat residual choledocholithiasis, and in these cases the procedure was one of choice, keeping in mind the morbidity and mortality associated with biliary surgical reintervention in these cases, as well as the frequency of mild stenosis of the papilla of Vater which would normally require an additional local operative procedure [16]. The choice between surgery or endoscopic sphincterotomy depends on the diameter of the bile ducts. If the bile duct diameter is less than 25 mm, it is logical to perform endoscopic sphincterotomy in the first instance. If the bile duct diameter is greater than 25 mm, a biliary-intestinal anastomosis is preferable, as this will ensure satisfactory biliary drainage. Finally, when endoscopic sphincterotomy has failed, or when the calculus is bigger than 30 mm, surgical intervention is indicated. Although in certain series of cases no residual calculi were noted after surgical sphincteroplasty, a comparative study between surgery and endoscopic sphincterotomy which has not been done so far, would be of great practical benefit [16, 18].

Endoscopic sphincterotomy was performed in 197 cases of choledocholithiasis, which was coexistent with gallstones in the gallbladder in 192 cases and without gallbladder stones in five cases. In this group surgical contraindications

Table 13.1. Indications for endoscopic sphincterotomy
(467 cases)

Choledocholithiasis		
Gallbladder stones also	197	
Retained after recent choledochotomy	60	409
Cholecystectomy some time ago	152	
Stenosis of the sphincter of Oddi		39
Tumours of the papilla of Vater		14
Hydatid cysts		2
Pancreatic lithiasis		3

were present in 91 per cent of the cases. These are, then, patients representing a high surgical risk because of age or the existence of associated cardiorespiratory disease, or because of the extent and gravity of the biliary affection. Cardio-respiratory affections are known to increase the operative risk, especially in the aged [13].

Endoscopic sphincterotomy was performed in 60 cases of choledocholith-iasis, diagnosed following surgical intervention with the aid of postoperative T-tube cholangiography. Flushing through the drain with the use of relaxants of the sphincter of Oddi, as well as the use of other solutions, should be performed first because in certain cases they can be quite successful [11, 14, 23, 31]. These medical methods are usually unsuccessful if the gallstone is large and also if there is associated stenosis of the papilla of Vater. Instrumental extraction of residual stones through a T tube has become more and more successful over the years, with the use of special instruments under x-ray control, as well as the more recent utilisation of a small calibre fibroscope which enables extraction to be made under direct vision [4, 29, 36]. These instrumental methods have two disadvan-tages, the first being a waiting period of 1–2 months to allow the development of a fibrous tract and also the inability of these methods to treat an associated stenosis of the papilla of Vater. Thus, in these cases, endoscopic sphincterotomy has the benefit that it can be used immediately after surgery, and also that it can deal with a stenosis of the papilla of Vater, but its disadvantage is that it is a more aggressive method with a small, but definite, risk of mortality and morbidity. This subject of removal of residual stones following surgery is also discussed in Chapter 5.

Endoscopic sphincterotomy was performed in 39 cases of mild stenosis of the sphincter of Oddi. In ten cases the patients had undergone a previous cholecys-tectomy and in 29 cases there was the coexistence of a stenosis of the papilla of Vater, together with gallbladder stones. The diagnostic criteria for stenosis of the papilla of Vater should be strict, in order to avoid unnecessary surgical interven-tions on the sphincter, as has been emphasised in Chapter 6. From a radiological standpoint stenosis of the terminal portion of the biliary tract cannot be made in all cases, but stasis of the contrast medium in a distended bile duct is a constant and important finding. Finally, diagnosis of stenosis of the papilla of Vater can only be verified by endoscopic gauge measurement of the papillary area, together with evidence of an elevated duodenobiliary pressure [32]. Endoscopic sphincterotomy is then suggested in those cases in which this stenosis is associated with disabling symptoms, such as repeated biliary colic, jaundice, or cholangitis.

In 14 cases endoscopic sphincterotomy was performed for tumours of the papilla of Vater. It may be performed as a first stage to drain the obstructed biliary tract, thereby improving the state of cholestasis and cholangitis and this stage can then be followed by excisional surgery when the patient is in a better condition. In cases where the tumour cannot be removed an endoscopic sphincterotomy may be performed instead of a surgical biliary bypass procedure.

Endoscopic sphincterotomy has also been practised for a miscellaneous number of affections which included extraction of hydatid cysts in the biliary system, for acute pancreatitis without gallstones, and in relapsing pancreatitis.

Endoscopic sphincterotomy is an absolute contraindication under two circumstances: first, in a long stenosis of the distal bile duct, and when there is a calculus impacted in the choledochus above the infundibulum of the bile duct.

Relative contraindications to endoscopic sphincterotomy include blood dyscrasias, although it is emphasised that sphincterotomy has been performed without complications on cirrhotic patients suffering from problems of haemostasis and portal hypertension; secondly, relative contraindications are calculi which exceed 3 cm in diameter and, finally, a papilla which cannot be located especially when placed at the base of a large duodenal diverticulum. In this regard it should be noted that acute gallstone pancreatitis, a precarious general medical condition, and the mere existence of a peripapillary duodenal diverticulum, are not in themselves contraindications to endoscopic sphincterotomy.

TECHNIQUE OF ENDOSCOPIC SPHINCTEROTOMY

We use a JFB3 Olympus duodenoscope which is designed for the use of high-frequency currents. The high-frequency generator should be powerful enough to be able to supply separately both a cutting, and a coagulation current.

The sphincterotome itself consists of a Teflon catheter inside which slides a conductor wire whose distal end is free from the insulating sheet. The sphincterotome is capable of sliding into the duct and, by passing the current, it is possible to section the papilla and the infundibulum region over a length that can be controlled. A number of sphincterotomes are available and Fig. 13.1 shows just

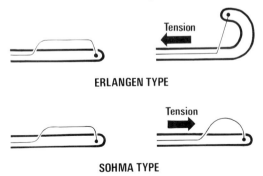

ERLANGEN TYPE

SOHMA TYPE

Fig. 13.1. Different types of sphincterotomes and their mode of action.

two of the different varieties [8]. The procedure is performed in the radiology department after premedication.

The papilla of Vater catheterisation is performed with the Erlangen type of sphincterotome which is shown in Fig. 13.1. The sphincterotome is inserted into the distal bile duct as far as possible, as seen in Fig. 13.2. The injection of contrast material enables one to locate the catheterised duct precisely and in 75 per cent of the cases, in fact the catheter does lie in the bile duct. Should there be any doubt about the position of the sphincterotome it is imperative to verify it with contrast radiology. Indeed, opacification of the biliary tract alone may not be a satisfactory test regarding the position of the sphincterotome as, on occasions, the sphincterotome may be in the pancreatic duct but contrast material does flow into the bile duct, misleading the operator. In these cases, it is important to look at all of the contrast radiographs and locate exactly the position of the sphincterotome in this way.

Opacification of the bile ducts confirms the diagnosis and will also detect the existence of possible contraindications to endoscopic sphincterotomy, such as an extended stenosis of the distal biliary tract which goes beyond its intraduodenal passage and, in which case, endoscopic sphincterotomy is unlikely to relieve the obstruction.

The sphincterotome is then slightly withdrawn until the metal wire appears just outside the papilla, as can be seen in the ERCP shown in Fig. 13.3. The wire of the sphincterotome is then tensed by pulling the handle of the sphincterotome

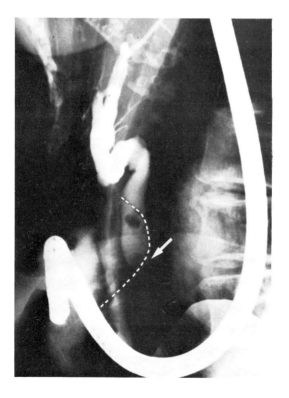

Fig. 13.2. Endoscopic retrograde cholangiogram showing the sphincterotome in place in the distal bile duct.

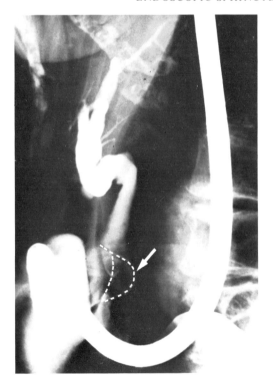

Fig. 13.3. Endoscopic retrograde cholangiogram showing the sphinctero- tome in position to com- mence endoscopic sphinc- terotomy. For details see text.

as shown in Fig. 13.1, and then the alternate application of the sectioning and coagulation current enables the sphincterotomy to be performed. It is known that this sphincterotomy or papilloinfundibulotomy has been completed when the lumen of the distal end of the common bile duct becomes visible. The view of the endoscopist at the beginning of sphincterotomy, as well as at the completion of the procedure, is shown in Fig. 13.4.

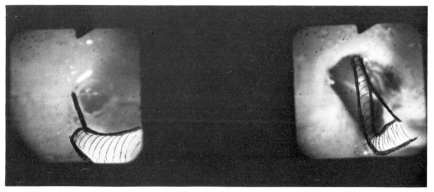

Fig. 13.4. The endoscopist's view of sphincterotomy. The sphincterotome has been accentuated by the line drawing. (*left*) The sphincterotome in position. (*right*) Sphincter- otomy (papillo-infundibulotomy) completed when lumen of distal bile duct becomes visible.

If it is not possible to place the sphincterotome into the bile duct then there are three other alternatives, which include a puncture of the bile duct infundibulum through the duodenum, a second attempt at sphincterotomy but using a single cut papillotomy, or thirdly, one can practise a descending duodenotomy [26]. These three techniques will now be described.

The principle of infundibulotomy consists of puncturing the infundibulum of the distal bile duct about 1 cm above the papilla, thereby obtaining direct entry into the bile duct which is then opacified through a contrast medium. An Erlangen type of sphincterotome is then inserted through such an opening and an incision is made with the sphincterotome in the upper part of the infundibulum and this then becomes an infundibulotomy (Fig. 13.5). In some cases, after the infundibulum has collapsed, the sphincterotome is inserted normally through the papilla to complete the incision. If, however, the choledochal infundibulum is not protruding into the duodenum another attempt should be made through the papilla 24 hours later as, not uncommonly, one can easily succeed with a second attempt at catheterisation and sphincterotomy of the biliary tract.

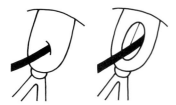

Fig. 13.5. Diagrammatic representation of infundibulotomy.

Should the second attempt at endoscopic sphincterotomy fail it is still possible to perform a limited incision, or a so-called precutting, by incising the upper portion of the papilla of Vater only, in order to separate the pancreatic orifice from the biliary orifice. Under these conditions it is then possible to catheterise the biliary tract either immediately, or a few days later, when the oedema has subsided. This limited incision is made either with the Erlangen sphincterotome or with the Sohma sphincterotome as shown in Fig. 13.1. If the Sohma type is used the sphincterotomy is performed by pushing on its handle, the cutting wire of which forms an arc applied in the direction of the bile duct under vision.

Finally, in a patient who has a T tube in place when access to the distal bile duct could not be obtained in the usual endoscopic way, it is sometimes possible to practise the technique of a 'descending sphincterotomy' [35]. In these cases the sphincterotome is inserted via the T tube from above down, across the papilla, and into the duodenum where a papilloinfundibulotomy is performed under endoscopic control.

Whatever the technique adopted the length of the incision varies according to the particular endoscopic anatomy of that patient, but in all cases it is necessary to cut the upper pole of the papilla, the hood, and the infundibulum of the bile duct. The length of the incision varies from 10 to 20 mm and it is essential at the end of the intervention to be able to see the opening of the distal common bile duct as shown in Fig. 13.6. Under these conditions the contrast from the bile duct

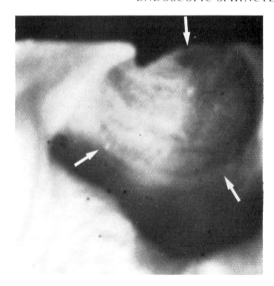

Fig. 13.6. Completion of sphincterotomy and the lumen of the distal bile duct is clearly visible.

will empty immediately. The total duration of the intervention is approximately 25 minutes in the average case. A diagrammatic representation of standard endoscopic sphincterotomy is shown in Fig. 13.7.

The endoscopic instrumental extraction of stones from the bile duct is not usually performed immediately, because it is a risky procedure and also because usually the stones will be evacuated spontaneously. The extraction is attempted immediately however, in cases where a calculus is impacted or when the calculus size is greater than 20 mm. Extraction of the stone is then performed under x-ray control using a flexible Dormia type of basket (Fig. 13.7).

If calculi are large and numerous it is advisable to use preventative antibiotics. The endoscopic insertion of transnasal biliary drainage, immediately after sphincterotomy, can also be done and it offers several advantages. The advantages of transnasal biliary drainage are the possibility of repeated cholangiography, thus avoiding the necessity for additional duodenoscopic intervention, and through it also antibiotics can be instilled or the bile duct can be lavaged with saline, or with chemical substances capable or reducing the size of the calculus [9].

If a gallstone remains in the bile duct it is necessary to perform a check endoscopy on the eighth day and an attempt is then made at extracting the

Fig. 13.7. Diagrammatic representation of endoscopic sphincterotomy shown left and centre. Instrumental extraction of a stone is shown on the right.

Fig. 13.8. The technique of per oral choledocoscopy. (*left*) The sphincterotomy is visible through the duodenoscope. (*middle*) The choledochoscope is introduced into the distal end of the bile duct. (*right*) The catheter is pushed ahead in the bile duct.

calculus should it still be there. At this check an endoscope of a larger diameter can be used to enable the usage of a larger type of Dormia basket.

The biliary system can now also be visualised, orally, through a choledocho-scope and under these circumstances stone extraction is operated under direct visual control [27]. This type of per oral choledochoscopy is shown in Fig. 13.8. Improvements are still needed in this area of per oral choledochoscopy, because at present the penetration into the biliary duct is restricted as only a small-calibre axial vision choledochoscope can be introduced. If the calculus size is clearly bigger than the size of the sphincterotomy there are two further choices, the first being a second sphincterotomy enlargement of the original incision or, secondly, an attempt can be made to fragment the calculus within the bile duct by means of an electrohydraulic probe which is coupled with a Dormia type of probe in order to avoid damage to the wall of the bile duct during calculus fragmentation [22].

RESULTS

Endoscopic sphincterotomy has been successful in 451 out of 457 attempts, that is, in 96.5 per cent of the series. An international survey conducted on 3853 attempts at endoscopic sphincterotomy showed a success rate of 93.9 per cent [33]. It is interesting to note that this very high percentage of success is even higher than that obtained for simple catheterisation of the bile duct in order to perform retrograde cholangiography and, in these cases, the success rate overall in various series is of the order of 85 per cent. Endoscopic cholangiography is the preliminary to sphincterotomy and the discrepancy in these two figures probably has one or more of several reasons: firstly, endoscopic sphincterotomy has been practised by endoscopists especially skilled in endoscopic cholangiography; secondly, that there are some favourable local conditions in this series, such as the spontaneous migration of microcalculi, or the possibility of choledochoduodenal fistulae which quickly get bigger in infundibulotomy; thirdly, previous surgical sphincterotomies; fourthly; the possibility of applying special techniques such as precutting of the papilla and puncturing the infundibulum of the bile duct [17, 26].

Thus, in 451 sphincterotomies we benefited from favourable local conditions described above in 16 cases or 3.5 per cent, of which six had previous surgical sphincterotomies, seven had choledochoduodenal fistulae, and three had a calculus wedged in the infundibulum. We applied special technical devices in 118 cases or 26 per cent, and this involved precutting of the papilla in 75 cases and puncturing of the infundibulum of the bile duct in 43 cases. Whenever possible we prefer to puncture the bile duct infundibulum because this enables us to perform the sphincterotomy at the same time [26].

In the presence of bile duct stones endoscopic sphincterotomy was successful in 394 of the 409 cases, that is in 96.3 per cent. The gallstones were successfully removed in 358 out of the 394 successful sphincterotomies, that is, in 90.8 per cent of the treated cases. The ways in which the bile ducts were cleared of gallstones is shown in Table 13.2. Thus, in two-thirds of cases, the stones evacuated spontaneously after endoscopic sphincterotomy, while in 17 per cent instrumental

Table 13.2. Choledocholithiasis in 394 cases. Evacuation of calculi after endoscopic sphincterotomy

	Number	%
Spontaneous evacuation	260	66
Instrumental evacuation	68	17.2
Postlavage evacuation	30	7.6
Failure of evacuation	36	9.2

evacuation was required and in 8 per cent evacuation occurred after lavage, and there was a failure of evacuation in 36 of the 394 cases, or in 9.2 per cent. These data compare favourably with the above-mentioned international survey, particularly for the percentage of failures in removing bile duct calculi which in that survey was about 9 per cent [33]. Failure to remove calculi, despite a properly performed endoscopic sphincterotomy, will obviously occur in cases of multiple gallstones or when the size of the gallstones is large, usually exceeding 20 mm in diameter. Failure can also be explained in some cases because of the occurrence of a bend in the distal bile duct that hinders the spontaneous drainage or extraction of calculi with instruments. Thus, it is now reasonable to recapitulate the steps we undertake when there is a failure of the calculus to clear from the bile duct, and this means a second endoscopic sphincterotomy if the opening is not of a maximal size and, secondly, fragmentation of the calculus within the bile duct [22].

The question of microlithiasis is interesting and we have encountered it in 20 cases out of the 358 lithiasis patients successfully treated. Endoscopic sphincter-otomy is recommended only when we have the correct clinical data, more commonly in association with cholangitis or acute biliary pancreatitis, as these calculi cannot be seen on x-rays. A diagnosis of microlithiasis can be made only after sphincterotomy and observation of drainage or removal of calculi which measure merely a few millimetres.

Endoscopic sphincterotomy was also performed on 18 cases of acute pan-creatitis of biliary origin, and acute pancreatitis does not constitute a contraindi-cation to performing endoscopic sphincterotomy as it has not been followed by complications. Endoscopic sphincterotomy has been done in eight cases at the peak of the pancreatitis. Drainage of bile duct calculi, in association with acute pancreatitis, has been obtained in all cases of patients who had an endoscopic sphincterotomy under this situation, because the stones were generally small in size.

Endoscopic sphincterotomy was successful in 38 out of 39 cases of mild stenosis of the sphincter of Oddi. Thus, the presence of sphincter of Oddi stenosis does not diminish the chances of success of an endoscopic sphincterotomy. Following sphincterotomy in all of these cases the symptoms vanished and there was a return to normal liver function, as well as a reduction in the diameter of the biliary ductal system as observed with the aid of endoscopic cholangiography.

Endoscopic sphincterotomy was successful in 14 cases involving tumours of the area of the papilla of Vater. In certain cases the excessive protuberance of the bulging infundibulum of the bile duct tilts the papilla downwards and this makes catheterisation of the papilla very difficult and recourse is then made to punctur-ing the infundibulum. The puncture of the infundibulum under these circum-stances is a particularly easy operation because of its considerable bulge into the duodenum. This approach into the biliary duct was performed in four cases. Endoscopic sphincterotomy preceded excisional surgery on six patients who presented with deep jaundice or intense cholangitis. Finally, endoscopic sphinc-terotomy was performed on eight patients with an inoperable cancer, and the procedure permitted the performance of an internal bile drainage without the need for an operation. The jaundice or cholangitis in these cases quickly subsided and the biliary duct resumed its normal diameter.

Endoscopic sphincterotomy was performed on two complicated cases of hydatid cysts which involved the biliary ductal system, and the sphincterotomy has helped the progress of the illness in these two cases. Sphincterotomy was also performed on three cases of acute pancreatitis who were in relapse, and in these the short-term results were excellent, but at present there is insufficient data to form an opinion regarding the value of this procedure in relapsing acute pancrea-titis when no gallstones are present.

COMPLICATIONS AND MORTALITY

The immediate complications and mortality of endoscopic sphincterotomy in this series is summarised in Table 13.3. Essentially, complications occurred in 9 per cent of cases requiring an urgent laparotomy in 2 per cent and the mortality rate was 1.1 per cent. The international survey of 3618 cases previously referred to, in which an endoscopic sphincterotomy was performed, gave a complication rate of 7 per cent requiring emergency laparotomy in 2.3 per cent and the mortality rate was 1.4 per cent [33].

Haemorrhage is the most frequent complication and it occurred in 19 cases or 4.2 per cent, requiring laparotomy in two cases with one death. Haemorrhage has always occurred immediately after sphincterotomy, and if it occurs after a bleeding-free interval a further emergency endoscopy should be performed because the bleeding may be due to another associated gastroduodenal cause, not related to the endoscopic sphincterotomy. This accident may result from the sectioning of an artery under the papilla which crosses over the front face of the bile duct, and in these cases it is unpredictable because the artery is not constant

Table 13.3. Endoscopic sphincterotomy in 451 cases. Complications and mortality

Complication	Number	Urgent Laparotomy	Death
Haemorrhage	19	2	1
Retroperitoneal perforation	5	3	1
Haemorrhage and perforation	2	2	1
Cholangitis	8	2	1
Pancreatitis	5	—	1
Cholecystitis	2	1	—
Total	41 (9%)	10 (2.1%)	5 (1.1%)

and its exact topography is variable. Haemorrhage is commonly observed after recutting the papilla following a previous surgical sphincterotomy, or after recutting the papilla following a previous endoscopic sphincterotomy in order to remove a large-size calculus. The present author, together with others, believes that the risk of haemorrhage is related to the length of the incision [5]. On the other hand the use of a cutting current during sphincterotomy does not necessarily predispose to the risk of haemorrhage, but we are in the habit of using a coagulation current alternatively with a cutting current during sphincterotomy, as this may minimise the incidence of haemorrhage. It is important to remember that blood dyscrasias do not constitute a contraindication to performing an endoscopic sphincterotomy. It should also be emphasised that haemostasis during surgery is also quite difficult, and surgical intervention should only be made when the haemorrhage cannot be controlled by blood transfusion.

Retroperitoneal perforation is diagnosed by noticing leakage of contrast medium outside the bile duct. Such a perforation occurred in five cases requiring a laparotomy in three cases, with one death. Perforation is the consequence of an endoscopic sphincterotomy which is too long and the perforation is usually situated at the point of entry of the bile duct into the duodenal wall [6]. This type of perforation does not always require surgical intervention, and in our practice two perforations were successfully treated medically. In the above-mentioned international survey 21 out of 40 cases of perforation also did not require surgical intervention [33]. Medical treatment should be started immediately and it consists of duodenal aspiration, intravenous therapy, antibiotics, and the use of atropine.

In two cases we have observed perforation accompanied by haemorrhage, requiring laparotomy in both cases and followed by one death. This rare complication is evidently due to an excessively long endoscopic sphincterotomy which well exceeds the infundibulum of the bile duct.

Cholangitis was observed in eight cases requiring urgent surgical intervention in two cases, followed by one death. In the previously mentioned international survey, cholangitis occurred 49 times in 3618 endoscopic sphincterotomies which required laparotomy in 21 cases, followed by 11 deaths [33]. Cholangitis is usually observed when it is not possible to perform an immediate sphincterotomy and only a precutting of the papilla is possible, or when large size or numerous calculi persist in the biliary duct after sphincterotomy. In such cases, the immediate extraction of calculi should be attempted, and in cases of failure one should perform transnasal biliary drainage endoscopically. Before surgical intervention is advised in these cases a further endoscopic examination is required and a new attempt is made at extracting the calculus or an attempt is made to break up the gallstones within the bile duct, or to enlarge the previous sphincterotomy if it is too narrow. We have thus succeeded in six cases, thereby avoiding surgical intervention.

Acute pancreatitis occurred in five cases, followed by one death. The international survey found acute pancreatitis occurring in 48 cases requiring laparotomy in three cases, with nine deaths [33]. While a rise of serum amylase is relatively frequent immediately following endoscopic sphincterotomy, clinical acute pancreatitis is rather uncommon as can be seen from our, and the international, series. Several mechanisms have been postulated regarding the cause of pancreatitis in these cases. Thus, sphincterotomy practised in the pancreatic duct, due to an unusual position of the sphincterotome, has been one hypothesis, while technical defects of the papillotomy causing the formation of a choledochopancreatic fistula during the flow of the current, has been another hypothesis [10, 20]. Excessive use of the coagulation current which diffuses widely into the tissues and repeated injection into the pancreatic duct with duct hyperpressure during attempts at catheterisation of the biliary ductal system, have also been hypothesised and the last two mentioned mechanisms are often associated, and are probably responsible for most of the postsphincterotomy pancreatitis seen. It is emphasised that acute pancreatitis following endoscopic sphincterotomy is much less severe than acute pancreatitis seen following a surgical sphincterotomy [25].

We have seen two cases of acute cholecystitis which occurred within 8 days of performing endoscopic sphincterotomy.

Immediate complications following endoscopic sphincterotomy could be reduced if certain rules were applied: avoid repeated injections into the pancreatic duct during catheterisation; check the sphincterotome for satisfactory functioning immediately before its use; strictly supervise the position of the sphincterotome inside the bile duct; use the coagulation and cutting currents judiciously; take time and patience to perform a sufficiently wide sphincterotomy; control the length of the sphincterotomy incision and thus avoid extending it beyond the infundibulum of the bile duct; attempt immediate extraction of large-size or multiple calculi.

If a complication occurs it is necessary to perform emergency duodenoscopy in order to diagnose the mechanism of the complication and attempt to treat it endoscopically. This means extraction of the calculus, recutting of the sphincterotomy, or institution of adequate biliary drainage. Thus, in our last 105 endoscopic sphincterotomies we observed only seven complications which included four haemorrhages, two cases of cholangitis, and one pancreatitis, requiring surgical intervention only in one case of haemorrhage, without a single death.

The choice between endoscopy and surgery is open for discussion in the treatment of certain biliary affections. Thus, the mortality rate of surgical sphincterotomy is of the order of 4.7 per cent according to the documented cases over the past 10 years [24]. The total mortality rate in cases of reintervention for residual bile duct stones is of the order of 10 per cent [3]. The mortality rate of biliary surgery varies with the age of the patient and it is estimated to be 2.4 per cent for stones in the bile duct for patients aged 60 or less, increasing to 12.8 per cent for patients over the age of 60 [34]. The operative mortality rate increases as soon as the bile ducts are explored, while for simple cholecystectomy the mortality rate remains low, of the order of 0–1.6 per cent [30]. The postoperative mortality rate for tumours of the papilla of Vater is of the order of 17 per cent [28].

Thus, one can conclude that endoscopic sphincterotomy is less dangerous than surgical sphincterotomy, endoscopy is less dangerous than surgery in cases of residual bile duct stones and in cases of bile duct stones in high-risk patients, or in patients suffering from tumours of the papilla of Vater.

The delayed complications of endoscopic sphincterotomy have not been fully defined because of insufficient data. We have re-examined 140 patients from 6 to 36 months after sphincterotomy with the following results: complete healing was observed in 130 cases or 93 per cent, while there was stenosis secondary to sphincterotomy in four cases, or 3 per cent. Gallstones recurred in six cases or 4 per cent. However, this may have been due to gallstones overlooked in the course of the previous endoscopic examination.

It is known that a properly performed surgical sphincterotomy or sphincteroplasty will not result in ascending cholangitis, and in this regard 1 year after an endoscopic sphincterotomy there was also no case of ascending cholangitis in 107 patients who were re-examined [15, 21].

CONCLUSION

Endoscopic sphincterotomy should be considered in difficult biliary problems. In most cases it is performed on patients who have already been operated on for affections of the biliary duct, or on patients who present a high surgical risk. The seriousness and the difficulty of biliary surgical intervention in these groups is well known and, therefore, endoscopic sphincterotomy represents the only alternative.

Endoscopic sphincterotomy should be performed only by fully trained and experienced endoscopists in close cooperation with surgeons. Further improvements in the existing equipment and instruments will enable considerable progress to be made in the future in this special branch of endoscopy.

REFERENCES

1. Acosta J.M. & Ledesma C. Gallstone migration as a cause of acute pancreatitis. *New Eng. J. Med.* **209**:484, 1974.
2. Barraya L., Pujol-Soler R. & Yvergneaux J.P. La région oddienne—anatomie millimétrique—presse méd. **79**:25, 1971.
3. Buffin R.P. La lithiase résiduelle et récidivante de la voie biliaire principale. Conclusions générales. *Ann. Chir.* **22**:1513, 1968.
4. Burhenne H.J. Non operative retained biliary tract stone extraction. A new roentgenologic technique. *Am. J. Roentgen.* **117**:388, 1973.
5. Classen M. & Ossenberg F.W. Non surgical removal of common bile duct stones. Progress report. *Gut* **18**:760, 1977.
6. Classen M. & Safrany L. Endoscopic papillotomy and removal of gallstone. *Br. Med. J.* **1**:371, 1977.
7. Classen M. & Demling L. Endosckopische sphincterotomie der papilli Vateri und steinextraktion aus dem ductus choledocus. *Dtsch. Med. Wschr.* **99**:496, 1974.
8. Coffin J.C. & Liguory C. Les sphinctérotomes. *Endoscopie digestive* 1979.
9. Cotton P.B. Transnasal bile duct catheterisation after endoscopic sphincterotomy. A method for biliary drainage, perfusion and sequential cholangiography. II. Symposium International d'Endoscopie Digestive, Paris 16–17 Oct 1978, Volume des résumés, p. 50.
10. Cremer M., Dony A., Toussaint J., Hermanus A. & de Toeuf J. Pancréatite aigue nécrosante résolutive: complication de la sphinctérotomie endoscopique. *Endoscopie digestive* **2**:191, 1977.
11. Debray Ch., Roux N., Lecanuet R. & Thomas J. Sur le traitement médical des calculs cholédociens oubliés. *Sem. Hop. Paris* **28**:433, 1959.
12. Doubilet H. & Muholland J.H. Recurrent acute pancreatitis: observations on etiology and surgical treatment. *Ann. Surg.* **128**:609, 1948.
13. Dowdy G.S. & Waldron G.W. Importance of coexistent factors in biliary tract surgery (analysis of 2285 operations). *Arch. Surg.* **88**:314, 1964.
14. Gardner B. Heparin for common duct stones. *New Eng. J. Med.* **289**:592, 1973.
15. Goignard P. & Pelissier G. Compte rendu d'une expérience de 8 années de sphinctérotomies. *Revue Internationale d'hépatologie* **16**:605, 1966.
16. Hivet M., Richarne J., Chevrel H.P. & Berlinsky M. 340 sphinctérotomies oddiennes. Techniques, indications, résultats immédiats et tardifs. *Ann. Chir.* **21**:1409, 1967.
17. Ikeda S. & Okada Y. Classification of choledochoduodenal fistula diagnosed by duodenal fibroscopy and its etiological significance. *Gastroenterology* **69**:130, 1975.

18. Jones S.A. & Smith L.L. A reappraisal of sphincteroplasty (non sphincterotomy). *Surgery* **71**:565, 1972.
19. Kawai K., Akasaka Y., Murakami K., Tada M., Koh L. & Nakajima M. Endoscopic sphincterotomy of the ampulla of Vater. *Gastrointest. Endoscopy* **20**:148, 1974.
20. Koch H. Endoscopic papillotomy. *Endoscopy* **7**:89, 1978.
21. Koch H., Rösch W., Schaffner O. & Demling L. Endoscopic papillotomy. *Gastroenterology* **73**:1393, 1977.
22. Koch H., Stolte M. & Walz V. Endoscopic lithotrypsy in the common bile duct. *Endoscopy* **9**:95, 1977.
23. Lansford C., Mehta S. & Kern S. The treatment of retained stones in the common bile duct with sodium cholate infusion. *Gut* **15**:48, 1974.
24. Lechat J.R., Leborgne J., Leneel J.C., Visset J. & Mousseau M. La place actuelle de la sphinctérotomie oddienne dans la chirurgie pour lésion bénigne de la voie biliaire principale chez l'adulte. Etude à propos de 100 cas de sphinctérotomies et d'une revue de la littérature des 10 dernières années. *Ann. Chir.* **30**:363, 1976.
25. Liguory C. & Leger L. Traitement perendoscopique des calculs de la voie biliaire principale. *Chirurgie* **102**:466, 1976.
26. Liguory C., Coffin J.C., Chiche B. & Leger L. Sphinctérotomies oddienne endoscopiques. *La nouvelle Presse Médicale* **8**:403, 1979.
27. Liguory C & Coffin J.C. Choledocoscopie per orale après sphinctérotomie endoscopique. II. Symposium International d'Endoscopie Digestive. *Paris* 16–17 Oct, 1978, Volume des resumes p. 51.
28. Marchal G. & Hureau J. *Les Tumeurs Oddiennes.* Masson, Paris, 1978.
29. Mazzariello R. Review of 220 cases of residual biliary tract calculi treated without reoperation: an eight year study. *Surgery* **73**:299, 1973.
30. Moreaux J. & Dufour P. Lithiase de la voie biliaire principale chez les sujets âgés. Modalités opératoire et choix de l'intervention. *Ann. Chir.* **20**:353, 1966.
31. Pribram B.O. Method for dissolution of common duct stones remaining after operation. *Surgery* **22**:806, 1947.
32. Rösch W., Koch H. & Demling L. Manometric studies during ERCP and endoscopic papillotomy. *Endoscopy* **8**:30, 1976.
33. Safrany L. Endoscopic treatment of biliary tract diseases. An international study. *Lancet* **4**:983, 1978.
34. Spohn K., Fux H.D. & Tewes G. Gallenwegserkrankungen. Chirurgie intra opérative diagnostik. *Therapiewoche* **9**:1033, 1975.
35. Wurbs D., Dammermann R., Ossenberg F.W. & Classen M. Descending sphincterotomy of the papilla of Vater through the T drain under endoscopic view: variants of endoscopic papillotomy (EPT). *Endoscopy* **10**:199, 1978.
36. Yamakawa T., Mieno K., Nogucki T. & Shikata J. An improved choledocofiberscope and non surgical removal of retained biliary calculi under direct visual control. *Gastrointest. endoscopy* **22**:160, 1976.
37. Zimmond P., Falkenstein D.B. & Kessler R.E. Management of biliary calculi by retrograde endoscopic instrumentation. *Gastrointest. endoscopy* **23**:2, 1976.

14. Biliary-Intestinal Operations

Operations that divert or augment biliary flow are performed for a wide variety of conditions. Many of these drainage procedures have already been discussed in the chapters dealing with bile duct physiology, gallstones, strictures, tumours, and cysts. This chapter summarises current knowledge regarding the indications, techniques, and results that one can expect from these operations. The following procedures are discussed in this chapter:
1. Sphincterotomy and sphincteroplasty.
2. Choledochoduodenostomy.
3. Cholecystojejunostomy.
4. Choledochojejunostomy and hepaticojejunostomy.

SPHINCTEROTOMY AND SPHINCTEROPLASTY

INDICATIONS

There are two main groups of indications for transduodenal division of the sphincter of Oddi:
1. Access to and exposure of the distal bile duct.
2. Improvement of biliary drainage.

ACCESS TO DISTAL BILE DUCT

Removal of gallstones. The usual indication in this category is the presence of gallstones or biliary debris in the distal duct which cannot be removed adequately by supraduodenal exploration. A further indication is when a probe cannot be made to pass through the sphincter of Oddi during bile duct exploration (Chapter 5). Gallstones in diverticula of the distal bile duct always require sphincterotomy for their removal (Chapter 5) [25].

Exposure of pancreatic duct. Transduodenal sphincterotomy may be necessary to gain access to the distal end of the pancreatic duct when this is explored in patients with chronic pancreatitis [1].

Tumours. Occasionally, probing of the bile ducts during exploration or examination of the papilla of Vater during laparotomy for jaundice arouses the suspicion of a benign or malignant tumour of the distal duct, or of the papilla. Under such circumstances a transduodenal sphincterotomy is performed.

Routine bile duct exploration? Enthusiastic reports have appeared in which all explorations of the bile ducts were carried out entirely through the transduodenal route [9, 14, 37, 38]. Transduodenal sphincterotomy, in most cases, carries a higher mortality than does supraduodenal exploration, and the authors believe that at present the indications for transduodenal exploration in the presence of choledocholithiasis should remain selective (Chapter 5).

IMPROVEMENT OF BILE FLOW

Complicated choledocholithiasis. It was shown in Chapter 5 that patients with primary bile duct stones, those who have multiple stones, and those who have had previous choledocholithotomies require not only the removal of these stones, but also a biliary drainage procedure in order to prevent recurrence and minimise the need for a further operation.

Stenosis of the papilla of Vater. This condition clearly requires an improvement of biliary drainage (see Stenosis of the papilla of Vater, Chapter 6).

Functional disorders and postcholecystectomy symptoms. Functional disorders of the sphincter of Oddi, particularly the hypertonic type, have been treated in the past with transduodenal division of the sphincter of Oddi. There is doubt about the very existence of these entities and there is also doubt that surgical intervention of this type influences the outcome (see Acalculous biliary disease, Chapter 12).

Chronic pancreatitis. Transduodenal sphincterotomy was at one time advocated as the treatment of choice for chronic relapsing pancreatitis. This was based on the assumption that the disease is caused by pancreatic reflux due to either sphincteric spasm or stenosis, and that sphincterotomy will prevent reflux by augmenting biliary flow. It was shown in Chapter 2 that reflux may well be a physiologic phenomenon, that sphincter spasm and stenosis prevent rather than aid reflux, and that a simple sphincterotomy will not augment biliary dynamics. For these reasons transduodenal sphincterotomy is not now recommended for the treatment of chronic pancreatitis [26, 46, 49, 50].

SPHINCTEROTOMY OR SPHINCTEROPLASTY?

A single-cut transduodenal sphincterotomy does not result in permanent alteration of biliary flow or in significant change of biliary dynamics (Chapter 2). This means that bile duct pressures, bile flow, and bile drainage remain unaltered; therefore, a sphincterotomy is unlikely to be of great value in permanently improving biliary drainage. However, this may not be true if the operation is performed for stenosis of the sphincter of Oddi, because here improvement of drainage may occur after the division of a stenotic sphincter. Also, duodenoscopy in a large series of cases, up to 9 years after a single-cut sphincterotomy, showed that the sphincter had healed without stenosis and that sphincteric activity had not been abolished [37]. There is also some evidence that, if a single-cut sphincterotomy is combined with a long T tube which remains in place for 6–8 weeks, a permanent increase in size of the lumen is obtained [4].

Transduodenal sphincteroplasty also does not alter the mechanism of bile emptying, but the sphincteric resistance is permanently lowered and the aperture of the sphincter is wider than normal when it is fully open [22, 26, 48]. This means that biliary drainage is improved, although bile flow is still intermittent, as in the normal subject. A growing body of clinical evidence also indicates improved biliary drainage with sphincteroplasty [21, 33, 39].

On present evidence, therefore, it appears that a single-cut sphincterotomy is satisfactory if the indication for its performance is access to the distal end of the bile duct; if the indication is a need to improve biliary drainage, however, a sphincteroplasty is probably the procedure of choice.

SURGICAL TECHNIQUE
EXPOSURE
The incision used and the exposure of the area are similar to those for cholecystectomy and for exploration of the bile duct (Chapter 5). The hepatic flexure of the colon may have to be mobilised downward to expose the duodenum. The duodenum and the head of the pancreas are fully mobilised. Many of these patients have already had a supraduodenal exploration, so the duodenum is frequently already mobilised (Fig. 14.1).

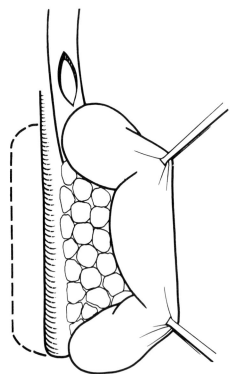

Fig. 14.1. Technique of transduodenal sphincterotomy. Duodenum and head of the pancreas are mobilised as a preliminary to duodenotomy. Dotted line indicates original position of duodenum.

DUODENOTOMY AND SPHINCTEROTOMY

If a supraduodenal choledochotomy has already been performed, it is best to pass a probe or Bakes dilator down the common bile duct and into the duodenum. This will localise the papilla of Vater. If this cannot be done the papilla can frequently be felt as a nipple-like structure through the duodenal wall.

The duodenotomy incision is best made in a longitudinal direction, because this can be easily extended up or down if required (Fig. 14.2). Two stay sutures of fine silk are inserted before the incision is made. The incision should be about 5

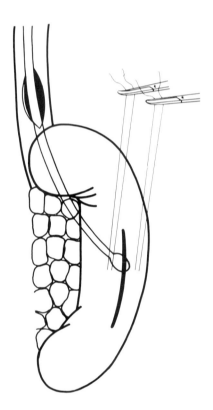

Fig. 14.2. Technique of transduodenal sphincterotomy. Site of duodenotomy incision is shown, after probe has been passed through the sphincter of Oddi.

cm long, centred on the probe or on the papilla of Vater, if this is palpable. If the position of the papilla is not known the incision is best commenced about the middle of the descending part of the duodenum, and carried downward. The commonest error is to make the incision too high in the second part of the duodenum.

The papilla of Vater is easily found if a probe passes through it. If a probe has not been passed the papilla may be seen or felt after duodenotomy as a firm nipple-like projection against the back wall of the duodenum, and the mucosa over it does not move as over the rest of the duodenum. As described in Chapter 1 the endoscopists describe the appearance of the papilla as a pink projection, above which there is a longitudinal fold with a transverse fold just above the papilla which may hide it from view and a distal longitudinal fold, or frenulum, leading up to the papilla from below. Also, if the biliary tract is intact, the gallbladder or the common bile duct can be squeezed and the papilla identified when bile appears from it. If a cholecystectomy and operative cholangiogram have been done, but the bile duct was not explored from above, saline can be syringed down the bile duct through the cholangiography catheter, if this has not been removed.

When the papilla is identified two stay sutures of fine silk are placed at its edge in the right upper quadrant, which is well away from the pancreatic duct opening. The stay sutures are lifted up and separated, and the papilla and the sphincter of Oddi are divided.

The division of the sphincter of Oddi may be performed in one of several ways. It may be possible to pass a probe or even a grooved director into the papilla and cut down on this with the scalpel. Alternatively, one blade of sharp, fine, pointed scissors is inserted into the papilla and the scissors are closed on this, thus cutting the papilla. The pointed type of angled Potts scissors used in vascular surgery are particularly suitable for this purpose. Lord Smith of Marlow (Rodney Smith) has devised special sphincterotomy scissors, which considerably facilitate the procedure (Fig. 14.3).

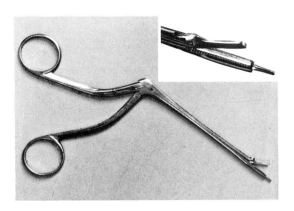

Fig. 14.3. Sphincterotomy scissors devised by Lord Smith of Marlow (Rodney Smith). Insert shows design of the blades (Heaton Grogan Co., London).

A technique has been devised in which a fine, rubber catheter is passed through the papilla after choledochotomy (Fig. 14.4). The end of the catheter is split into two halves, each of which is retracted to either side, thus facilitating division of the sphincter [17]. Another useful technique is to cut a longitudinal window in a rubber catheter and pass this through the papilla after choledochotomy and then cut the sphincter above. The catheter will protect the pancreatic duct [27].

The length of a single-cut sphincterotomy is usually about 1.5–2 cm.

SPHINCTEROPLASTY
Sphincteroplasty is performed in a way similar to sphincterotomy, but when the sphincteric muscle has been divided the mucosa of the bile duct is sutured to the

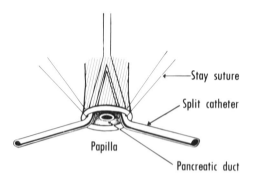

Fig. **14.4.** Technique of sphincterotomy or sphincteroplasty. Urethral catheter passed down the choledochotomy is split and each half retracted laterally, facilitating sphincterotomy and sphincteroplasty and also making pancreatic duct opening easily visible. Modified from Hutchison [17].

duodenal mucosa by four to six interrupted sutures of fine, chromic catgut, carried on an atraumatic needle. The sutures are placed in the upper half of the cut, in order to avoid the opening of the pancreatic duct, which should be identified (Fig. 14.5). Cutting of the sphincter and insertion of the sutures is best performed step by step, so that the last two sutures can be held up and used as traction on the area to facilitate further division of the sphincter. The sphincteric muscle retracts, and the sutures convert the sphincterotomy incision into a trough-like stoma.

The adequate length of a sphincteroplasty incision is difficult to state with certainty. Various surgeons have recommended incisions ranging from 1.5 to 3 cm, although one doubts whether the length of these cuts is ever accurately measured [14, 48]. In Chapter 1 it was shown that the sphincteric area has a variable extent in different subjects, with a range of 7 to 38 mm, though in the majority the range is 10 to 30 mm. In actual practice it is difficult to be sure that the surgeon has incised all the sphincteric area. On the other hand, if the incision is carried too far proximally, there is a risk of leakage. The authors, therefore, recommend that the incision include the whole of the projecting papilla, and that it be extended upward for a further distance of about 1 cm. Stitches are then inserted, and the size of the stoma so produced is examined with probes. If significant narrowing is still present the incision is cautiously extended upward

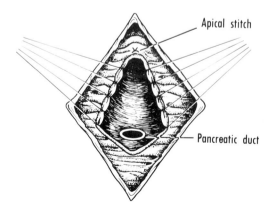

Fig. **14.5.** Completed sphincteroplasty. Note apical stitch, which is put at completion. Modified from Logerfo and Harrower [27].

until the bile duct suddenly widens out. This sudden widening of the bile duct is the critical part of the operation, because it means that the stoma of the sphincteroplasty equals the size of the common duct above the sphincter and, therefore, that the sphincter has now been completely divided. At this stage some surgeons advise the use of an 'apical stitch' to protect against leakage (Fig. 14.5) [22, 27]. It is rarely necessary for the total length of the incision to be any longer than 3 cm. When the sutures have been inserted the bile duct may be explored through the newly created stoma.

If a supraduodenal exploration has also been performed the insertion of a short-arm T tube is advised. A splint through the stoma appears to be unnecessary in humans, as evidenced by re-examination of the stoma at a later date, although in dogs a permanent reduction of sphincter resistance was obtained only when sphincteroplasty was combined with the use of a long T tube [26, 51].

CLOSURE OF DUODENOTOMY

In the past it was advocated that the duodenotomy incision be closed transversely in order to prevent duodenal obstruction. However, if the duodenotomy is carefully closed in two layers in the longitudinal direction, duodenal obstruction has not been reported [33]. The authors close the incision longitudinally, and so far no complications have occurred as a consequence.

RESULTS

MORTALITY

Transduodenal sphincterotomy or sphincteroplasty has been reported to have a relatively low mortality of from 1 to 6 per cent [9, 14, 22, 33, 38, 47]. However, the very low mortality rates of 1–2 per cent, which would favourably compare with supraduodenal exploration, only come from surgical centres where transduodenal sphincterotomy is commonly performed and, therefore, where the surgeons involved have special skill and experience with this relatively meticulous operation. There is evidence, however, that the *addition* of transduodenal sphincterotomy to supraduodenal exploration does increase the mortality rate [4, 7, 42, 38]. Patients requiring both modes of bile duct exploration are clearly not comparable to those who need one modality of exploration only, because the two groups will have different disease characteristics, and as a randomised controlled trial has not ever been performed such comparisons are not valid.

The most common cause of death is postoperative pancreatitis, but septic and chest complications are also responsible.

MORBIDITY

Early complications. Postoperative pancreatitis is the most important early complication. The frequency of postoperative pancreatitis after sphincterotomy or sphincteroplasty is uncertain because of difficulties in the diagnosis of mild cases. Review of the literature indicates that severe pancreatitis occurs in about 5 per cent [4, 9, 14, 22, 33]. The cause of pancreatitis is not clear. Duodenal leakage or gastrointestinal haemorrhage from the suture lines occurs in less than 1 per cent of cases, so that these complications are not common in practice.

Late complications. Reflux of duodenal contents following sphincteroplasty has been demonstrated on occasion in all the reported series. As discussed in Chapter 9, previously, it is obstruction or stasis to bile flow and not reflux which is responsible for cholangitis, so that postsphincteroplasty reflux in itself cannot be held responsible for postoperative morbidity [37, 38].

Stenosis of an adequately constructed sphincteroplasty appears to be an uncommon delayed complication, present in less than 1 per cent of cases [14, 22, 33, 39].

CHOLEDOCHODUODENOSTOMY

INDICATIONS

Choledochoduodenostomy is usually employed for augmentation or improvement of bile flow; the indications, therefore, are similar to those for sphincteroplasty. It is also sometimes used in bile duct reconstruction and for the bypass of malignant obstruction. A number of papers report enthusiastically on these various indications for choledochoduodenostomy [8, 19, 29, 30, 31, 41].

CHOLEDOCHOLITHIASIS
Choledochoduodenostomy is principally advocated in those cases in which the risk of recurrent or overlooked gallstones is high. These are patients with primary bile duct gallstones, those with multiple gallstones or extensive biliary debris, and those with previous choledocholithotomies (see Exploration of the Bile ducts in Chapter 5).

STENOSIS OF THE PAPILLA OF VATER
In the presence of fibrotic stenosis of the papilla of Vater, choledochoduodenostomy has been used to relieve the obstruction to bile flow (see Stenosis of the Papilla of Vater in Chapter 6).

CHRONIC PANCREATITIS
In company with other bypass procedures choledochoduodenostomy is of little value in relieving the pain of chronic pancreatitis [49, 50]. It is a valuable procedure in those patients who have chronic pancreatitis, but whose principal symptom is obstructive jaundice with little or no pain. In a number of these choledotholithiasis is also present, and a few also have stenosis of the papilla of Vater (Chapter 6).

MALIGNANT TUMOURS
For malignant obstruction of the distal common bile duct choledochoduodenostomy has been advocated as a palliative bypass measure. However, choledocho-

jejunostomy or cholecystoenterostomy is preferred in these cases, because the anastomosis is less likely to be compromised by tumour growth following the bypass. However, if the gallbladder has already been removed or contains gallstones, a choledochoduodenostomy may be preferred to a choledochoje-junostomy as a palliative procedure [23].

SURGICAL TECHNIQUE

Only side-to-side choledochoduodenostomy is described in this section. Division of the common bile duct and an end-to-side choledochoduodenostomy is occasionally performed after operative injuries to the duct and the surgical technique of this is described in Chapter 6 (Fig. 6.15).

The exposure of the operative area is similar to that used for exploration of the common bile duct and for transduodenal sphincterotomy or sphincter-oplasty. The gallbladder is removed first, though in many patients it has already been removed previously. The duodenum is completely mobilised in order to relieve tension on the anastomosis.

SIZE OF STOMA

Failure of choledochoduodenostomy is usually attributed to a stoma that is too small. The various advocates of this operation recommend stomas that vary from 1.5 to 3 cm [6, 8, 16, 29, 41]. Recent evidence shows that a stoma of 2.5 cm is necessary for the success of the operation [18, 19, 20].

The authors are amazed at the naïvety of surgeons who recommend large stomas of arbitrary size and ignore the diameter of the common bile duct. It is clear that the effective size of the opening can never be wider than the diameter of the common bile duct, irrespective of the size of the anastomotic stoma. Thus, a stoma which is about 8–10 mm wider than the common duct is created in order to allow for a possible postoperative narrowing of the anastomosis. The operation is contraindicated in undilated bile ducts, although in one recent report it was concluded that the size of the bile duct was not important [6, 11, 16, 36, 41]. However, the weight of evidence is that the operations should not be performed unless the bile duct is at least 1.5 cm in diameter.

THE ANASTOMOSIS

The steps of the operation are shown in Figs. 14.6 and 14.7. A longitudinal incision is made in the supraduodenal common bile duct, and this is followed by exploration of the bile ducts in the usual manner. An incision of similar size, either transverse or longitudinal, is made in the duodenum opposite (Fig. 14.6). If the first part of the duodenum is unduly tethered the bile duct incision is made on the lateral side and the duodenal one slightly more distally.

Some surgeons advocate a one-layer anastomosis, others a two-layer anasto-mosis, yet both obtain comparable results. The authors perform a two-layer anastomosis whenever possible because this may prevent a biliary leak. In some cases the bile duct will not accept an outer layer of sutures; then the anastomosis consists of only a single layer of interrupted sutures. Whatever the method used it

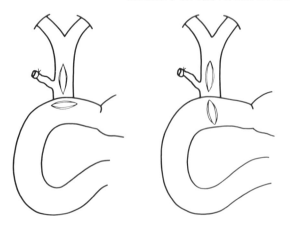

Fig. 14.6. Technique of side-to-side choledocho-duodenostomy. The two types of duodenal incision that may be used are shown.

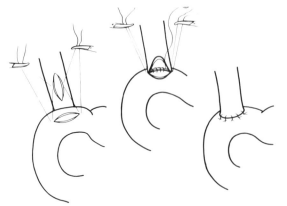

Fig. 14.7. Technique of side-to-side choledocho-duodenostomy, showing the steps in the construction of the anastomosis. Modified from Madden *et al* [29].

is essential to obtain accurate mucosa-to-mucosa apposition. The outer layer is of interrupted fine silk, and goes through the seromuscular layer of the duodenum and the adventitial layer of the bile duct. The inner layer is an all-coats continuous suture of fine, chromic catgut carried on an atraumatic needle (Fig. 14.7). When the anastomosis is completed the abdomen is closed with drainage of the operative area.

RESULTS

MORTALITY

Choledochoduodenostomy is a safe operation, with a low mortality, of the order of 3 per cent [8, 18, 20, 29, 31, 36, 47]. An analysis of these deaths shows that they occurred mostly in elderly patients and were not usually directly due to a complication of the choledochoduodenostomy itself.

MORBIDITY

Early complications. Temporary leakage of bile and wound infection is sometimes recorded. In general, early complications specific to choledochoduodenostomy are uncommon. In contradistinction to sphincterotomy and sphincter-oplasty postoperative pancreatitis is not a problem.

Late complications

Duodenal reflux. Reflux of duodenal contents through the stoma occurs in all cases. Advocates of this procedure have clearly shown that reflux in itself is never responsible for cholangitis, so long as the refluxed material can be rapidly cleared from the biliary tract [6, 18, 29, 30]. Reflux of barium and its rapid removal constitute, in fact, a standard method of testing the patency of the anastomosis (Fig. 14.8). Similarly, a 'gas choledochogram', shown in Fig. 14.9, is valuable in checking the patency of a choledochoduodenostomy. In this investigation the patient is given an effervescent drink and then placed in the supine position with his right side up in order to get the gas to enter the biliary system.

The only possible symptom which may be attributable to duodenal reflux is severe short-lived pain in the upper abdomen, which lasts for 1 or 2 minutes and immediately follows a meal. This symptom is commonly noted after a choledo-choduodenostomy, but it usually disappears 3 or 4 months post surgery.

Cholangitis—anastomotic stenosis. It has been shown that duodenal reflux after choledochoduodenostomy is normal, and in itself *does not cause cholangitis.*

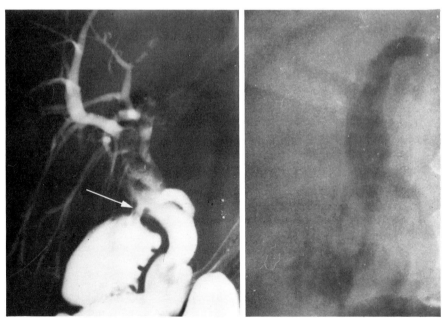

Fig. 14.8. (*left*) Barium meal examination to check patency of a previous choledochoduo-denostomy shown by arrow. Anastomosis was patent and refluxed barium was rapidly cleared from the ducts.

Fig. 14.9. (*right*) Gas choledochogram to outline bile ducts and thus check the patency of a previous choledochoduodenostomy. Note gas outlining the biliary tree.

Recurrent cholangitis attacks following choledochoduodenostomy do occur in up to 4 or 5 per cent of cases [6, 8, 12, 19, 30]. In these cases the cholangitis is usually caused by a combination of a stenotic choledochoduodenostomy, sumping of infected bile and biliary debris in the distal end of the common bile duct, and a high degree of distal bile duct obstruction (Fig. 14.10).

Anastomotic stenosis of a choledochoduodenostomy does occur, but its exact incidence is uncertain, because in a number of cases the anastomosis has become stenotic, but as bile is draining normally through the sphincter of Oddi the patient experiences no symptoms. Careful recent studies indicate that if the operation is done when the bile duct is dilated to 1.5 cm or more and when the

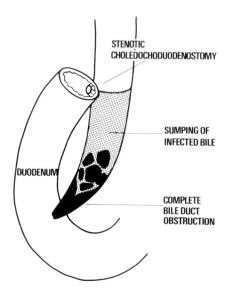

Fig. 14.10. Stenotic choledochoduodenostomy which is producing the symptoms of cholangitis.

stoma is 2.5 cm or larger the risk of an anastomotic stricture is of the order of 3 per cent [6, 18, 19, 20, 45].

The assessment of anastomotic stenosis is especially important in patients with recurrent symptoms severe enough to contemplate reoperation. Markedly delayed emptying of barium from the bile duct is the most important criterion, but even then this must be taken in conjunction with the clinical picture. Transnasal selective catheterisation of the bile duct via the stoma followed by contrast radiology was introduced by Ham and Sorby in Australia in 1973 and has become an accurate means of measuring stoma size (Fig. 14.11) [13].

A phenomenon peculiar to choledochoduodenostomy is the passage into and the retention within the distal bile ducts of tomato skins, vegetable fibres, and other food debris. While this complication is most uncommon and it is usually associated with a stenotic choledochoduodenostomy, nevertheless, it is a wise precaution to advise patients against eating tomato skins, grape pips, and similar fibre matter.

Thus, late failures of a choledochoduodenostomy are due to one or several of

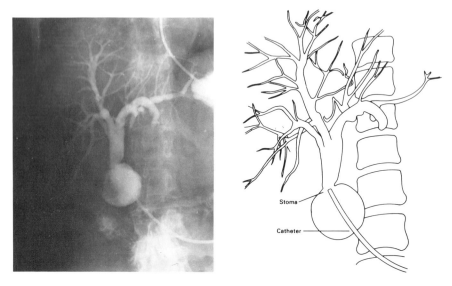

Fig. 14.11. Method of selective transnasal catheterisation and measurement of choledo-choduodenostomy stoma size described by Ham and Sorby [13]. Courtesy of Professor John M. Ham, Sydney, Australia.

the following: anastomotic stenosis, retention of gallstone, retention of biliary debris or vegetable fibres in the distal common bile duct, and the presence of infected bile. In any one case it may be difficult to untangle the importance of any of these factors, though usually anastomotic stenosis is the principal culprit.

In collected series a superficial inspection of late failures severe enough to warrant reoperation is low, of the order of 2 per cent. However, a careful search of the indications shows that in a significant number of cases the procedure was unnecessary and, therefore, the final result would have been equally satisfactory without the addition of choledochoduodenostomy. These unnecessary proce-dures clearly dilute the incidence of late failures. With this in mind the corrected incidence of late failures is probably of the order of 4 per cent.

SPHINCTEROPLASTY OR CHOLEDOCHODUODENOSTOMY?

In biliary-pancreatic surgery there are certain absolute indications and contra-indications for transduodenal sphincteroplasty and for choledochoduodenos-tomy, while under some other circumstances a choice is possible between the two procedures, should they need to be performed.

NO CHOICE POSSIBLE

Table 14.1 sums up these circumstances.

Table 14.1. Sphincteroplasty and choledochoduodenostomy—absolute indications and contraindications

	Sphincteroplasty (sphincterotomy)	Choledochoduodenostomy
Absolute indications	1. Stone impacted in distal common bile duct 2. Malignant tumour of distal common bile duct or papilla of Vater—for biopsy	
Absolute contraindications	Long benign stricture of distal common bile duct involving retropancreatic portion of the duct (Chapter 6)	Bile duct smaller than 1.5 cm in diameter.

A CHOICE CAN BE MADE

When the bile duct is bigger than 1.5 cm in diameter there is no stone or tumour in relation to the distal duct, and where there is no long, distal choledochal stricture a choice between the two procedures is possible if there is an indication to improve biliary drainage. Under these circumstances both procedures have their enthusiastic advocates, but up to now a comparison of *matched* groups of cases is not available.

Table 14.2 is a summary of an extensive literature survey of postoperative mortality, early postoperative morbidity, and late results, comparing the two operations.

The evidence indicates that the operative mortality is slightly higher after sphincteroplasty, but the long-term late results are more satisfactory than with

Table 14.2. Sphincteroplasty and choledochoduodenostomy—mortality, early and late morbidity

	Operative mortality	Early postoperative morbidity	Reoperation needed years later
Sphincteroplasty	5% (Elderly patients, pancreatitis)	15% (Pancreatitis, infection)	1%
Choledochoduodenostomy	3% (Elderly patients, general causes)	10% (Infection, general causes)	4%

choledochoduodenostomy. In sphincteroplasty the greatest postoperative danger is the onset of pancreatitis, and we know that younger patients can withstand this complication better than older subjects.

Because of the quoted evidence, when an indication is present for improved bile drainage and when a choice exists between sphincteroplasty and choledocho-duodenostomy, the authors prefer sphincteroplasty in the younger and fit patient, because the long-term results are better and because such a patient is more able to withstand an attack of postoperative pancreatitis, should it occur. A side-to-side choledochoduodenostomy is, however, preferred for the older, poorer-risk patient because the operative mortality is smaller, but then the patient must accept a somewhat higher rate of a late failure. Of course, a number of these elderly patients are dead from unrelated causes long before an anas-tomotic stricture becomes evident.

CHOLECYSTOJEJUNOSTOMY

INDICATIONS

Theoretically, a cholecystojejunostomy may be performed in order to bypass a bile duct obstruction located in the common bile duct below the level of insertion of the cystic duct. Cholecystojejunostomy is not used if the gallbladder is diseased or if the duct obstruction involves the cystic duct opening. Cholecystoje-junostomy does not always provide satisfactory drainage of bile, even when the above criteria have been satisfied. Some patients still have residual obstruction and bile duct infection after cholecystojejunostomy. The probable reasons for this are the narrow calibre and the tortuous course of the cystic duct, as well as the presence of a 'blind' stagnant segment of bile duct, distal to the cystic duct, in which organisms may proliferate (Fig. 14.12).

Cholecystojejunostomy has been virtually abandoned for all non-malignant

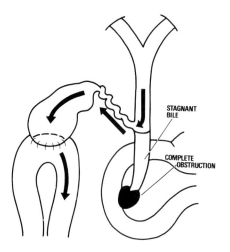

STAGNANT
BILE

COMPLETE
OBSTRUCTION

Fig. 14.12. Probable reasons for inade-quate long-term biliary drainage some-times seen after cholecystojejunostomy. There is a stagnant column of bile and drainage is through a tortuous channel passing through a convoluted, narrow cystic duct.

obstructive lesions of the distal bile duct, because in a significant proportion of cases it does not provide adequate long-term biliary drainage.

Cholecystojejunostomy finds its commonest use in the palliative decompression of malignant obstructions of the distal bile duct caused by carcinoma of the head of the pancreas. It is a useful procedure in these cases, because long-term palliation is not usually required and because the operation is quick and relatively simple to perform. However, even under these circumstances, it has been found that by employing the common duct rather than the gallbladder for a bypass a more satisfactory palliation of symptoms is obtained [5, 10]. The procedure is also used as a first-stage decompressive measure in patients who have a resectable malignant obstruction of the distal bile duct, but in whom it is elected to perform the resection in two stages.

A side-to-side cholecystojejunostomy is the type usually performed (Fig. 14.13). The stoma of the anastomosis is usually 2–3 cm wide. It is unnecessary to make

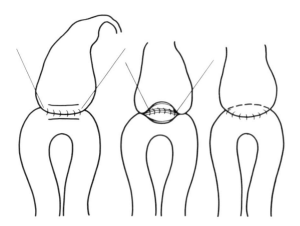

Fig. 14.13. Technique of side-to-side cholecystoje-junostomy. For details see text.

the stoma any larger, because drainage is governed by the very narrow cystic duct.

The authors use a two-layer anastomosis, though some surgeons prefer a single-layer technique. The outside layer is of continuous, fine silk, piercing the seromuscular layer of the gut and only the peritoneal coat of the gallbladder. The inner layer is an all-coats continuous suture employing fine chromic catgut on an atraumatic needle. This two-layer anastomosis is a possible safeguard against a biliary leak.

In the past a proximal jejunojejunostomy was performed in order to prevent reflex. In fact, jejunojejunostomy does not usually prevent reflux. As reflux in itself, in the absence of obstruction, does not produce cholangitis a jejunojejunostomy is unnecessary. For these reasons also a Roux-en-Y cholecystojejunostomy is unnecessary, particularly as the procedure is usually used only as either a palliative or a temporary measure.

CHOLEDOCHOJEJUNOSTOMY AND HEPATICOJEJUNOSTOMY

INDICATIONS

TRAUMATIC BILIARY STRICTURES

Hepaticojejunostomy or choledochojejunostomy is frequently indicated for the repair of traumatic biliary strictures, but the principles involved in the surgical technique are no different to the cases when these operations are performed on a normal bile duct. The reader should refer to Chapter 6.

PANCREATIC RESECTION

Choledochojejunostomy is one of the anastomoses following pancreaticoduo-denectomy or following total pancreatectomy, but a detailed consideration of these procedures is outside the scope of the book.

RECURRENT CHOLEDOCHOLITHIASIS AND FAILURE OF SPHINCTEROPLASTY OR CHOLEDOCHODUODENOSTOMY

There is a very small group of patients who have recurrent choledocholithiasis, frequently with intrahepatic gallstones, and many with associated stenosis of the papilla of Vater. Almost all these patients have had two or more previous simpler operations to rid them of their stones and to provide an alternative form of biliary drainage, such as sphincteroplasty or side-to-side choledochoduodenos-tomy, and have failed. These patients require a transection of the common bile duct and a choledochojejunostomy Roux-en-Y. The decision to divide the bile duct is a serious one, and it should not be entertained unless other simpler forms of drainage have failed.

CHRONIC PANCREATITIS

Roux-en-Y choledochojejunostomy has been advocated as a method of diver-sion of the biliary stream in the presence of chronic pancreatitis [3]. The useful-ness of this procedure, just as with choledochoduodenostomy, is confined to those cases in which the predominant symptom is obstructive jaundice rather than pain [49, 50].

CHOLEDOCHAL CYSTS

The indications for choledochal-cystojejunostomy or for cyst excision and hepa-ticojejunostomy are described in Chapter 8.

MALIGNANT OBSTRUCTION

Choledochojejunostomy or hepaticojejunostomy may be used as a method of palliative bypass procedure in patients with malignant obstruction of the extra-hepatic bile ducts, or following resection of such a tumour (Chapter 7).

SURGICAL TECHNIQUE

METHODS OF CHOLEDOCHOJEJUNOSTOMY

This procedure may be performed in one of several ways, according to whether a loop of jejunum or the Roux-en-Y method is used, and whether the bile duct is divided or left in continuity. The different types of choledochojejunostomy fall into two groups (Fig. 14.14):

1. Loop choledochojejunostomy (or hepaticojejunostomy) with division of the bile duct (Fig. 14.14a), or much less commonly without bile duct division (Fig. 14.14b). For extensive and unresectable bile duct carcinoma a very simple form of choledochojejunostomy has been described in which a T tube is thrust through

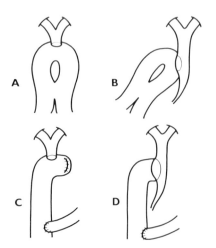

Fig. 14.14. Various types of choledocho-jejunostomy or hepaticojejunostomy. (a) Loop with entero-anastomosis and divi-sion of bile duct. (b) Loop with entero-anastomosis and bile duct in continuity. (c) Roux-en-Y and division of bile duct (preferred method). (d) Roux-en-Y and bile duct in continuity.

the tumour and into the jejunum to create what amounts to an internal fistula, because an exact anastomosis cannot be done [40]. A jejunojejunostomy is usually also employed, although this has little effect in preventing reflux of jejunal contents into the biliary tract as noted in subsequent barium meal examinations [52].

2. Roux-en-Y choledochojejunostomy (or hepaticojejunostomy), usually with division of the bile duct (Fig. 14.14c) or, much less commonly, without bile duct division (Fig. 14.14d).

The authors prefer division of the bile duct and choledochojejunostomy Roux-en-Y, because this appears to provide the most adequate form of long-term bile drainage [16, 24, 35, 43, 44]. The Roux-en-Y procedure also has other advantages over a loop, namely, there is no intestinal reflux, and if a postopera-tive fistula occurs it is merely a biliary fistula, rather than the more serious biliary and jejunal fistula. Finally, reoperations are easier with a Roux-en-Y than with a loop.

ROUX-EN-Y CHOLEDOCHOJEJUNOSTOMY

If the Roux-en-Y method is used the isolated segment of jejunum should be at least 40 cm long in order to minimise the incidence of reflux.

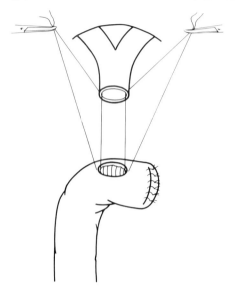

Fig. 14.15. Choledochojejunostomy, hepaticojejunostomy Roux-en-Y. Note stay sutures and that the end of the jejunum is closed and a new opening is made in its side nearby.

The steps in the operation of choledochojejunostomy or hepaticojejunostomy Roux-en-Y are shown in Figs. 14.15 and 14.16, and have also been described in the section dealing with traumatic strictures (Chapter 6 & Figs. 6.22–6.25). Note that the end of the jejunum is first closed. A new opening of the required size is then made in the side of the jejunum near the closed end (Fig. 14.15). A single layer of carefully placed interrupted fine, silk sutures are usually used, though some surgeons prefer fine, chromic catgut. Accurate apposition of the two surfaces is most important (Fig. 14.16). A two-layer anastomosis is only sometimes possible. A tube is not always necessary.

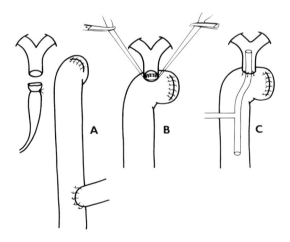

Fig. 14.16. Steps taken in choledochojejunostomy or in hepaticojejunostomy Roux-en-Y. (a) Construction of isolated jejunal segment which should be at least 40 cm long to eliminate gastrointestinal reflux. (b) The anastomosis. (c) Anastomosis completed and T tube in place as a temporary splint (T tube not always used).

RESULTS

The results of biliary-jejunal anastomoses are entirely different when the bile duct is of relatively normal quality, compared to cases in which the bile duct is of poor quality, such as in traumatic biliary strictures. Thus, the postoperative mortality and morbidity and the frequency of anastomotic stenosis is much higher with traumatic stricture repair. This is not a fault of the anastomosis, but rather a feature of the underlying condition (Chapter 6). The present discussion is restricted to instances in which the bile duct used for the anastomosis is of relatively normal quality.

MORTALITY

Bowers, in 1964, reported on 40 cases of choledochojejunostomy Roux-en-Y (this excludes pancreaticoduodenectomy and traumatic strictures) with two postoperative deaths, or a mortality of 5 per cent, while more recently Bismuth reported 123 consecutive cases without mortality [2, 3].

MORBIDITY

A temporary leakage of bile occasionally follows this operation, but in practice this is not a common problem.

There is some evidence that one of the long-term complications of a choledochojejunostomy is the development of a chronic peptic ulcer [3, 34]. The cause of this is not clear, but it may be due to a combination of bypass of alkaline bile from

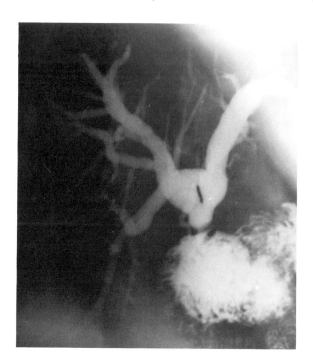

Fig. 14.17. Barium meal cholangiogram popularised by Robert Wise of Boston, to test the patency of a loop choledochojejunostomy. In this case barium entered and left the bile duct quickly, signifying that there is no stenosis. (This investigation is unsuitable after Roux-en-Y procedures.)

the duodenum and a secondary gastric hypersecretion [34]. It is also argued that
when an ulcer develops there is also some chronic pancreatitis as well, thereby
further reducing the alkalinity of the duodenum [2]. If a peptic ulcer does develop
it is treated along conventional lines.

Reflux of jejunal contents will occur regularly following loop jejunostomy,
and sometimes even with a Roux-en-Y anastomosis [32, 52]. Biliary-jejunal
anastomoses are similar to other biliary-intestinal procedures in that reflux in
itself is not responsible for bile duct infection, provided there is no anastomotic
stenosis and provided the refluxed material is rapidly cleared. Indeed, the reflux
of barium through a hepaticojejunal anastomosis has been used as a method of
testing its patency (Fig. 14.17) [52]. The symptoms of cholangitis signify anastomotic stenosis and not reflux.

The frequency of anastomotic stenosis following choledochojejunostomy in
which the bile duct was of relatively normal quality was one case in 77, or an
incidence of 1.3 per cent, as reported by Bowers [3]. A similar low incidence of
choledochojejunal anastomotic stricture formation was found by Warren, Kune,
and Poulantzas in 1966, when they reviewed 82 cases of pancreaticoduodenectomy performed at the Lahey Clinic for chronic relapsing pancreatitis [50]. In
that series only one patient developed an anastomotic stricture, an incidence of
1.2 per cent. This low incidence of anastomotic stenosis, when the duct is normal,
is in marked contrast with the high incidence of recurrent stricture formation in
patients whose operation is performed for a traumatic biliary stricture.

REFERENCES

1. BARTLETT M.K. & CARTER E.L. The technic of pancreatic duct exploration for
   recurrent pancreatitis. *Am. J. Surg.* **105:**755, 1963.
2. BISMUTH H., FRANCO D. & CORLETTE M.B. Longterm results of Roux-en-Y hepaticojejunostomy. *Surg. Gynec. Obstet.* **146:**161, 1978.
3. BOWERS R.F. Morbid conditions following choledochojejunostomy. *Ann. Surg.*
   159:424, 1964.
4. BRAASCH J.W. & McCANN J.C. JR. Observations on single section of the sphincter of
   Oddi. *Surg. Gynec. Obstet.* **125:**355, 1967.
5. BUCKWALTER J.A., LAWTON R.L. & TIDRICK R.T. Bypass operations for neoplastic
   biliary tract obstruction. *Am. J. Surg.* **109:**100, 1965.
6. CAPPER W.M. External choledochoduodenostomy. An evaluation of 125 cases. *Br. J.
   Surg.* **49:**292, 1961.
7. COLCOCK B.P. & PEREY B. Exploration of the common bile duct. *Surg. Gynec. Obstet.*
   118:20, 1964.
8. DEGENSHEIN G.A. Choledochoduodenostomy: an 18 years study of 175 consecutive
   cases. *Surgery* **76:**319, 1974.
9. DROUIN J.P. Cholecystectomy with routine sphincteroplasty. *Canad. J. Surg.* **7:**367,
   1964.
10. ELMSLIE R.G. & SLAVOTINEK A.H. Surgical objectives in unresected cancer of the
    head of the pancreas. *Br. J. Surg.* **59:**508, 1972.
11. ENGIN A., HABERAL M. & SANAC Y. Side-to-side choledochoduodenostomy in the
    management of choledocholithiasis. *Br. J. Surg.* **65:**99, 1978.
12. FREUND H., CHARUZI I., GRANIT G. & BERLATZKY Y. Choledochoduodenostomy in
    the treatment of benign biliary tract disease. *Arch. Surg.* **112:**1032, 1977.

13. HAM J.M. & SORBY W. Measurements of stoma size following choledochoduodenostomy by transduodenal cholangiography. *Br. J. Surg.* **60:**940, 1973.

14. HARDY E.G. & DAVENPORT T.J. The transduodenal approach to the common bile duct. *Br. J. Surg.* **56:**667, 1969.

15. HERZOG K.H. Choledochoduodenostomy: indications and technique. *Chirurg.* **37:**486, 1966.

16. HESS W. *Surgery of the biliary passages and the pancreas.* Van Nostrand, Princeton, N.J., 1965.

17. HUTCHISON D.E. Sphincteroplasty of ampulla of Vater. A safe technique. *Br. J. Surg.* **56:**593, 1969.

18. JOHNSON A.G. & STEVENS A.E. Importance of the size of the stoma in choledochoduodenostomy. *Gut* **10:**68, 1969.

19. JOHNSON A.G. & RAINS A.J.H. Choledochoduodenostomy. *Br. J. Surg.* **59:**277, 1972.

20. JOHNSON A.G. & RAINS A.J.H. Prevention and treatment of recurrent bile duct stones by choledochoduodenostomy. *World J. Surg.* **2:**487, 1978.

21. JONES S.A., STEEDMAN R.A., KELLER T.B. & SMITH L.L. Transduodenal sphincteroplasty (not sphincterotomy) for biliary and pancreatic disease. Indications, contraindications and results. *Am. J. Surg.* **118:**292, 1969.

22. JONES S.A. & SMITH L.L. A reappraisal of sphincteroplasty (not sphincterotomy). *Surgery* **71:**565, 1972.

23. KAMINSKI D.L., BARNER H.B., CODD J.E. & WOLFE B.M. Evaluation of choledochoduodenostomy in the treatment of malignant obstruction of the biliary tree. *Am. J. Surg.* **132:**565, 1976.

24. KEHNE J.H. & CAMPBELL R.E. Choledochojejunostomy en Roux Y. *A.M.A. Arch. Surg.* **73:**12, 1956.

25. KUNE G.A. Gallstones in diverticula of the lower common bile duct. *Gut* **6:**95, 1965.

26. KUNE G.A. The influence of structure and function in the surgery of the biliary tract. Arris and Gale Lecture, April, 1970. *Ann. R. Coll. Surg. Eng.* **47:**78, 1970.

27. LOGERFO F.W. & HARROWER H.W. A simple technique for total sphincteroplasty. *Surg. Gynec. Obstet.* **141:**615, 1975.

28. LOUW J.H., MARKS I.N. & BANKS S. The management of severe acute pancreatitis. *Postgrad. Med. J.* **43:**31, 1967.

29. MADDEN J.L., CRUWEZ J.A. & TAN P.Y. Obstructive (surgical) jaundice: an analysis of 140 consecutive cases and a consideration of choledochoduodenostomy in its treatment. *Am. J. Surg.* **109:**89, 1964.

30. MADDEN J.L., CHUN J.Y., KANDALAFT S. & PAREKH M. Choledochoduodenostomy. An unjustly maligned surgical procedure. *Amer. J. Surg.* **119:**45, 1970.

31. MAGAREY J.R. Biliary fenestration. *Br. J. Surg.* **53:**41, 1966.

32. MAINGOT R. Injuries of the biliary tract, including operative and postoperative complications. In R. Smith & S. Sherlock (eds.), *Surgery of the Gallbladder and Bile Ducts.* Butterworth, London, 1964.

33. MARSHALL R.D. Transduodenal ampulloplasty in the surgery of the common bile duct. *Aust. New Zeal. J. Surg.* **32:**160, 1962.

34. MCARTHUR M.S. & LONGMIRE J.P. JR. Peptic ulcer disease after choledochojejunostomy. *Am. J. Surg.* **122:**155, 1971.

35. MORGENSTERN L. & SHORE J.M. Selection of an optimal procedure for decompression of the obstructed common bile duct. Experimental and clinical observations. *Am. J. Surg.* **119:**38, 1970.

36. ORR K.B. External choledochoduodenostomy for retained common duct stone: reappraisal of an old technique. *Med. J. Aust.* **2:**1027, 1966.

37. PEEL A.L.G., HERMON-TAYLOR J. & RITCHIE H.D. Technique of transduodenal exploration of the common bile duct. *Ann. R. Coll. Surg. Eng.* **55:**236, 1974.

38. PEEL A.L.G., BOURKE J.B., HERMON-TAYLOR J., MACLEAN A.D.W., MANN C.V. & RITCHIE H.D. How should the common bile duct be explored? *Ann. R. Coll. Surg. Eng.* **56:**124, 1975.

39. ROTHWELL-JACKSON R.L. Sphincteroplasty in the treatment of biliary and pancreatic disease. *Br. J. Surg.* **55:**616, 1968.

40. SAYPOL G.M. Biliary-intestinal anastomosis. *Ann. Surg.* **152:**103, 1960.

41. SCHEIN C.J., SHAPIRO N. & GLIEDMAN M.L. Choledochoduodenostomy as an adjunct to choledocholithotomy. *Surg. Obstet. Gynec.* **146:**25, 1978.

42. SHIEBER W. Duodenotomy with common duct exploration. *Arch. Surg. (Chicago)* **85:**944, 1962.

43. SMITH R. The short-circuiting operations in biliary tract surgery. In R. Smith & S. Sherlock (eds.), *Surgery of the Gallbladder and Bile Ducts.* Butterworth, London, 1964.

44. SMITH R. Hepaticojejunostomy with transhepatic intubation. A technique for very high strictures of the hepatic ducts. *Br. J. Surg.* **51:**186, 1964.

45. STUART M. & HOERR S.C. Late results of side-to-side choledochoduodenostomy and of transduodenal sphincterotomy for benign disorders: 20 year comparative study. *Am. J. Surg.* **123:**67, 1972.

46. THISTLETHWAITE J.R. & SMITH D.F. Evaluation of sphincterotomy for the treatment of chronic recurrent pancreatitis. *Ann. Surg.* **158:**226, 1963.

47. THOMAS C.G., NICHOLSON C.P. & OWEN J. Effectiveness of choledochoduodenostomy and transduodenal sphincterotomy in the treatment of benign obstruction of the common duct. *Ann. Surg.* **173:**845, 1971.

48. VAJCNER A., GROSSLING S. & NICOLEFF D.M. Physiologic evaluation of sphincteroplasty. *Surgery* **62:**589, 1967.

49. WARREN K.W. Surgical management of chronic relapsing pancreatitis. *Am. J. Surg.* **117:**24, 1969.

50. WARREN K.W., KUNE G.A. & POULANTZAS J.K. Surgical treatment of chronic pancreatitis. *Proceedings of the Third World Congress of Gastroenterology, Vol. 4,* Third World Congress of Gastroenterology, Tokyo, 1966, p. 385.

51. WEBB W.R., DEGUZMAN V.C., HOOPES J.E. & DOYLE R.E. Experimental evaluation of sphincteroplasty with and without long-arm T tubes. *Surg. Gynec. Obstet.* **119:**62, 1964.

52. WISE R.E. & KEEFE J.P. Radiologic evaluation of hepaticojejunal anastomoses. *Surgical Clin. N. Amer.* **48:**579, 1968.

15. Hepato-Biliary Hydatid Disease

BY BARRIE J. AARONS & SAMUEL C. FITZPATRICK

LIFE CYCLE

The life cycle of *Taenia Echinococcus* (*E. granulosus*) is well established (Fig. 15.1). Humans, like sheep, ingest the tapeworm ova excreted in the faeces of the tapeworm-infested dog. The ova reach the stomach, hatch, the oncospheres are released, become activated, penetrate the wall of the intestine and pass via the portal blood vessels to the liver. Some develop there while others are destroyed or pass on to the lungs or other sites. Development is slow and, for example, the liver cysts of sheep are only 4–5 mm in diameter when 3 months old and reach 10 mm by 4–5 months [2].

PATHOLOGY AND NATURAL HISTORY OF LIVER HYDATIDS

SITES OF CYSTS AND GROWTH RATES

Two-thirds of all hydatid cysts in man occur in the liver. In 75 per cent the cyst is solitary, but in 25 per cent there is more than one cyst in the liver. In 40 per cent of liver hydatids there are cysts elsewhere in the body.

Rate of growth seems to depend on the resistance offered by the enveloping structures. Cysts near the surfaces of the liver, especially in the left lobe, seem to grow more rapidly than centrally placed cysts and pulmonary and peritoneal hydatids grow much faster than liver cysts. As an approximation, liver cysts increase their diameter by 2–4 cm per year.

EFFECT ON BILE DUCTS AND LIVER

As the cyst enlarges it compresses adjacent liver and stretches the bile channels in its immediate vicinity. Lateral openings develop in these overstretched ducts, producing fistulae when the hydatid itself ruptures (Fig. 15.2).

If the cyst is in the vicinity of the hilum of the liver it may cause obstructive jaundice by extrinsic obstruction of the main bile ducts, but by far the commonest cause of obstructive jaundice is rupture of cyst elements into the biliary tree (Fig. 15.3).

As the cyst enlarges and compresses the liver, atrophy occurs in the adjacent liver, presumably due to compression of the blood supply. Compensatory hyper-

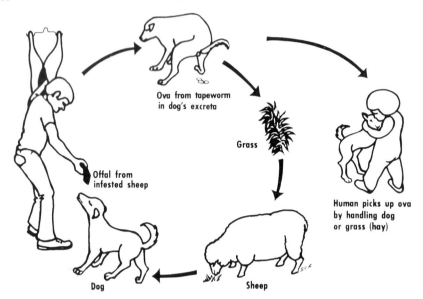

Fig. 15.1. The life cycle of the hydatid parasite *E. granulosus.*

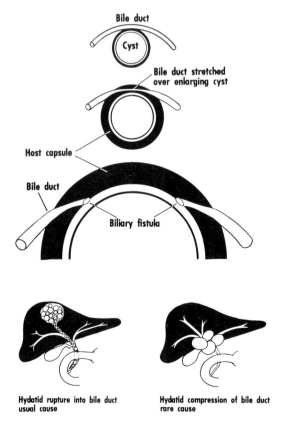

Fig. 15.2. The mode of development of cyst-biliary connections.

Fig. 15.3. Diagram illustrating the ways in which hydatids can cause obstructive jaundice. (*left*) Usual cause—hydatid rupture into the bile duct. (*right*) Rare cause—hydatid cysts compress bile ducts in the porta hepatis.

trophy of healthy liver occurs elsewhere. The host capsule in the liver tends to calcify after many years and, radiologically, a complete or an interrupted opaque ring may be seen (Figs. 15.5 & 15.6).

EFFECT ON ADJACENT STRUCTURES

When cysts present on the liver surface adhesions to adjacent structures may develop. Complicated cysts or previous surgery are more frequently associated with adhesions. Cysts presenting on the dome of the right lobe of the liver usually elevate the right hemidiaphragm. As enlargement continues without rupture, atrophy occurs of the diaphragm muscles stretched over the cyst, and if adhesions form, subsequent rupture of the cyst into the right pleural cavity may occur. If pulmonary adhesions precede rupture, cyst contents discharge into the lung, and even into the bronchial tree.

PATHOLOGY

PRIMARY CYST

This consists of a single sac of fluid within a host capsule which is compressed liver and fibrous tissue (Fig. 15.4). The wall of the sac consists of the laminated membrane layer lined internally by germinal cells which give rise to brood capsules, each containing 15–20 protoscolices. Each proscolix resembles a tapeworm head and is capable of developing in the intestine of the dog into a hydatid tapeworm. Experiments in Australia have failed to implant *E. granulosus* in the cat or fox, but the Australian dingo has been shown to act as a definitive host [2]. Some of these brood capsules drop off into the fluid as 'hydatid sand' and by disintegration set free protoscolices capable of forming new cysts when disseminated in the host.

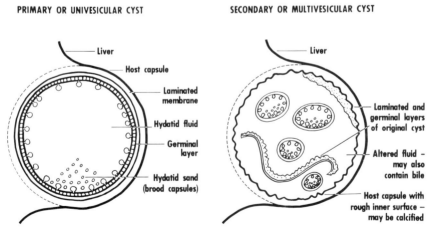

PRIMARY OR UNIVESICULAR CYST   **SECONDARY OR MULTIVESICULAR CYST**

Fig. 15.4. (*left*) Pathological features of the primary cyst. (*right*) Pathological features of the secondary cyst.

SECONDARY CYST

If the sac of the primary cyst ruptures, remaining scolices and pieces of germinal layer may form daughter cysts, each in every respect similar to the mother cyst, but not having individual host capsules if they remain within the original host capsule in the liver (Fig. 15.4). The collection of daughter cysts in such a host capsule together with remnants of the mother cyst membrane is referred to as a secondary or multivesicular cyst.

After rupture the host capsule becomes thicker, often begins to calcify, and adhesions tend to form to surrounding structures. If a bile leak is present some or all of the cyst contents may be bile stained. Otherwise, mother and daughter cyst walls are pure white. If the surgeon fails to eliminate all living elements of the primary cyst then a secondary cyst, identical to that described above, may form, filling and even expanding the original host capsule.

SECONDARY IMPLANTATION

When hydatid fluid containing protoscolices and pieces of laminated membrane containing brood capsules is spilled into the serous cavities, secondary implantation and growth may occur, usually forming univesicular cysts surrounded by host capsules of fibrous tissue and peritoneum. However, in many situations this is visceral peritoneum and so the wall of gut, bladder, uterus, or omentum may become involved in the host capsule. The spillage of living hydatid germinal elements is not always followed by secondary implantation and growth. In some cases where frank rupture has occurred some months prior to laparotomy, small white specks may be seen scattered throughout the peritoneal cavity resembling miliary tuberculosis. These when examined histologically, show that they are suppressed hydatid protoscolices in dense capsules of fibrous tissue. At subsequent laparotomy, a year or two later, no sign of these may remain.

NATURAL HISTORY

The natural history of liver hydatids is continuing growth and with time the onset of complications, of which rupture is the most important and potentially most serious.

RUPTURE

Cyst rupture is the commonest complication. This may mean cyst death because of complete extrusion of the cyst's contents and sac into the biliary tree and thence to the gut with evacuation in the faeces, or evacuation into the peritoneal cavity where host immune reaction may prevent further development, or into the bronchial tree, and expectoration. Unfortunately all of these are rare and most cysts not only survive rupture but usually also multiply and disseminate as a result.

Rupture may mean rapid death of the patient from anaphylactic shock or less severe but uncomfortable anaphylactic reactions, such as urticaria, bronchospasm, or angioneurotic oedema. Usually rupture produces abdominal pain either due to peritoneal irritation or in the case of intrabiliary rupture to obstruction of the bile duct by hydatid elements. This latter is usually associated with transient, though often repeated, obstructive jaundice. In the long term, rupture may give rise to secondary hydatidosis usually in the peritoneal cavity, but occasionally in the pleural, and rarely in the pericardial spaces.

SUPPURATION

Suppuration occurring in a liver hydatid which has not been treated surgically is an uncommon complication [12]. Previously it was thought to be more common, but what was thought to be pus was a thick bile-stained material containing leucocytes, but no bacteria. Usually these were cysts that had ruptured into bile ducts and were no longer viable. It is important to distinguish the true infected cyst, as its management is different. Suppuration more commonly follows surgical treatment especially when external or internal drainage is utilised. As will be shown, external drainage of a non-suppurating cyst is neither necessary nor desirable.

DEATH OF CYST

Death of the cyst in the liver may occur spontaneously. Usually the cyst has communicated with the biliary tree and it is thought that the bile kills the cyst. When death does occur the cyst's host capsule calcifies and this calcified capsule tends to appear irregular in outline (Fig. 15.5). However, it is important to note that minimal calcification does *not* mean death of the cyst.

DIAGNOSIS OF LIVER HYDATIDOSIS

CLINICAL FEATURES

The disease presents various clinical pictures. In a personal series of the authors of over 200 cases the following was the frequency of various modes of presentation:

1. Enlargement of the liver—66 per cent.
2. Latent unexpected finding on laparotomy, on radiology, or on liver imaging—13 per cent.
3. Biliary colic usually with transient jaundice (due to intrabiliary rupture)—10 per cent.
4. Secondary peritoneal hydatidosis (abdominal masses)—8 per cent.
5. Acute abdomen (due to intraperitoneal rupture of cyst, either spontaneous, or posttraumatic)—2.5 per cent.
6. Lung base problem—1.5 per cent.
7. Other rare presentations—1 per cent.

We therefore emphasise that the common mode of presentation of liver hydatids is a palpable mass in the abdomen and this is usually in the liver. Biliary colic, with or without jaundice, in the absence of gallstones should cause one to think of the possibility of a liver hydatid discharging into the biliary tree. If in

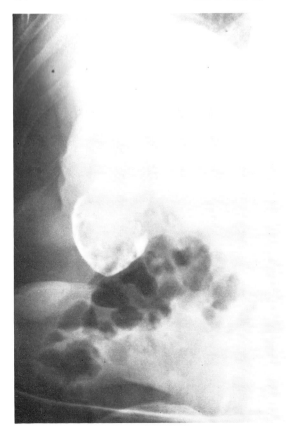

Fig. 15.5. Dead hydatid producing extensive calcification, which is irregular in outline.

doubt about the cause of hepatic enlargement or upper abdominal pain, serology should be done.

IMMUNOLOGICAL STUDIES

Immunoelectrophoresis (IEP). This test is based on the presence of the ARC 5 as its criterion of positivity. It is the test of choice for immunological diagnosis of active hydatid disease in humans. So specific is this test that the hydatid complement fixation test and Casoni tests with their high incidence of false results can no longer be recommended as diagnostic aids. A positive IEP test confirms hydatid disease, but although a negative test would not rule out the possibility of infection, false negatives in active liver hydatidosis are very uncommon. In these cases the latex agglutination (LA) and indirect haemagglutination tests (IH) may be positive, adding support to the possibility of hydatid disease suggested clinically. The observation of three or more bands in the IEP test in the absence of an ARC 5 band suggests, but does not confirm, hydatidosis.

Latex agglutination (LA). This test is recommended as a screening test, as it is relatively easy to perform and requires no specialised equipment. It has a low rate of false positive results, but immunological confirmation by IEP is necessary. It is therefore recommended that the serum of patients suspected of harbouring active hydatid cysts should be tested by both the IEP and LA methods as a routine.

RADIOLOGY

This is of value in the preoperative diagnosis of hydatids of the liver only when finding a calcified ring in the liver area in plain x-rays of the chest or abdomen (Fig. 15.6). A thin round or oval dense line with smooth or irregular contour may represent calcification in the host capsule of a living or a dead cyst. Immunological studies and liver imaging are necessary to confirm the diagnosis.

Fig. 15.6. Radiograph of the liver area showing a calcified ring caused by a hydatid.

LIVER IMAGING

Liver imaging is essential for the diagnosis of liver hydatids. Radionuclide scanning of the liver remains a useful screening test for the presence of a liver hydatid (Fig. 15.7). However, ultrasound examination of the liver can give more precise information on the location and nature of the hydatid (Fig. 15.8). The ultrasound can also outline the biliary ductal system if jaundice is also present (Chapter 4). Computed tomographic scanning appears to be the most precise means at present of determining the nature and extent of a mass lesion in the liver, including a liver hydatid, and the films obtained can be very useful in the planning of the surgical approach to the hydatid (Fig. 15.9).

Fig. 15.7. Radionuclide scan of the liver with a large hydatid in the right lobe.

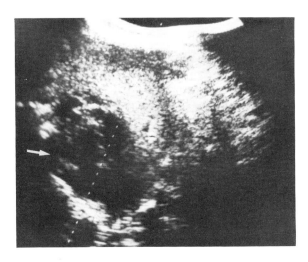

Fig. 15.8. Ultrasonography showing a large hydatid cyst in the liver with internal reflections created by daughter cysts.

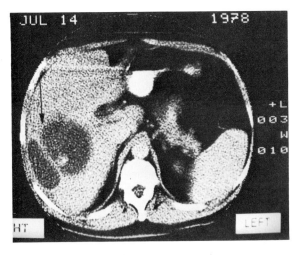

Fig. 15.9. Computed tomographic scan of the abdomen outlining the precise location and nature of this large multivesicular hydatid, which was also complicated by intrahepatic rupture and jaundice. The scan helped to plan surgical exposure of the cyst.

OPERATIVE DIAGNOSIS

The cyst is usually felt as a rounded mass presenting on one or two surfaces of the liver. The presenting surface is usually light brown, yellowish, or white and may be adherent to adjacent structures. It is not usually possible to detect fluctuance unless the cyst has recently leaked, because it is tense and there is a dense host capsule around it. Aspiration of the cyst is usually diagnostic, producing clear fluid, but must not be carried out without due precautions, since spillage of fluid may lead to anaphylaxis or dissemination, or both. The laminated membrane wall of the cyst or the daughter cysts are readily identified macroscopically and confirmed histologically. Sometimes bile leaking into or around the cyst colours the normally pure white membrane yellow. If the fluid has escaped from a ruptured cyst via the biliary tree all that may be found within the host capsule is some yellow membrane and sometimes some thick, yellow pultaceous material.

It is to be noted that calcification when present is in the host capsule and not in the parasite. The parasite wall is never adherent to the host capsule.

Operative choledochography is useful to assist in localising a cyst which has ruptured into a bile duct (Figs. 15.10 & 15.11). This would have been suspected

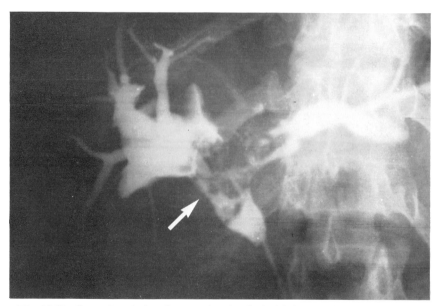

Fig. 15.10. Operative cholangiogram showing hydatid elements in the biliary tree.

preoperatively by the history of biliary colic, jaundice, bilirubinuria, and bilirubinaemia, and especially the finding of laminated membrane in the faeces.

POST-SURGERY FOLLOW-UP DIAGNOSIS OF RECURRENT DISEASE

The diagnosis of residual or recurrent cysts is a most important duty of the treating surgeon. A thorough clinical examination for associated cysts, for

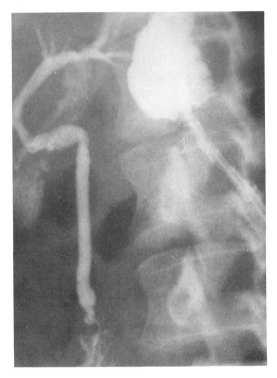

Fig. 15.11. Operative cholangiogram of a patient
whose hydatid cyst had
ruptured into the bile duct
and then became infected.
There is a communication
with the left hepatic duct,
but there are no intrabiliary hydatid elements pre-
sent.

example in the lung, should have been made prior to surgery. However, if the
diagnosis was first made at operation, this examination should be made in the
early convalescent period. Associated intraperitoneal or renal cysts should have
been excluded at laparotomy. A chest x-ray should clarify the pulmonary
situation and physical examination will eliminate peripheral, usually intramuscular cysts, and unless there are clinical indications to suggest the possibility of
intracranial cysts, it is not warranted to carry out sophisticated investigations,
such as computerised axial tomography of the brain or bone scans.

In the long term it is essential to follow-up all hydatid patients since recurrent
cysts or further development of undetected associated cysts is common. These
people should be re-examined 6 months and 1 year postoperatively and at the
annual check an IEP should be done. Current indications suggest that in most
cases this will be negative 12 months after successful treatment. Currently, a
combined investigation is being carried out in Argentina and Australia to
evaluate the IEP test in this respect [3].

If the IEP test is positive at that stage, and clinical examination and chest
x-ray fail to indicate cysts, then liver imaging should be done.

It is not yet known how long cases should be followed up with the IEP test.
Prior to the availability of the test, we have found recurrent or residual active
cysts as long as 9 years after the first operation. It is thought possible that if the
IEP test remains negative for 2 successive years following surgery, then unless
further exposure to infestation occurs, the patient is cured.

TREATMENT

DEAD CYSTS—NO TREATMENT

It is both unnecessary and unwise to interfere with dead cysts, as this may lead to bacterial infection with possible disastrous results, such as the development of cholangitis, or of a biliary fistula. The finding of a negative IEP test in a patient with a calcified liver cyst is an indication for 'masterly inactivity' unless infection has already intervened.

MEDICAL TREATMENT

Mebendazole is a drug currently being evaluated with regard to effectiveness, and may be available for general use in the near future [4, 5, 9, 10].

Mebendazole is a potent oral antihelminthic which was found to have a marked effect on cysts of *E. granulosus* in mice [9, 11]. Chevis believes that Mebendazole damages the cyst wall which then ceases producing the antigenic material. There is then a fall in osmotic pressure and the cyst collapses and the cyst wall then breaks up [6]. Other workers have suggested that Mebendazole causes the cysts to rupture but Chevis' theory is supported by the fact that in over 150 human treatments around the world, including 14 patients by Goodman in Australia, no adverse reactions have yet occurred [8]. This method of treatment looks promising, but as yet it is not known whether the drug reaches all cysts in sufficient amounts to be effective. Also, possible side effects have not been fully evaluated.

Mebendazole may find its greatest use in cases in which the disease is very widespread or recurrent after multiple previous operations, when surgery is contraindicated because of the poor general condition of the patient, or when preoperative or peroperative spillage has occurred.

OPERATIVE TREATMENT

At present the recommended treatment for all living hydatid cysts of the liver is surgical removal of the cyst. This certainly applies to symptomatic and complicated cysts, but it also applies to the symptomless cysts, in order to prevent the onset of complications.

The surgical approach to the operation depends on the size and position of the cyst. Cysts in the left lobe of the liver and low on the right lobe can be approached abdominally, but cysts high in the right liver lobe usually require a thoracoabdominal approach, but at times a thoracic approach only is adequate.

The cardinal principles of treatment are:
1. Prevention of spillage.
2. Removal of all living cyst elements.
3. Closure of biliary communications.
4. Sterilisation of the cavity, and closure.
5. Treatment of complicated cysts.

PREVENTION OF SPILLAGE

In the past, surgeons have relied on packing around the cyst and prior aspiration with or without instillation of scolicides. In 1971, Saidi and Nazarian described both the use of a cryogenic cone adhered to the cyst surface by freezing, and the use of 0.5 per cent silver nitrate as a better scolicide than others currently in use [13]. Cetrimide (1 per cent) is a suitable alternative. Such a cone eliminates the risk of spillage, provided that complete and continuous adhesion is maintained. Recently, one of us (B.J.A.) has designed a suction cone with a variable angle of attitude which has been used successfully in cases known to be highly sensitive to hydatid fluid even where a cyst was situated high on the liver and difficult of access (Fig. 15.12).

The use of an adherent cone eliminates the need for aspiration and instillation of a scolicide prior to opening the cyst, and virtually eliminates the risk of anaphylaxis. If a suction or cryogenic cone is not available then every effort must

Fig. 15.12. Hydatid suction cone with a variable angle of attitude. Devised by Barrie J. Aarons.

be made to prevent spillage by careful packing and aspiration of univesicular cysts with a fine trochar and cannula attached to suction prior to opening the cyst. Also, it is advisable to leave the cyst undisturbed for 5 minutes after packing before inserting the trochar and cannula, to allow time for living cyst elements free in the cyst fluid to settle to the bottom [7]. If the cyst contains daughter cysts, prior aspiration is impossible. As daughter cysts are prone to rupture during removal it is recommended that they be carefully removed with a spoon or with a wide-bore sucker using wide-bore tubing to the trap bottle, to avoid blockage at connections.

In patients known to be very sensitive to hydatid fluid, that is, cases exhibiting previous anaphylaxis or a strong reaction to a half dose Casoni test, preoperative desensitisation to hydatid fluid is recommended. This is done in a manner similar to desensitisation against pollens, using four dilutions of hydatid fluid in gradually increasing doses and with the usual precautions. However, if a hydatid cone is available, desensitisation is probably unnecessary.

REMOVAL OF ALL CYST ELEMENTS

In order to prevent recurrence in the cyst cavity it is necessary to remove all cyst elements or kill the remaining ones. Laminated membrane and daughter cysts are never adherent to the host capsule, but laminated membrane tends to fragment and pieces of this material or small daughter cysts may be secreted in folds of the collapsing host capsule. Adequate lighting and spreading of the host capsule wall with sponges assist in locating these elusive pieces. In cases of multiple liver cysts it is often possible to remove adjacent cysts through the one cavity. Such juxtaposition should be carefully sought by palpation with the finger inserted into the cavity and subsequently confirmed by inspection of suspected areas. These areas tend to bulge into the cavity and may feel fluctuant since there is no thick host capsule overlying them. Further confirmation may be obtained by needle aspiration.

In liver hydatidosis of the *E. granulosus* variety, excision of the host capsule, or segmental hepatic resection is usually unnecessary and not advocated by us. The host capsule is part of the liver and in itself is not infectious. By leaving the properly treated host capsule, surgery of liver hydatids should be bloodless and recurrences should be rare.

CLOSURE OF BILIARY COMMUNICATIONS

When a significant opening into a bile duct has occurred by pressure necrosis and stretching occasioned by the enlarging cyst, leakage of bile into the cyst cavity has usually occurred by the time of surgery (Figs. 15.2 & 15.11). This may result in total bile staining of the collapsed cyst elements and usually means death of the cyst, or merely a yellow stain on the otherwise pure white laminated membrane, or on several daughter cysts. In any case it is necessary after removing the cyst elements to carefully inspect the host capsule for bile leaks. These are then sutured with fine material on atraumatic needles. As the cavity has not yet been sterilised, gloves and instruments used inside the cavity should be discarded or sterilised by soaking in 0.5 per cent silver nitrate solution for 2 minutes. Remaining suture material should be discarded.

STERILISATION OF THE CAVITY AND CLOSURE

Formol solution (1 per cent) has not proved to be a satisfactory scolicidal agent in practice. It was replaced by 17 per cent sodium chloride in 1961, but similarly this has not proved to be satisfactory [1]. Following the work of Saidi and Nazarian, which showed excellent scolicidal activity of 0.5 per cent silver nitrate and absence of side-effects with clinical use, this solution has been used by us since 1973 [13]. To this date no cavity so sterilised has been shown to regrow hydatids, and in eight out of ten of these cases the IEP is negative. In the two cases where the IEP, was positive one had a further cyst in the superior pole of the spleen previously concealed by adhesions and has now had a splenectomy. The other was thought to have recurred in a large liver cyst shown by scan to persist 5 years after surgery, as no other evidence of cysts was found. However, at operation the cyst cavity was sterile, containing only bile stained fluid and no cyst elements.

The surgical objectives to be achieved in simple cysts, and the appearance of the liver at the completion, is presented in diagrammatic form in Fig. 15.13.

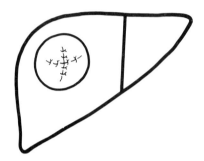

REMOVE ALL LIVING CYST ELEMENTS

PREVENT SPILLAGE

CLOSE BILIARY COMMUNICATIONS

STERILIZE CAVITY

CLOSE WITHOUT DRAINAGE

Fig. 15.13. Summary of surgical objectives and appearance of liver at completion of surgery for a simple hydatid cyst.

TREATMENT OF COMPLICATED CYSTS

Anaphylaxis. Prevention is the golden rule. Patients with a history of allergic rash should have a half dose Casoni test carried out. If a marked local reaction occurs within an hour (a palpable weal exceeding 3 cm in diameter) then consideration should be given to desensitisation against hydatid fluid.

All patients should have an antihistamine with the premedication for general anaesthesia, and intravenous hydrocortisone 100 mg ampoules should be available close to the anaesthetist and be administered at the first sign of unexpected collapse during the operation. A rapid infusion of 1–2 litres of plasma-expanding solution may be required and, therefore, an intravenous infusion should be running prior to the commencement of surgery. Bronchospasm should be treated with intravenous aminophylline.

Prevention of spillage is of prime importance, especially in sensitive subjects, and methods to avoid this have already been described. Unless there has been considerable blood loss during surgery the most likely cause of the shock state is anaphylaxis. Blood transfusion is contraindicated in anaphylactic shock, as is the infusion of large quantities of crystalloid solution. Only plasma-expanding solution should be used in conjunction with the drugs described above.

Rupture into bile ducts. This is often associated with transient jaundice. If preoperative jaundice has occurred an operative cholangiogram is essential to exclude the presence of retained material in the common bile duct which would then require choledochotomy (Fig. 15.14). If the cyst presents on the surface of the liver it is dealt with in the usual manner, being careful to identify and suture the biliary communication. The cavity should *not* be drained, but closed after filling with normal saline. When the cyst is deeply situated and, therefore, inaccessible from the surface the operative cholangiogram may indicate its position in relation to hepatic ducts. In such cases it may then be possible to pass bile duct forceps, or an open-ended suction catheter, or a Fogarty biliary balloon catheter, up the hepatic duct into the cyst cavity to extract remaining elements. It is not usually possible to ensure complete emptying of such a cavity and instillation of scolicidal agents is difficult and probably undesirable. A transduodenal sphincteroplasty is then a wise precaution against future obstructive jaundice. Choledochoscopy is useful at the completion of bile duct exploration to be sure that the bile ducts have been cleared of all hydatid elements.

The surgical objectives and the procedures performed are shown in Fig. 15.14.

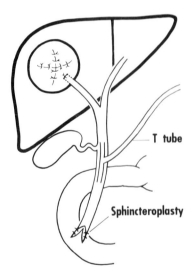

AS FOR SIMPLE CYSTS

PLUS
OPERATIVE CHOLANGIOGRAM
BILE DUCT EXPLORATION
T TUBE INSERTION
CHOLEDOCHOSCOPY
SPHINCTEROPLASTY SOMETIMES

T tube

Sphincteroplasty

Fig. 15.14. Summary of surgical objectives and the operation when a hydatid cyst ruptures into the bile ducts.

Biliary fistula. Small biliary openings are dealt with prior to sterilisation of the cavity as described above. Provided the cyst capsule is closed without drainage, and no infection supervenes, biliary fistula will rarely occur. Occasionally, a large biliary communication resists closure due to the rigidity of the walls by calcification. In such cases, omentoplasty, suturing a pedicle of omentum into the cavity about the biliary opening suffices. Alternatively, the cyst has in some cases been anastomosed to a Roux-en-Y segment of jejunum.

The commonest cause of a biliary fistula is unnecessary drainage of the host cavity, with secondary infection as a common accessory cause. Such fistulae can usually be treated expectantly since most will close within 3 months, provided there is no obstruction to the common bile duct. If such a fistula persists beyond this time in the absence of common bile duct obstruction, consideration should be given to internal drainage of the fistula, usually into the jejunum.

Infection. This is also a rare complication of hydatid cysts and is more usually postoperative rather than spontaneous. If infection of the cyst is confirmed by Gram's stain during surgery, then the cavity should not be closed as described earlier, but opened widely and omentum either as a flap or free graft should be laid into the cavity after first irrigating it with an antibiotic solution. Many old cysts appear to be infected, but are merely undergoing degeneration and invasion by polymorphonuclear leucocytes. No bacteria can be seen in a smear or grown on culture. If such patients do not have preoperative features of infection and a Gram's stain during operation is negative, the cavity may be treated as for uncomplicated cysts. If in doubt, omentoplasty is a reasonable method of treatment. Fig. 15.15 is a summary of the operation and of the surgical objectives when an infected liver hydatid is encountered.

Postoperative infection of a cyst cavity may lead to cholangitis, liver abscess, peritonitis, or biliary fistula. The management of these consists of administration of the appropriate antibiotics and drainage of the cavity, together with omentoplasty if this is still feasible.

Rupture into peritoneal cavity. This may lead to early laparotomy, as for a perforated viscus. The surgeon may find clear fluid, and/or pieces of membrane, or daughter cysts, or even an intact univesicular cyst free in the peritoneal cavity. The ruptured cyst should be readily found by palpation and the incision extended, if necessary, to gain access. In the case of a cyst high on the dome of the right lobe of the liver, or posteriorly in that lobe, a transthoracic approach may be necessary. If this is not feasible, improved access may be obtained by extending the incision up over the right lower costal cartilages, dividing 2 or 3 of these cartilages and elevating the lower ribs with a strong retractor. The ruptured cyst is dealt with as for the unruptured cyst. In addition, the peritoneal cavity should be searched for visible hydatid elements and free fluid aspirated, especially from the pouch of Douglas, the lesser sac, and the perihepatic spaces. In general, scolicides should not be instilled into the general peritoneal cavity. However, 1 per cent cetrimide may be used, provided it is lavaged after 5 minutes with normal saline.

Rupture into the pleural or pericardial cavity. This is a rare complication and demands careful toilet of those serous cavities and irrigation with normal saline solution. We have used 0.5 per cent silver nitrate in the pleural cavity, but not in the pericardium. There was no untoward toxic reaction in the pleura, but

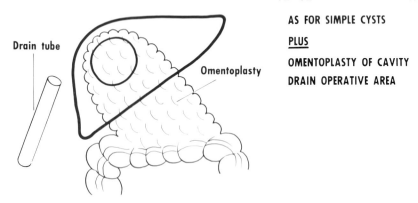

Drain tube

Omentoplasty

AS FOR SIMPLE CYSTS

PLUS

OMENTOPLASTY OF CAVITY
DRAIN OPERATIVE AREA

Fig. 15.15. Summary of the operation and of the surgical objectives in the presence of an infected hydatid cyst of the liver.

adhesions must be expected to occur. The pericardial sac, if opened, should be left open to drain into the pleural cavity from whichever side it was approached and the latter should always be drained for at least 48 hours. The liver cysts should be accessible through the diaphragm and would be treated in the usual manner.

Secondary peritoneal hydatidosis. Not uncommonly, leakage of a liver hydatid has preceded laparotomy by months or years and led to secondary peritoneal hydatidosis, or these peritoneal cysts may have resulted from dissemination by spillage at previous surgery. The surgeon should never despair at the sight of multiple peritoneal hydatids as they are readily treated. Hydatidosis due to *E. granulosus* is not a malignant condition and all cases are potentially curable. Most peritoneal hydatids may be removed with their host capsule intact, but where this is not feasible, as for example where bladder, bowel, or other viscera are involved in the host capsule, the cyst should be treated in a fashion identical to primary liver cysts.

REFERENCES

1. AARONS B.J. *Proceedings, 'Symposium on Recent Advances in Hydatid Disease'.* Hamilton, Victoria, Australia, 1973.
2. ARUNDEL J.H. *Proceedings, 'Symposium on Recent Advances in Hydatid Disease'.* Hamilton, Victoria, Australia, 1973.
3. ARUNDEL J.H. Pers. Commun., 1977.
4. BEARD T.C., RICKARD M.D. & GOODMAN H.T. Medical treatment for hydatids. *Med. J. Aust.* **1**:633, 1978.
5. BEKHTI A., SCHAAPS J.P., CAPRON M., DESSAINT J.P., SANTORO F. & CAPRON A. Treatment of hepatic hydatid disease with mebendazole: preliminary results in four cases. *Br. Med. J.* **2**:1047, 1977.
6. CHEVIS R.A.F. Pers. Commun., 1977.

7. FITZPATRICK S.C. Sedimentation of brood capsules. *Aust. New Zeal. J. Surg.* **24:**109, 1954.
8. GOODMAN H.T. *Pers. Commun.*, 1977.
9. HEATH D.D., CHRISTIE M.J. & CHEVIS R.A.F. The lethal effect of mebendazole on secondary Echinococcus Granulosa, Cysticirci of Taenia and Tetrathyridia of Meso-cestoides corti, *Parasitology* **70:**273, 1975.
10. HEATH D.D. & CHEVIS R.A.F. Mebendazole. *Med. J. Aust.* **2:**179, 1974.
11. KAMMERA W.S. & JUDGE D.M. Chemotherapy of Hydatid disease in mice with mebendazole and bithionol. *Am. J. Tropical Med. Hyg.* **25:**714, 1976.
12. KUNE G.A., JUDSON R. & HILL P. Solitary liver abscess: A continuing medico-surgical problem. *Med. J. Aust.* **1:**151, 1979.
13. SAIDI F. & NAZARIAN T. Surgical treatment of hydatid cysts by freezing of cyst wall and instillation of 0.5% silver nitrate solution. *New Eng. J. Med.* **284:**1346, 1971.
14. TANNER C.E. *Pers. Commun.*, 1978.

16. Paediatric Aspects of Biliary Disease

BY PETER G. JONES

Developmental anomalies and acquired disease of the bile ducts form a relatively small but important part of the surgery of infancy and childhood.

Most of the variations in anatomy and malformations are similar to their counterparts in adults, such as absent or double gallbladder, but others differ significantly, are more complex and by the nature of the effects, such as duodenal obstruction, they are confined to the paediatric age group, and most present as abdominal emergencies in the newborn.

In this chapter the following conditions will be considered:
1. Developmental abnormalities of the bile ducts:
    (a) Duodenal atresia-stenosis and annular pancreas.
    (b) Duodenal septum.
    (c) Cystic dilatations of the extrahepatic bile ducts, choledochal cysts.
    (d) Congenital cystic dilatation of the intrahepatic ducts (Caroli's disease).
    (e) Preduodenal portal vein.
2. Perinatal diseases:
    (a) Atresia of the extrahepatic bile ducts.
    (b) Spontaneous perforation of the bile ducts.
3. Acquired biliary disease:
    (a) Cholelithiasis.
    (b) Acute acalculous cholecystitis.
4. Neoplasms of the liver and bile ducts:
    (a) Hepatoblastoma.
    (b) Hepatocarcinoma.
    (c) Rhabdomyosarcoma of the bile ducts.
5. Traumatic injuries.

DEVELOPMENTAL ANOMALIES

Variations in the number and course of the bile ducts, the hepatic artery and its branches, and divisions of the portal vein are so common that they are a potential technical hazard in every operation on the biliary tract. In many cases the only safe course is to dissect, trace, and identify all structures encountered in the gastrohepatic ligament. This applies particularly in atresia of the extrahepatic bile ducts, in which no two examples are ever exactly the same.

417

DUODENAL ATRESIA-STENOSIS, ANNULAR PANCREAS

These entities are often coexistent and, together with 'duodenal septum', constitute one of the commonest causes of neonatal intestinal obstruction, without apparent interference with the flow of bile [36, 63, 65]. An awareness of the variability of the course and opening of the common bile duct in this condition is essential to avoid damage during surgical relief of duodenal obstruction.

In almost all cases of annular pancreas the anomalous uncinate process of the pancreas coincides with, and overlies, a malformation causing interruption of the wall of the second part of the duodenum. The duodenum proximal and distal to this obstruction communicates via a narrow segment of 'bile duct' into which the common bile duct and the main pancreatic duct open (Fig. 16.1a,b,c). An irregularity or a flap of mucosa just above this point is often present and may cause confusing evidence of intermittent patency, such as the passage of air into the distal small bowel and the presence of bile in the vomitus [12, 51, 72].

EMBRYOLOGY

Bland-Sutton's theory that congenital narrowings and obstruction of the alimentary canal occur at the site of embryological events is supported by the occurrence of duodenal atresia-stenosis at the site of its junction with the developing biliary and pancreatic ducts [14].

Tandler described the duodenum at the 8-mm stage as an endodermal tube with a lumen, which becomes invested by mesenchymal tissue and then enters a phase of rapid proliferation in which the lumen is obliterated, the so-called 'solid phase'. The primitive bile and pancreatic ducts then develop, but end blindly in the 'solid' duodenum [84].

In the next phase, described by Boyden, vacuoles appear in the solid duodenum, and coalesce to form two separate channels [16]. There is a larger dextral cavity following the convexity of the duodenum, and a smaller sinistral passage along its concavity. The biliary and pancreatic ducts then bifurcate so that each duct opens into each duodenal passage.

Simplification then occurs, in which the terminal common bile duct and pancreatic duct become fused together, in parallel, and open jointly via the papilla of Vater into the sinistral channel. Finally, the 'septum' between the dextral and sinistral channels is absorbed, forming a single lumen. The bifurcated second orifice of the common bile duct disappears, while the second pancreatic orifice may persist as the accessory pancreatic duct of Santorini.

INCIDENCE

The incidence of anomalous biliary ducts in patients with duodenal obstruction varies greatly in reported series, from 19 per cent to 78 per cent [35, 73]. An explanation lies in the different nature of the series, that is, whether predominantly collected operative cases or whether they are anatomical dissections of autopsy material [35, 69, 73, 74].

From the information available the commonest malformation encountered

(21 out of 27 specimens reported by Gourevitch and 8 out of 10 by Noblett and Paton) is depicted diagrammatically in Fig. 16.1 [35, 42, 69].

1. The duodenum is atretic in that a segment of its wall is missing.

2. There is a narrow communication (stenosis) between the proximal and distal parts of the duodenum, by means of a segment of bile duct.

3. The common bile duct opens into the segment as an L, T, or Y junction and the pancreatic duct also enters at the same level.

4. This level corresponds to the area where the bile and pancreatic ducts normally enter the duodenum.

5. Intermittent complete obstruction may be caused by a flap valve or irregularity of the mucosa which may, at times, allow some air to enter the distal duodenum and small bowel, and some bile to appear in the vomitus (Fig. 16.1a).

6. The pancreas is frequently wrapped around this area of stenosis, giving rise to the term 'annular pancreas' which has been mistakenly blamed for the obstruction, whereas it is only one part of the complex [33].

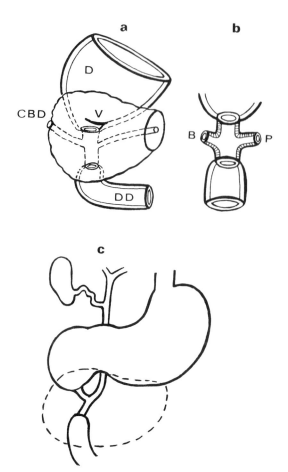

Fig. 16.1. Duodenal atresia-stenosis.
(a) Lack of mural continuity and obstruction between proximal duodenum (D) and distal duodenum (DD) which are connected only by a segment of 'bile duct' into which the common bile duct (CBD) and pancreatic duct open [35, 69]. A flap-value (V), commonly present can cause intermittent complete obstruction [69].
(b) Detail indicating extent of bile duct epithelium. Bile duct (B) and pancreatic duct (P) indicated.
(c) Variation reported by Jona [42]. The outline of an annular pancreas is indicated, though not always present.

The 'annular pancreas' occasionally seen as an incidental symptomless finding is obviously a different anomaly, presumably without any duodenal component.

The histology of atresia-stenosis has been studied by Gourevitch, who found
that the muscular coat and lining epithelium of the narrow communication is the
same as that of the normal bile duct and not that of the duodenum or small bowel
[35].

It is of interest that usually there is no fibrosis or scarring to suggest infection,
nor evidence of a vascular accident such as intrauterine infarction, antecedents
widely accepted as the probable causes of atresia or stenosis at other sites in the
bowel [67].

TREATMENT

Decompression of the stomach and duodenum via a nasogastric tube is a matter
of urgency in order to remove the risk of inhaling vomitus. This is even more
important when contemplating transport of a neonate to a paediatric centre.
Rehydration, correction of fluid, and electrolyte losses and of the circulating
blood volume, is equally important in preparing the infant for operation.

Plain films of the abdomen typically demonstrate the 'double bubble' of
duodenal obstruction. Contrast studies with barium or gastrograffin are not
essential in typical cases.

The association of Down's syndrome with suprapapillary duodenal atresia
and obstruction should be borne in mind.

Laparotomy via an upper right transverse incision, and bypass of the
obstruction by duodenoduodenostomy or duodenojejunostomy is the usual
treatment. The best prognosis is obtained in a paediatric institution where, in
addition to surgical skills, there are facilities for and expertise in managing fluid
and electrolytes, ventilatory support, and parenteral alimentation.

DUODENAL SEPTUM

A rigid septum composed of duodenal mucosa is one of the causes of intestinal
obstruction in the neonatal period (Fig. 16.2). In some examples the septum is
perforated (Fig. 16.2a) or thinned out and elongated as a cylindrical structure (a
'wind-sock') in which the orifice is often eccentric, stenotic, or both (Fig. 16.2d),
causing obstruction in the neonatal period [36, 63]. At times it is recognised later
when semi-solid or solid foods are introduced.

The attachment of the septum to the wall of the duodenum is usually in its
second or third part and, when in the second part, the lower end of the common
bile duct may open into the free edge of the septum (Fig. 16.2a), or birfurcate so
that one opening lies on either side of it, usually in the left or the posterior
quadrants (Fig. 16.2c). This last area is to be avoided when excising a septum to
relieve the obstruction.

One of the technical difficulties with the 'wind-sock' type of septum is that its
orifice may become thin, elastic, stenotic, or eccentric, and may be situated
several centimetres from its mural attachment (Fig. 16.2e).

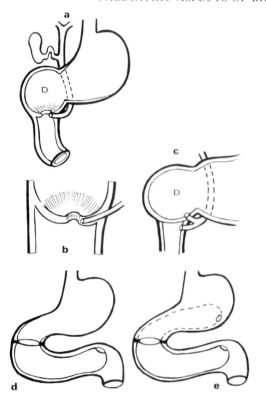

Fig. 16.2. Duodenal septum.
(a) Rigid septum of the duodenum (D) with central perforation and the common bile duct opening into its free edge.
(b) Detail of (a).
(c) Complete septum with bifid bile ducts opening both above and below the septum. After Jona [42].
(d) 'Wind-sock' septum with eccentric stenotic orifice. The dotted lines (e) indicate the situation which may occur when turned inside out during operative exploration.

CHOLEDOCHAL CYST

Cysts and cystic dilatations of the biliary tract are described in Chapter 8, and the section which follows is confined to some observations on choledochal cysts as they occur in infancy and childhood.

ANATOMY

In the great majority of those seen in childhood (Fig. 16.3a), the lower third of the common bile duct is the segment chiefly affected (Alonso-Lej Type I) [3]. By the time the diagnosis is made in children it has usually enlarged to a capacity of 100–200 ml, and drawn the cystic duct into its wall. The cyst extends upwards behind the common hepatic duct, which is distended to three to five times its normal diameter. When the cyst is tense and distended it displaces the second part of the duodenum downwards, forwards, and to the left, giving rise to a typical radiological appearance in a contrast study of the stomach and duodenum. This may be absent during non-obstructive phases when the choledochal cyst is lax and collapsed.

AGE

A choledochal cyst has been described as a cause of prolonged jaundice in the newborn, and two entities should be distinguished:

1. A choledochal cyst in an infant 1–3 months of age, accompanied by atresia of the extrahepatic bile ducts (Fig. 16.5e). This may be as large as 6 cm in diameter and contain 'white bile', because the duct above or below the cyst is completely atretic. In reality this is a type of atresia of the bile ducts and can be either correctable when the atresia segment lies distal to the cyst, or uncorrectable but operable when the atresia affects the hepatic ducts above the cystic structure. The treatment for this type is as for biliary atresia described later in this chapter.

2. A true choledochal cyst presenting in infancy, which can be confirmed by an operative cholangiogram. The findings are similar to those seen in older children or adults, and the treatment is along the same lines (Chapter 8).

The important point is to make this distinction, for superficially the two conditions resemble each other. Careful dissection is required to differentiate them, although cholangiography may be conclusive.

AETIOLOGY

Many possibilities have been advanced; Saito and Ishida reviewed the theories suggested, but no finality has been reached, except that obstruction alone, at the papilla, would not account for the focal localisation of the dilatation, and less or little distension of the proximal duct system [75].

Episodes of almost complete obstruction, possibly the result of infection and oedema, would account for the recurring episodes of increased tension and dilatation of the cyst, causing abdominal pain, nausea, vomiting, occasionally jaundice, and the appearance of a palpable abdominal mass [31].

COMPLICATIONS

Secondary changes, such as cholangitis and fibrosis, occur in the proximal and intrahepatic ducts causing hyperaemia and fibrosis in pericystic tissues, hepatic fibrosis, cirrhosis, and portal hypertension [39]. Less commonly, spontaneous or post-traumatic rupture and biliary peritonitis may occur [83].

PRESENTATION

Excluding those with jaundice in early infancy, symptoms usually appear in the first 5 years of life as recurring and initially transient and infrequent episodes of abdominal pain lasting 1–3 days at intervals of 6–12 months. Unless jaundice draws attention to the biliary tract in the first few attacks, diagnosis is often delayed for years. In our experience the mean age at the onset of symptoms was 5 years, and the average age at diagnosis less than 10 years of age [22]. The diagnostic triad of pain, an abdominal mass, and jaundice coexist in only one-third of the patients [45, 88].

DIAGNOSIS

Once suspected, the diagnosis can be confirmed by contrast studies of the gastrointestinal tract, or by ultrasonography when the cyst is small or collapsed, in a symptomless phase (Fig. 8.3).

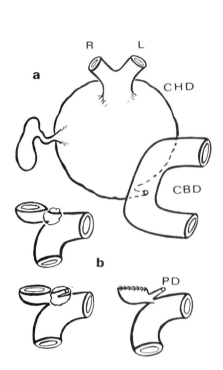

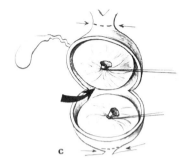

Fig. 16.3. Choledochal cyst.
(a) The usual anatomy; the area maximally involved is the common bile duct. The cystic and common hepatic ducts (CHD) are drawn into the wall of the cyst. Distal common bile duct (CBD) opening shown.
(b) A method of avoiding injury to the pancreatic duct (PD) by leaving a segment of the wall of the cyst, and closing it without dissecting the pancreatic duct.
(c) Alternative technique, developing plane between lining and adventitia suggested by Lilly [93].

Cholecystography and intravenous cholangiography usually fail to opacify the duct system because of dilution of the contrast material by the large volume of fluid in the cyst, but it can show up a cyst in some cases (Fig. 8.4). Transhepatic cholangiography or endoscopic retrograde cholangiography can provide further information concerning the proximal and intrahepatic ducts (Fig. 8.5).

TREATMENT

An operative cholangiogram provides the clearest picture of the anatomy and the relation of the cyst to adjacent structures [26].

Surgical treatment has evolved from drainage procedures, to an anastomosis to the duodenum or jejunum, or a Roux-en-Y choledochocystojejunostomy, to total excision of the cyst and the gallbladder, followed by anastomosis of the common hepatic duct to the end, or to the antimesenteric border of a Roux-en-Y loop of jejunum [45, 48, 61, 90].

In the paediatric age group there is still, in most cases, an areolar non-fibrotic plane around the cyst which permits dissection and complete removal, which may not be feasible because of hyperaemia or fibrosis in older patients. There is little doubt that this operation has the advantage of the least incidence of postoperative symptoms, and the best long-term prognosis, important considerations in paediatric surgery [45]. The small, but recognised, incidence of carcinoma arising in a retained choledochal cyst is a further reason for excision of the cyst whenever possible [29].

Temporal external drainage may still have a place as a preliminary step when there is severe cholangitis, sepsis, fever, or malnutrition at the time of diagnosis, or when acute inflammation in and around the cyst is found at laparotomy. In both circumstances the aim is to excise the cyst eventually.

Particular attention is paid to the site of the pancreatic duct to avoid damaging it during dissection of the lower medial aspect of the cyst, and a small cuff of the cyst wall is left *in situ* and oversewn (Fig. 16.3b) [45, 48].

The prohibitive mortality of total excision predicted by Dickson-Wright and Gross has long since been overcome, and may have reflected ill-advised attempts to remove a choledochal cyst without recognising its nature, and lacking the information obtainable by an operative cholangiogram at a time when anaesthetic techniques and facilities for resuscitation and transfusion were as yet undeveloped [26, 37].

PROGNOSIS

The outcome is very satisfactory when surgery is performed before there are secondary and possible irreversible parenchymatous changes in the liver, or in the intrahepatic ducts.

In infants with a cystic structure associated with atresia of the common hepatic or common bile duct (Fig. 16.5e), the outcome is much less hopeful. Long-term survival was reported by Kasai in only three of eight such infants, a success rate in keeping with the long-term results currently obtained in biliary atresia, as described later in this chapter [48].

CONGENITAL DILATATION OF THE INTRAHEPATIC BILE DUCTS

In this condition, also known as Caroli's disease, there are multiple, irregular, saccular dilatations of the intrahepatic bile ducts, the loculi being connected by short segments of normal or stenotic ducts [21].

Caroli's disease may be an intrahepatic variant of the same malformation, as seen in choledochal cysts, and is sometimes demonstrated in association with a choledochal cyst when the intrahepatic ducts have been adequately filled [57, 86].

DIAGNOSIS

The clinical picture is very similar to that of a choledochal cyst and may only be distinguishable by the distribution and extent of the dilatation found on operative cholangiography. Preoperative transhepatic cholangiography and ultrasonography may be diagnostic (Fig. 3.23).

TREATMENT

Treatment depends upon the distribution, and whether there is a co-existent choledochal cyst, which should be treated along the lines described earlier [61].

Hepatic lobectomy has been recommended for Caroli's disease when grossly dilated intrahepatic ducts are confined to one lobe [64]. The outcome and results are affected by the high incidence of coexisting cystic renal disease (medullary sponge kidney) and congenital hepatic fibrosis and, on rare occasions, cholangiocarcinoma [21, 44].

The embryology and observed associations indicate no clear reasons why this abnormality should be related to anomalies or diseases of the bile duct [15]. However, Wakayama *et al.* found that 10 out of 55 cases of preduodenal portal vein in the literature also had atresia of the extrahepatic bile ducts [89]. On the other hand only two cases have been found in 65 cases of biliary atresia explored at the Royal Children's Hospital, Melbourne. The abnormal position of the vein not only added difficulties to the dissection, but made it more difficult to determine where the remnants of the hepatic ducts might be, for example posterior to the bifurcation of the portal vein instead of anterior or superior to it (Fig. 16.6c).

Other unusual malformations, occasionally associated with biliary atresia, have been reported by Lilly and Chandra, for example absence of the inferior vena cava, situs inversus, 'symmetrical liver', malrotation, and malfixation with a subhepatic caecum [58].

SPONTANEOUS PERFORATION
OF THE EXTRAHEPATIC BILIARY DUCTS

This extremely rare catastrophe occurs in infants, mostly in the first 3 months of life. The perforation is typically in the common bile duct at its junction with the cystic duct, suggesting the possibility of a congenital deficiency in the wall at this point.

Although perforation may lead to acute symptoms, more often the onset is undramatic, with progressive abdominal distension, low-grade fever, jaundice, ascites, failure to thrive, and mildly elevated levels of serum bilirubin [60, 71].

DIAGNOSIS
The diagnosis can be confirmed by an intravenous cholangiogram or an ^{131}I-rose bengal scan, both of which show leakage of bile into a pseudocyst or into the peritoneal cavity.

At operation there is bile-stained ascites and a fibrinous 'pseudocyst' occupying the area. An operative cholangiogram via the gallbladder will display the anatomy and indicate the size and site of the perforation, and many have been reported to falsely indicate obstruction of the lower end of the common bile duct [57, 60].

It is important to distinguish the pseudocyst in this condition from traumatic rupture of a choledochal cyst, because an intestinal anastomosis to the wall of a 'pseudocyst' carries a high mortality [57, 60].

TREATMENT
Cholecystostomy and simple drainage of the area of perforation is recommended as the best treatment, because the perforation can be expected to close spontaneously [57, 60].

Antibiotics and prolonged local drainage until cholangiography via the cholecystostomy shows a normal duct system are the basis of treatment.

ATRESIA OF THE EXTRAHEPATIC BILE DUCTS

Although the aetiology of this condition remains an enigma the macroscopic and microscopic findings are in accord with the suggestion that it is the result of a destructive inflammatory, and possibly infective, condition usually occurring late in intrauterine life, but occasionally in the perinatal period [55].

Other conditions which have caused diagnostic confusion in the past, such as alpha$_1$-trypsin deficiency, have gradually been identified and excluded, but there remains a 'hard core' of jaundiced infants with either atresia or severe 'obstructive' neonatal hepatitis, in which their differentiation still presents difficulties. Scarcely a year has passed without the introduction of a new preoperative investigation predicted to distinguish between these two conditions, only to find that the incidence of false positive or negative results rendered it unreliable.

As a result of a prospective study of these patients at the Royal Children's Hospital, Melbourne, over more than 15 years, reliance is placed on percutaneous needle biopsy of the liver to guide management and to identify those with atresia who require laparotomy. Fig. 16.4 shows the general plan, with repetition of the biopsy when the histological findings are equivocal or inconclusive.

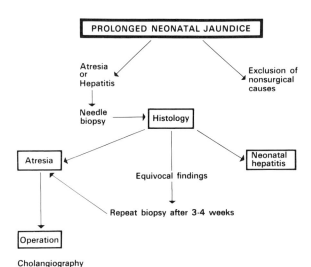

Fig. 16.4. The diagnostic pathway in cases of prolonged neonatal jaundice.

The optimum time for exploration is still the subject of debate, but there is ample evidence that the age at the time of operation is an important factor in the prognosis and, ideally, surgery should be undertaken as soon after 4 weeks of age as possible [47].

Unquestionably, fluctuations in the degree of jaundice, its mild appearance, variations in the level of serum bilirubin, and misleading colouration of the stools by bile pigments excreted in colonic mucus, are all potentially misleading and favour procrastination.

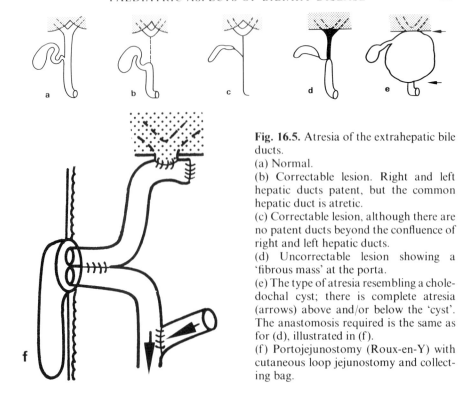

Fig. 16.5. Atresia of the extrahepatic bile ducts.
(a) Normal.
(b) Correctable lesion. Right and left hepatic ducts patent, but the common hepatic duct is atretic.
(c) Correctable lesion, although there are no patent ducts beyond the confluence of right and left hepatic ducts.
(d) Uncorrectable lesion showing a 'fibrous mass' at the porta.
(e) The type of atresia resembling a chole-dochal cyst; there is complete atresia (arrows) above and/or below the 'cyst'. The anastomosis required is the same as for (d), illustrated in (f).
(f) Portojejunostomy (Roux-en-Y) with cutaneous loop jejunostomy and collecting bag.

Given time, the jaundice in most infants with infective hepatitis will disappear, but this waiting period carries an unacceptable penalty, and the results of surgery for atresia are progressively worse when undertaken at 30, 60 and 90 days [46, 50]. Beyond the age of 100–120 days operation is almost invariably unsuccessful, even when a potentially remediable abnormality is found, because of the extent of periductal fibrosis and deterioration of the parenchyma [50].

CLASSIFICATION

Two kinds of abnormality are found, depending on which portions of the extrahepatic bile ducts are occluded or absent. Traditionally, these have been termed 'correctable' and 'uncorrectable', depending on whether the individual type was amenable in the past to surgical correction. This terminology has persisted even though there is now an operation applicable to 'uncorrectable' types which are, paradoxically, 'operable'.

CORRECTABLE BILIARY ATRESIA
In this group the important point is that some part of the extrahepatic ducts system remains patent and communicates with patent intrahepatic ducts (Fig. 16.5b,c). The incidence of this group varies in reported series from 4 per cent to nearly 40 per cent, and an average figure may be approximately 10 per cent [57].

In theory an anastomosis of the proximal patent ducts, preferably to the antimesenteric aspect of a Roux-en-Y loop of jejunum, that is, a choledochoje-junostomy (Fig. 16.5f), should be curative, but this is not always the case, partly because of the adverse effects on the liver before surgical relief, and also because of the occurrence of progressive biliary cirrhosis after operation [10]. An additional factor is the incidence of attacks of cholangitis with cumulative hepatic fibrosis, which occurs after operation in both correctable and uncorrectable forms of biliary atresia [6, 7, 10, 57].

UNCORRECTABLE BILIARY ATRESIA

This is the usual type of case, comprising about 90 per cent of all cases of biliary atresia and, by definition, no portion of the extrahepatic ducts communicates with ducts in the liver. There are many variations on this anatomical theme, and some of the types encountered are shown in Fig. 16.5d,e. It will be apparent that patency of the gallbladder, cystic or common bile duct is irrelevant when the common hepatic duct is represented by a fibrous cord, or is totally absent. This group was 'uncorrectable' until Kasai devised his operation, first described in English in 1968 and now known as hepatic portojejunostomy [46]. The rationale of this procedure is based on the observation that the 'fibrous mass' at the porta, anatomically the right and left hepatic ducts and the adjacent common hepatic duct, is found on microscopy to contain many tiny ducts, varying in size and number, in a collagenous stroma (Fig. 16.6a). There is evidence that these small ductules are most numerous in patients 1–2 months of age, and in most cases they have disappeared by the age of 4 months [47, 70].

The size and shape of the 'fibrous mass', as seen macroscopically, varies from patient to patient, but is usually conical, 4–10 mm in circumference at its attachment to the liver and is up to 1 cm in length or height (Fig. 16.6a).

OPERATION

Following diagnosis by means of needle biopsy exploration is commenced via a right upper transverse laparotomy and an operative cholangiogram via the fundus of the gallbladder is performed. Not infrequently, the gallbladder or the cystic duct or both have no lumen, in which case cholangiography is abandoned.

In another group of patients the gallbladder, cystic duct, and common bile duct are virtually normal with a good flow of contrast into the duodenum. A second film should be taken with a non-crushing clamp on the gastrohepatic ligament close to the duodenum, in an attempt to force contrast material up the common hepatic duct and into the intrahepatic ducts. When this fails, dissection is commenced.

The incision is extended from the midline to the costal margin. The gallbladder is freed from its bed, and the cystic duct followed to its junction with the common hepatic duct or what remains of it, that is, a fibrous cord or strand. This is then followed upwards towards the porta, clearing the hepatic artery and its branches which are held aside for better exposure.

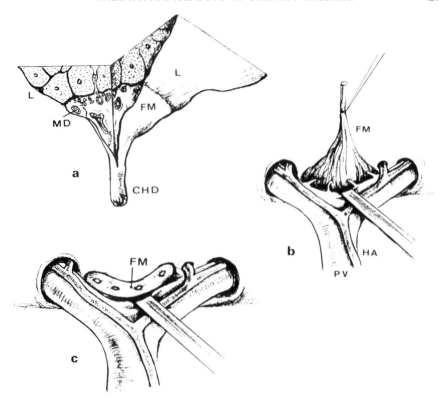

Fig. 16.6. Atresia of bile ducts. The Kasai operation.
(a) Diagrammatic concept of the 'fibrous mass' (FM), attached to the liver (L) at the porta, containing multiple minute ducts (MD) and obliterated common hepatic duct (CHD).
(b) Separation of posterior aspect from the portal vein (PV). Note the small vessels between these structures, and close relationship to branches of the hepatic artery (HA).
(c) Depressing the bifurcation of the portal vein to display the outline of the excised fibrous mass; the probable sites of intrahepatic ducts (not visible at operation) are indicated diagrammatically. After Kimura [53].

The attachment at the porta is defined anteriorly and the remnant of the common hepatic duct is divided and held forwards to display the posterior aspect of the fibrous mass and its close relationship to the portal vein (Fig. 16.6b) [56].

The portal vein is then cleared, and on depressing it gently downwards and posteriorly, one to three small vessels are usually seen running between the fibrous mass and the portal vein. These are divided and ligated. The bifurcation is then retracted downwards to delineate the posterior margin of the fibrous mass at its junction with the capsule of the liver.

The fibrous mass is then excised, cutting it off flush with the capsule of the liver, and the somewhat elliptical outline of its attachment (Fig. 16.6c) represents the hepatic side of the anastomosis which follows. The fibrous mass is preserved for histological examination and serial sections are made in the plane of its attachment.

A suitable loop of jejunum is selected, and the vertical arm of a Roux-en-Y is brought up to the porta, through the root of transverse mesocolon if desired. The end of the loop is closed; a stoma of appropriate size is made in the antimesenteric border and an anastomosis to the porta is made. Some five or six absorbable sutures (4/0 polyglychollic acid) are placed as the posterior layer, tying the knots on the inside and an anterior series of full thickness sutures tied on the outside, that is, a single-layer anastomosis.

The loop of jejunum is made long enough to bring up to the abdominal wall as a double-barrelled cutaneous jejunostomy through a second stab incision in the nipple line (Fig. 16.5f) [81]. Continuity of the small bowel is restored by jejunojejunostomy, and the abdomen closed with two drains, one anterior and the other posterior to the anastomosis.

Postoperative treatment includes nasogastric suction, intravenous fluids, antibiotics (e.g. penicillin and gentamicin) and a urine-collecting bag over the jejunostomy to collect and measure bile if and when it appears, from 3 to 30 days after operation (Fig. 16.5f).

Several modifications of this technique have been devised. For example, a double Y-Roux loop, the use of the antrum of the stomach or a gastric tube instead of jejunum, dissection extended into the substance of the liver, using microsurgical techniques to identify what remains of the right and left hepatic ducts (Fig. 16.7a,b) [40, 75, 81, 82].

Theoretically the gallbladder, when patent, may be used as a conduit, that is,

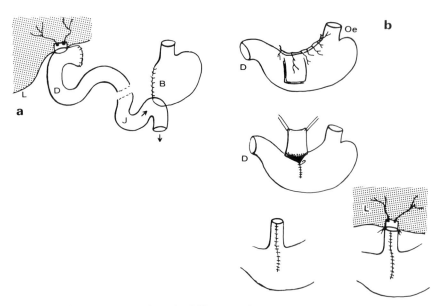

Fig. 16.7. Alternative operations for biliary atresia.
(a) Gastric transection with hepatic porto-duodenostomy (or porto-antrostomy) and gastrojejunostomy.
(b) Hepatic porto-gastrostomy (antrostomy) using a flap of gastric wall to fashion a tube.
After Ikeda [40].

hepatic portocholecystostomy, but in a number of cases this has not proved to be effective, and a further operation has been necessary because of leakage of bile, via a cutaneous fistula [7, 47]. A subsequent portojejunostomy has been required in the majority of patients treated, initially, by portocholecystostomy. The irreversible changes in the liver and the predictable death of infants in whom portojejunostomy is unsuccessful, warrants consideration of transplantation of a donor liver. Starzl's group have transplanted a liver in several such cases and the results are promising [59, 78].

RESULTS

The criteria of a successful operation are an adequate flow of bile (150–350 ml/day) from the cutaneous jejunostomy, clearance of jaundice, and return of the serum bilirubin to normal in the course of 1–3 months.

This is achieved in approximately 60 per cent of cases and up to 80 per cent when operation is performed in patients less than 8 weeks of age [50, 57].

The impossibility of a mucosa-to-mucosa anastomosis is a potential source of 'stenosis' and interference with bile flow and this, together with recurring attacks of cholangitis, usually due to enterobacteria (*Klebsiella, Strep. faecalis* and *E. coli*), are the cause of hepatic fibrosis, nodular reparative cirrhosis, and portal hypertension [67]. Unfortunately, only some 50 per cent of those with an initially adequate bile flow are in reasonable health and free of jaundice 5 years after operation [41, 50, 57, 88].

Late complications responsible for the small number of long-term survivors include cirrhosis and liver failure, bleeding from oesophageal varices due to portal hypertension and, rarely, cholangiocarcinoma [6, 50, 54, 57, 67].

CHOLELITHIASIS IN CHILDHOOD

In general, biliary calculi are rare in children, and the incidence in a particular community depends to a large extent on its ethnic composition and the dietary patterns. Their rarity in paediatric practice leads to a low index of suspicion and to delay in diagnosis, even when symptoms would suggest the possibility of gallstones. In many adults found to have gallstones, the symptoms in retrospect commenced at puberty or even earlier.

Further, diagnosis in childhood is made more difficult by the prevalence of recurrent abdominal pain of non-calculous and psychosomatic origin [8]. However, earlier diagnosis and removal of gallstones can prevent months or years of ill health in children.

AETIOLOGY

Although excess haemolysis, rather than metabolic derangement, has been said to be the commonest cause of biliary calculi [7] this is not the case in most Western nations today [67, 77, 80]. This is borne out in the experience of the

Royal Children's Hospital, Melbourne, where non-haemolytic (non-pigment) biliary calculi constitute the majority and the major component of the increased incidence in subsequent years (Table 16.1) [76].

Table 16.1. Cholelithiasis in children (Royal Children's Hospital, Melbourne 1952–76; 47 cases)

Non-haemolytic calculi		
Haemolytic calculi		
Spherocytosis	6	15
Thalassaemia major	9	

Conditions reported to contribute to, or actually cause, cholelithiasis in children are:
1. Developmental anomalies.
2. Metabolic disorder (ethnic, genetic, familial, and dietary factors).
3. Obesity.
4. Excess haemolysis, such as familial spherocytosis, thalassaemia major and sickle-cell disease [13, 19, 20].

Forshall and Rickham drew attention to latent developmental abnormalities, especially in the cystic duct, only identified by careful dissection and serial sections of operative specimens [32]. These were present in all three of their cases in which the specimen was examined in such detail, and included bifid cystic duct, stenotic cystic duct and, in one patient, multiple small channels instead of a single lumen in one segment of the cystic duct.

Biliary calculi are also occasionally found in children with a choledochal cyst, and as a late complication in adolescence in patients operated on successfully for duodenal atresia-stenosis in infancy.

It will be apparent that the relative importance of the aetiological factors is influenced by the genetic and ethnic composition of the community, the dietary habits and, possibly, prevailing level of nutrition.

In the paediatric age group non-haemolytic biliary calculi are twice or three times as common in girls as in boys, reflecting the greater incidence in adult females. Most girls affected are intra- or postpubertal, whereas the average age of the boys affected is less. Slight to moderate obesity has been noted in both sexes [77]. The weight of 14 out of 27 children with non-haemolytic calculi was greater than the seventy-fifth centile [76].

SYMPTOMS AND PRESENTATION

Abdominal pain is predictably the commonest symptom and in children this was indicated in the epigastrium as often as in the right hypochondrium. In seven of 27 cases the pain was also referred to the back (Boas' sign). Nausea and vomiting occurred in 22 of 27 patients, but jaundice was observed or reported in only seven, and a palpable gallbladder in only four patients. A history of gallstones in the immediate family was found in 12 of 27 patients [27].

INVESTIGATIONS

Opaque calculi were demonstrated in plain films of the abdomen in 63 per cent of patients, in accord with other series and in three patients this, as an incidental finding, first suggested the diagnosis.

Translucent calculi were demonstrated as filling defects in 10 patients. There were gallstones in the bile ducts in five patients of whom only one was jaundiced at the time. This incidence of 18 per cent of ductal calculi in children with cholelithiasis is greater than usually reported. Oral cholecystography should be performed in all cases and, if this fails to demonstrate the duct system it should be followed by an intravenous cholangiogram.

SURGICAL TREATMENT

Operation is conducted along the same lines as for adults, as described in Chapter 5, that is, cholecystectomy. The indications for an operative cholangiogram and exploration of the common duct are also as for adults, as described in Chapter 5. Experience has shown that operative exploration of the duct system will be indicated in approximately 44 per cent of children undergoing cholecystectomy for cholelithiasis [76].

In children, the debate concerning cholecystectomy versus cholecystostomy and removal of calculi is confined to patients with familial spherocytosis undergoing splenectomy, which can be expected to prevent further haemolysis. This is not the case in thalassaemia major nor in those with cholesterol calculi. It is, therefore, the accepted practice to remove pigment stones via a cholecystostomy without cholecystectomy when the gallbladder is otherwise normal, and when calculi are due to excessive haemolysis in children with familial spherocytosis.

ACUTE ACALCULOUS CHOLECYSTITIS IN CHILDREN

This is rare in the paediatric age group, but acute acalculous cholecystitis appears to be more common in childhood than cholecystitis arising as a complication of cholelithiasis [11, 18, 24, 38, 68].

Experience at the Royal Children's Hospital confirms this, in that there have been eight cases of acute acalculous cholecystitis in the same period as there were 27 children with non-haemolytic gallstones, only two of whom had any evidence of complicating cholecystitis [76].

SYMPTOMS AND DIAGNOSIS

The diagnosis is seldom made before operation. A review of the literature indicates that the pain is frequently periumbilical and fever, toxaemia, and leucocytosis are usual, while jaundice is surprisingly common (26–45 per cent) despite the absence of biliary calculi [87].

Brenner found no calculi in 72 per cent of 81 children with acute cholecystitis and in 244 children with acute cholecystitis, there was no associated condition or obvious cause in 53 [22 per cent].

Trauma is also recognised as a contributory factor in acalculous cholecystitis, in the form of external violence to the abdomen, but also following abdominal operations not directed to the liver and bile ducts [34, 85, 92].

TREATMENT

Cholecystectomy is regarded as the most appropriate treatment and, whenever feasible, an operative cholangiogram should be performed to exclude an underlying cause or latent calculi.

Culture of the contents of the gallbladder should be performed because of the well-known association of acute cholecystitis with typhoid fever. Salmonella typhimurium is also known to cause acute cholecystitis.

Cholecystostomy instead of cholecystectomy should be considered when appropriate, depending on the condition or on the age of the patient [11].

TUMOURS OF THE LIVER AND BILE DUCTS

HEPATOBLASTOMA, HEPATOCARCINOMA

The most common tumour of the liver in the paediatric age group is the hepatoblastoma, an embryonal tumour predominantly sarcomatous in its behaviour, typically presenting in children less than 5 years of age, and very rarely causes obstruction of the bile ducts or jaundice [43, 49, 52].

Hepatocarcinoma, in contrast, arises in a significantly older age group (10 years or older), most often in a cirrhotic liver, as a multicentric tumour. A far more invasive tumour, it shows a propensity to grow along tubular structures in the liver, such as the bile ducts, and subdivisions of the portal vein. Extensions of the tumour down the right or left hepatic duct, or metastases in the lymph nodes in the porta can give rise to obstructive jaundice which is sometimes the mode of presentation.

Surgical treatment of both these tumours is determined by the site, the size, and extent of the tumour, and the feasibility of hepatic lobectomy.

RHABDOMYOSARCOMA OF THE BILE DUCTS

This is the only primary malignant tumour of the extrahepatic ducts in children. It usually arises in the common bile duct in patients between 2 and 6 years of age, as a yellowish, grapelike polypoid mass, causing obstructive jaundice, haemorrhage, necrosis, and perforation [2, 25].

MODE OF PRESENTATION

The common picture is a young child with fever, malaise, abdominal pain, jaundice, and a mass palpable in the right hypochondrium.

INVESTIGATION

A plain film of the abdomen should show the outline of the mass, while a barium study may show indentation, displacement, and possibly obstruction, of the stomach and duodenum.

A cholecystogram or intravenous cholangiography may fail to provide any information when there is complete biliary obstruction.

Ultrasonography may confirm dilation of the proximal and intrahepatic bile ducts, while a computerised tomographic scan should confirm the presence of a mass in the region of the gastrohepatic ligament, and possibly duodenal obstruction.

DIAGNOSIS

The diagnosis can only be made with certainty at laparotomy and, because of the rarity of the condition, frozen sections or an interim drainage procedure while awaiting paraffin sections are often required.

TREATMENT

Surgery. Total excision may be feasible if the operative findings, radiographs of the chest, and a radionuclide bone scan, exclude distant metastases. As diagnosis is often made at a late stage, total excision is usually required, that is, pancreaticoduodenectomy and a Roux-en-Y hepaticojejunostomy.

Chemotherapy and radiotherapy. Even when total excision is possible, adjuvant chemotherapy and radiotherapy are indicated. Although there have been no recent reports of their use in patients with this tumour, from experience of rhabdomyosarcomas in other areas, the most appropriate chemotherapy would probably be VAC (vincristine, actinomycin D and cyclophosphamide) in recurring pulses for 2 years, possibly with the addition of adriamycin, combined with radiotherapy in a dose of approximately 4000 to 4500 rads.

In patients less than 2 years of age both chemotherapy and radiotherapy would have to be greatly modified and, if possible, omitted.

The results reported in the literature are very poor, with only an occasional long-term survivor free of disease [25, 30].

INJURIES TO THE EXTRAHEPATIC BILE DUCTS

Isolated injuries of the bile ducts are rare, and more often associated with damage to the liver or the pancreas, the result of either penetrating injuries or blunt trauma [79].

At exploration for upper abdominal trauma the possibility of laceration or avulsion of part of the biliary tree should be borne in mind. However, bizarre and inexplicable closed injuries in children may not be detected early, especially when abdominal findings are obscured by an associated head injury.

CLASSIFICATION
Ahmed analysed 33 such cases and classified the injuries reported into two categories:
1. Transection, or complete rupture, of one of the bile ducts; and
2. Perforation, or incomplete rupture, which occurred in approximately equal numbers (Table 16.2).

Table 16.2. Trauma to gallbladder and bile ducts (closed injuries, 45 collected cases) [1]

Rupture of the gallbladder		12
Complete rupture		
Common bile duct	13	16
Left hepatic duct	3	
Incomplete rupture		
Common bile duct	6	
Common hepatic duct	7	17
Left hepatic duct	1	
Unidentified site	3	

CLINICAL FEATURES
The clinical picture can also be divided into two types:
1. Those presenting soon after the injury with signs of an 'acute abdomen', leading to early exploration and the opportunity for early diagnosis, but the injury to the bile duct may be overlooked, particularly when there is also major injury to other viscera.
2. Delayed appearance of symptoms and signs for days, weeks, or even months after the injury. This is the more likely course when a bile duct alone is injured, and when the injury is a laceration or perforation rather than complete transection or avulsion.

The development of malaise, fever, haemoperitoneum, biliary ascites, ileus, and a vague upper abdominal mass or acholic stools may be the first indication of rupture of the bile ducts in a child [1].

TREATMENT
A partial transection is repaired when possible, and the site drained. More severe injuries may require the use of a T tube, with reconstitution when feasible, or an anastomosis, such as a hepaticojejunostomy Roux-en-Y (Fig. 16.8).

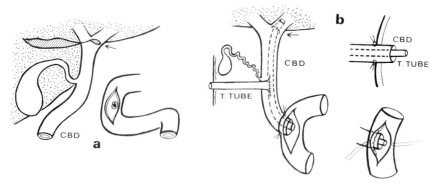

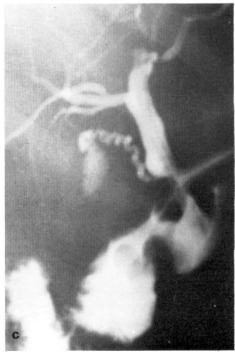

Fig. 16.8. Injuries to the bile ducts.

(a) Laceration of the liver and left hepatic duct, combined with avulsion of the common bile duct from the papilla, due to closed abdominal trauma in a 5-year-old girl.

(b) The method of repair using a T tube, re-implanting the common bile duct at a new site and suture of lacerated left hepatic duct.

(c) Postoperative cholangiogram before removing T tube, 4 weeks after repair. No symptoms in subsequent 3 years.

REFERENCES

1. AHMED S. Bile duct injuries from non-penetrating abdominal trauma in childhood. *Aust. New Zeal. J. Surg.* **46:**209, 1976.
2. AKERS D.R. & NEEDHAM M.E. Sarcoma botryoides (rhabdomyosarcoma) of the bile ducts with survival. *J. Pediat. Surg.* **6:**474, 1971.
3. ALONSO-LEJ F., REVER W.B. & PESSAGNO D.J. Congenital choledochal cyst with a report of two and an analysis of 94 cases. *Int. Abstr. Surg.* **108:**1, 1959.
4. ALTMAN R.P. Portal decompression by interposition mesocaval shunt in patients with biliary atresia. *J. Pediat. Surg.* **11:**809, 1976.
5. ALTMAN R.P. & POTTER B.M. Portal decompression in infants and children with the interposition mesocaval shunt. *Amer. J. Surg.* **135:**65, 1978.

6. ALTMAN R.P., CHANDRA R. & LILLY J.R. Ongoing cirrhosis after successful porti-
   coenterostomy in infants with biliary atresia. *J. Pediat. Surg.* **10**:685, 1975.

7. ALTMAN R.P. & LILLY J.R. Technical details in the surgical correction of extrahepatic
   biliary atresia. *Surg. Gynec. Obstet.* **140**:952, 1975.

8. APLEY J. *The Child with Abdominal Pains*, (2e). Blackwell Scientific Publications,
   Oxford, 1975.

9. ARIMA E. & AKITA H. Congenital biliary tract dilatation and anomalous junction of
   the pancreatico-biliary duct system. *J. Pediat. Surg.* **14**:9, 1979.

10. ARIMA E., FONKALSRUD E.W. & NEERHOUT R.C. Experiences in the management of
    surgically correctable biliary atresia. *Surgery* **75**:229, 1974.

11. ARNSPIGER L.A., MARTIN J.G. & KREMPIN H.O. Acute noncalculous cholecystitis in
    children: report of a case in a 17 day old infant. *Am. J. Surg.* **100**:103, 1960.

12. ASTLEY R. Duodenal atresia with gas below the obstruction. *Br. J. Radiol.* **42**:351,
    1969.

13. BATES G.C. & BROWN C.H. Incidence of gallbladder disease in haemolytic anaemia
    (spherocytosis). *Gastroenterology* **21**:104, 1952.

14. BLAND-SUTTON J. Imperforate ileum. *Am. J. Med. Sci.* **98**:456, 1889.

15. BOWER R.S. & TERNBERG J.L. Preduodenal portal vein. *J. Pediat. Surg.* **7**:579, 1972.

16. BOYDEN E.A., COPE J.G. & BILL A.H. Anatomy and embryology of intrinsic obstruc-
    tion of the duodenum. *Am. J. Surg.* **114**:190, 1967.

17. BRENNER R.W. & STEWART C.F. Cholecystitis in children. *Rev. Surg.* **327**, Oct 1964.

18. BROWN H.W. & XIMENES J.O. Cholelithiasis and cholecystitis in childhood.
    Case reports of twin sisters and review of literature. *International Surgery* **49**:547,
    1968.

19. BURRINGTON J.D. & SMITH M.D. Elective and emergency surgery in children with
    sickle cell disease. *Surg. Clin. N. Amer.* **56**:55, 1976.

20. CAMERON J.L., MADDREY W.C. & ZUIDEMA G.D. Biliary tract disease in sickle cell
    anaemia: surgical considerations. *Ann. Surg.* **174**:702, 1971.

21. CAROLI J., SOUPAULT R. & KASSABOWSKI J. La dilatation polykystique congénitale
    des voies biliaire intrahépatique: essai de classification. *Semin. Hôp. Paris* **34**:488,
    1958.

22. CLARKE A.M. Choledochal cyst. *Med. J. Aust.* **2**:669, 1961.

23. CLATWORTHY H.W. JR., WALL T. & WATMAN R.N. A new type of portal-to-systemic
    venous shunt for portal hypertension. *Arch. Surg.* **71**:588, 1955.

24. CRYSTAL R.F. & FINK R.L. Acute acalculous cholecystitis in childhood. *Clin. Pediat.*
    10:423, 1971.

25. DAVIS G.L., KISSANE J.M. & ISHAK K.G. Embryonal rhabdomyosarcoma (sarcoma
    botryoides) of the biliary tree. *Cancer* **24**:333, 1969.

26. DICKSON-WRIGHT A. X-ray appearances produced by congenital dilatation of the
    common bile duct. *Br. J. Radiol.* **8**:227, 1935.

27. DIXON C.T. & OWEN H.W. Cholelithiasis: familial predisposition. *Surg. Clin. N.
    Amer.* **32**:1177, 1952.

28. DRAPANAS T. Interposition mesocaval shunt for the treatment of portal hypertension.
    Ann. Surg. **176**:435, 1972.

29. FLANIGAN D.P. Biliary cysts. *Ann. Surg.* **182**:635, 1975.

30. FLAMMAND F. Institut. Gustave Russey (Pers. Commun.), 1978.

31. FONKALSRUD E.W. & BOLES E.T. Choledochal cysts in infancy and childhood. *Surg.
    Gynec. Obstet.* **121**:733, 1965.

32. FORSHALL I. & RICKHAM P.P. Cholecystitis and cholelithiasis in childhood. *Br. J.
    Surg.* **42**:161, 1954.

33. GILROY J.A. & ADAMS A.B. Annular pancreas. *Radiology* **75**:568, 1960.

34. GLENN F. & WANTZ E.W. Acute cholecystitis following surgical treatment of unre-
    lated disease. *Surg. Gynec. Obstet.* **102**:145, 1956.

35. GOUREVITCH A. Duodenal atresia in the newborn. *Ann. R. Coll. Surg. Eng.* **48**:141,
    1971.

36. GROSFELD J.L. Alimentary tract obstruction in the newborn. In *Current Problems in Pediatrics*. Year Book Medical Publishers Inc., Chicago, 1975.
37. GROSS R.E. The Surgery of Infancy and Childhood. Saunders, Philadelphia, 1953.
38. HANSON B.A., MAHOUR G.H. & WOOLLEY M.W. Diseases of the gallbladder in infancy and childhood. *J. Pediat. Surg.* **6:**277, 1971.
39. HAYES D.M., GOODMAN G.N., SNYDER W.H. & WOOLEY M.M. Congenital cystic dilatation of the common bile duct. *Arch. Surg.* **98:**457, 1969.
40. IKEDA K. & SUITA S. Hepatic portogastrostomy using a gastric tube for the treatment of congenital biliary atresia. *Zeitschr. für Kinderchirurg.* **17:**360, 1975.
41. IZANT R.J. Biliary atresia survey. Surgical Section. Proceedings of the American Academy of Pediatrics, 1965.
42. JONA J.Z. & BELIN R.P. Duodenal anomalies and the ampulla of Vater. *Surg. Gynec. Obstet.* **143:**565, 1976.
43. JONES P.G. & CAMPBELL P.E. (eds.), Tumours of the liver and bile ducts. In *Tumours of Infancy and Childhood*. Blackwell Scientific Publications, Oxford, 1976.
44. JONES A.W. & SHREEVE D.R. Congenital dilatation of the intrahepatic biliary ducts with cholangiocarcinoma. *Br. Med. J.* **2:**277, 1970.
45. JONES P.G., SMITH E.D., CLARKE A.M. & KENT M. Choledochal cyst: experience with radical excision. *J. Pediat. Surg.* **6:**112, 1971.
46. KASAI M., KIMURA S., ASAKURA Y., SURUKI H., TAIRA Y. & OHASHI E. Surgical treatment of biliary atresia. *J. Pediat. Surg.* **3:**665, 1968.
47. KASAI M. Treatment of biliary atresia with special reference to hepatic portoenterostomy and its modifications. *Prog. Pediat. Surg.* **6:**5, 1974.
48. KASAI M., ASAKURA Y. & TAIRA Y. Surgical treatment of choledochal cysts. *Ann. Surg.* **172:**844, 1970.
49. KASAI M. & WATANABE I. Histologic classification of liver cell carcinoma in infancy and childhood and its clinical classification. *Cancer* **25:**551, 1970.
50. KASAI M., WATANABE I. & OHI R. Follow up studies of long-term survivors after hepatic portoenterostomy for non-correctable biliary atresia. *J. Pediat. Surg.* **10:**173, 1975.
51. KASSNER E.G., SUTTON A.L. & DE GROOT T.J. Bile duct anomalies associated with duodenal atresia; paradoxical presence of small bowel gas. *Am. J. Roentgen.* **116:**577, 1972.
52. KEELING J.W. Liver tumours in infancy and childhood. *J. Path.* **103:**69, 1971.
53. KIMURA K., TSUGAWA C., KUBO M., MATSUMOTO Y. & ITOH H. Technical aspects of hepatic portal dissection in biliary atresia. *J. Pediat. Surg.* **14:**27, 1979.
54. KULKARNI P.B. & BEATTY E.C. Cholangiocarcinoma associated with biliary cirrhosis due to congenital biliary atresia. *Am. J. Dis. Child.* **131:**442, 1977.
55. LANDING B. Considerations of the pathogenesis of neonatal hepatitis, biliary atresia cholangiopathy and choledochal cyst: the concept of infantile obstructive cholangiopathy. University Park Press, Baltimore, 1972.
56. LILLY J.A. & ALTMAN R.P. Hepatic portoenterostomy (the Kasai operation) for biliary atresia. *Surgery* **78:**76, 1975.
57. LILLY J.R. & ALTMAN R.P. The biliary tree. In M.M. Ravitch, K.J. Welch *et al.* (eds.), *Pediatric Surgery*. Year Book Medical Publisher Inc., Chicago, 1979.
58. LILLY J.R. & CHANDRA R.S. Surgical hazards of co-existing anomalies in biliary atresia. *Surg. Gynec. Obstet.* **139:**49, 1974.
59. LILLY J.R. & STARZL T.E. Liver transplantation in children with biliary atresia and vascular anomalies. *J. Pediat. Surg.* **9:**707, 1974.
60. LILLY J.R., WEINTRAUB W.H. & ALTMAN R.P. Spontaneous perforation of the extrahepatic bile ducts and bile peritonitis in infancy. *Surgery* **75:**664, 1974.
61. LONGMIRE W.P., MANDIOLA S.A. & GORDON H.E. Congenital cystic disease of the liver and biliary system. *Ann. Surg.* **174:**711, 1971.
62. LOUW J.H. & BARNARD C.N. Congenital intestinal atresia: observations of its origin. *Lancet* **2:**1065, 1955.

63. LYNN H.B. Duodenal obstruction: atresia, stenosis and annular pancreas. In M.M. Ravitch, K.J. Welch *et al.* (eds.), *Pediatric Surgery*, Vol 1:902. Year Book Medical Publishers Inc., Chicago, 1979.

64. MERCADIER M. Nouvelle observation de dilatation congénitale de voies biliaires intrahépatiques. *Semin. Hôp. Paris* **44**:3283, 1968.

65. MERRILL J.R. & RAFFENSPERGER J.G. Pediatric annular pancreas: 20 years experience. *J. Pediat. Surg.* **11**:921, 1976.

66. MIYANO T., SURUGA K. & SUDA K. Abnormal choledochopancreatic ductal junction related to etiology of infantile obstructive jaundice diseases. *J. Paediat. Surg.* **14**:16, 1979.

67. MIYATA M., SATANI M., UEDA T. & OKAMOTO E. Longterm results of hepatic portoenterostomy for biliary atresia: special reference to postoperative portal hypertension. *Surgery* **76**:234, 1974.

68. NEWMAN W.H. & HALL W.B. Acute cholecystitis in children. *North Carolina Med. J.* **28**:520, 1967.

69. NOBLETT R.N. & PATON C. Intrinsic duodenal obstruction associated with interposition of the pancreas. *Proc. International Paed. Surg. Congress, Melbourne* **2**:392, 1970.

70. ODIÈVRE M. & VALAYER J. Hepatic portoenterostomy or cholecystostomy in the treatment of extrahepatic biliary atresia. *Prog. Paediat. Surg.* **3**:187, 1976.

71. PRÉVOT J. & BABUT J.M. Spontaneous perforations of the biliary tract in infancy. *Prog. Paediat. Surg.* **3**:187, 1971.

72. RAINE P.M. & NOBLETT H.R. Duodenal atresia and unusual gas patterns. *J. Pediat. Surg.* **12**:763, 1977.

73. REID I.S. Biliary tract abnormalities associated with duodenal atresia. *Arch. Dis. Childh.* **48**:952, 1973.

74. RICKHAM P.P. *Neonatal Surgery*, (2e), p. 355. Churchill Livingstone, Edinburgh, 1978.

75. SAITO S. & ISHIDA M. Congenital choledochal cyst (cystic dilatation of the common bile duct). *Prog. Paediat. Surg.* **6**:63, 1974.

76. SOLOMON J.R. Royal Children's Hospital. Unpublished data, 1979.

77. SÖDERLUND S. & ZETTERSTROM B. Cholecystitis and cholelithiasis in children. *Arch. Dis. Childh.* **37**:174, 1962.

78. STARZL T.E. Liver replacement in children. In S.R. Berenberg (ed.), *Liver Diseases in Infancy and Childhood*. Nijhoff Medical Division, The Hague, 1976.

79. STONE H. & ASTLEY J.D. Management of liver trauma in children. *J. Pediat. Surg.* **12**:3, 1977.

80. STRAUSS R.G. Cholelithiasis in childhood. *Am. J. Dis. Child.* **117**:689, 1969.

81. SURUGA K., KONO S., MIYANO T., KITAHARA T. & SOUL-CHIN S. Treatment of biliary atresia: microsurgery for hepatic portoenterostomy. *Surgery* **80**:558, 1976.

82. SURUGA K., NAGASHIMA K., KOHNO S., MIYANO T., KITAHARA T. & INVI M. A clinical and pathological study of congenital biliary atresia. *J. Pediat. Surg.* **7**:665, 1972.

83. TAGART R.E. Perforation of a congenital cyst of the common bile duct. *Br. J. Surg.* **44**:18, 1956.

84. TANDLER J. Zür Entwicklungsgeschichte des menschlichen Duodenums im frühen Embryonalstadien. *Morph. Jahrb.* **29**:187, 1900.

85. THOMPSON J.W., FERRIS D.O. & BAGENSTOSS A.H. Acute cholecystitis complicating operations for other diseases. *Ann. Surg.* **155**:489, 1962.

86. TSUCHIDA Y. & ISHIDA M. Dilatation of the intra-hepatic bile ducts in congenital cystic dilatation of the common bile duct. *Surgery* **69**:776, 1971.

87. ULIN A.N., NOSAL J.L. & MARTIN W.L. Cholecystitis in childhood: associated obstructive jaundice. *Surgery* **31**:312, 1952.

88. VALAYER J. Hepatic portoenterostomy surgical problems and results. In S.R. Berenberg (ed.), *Liver Diseases in Infancy and Childhood*. Martinus Nijhoff Medical, The Hague, 1976.

89. WAKAYAMA M. Preduodenal portal vein associated with congenital biliary atresia. *Jap. J. Pediat. Surg. Med.* **8**:229, 1976.

90. WARREN K.W., KUNE G.A. & HARDY K.J. Biliary duct cysts. *Surg. Clin. N. Amer.* **48:**567, 1968.
91. WARREN W.D., SALAM A.A., HUTSON D. & ZEPPA R. Selective distal splenorenal shunt: technique and results of operation. *Arch. Surg.* **108:**306, 1974.
92. WINEGARNER F.G. & JACKSON G.F. Post traumatic acalculous cholecystitis: a highly lethal complication. *J. Trauma* **11:**567, 1971.
93. LILLY J.R. Surgery of coexisting biliary malformations in choledochal cyst. *J. Paediat. Surg.* **14:**164, 1979.

17. The Liver in Biliary Disease

BY JOHN M. HAM

There is little information in the surgical literature on the assessment of the liver in patients having operations for biliary disease. This is a surprising omission since pathological changes in the liver (and in the pancreas) are often found in these patients. The surgeon should be able to make an excellent assessment of the extent and severity of liver disease from the gross findings. This assessment complements the assessment of the physician, surgeon, and gastroenterologist from the clinical features, biochemical results, and liver imaging, and the assessment of the pathologist from the operative liver biopsy (Fig. 17.1).

LIVER DISEASE AND BILIARY SURGERY

Liver disease may be encountered during biliary operations under the following circumstances.

Secondary to biliary disease. The obvious examples are abscesses associated with cholangitis, secondary tumour, and biliary cirrhosis.

Simultaneous disease at both sites. Congenital disorders of the bile ducts and sclerosing cholangitis frequently affect both intrahepatic and extrahepatic bile ducts. A hydatid cyst which ruptures into a bile duct may present with extrahepatic biliary obstruction.

Unrelated liver disease. The commonest examples are hepatitis (either viral or alcoholic), the various forms of cirrhosis, and liver tumours. It is important to remember that under these circumstances the cause of the patient's symptoms may be the liver disease rather than that in the biliary tract.

Biliary disease reflected solely in the liver. The classic example in this category is that of an intrahepatic bile duct carcinoma.

Liver disease which does not correlate with the biliary disease. Occasionally, the gross findings in the liver are less abnormal than expected and this should alert the surgeon to the possibility of a diagnosis other than that made preoperatively. For example, complete biliary obstruction usually is associated with an enlarged, firm, and often green liver. The absence of these changes in the liver should

442

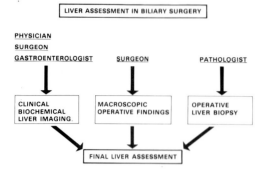

Fig. 17.1. Flow chart of the manner in which a complete assessment of the liver is obtained in patients operated on for biliary disease.

suggest either that the patient's jaundice was not due to obstruction, or that there was disease of the liver which prevented its enlargement, such as cirrhosis.

Thus, operative assessment of the liver may have considerable prognostic significance. Hepatic decompensation after operation is common in patients with biliary obstruction and sepsis, in patients with viral or alcoholic hepatitis, and in patients with chronic liver disease. Recognition of the disorder will prompt appropriate treatment to minimise the risk of decompensation.

ASSESSMENT OF THE LIVER AT OPERATION

DISORDERS AFFECTING THE WHOLE LIVER

The most common abnormalities are those associated with biliary obstruction. Classically, the liver is enlarged, tense, and green. If the obstruction has been long-standing and complete, the liver may be almost black and there may be scarring due to secondary biliary cirrhosis. By contrast, intermittent obstruction, even though longstanding, may be accompanied by little gross change in the liver and the only evidence of obstruction is provided by microscopic examination.

Another frequent liver abnormality is yellowish discolouration due to fatty infiltration. The causes include alcohol, drugs, diabetes, and morbid obesity. It is not necessarily a bad prognostic sign; however, if there is evidence of hepatitis as well (the liver being then best described as 'angry yellow'), the patient may have alcoholic hepatitis—a condition which carries a high risk of hepatic decompensation after any operation.

Alcoholic hepatitis is also frequently seen in conjunction with micronodular cirrhosis. In this form of cirrhosis the liver surface shows diffuse nodules up to 5 mm in diameter, together with fine fibrosis. In the macronodular cirrhosis which follows severe liver necrosis, there are broad deep fibrotic scars and large smooth regenerative nodules on the liver surface. The same pattern is frequently seen in patients with chronic active hepatitis and cirrhosis.

A variety of other less common diffuse liver disorders may be recognised, macroscopically, and their features have been discussed in detail by Cammerer and co-workers [3].

SPACE-OCCUPYING LESIONS

Metastatic tumour is, of course, the commonest space-occupying lesion of the liver. In the great majority of patients the operative diagnosis is obvious. However, there are a number of other liver lesions which may mimic metastases, either on a liver scintiscan or at operation. It is, therefore, important that biopsy confirmation of a presumed metastasis be obtained.

The usual features of the lesions which may be confused with metastases are summarised in Table 17.1. The variations in their macroscopic and microscopic appearances have been discussed by Scheuer [12].

Liver abscesses associated with biliary disease are usually small and multiple, and often resemble small metastases. In most patients they are due to cholangitis complicating gallstones, but occasionally may follow malignant obstruction. In patients who have had previous biliary bypass operations, for either benign or malignant disease, recurrence of biliary obstruction is commonly associated with sepsis and abscesses. Under these circumstances they may easily be confused with metastases. Solitary liver abscess, in association with biliary disease, is much less

Table 17.1. Liver lesions which may mimic metastases

Lesion	Usual appearance	Usual size	Single or multiple	Remainder of liver
Abscesses	Pale yellow nodules	< 1 cm	Multiple	Evidence of obstruction
Microhamartoma	Pale or brownish nodules or cysts	< 1 cm	Single or multiple	Normal
Bile cysts	Pale yellow or grey thin-walled cysts	Variable —may be very large	Single or multiple	Normal
Focal nodular hyperplasia	Pale nodule —may have central scar 'focal cirrhosis'	< 10 cm	Usually single	Normal
Hepatic adenoma	Encapsulated vascular tumour	Often large	Single	Normal
Bile duct adenoma	Demarcated pale nodules, usually subcapsular	< 2 cm	Single or multiple	Normal
Malignant hepatoma	Vascular tumour	Large	May be multiple foci	Normal or cirrhosis

common; it usually follows obstruction of a lobar or segmental bile duct or direct liver surgery [10].

Bile cysts, either single or multiple, may feel like metastases, but the diagnosis is usually quite obvious when they can be seen. Microhamartomata present as pale nodules, either single or multiple, a few millimetres in diameter and may also resemble small metastases.

The conditions of hepatic adenoma and focal nodular hyperplasia have been the subject of a number of recent papers in view of their possible relationship to oral contraceptive medication [2, 5, 9]. Hepatic adenomas are circumscribed vascular tumours which may be large and which may be impossible to distinguish from a hepatoma. The appearances of focal nodular hyperplasia are best described as resembling an area of focal cirrhosis; there is often a central scar with radiating fibrous septa.

Finally, hydatid disease may be found incidentally, or it may be the cause of the biliary tract disease due to rupture of a cyst into the biliary tract. The presence of one or more cysts in the liver is usually obvious, although quite large cysts may be hidden within the liver substance with only a small portion of the white cyst wall visible on the liver surface (Chapter 15).

LOCALISED ABNORMALITIES OF THE LIVER SUBSTANCE

Most surgeons experienced in the surgery of the liver and biliary tract have observed localised hypertrophy or atrophy of the liver substance. These abnormalities are uncommon, but are important, since they may create considerable diagnostic and therapeutic problems. Enlargement of a liver segment or lobe may represent true hypertrophy because of disease of the remaining liver, or may be due to obstruction of its venous outflow. Atrophy of a liver segment or lobe may be partial or complete. It is commonly associated with severe liver damage and cirrhosis, but may be caused by obstruction of the vascular inflow or biliary drainage of that segment or lobe.

In a personal series of 34 patients with various forms of liver atrophy, 17 had complete atrophy of a liver segment or lobe and 17 had partial atrophy (defined as a reduction of 50 per cent or more in the size of that segment or lobe [7]. Half the patients had cirrhosis due to primary hepatocellular disease. In the remaining patients the atrophy was caused by hydatid disease, bile duct carcinoma, sclerosing cholangitis, viral hepatitis, hepatocellular carcinoma, secondary biliary cirrhosis, and congenital hepatic fibrosis. Thus, there is a wide variety of possible causes, and the presence of atrophy indicates severe liver disease.

The diagnosis may be made before operation on the basis of the appearances on a liver scintiscan, or by hepatic angiography [7]. The macroscopic features of complete atrophy may be summarised as follows: the affected lobe or segment is shrunken, firm, and pink, and is well demarcated from the surrounding liver tissue. Depending on the cause of the atrophy there may or may not be hypertrophy of the remaining liver tissue. Microscopically, the affected region shows almost complete disappearance of hepatocytes, bile duct proliferation, and fibrosis. The features of partial atrophy are similar, though less marked.

These lesions are easily recognised at laparotomy or laparoscopy. In most patients the remainder of the liver will be cirrhotic. If, however, the other liver tissue is normal or hypertrophied then the most likely cause of the atrophy is a space-occupying lesion or obstruction of a lobar or segmental bile duct. In either of these situations surgical treatment is possible and, therefore, the cause of the atrophy should be established by full investigation. The principles of the surgical management of these patients have been discussed previously [1, 6, 7].

MICROSCOPIC ASSESSMENT OF THE LIVER IN BILIARY DISEASE

It is clear from the preceding discussion that a reasonable assessment of liver disorders may be made macroscopically. However, the diagnosis should be confirmed histologically. The surgeon has the opportunity of taking biopsies from one or more obviously diseased areas of the liver and may, therefore, avoid the sampling errors which occur with percutaneous needle biopsy [13]. It is unfortunate that operative liver biopsy is not yet regarded by surgeons as a procedure frequently required as part of a biliary tract operation.

INDICATIONS FOR OPERATIVE LIVER BIOPSY

The most important indications for operative liver biopsy in patients having biliary surgery are as follows:

1. Patients who are, or have been, jaundiced. Gallstones are common, and will frequently be associated by chance with other causes of jaundice or liver disease. It is also well recognised that the incidence of jaundice in patients with stones in the gallbladder is higher than the operative yield of stones in the common bile duct. Thus, biopsy confirmation of biliary obstruction is necessary to exclude other causes of the jaundice. The demonstration that the liver is normal is an important part of the diagnosis of bilirubin-conjugation defects. These disorders may present with jaundice and gallbladder stones (Chapter 4).

2. Patients with macroscopic diffuse liver disease.

3. Patients with any abnormality of the extrahepatic bile ducts. This category includes patients with stones, tumours, and inflammatory changes who have had liver disease as well.

4. Patients with biliary disease and pancreatitis. In the majority of these patients obstructive changes will be evident in the biopsy [8]. In some, the biopsy may demonstrate alcohol-induced liver disease, a finding of obvious diagnostic and therapeutic significance.

5. Patients with presumed functional biliary disorders (Chapter 12).

6. Patients with presumed metastases. It has already been stressed that biopsy confirmation of metastatic disease is important. In the review of 520 biopsies, mentioned earlier, there were 65 patients who had biopsies of presumed metastases. In five of the 65 the pathologist found a lesion other than secondary malignancy.

TECHNIQUE OF OPERATIVE LIVER BIOPSY

It is essential that the biopsy be obtained as soon as possible after the abdomen has been opened. Biopsies taken later in the course of an operation demonstrate an acute inflammatory cell infiltrate which may confuse the histological findings [4].

The site of biopsy should be selected carefully to include obviously abnormal tissue and, if possible, apparently normal liver as well. The type of biopsy depends on the macroscopic appearance of the liver and, frequently, more than one is indicated. Needle biopsy is the most common method and gives good results provided an adequate 'core' is obtained. Wedge biopsies give better sampling of portal tracts, an important advantage in the assessment of biliary disease. However, it must be emphasised that wedge biopsies may be misleading if they are taken from areas with considerable subcapsular fibrosis, or if they are too superficial. A wedge biopsy should be at least 12 mm deep and preferably more. Biopsy of metastases, or other space-occupying lesions, is usually by the wedge technique, or by complete excision.

During laparoscopy, biopsies of suspicious areas may be obtained using biopsy forceps, or by guided needle biopsy.

MICROSCOPIC ASSESSMENT OF THE BIOPSY

A detailed discussion of the assessment of microscopic changes in the liver is beyond the scope of this section. The important features of obstructive biliary disease have been outlined elsewhere and the whole subject is discussed in the monograph by Scheuer [8, 12].

THE RISKS OF OPERATIVE LIVER BIOPSY

We have recently reviewed 520 operative liver biopsies carried out in our Gastrointestinal Surgical Unit in patients with hepatobiliary and pancreatic disorders. There were no deaths related to the procedure; two patients had leakage of bile through a drainage tube and in one of these biliary obstruction could not be relieved at operation. One other patient was thought to have bled from the biopsy site, but did not require re-exploration. There were no other complications. The risk is therefore low. Theoretically, the risk of needle biopsy is greater than that of wedge biopsy, because puncture of a major vessel or bile duct is more likely with the former, and control of bleeding or bile leak may be more difficult. It is wise to avoid needle or laparoscopic biopsies if biliary obstruction cannot be relieved, or if control of bleeding is in doubt, for example, with a very vascular tumour.

REFERENCES

1. BRAASCH J.W., WHITCOMB F.F. & WATKINS E. *et al.* Segmental obstruction of the bile duct. *Surg. Gynec. Obstet.* **134:**915, 1972.
2. BRITTON W.J., GALLAGHER N.D. & LITTLE J.M. Liver tumours associated with oral contraceptives. *Med. J. Aust.* **2:**223, 1978.

3. CAMMERER R.C., ANDERSON D.L. & BOYCE H.W. Laparoscopy in hepatology. In G. Berci (ed.), *Endoscopy*. Appleton-Century-Crofts, New York, 1976.

4. EDLUND Y.A. & ZETTERGREN L.S.W. Microstructure of the liver in biliary tract disease and notes on the effect on the liver of anaesthesia, intubation and operation trauma. *Acta Chir. Scand.* **113**:201, 1957.

5. EDMONDSON H.A., HENDERSON B. & BENTON B. Liver-cell adenomas associated with the use of oral contraceptives. *New Eng. J. Med.* **294**:470, 1976.

6. HAM J.M. Segmental and lobar atrophy of the liver. *Surg. Gynec. Obstet.* **139**:840, 1974.

7. HAM J.M. Partial and complete atrophy of liver segments and lobes. *Br. J. Surg.* **66**:333, 1979.

8. HAM J.M., BOLIN T.D., STEVENSON D., JEFFERIES S. & LIDDELOW A.G. Operative liver biopsy abnormalities in patients with functional disorders of the biliary tract. *Aust. New Zeal. J. Surg.* **48**:499, 1978.

9. HAM J.M., STEVENSON D. & LIDDELOW A.G. Hepatocellular carcinoma possibly induced by oral contraceptives. *Am. J. Dig. Dis.* **23**:38s, 1978.

10. KUNE G.A., JUDSON R. & HILL P. Solitary liver abscess: a continuing medicosurgical problem. *Med. J. Aust.* **1**:151, 1979.

11. MAYS E.T., CHRISTOPHERSON W.M. & BARROWS G.H. Focal nodular hyperplasia of the liver. Possible relationship to oral contraceptives. *Am. J. Clin. Pathol.* **61**:735, 1974.

12. SCHEUER P.J. *Liver Biopsy Interpretation* (2e). Bailliere Tindall, London, 1973.

13. SOLOWAY R.D., BAGGENSTOSS A.H., SCHOENFIELD L.J. & SUMMERSKILL W.H.J. Observer error and sampling variability tested in evaluation of hepatitis and cirrhosis by liver biopsy. *Am. J. Dig. Dis.* **12**:1082, 1971.

Index